BIOTECHNOLOGY AND THE CHALLENGE OF PROPERTY

Medical Law and Ethics

Series Editor
Sheila McLean, Director of the Institute of Law and Ethics in Medicine,
School of Law, University of Glasgow

The 21st century seems likely to witness some of the most major developments in medicine and healthcare ever seen. At the same time, the debate about the extent to which science and/or medicine should lead the moral agenda continues, as do questions about the appropriate role for law.

This series brings together some of the best contemporary academic commentators to tackle these dilemmas in a challenging, informed and inquiring manner. The scope of the series is purposely wide, including contributions from a variety of disciplines such as law, philosophy and social sciences.

Forthcoming titles in the series

Medical Self-Regulation
Crisis and Change
Mark Davies
ISBN 978 0 7546 4459 0

The Jurisdiction of Medical Law
Kenneth Veitch
ISBN 978 0 7546 49441

Ethical and Regulatory Aspects of Human Genetic Databases
Edited by Bernice Elger, Nikola Biller-Andorno, Alexandre Mauron and Alexander M. Capron
ISBN 978 0 7546 7255 5

Altruism Reconsidered
Exploring New Approaches to Property in Human Tissue
Edited by Michael Steinmann, Peter Sykora, and Urban Wiesing
ISBN 978 0 7546 7270 8

Bioequity – Property and the Human Body
Nils Hoppe
ISBN 978 0 7546 7280 7

Biotechnology and the Challenge of Property
Property Rights in Dead Bodies, Body Parts, and Genetic Information

REMIGIUS N. NWABUEZE
University of Southampton, UK

Published by
Ashgate Publishing Limited
Gower House
Croft Road
Aldershot
Hampshire GU11 3HR
England

Ashgate Publishing Company
Suite 420
101 Cherry Street
Burlington, VT 05401-4405
USA

Ashgate website: http://www.ashgate.com

British Library Cataloguing in Publication Data
Nwabueze, Remigius N.
    Biotechnology and the challenge of property : property
    rights in dead bodies, body parts and genetic information.
    - (Medical law and ethics)
    1. Donation of organs, tissues, etc. - Law and legislation
    2. Genetic engineering - Law and legislation
    I. Title
    344'.04194

Library of Congress Cataloging-in-Publication Data
Nwabueze, Remigius N., 1968-
    Biotechnology and the challenge of property : property rights in dead bodies, body
parts, and genetic information / by Remigius N. Nwabueze.
        p. cm. -- (Medical law and ethics)
    Includes bibliographical references and index.
    ISBN 978-0-7546-7168-8
    1. Biotechnology industries--Law and legislation. 2. Genetic engineering--Law and
legislation. 3. Body, Human--Law and legislation. I. Title.

    K3925.B56N83 2007
    344.04'194--dc22
                                                                2007005507

ISBN 978-0-7546-7168-8

Printed and bound in Great Britain by TJ International Ltd, Padstow, Cornwall.

Contents

Preface

The concept of 'property' is at once both obvious and elusive. People commonly know the objects that are theirs and others, and can usually understand the abstract ideas, designs and texts they have created that they consider 'theirs'. In contrast, they consider themselves not to be property, unlike slaves, but to be owners, possessors, lenders and/or borrowers of property. Property concepts govern and define relationships between people and things, particularly objects and land but also people's creations and expressions of ideas. More difficult to determine are individuals' relationships to the materials that constitute their bodies. They are the people who occupy, operate, motivate and protect their bodies, without which they would not exist. Their internal organs and their limbs, tissues and bones are them, not just property they own. They do not consider themselves as owners or possessors of the skeletons, organs, limbs or tissues that embody them.

Lawyers, certainly in the Anglo-Saxon common law tradition and often beyond, prefer to understand 'property' as legally protected interests that entities such as people and corporate institutions have in material objects, in places, and in ideas, rather than as the objects, places and ideas themselves. Legally protected and enforceable property interests can be recognized in a limitless range of objects, places, ideas and influences, such as daylight entering a window, electrical currents, ways of manufacturing objects or rendering services, and, for instance, in the eighteenth floor accommodation of a building that has yet to be built on open or reclaimed land.

The concept of property may accordingly apply to human organs and other body products from both deceased and living people. In law, property interests are often seen to protect value. Therefore, a worthless object, such as a dead leaf fallen from a tree, is not amenable to theft since, having no value, it is not governed by criteria of ownership or possession. A person who enters land to acquire such a non-larcenable item may be liable for trespass, but not theft. However, an accumulation of leaves in a compost pile is property, because it has value. Value often arises from utility, which may be purely utilitarian, as with tools, spiritual, as with religious relics or icons, or, for instance, aesthetic, as with an artistic design, a melody or the pleasing amenity of a location. Wild creatures, including flying birds and swimming fish, are not property in some legal systems, but they become property on being caught, even by trespassers. By historical common law jurisprudence, dead bodies are not property, and still cannot be bequeathed by will, because they had no use, or value. Exceptionally, a preserved body may have value, such as the embalmed body of Jeremy Bentham possessed by University College London, because of its celebrity and curiosity interest.

This study by Dr Nwabueze shows how modern developments in biotechnology have given utility and therefore value to human bodily materials derived from cadaveric and living sources. It addresses how property law is being and could be advanced and moulded to shape legal regimes of control of the interests that have been and will be recognized through the engineering of human tissues, and means to induce regeneration of cells and tissues within the bodies, for instance, of persons with congenitally inherited or traumatically suffered disabilities. The study explains the various legal regimes of commercial, industrial and intellectual property that may be applied to protect interest in biotechnology and genetic knowledge, including genetic data and tissue (DNA) banks.

A distinctive merit of this study is its comparative component. To place prevailing legal regimes that govern interests in biotechnological processing of human tissues in industrialized legal systems in a comparative context, Dr Nwabueze goes to the dimension not of time, looking to history, but of place. He considers the culture of the Ibo people of south-eastern Nigeria, which is essentially spiritual, in contrast to the materialistic, utilitarian culture of westernized, industrially and scientifically advanced cultures in which property law is now being applied to bioengineering and biotechnology.

Spiritual convictions among the Ibo have pre-Christian roots, but are congruent with, and often integrated into, Christian beliefs. There is acceptance of supernatural authority and agency, and that life does not end with death but that death is a prelude to reincarnation, a form of resurrection or new embodiment. This system of belief affects how it is considered proper to treat bodies of deceased family members.

Through the medium of Ibo culture, the study relates to the customary, traditional beliefs of many other peoples in Africa and other continents, including the Americas and Asia. It addresses the impact of modern biotechnology, and means of its legal accommodation, on the customary conduct and traditional beliefs by which people in different societies have understood the world and organized their lives and communities. The text provides an introduction to the legal means by which technologically advanced societies may regulate development, exploitation and protection of interests in evolving uses of human tissues, and also to the threat and promise of these legal means to traditional knowledge, beliefs and cultures.

Bernard M. Dickens
Faculty of Law, Faculty of Medicine and Joint Centre for Bioethics
University of Toronto

Acknowledgements

The chaotic ideas presented in the initial draft of this book were significantly streamlined and developed into a more accessible and readable quality with the help of a good number of colleagues and friends. This book would have been poorer without their kind suggestions. Accordingly, I am exceedingly grateful for the constructive criticism and helpful suggestions of Professors Peter Sparkes, Jonathan Montgomery and Mr Nick Hopkins, all of the University of Southampton; Professors Trudo Lemmens, Bernard Dickens, Abraham Drassinower, Kerry Rittich and Lisa Austin, all of the Faculty of Law, University of Toronto; Professor DeLloyd G. Guth of the Faculty of Law, University of Manitoba; and Professor Carlos Correa, University of Buenos Aires, Argentina. Many thanks to my former colleagues at the Faculty of Law, University of Ottawa, Canada, especially Professors Ruth Sullivan and Jamie Benidickson, for their intellectual support and encouragement. I continue to be grateful for the friendship and support of Mr James C. Ezike, a legal practitioner in Lagos, Nigeria.

Finally, I am grateful for the love and support of my family members, especially my wife, Nkasiobi Nwabueze; my daughter, Chinemere Nwabueze; my sister, Clara Asams and her husband, Jacob Asams; and my mother-in-law, Dorothy Muonago.

Table of Cases

Table of Statutes

To the memory of my father,
Chief Michael M. Nwabueze (1927–2002);
an achiever and lover of knowledge

Introduction

Human body and body parts are used by biotech companies in the production of biomedical goods and services, and in academic and commercial research. Parts of the human body are used in transplant operations, fertility treatments, artistic casts and medical education. Biotechnology has also converted some medicinal plants, mainly from developing countries, and associated traditional knowledge into useful pharmaceutical compounds and products. Modern biotechnology has made possible the scientific and industrial use of new or uncommon raw materials in the production of goods and services that have implications for human health, well-being and the creation of wealth.

Biotechnological advances have in turn posed many challenges to the law of property, whose concepts were formulated in the period pre-dating most modern biotechnological applications. Thus, questions arise as to the relevance and implication of property concepts for new forms of technology and innovations utilizing human body parts, biologic raw materials and products. For instance, some biotech companies argue that they have property rights in their products that utilize body parts or other biologic materials, and that patents should be available to protect life forms and other products of biotechnology. The use of the concept of property in these areas is not without controversy. Within certain cultures and legal systems, people may be offended by the application of property concepts to the human body and parts. Religious, spiritual, economic and technological considerations largely influence discussions and debate on the application of property law to the human body.

In addition to advances in technology, traditional knowledge also poses challenges to the law of property. Traditional knowledge, including folklore, folk agriculture and folk medicine, is generally regarded or presumed as being outside the contemplation of conventional property and intellectual property law. The difficulties inherent in the application of property concepts to traditional knowledge ensure that modernity as well as antiquity has challenged property.

Traditional knowledge is part of a people's cultural heritage, and is a veritable means of social and cultural identity. Traditional medicine is the main source of health care for many developing countries' populations. In Africa about 80 per cent of the population depends on traditional medicine.[1] Access to conventional health care in developing countries is limited by many factors, including religion, culture, geography, illiteracy and poverty, so traditional medicine provides the main source of care. While being a source of cultural identity, and often the sole basis for local health care, some traditional knowledge products, such as folk art, folk music and folk medicine, also have commercial value. For instance, some indigenous images

---

1   World Health Organization (WHO), *WHO Traditional Medicine Strategy 2002-2005* (Geneva: WHO, 2002), at 1.

have been appropriated in the marketing of various types of products, including T-shirts, automobiles and souvenirs.[2] Some traditional medical products are becoming popular in some developed countries and generate significant revenue domestically and internationally. Products associated with traditional medicinal knowledge have been useful leads in drug discovery efforts of some pharmaceutical corporations, especially in the developed countries.

Unfortunately, some uses of traditional knowledge debase the spirituality and culture of its holders. Some traditional knowledge holders also complain that they have not been adequately compensated nor benefited from the commercial and profitable utilization of traditional knowledge by some Western corporations. Holders of traditional knowledge complain against the inequity in the present system of reward for traditional knowledge utilization, which largely favours patentees and producers of traditional knowledge-based products mainly in the West. Hence the growing demands from indigenous peoples, non-governmental organizations, developing countries and scholars from both developed and developing countries, for an effective protection of traditional knowledge.

Some proponents of traditional knowledge protection have sought to make use of existing property regimes, and arguably intellectual property, possibly in modified forms, to secure property and intellectual property rights (IPR) over traditional knowledge and genetic resources. Others find existing property and intellectual property tools inherently unsuitable for the protection of traditional knowledge and envisage the need for the formulation of a sui generis framework. Yet another school of thought believes that non-IPR regimes, non-monopolistic in character, should be employed in the protection of traditional knowledge, to secure it against misappropriation and to ensure consent and compensation for its use.

A special response of property law is needed to reconcile differences and demands of important stakeholders, whether they are individuals, scientific researchers, public and private institutions, or indigenous peoples and developing countries. It is submitted that property will more readily respond to the challenges posed by advances in technology, economic and cultural dynamics of any society, and issues raised by the protection of traditional knowledge, if it is evolutionary, flexible and capable of continuous adaptation to changing needs and circumstances.

This book, thus, attempts to show that in contemporary legal scholarship 'property' is increasingly used as a flexible and evolutionary legal concept in contradistinction to its popular thinghood conception and that these features have made it possible to deploy property to some areas that were not within its original contemplation, such as human body, body parts and traditional knowledge. The flexibility and evolutionary nature of property has contributed to useful analytical legal discourses. For instance, Harris embodied and propertized 'whiteness' to explain the privileges claimed and expected by white people in the USA during the epoch of slavery, and also during the period before the regime of affirmative action.[3] Reich propertized wages and social welfare benefits in a modern state to secure stability in employment and enhance

---

2   Christine Haight Farley, 'Protecting Folklore of Indigenous Peoples: Is Intellectual Property the Answer?' (1997) 30 *Conn. L. Rev.* 1–57.

3   Cheryl I. Harris, 'Whiteness as Property' (1993) 106 *Harv. L. Rev.* 1709.

economic security.[4] Michel Foucault's postmodern reconceptualization of the human body as a medical, legal and cultural construct lacking naturalness or physicality underpins considerable feminist discourse and illustrates the disaggregation of property as legal rights rather than the things themselves.[5] Furthermore, Radin's personhood conception of property has shed light on many issues concerning the commodification of the human body.[6] Radin believes that certain objects, including the human body, which are essential for human flourishing, partake of our personhood and ought to be protected by a regime of market-inalienability. In other words, such objects are property but should not be bought and sold in the market.

The evolutionary and flexible character of property is clearly manifest in the area of intellectual property law. Intellectual property (IP) promotes and protects creations of the mind. Since the categories of the mind's creativity are not closed, intellectual property would by sheer logic be evolutionary and flexible enough to protect new creations. IP law has consistently evolved and adapted to technological, economic and cultural changes.[7] In the 1950s and 1960s, IP evolved to recognize and confer protection on new plant varieties through a *sui generis* framework. Today, many developed countries including Canada, the USA and Australia have plant breeders' legislation. In the 1980s, IP fashioned layout designs for integrated circuits to protect producers of semiconductors. In the 1970s and 1980s, IP law in some jurisdictions started conferring patent protection on life-forms, biological materials and other living organisms. The information age brought with it questions relating to the copyrightability of computer software. IP responded by conferring protection on computer software in the 1980s.

Further evolution in IP law was evident in 1996 when the so-called 'internet treaties' were concluded to respond to questions raised by digital technology and the Internet, commonly referred to as the 'digital agenda'. These treaties are the WIPO Copyright Treaty, 1996 (WCT), and the WIPO Performances and Phonograms Treaty, 1996 (WPPT). Each of these treaties will come into force when ratified by 30 countries. Currently, the IP debate concerns the means of crafting proper and effective protection for traditional knowledge. Regardless of one's view on whether

---

4   Charles A. Reich, 'The New Property' (1964) 73 *Yale L.J.* 733; Tom Allen, *The Right to Property in Commonwealth Constitutions* (Cambridge: Cambridge University Press, 2000), at 153–61.

5   Michel Foucault, *The History of Sexuality* (New York: Vintage Books, 1990. Robert Hurley Trans.). Note, however, that women's corporeity is still significant as a symbol of sexuality, identity and individuality, and provides a medium of social control over reproductive activity. See, Franca Pizzini, 'The Medicalization of Women's Body' http://www.women.it/ quarta/workshop/epistemological4/pizzini.htm (last accessed: 2 August 2005).

6   Margaret Jane Radin, *Contested Commodities* (Cambridge, Mass.: Harvard University Press, 1996); Margaret Jane Radin, *Reinterpreting Property* (Chicago: The University of Chicago Press, 1993); Margaret Jane Radin, 'Reflections on Objectification' (1991) 65 *S. Cal. L. Rev.* 341; Margaret Jane Radin, 'Market-Inalienability' (1987) 100 *Harv. L. Rev.* 1849; Margaret Jane Radin, 'The Consequences of Conceptualism' (1986) 41 *U. Miami L. Rev.* 239.

7   Carlos A. Primo Braga, *et al.*, *Intellectual Property Rights and Economic Development* (Washington, D.C.: The World Bank: World Bank Discussion Paper No. 412, 2000), 1–53.

existing IPRs protect traditional knowledge or not, it is possible that intellectual property law will evolve fully in the future to give comprehensive protection to traditional knowledge.

It is proposed, therefore, to examine some of the challenges posed to the law of property both by advances in modern biotechnology utilizing the human body and parts and by the issues raised in the protection of traditional knowledge. One of the issues that call for exploration is the extent to which the flexibility and evolutionary nature of property is capable of accommodating certain innovations and knowledge, for instance, biotechnological products and raw materials: human body parts, and traditional knowledge and associated products. In brief, the conclusions are that a limited property framework should be adopted with respect to the human body and parts, and that while a property framework significantly contributes to the debate on the protection of traditional knowledge, developing countries may wish to adopt a *sui generis* form of protection.

Chapter 1 examines the meaning and nature of property and its function as both a legal and social institution. It traces the evolution of property through different forms of wealth, and makes a distinction between a layperson's understanding of property and its meaning in law. Chapter 1 significantly explores the theory of property and emphasizes its flexible and evolutionary qualities. Chapter 2 examines the application of property law in the area of the human body and parts. This chapter suggests that modern biotechnological applications have challenged the application of traditional property law concepts, and recommends four ways of finding a limited property interest in the human body and body parts. Chapter 2 has three objectives that put its thematic framework in bold relief.

First, the chapter attempts to provide an analytical structure for examining recent medical research scandals, in which some medical researchers were alleged to have illegally harvested body parts and organs from deceased persons, as witnessed in the United Kingdom, Canada, Australia and the USA. Second, it provides an analysis of the appropriate remedial legal framework for the conversion or unlawful withholding of biomedical inventions, like scientifically preserved cadavers for medical education or exhibition, frozen embryos, frozen human eggs and sperm, stored tissue samples, transplantable organs, and cultured human cell lines. Third, Chapter 2 suggests that the propertization of human body and parts probably gives the fullest protection to living relatives against the despoliation of a dead relative's grave, and provides the desired deterrence against biotechnological invasion of the human body. To realize these objectives, Chapter 2 starts with a historical analysis of dead bodies jurisprudence, which shows that despite the USA's fictional and parochial quasi-property rule and Australia's fairly advanced property rule in dead bodies, many jurisdictions still follow the dominant and ecclesiastically influenced English no-property rule in dead bodies and body parts. Efforts are made to highlight recent judicial developments in England, Canada and the USA, which potentially promise to consign the general no-property rule in dead bodies and body parts to its historical past. With little historical support for a property-rule in the human body, Chapter 2 turns to property theories. Analysis of the dominant concepts of property (right to a thing, and a bundle of rights) suggests that neither theory rationalizes decisively the proprietary interest in the human body and parts of it. This is hardly surprising since most property theories are cast in the mould of common law, which at its formative stages hardly had the opportunity to address the human body and parts. Using biotechnology as a contemporary historical fact, it is suggested that current jurisprudence on cadavers and body parts has become anachronistic, and ought to respond to recent biomedical and economic realities. Accordingly, Chapter 2 proposes four analogies that may appeal to judicial creativity in finding a limited property interest in the human body and parts of it.

Chapter 3 furthers the analysis in Chapter 2 by examining the human body jurisprudence in the context of a developing country like Nigeria, where issues such as religion, culture and worldview further complicate the analysis of cadaver jurisprudence. With the opening of the borders of many developing and culturally sensitive societies to biotechnology, biomedical research and international trade, the traditional conflict between science and religion is likely to be more intense. The potential impact of new technological advances on some culturally and communally oriented societies in Africa would likely motivate the reconsideration or reconceptualization of their legal order in the light of contemporary biomedical reality. How can the Nigerian legal order (or a similarly situated legal system) respond to such challenges as, for instance, proprietary control over the human body and its parts? This chapter tries to suggest some answers by analyzing the jurisprudence on the human body in the context of Nigeria's tripartite legal order: received English law, customary law and Nigerian legislation.

Chapter 4 explores legal issues and policy questions relating to micro or less visible body parts, such as genes, DNA and genetic information. It examines some problems arising from the use of DNA samples for forensic purposes, and in connection with population-based genetic studies. While a whole range of problems is encountered, Chapter 4 concentrates on property issues, such as the proprietorial character of genetic information. Chapter 4 provides the analysis of some case studies relating to population-based genetic studies in Iceland, Estonia, Newfoundland and Labrador, and the Kingdom of Tonga, which involved states' establishment and commercialization of DNA banks generated from biologic samples and medical information of their citizens. The manner in which property questions over samples in DNA banks are resolved by the relevant statutes is considered. Absent statutory establishment of a DNA bank, Chapter 4 considers, theoretically, how courts would resolve ownership disputes over DNA samples. Chapter 5 examines the various remedies potentially available to a plaintiff complaining of interference with a dead body or body parts. These remedies are both proprietary and non-proprietary. It provides a more detailed exploration of the difficulties associated with non-property remedies. These difficulties were highlighted in the previous chapters and projected as some of the justificatory bases for a limited property framework for dead bodies and body parts. These non-property remedies include negligence action for nervous shock or infliction of psychiatric injury; consent and informed consent; privacy; human right or constitutional right action; and unjust enrichment. Chapter 5 juxtaposes analysis of a property-based remedy in conversion with the non-property remedies to highlight their comparative advantages and weaknesses. The chapter, however, suggests that these remedies are not mutually exclusive and should be pursued simultaneously by a plaintiff. A reader who wants to see immediately why this book supports the recognition of a limited property interest in the human body might want to read Chapter 5 first before reading the other chapters. This would give a preview of the remedial problems that abound in this area of law and which support the recognition of a limited property interest in the human body. But if read in order, Chapter 5 provides a remedial demonstration of the arguments progressively developed in the previous chapters. Whether read in order or out of order, however, Chapter 5 provides a systematic remedial analysis of the need for a property framework which will be beneficial to all stakeholders: tissue sources, biotechnology industries and medical institutions.

From property questions relating to the human body, Chapter 6 segues to property and policy issues relating to the protection of traditional knowledge. This chapter raises more questions than it answers. The legal protection of traditional knowledge is a question of intense debate that has attracted considerable attention nationally and internationally. As in the area of biotechnology, an intellectual property regime has been suggested by some as a suitable mechanism for traditional knowledge protection. Some commentators, however, have argued against the use of a conventional intellectual property framework in the protection of traditional knowledge, and have suggested non-IPR measures, including the use of a *sui generis* regime. Thus, this chapter examines the subject matter captured by the term 'traditional knowledge' (TK) and the possible objectives of a protective regime. It examines the different tools and options potentially available for the protection of traditional knowledge, for instance, an existing IPR regime (patent, copyright, trademark, industrial design, geographical indication, trade secret, moral rights), a *sui generis* regime, a misappropriation regime, and the use of private contracts. Chapter 6 examines, by reference to decided cases, how holders of traditional knowledge could qualify as 'inventors' under patent statutes. Finally, Chapter 6 considers some of the international forums where issues relating to the protection of traditional knowledge have been explored.

This book draws attention (in the different chapters) to the increasing analytical uses of the property metaphor, made possible by the flexibility of property. It recommends the adoption of a limited property framework in the protection of cadavers and body parts, and suggests that a property framework provides some insights that might be helpful in the debate on the protection of TK. Of course the same issues may arise in civil law jurisdictions, but the focus of this book, at this time, is on countries whose legal systems are based on the common law, such as England, Nigeria, the USA, Canada and Australia.

Chapter 1

The Nature, Uses and Meaning
of Property

Introduction

The purpose of this chapter is to clarify the use and evolution of the concept of property. A legal conception of property as rights gives it some flexibility which, despite difficulties such a conception might create,[1] is potentially useful in analysing legal issues arising from modern technology.[2] Malleability is an important feature of property which makes its framework suitable for analysis of some aspects of the legal challenges posed by claims relating to dead human bodies, body parts and traditional knowledge.

In order to clarify the flexibility imbedded in the legal notion of property, it is necessary to sketch briefly the development of the concept of property, through an analysis of the different forms of property and the changes in these forms of property. This chapter highlights the factors that contribute to such changes, such as transitions in economic pattern, societal organization and technological change. Some of the functions of property are also explored. It will be important to elaborate, for instance, how property has been used as a basis of expectation, and the way property attempts to protect changing legitimate expectations of a given society. In addition, this chapter examines the differences between a layperson's conception of property as things and its legal conception as rights. In other words, rather than being the thing itself, property is the right exercised with (or without) respect to a thing. The legal conception of property as rights seems to underpin the meaning of property even in some non-Western societies.[3] For instance Gluckman observed:

---

1   Instances of such difficulties were provided by Penner, who stridently criticized the bundle of rights metaphor of property as an amorphous and confused concept that lacks any logical structure or consistency by reference to which rights of property are determined. He analogized the bundle of rights metaphor to a slogan that conjures up an image that gives a general sense of direction but is lacking in specificity and masks the real problems that cry for some solutions. J.E. Penner, 'The "Bundle of Rights" Picture of Property' (1996) 43 *UCLA L.Rev.* 711–820.

2   Richard H. Stern evinced similar analytical optimism for technological advances in noncoded aspects of computer programs, and recombinant DNA technology. See Richard H. Stern, 'The Bundle of Rights Suited to New Technology' (1986) 47 *U. Pitt. L. Rev.* 1229–67.

3   Bhalla argued, however, that the teleological idea that underpins the institution of property, and which is common to all ages, is the provision of means of subsistence for individual members of a given society. From that premise, Bhalla contended that the essence of ownership was to allow a personal use of property through the conferment of absolute

'Property law in tribal society defines not so much rights of persons over things, as obligations owed between persons in respect of things.'[4] Thus, this chapter suggests that the flexibility inherent in the legal conception of property could be exploited for analytical purposes.

The Relations of Property

It might be useful to point out this early that the nature and extent of legal relations created by property rights is a bit controversial and, perhaps, a summary account of this controversy is necessary. Generally speaking, property rights create legal relations between a person and a thing, between persons with respect to things, and between persons without reference to things. Accordingly, property relation is tripodic although some commentators would rather accept the existence of only a unidimensional or monistic relation. For instance, the person-object relation of property is not generally accepted because things are not, strictly speaking, right-bearing entities. It seems, nevertheless, that persons can have relationships with things. As Honoré observed: 'There can, obviously, be relations between persons and things, not merely between persons and persons. To argue that legal relations can only subsist between persons is either arbitrarily to restrict the definition of "legal relations" or obscurely to reflect the truism that legal claims can only be enforced by proceedings brought against persons.'[5] Despite Honoré's forceful assertion, right-bearing entities are generally regarded in Western legal thought as those entities capable of having interests and making choices. Only living human beings, non-human persons and, arguably, certain animals, fit this criterion.[6]

While Stephen Munzer's description of right-bearing entities might be adequate for Western jurisprudence, it fails to capture the more embracing position that exists in some non-Western societies, where perspective on right holding is conditioned by prevailing worldviews. For instance, some Native American Indians in the USA and Canada, and some traditional African communities regard some inanimate entities, like dead bodies of ancestors and sacred forests, as spiritual and organic entities capable of having relationships with living human beings.[7] Even in Western

---

physical control over the object of sustenance on the owner. In other words, ownership was hardly different from physical control of an object. This medieval view of ownership emphasizes the materiality of property rather than its more modern disaggregation as a bundle of rights. See R.S. Bhalla, 'The Basis of the Right of Property' (1982) 11 *Anglo-American L. Rev.* 57–73. Whatever merit is ascribable to Bhalla's contention, the more persuasive view in African traditional societies is that property refers more to rights than things.

4   Max Gluckman, 'Property Rights and Status in African Traditional Law', in Max Gluckman, ed., *Ideas and Procedures in African Customary Law* (Oxford: Oxford University Press, 1969), at 262.

5   A.M. Honoré, 'Rights of Exclusion and Immunities Against Divesting' (1960) 34 *Tulane Law Rev.* 453, at 463.

6   Stephen R. Munzer, *A Theory of Property* (New York: Cambridge University Press, 1990), at 42.

7   For instance, in a Canadian case, *Poplar Point Ojibway Nation v. Ontario* (1993) O.J. No. 601, it was contended by an aboriginal group that the disturbance of an ancient

jurisprudence, some scholars are increasingly arguing for a reconceptualization of property to take account of individuals' peculiar relationship with things that are constitutive of their personality.[8] Similar arguments have been made for a new concept of property that promotes an environmental ethic by recognizing the physicality and features of our natural environment.[9] Furthermore, J.W. Harris, in one of his articles, made numerous references to the person-thing property relationship and seems to support its existence.[10] Finally, there seems to be some archaeological support for the person-object relation of property. Some emerging archaeological theories posit that the dead body itself is capable of having an agency that is of considerable social and mnemonic importance to the living.[11] In other words, the dead (supposedly a thing) can in certain circumstances have a relationship with the living.

Another controversial property relation is that alleged to exist between persons without reference to things. As Arnold Weinrib puts it: 'The realization that property consists only of legal relations between people makes it clear that there is no need for any tangible object to serve as the object of those relations.'[12] Unquestioningly, the dephysicalization of property resulting from this perspective of the bundle of rights' theory imbues it with some flexibility that is amenable to judicial and analytical creativity, and also creates an important opportunity for the propertization of rights and interests on the fringes of property law, such as dead bodies, body parts and traditional knowledge. Because property is conclusory rather than criterial, its outer limits would remain largely undefined, allowing for property protection to be accorded to every valuable interests according to the socio-economic dictates of any legal system. There is also growing evidence of the instrumentality of the fragmentation of property and the analytical utility of its malleability. The flexibilization of property has facilitated analyses of myriad situations of legal significance; for instance, the existence of a property right in one's employment, in one's race, in one's person, in one's body, in cadavers, and in one's knowledge. Thus, property potentially includes every valuable interest and right (the implication of this conceptual imperialism is explored at the end of this chapter), and the characterization of an interest as valuable paves the way for a property protection. Some scholars (like Radin, Harris and Reich) have made interesting analytical uses of the flexible conception of property

---

burial ground to make way for a hydroelectric generating station unduly interfered with their communication and communion with their ancestors. For a more detailed discussion of such transcendental relationships, R.N. Nwabueze, 'Spiritualising in the Godless Temple of Biotechnology: Ontological and Statutory Approaches to Dead Bodies in Nigeria, England, and the USA' (2002) *Manitoba Law Journal* 171.

8   For instance, Margaret Jane Radin, *Reinterpreting Property* (Chicago: The University of Chicago Press, 1993).

9   Craig Arnold, 'The Reconstitution of Property: Property As A Web Of Interests' (2002) 26 *Harvard Environmental L.R.* 281.

10   J.W. Harris, 'Who Owns My Body' (1996) 16 *Oxford Journal of Legal Studies* 55, at 57–9.

11   Harold Williams, 'Death Warmed Up: The Agency of Bodies and Bones in Early Anglo-Saxon Cremation Rites' (2004) 9 *Journal of Material Culture* 263–91.

12   Arnold S. Weinrib, 'Information and Property' (1988) 38 *U.T.L.J.* 117, at 120.

as a bundle of rights or a set of legal relations. The use of property metaphor as a tool of intellection and analysis is on the increase.

The abstraction of property and its dialectical deployment as a framework of intellection devoid of thingness (in contradistinction to its real world, pragmatic signification) is evident in some seminal works attributing property to odd and traditionally non-proprietorial entities or concepts like whiteness,[13] and racial identity.[14] Similar methodology undergirds Radin's conception of personhood property. This refers to objects socially mediated as constitutive of our personalities.[15] It also seems that Reich's recommended propertization of social and welfare benefits[16] in a modern state inexorably captures the modern dialectical applications of the property metaphor.[17] The above analytical uses of the property metaphor were made possible by, and trace their provenance to, the bundle of rights metaphor's flexibility, its abstraction and disaggregation of property.

Despite the advantages of a fragmented and thingless conception of property, some scholars would rather confine property to its traditional, physical, and parochial manifestations. Although such scholars accept that property rights create a legal relationship between a person and a thing or between persons with respect to things, they deny that property relation exists between persons without reference to things. Nevertheless, some apologists of the bundle of rights' theory posit property as creating a legal relation among persons without reference to things. Craig Arnold has highlighted this aspect of the bundle of rights metaphor of property (that is, simply creating a set of legal relationships among people and not necessarily with reference to things):[18]

> The central premise of the bundle of rights conception of property is that property is a set of legal relationships among people, and therefore most emphatically is neither ownership of things nor relationships between owners and things. Some scholars insist that the definition of property has nothing to do with things and everything to do with social relationships. Other scholars, unable to move entirely away from the idea that there must be some object of the rights in the bundle, state that property is about legal relationships among people with respect to things. Nonetheless, these scholars give little attention to the thingness of property. Some scholars have attempted to bridge the inattention to objects of property rights and the bare acknowledgement of property rights in things by asserting that the rights in the bundle involve relationships among people with respect to valuable

---

13 Cheryl I. Harris, 'Whiteness As Property' (1993) 106 *Harvard Law Review* 1709.

14 Jim Chen, 'Embryonic Thoughts on Racial Identity as New Property' (1997) 68 *U. Colo. L. Rev.* 1123.

15 Radin, *supra*, note 8, at 1–71.

16 Social welfare benefits are not regarded as property in some legal systems. As Allen observed: 'Commonwealth courts have ruled against treating access to the state's resources as constitutional property, primarily because of a formal analysis of the rights held by the claimant. In general, these rights are neither exclusive nor transferable; hence according to either one of these formal criteria, the claimant has no property.' Tom Allen, *The Right to Property in Commonwealth Constitutions* (Cambridge: Cambridge University Press, 2000), at p. 154.

17 Charles A. Reich, 'The New Property' (1964) 73 *Yale L.J.* 733.

18 Arnold, *supra*, note 9, at 285–6.

resources. However the definition gives little useful guidance about which resources are objects of property, and the primary, almost exclusive, attention falls on market and power relationships among people. Overall, the bundle of rights conception is, at its core, anti-thingness.

Similarly, Kenneth Vandevelde suggests that a distinction exists between property as rights to things, creating a set of legal relations between persons and things or between persons with reference to things, and property as a set of legal relations existing among persons with or without reference to things.[19] In analysing the distinction between Blackstone's definition of property as a right to a thing and Hohfeld's analysis of property as a set of legal relations that need not have any reference to things, Kenneth Vandevelde observed:

> Blackstone...equated property not with things, but with rights over things. This was the second manifestation of the old property's obsession with things. Hohfeld also disputed this definition of property by arguing that legal relations were between people, not between people and things. Hohfeld, by denying that property was things or rights over things, had rejected both of the plausible interpretations of Blackstone's definition of property. Whether property was the thing or the right over the thing, Blackstone had made clear that property could exist only in relation to something. Hohfeld rejected even this minimal association with tangible objects, arguing that property could exist whether or not there was any tangible thing to serve as the object of the rights.[20]

Vandevelde's observation seems to support the contention that legal relations arising from property rights might exist in three forms: a set of legal relations may exist between a person and a thing;[21] between persons with reference to things; and between persons without reference to things. The bundle of rights metaphor is alleged to capture the meaning of property in the last sense.[22] The implication of these different senses or forms of property relations seems to be that a definition of property rights without reference to things is more expansive than its definition with reference to things. The tripodic formulation of property relation is debatable and not every property scholar would agree that property rights can give rise to a set of legal relations existing without reference to things. Even some of the scholars that accept the bundle of rights' definition of property as a set of legal relations still insist that the legal relationships exist with reference to things (Craig Arnold, in the quotation above, tried to make a similar point). For instance, Stephen Munzer observed:

---

19 Kenneth J. Vandevelde, 'The New Property of the Nineteenth Century: The Development of the Modern Concept of Property' (1980) 29 *Buffalo L.R.* 325–67.

20 *Ibid.*, at 360.

21 This type of property relation is denied by scholars like Cohen: Morris Cohen, 'Property and Sovereignty' (1927) 13 *Cornell L.Q.* 8, at 12. K.A.B. Mackinnon, 'Giving It All Away? Thomas Reid's Retreat from a Natural Rights Justification of Private Property' (1993) 2 Can. J.L. & Juris. 367, at 372.

22 Pavlos Eleftheriadis, 'The Analysis of Property Rights' (1996) 16 *Oxford Journal of Legal Studies* 31–54 (defending Hohfeld's definition of property as a set of legal relations between persons).

These contrasts between the no-property world and the actual world suggest two different ways of understanding property. One is the popular conception of property. It views property as *things*. For the most part, property is tangible things – land, houses, automobiles, tools, factories. But it also includes intangible things – copyrights, patents, and trademarks. Many of these would not exist in a no-property world. The other way of understanding property is the sophisticated conception. One might almost call it the legal conception, for it is very common among lawyers. It understands property as *relations*. More precisely, property consists in certain relations, usually legal relations, among persons or other entities with respect to things. A metaphorical way of stating the sophisticated conception is that property is a bundle of 'sticks.'[23] (Italics in the original)

Stephen Munzer did not seem to think that the bundle of rights perspective of property creates legal relations that could exist without reference to things:

> Earlier thinkers confronting the question, what is property?, answered it in different ways. Some hold that property is things; others maintain that it is relations between persons and things, or relations among persons with respect to things; yet others claim that it is a basis of expectations with respect to things…It is perfectly sound to think of property both as things (the popular conception) and as relations among persons or other entities with respect to things (the sophisticated conception) – provided that the context makes clear which conception is meant.[24]

We need not be detained by this debate as to whether the bundle of rights definition of property refers to the existence of legal relations between persons and things (or between persons with reference to things) or simply refers to a set of relations existing among persons without reference to things. This debate is highlighted here to simply introduce the reader to some of the controversies that could arise from the definition of property in terms of rights rather than its popular conception as things. The important point for this book is that, whatever one's view as to the nature and scope of the bundle of rights metaphor, property has a legal meaning which is different from a layperson's conception of it as things. That legal meaning is that property refers more to rights (which could be exercised with or without reference to things) rather than the things themselves. The later part of this chapter will further consider the meaning and concept of property.

The Characteristics and Forms of Property

Although the introduction of this book mentioned the characteristics, forms and dynamics of property, these issues are further examined here in some detail and with more illuminating examples to underscore the changeability of property and its relevance for emerging new forms of property. Property may refer to an institution,[25] a method, an expectation, an interest, a right, or an innate quality, such

---

23 Munzer, *supra*, note 6, at 16.

24 *Ibid.*, at 17.

25 J.W. Harris has explored what it means to say that property is a legal and social institution: Harris, *supra*, note 10, at 56–7; Reich, *supra*, note 17, at 771: 'Property is a legal

as the property of a metal.[26] This generality of property hardly qualifies it as a word of art. It seems, however, that the variability or malleability of property probably bodes well for legal analysis since it gives much freedom to characterize some new things or intangibles as property, or to accord property protection as necessitated by the dictates of time and circumstances.[27] Thus, the expansivity and flexibility of property provides a useful tool of analysis for some of the legal, political and socio-economic problems that confront society.[28] Property is a well-known analytical tool in the social and political science disciplines.[29] For instance, in a preface to Larkin's dated but important book on property, Professor J.L. Stocks states: 'The conviction of the cardinal importance of property for social and political analysis seems to be a distinguishing characteristic of the modern world.'[30] The possible analytical deployment of property in a legal context relating to human bodies and traditional knowledge is a theme pursued in this book.

Property is dynamic.[31] What is property today may not qualify as property tomorrow. Any anthropological or cultural museum is capable of capturing the changing conceptions of property and the profound and fascinating generational changes that have taken place in its forms.[32] Property is in a state of flux.[33] The relativity of property is captured by Vogt, who observed that 'property rights may vary considerably from one society to another, and in a particular society from one period to another, because they are.historically determined'.[34] The property of one epoch may be viewed with disdain, and depropertized, by another epoch.

---

institution the essence of which is the creation and protection of certain private rights in wealth of any kind. The institution performs many different functions.'

26 Marcus Cuncliffe, *The Right to Property: a Theme in American History* (Leicester: Leicester University Press, 1974), at 10.

27 As Alan Brudner observed:

> From a premise of juristic reasoning, property becomes a conclusion of practical reasoning. The law does not protect something because it exemplifies a mysterious essence called property; rather something is property because the law protects an interest in its exclusive possession, and the law protects this interest because doing so enhances the general welfare. Property is thus infinitely malleable.

Alan Brudner, 'The Unity of Property Law' (1991) 4 *Canadian J.L. & Juris.* 3, at 11.

28 For instance, Weinrib used the flexibility inherent in the concept of property to argue for the recognition of property rights in information: Weinrib, *supra*, note 12.

29 For the value of property in law and economic analysis, see Robert P. Merges, 'A Transactional View of Property Rights' (2005) Berkeley Center for Law & Technology, Paper 8 (also posted on http://repositories.cdlib.org/bclt/lts/8).

30 J.L. Stocks, 'Preface', in Paschal Larkin, *Property in the Eighteenth Century: With Special Reference to England and Locke* (Dublin: Cork University Press, 1930), at v.

31 James W. Ely, *The Guardian of Every Other Right* (Oxford: Oxford University Press, 1992), at 6.

32 Francis S. Philbrick, 'Changing Conceptions of Property in Law' (1938) 86 *U. PA. L. Rev.* 691.

33 Roy Vogt, *Whose Property? The Deepening Conflict Between Private Property and Democracy in Canada* (Toronto: University of Toronto Press, 1999), at 8, observing that 'property rights in any society are changing all the time'.

34 *Ibid.*, at 17.

An instance is slavery (human ownership), which was practised by different legal systems of the world many years ago.[35] Slaves could not own property; rather, they were objects of property.[36] Today, it is generally agreed that ownership of human beings is unacceptable and this is reflected in the constitutions and laws of almost every country.[37] In medieval England and many other places of the world, land was the main form of wealth and probably the most significant item on the contemporary property list of the medieval world.[38] That land was the prevailing property model

---

35   For an excellent account of slavery in the USA: Cheryl I. Harris, 'Bondage, Freedom and the Constitution: The New Slavery Scholarship and its Impact on Law and Legal Historiography. Part II Contribution: Private Law and United States Slave Regimes' (1996) 18 *Cardozo L. Rev.* 309.

36   Willam H. Taft, 'The Right of Private Property' (1894) 3 *Mich. L. J.* 215. Harris analysed the situation of slavery in America:

> Even though there was some unease in slave law, reflective of the mixed status of slaves as humans and property, the critical nature of social relations under slavery was the commodification of human beings. Productive relations in early American society included varying forms of sale of labor capacity, many of which were highly oppressive; but slavery was distinguished from other forms of labor servitude by its permanency and the total commodification attendant to the status of the slave. Slavery as a legal institution treated slaves as property that could be transferred, assigned, inherited, or posted as collateral. For example, in *Johnson v. Butler* (4 Ky. – 1 Bibb – 1815, 97), the plaintiff sued the defendant for failing to pay a debt of $496 on a specified date. Because the covenant had called for payment of the debt in 'money or Negroes,' the plaintiff contended that the defendant's tender of one Negro only, although valued by the parties at an amount equivalent to the debt, could not discharge the debt. The court agreed with the plaintiff. The use of Africans as a stand-in for actual currency highlights the degree to which slavery 'propertized' human life.

Cheryl I. Harris, 'Whiteness As Property' (1993) 106 *Harv. L. Rev.* 1709, at 1720. Harris, *supra*, note 35.

37   The decision of the Canadian Federal Court of Appeal in *President and Fellows of Harvard College v. Canada (Commissioner of Patents)* (2000) 189 D.L.R. (4th) 385 touches upon this point. Justice Rothstein observed:

> Strictly, the question does not arise here, because the patent claims are restricted to non-human mammals. However, the potential extension to human beings is an obvious concern. The answer is clearly that the *Patent Act* cannot be extended to cover human beings. Patenting is a form of ownership of property. Ownership concepts cannot be extended to human beings. There are undoubtedly other bases for so concluding, but one is surely section 7 of *the Canadian Charter of Rights and Freedoms* which protects liberty. There is, therefore, no concern by including non-human mammals under the definition of 'invention' in the *Patent Act*, that there is any implication that a human being would be patentable in the way that the oncomouse is.

Although the decision of the Court of Appeal was overturned by the majority decision of the Supreme Court of Canada: *Harvard College v. Canada (Commissioner of Patents)* (2002) SCC 76, the above observation of the Court of Appeal was left intact.

38   Bernard Rudden, 'Things as Things and Things as Wealth' (1994) 14 *Oxford Jour. L. Stud.* 81, at 82. Nwakamma Okoro, *The Customary Laws of Succession in Eastern Nigeria and the Statutory and Judicial Rules Governing their Application* (London: Sweet & Maxwell,

is partly attributable to the feudal system in England and the agrarian economy that characterized many production systems in the past.

The industrial revolution changed the production systems of a significant part of the Western world with the result that new forms of property emerged to diminish the dominating value of land.[39] In pre-colonial African societies, land was generally held in common and vested in the family or the political unit.[40] The advent of colonialism, which substantially altered the means of production, distribution and exchange, instigated changes in the land tenure systems of many colonial African countries, with the result that now individual and private ownership of land is the norm in many African countries.[41] According to Demsetz, some Native American Indians of the Labrador Peninsula generally used land for hunting and there was no trace of, or incentive for, private ownership.[42] Things changed with the initiation of the lucrative North American fur trade. The fur trade provided incentives (for the Indians) for the husbanding of fur-breeding animals and the creation of private property rights in land to aid such husbanding and prevent poaching.[43] In other words, the introduction of modern commerce in many parts of Africa and North America brought about changes in forms of property and patterns of ownership.

Technological and social innovations usually bring changes to forms of wealth and property. In a seminal 1964 journal article, Charles Reich observed the emergence

---

1966), at 2: 'Land forms the greater bulk of wealth in Eastern Nigeria and group ownership of land is a characteristic feature of land tenure in the region.' Similar comments were made with respect to Ghana in West Africa. See, Kwamena Bentsi-Enchill, *Ghana Land Law: An Exposition, Analysis and Critique* (London: Sweet & Maxwell, 1964), at 3:

> Whether he has any land for his own use, how he holds it, what he gets out of it – these condition to a great extent the measure of a man's material wealth and also the character of his social relationships. Small wonder then that our ancestors viewed the land with such religious awe. For land is the primary capital asset...

39 Jonathan R. Macey, 'Property Rights, Innovation, and Constitutional Structure', in Ellen F. Paul, *et al.*, eds, *Property Rights* (New York: Cambridge University Press, 1994), at 181 observed that: 'The Industrial Revolution caused an expansion of our ideas of property to include other forms of wealth, such as innovations and productive techniques. And the modern age has caused a further expansion of our ideas of property to include inchoate items, particularly information.'

40 Detailed treatment of land tenure under the customary laws of some African countries could be read in: T.O. Elias, *The Nature of African Customary Law* (Manchester: The University of Manchester Press, 1956), at 162–75; G.B.A. Coker, *Family Property Among the Yorubas* (London: Sweet & Maxwell, 1966); T.O. Elias, *Nigerian Land Law* (London: Sweet & Maxwell, 1971); N.A. Ollennu, *Principles of Customary Land Law in Ghana* (London: Sweet & Maxwell, 1962); Bentsi-Enchill, *supra*, note 38.

41 For the situation in Nigeria: Remigius N. Nwabueze, 'The Dynamics and Genius of Nigeria's Indigenous Legal Order' (2002) 1 *Indigenous L. J.* 153–99, at 164–5.

42 Harold Demsetz, 'Toward A Theory of Property Rights' (1967) 57 *Am. Ec. Rev.* 347, at 350–59.

43 *Ibid.* However, the Supreme Court of the USA held in *Johnson v. McIntosh* (1823) 21 U.S. 543, that Native Americans do not have an indefeasible right to their lands based on natural law. For a good analysis of this case that puts it in historical context: Robert Williams, *The American Indian in Western Legal Thought* (Oxford: Oxford University Press, 1990).

of new forms of wealth in the USA that entailed significant dependence on the government (such as income and benefits, jobs, occupational licences, franchises, government contracts and subsidies, use of public resources, and government services) and argued for their legal protection as new forms of property.[44] The impact of technological development on property forms could be profound. For instance, the rail technology in the nineteenth century antiquated canals, while twentieth-century air travel has taken a significant part of rail transport business.[45] Aviation has itself triggered claims to uncommon forms of property, for instance a property right to airspace above an owner's land.[46] Before the dawn of air transportation, a landowner's claim to airspace above his or her property arose in connection with interferences occurring at a height within which the landowner could make an ordinary use and enjoyment of his or her land.[47] Thus, the old cases dealing with property claims over airspace concerned structures on one's property which extended over a neighbouring property, for instance, overhanging branches of trees, overhanging buildings, signs or telegraph wires.[48] However, the routine use of air transportation has challenged modern courts to find an appropriate balance between the rights of a landowner and an aviator.[49] One of the earliest Canadian cases on the subject is *Atlantic Aviation Ltd., v. N.S. Light & Power Co.*,[50] which seems to have tilted the balance in favour of a landowner.[51] The court held, though *obiter*, that aviation at any height constituted a trespass to property except the overflight was privileged. It is privileged, the court held, only if it is done for a legitimate purpose, in a reasonable manner and at a height that does not unreasonably interfere with a landowner's use of his or her land.[52] The decision in *Atlantic Aviation Ltd.*

---

44 Reich, *supra*, note 17.

45 Ely, *supra*, note 31, at 6–7.

46 For Professor Gray's illuminating analysis: Kevin Gray, 'Property in Thin Air' (1991) 50 *Cambridge L.J.* 253–307.

47 Jack E. Richardson, 'Private Property Rights in the Air Space at Common Law' (1953) 31 *Can. Bar Rev.* 117; H. W. Silverman and J. D. Evans, 'Aeronautical Noise in Canada' (1972) 10 *Osgoode Hall L.J.* 607; J. Irvine, 'Some Thoughts on Trespass to Airspace' (1986) 37 *C.C.L.T.* 99.

48 *Gifford v. Dent* (1926) W.N. 336; *Pickering v. Rudd* (1815) 4 Camp. 219; *Kelsen v. Imperial Tobacco Co. (of Great Britain and Ireland) Ltd.* (1957) 2 Q.B. 334; *Big Point Club v. Lozon* (1943) 4 D.L.R. 136 (Ont. H.C); *Dahlberg v. Naydiuk* (1969) 10 D.L.R. (3d) 319 (Man. C.A.).

49 It should be noted that the right of the public or the public interest is implicated in this balance. The public has a legitimate interest in air transportation and has a right to take advantage of all that science offers in the use of air space. *Bernstein v. Skyviews & Gen.* (1978) Q.B. 479.

50 *Atlantic Aviation Ltd. v. N.S. Light & Power Co.* (1965) 55 D.L.R. (2d) 554 (Nova Scotia S.C.).

51 Other Canadian cases on the subject include *Lacroix v. R.* (1954) 4 D.L.R. 470 (Ex Ct.); *The Queen in Right of Man. v. Air Can.* (1980) 111 D.L.R. (3d) 513 (SCC); *Didow v. Alta. Power Ltd.* (1988) 5 W.W.R. 606 (Alta. C.A.); *Kingsbridge Development Inc. v. Hanson Needler Corp.* (1990) 71 O.R. (2d) 636 (H.C).

52 *Atlantic Aviation Ltd.*, *supra*, note 50.

contrasts with the decision of an English court in *Bernstein v. Skyviews & Gen.*,[53] where Griffiths, J. held that the rights of a landowner in the airspace above his or her land is limited to the height necessary for the ordinary use and enjoyment of the land and structures on it, and beyond this zone the landowner can make no valid property claims.[54] The point is that air transportation technology brought with it new forms of property or property claims.

Developments in medicine also had an impact on the use of the concept of property in the context of the human body. The standardization of the practice of anatomy in the early nineteenth century opened a whole new jurisprudence on dead bodies. Before anatomy emerged as a recognized branch of medical practice, dead bodies had no commercial or medical value and, as such, disputes concerning their ownership hardly arose. With the emergence of anatomy as a separate and recognized branch of medicine, physicians began to need dead bodies to practise dissection and perfect the art of surgery. Initial supply came illegally from a class of infamous men known as the 'resurrectionists' or 'Body-Snatchers'.[55] This group specialized in stealing newly buried dead bodies from their graves and selling the stolen corpses to physicians.[56] The emerging commercial value of dead bodies sustained the activities of the resurrectionists for many years. Body-snatching prevailed in the period that the common law did not recognize a property right in dead bodies. The common law's depropertization of dead bodies made it difficult to prosecute body-snatchers for stealing.[57] Public concern regarding the inhuman activities of the resurrectionists, and the urgent medical demand for corpses for the purpose of dissection, inspired the development of a legal governance regime, including the use of anatomy legislation. Part of the solution, suggested by some cases and scholars,[58] is to consider corpses as limited property. Thus, interference with corpses may be considered a meddling with property rights.[59] Property issues and problems relating to dead bodies are treated in detail in Chapters 2 and 3 but are mentioned here to underscore the point that changes in biomedical technology and medical innovations can affect our conceptions of property or property rights.

More recently, the emergence of information technology has endowed certain pieces of information and data with a greater value than was previously attributed to them and today some categories of information have attained the status of property.[60] The increased value attached to confidential information and the impact of this

---

53 *Bernstein v. Skyviews & Gen.* (1978) Q.B. 479.

54 *Ibid.*

55 M.P. Hutchens, 'Grave Robbing and Ethics in the 19th Century' (1997) 278 *JAMA* 1115; S.M. Shultz, *Body Snatching: The Robbing of Graves for the Education of Physicians* (North Carolina: McFarland & Co., 1992).

56 *Ibid.*

57 Alan Ryan, 'Self-Ownership, Autonomy and Property Rights', in Paul, *supra*, note 39, at 254. However, the common law made it a misdemeanor to disinter a corpse. As argued in Chapter 2, common law originally recognized property rights in corpses.

58 The relevant materials are considered in Chapters 2 and 3.

59 This is in addition to whatever criminal sanction the law may provide.

60 Weinrib, *supra*, note 12; Wendy J. Gordon, 'On Owning Information: Intellectual Property and the Restitutionary Impluse' (1992) 78 *Va. L. Rev.* 149. Macey observed:

development on the concept of property also plays out in the context of medicine. For instance, a gene contains complete genetic information relating to a particular person and this information could be used in a wide variety of medical applications, and in forensic contexts.[61] Many patent applications have claimed ownership of, or patent rights over, an isolated and purified gene.[62] The purification and isolation of a gene is generally considered to amount to an invention justifying patent protection under the law.[63] However, it has been strongly argued that what is important in a gene is not its isolation and purification, but the information it contains.[64] Since a person's genetic information is the same even after isolation of the person's gene, it seems to follow that patents on genes have the effect of protecting discoveries, contrary to traditional legal wisdom on patentability.[65] Note that this argument against the patentability of genes assumes that allowing patent on human genes has the tendency of legitimizing

---

> Consistent with the view that property is an expansive concept, the Supreme Court (USA) has held that inside information about corporate take-overs is property, and the Securities and Exchange Commission (SEC) rules against insider trading must therefore be construed to protect property rights in information. Similarly, the court has held that medical researchers may decide whether and to whom to release their raw data (see, *Forsham v. Harris* (1980) 445 U.S. 169); television manufacturers have property rights in information about their products, including a limited right to confidentiality with respect to accident reports (see, *Consumer Product Safety Commission v. GTE Sylvania, Inc.* (1980) 447 U.S. 102); and the property interest reflected by shares of a stock in a corporation includes the potential to control that corporation (see, *Manges v. Camp* (1973) 474 F.2d 97).

Paul, *supra*, note 39, at 181. See also, Jonathan R. Macey, 'From Fairness to Contract: The New Direction of the Rules Against Insider Trading' (1984) 13 *Hofstra Law Rev.* 9.

61 The social, ethical and legal implications of genetic technology have been the subject of inquiry in some jurisdictions, such as Canada and the United Kingdom. See, Human Genetics Commission, *Inside Information: Balancing Interests in the Use of Personal Genetic Data* (A Report by the Human Genetics Commission (UK), May 2002); Ontario Report to Premiers, *Genetics, Testing and Gene Patenting: Charting New Territory in Healthcare* (Toronto: Ontario Government, 2002).

62 D.J. Willison and S.M. Macleod, 'Patenting of Genetic Material: Are The Benefits To Society Being Realized?' (2002) 167 *Can. Med. Assoc. J.* 259–66; R. M. Cook-Deegan and S.J. McCormack, 'Patents, Secrecy, and DNA' (2001) 293 *Science* 217; A.R. Willamson, 'Gene Patents: Socially Acceptable Monopolies or an Unnecessary Hindrance to Research?' (2001) 17 *Trends in Genetics* 670.

63 Sources cited above. Note, however, that isolation and purification of a gene amounts to a patentable invention only on the satisfaction of other patent criteria, such as utility, non-obviousness and industrial application.

64 World Health Organization, *Genomics and World Health* (Geneva: WHO, 2002), at 136:

> It is argued that a normal or abnormal gene sequence is, in effect, naturally occurring information which cannot therefore be patentable. The counter-argument which has been widely used by patent lawyers, that DNA sequence identification is a form of purification 'outside the body,' and therefore analogous to the purification of naturally occurring pharmacological agents, is specious; the DNA molecule is not, in this context, important as a substance and its value resides in its information content.

65 *Ibid.*

ownership of genetic information relating to a person.[66] It seems that the debate on gene patents indirectly bears on whether human genetic information could be owned and, if so, how the law could structure the prerequisites for such ownership.[67]

It is not uncommon now to talk of ownership of information.[68] Arnold Weinrib warned that 'a legal system that fails to recognize that information itself can be stolen is simply out of touch with the role of information in modern commercial practice'.[69] In the area of genetics, an example could be drawn from the emergence of DNA banks in some jurisdictions, such as the United Kingdom, Iceland, Estonia, the Kingdom of Tonga, and Newfoundland in Canada. Population-wide DNA banks came in the wake of the human genome project that was partly aimed at producing a complete map of the genes in the human body.[70] Sequencing of the human genome was successfully completed in 2000 and published in 2001, knowledge of which promises to revolutionize medical practice.[71] Population geneticists believe that linkage studies can provide genetic bases for certain diseases prevalent in a group, such as

---

66 The Ontario Report to Premiers alluded to the potentials of a broadly drawn gene patent to confer proprietory control over genetic information:

> the effect of fully enforced, broad scope gene patents may challenge certain principles of patent law by in effect patenting genetic *information* rather than simply genetic inventions, products or utilities. To remedy this problem, the scope of patents over genetic material may need to be more rigorously defined to separate the chemical or structural nature of genetic material from its informational content. Patents should only prevent the making, using, selling, and importation of genetic material when that material is used as a chemical, but should not unduly limit access and use of the particular information content of a naturally occurring sequence, regardless of whether the sequence is being used in natural or artificial form (italics in original).

Ontario Report to Premiers, *supra*, note 61, at 49.

67 *Ibid.*

68 D.F. Libling argued that commercially valuable information obtained by the expenditure of time, effort, labour and money amounts to property: D.F. Libling, 'The Concept of Property: Property in Intangibles' (1978) 94 *Law Quarterly Rev.* 103–19. In *International News Service v. Associated Press* (1918) 248 U.S. 215, the issue was whether one could have property rights in news. The majority of the US Supreme Court upheld a quasi-property right in news by holding that a news gatherer was entitled to an injunction prohibiting others from selling the news for a limited time. See a review of this case by Walter W. Cook, 'Comment: The Associated Press Case' (1919) 28 *Yale L.J.* 387.

69 Weinrib, *supra*, note 12, at 142.

70 For an account of the history and objectives of the human genome project, see, F.S. Collins and V.A. McKusick, 'Implications of the Human Genome Project for Medical Science' (2001) 285 *JAMA* 540.

71 *Ibid.*, at 544, predicting that:

> By 2020, the impact of genetics on medicine will be even more widespread. The pharmacogenomics approach for predicting drug responsiveness will be standard practice for quite a number of disorders and drugs. New gene-based 'designer drugs' will be introduced to the market for diabetes mellitus, hypertension, mental illness, and many other conditions. Improved diagnosis and treatment of cancer will likely be the most advanced of the clinical consequences of genetics, since a vast amount of molecular information already has been collected about the genetic basis of malignancy. By 2020, it is likely that every tumor will have a precise molecular

obesity and diabetes. As a result, some countries mentioned above,[72] in conjunction with entrepreneurs, have established DNA banks for the collection of tissue samples and medical information. These DNA banks hold prospects of commercial profits to the participating private entities.[73] Though DNA banks are of potential benefit to the entire community, there is a debate concerning the justification of demanding citizens to freely give their tissues even when a participating corporation derives commercial profits from the medical application of those tissues. Some suggest that the commercial nature of some DNA banks warrants that tissue donors should receive sufficient remuneration for their tissues.[74] But on what legal basis can donors of tissues and medical information claim such compensation? Can the concept of property afford a remedial framework? These are some of the questions treated in more detail in Chapter 4, but mentioned here to emphasize the point that the emergence of DNA banking and genetic technology has given rise to new property claims over genes and genetic materials.

The twenty-first century has continued to witness the dynamism and transitions of property. New forms of property have emerged in the wake of biotechnology. Biotech forms of property challenge traditional property law regimes, for instance patent law. Questions have arisen as to whether human body parts, cell-lines based on human body parts, biological specimens, genes, and products of traditional knowledge are patentable and admissible to the category of property.[75] The emergence of plant-based medicines and the increasing commodification of traditional knowledge and articles of culture have also ignited a heated controversy on the protection of traditional knowledge and symbols of certain cultures.[76] This controversy was hardly noticeable many decades ago. Challenges to property in the area of traditional knowledge are more fully explored later.

---

fingerprint determined, cataloging the genes that have gone awry, and therapy will be individually targeted to that fingerprint.

However, the World Health Organization has cautioned that there is no certainty as to the realization of the promises held by genomics nor the time-scale for their realization: World Health Organization, *Genomics and World Health* (Geneva: WHO, 2002).

72 It does appear that in the case of Newfoundland, Canada, the tissue collection there was entirely undertaken by a private company without governmental involvement.

73 H. Rose, *The Commodification of Bioinformation: The Icelandic Health Sector Database* (London: The Wellcome Trust, 2001).

74 J.C. Bear, *What is a Person's DNA Worth? Fair Compensation for DNA Access* (Vienna: 10th International Congress of Human Genetics, 2001).

75 For instance, L. Andrews and D. Nelkin, 'Whose Body Is It Anyway? Disputes Over Body Tissue in a Biotechnology Age' (1998) 351 *Lancet* 53–7; Stephen R. Munzer, 'An Uneasy Case Against Property Rights in Body Parts' in Paul, *supra*, note 39, at 259–86; Stephen R. Munzer, 'Kant and Property Rights in Body Parts' (1993) 6 *Can. Jour. L. Jur.* 319–41; Charles P. Wallace, 'For Sale: The Poor's Body Parts', *Los Angeles Times*, 27 August 1992, at A1. For traditional knowledge, Carlos M. Correa, *Traditional Knowledge and Intellectual Property* (Geneva: The Quaker United Nations Office, 2001).

76 Michael F. Brown, 'Can Culture Be Copyrighted?' (1998) 39 *Current Anthropology* 193; Carlos M. Correa, *Protection and Promotion of Traditional Medicine: Implications for Public Health in Developing Countries* (Geneva: South Centre, 2002).

In addition to changes in the form of property brought about by changes in technology, the need to protect certain societal expectations may lead to the emergence of new forms of property.[77] Because our expectations change, new expectations may deserve new property protection or make property protection unsuitable. For instance, it is arguable that a good section of the public expects that the human body and its parts should not be the object of commerce. This is a legitimate expectation for which the global community is still considering the appropriate form of protection. The current debate concerning the existence of a property interest in the human body partly reflects this expectation. If any legal system protects its societal expectation relating to the human body and its parts, by recognizing the existence of a property right in the human body, then it would have recognized a new form of property in the human body.[78] Our expectations could

---

77 The connection between property and expectation is not very clear. In a sense, it simply means that property is the basis of certain expectations that the law will protect and enforce. Bentham asserted that: 'Property is nothing but a basis of expectation', Jeremy Bentham, 'Security and Equality of Property', in C.B. Macpherson, ed., *Property: Mainstream and Critical Positions* (Toronto: University of Toronto Press, 1978), at 51. Similarly, Demsetz observed that:

> Property rights are an instrument of society and derive their significance from the fact that they help a man form those expectations which he can reasonably hold in his dealings with others. These expectations find expression in the laws, customs, and mores of a society. An owner of property rights possesses the consent of fellowmen to allow him to act in particular ways. An owner expects the community to prevent others from interfering with his actions, provided these actions are not prohibited in the specifications of his rights.

Demsetz, *supra*, note 42, at 347. In another sense, expectation itself may be regarded as property. John A. Powell, 'New Property Disaggregated: A Model to Address Employment Discrimination' (1990) 24 *U.S.F.L. Rev.* 363, at 366, observed that the law 'has recognized and protected even the expectation of rights as actual legal property'. Similarly, Harris stated: 'Because the law recognized and protected expectations grounded in white privilege (albeit not explicitly in all instances), these expectations became tantamount to property that could not permissibly be intruded upon without consent.' Harris, *supra*, note 13, at 1731. However, Munzer has suggested that an expectation does not amount to property but could be part of the psychological aspects of property. See, Munzer, *supra*, note 6, at 30.

78 Powell, *supra*, note 77, at 374: 'Expectations are an important part of modern property theory.' A case illustrating property protection of expectations is *Local 1330, United Steel Workers v. United States Steel Corp.* (1980) 631 F. 2d 1264. At the pretrial hearing of this case, the District Judge observed as follows:

> Everything that has happened in the Mahoning Valley has been happening for many years because of steel. Schools have been built, roads have been built. [The]Expansion that has taken place is because of steel. And to accommodate that industry, lives and destinies of the inhabitants of that community were based and planned on the basis of that institution…We are talking about an institution, a large corporate institution that is virtually the reason for the existence of that segment of this nation [Youngstown]. Without it, that segment of this nation perhaps suffers, instantly and severely. Whether it becomes a ghost town or not, I don't know. I am not aware of its capability for adapting…But what has happened over the years between U.S. Steel, Youngstown and the inhabitants? Hasn't something come out of that relationship, something that

be based on a mix of socio-economic and political circumstances, and it might be the province of property to identify those expectations that deserve protection.[79] It seems in some cases that when a legal system protects a certain expectation,

out of which – not reaching for a case on property law or a series of cases but looking at the law as a whole, the Constitution, the whole body of law, not only contract, but tort, corporations, agency, negotiable instruments – taking a look at the whole of American law and then sitting back and reflecting on what it seeks to do, and that is to adjust human relationships in keeping with the whole spirit and foundation of the American system of law, to preserve property rights. It would seem to me that when we take a look at the whole body of American law and the principles we attempt to come out with – and although a legislature has not pronounced any laws with respect to such a property right, that is not to suggest that there will not be a need for such a law in the future dealing with similar situations – *it seems to me that a property right has arisen from this lengthy, long-established relationship between United Steel, the steel industry as an institution, the community in Youngstown, the people in Mahoning County and the Mahoning Valley in having given and devoted their lives to this industry.* Perhaps not a property right to the extent that can be remedied by compelling U.S. Steel to remain in Youngstown. But *I think the law can recognize the property right to the extent that U.S. Steel cannot leave that Mahoning Valley and the Youngstown area in a state of waste, that it cannot completely abandon its obligation to that community, because certain vested rights have arisen out of this long relationship and institution* (italics in the original).

Ibid., at 1279–80. Following the above pretrial ruling, the plaintiffs' lawyer amended the claim as follows:

52. A property right has arisen from the long-established relation between the community of the 19th Congressional District and plaintiffs, on the one hand, and Defendant on the other hand, which this Court can enforce. 53. This right, in the nature of an easement, requires that Defendant: a. Assist in the preservation of the institution of steel in that community; b. Figure into its cost of withdrawing and closing the Ohio and McDanold Works the cost of rehabilitating the community and the workers; c. Be restrained from leaving the Mahoning Valley in a state of waste and from abandoning its obligation to that community.

Ibid., at 1280. In rejecting this community property claim, the Court of Appeal held:

Our problem in dealing with plaintiffs' fourth cause of action is one of authority. Neither in brief nor oral argument have plaintiffs pointed to any constitutional provision contained in either the Constitution of the United States or the Constitution of the State of Ohio, nor any law enacted by the United States Congress or the Legislature of Ohio, nor any case decided by the courts of either of these jurisdictions which would convey the authority to this court to require the United States Steel Corporation to continue operations in Youngstown which its officers and Board of Directors had decided to discontinue on the basis of unprofitability…Whatever the future may bring, neither by statute nor by court decision has appellant's claimed property right been recognized to date in this country.

Ibid., at 1280–81.

79 Joseph L. Sax, 'Liberating the Public Trust Doctrine From Its Historical Shackles' (1980) 14 *U.C. Davis L. Rev.* 185, at 186–7: 'The essence of property law is respect for reasonable expectations. The idea of justice at the root of private property protection calls for identification of those expectations which the legal system ought to recognize.'

it elevates it to a status of property.[80] The elevation of certain expectations to the status of property is exemplified by the rationalization of 'whiteness' as property.[81] Some legal race scholars have drawn attention to the connection between race and property.[82] Harris has argued, in the historical context of the USA, that the status of being white conferred some racialized privileges and advantages. Whiteness, she argued, was also the basis of certain expectations of benefits and privilege, which the law directly and indirectly legitimated and enforced.[83] She reasoned that the legal

---

80 Jack L. Knetsch, *Property Rights and Compensation: Compulsory Acquisition and other Losses* (Boston: Butterworths, 1983), at 1, observing with reference to property rights: 'In a sense, entitlements can be considered as expectations of how actions or behaviour will be tolerated or treated. Some expectations receive strong community support and remain almost invariable over time – although specific rights that receive such sanction vary widely among societies – while others are more tentative, and are recognized as being so.'

81 In *Plessy v. Ferguson*, 163 U.S. 537, the plaintiff was a black man (only one-eighth black) but appeared white. The plaintiff was prevented from boarding a 'white' railway car based on the prevailing segregation statute. The plaintiff argued that he possessed a property interest in his reputation of being white. Though the court rather decided the case on constitutional grounds, it nevertheless held that:

> If he (plaintiff) be a white man and assigned to a colored coach, he may have his action for damages against the company for being deprived of his so-called property. Upon the other hand, if he be a colored man and be so assigned, he has been deprived of no property, since he is not lawfully entitled to the reputation of being a white man.

Ibid., at 549. The prevalence of property right claims over whiteness in the nineteenth and early twentieth centuries was noted by Francis J. Swayze 'The Growing Law,' (1915) 25 *Yale L.J.* 1, at 11: 'but the courts have frowned upon the contention that the reputation in the South of belonging to the white race is a right of property.'

82 J. Allen Douglas, 'The "Most Valuable Sort of Property": Constructing White Identity in American Law, 1880-1940' (2003) 40 *San Diego L. Rev.* 881 (tracing the connection between race, reputation and property); Harris, *supra*, note 13; Ariela J. Gross, 'Litigating Whiteness: Trials of Racial Determination in the Nineteenth-Century South' (1998) 108 *Yale L.J.* 109; Harris, *supra*, note 35; Sally Ackerman, 'The White Supremacist Status Quo: How the American Legal System Perpetuates Racism as Seen Through the Lens of Property Law' (1999) 21 *Hamline J. Pub. L. & Pol'y* 137 (suggesting that the idea of whiteness as property was developed from the concept of white supremacy); Patricia J. Williams, 'The Obliging Shell: An Informal Essay on Formal Equal Opportunity' (1989) 87 *Mich. L. Rev.* 2128, at 2145: 'black...and white are every bit as much "properties" as the buses, private clubs, neighborhoods and schools which provide the extra-corporeal battlegrounds of their expression.' Margalynne Armstrong, 'Race and Property Values in Entrenched Segregation' (1998) 52 *U. Miami L. Rev.* 1051; Thomas Ross, 'The Rhetorical Tapestry of Race: White Innocence and Black Abstraction' (1990) 32 *Wm. & Mary L. Rev.* 1.

83 Harris, *supra*, note 13, at 1713–14:

> In ways so embedded that it is rarely apparent, the set of assumptions, privileges, and benefits that accompany the status of being white have become a valuable asset that whites sought to protect and that those who passed (pretended to be white) sought to attain – by fraud if necessary. Whites have come to expect and rely on these benefits, and over time these expectations have been affirmed, legitimated, and protected by the law. Even though the law is neither uniform nor explicit in all instances, in protecting

and social deployment of whiteness in the USA supported underlying assumptions that it was a property right. The point is that certain societal expectations can give rise to property, such as limited property rights in the human body or parts of it. Since societal expectations are not fixed and can change from time to time, property law would remain flexible enough to accommodate those expectations.

The Meaning of Property

The meaning of property,[84] like forms of property, is not constant and changes from time to time in response to changes in the socio-economic circumstances of a particular society. The concept of property does not operate in a social vacuum but is conditioned by the dynamics of a given society.[85] This situation makes a precise and clear definition of property difficult. It seems that C.B. Macpherson's analysis provides a good approach, or starting point, to the definition of property.[86] Macpherson drew a distinction between a layperson's understanding of property as a physical thing and its legal meaning as rights to things: 'In current common usage, property is *things*; in law and in the writers, property is not things but *rights*, rights in or to things.'[87] He suggested that once a particular society acknowledges that a person may have the physical possession of a thing without being the property owner, then that society has defined property as rights and not the thing itself.[88]

---

settled expectations based on white privilege, American law has recognized a property interest in whiteness that, although unacknowledged, now forms the background against which legal disputes are framed, argued, and adjudicated.

84 What I have done here, in relation to the meaning of property, is akin to what R.C. Nolan characterized as a descriptive exercise (descriptions of rights) rather than a justificatory one. See, R.C. Nolan, 'Property in a Fund' (2004) 120 *L.Q.R.* 108. Accordingly, I have not treated at all, or in any detail, common justificatory theories of property, such as the labour theory, the occupation theory, the personhood theory and the economic theory of property. For a justificatory account of property, including those in some of the sources already cited in this chapter, see S. Coval, J.C. Smith and Simon Coval, 'The Foundations of Property and Property Law' (1986) 45 *Cambridge L.J.* 457–75.

85 See, generally, Joseph W. Singer and Jack M. Beermann, 'The Social Origins of Property' (1993) 6 *Can. J.L. & Juris.* 217.

86 Macpherson, *supra*, note 77.

87 *Ibid.*, at 2. Bruce Ackerman similarly observed that: 'If there is anything a lawyer remembers from his legal education, it is that laymen are deeply confused in their property talk; that the law of property concerns itself with bundles of user-rights, not with the awkward idea that things "belong to" particular people.' Bruce A. Ackerman, *Private Property and the Constitution* (New Haven: Yale University Press, 1977), 115. Munzer, *supra*, note 6, at 16.

88 Macpherson, *supra*, note 77, at 3:

As soon as any society, by custom or convention or law, makes a distinction between property and mere physical possession it has in effect defined property as a right. And even primitive societies make this distinction. This holds both for land or flocks or the produce of the hunt which were held in common, and for such individual property as there was. In both cases, to have a property is to have a right in the sense of an enforceable claim to some use or benefit of something, whether it is a right to a share in some common resource or an individual right in some particular things.

Macpherson opined that the conception of property as rights over things was the classical understanding of the term and this meaning of property prevailed up to the late part of the seventeenth century when the layperson's definition of property as a 'thing' emerged.[89] He argued that the misusage of property as the thing itself was due to certain socio-economic factors:

> The change in common usage, to treating property as the things themselves, came with the spread of the full capitalist market economy from the seventeenth century on, and the replacement of the old limited rights in land and other valuable things by virtually unlimited rights. As rights in land became more absolute, and parcels of land became more freely marketable commodities, it became natural to think of the land itself as the property. And as aggregations of commercial and industrial capital, operating in increasingly free markets and themselves freely marketable overtook in bulk the older kinds of moveable wealth based on charters and monopolies, the capital itself, whether in money or in the form of actual plant, could easily be thought of as the property. The more freely and pervasively the market operated, the more this was so. It appeared to be the things themselves, not just rights in them that were exchanged in the market.[90]

It is important to note that in addition to identifying property as rights in things, Macpherson recognized that property rights create and maintain certain relations between people.[91] Accordingly, Macpherson observed:

> We may notice here one logical implication of the definition of property as an enforceable claim: namely, that property is a political relation between persons. That property is political is evident. The idea of an enforceable claim implies that there be some body to enforce it. The only body that is extensive enough to enforce it is a whole organized society itself or its specialized organization, the state; and in modern (i.e., post-feudal) societies the enforcing body has always been the state, the political institution of the modern age. So property is a political phenomenon. That property is a political relation between persons is equally evident. For any given system of property is a system of rights of each person in relation to other persons. This is clearest in the case of modern private property, which is my right to exclude you from something, but is equally true of any form of common property, which is the right of each individual not to be excluded from something.[92]

---

89 Macpherson, *supra*, note 77, at 7:
   In ordinary English usage, at least through the seventeenth century, it was well understood that property was a right in something. Indeed, in the seventeenth century, the word property was often used, as a matter of course, in a sense that seems to us extraordinarily wide; men were said to have a property not only in land and goods and in claims on revenue from leases, mortgages, patents, monopolies, and so on, but also a property in their lives and liberties. It would take us too far afield to try to trace the source of that very wide use of the term, but clearly that wide sense is only intelligible while property *per se* is taken to be a right not a thing.

90 *Ibid.*

91 *Ibid.*, at 1 (observing that property 'creates and maintains certain relations between people'.)

92 *Ibid.*, at 4.

The relational aspect of property is extremely important for communitarian societies where the exchange of gifts or items of property symbolizes the creation of a new relationship, or the fortification of an already existing one. For instance, a marriage relationship in many African communities is crystallized by the payment of a 'bride price'[93] by a man and his family to the family of the woman to be married. The bride price can take the form of money (which is usually the case these days where many economies encourage the use of money as a valuable means of exchange), cattle, palm wine, or other forms of wealth. Upon the payment of a bride price or transfer of property from the suitor to the woman's family, and coupled with the performance of other traditional rites, a new relationship of marriage is created not only between the man and woman but also between their families. Early colonial English judges in many African countries misunderstood this phenomenon and the symbolism of property in the African marital setting. This ignorance resulted in judicial characterization of African marriages as 'wife purchase'.[94] It appears, therefore, that the bundle of rights metaphor captures the instrumentalism of property in some traditional societies and could be used to analyse some of their social institutions. This potential cross-cultural application of the bundle of rights metaphor is evident in Hoebel's analysis of 'ownership' among the traditional Yurok Indian Society in northern California.[95]

Apart from illuminating the distinction between a layperson's conception of property as 'things' and its legal signification as rights to or in things, Macpherson's analysis draws useful attention to the flexibility inherent in the meaning of property as rights.[96] Though clear and useful, Macpherson's definition evinces a conceptual entrapment to the physicality of property, which the modern bundle of rights metaphor tries to disavow.[97] Defining property as rights in, and over, things would presumably require a comprehensive list of 'things' that constitute the criterial objects of property rights. As Munzer aptly observed, 'the idea of property will remain open-ended until one lists the kinds of "things" open to ownership. In a legal system, it will be mainly a descriptive task to compile the list.'[98] Not only does such a list not exist, we do not also have an explanatory model as to what 'things' rightly belong to property and the ones that are outside that category. If, as Macpherson argued, property rights exist in or over things, how then do we talk of property right in one's job (a concept that is gaining currency in employment law) or to the professional qualification of a

---

93 The meaning of this term is culturally dependent and I use it here with some trepidation.

94 See *R v. Amkeyo* (1917) 7 E.A.L.R. 14; *Abdul Rahman Bin Mohamed and Another v. R.* (1963) E.A.L.R. 188. Elsewhere I made a trenchant criticism of these two cases: Nwabueze, *supra*, note 41, at 176–8.

95 E. A. Hoebel, 'Fundamental Legal Concepts as Applied in the Study of Primitive Law' (1942) 51 *Yale L.J.* 951.

96 Macpherson's definition of property bears significant analytical resemblance to the framework adopted by Cohen. See Cohen, *supra*, note 21, at 11–12.

97 Wesley N. Hohfeld, 'Fundamental Legal Conceptions as Applied in Judicial Reasoning' (1917) 26 *Yale L.J.* 710; Wesley N. Hohfeld, 'Some Fundamental Legal Conceptions as Applied in Judicial Reasoning' (1911) 23 *Yale L.J.* 16.

98 Munzer, *supra*, note 6, at 23.

spouse?[99] In the employment context or relationship, there is obviously no referential object of a property right. In the case of a professional qualification or degree, its value lies not in the paper on which the degree is written but in the intangible training and skills acquired over a period of time. Similarly, where lies the object of property in the case of uncrystallized floating charge and, to some extent, a beneficiary's interest in a trust fund?[100]

The limitations inherent in Macpherson's thingification of property rights require further rational justification before their adoption.[101] Otherwise, we would unwittingly be excluding new and emerging forms of property rights that have no reference to things. These types of property, such as wages, professional qualification and genetic information, are increasingly characteristic of our global economy that is knowledge-based. It is important that a definition of property as rights (as Macpherson did) should not be inexorably linked to things; here lies the beauty of the bundle of rights metaphor. Penner, however, has made some spirited attempts to defend the thinghood conception of property, by considering 'things' as part of the essential and distinguishing criteria of property.[102] Though he did not see the need or practicality of devising a list of things of property, he proffered a criterion of thinghood that was optimistically projected to be good for all times.[103] With respect to what he calls 'personality-rich'[104] relationships that are not properly thingifiable, he opined that it is 'the conceptual impossibility of separating particular things from the person who has them, to deliver a free-standing thing that anyone else might just as well "own," that removes them from the realm of things that can be property.'[105] Similarly, Arnold's recent suggestion that a concept of property (which he called a web of interests) needs to capture the physical nature and features of our natural environment provides some conceptual support for Macpherson's definitional framework.[106]

Even if the thinghood doctrine was utterly rejected, the disaggregation of property as rights brings its own wrinkles to the analysis. For instance, which rights are property rights and why are others excluded? If for policy reasons, an employee's right to her job is regarded as a property right, why should we divest human rights and right to the professional qualification of one's spouse of their proprietorial nature? Is a right to marry a property right? What of one's personal rights to one's body? Is

---

99 Further treated in Chapter 2 with illuminating cases.

100 Nolan, *supra*, note 84. Intricacies of the contextual and transformatory nature of the object of property in trust relations are also analysed by Rudden, *supra*, note 38.

101 But various writers are increasingly drawing attention to the thingness of property. For instance, see Thomas W. Merrill and Henry E. Smith, 'What Happened to Property in Law and Economics?' (2001) 111 *Yale L.J.* 357; Arnold, *supra*, note 9; Penner, *supra*, note 1.

102 Penner, *supra*, note 1, at 802–807.

103 'Thus, in respect of what things can be treated as property, "thinghood" is a conceptual criterion: For a thing to be held as property, we must not conceive of it as an aspect of ourselves or our ongoing personality-rich relationships to others.' *Ibid.*, at 807.

104 *Ibid.*, at 804.

105 *Ibid.*, at 805.

106 Arnold, *supra*, note 9.

there a rational distinction between rights of property and non-property rights?[107] Some of these questions underpin understandable frustrations with the bundle of rights picture of property; and the frustrations are so intense as to lead to suggestions that the disaggregation of property has made it a useless tool for moral and political analysis,[108] or that it is a slogan without any internal coherence or logical structure necessary for analysis of real life problems.[109] Paul Kohler, however, has offered some admirable defence of the disaggregation of property.[110] He suggested that current scepticism concerning the complexity and analytical relevance of property is often exaggerated. While he conceded that overly broad definition of a term like property poses conceptual problems, nevertheless, 'it is simply wrong to assert that we have, as yet, reached that point in respect of property'.[111] Kohler opined that it is possible to isolate property from non-property rights by adopting an approach that is intuitive, pragmatic and policy-based. Accordingly, he submitted that: 'Faced with such a pragmatic approach to property there really is no point in offering a characterisation which seeks to transcend that reality. Property is no more than a normative set of relations which might be attached to whatever society deems it necessary or beneficial to make the subject of property.'[112]

The point is that though this book supports the disaggregation of property as an associated bundle of rights, its tendency or potential to consume all other rights smacks of conceptual imperialism. Accordingly, this book suggests that it is possible to analytically deploy the flexibility of property, despite the difficulties to which it is susceptible, to capture new and emerging forms of property, and that the state could regulate property rights granted with respect to such new forms of property. Another point is that if the meaning of property were restricted to a layperson's understanding of the term as referring to things, it would have been difficult to consider the application of property protection to new and non-traditional forms of property.

William Blackstone, in his *Commentaries on the Law of England*, provided another useful definition of property, which underpinned property scholarship for many years.[113] It seems that though Blackstone's definition of property is thing-focused, it arguably makes an implicit (if not explicit) distinction between a 'thing'

---

107 Kenneth Campbell made a more or less successful attempt to proffer a distinction: K. Campbell, 'On the General Nature of Property Rights' (1992) 3 *Kings C.L.J.* 79–97.

108 Thomas C. Grey, 'The Disintegration of Property', in J. Roland Pennock and John W. Chapman, eds, *NOMOS XXII: Property* (New York: New York University Press, 1980).

109 Penner, *supra*, note 1. But see Alan Brudner, arguing that the framework of dialogic community brings internal coherence and unity to property law: Brudner, *supra*, note 27. Similarly, Harris does not seem to share the general scepticism concerning the utility of the concept of property. Accordingly, he locates the essence of property in the interaction of trespassory rules and ownership spectrum. See Harris, *supra*, note 10.

110 Paul Kohler, 'The Death of Ownership and the Demise of Property' (2000) 53 *Current Legal Problems* 237–82.

111 *Ibid.*, at 241.

112 *Ibid.*, at 242–3.

113 Duncan Kennedy, 'The Structure of Blackstone's Commentaries' (1979) 28 *Buffalo L. Rev.* 209; Vandevelde, *supra*, note 19.

and rights exercised with respect to a thing, which qualify as property rights.[114] William Blackstone stated:

> There is nothing which so generally strikes the imagination, and engages the affections of mankind, as the right of property; or that sole and despotic dominion which one man claims and exercises over the external things of the world, in total exclusion of the right of any other individual in the universe.[115]

It is important that Blackstone's definition above should not be misread or misinterpreted. For instance, Blackstone should not be taken to mean that property rights are absolute.[116] Rights of property are usually subject to limitations dictated by the socio-economic and political circumstances of a particular legal system.[117] Through legislation or regulation, governments may limit the exercise of an owner's property rights. Instances include taxation on property, and the power of eminent domain.[118]

Limitations on property rights vary from jurisdiction to jurisdiction. Moral considerations are a significant part of private property limitation, though their impact on the operation of the institution of property rarely receives scholarly consideration or thoughtful reflection from the public.[119] Only a little reflection will reveal that considerations of public morality infuse and underpin the non-propertization of socially valuable resources needed for human flourishing and interdependence, such as air and water. For similar reasons, an owner of private property where a public activity takes place cannot generally exclude the public or a neighbouring landowner from the visual[120] or photographic[121] appropriation of the events thereon. In other words, a spectacle is not property and cannot be owned. The exercise of basic and fundamental freedoms that underscore our humanness and dignity, such as freedom of expression, entail moral limitations on the right of private property owners to curtail expressive activities on their property that take on public features, such as a shopping mall.[122] Jeremy Waldron was, therefore, right when he suggested that the moral reputation of the concept of property determines the type and number of limitations that would be imposed by a regulator.[123]

---

114 For the view that common law has, at least since the sixteenth century, recognized property rights in intangibles, Libling, *supra*, note 68.

115 William Blackstone, *Commentaries on the Laws of England, vol 2* (London: A. Strahan, 1809), at 2.

116 Carol M. Rose, 'Canons of Property Talk, or, Blackstone's Anxiety' (1998) 108 *Yale L.J.* 601. Ackerman, *supra*, note 87, at 97–103.

117 Ely, *supra*, note 31, at 17–25.

118 Cohen, *supra*, note 21, at 21–30.

119 Gray, *supra*, note 46.

120 *Victoria Park Racing and Recreation Grounds Co. Ltd. v. Taylor* (1937) 58 C.L.R. 479.

121 *Sports and General Press Agency Ltd. v. 'Our Dogs' Publishing Co. Ltd.* (1917) 2 K.B. 125.

122 The dissenting judgement in *Harrison v. Carswell* (1976) 62 D.L.R. (3d) 68.

123 Jeremy Waldron, 'Property, Justification and Need' (1993) 2 *Can. J.L. & Juris.* 185, at 188–9.

Considering the various property topics and limited interests in land which Blackstone treated in the two volumes of his *Commentaries on the Laws of England*, he obviously appreciated that ownership is not always united in one individual alone. For instance, A may own the fee simple interest in Whiteacre; B may be a lessee of Whiteacre; and C may be a sub-lessee of Whiteacre; D may have a right of easement over Whiteacre. A, B, C and D all have proprietary interest in Whiteacre but none is absolute. Blackstone's reference to a 'sole and despotic dominion' over an item of property should be understood as referring to an owner's right of alienation which is not dependent on the performance of any social function. Macpherson suggested a similar interpretation, although he was not directly concerned with the Blackstonian definition. According to Macpherson:

> Modern private property is indeed subject to certain limits on the uses to which one can put it: the law commonly forbids using one's land or buildings to create a nuisance, using any of one's goods to endanger lives, and so on. *But the modern right, in comparison with the feudal right which preceded it, may be called an absolute right in two senses: it is a right to dispose of, or alienate, as well as to use; and it is a right which is not conditional on the owner's performance of any social function.*[124] (Italics supplied)

Despite criticisms to which the Blackstonian definition is vulnerable,[125] it brought measurable certainty to the meaning of property and established a criterion for distinguishing property rights from non-property rights, for instance human rights.[126]

An interesting judicial example of the meaning of property, which highlights its flexibility, is the Canadian Supreme Court case of *Harrison v. Carswell*.[127] Although the judgement never mentioned any particular property theory, the minority judgement intuitively considered property from a bundle of rights perspective. The facts of the case were that the Respondent, an employee of a tenant of a shopping centre, lawfully participated in a picket on the sidewalk of the shopping centre, in front of the tenant's premises.[128] The Respondent continued the picketing after being asked not to do so by the owner of the shopping centre and was, therefore, prosecuted under the *Petty Trespasses Act, R.S.M. 1970, c. P-50.* On behalf of the owner of the shopping centre, it was contended that the shopping centre was a private property, even though open to members of the public, and that unauthorized acts

---

124 Macpherson, *supra*, note 77, at 10.

125 For instance, see Vandevelde, *supra*, note 19.

126 The distinguishing criterion is the presence of a 'thing' over which property rights are exercised. Accordingly Grey inquired:

> What, then, of the idea that property rights must be rights in things? Perhaps we no longer need a notion of ownership, but surely property rights are a distinct category from other legal rights, in that they pertain to things. But this suggestion cannot withstand analysis either; most property in a modern capitalist economy is intangible.

Grey, in Pennock and Chapman, *supra*, note 108, at 70.

127 *Harrison, supra*, note 122.

128 *Ibid.*, at 69–70.

amount to trespass.[129] The Respondent was convicted by the County Court, but the Manitoba Court of Appeal set aside the conviction.[130] The Appellant then appealed to the Supreme Court of Canada. The majority judgement, delivered by Dickson, J., stressed the similarity of the case before the court to the previous judgement of the Supreme Court in *R v. Peters*.[131] Following the previous decision in *Peters'* case, the majority allowed the appeal of the shopping centre owner. After a detailed discussion of the rule of judicial precedent, the majority judgement observed:

> Anglo-Canadian jurisprudence has traditionally recognized as a fundamental freedom, the right of the individual to the enjoyment of *property* and the right not to be deprived thereof, or any interest therein, save by due process of law. The Legislature of Manitoba has declared in the *Petty Trespasses Act* that any person who trespasses upon *land*, the *property* of another, upon or through which he has been requested by the *owner* not to enter, is guilty of an offence. If there is to be any change in this statute law, if A is to be given the right to enter and remain on the *land* of B against the will of B, it would seem to me that such must be made by the enacting institution, the Legislature, which is representative of the people and designed to manifest the political will, and not by this court.[132] (Italics supplied)

Judging by the tenor and text of the above quotation, and highlighted by the italics, it appears that the majority largely thought of the property in that case (land and the shopping centre) as a physical thing, the invasion of which was protected by the law of trespass. Of course, it is possible for the reader to give the passage a different interpretation. However, it was the minority judgement delivered by Laskin, C.J.C. that probably came closer to the application of 'property' as a bundle of rights.

Laskin, C.J.C. realized that the court was being asked to apply an old doctrine of property law (trespass) to economic and social circumstances that post-dated it.[133] Apparently recognizing that application of the thinghood conception of property to the facts of that case might lead to the suppression of a lawful activity (picket), Laskin, CJ.C. resorted, at least intuitively, to the flexible conception of property as a bundle of rights. Two quotations seem to make this clearer. First, he began by ascertaining what it was that the shopping centre owner owned, or what was the property that was invaded? He asked: 'What does a shopping centre *owner* protect, for what invaded *interest* of his does he seek vindication in ousting members of the public from sidewalks and roadways and parking areas in the shopping centre?'[134] This semantic formulation seems to suggest that the 'property' of a shopping centre owner amounts to 'interests', rather than the physical structure that constitutes the shopping centre. Another passage seems to support this construction:

---

129 *Ibid.*, at 73.

130 *Ibid.*, at 78.

131 *R v. Peters* (1971) 17 D.L.R. (3d) 128.

132 *Harrison, supra,* note 122, at 83. For a criticism of the majority judgement: J. Colangelo, 'Labour Law: *Harrison v. Carswell*' (1976) 34 *U. of T. Fac. L. R.* 236.

133 *Harrison, supra,* note 122, at 69 and 73.

134 *Ibid.*, at 73–4.

If it was necessary to categorize the legal situation which, in my view arises upon the opening of a shopping centre, with public areas of the kind I have mentioned...I would say that the members of the public are *privileged* visitors whose *privilege* is revocable only upon misbehaviour...or by reason of unlawful activity.[135] (Italics supplied)

It seems that the judgement of Laskin, C.J.C., although not expressly employing any property metaphor, reflects the conception of property as a flexible bundle of rights.[136]

Another Canadian Supreme Court case, which is not directly on point but similar to the facts of *Harrison's* case, is *Committee for the Commonwealth of Canada v. Canada*.[137] In that case, the members of the Respondent (Committee) went to the Montréal airport in Dorval and, by means of leaflets and discussions with members of the public, disseminated the Committee's goals and objectives.[138] The members of the committee were asked to stop their political propaganda by an RCMP officer and the airport's assistant manager, purportedly acting under the relevant airport regulation. The Respondent members brought an action for a declaration that the Appellant had infringed their fundamental freedom of expression. The Respondent members were successful both at the trial court and Court of Appeal. The Appellant appealed to the Supreme Court. The case, however, turned on judicial analysis of a person's charter rights to use a public place for some expressive activity. Nevertheless, Lamer, C.J., in his own contribution, observed that it would be wrong to proceed solely on the basis that since the airport in that case was the government's property, the Appellant had unlimited rights over it.[139] He held that such an approach ignores the fact that the exercise of a freedom of expression needs a physical space.[140] Thus, he held that the function of the court in such situations is to balance the competing interest of the person seeking to communicate and the interest of the government. He, therefore, concluded that 'as a consequence of its special nature, the government's right of ownership cannot itself authorize an infringement of the freedom guaranteed by s. 2(b) of the Charter'.[141] What is interesting, though, is that 'ownership' of the physical structure of the airport did not exhaust property analysis in that case. Because 'property' was probably considered to be in the nature of 'rights', the Supreme Court of Canada was able to conduct the balancing exercise that it did.

Conclusion

Property is an expansive, malleable and flexible concept. It is dynamic and has considerable uses and values. It comes in different forms that continue to change over

---

135 *Ibid.*, at 74.

136 Bruce Welling, *Property in Things in the Common Law System* (Gold Coast, Australia: Scribblers Publishing, 1996), at 3–20.

137 *Committee for the Commonwealth of Canada v. Canada* (1991) 1 S.C.R. 139 (S. Ct.).

138 *Ibid.*, at 158.

139 *Ibid.*, at 154

140 *Ibid.*, at 155.

141 *Ibid.*

time. What is property in one age may cease to be property in another age. Likewise, forms and standards of property may vary from country to country. Changes in technology, economic system, social and political patterns are some of the factors that instigate changes in forms of property or concepts of property. Property also serves useful functions as the basis of expectations.

There are noticeable differences between a layperson's understanding of property and its legal conception. While laypersons see property as things, it is regarded in law as rights to things or a bundle of rights, which create a set of legal relations. As we have seen, the concept of property has now evolved to the point that it is no longer defined only with reference to things. The disaggregation of property is useful for intellectual analysis. It enables valuable interests to be protected by treating them as property rights.[142] This analytical function may be helpful in designing protection for rights relating to the human body and traditional knowledge, without prejudice to other methodological approaches. However, the fragmentation of property as a set of legal relations or as a bundle of rights has its own problems relating to legal certainty.

The bundle of rights perspective of property potentially embraces all rights, including human rights. This generality of property rights makes it difficult to differentiate property rights from non-property rights. The all-embracing nature of property rights potentially leads to conceptual imperialism.[143] In an attempt to free property from the narrowness of the Blackstonian thinghood conception, the bundle of rights perspective has seemingly introduced a limitless flexibility. If we must make a distinction between property rights and non-property rights, then we need to establish some distinguishing criteria. But upon what basis do we make property rights unique or ascertain the uniqueness of property rights? Even when we accept that a right, such as rights relating to dead bodies and body parts, should be treated as a property right on the basis of the bundle of rights conception of property, should there be any limit to the exercise of such rights? Should the limitation be based on public policy or statute or intuition? These questions show that, though this book supports a flexible conception of property as rights rather than things, such a conception is not without difficulties. Accordingly, it is suggested that, despite the difficulties associated with a flexible conception of property as rights, it is a potentially useful tool to analyse emerging and non-traditional forms of property.

---

142 For instance, Dean G. Acheson, 'Book Review' (1919) 33 *Harv. L. Rev.* 329, at 330, observed: 'the all-absorbing legal conception of the (19th) century (was) that of property right. Everything was thought of in terms of property – reputation, privacy, domestic relations – and as new interest required protection, their viability depended upon their ability to take on the protective coloring of property.'

143 As Vandevelde observed: 'This dephysicalization was a development that threatened to place the entire corpus of American law in the category of property. Such a conceptual imperialism created severe problems for the courts.' Vandevelde, *supra*, note 19, at 329.

Chapter 2

Biotechnology and the Property Jurisprudence on the Human Body and Parts

Introduction

Chapter 1 provided an overview of the concept of property. This chapter attempts to apply the concept of property to the area of dead bodies and body parts. Recent developments have brought into bold relief the necessity for re-examination of the legal attitude towards property rights in a corpse and body parts.[1] Some medical researchers in Canada,[2] Australia,[3] Germany[4] and England[5] stand accused of harvesting

---

1   Donna M. Gitter, 'Ownership of Human Tissue: A Proposal for Federal Recognition of Human Research Participants' Property Rights in their Biological Material' (2004) 61 *Wash. & Lee L. Rev.* 257; Roy Hardiman, 'Comment, Toward the Right of Commerciality: Recognizing Property Rights in the Commercial Value of Human Tissue' (1986) 34 *UCLA L. Rev.*, 207, 228; Julia D. Mahoney, 'The Market for Human Tissue' (2000) 86 *Virginia L. Rev.* 163; C.M. Thomas, *Should the Law Allow Sentiment to Triumph Over Science? The Retention of Body Parts* (Auckland: Massey University School of Accountancy Discussion Paper Series 210, 2002).

2   Charlie Gillis, 'Doctor Left Autopsies Unfinished in Halifax: Children's Organs Found in Warehouse', *National Post*, Tuesday, 3 October 2000, A8.

3   Michael Perry, 'Body-Parts Supermarket Causes Uproar in Australia', *National Post*, 20 March 2001, A13; Roger Maynard, 'Row Over Body Parts Erupts in Australia', *The Times*, 2 February 2001.

4   D.T. Tilmann, 'German Prosecutor Investigates the Removal of Dead Babies' Organs' (2000) 320 *BMJ* 77.

5   Stephen White, 'The Law Relating To Dealing With Dead Bodies' (2000) 4 *Medical Law International* 145. In the United Kingdom, some medical researchers at Alder Hey Hospital and Bristol Royal Infirmary retained thousands of organs harvested from deceased infants without the consent of the infants' living relatives. The public disapproval of this incident led to the establishment of a public inquiry chaired by Michael Redfern, QC. Redfern's commission has issued a report, which condemned the practice of obtaining and retaining cadaveric organs without consent. The report was especially critical of the conduct of Professor van Velzen, the pathologist at Alder Hey Hospital, and recommended that Professor van Velzen should not be allowed to practise medicine again. See House of Commons (UK), *The Royal Liverpool Children's Inquiry* (The House of Commons, 2001). Also, the parents of the affected deceased infants have brought a class action for compensation against the accused hospitals. See Clare Dyer, 'Group's Legal Action Launched Over Retained Organs' (2001) 322 *BMJ* 1202. A similar incident occurred in England in 1987. Cyril Isaacs committed

organs and body parts from cadavers without the consent of living relatives. For example, a husband, apparently alleging a property right in the corpse of his wife, brought an action against a research foundation for removing her brain tissues.[6] In another incident, Ashkenazi Jews collaborated with researchers investigating Canavan's disease by providing their bodily tissues and pedigree information.[7] When the research results were subsequently patented, however, the research subjects complained that the patent was unfair and amounted to a conversion of property rights in their bodily tissue.[8] More recently, the director of the UCLA Willed Body Program (Mr Henry Reid) was accused of illegally harvesting cadaver parts and selling them to some biotechnology and pharmaceutical companies, including a subsidiary of Johnson & Johnson, through a middleman named Ernest Nelson.[9] The living relatives have filed claims in court, claiming damages for the desecration and

---

suicide and his brain was retained for mental health research after a post-mortem examination at Prestwich Hospital mortuary. The consent of Cyril Isaacs' family was neither sought nor obtained for the retention of the brain tissue. The UK government commissioned an inquiry into this incident. The inquiry was chaired by Dr Jeremy Metters, Her Majesty's Inspector of Anatomy. Metters' report shows that more than 21,000 brains collected between 1970 and 1999 were still being held at various medical research centres throughout England. The report also found that most of the brains were held for proper diagnostic investigation into the cause of death, but that a smaller number of the brains were retained for medical research and teaching. However, the report found that the consent of living relatives was neither sought nor obtained for the research and educational uses of those brain tissues. See Department of Health, *Isaacs Report: The Investigation of Events that Followed the Death of Cyril Mark Isaacs* (England: The Department of Health, 2003). Pursuant to these scandals, the UK now has a comprehensive legislation dealing with the taking, storage and use of human tissues: *Human Tissue Act 2004, c. 30.*

6   Paul Waldie, 'Husband Sues After Brain Tissue Taken From Dead Wife', *National Post*, 29 January 2000, A13. I am not aware of the present position of this case, despite my efforts to follow it up.

7   Peter Gorner, 'Parents Suing over Patenting of Genetic Test: They Say Researchers They Assisted Are Trying to Profit from a Test for a Rare Disease', *Chicago Tribune*, 19 November 2000, A1.

8   The case, *Greenberg v. Miami Children's Hospital Res. Inst.* 264 F.Supp.2d 1062 (S.D.Fla. 2003) has now been decided by the United States District Court of Florida. The court dismissed the plaintiffs' conversion action on the ground that they made voluntary donations of their genetic samples and familial information without any contemporaneous expectations of return. The court, however, upheld the plaintiffs' claim for unjust enrichment.

9   Alan Zarembo and Jessica Garrison, 'Illegal Profits Drive Trade in Body Parts', *The Seattle Times*, 8 March 2004 (page unknown); Charles Ornstein, 'Sale of Body Parts at UCLA Alleged', Los Angeles Times, 6 March 2004: www.latimes.com/news/local/la-me-ucla6mar06,1,7774556.story?coll=la-home-headlines.

mutilation of the (donated) corpses of their beloved ones.[10] These claims aggressively impugn the general proposition that there are no property interests in corpses.[11]

In contrast to the historic jurisprudence on dead bodies,[12] some current judicial decisions favour the recognition of property rights in the human body and its parts.[13] For instance, in 1992 Judge Cowen of the United States Court of Appeals, Third Circuit, observed: 'human remains can have significant commercial value, although they are not typically bought and sold like other goods…Although remains which are used for these medical and scientific purposes are usually donated, rather than bought or sold, this does not negate their potential commercial value.'[14] Even

---

10 Jean Guccione, 'Body Parts Suit Enters Murky Area of the Law', *Los Angeles Times*, 13 March 2004: www.latimes.com/news/local/la-me-ucla13mar13,1,56360.story?coll=la-home-headlines. The suit was filed on 9 March 2004 in the Superior Court of California (for the County of Los Angeles) and styled: *Beatrice Cohen, et al. v. Johnson & Johnson et al. Case Number BC311865*. In a preliminary ruling delivered by Judge Kuhl on 5 April 2005, the court rejected the defendants' contention that (1) it is not unlawful for the Regents of the University of California to sell, or for a third party to purchase, cadaveric materials for use in education or research; and (2) the Regents are not subject to any constraints in exercising their discretion to sell or otherwise reallocate donors' remains for education or research beyond the document of gift. On the first contention, the court held that while it is true that the relevant California Code does not expressly preclude sale of body parts for research and education, yet not all sales of body parts for education and research are legally permitted. The court demonstrated this with the example of a purchased organ that is used in an organ transplantation experiment. The use of such organ, according to the court, is legally prohibited though it was for education and research. On the second contention, the court held that though the right of a donee of body parts is superior to that of third parties, such rights are nevertheless constrained by limitations in other legal provisions. A copy of the courts preliminary ruling on 5 April 2005 is available on the website of Kiesel, Boucher & Larson, LLP: http://kbla.com/active/ucla.php.

11 The Queensland Law Reform Commission, *A Review of the Law in Relation to the Final Disposal of a Dead Body* (Queensland: Queensland Law Reform Commission, Working Paper No 58, 2004), at 15–19; B. Dickens, 'The Control Of Living Body Materials' (1977) *Uni. of Tor. L. Jour.* 142, at 143.

12 The traditional rule is that there is no property interest in a corpse or parts of it. Paul Matthews argued that it is possible to consider a corpse as a physical object and therefore entitled to the characterization of property, and protection of the law as such: 'Whose Body? People As Property' (1983) 36 *Current Legal Problems* 193. Dickens, however, in a discussion of living body and parts, suggested: 'A better approach, therefore may be to consider the human source as having an inchoate right of property in materials issuing from his body.' *Supra*, note 11, at 183; earlier, he suggested that a property approach might have changed the outcome of cases like *Mokry v. University of Texas Health Science Center at Dallas* 592 S.W. 2d 802 (1975) and *Brooks v. South Broward Hospital District* 32 So. 2d 479 (1975); *supra*, note 11, at 149.

13 Matthews, *supra*, note 12, at 198. But see Randy W. Marusky and Margaret S. Swain, 'A Question of Property Rights in the Human Body' (1989) 21 *Ottawa L. R.* 351–86 (arguing that property rights in the human body should not be recognized by law).

14 *Onyebuchi Onyeanusi v. Pan Am* 952 F. 2d 788, at 792 (1992); this contrasts with the holding of Stamp, J., that, 'it would be a distortion of the English language to describe the living or the dead as goods or materials', in *Bourne v. Norwich Crematorium Ltd.* (1967) All E.R. 576. In the Court of Appeals decision in *John Moore v. The Regents of the University of*

recently, the British Court of Appeals accepted that there are property interests in the human body.[15]

The non-market view of the human body and tissue, without its moral, philosophical[16] and religious underpinnings,[17] has been progressively challenged.[18] Advances in biomedical technology and research have brought the issues of property rights in human bodies and tissues to the forefront.[19] These issues are important to biomedical researchers, as well as society in general.[20]

Governmental agencies have also expressed concerns about how laws creating property interests in dead human bodies and tissue will impact biomedical research.[21] For instance, the US Office of Technology Assessment observed:

California, et al. 249 Cal. Rptr. 494, at 504 (1988), Justice Rothman observed: 'Until recently, the physical human body, as distinguished from the mental and spiritual, was believed to have little value, other than as a source of labor. In recent history, we have seen the human body assume astonishing aspects of value...For better or worse, we have irretrievably entered an age that requires examination of our understanding of the legal rights and relationships in the human body and cell.'

15 *Dobson v. North Tyneside Health Authority* (1997) 1 W.L.R. 596, at 601.

16 For analysis and criticism of the Kantian philosophical approach to the human body and parts of it, see Stephen R. Munzer, 'Kant and Property Rights in Body Parts' (1993) 6 *Can. J.L.& Juris.* 319–41. Munzer later modified his suggestion as to the existence of property rights in body parts. See Stephen R. Munzer, 'An Uneasy Case Against Property Rights In Body Parts', in Ellen Frankel Paul, *et al.*, eds, *Property Rights* (Cambridge: Cambridge University Press, 1994), at 259–86. Peter Halewood, 'Law's Bodies: Disembodiment and the Structure of Liberal Property Rights' (1996) 81 *Iowa L. Rev.* 1331 (blaming liberal philosophy's subject/ object dichotomy for the potential objectification and commodification of the human body).

17 For instance, D.G. Gareth Jones, 'The Human Cadaver: An Assessment of the Value We Place on the Dead Body' (1995) 47 *Perspectives on Science & Christian Faith* 43–51.

18 Margaret Somerville, 'The President, the Prime Minister, the Pope and the Embryo', *National Post*, 21 September 2000, A18 (commenting on the therapeutic and commercial usage of the human embryo and its corollary ethical question); Mahoney, *supra*, note 1 (arguing that propertization and commodification are already part of current social and economic realities).

19 M.T. Meulders-Klein's observations many years ago, that new developments in biomedical technology drive and mediate the rights exercisable over the human body, accurately describe the situation today. Meulders-Klein noted that the debate concerning the extent of right over one's own body is underpinned by an apparent conflict between a person's right to self-determination and the principle of inviolability of the person. This conflict is resolved more or less differently by many countries according to their peculiar socio-economic and legal circumstances, and level of technological development. See M.T. Meulders-Klein, 'The Right Over One's Own Body: Its Scope and Limits in Comparative Law' (1983) 6 *Boston College Int'l. & Comp. L. Rev.* 29–79. See, also, J.-G. Castel, 'Legal Implications of Biomedical Science and Technology in the Twenty-First Century' (1973) 11 *Can. Bar Rev.* 119.

20 Joan M. Gilmour, '"Our" Bodies; Property Rights in Human Tissue' (1993) 8 *Can. J.L. & Soc.* 113, at 113, observing that: 'The decision in Moore is but one example of the range of new legal problems created by the many and rapid advances in biotechnology and of the attempts courts are making to respond.'

21 *Moore v. Regents of the University of California* 249 Cal. Rptr. 494, at 508 (1988).

[There exists an uncertainty about] how courts will resolve disputes between specimen sources and specimen users and the infant biotechnology industry, particularly when the rights are asserted long after the specimen was obtained. The assertion of rights by sources would affect not only the researcher who obtained the original specimen, but perhaps other researchers as well. Biological materials are routinely distributed to other researchers for experimental purposes, and scientists who obtain cell lines or other specimen-derived products, such as gene clones, from the original researcher could also be sued under certain legal theories. Furthermore, the uncertainty could affect product developments as well as research. Since inventions containing human tissues and cells may be patented and licensed for commercial use, companies are unlikely to invest heavily in developing, manufacturing, or marketing a product when uncertainty about clear title exists.[22]

This chapter explores the laws on dead bodies and body parts in historical, modern, and comparative contexts. In addition, it examines how these laws accord with current scientific and economic realities. The second section deconstructs the traditional concepts of property and assesses the suitability of their application to human corpses and body parts. The final section argues that there should be a limited property interest in human corpses and tissue.

Framework of Analysis: Property, Tort, Consent or Human Rights?

This chapter recommends a limited property framework. Legislation is proposed to eliminate some of the incidents of property with respect to corpses and body parts, for instance, the right to sell or transfer cadavers or their parts for value. In other words, this chapter does not suggest the existence of a market in cadavers. It may be wondered why the property framework is still engaged after eliminating some of the rights that constitute the property bundle. For instance, in the case of *Moore v. Regents of the University of California*,[23] the Supreme Court of California, in refusing to uphold the existence of property rights in Moore's excised spleen, reasoned that the relevant legislation in California had so weakened a patient's right of control over his or her excised tissue that whatever rights that remained did not qualify as property rights.[24] This problem will be explored later.

The choice of a property framework is deliberate and strategic, and based on this book's objectives. One of the objectives is to find for potential plaintiffs, complaining of interference with the corpses of their relatives, a strong legal basis

---

22 US Congress: Office of Technology Assessment, New Developments in Biotechnology; Ownership of Human Tissues and Cells, 1987, 27; quoted in *Moore v. Regents of the University of California* 793 P. 2d 479 at 493–4 (1990) (California Supreme Court).

23 *Moore v. Regents of the Univ. of Cal.* 793 P. 2d 479 (1990).

24 *Moore v. Regents, supra*, note 14, at 492: '[t]he statute's (California Health and Safety Code) practical effect is to limit, drastically, a patient's control over excised cells. By restricting how excised cells may be used and requiring their eventual destruction, the statute eliminates so many of the rights ordinarily attached to property that one cannot simply assume that what is left amounts to "property" or "ownership" for purposes of conversion law.'

to have standing in court and obtain the desired judicial remedy.[25] In other words, the property framework that this chapter proposes should be used as a remedial framework, rather than as a basis for an open market in cadavers and body parts. Bernard Dickens seems to make the same point when, in reference to the decision in *Moore v. The Regents of the University of California*,[26] he observed: 'Their judgment could in fact be used as a basis for defending living individuals' property claims in their tissues so as to permit their protection against abuse, although not necessarily for commercial exploitation.'[27]

Other scholars, however, may want to reach the same objectives through other legal categories. Accordingly, Jennifer Nedelsky has observed that the choice of legal categories is strategic and there is nothing in one category that makes it inherently better than the other.[28] Nedelsky's analysis partly answers the question: why not tort, criminal law, constitutional law, or human rights frameworks? The choice of property framework does not mean that it is the only available framework or the best framework to deal with the problems that this chapter highlights.[29] The

---

25 In commenting on the efficacy of a limited property framework with respect to the human body, Jane Churchill observed: 'Under the past and present common law (of Canada), nothing was afforded greater protection than a person's property; one needs only to look at the requirements to prove, and the severity of penalties for, property offences compared to those for offences against the person in the Criminal Code of Canada (Parts IX and VIII, respectively). Since this is the legal system we are attempting to function in, it only seems reasonable to protect what is most precious, the human body, under the classification which affords it the greatest protection – property.' Jane Churchill, 'Patenting Humanity: The Development of Property Rights in the Human Body and the Subsequent Evolution of Patentability of Living Things' (1994) 8 *I.P.J.* 249, at 281.

26 *Moore v. Regents, supra*, note 23.

27 Bernard M. Dickens, 'Morals and Legal Markets in Transplantable Organs' (1994) 2 *Health L.J.* 121, at 126.

28 Jennifer Nedelsky, 'Property in Potential Life? A Relational Approach to Choosing Legal Categories' (1993) 6 *Can. J. L. & Juris.* 343, at 44:

> The choice of a legal category is essentially a strategic choice. There is no one concept, such as property, which is intrinsically appropriate or inappropriate. The choice must be based on judgments about the probable consequences of different concepts and there are various ways of framing those judgments. For example, conventional liberal theory might ask which category will best facilitate individual autonomy. A more 'economic' version would move quickly to the question of which would facilitate exchange and innovation (which are thought in turn to foster autonomy and maximize preferences/utility). Feminists might ask which category is most likely to contribute to the empowerment of women, to mitigate their current systemic subordination – to focus on the ways an enhanced scope of choice for some women may come at the expense of the exploitation of others. Feminists might also focus on the probable effects of a given legal approach on our collective conceptions of motherhood and, more broadly our society's stance toward children – the way they are valued, the understanding of the nature they require, and the priority accorded to that nature.

29 Alexandra George, *Property in the Human Body and Its Parts: Reflections on Self-Determination in Liberal Society* (San Domenico, Italy: European University Institute, 2001), arguing that the language of property, as applied to the human body, obscures certain

regime of property is adopted on the basis of its practical utility compared to the other frameworks.[30] Furthermore, some of the relevant tort remedies, for instance, conversion and detinue, depend on the proof of the existence of a property right.[31]

The tort action for intentional infliction of emotional distress is hedged with so many difficult requirements that it is hardly of any avail to some plaintiffs complaining of interference with their relative's dead body.[32] These requirements include proving physical or monetary loss.[33] In *Lynch v. Knight*,[34] Lord Wensleydale of the British House of Lords observed:

> Mental pain or anxiety the law cannot value, and does not pretend to redress, when the unlawful act complained of causes that alone; though where a material damage occurs, and is connected with it, it is impossible a jury, in estimating it, should altogether overlook the feelings of the party interested.[35]

A person complaining of the desecration or mutilation of a dead relative's body hardly suffers any visible physical injury.[36] Some of these difficulties could be illustrated with the recent decision of the Ontario Superior Court of Justice in *Bastien et al. v. Ottawa Hospital (General Campus) et al.*[37] The plaintiff, in that case, gave birth to premature twins that died shortly after their delivery. Subsequently, the plaintiff permitted the defendants to bury the deceased twins. Unknown to the plaintiff, the defendants buried the twins in a common casket containing the bodies of sixteen

---

fundamental questions arising from liberal philosophy, such as whether individuals should be permitted to trade their body parts if they so desire.

30 Churchill, *supra*, note 25.

31 For instance, *Moore v. Regents of the Uni. Of Cal.*, *supra*, note 23.

32 Cases illustrating this difficulty are examined later.

33 See *Wilkinson v. Downton* (1897) 2 Q.B. 57; *Purdy v. Woznesensky* (1937) 2 W.W.R. 116 (Sask C.A); *Bielitski v. Obadiak* (1922) 65 D.L.R. 627 (Sask. C.A); *Radovski v. Tomm* (1957) 9 D.L.R. (2d) 751 (Man. Q.B); *Clark v. Canada* (1994) 20 C.C.L.T. (2d) 241 (Fed Ct.); *Prinzo v. Baycrest Centre for Geriatric Care* (2002) 215 D.L.R. (4th) 31.

34 *Lynch v. Knight* (1861) 11 All E.R. 854 (H.L.).

35 *Ibid.*, at 863. Paula Giliker, 'A "New" Head of Damages: Damages for Mental Distress in the English Law of Torts' (2000) 20 *Legal Studies* 19–41 (suggesting that the law should allow the recovery of damages for pure emotional distress).

36 In discussing problems relating to the recovery of damages for emotional distress or nervous shock, Estey J. of the Supreme Court of Canada observed in *Guay v. Sun Publishing Co.* (1953) 2 S.C.R. 216, at 238:

> Moreover, it is important to keep in mind what must be proved in order that damages may be recovered, as stated in Pollock on Torts, 15th ed., 37-8, as follows; 'A state of mind such as fear or acute grief is not in itself capable of assessment as measurable temporal damage. But visible and provable illness may be the natural consequence of violent emotion, and may furnish a ground of action against a person whose wrongful act or want of due care produced that emotion…In every case the question is whether the shock and the illness were in fact natural or direct consequences of the wrongful act or default; if they were, the illness, not shock, furnishes the measurable damage, and there is no more difficulty in assessing it than in assessing damages for bodily injuries of any kind.'

37 *Bastien et al. v. Ottawa Hospital (General Campus) et al.* (2002) 56 O.R. (3d) 397.

other deceased infants. The plaintiff discovered this fact when she made inquiries about the disinterment of the twins, eight years after their burial. The plaintiff brought a tort action against the defendants, seeking damages for the infliction of emotional distress. The defendants filed a preliminary objection asking the court to dismiss the plaintiff's action for disclosing no reasonable cause of action. In support of this preliminary objection, the defendants argued that the plaintiff failed to prove any psychiatric injury or damage that would warrant the trial of the case. In dismissing the defendants' objection to the plaintiff's suit, Polowin, J. approved the following observation of Justice Molloy in *Mason v. Westside Cemeteries Ltd.*:[38]

> In tort cases, courts have for the most part refused to award damages for emotional upset unless this has caused physical symptoms or some recognizable psychiatric illness. It has repeatedly been said that grief alone is not compensable in damages...Where damages for mental shock have been awarded, this has tended to be in addition to damages for physical injuries sustained or as a result of somebody having witnessed the injury or death of a loved one...It is difficult to rationalize awarding damages for physical scratches and bruises of a minor nature but refusing damages for deep emotional distress which falls short of a psychiatric condition. Trivial physical injury attracts trivial damages. It would seem logical to deal with trivial emotional injury on the same basis, rather than by denying the claim altogether. Judges and juries are routinely required to fix monetary damages based on pain and suffering even though it is well-known that the degree of pain is a subjective thing incapable of concrete measurement. It is recognized that emotional pain is just as real as physical pain and may, indeed, be more debilitating. I cannot see any reason to deny compensation for the emotional pain of a person who, although suffering, does not degenerate emotionally to the point of actual psychiatric illness. Surely emotional distress is a more foreseeable result from a negligent act than is a psychiatric illness.

The *Bastien* and *Mason* cases suggest that some Canadian courts are prepared to sustain a cause of action for the infliction of emotional distress, probably resulting from an interference with a corpse, even when there is no visible physical harm.

A human rights framework is arguably inapplicable to dead bodies.[39] For instance, in *Silkwood v. Kerr-McGee Corp*, the court held that 'the civil rights of a person cannot be violated once that person has died'.[40] This makes it difficult to bring an action for interference with a dead person's constitutional rights to privacy[41] and dignity. As with privacy, the framework of consent is obviously inapplicable to dead bodies. Consent can only be given by, or on behalf of, living persons. Though the law

---

38 *Mason v. Westside Cemeteries Ltd.* (1996) 135 D.L.R. (4th) 361, at 379–80.

39 Bernard Dickens, *supra*, note 27, at 126: 'It is uncertain whether human rights have a posthumous dimension, because human rights may attach to human beings rather than to their remains and estates.'

40 *Silkwood v. Kerr-McGee Corp.* 637 F. 2d 743, at 749 (1980).

41 With respect to privacy, Hartz, J., in *Smith v. Artesia* 108 N.M. 339, at 341 (1989), observed: '[t]he right protected by the action for invasion of privacy is a personal right peculiar to the individual whose privacy is invaded. The cause of action is not assignable, and it cannot be maintained by other persons such as members of the individual's family, unless their own privacy is invaded along with his...We also note that no special rule provides relatives with a right of privacy in the body of a deceased person.'

on consent can provide some protections in the case of interference with the body of a living person, there are difficulties in the use of a consent framework where a body part is already excised from the body. This is mainly due to the fact that consent does not provide a continuing control over an excised body part. The complexities in this area are further examined in Chapter 4. Similarly, remedies under criminal law may not be sufficient.[42] In some legal systems, such as Canada, criminal law provides some statutory protection to dead bodies.[43] The British common law also makes it a criminal offence (misdemeanour) to disinter a dead body, and recent English decisions show that there could be a theft of scientifically preserved cadavers. These criminal protections are considered later. It suffices to say that the protections given by criminal law vindicate the interest of the state as the repository of public interest. Criminal law does not usually grant the type of compensation and other civil remedies available in a civil suit.

Some constitutional law protections that could be extended to dead bodies are available only on proof of a property interest in a dead body. For instance, the 14th Amendment of the US Constitution provides that no state shall 'deprive any person of life, liberty, or property, without due process of law', and the 5th Amendment provides that no 'private property be taken for public use, without just compensation'. Some cases alleging that interference with dead bodies amounted to deprivation of rights secured under the 14th Amendment of the US Constitution failed for failure to prove a property interest in a corpse.[44] These cases are analysed later.

The limited property framework suggested in this chapter may potentially be applicable in the organ donation context and could be used to argue for increased supply of organs needed for transplantation.[45] It is emphasized, however, that this chapter is not particularly concerned with problems arising in the area of organ transplantation, or intended to design an appropriate framework that can boost the

---

42 Under the general common law no-property rule, a person cannot be charged with theft of a corpse.

43 For instance, see section 182 of the *Criminal Code* (*Criminal Code, R.S.C. 1995, c. C-46*): '182. Every one who (a) neglects, without lawful excuse, to perform any duty that is imposed on him by law or that he undertakes with reference to the burial of a dead human body or human remains, or (b) improperly or indecently interferes with or offers any indignity to a dead human body or human remains, whether buried or not, is guilty of an indictable offence and liable to imprisonment for a term not exceeding five years.' Canadian cases interpreting this section include: *R v. Ladue* (1965) 4 C.C.C. 264 (Yukon Territory C.A.); *R. v. Mills* (1992) M.J. No. 505 (Man. C.A.)

44 For a good analysis of constitutional claims relating to dead bodies: Michael H. Scarmon, 'Brotherton v. Cleveland: Property Rights in the Human Body – Are the Goods Oft Interred with their Bones' (1992) 37 *South Dakota L. Rev.* 429.

45 For instance, Christopher Gates, 'Property in Human Tissues: History and Possible Implementations' (1998) 4 *Appeal* 32–43 (supporting the use of a property framework to increase the supply of organs for transplantation). See also, Dickens, *supra*, note 27; Bernard M. Dickens, 'Living Tissue and Organ Donors and Property Law; More on Moore' (1992) 8 *J. Contemp. H. L. & Pol'y* 73–93.

supply of organs.[46] Nevertheless, the limited property framework that this chapter proposes may be of assistance to a living donor who claims that his or her donated organ was mistreated or deliberately given to a person not designated as the recipient. In this context property serves as a framework against abuse of bodily integrity, rather than as a foundation for a market in body parts.[47]

Historical Background of the No-Property Rule in Dead Bodies

A historical sketch of the no-property rule in dead bodies is necessary to appreciate the recent changes in case law on the subject and the various suggestions outlined in this chapter.

United Kingdom

Before the early nineteenth century, British common law recognized a property interest in dead bodies.[48] Old British cases held that a creditor could arrest the body of a deceased debtor for debts owed.[49] Forbearance of the arrest was sufficient consideration for a contract.[50] These cases demonstrate that the British regarded a corpse as property. However, in *Jones v. Ashburnham*[51] Lord Ellenborough C.J. condemned the practice as being contrary to 'every principle of law and moral feeling'.[52] By the mid-nineteenth century, it was reasonably settled that a dead body was not property that could be arrested in execution of a debt or judgement.[53]

---

46 For some of the debates in this area: Madhav Goyal, *et al.*, 'Economic and Health Consequences of Selling a Kidney in India' (2002) 288 *JAMA* 1589–93; David J. Rothman, 'Ethical and Social Consequences of Selling a Kidney' (2002) 288 *JAMA* 1640–41; Richard M. Boyce, 'Organ Transplantation Crisis; Should the Deficit be Eliminated Through Inter Vivos Sales?' (1983) 17 *Akron L. Rev.* 283–302; Marvin Brams, 'Transplantable Human Organs: Should their Sale be Authorized by State Statutes?' (1977) 3 *Am. Jour. L. & Med.* 183–95; Keith N. Hylton, 'The Law and Economics of Organ Procurement' (1990) 12 *Law & Policy* 197–224; Clifton Perry, 'Human Organs and the Open Market' (1980) 91 *Ethics* 63–71; C.R. Stiller and C. Abbot, 'What Will Increase the Number of Organs for Transplantation? Some Strategies to Consider' (1994) 150 *Can. Med. Assn. J.* 1401; Lloyd R. Cohen, 'Increasing the Supply of Transplant Organs; The Virtues of a Futures Market' (1989) 58 *George Washington Law Review* 1–51; Henry Hansmann, 'The Economics and Ethics of Markets for Human Organs' (1989) 14 *Journal of Health Politics, Policy, and Law* 57–85; Calvin Lantz, 'The Anencephalic Infant as Organ Donor' (1996) 4 *Health L. J.* 179-95. Dickens, *supra*, note 27.

47 Dickens, *supra*, note 27, at 126, stated: 'A tissue donor may accordingly retain some property-based rights of control over separated tissues, for instance to influence their use for the purpose for which they were given and ensure that the intended recipient obtains the chance to benefit from the donation.'

48 *Quick v. Coppleton* (1803) 83 E.R. 349; *R v. Cheere* (1825) 107 E.R. 1294.

49 *Cheere, ibid.*, at 1297.

50 *Quick, supra*, note 48, at 349.

51 (1804) 102 E.R. 905.

52 *Ibid.*, at 909.

53 *R v. Francis Scott* (1842) 114 Eng. Rep. 97.

Consequently, in *R v. Fox*[54] the court issued a mandatory injunction against a correctional officer, compelling the release of a prisoner's corpse detained for an alleged debt.[55] The point is that those cases, which upheld the arrest of dead bodies of deceased debtors, are rationally and legally justifiable on the basis of the existence of a property interest in corpses. Otherwise, why were the bodies arrested?

While the provenance of the subsequent no-property rule in dead bodies cannot be traced with certainty,[56] some points are clear. The establishment of Christianity in England favoured burial in consecrated grounds rather than in caves or city outskirts.[57] The Ecclesiastical Courts assumed complete jurisdiction over dead bodies and applied canon law, that is, a religious law, as the substantive law. Property jurisdiction was mainly vested in common law courts. As a result, the common law of England, formed in non-ecclesiastical courts, did not have the opportunity to develop comprehensive rules on dead bodies.[58] Common law's jurisdiction and control over dead bodies started to take significant shape only by the middle of the nineteenth century, partly due to the increase in the practice of burial in unconsecrated grounds.[59]

Despite the no-property rule, the common law, however, offered some criminal law protection for buried and unburied bodies in unconsecrated grounds.[60] Under the common law, it was a misdemeanour to exhume a dead body, even for honourable reasons, without the authority of a court.[61] It was also a misdemeanour to prevent the burial of a corpse.[62] For that purpose common law recognized a duty on certain persons, that is, executors, administrators, occupiers of buildings, and next of kin, to bury a deceased person.[63] Beyond this, the common law did not provide any civil remedy to relatives of a deceased person for the indignities that might be inflicted

---

54 *R v. Fox* (1841) 114 E. R. 95.

55 *Ibid.*, at 96.

56 Skegg traced the no-property rule to Coke's Institutes, first published in 1644, but doubted the accuracy of Coke's statement on the existence of the no-property rule in dead bodies: P.D.G. Skegg, 'Human Corpses, Medical Specimens and the Law of Property' (1975) 4 *Anglo-American Law Rev.* 412.

57 *John Andrews v. Thomas Cawthorne* (1744) 125 E.R. 1308; *Gilbert v. Buzzard* (1820) 161 E.R. 761. It appears that cremation was a prevalent mortuary practice in medieval England in the fifth and sixth centuries AD. Subsequently, the practice of cremation lapsed, only to resurface in the late nineteenth and early twentieth centuries. See Howard Williams, 'Death Warmed Up: The Agency of Bodies and Bones in Early Anglo-Saxon Cremation Rites' (2004) 9 *Journal of Material Culture* 263–91.

58 *Phillips v. Montreal General Hospital* (1908) XIV La Revue Legale 159.

59 Skegg, *supra*, note 56, at 414.

60 Alec Samuels, 'Whose Body is it Anyway?' (1999) 39 *Med. Sci. Law.* 285–6.

61 *R v. Lynn* (1788) 100 Eng. Rept. 394, at 394–5; *R v. Sharpe* (1857) 169 Eng. Rep. 959, at 959.

62 *R v. Feist* (1858) 169 E.R. 1132; *R v. Hunter* (1974) 1 Q.B. 95; Michael Hirst, 'Preventing the Lawful Burial of a Body' (1996) *Crim. L. Rev.* 96.

63 *R v. Stewart* (1840) 113 E.R. 1007. Some Canadian cases have also observed that instead of allowing rights in corpses, the Canadian law imposes duties on certain persons, for instance, executors and administrators, towards a corpse. See *Abeziz v. Harris Estate* (1992) O.J. No. 1271 (O.C.G.D.); *Saleh v. Reichert* (1993) O.J. No. 1394 (O.C.G.D.).

upon a corpse.[64] The right, actually a duty, of the next of kin to possession of a corpse for the purpose of burial is a significant one, and is judicially enforceable.[65] Judicial enforcement of this right indirectly produces a result obtainable under a property rule. For instance, the next of kin can recover a corpse or parts of it from a person unlawfully in possession.[66] There is, however, no judicial remedy where lawful possession is lost by a person who has no duty of burial.[67] Only a property rule would mitigate the harshness of such outcomes. The right of possession for the purpose of burial is also of no avail with respect to interferences with cadaver organs and tissues used as anatomical specimens in medical schools.[68]

The common law no-property rule in dead bodies, despite its obvious shortcomings, is most clearly espoused by W. Blackstone who said, '[t]hough the heir has a property interest in the monuments and escutcheons of his ancestors, yet he has none in their bodies or ashes; nor can he bring any civil action against such as indecently at least, if not impiously, violate and disturb their remains, when dead and buried'.[69] Although William Blackstone has been criticized for his etymological quibbling about the Latin word 'cadaver',[70] his proposition articulated a rule that lasted more than 200 years and settled many cases in the United Kingdom.[71] Recently, this has been diluted by a significant exception introduced by the English Court of Appeal in *Dobson v. North Tyneside Health Authority*,[72] and *R v. Kelly*,[73] to the effect that an application of scientific skill and labour on a corpse or a part of the body transforms it into an object of property capable of being owned or stolen. This exception is more fully explored later in this chapter.

Statutorily, the United Kingdom has been active in this field since 1752 with pieces of legislation that directly or indirectly deal with property issues in the body. These statutes include the *Anatomy Act, 1752*,[74] *Anatomy Act, 1984*[75] (which

---

64 *Williams v. Williams* (1882) 20 Ch. D. 659, at 663–4.

65 Robert A. Brazener, 'Liability in Damages for Withholding Corpse from Relatives' 48 *A.L.R* (3d) 240 (1973).

66 I included parts of a corpse within the rubric of the next of kin's right of possession because the right of possession includes the right of the next of kin to receive the corpse the way it was when life left it.

67 Skegg, *supra*, note 56, at 418.

68 *Ibid.*, at 418. Though such cases are likely to be covered by statutory provisions, and the emerging exception that the application of scientific work and skill on a corpse or its parts translates to a property right.

69 W. Blackstone, *Commentaries on the Laws of England, Vol.2.* (Chicago: The University of Chicago Press, 1979), at 429.

70 21 *American Law Reports* 2d 472, at 480.

71 For example, *Williams v. Williams* (1882) 20 Ch. D. 659; *R v. Sharpe* (1857) 169 E.R. 959; P.D.G. Skegg, 'The No-Property Rule and Rights Relating to Dead Bodies' (1997) 5 *Tort L. Rev.* 222.

72 (1997) 1 W.L.R. 596.

73 (1998) 3 All E.R. 741. Also *AB v Leeds Teaching Hospital NHS* (2005) 2 W.L.R. 358 (Q.B.D.)

74 *Anatomy Act, 1752 (U.K.) 25 Geo. 11, c.37, vol. 20.*

75 *Anatomy Act, 1984, c.14.*

replaced the *1832 Anatomy Act*), *Human Tissue Act, 1961,*[76] *Corneal Tissue Act, 1986,*[77] *Human Organ Transplant Act, 1989,*[78] *Human Fertilization and Embryology Act, 1990,*[79] and the *Human Tissue Act, 2004.*[80] Chapter 3 attempts an analytical and comparative examination of the property implications of some of the above statutes. What is noticeable, though, is that legislation in this field has largely arisen in response to scandals that animated them.

Take for instance the *Anatomy Act of 1752*. It was a legislative response to the prevalent murderous violence of the era. The legislation sought to forestall murder by creating a supplementary sentence of dissection, so that a person sentenced to death for murder would have his or her body submitted to a medical school for dissection. It seems to be the first instance of legislative objectification of the body in the United Kingdom. The *Anatomy Act of 1832* (now 1984) was a statutory reaction to another scandal, the infamous acts of body-snatchers and resurrectionists in the eighteenth and nineteenth centuries. The Act tried to undermine the cadaver trade by establishing a gift-oriented framework for the supply of bodies for dissection. The *Human Tissue Act (1961)* responded to the need for more effective supply of body tissues or organs for medical education and training, and the *Human Organ Transplant Act* sought to address the potentially scandalous market in transplantable body organs. Within that genre is the new *Human Tissue Act (2004)*, which is a direct legislative response to Alder Hey and related scandals that rocked the United Kingdom in the early twenty-first century. They involved the non-consensual harvesting and retention of body organs of deceased children. The implication of this parochial legislative preoccupation is that, while immediate problems arising from a specific scandal were dealt with by the relevant legislation, broader issues or problems were left unattended in any principled, logical or theoretical manner. The *Human Tissue Act, 2004* is a good example of such a response, although this is not the place for a detailed study of the provisions of the Act and their far-reaching implications.[81]

The Alder Hey scandal in 2000–2001 galvanized the British public and brought enormous negative attention to the practice of medicine and medical research which the profession was happy to avoid since the end of resurrectionism. The debate that ensued was understandably laden with emotion, and the travails of the parents of the deceased children were, quite rightly, treated with a high degree of sensitivity, care and understanding. The medical profession, taking it in a broader sense, played the role of the guilty and was not quite forthcoming in protesting suggested policy moves that would be detrimental to the practice of medicine and medical research.[82]

---

76 *Human Tissue Act, 1961, c. 54.*

77 *Corneal Tissue Act, 1986, c.18.*

78 *Human Organ Transplant Act, 1989, c. 31.*

79 *Human Fertilization and Embryology Act, c.37.*

80 *Human Tissue Act, 2004, c. 30.*

81 For a good analysis of the Act: Kathleen Liddel, *et al.*, 'Beyond Bristol and Alder Hey: The Future Regulation of Human Tissue' (2005) 13 *Med. Law Rev.* 170.

82 Note that some professional medical bodies and individual practitioners made useful contributions to the debate. See, for instance, Colin Roberts, 'Human Tissue Act 2004 and Medical Microbiology' (2004) 126 *RCPath Bulletin* 23–6; Royal College of Physicians of

As a result, the initial Bill that preceded the *Human Tissue Act* was mainly victim-oriented,[83] though the final Act tried to strike an appropriate balance.

The *Human Tissue Act of 2004* is a comprehensive legislation that repealed all the statutes mentioned above, except the *Human Fertilization and Embryology Act, 1990*, but recast their provisions in a single statute, making for a more harmonized and consistent framework.[84] The Act deploys the framework of consent and makes it a criminal offence to take, remove, store and use a human tissue or cadaver for a scheduled purpose without appropriate consent.[85] The scheduled purposes include anatomical examination, determination of the cause of death, public display of cadavers, post-mortem determination of the efficacy of drug or treatment, obtaining scientific or medical information about a living or deceased person which may be relevant to any other person, transplantation, and research in connection with disorders, or functioning of the human body.[86] However, consent is not required for the storage and use of residual tissues obtained in the course of treatment or diagnosis if the storage and use are in connection with a research that is ethically approved, and the identity of the donor is safeguarded.[87] Storage and use of residual tissues (that is, from living persons) do not also require consent if it is in connection with clinical audit, education or training relating to human health, performance assessment, public health monitoring and quality assurance.[88] The Act made detailed provisions relating to consent, substitute consent, and attendant penalties for non-compliance.[89] The Act established a regulatory authority, the Human Tissue Authority, to oversee the operation of the legislation and with responsibility for licensing and drawing up codes of practice in relation to various issues dealt with in the legislation.[90] The *Human Tissue Act* left beyond cavil its preference for a consent framework to a property regime.[91] In fact, property right to the human body was only mentioned once in the Act, s. 32(9), in relation to prohibition on commercialization of transplantable materials. Section 32(9) exempts from that prohibition bodily materials that were the subject of scientific skill and labour. This is a statutory incorporation of the judicially crafted exception in *R v. Kelly*.

Edinburgh, *Comments on DOH: The Removal, Retention and Use of Human Organs and Tissue; the Law in England and Wales*, posted on www.rcpe.ac.uk/news/consultation_docs/removal_human_organs.html (last accessed on 17 December 2004); Paul van Diest and Julian Savulescu, 'For and Against: No Consent Should be Needed for Using Leftover Body Material for Scientific Purposes' (2002) 325 *BMJ* 648–51.

83 S. Dewar and P. Boddington, 'Returning to the Alder Hey Report and its Reporting: Addressing Confusions and Improving Inquiries' (2004) 30 *J. of Med. Ethics* 463–9.

84 *Human Tissue Act, 2004, c. 30*, s. 57, schedule 7.

85 *Ibid.*, s. 1.

86 *Ibid.*, schedule 1, part 1.

87 *Ibid.*, s. 1(7)(8).

88 *Ibid.*, s. 10.

89 *Ibid.*, ss. 2–7

90 *Ibid.*, ss. 13–29.

91 Cambridge Genetics Knowledge Park and the Public Health Genetics Unit, *A Critique of the Human Tissue Bill: A Discussion Paper* (CGKP, 2004); Department of Health, *Proposals for New Legislation on Human Organs and Tissue* (London: DOH, 2003).

In an illuminating essay, the chairperson of the Retained Organs Commission, established in the wake of the Alder Hey scandal, gave useful insights into the rejection of a property framework which, according to her, appeared to be only superficially attractive.[92] She reasoned that a property framework would import the language of ownership, enabling people to talk of owning, in a full property and market sense, the corpse of their child, spouse, relative, or parts of their bodies. Accordingly, she thought that: 'If my relative's body is *mine*, be she child, mother, or sister, I may do with my property as I wish. I may elect to sell her component parts in public auction. I may donate her for display as a plastinated exhibit.'[93] Though Professor Brazier recognized the legal certainty and other advantages that a property framework confers, she regretted that it 'authorises not just a right to say NO but grants untrammelled rights of disposal to the "owner"'.[94] I regret that these are insufficient reasons for the rejection of a property approach despite its enormous advantages. Although Professor Brazier was legitimately worried about the consequences of a property approach, the incidence of a market need not be the inexorable outcome of a property rule. The argument in this book is that a property framework could be structured to eliminate a market in body parts or cadavers. That is why this book proposes a limited but market-inalienable type of property right in the body, which is explored further at the end of this chapter.

One of the consequences of avoiding a property regime and tailoring the *Human Tissue Act, 2004* to specifically meet the needs of the Alder Hey scandal is that potential problems relating to a patient's right to share in the proceeds of research utilizing his or her body tissues remain unaddressed by the new Act. The problem arose in the USA in the case of *Moore v. Regents of the University of California*,[95] and despite the rejection of a property approach by the majority of the Supreme Court of California in *Moore's* case, the debate is still open and the law continues to evolve in the USA. A similar debate in the UK is hardly resolvable on the basis of consent under the new Act and the opportunity to do so which the legislation presented was, pitiably, not brought to fruition. Perhaps the UK needs another scandal of *Moore's* proportion to directly confront the need of vesting a patient or donor with a limited property right in the body that would facilitate the award of appropriate and sufficient judicial remedy.

Canada

Canada, like Great Britain, has its own tales of grave-robbing or body-snatching. Grave-robbing in Canada was significantly accentuated with the establishment of

---

92 Margaret Brazier, 'Organ Retention and Return: Problems of Consent' (2003) 29 *J. Med. Ethics* 30–33.

93 *Ibid.*, at 32.

94 *Ibid.*

95 *Moore v. Regents of the University of California* 793 P. 2d 479 (1990, Supreme Court of California decision).

Canada's first medical school in Montreal in 1822.[96] An interesting and peculiar aspect of the history of anatomy in Canada is that grave-robbing was largely carried out, not by professional resurrectionists, but by medical students who were doubly motivated by the allure of the science of anatomy and surgery, and the need to sufficiently fund their medical education from the filthy lucre of their horrible trade.[97] Grave-robbing suffered near extinction in Canada by the end of the nineteenth century due to the establishment of a legislative mechanism allowing medical schools access to dead bodies of the destitute in public institutions.[98] Though ethically and morally problematic, Canada was not the only country that conscripted dead bodies of the poor and socially oblivious to the service of medicine.[99] Gareth Jones estimated that even after 100 years of the passage of the *Anatomy Act* in England, more than 95 per cent of cadavers for dissection came from institutions housing the poor, such as workhouses and asylums.[100] Similar public institutions were a major source of cadavers for medical schools in New Zealand.[101]

Although Canada, like most other common law countries, was politically dependent on Britain, it did not have state-established ecclesiastical courts.[102] This provided an opportunity to adopt a radical and different approach to the British law that was formulated in the context of an ecclesiastical jurisdiction. The opportunity was not seized, however, as some court rulings in Canada remained faithful to the English no-property rule. For example, in *Davidson v. Garret*,[103] (decided by the Divisional Court, High Court of Justice, Ontario, and probably the first Canadian case on the subject) the plaintiff brought an action for damages against some practising physicians for conducting an unauthorized dissection on his deceased wife's body.[104] The defendants claimed justification for the act, on the authority of a post-mortem direction given orally by the coroner.[105] Though the case turned on the legality of the oral direction given by the coroner, and whether it legally justified the trespass to the plaintiff's home, Meredith, C.J. nevertheless held *in obiter*:

> The action of the plaintiff, as presented in the pleadings, at the trial, and in the argument before us, is one of trespass *quare clausum fregit*, and the cutting and mutilating of the dead body of the plaintiff's wife are alleged in aggravation of the damages which the plaintiff seeks to recover for the alleged trespass, probably because, according to the law of England as introduced into this Province, there is no property in a dead body, and a trespass cannot be committed in respect of it.[106]

---

96 Royce MacGillivary, 'Body-Snatching in Ontario' (1988) 5 *Can. Bull. Med. Hist.* 51–60; Francis Deepa, 'Bodysnatching in Canada' (2001) 164 *JAMC* 530.

97 *Ibid.*

98 MacGillivary, *supra*, note 96.

99 Jones, *supra*, note 17.

100 *Ibid.*

101 *Ibid.*

102 *Phillips v. Montreal Gen. Hosp.* XIV (1908) La Revue Legale 159, at 164; *Miner v. C.P.R.* (1911) Alta. L.R. 408, at 413.

103 (1899) 5 C.C.C. 200.

104 *Ibid.*, at 202–203.

105 *Ibid.*, at 203.

106 *Ibid.*, at 202–203.

Similarly, in *O'Connor v. City of Victoria*,[107] three plaintiffs brought an action in trespass against the City of Victoria for authorizing, without the consent of the plaintiffs, the disinterment and reburial of bodies in plots belonging to the plaintiffs, in order to make room for a road construction. Hunter, C.J. held that only two of the plaintiffs with title to the burial plot were entitled to succeed. Consequently, he dismissed the action of the third plaintiff. He further held that the successful plaintiffs were entitled to punitive damages, because the trespass involved an interference with human remains.

The above cases show that earlier Canadian decisions on the topic largely adopted the approach of trespass to land, because of the general rule that there is no property in a corpse. In those cases, the mutilation or interference with a corpse was only regarded as a factor aggravating the damages awarded for trespass to land. Trespass to land remained the main cause of action. The major limitation of this approach is that while the owner of a burial plot can easily prove a claim, other relatives of the deceased without title to the burial plot, but who were nevertheless aggrieved by the interference, would not succeed. That was exactly why one of the plaintiffs failed in *O'Connor's* case. The absurdity of the trespass framework and no-property rule is accentuated if we imagine a scenario where the burial plot belongs to a complete stranger to the deceased's family. Absent a trespass claim by the plot owner in the event of mutilation of the deceased buried therein, are we to hold that the deceased's spouse, parent, child or relative has no cause of action? It is in this connection that the judicial recognition of possessory and custodial rights over a corpse (considered below) has become very meaningful.

Possession and Custody Rights In 1930, in *Edmonds v. Armstrong Funeral Home*,[108] the Alberta Supreme Court accepted the British no-property rule with its narrow exception for possession and custody rights for burial.[109] In *Edmonds*, the undertaker, who was hired by the plaintiff to bury his wife, conspired with surgeons to harvest organs from the body of the corpse.[110] Harvey, C.J.A. approvingly referred to, and accepted,[111] the British decisions upholding the no-property rule. However, the court held that the defendants' acts were an interference with the plaintiff's right of custody and possession in his deceased wife's body for burial.[112]

In contrast, Quebec adopted a contrary rule, recognizing the existence of a property right in a dead body.[113] This emanates from the decision in *Phillips v.*

---

107 *O'Connor v. City of Victoria* (1913) 11 D.L.R. 577 [BCSC].

108 *Edmonds v. Armstrong Funeral Home* (1931) D.L.R. 676.

109 *Ibid.*, at 680.

110 *Ibid.*, at 681.

111 *Ibid.*, at 679–80.

112 *Ibid.*, at 680. See, also, *Hunter v. Hunter* (1930) 65 O.L.R. 586, at 594, noting that: 'The Law as to who has the right to the possession of a dead body for the purposes of burial, as distinguished from the question of upon whom a duty of burial devolves, may not be entirely well-settled.'

113 *Phillips* (1908) XIV La Revue Legale, at 165 (holding that a widow had a cause of action against a defendant who performed an unauthorized autopsy on her deceased husband's

Montreal General Hospital,[114] where a widow of the deceased claimed damages against the defendant for conducting an unauthorized autopsy on the deceased's body.[115] Davidson, J., in *Phillips*, confined the English decisions to their historical context[116] and sought guidance from the more revolutionary US cases on point.[117] The court observed:

> There is marked sterility of discussion, or even reference, as respects this subject in the French books. I do not account for the cause of this. *The Pandectes Belges vo.* 'cadaver' contains an interesting collaboration on the subject. It can be seen, according to this authority, that under the civil law a person may, during his life, dispose of his remains in whole or part, so long as the disposition does not offend against public order or police regulations. Thus, he might will his body to a school of anatomy. Gentry left his heart to the town of Lille. Judicial operation was given in 1823 to the legacy. In the absence of personal directions, the remains are the property of the family, just as is the body of an animal.[118]

Damages A similar radical approach was taken in the Alberta case of *Miners v. C.P.R.*[119] The plaintiff brought an action against the defendant for damages for mental distress, arising from the defendant's negligence in delaying delivery of the corpse of the plaintiff's son.[120] The defendant contracted to transport the corpse from British Columbia to Alberta.[121] The plaintiff's tort action for negligent infliction of emotional distress was based on the mistreatment of a corpse. The defendant argued that the plaintiff had no cause of action, because there was no property interest in a corpse and that the damage alleged by the plaintiff was not legally recognizable.[122] The trial judge, Beck, J., extensively reviewed the old English authorities on the point and concluded that they were based on weak precedent and juristic authority.[123] The court found the absence of ecclesiastical jurisdiction in Canada as further ground to depart from the English decisions.[124] Consequently, the court held 'the law recognises [a] property [interest] in a corpse…'[125] and, therefore, awarded both special and general damages to the plaintiff.[126] On appeal, however, the court addressed the issue of whether general damages for mental distress were permitted.[127] The court set aside

---

body). It appears that the property interest in a corpse recognized in *Phillip's* case does not carry the full incidents of property, such as the right to sell a corpse.

114 (1908) XIV La Revue Legale 159.
115 *Ibid.*
116 *Ibid.*, at 164.
117 *Ibid.*
118 *Ibid.*, at 165.
119 (1910) 3 Albt. L.R. 409.
120 *Ibid.*
121 *Ibid.*, at 409.
122 *Ibid.*
123 *Ibid.*, at 409–13.
124 *Ibid.*, at 413.
125 *Ibid.*, at 414.
126 *Ibid.*, at 417.
127 *Ibid.*, at 418.

the award of general damages for mental distress, on the ground that it was not accompanied by any physical harm.[128]

Recovery of damages for mental distress resulting from the mistreatment of a corpse is often a huge litigational hurdle that many plaintiffs fail to cross. As in *Miner's* case, the plaintiffs in *McNeil v. Forest Lawn Memorial Services Ltd*[129] failed to recover damages for mental distress suffered by them when the defendant, a funeral director, negligently failed to afford the plaintiffs a view of their deceased daughter's body before it was cremated, contrary to agreement between the parties. Notwithstanding that the mental distress in *McNeil's* case was reasonably foreseeable and was accompanied by a nominal pecuniary loss, Gould, J. of the British Columbia Supreme Court held that such claims were not legally compensable.

In *Mason v. Westside Cemeteries*,[130] however, an Ontario court held that damages were recoverable, even in the absence of physical harm.[131] In *Mason*, the defendant negligently lost urns containing the cremated remains of the plaintiff's parents.[132] The plaintiff successfully claimed damages in both bailment and negligence, but only nominal damages were awarded.[133] The case provided a useful insight into the court's treatment of the no-property rule. Though the court affirmed the general British rule that there was no property interest in a dead body,[134] the court found in favour of bailment. As the learned judge rightly stated,[135] bailment is a legal cause of action that seeks to redress the plaintiff's property rights in a thing in possession of a bailor.[136] Consequently, a bailment cause of action does not aid a plaintiff, except when a property right is implicated.[137] In finding for the plaintiff on bailment, the judge paradoxically or implicitly accepted the existence of a property right in a corpse or human remains.[138]

As illustrated, while some Canadian courts remain faithful to the British no-property rule, it does not justify arguing that the Canadian decisions reflect an unquestioning and unwavering application of the British rule.

---

128 *Ibid.*, at 419–422.
129 *McNeil v. Forest Lawn Memorial Services Ltd* (1976) 72 D.L.R. (3d) 556 [BCSC].
130 (1996) 135 D.L.R. (4th) 361.
131 *Ibid.*, at 379–380.
132 *Ibid.*, at 364.
133 *Ibid.*, at 382.
134 *Ibid.*, at 368.
135 *Ibid.*, at 367.
136 *Ibid.*, at 369.
137 *Ibid.*, at 367.
138 As the court noted:

> At first blush it may seem odd to apply the principles of bailment to a situation involving the burial of a dead person's remains in a cemetery. One does not normally think of a cemetery owner as being the bailee of all of the bodies buried in the cemetery. On reflection, however, I have come to the conclusion that there is a relationship of bailment created in these situations.

Ibid., at 368.

Criminal Statutes   Apart from the civil law protections given to a dead body, Canada has a well-defined criminal law provision intended to protect the dignity of a corpse.[139] Section 182 of the *Canadian Criminal Code*[140] states:

182 Every one who

   a. neglects, without lawful excuse, to perform any duty that is imposed on him by law or that he undertakes with reference to the burial of a dead human body or human remains, or

   b. improperly or indecently interferes with or offers any indignity to a dead human body or human remains, whether buried or not, is guilty of an indictable offence and liable to imprisonment for a term not exceeding five years.[141]

Although this section does not literally or expressly refer to the prevention of burial, which is a misdemeanour under common law, the terms are broad enough to cover cases of preventing burial.[142] This linguistic construction is more apparent and compelling when the next of kin, who is entitled to the disposition of the corpse, prevents burial. In that case, it is a clear breach of duty under Section 182(a).[143] Problems of interpretation arise when a third party, who owes no duty to the corpse,[144] prevents burial. Preventing the burial of a deceased person is an interference and indignity to a human corpse under Section 182(b).[145] It seems that the common law offence of preventing burial, with all its ambiguous elements,[146] is inapplicable in Canada because it has been statutorily supplanted.

Section 182(a) also addresses the infraction of voluntary obligations towards a corpse. A complete stranger with no relationship whatsoever to a corpse might be convicted under the section if she voluntarily undertook to bury a corpse but failed to do so or did it indecently. In *Queen v. Newcomb*,[147] the accused was the biological father of a deceased infant female child. Because the deceased child was considered illegitimate under the prevailing law, the accused was not under any legal duty towards the corpse. The child, however, died in the house of another person (who legally had the duty of burial) and the accused undertook to possess her body for the purpose of burial. Unfortunately, the accused wrapped the body in a blanket and threw it into a bush, leaving it on the surface of the ground. The court held that the burial was grossly indecent and that the accused also breached the duty of burial which he had voluntarily assumed. Thus, the accused was convicted under

---

139 *Criminal Code, R.S.C, 1985, c. C-46.*

140 *Ibid.*

141 *Ibid.*

142 *Ibid. R v. Hunter* (1974) 1 L.R.Q.B. 95, at 98.

143 *Ibid.*

144 As in *R v. Hunter* (1974) 1 Q.B. 95, where the accused persons, as friends of the deceased and all under 20 years old, hid the deceased's body after she died in the course of horseplay.

145 *Criminal Code, supra*, note 139, Section 182(b).

146 Michael Hirst, 'Preventing the Lawful Burial of a Body' (1996) *Crim. L. Rev.* 96 (discussing some of the ambiguities of the common law offence of preventing burial).

147 *Queen v. Newcomb* (1898) 2 C.C.C. 255 [County Court].

both limbs of Section 206 of the *Criminal Code, 1892*, the predecessor of current Section 182.

It is useful to point out that while Section 182(a) is directly concerned with criminal omissions towards a corpse, such as intentional and malicious omission by an executor to bury a corpse, Section 182(b) addresses acts of indignity towards a corpse. It is difficult to state precisely what amounts to indignity to a dead body. The circumstances of some cases, however, would be too clear on the question of indignity to a corpse to merit any serious analysis. For instance, in *R v. McKenzie*,[148] the accused confessed to killing a 12-year-old girl by running her over in his van. The accused burnt the deceased infant's body in a pit and threw the remains off a bridge. He was charged and convicted for manslaughter and interference with human remains. The Alberta Court of Appeal confirmed the conviction on both counts. In *R v. Ladue*,[149] the accused was charged under Section 167(b) of the *Criminal Code* (now Section 182(b)) for having sexual intercourse with a dead woman. The accused alleged in his defence that he was too drunk to know that the woman was dead and he thought that the woman was only unconscious. On appeal against his conviction by the High Court, the Court of Appeal proceeded on the assumption that the acts alleged against the accused came within the meaning of an 'indignity' to a corpse. Accordingly, the Court of Appeal decided to focus on the question of whether the appropriate *mens rea* was established. It held that knowledge that the body was dead was not a specific ingredient of the offence (because the fact of death would be generally obvious), and that it was enough to establish an intentional interference with a body that was in fact dead. In holding that proof of general criminal intent is sufficient for conviction under the section, the Court of Appeal observed that the accused's admission of rape in his defence (by believing that he was having sex with a living but unconscious woman) ensured his conviction.

Other cases of indignity to a corpse might, in contrast to the above, not be so clear-cut. In *R v. Mills*[150] the question was whether the collapse of a coffin in the course of, or immediately after, backfilling a grave amounted to an indignity to a corpse if it was proved that damage to the coffin itself was intentional. Though the High Court considered the act to come within the terms of Section 182(b), the Court of Appeal disagreed, holding that while intent to damage the coffin could be inferred, that would not amount to offering indignity to a corpse.[151] Helper, J.A, in his dissenting judgement, gave useful insights into the concept of indignity towards a corpse. He opined that indignity to a corpse would embrace 'acts of abuse, defilement or callous disrespect'.[152] The Supreme Court of Canada disagreed with the majority of the Court of Appeal and restored the High Court judgement (and that of the minority of the Court of Appeal), holding that the accused's conduct amounted to offering an indignity to a corpse.[153]

---

148 *R v. McKenzie* (2001) A.J. No. 1540 [ABCA].
149 *R v. Ladue* (1965) 4 C.C.C. 264 [CA].
150 *R v. Mills* (1992) M.J. No. 505 (CA).
151 *Ibid.*
152 *Ibid.*
153 *R v. Mills* (1993) 4 S.C.R. 277 (SCC).

The Supreme Court of Canada in *R v. Moyer*[154] further interpreted Section 182(b).[155] The accused, a white supremacist and neo-Nazi, committed indignities to corpses buried in a Jewish cemetery.[156] This was done by taking photographs depicting a simulated urination on one of the gravestones and an exhibition of a male genital organ on another gravestone.[157] The accused argued that the standard under Section 182(b) was not met because the indignity resulted from a photographic depiction without physical interference with the buried corpses.[158] Lamer, C.J. dismissed this argument, holding that although physical interference was a sufficient element of the offence, it was not necessary for its commission.[159] The Chief Justice also considered it immaterial that the indignity was offered to the gravestones marking the remains, instead of the remains themselves. The court did, however, emphasize that there must be human remains beneath the gravestone. Thus, if a gravestone were erected some distance from the human remains, any indignity toward such a gravestone would not amount to an offence under the section.[160]

One need not share the distinction between a gravestone under which there are human remains and that without human remains. In rejecting the element of physical interference, however, *Moyer* provided significant legal protection to the dead and the feelings and memories of the living. The distinction *Moyer* sought to draw did not reflect the apparent legislative intention that indignities deliberately and consciously committed on corpses should be punished. Where a wilful contempt is present, it should not matter that a gravestone was only artificially erected or simulated by the perpetrator of such indignities.

It should also be mentioned that under *The Coroners Act RSC 1980, c. 93*, a coroner has lawful possession of the dead body of a person who died in suspicious circumstances. The possession is for coronial inquisition and, for that purpose, the coroner may order exhumation of a corpse already buried. The coroner can also order a post-mortem examination of unburied corpses. Such lawful exercise of authority by a coroner does not amount to abuse of, or interference with, a dead body; neither does it give living relatives a civil cause of action.[161]

United States of America

From the beginning, US courts openly showed their aversion to the British no-property rule, because of its conceivable injustice to a plaintiff whose dead relative's body was the object of abuse or desecration by a defendant. Most US courts have made advantageous use of their non-ecclesiastical history, which was traditionally used as a basis for rejection of the ecclesiastically influenced British rule. The US

---

154 (1994) 2 S.C.R. 899.

155 *Ibid.*, at 907–909.

156 *Ibid.*, at 902.

157 *Ibid.*, at 902–903.

158 *Ibid.*, at 900.

159 *Ibid.*, at 907.

160 *Ibid.*, at 908–909.

161 *Sheng v. Ontario (Ministry of the Solicitor General and Correctional Services)* (1997) O.J. No. 3535 [CA].

courts of equity assumed jurisdiction with respect to dead bodies and were prepared to grant relief.[162] Consequently, a probate court did not have jurisdiction to entertain an action on interment and re-interment of a dead body because a corpse 'forms no part of the estate'[163] of a deceased person.

In *Ritter v. Couch*,[164] the court made a forceful declaration representative of the US judicial sentiment and aversion to the British rule:[165]

> The dogma of the English ecclesiastical law, that a child has no such claim, no such exclusive power, no peculiar interest in the dead body of its parent, is so utterly inconsistent with every enlightened perception of personal right, so inexpressibly repulsive to every proper moral sense, that its adoption would be an eternal disgrace to American jurisprudence.

The US courts were challenged in finding a legal basis to grant a remedy. Confusion, inconsistent approaches and legal fictions demonstrate the severity of this problem in numerous US cases on the subject.[166] The best practicable, and analytical, approach is to treat the various routes adopted by US courts under some general categories. For example, a remedy based on trespass to land presented no problem because it usually involved the desecration of the corpse of a plaintiff's relative, which was buried in, or lay on, land owned by the plaintiff or to where the plaintiff had some recognizable title.[167]

Claims Based in Tort   A widely used method relating to dead bodies was claims based in tort.[168] Most claims relating to dead bodies were formulated in tort. Tort claims, however, lacked consistency. This resulted in five distinct causes of action: intentional infliction of emotional distress,[169] intentional mishandling of a dead body,[170] abuse of a dead body,[171] negligent infliction of emotional or mental distress,[172] and negligent or wrongful interference with a dead body.[173]

---

162 *Home Undertaking Co. v. Joliff* 19 P. 2d 654, at 656 (1933); *Glatzer v. Dinnerman* 59 A. 2d 242, at 243 (1948).

163 *Fischer's Estate v. Fischer* 117 N.E. 2d 855, at 858–9 (1954). *Finn v. The City of New York* 335 N.Y.S. 2d 516, at 520 (1972). But such jurisdiction is now statutorily given to a probate court in Illinois: *In Re Estate of Medlen* 677 N.E. 2d 33, at 36 (1997).

164 *Ritter v. Couch* 76 S.E. 428, at 430 (1912).

165 *Ibid.*, at 430.

166 Michelle B. Bray, 'Note, Personalizing Personality: Toward a Property Right in Human Bodies' (1990) 69 *Tex. L. Rev.* 209, at 220.

167 *Meagher v. Driscoll* 99 Mass 281 (1868); *Thirkfield v. Mountain View Cemetery Assn.* 41, at 564 (1895).

168 Radhika Rao, 'Property, Privacy, and the Human Body' (2000) 80 *B.U.L. Rev.* 359, at 386.

169 *Jaynes v. Strong-Thorne Mortuary Inc.* 954 P. 2d 45 (1997).

170 *Culpepper v. Pearl Street BLDG. Inc.* 877 P. 2d 877 (1994).

171 *Carney v. Knollwood Cemetery Assn.* 514 N.E. 2d 430 (1986).

172 *Janicki v. Hospital of St Raphael* 744 A. 2d 963 (1999); *Wallin v. University of Cincinnati Hospital* 698 N.E. 2d 530 (1998); *Green v. Southern Transplant Service* 698 So. 2d 699 (1997).

173 *Ramirez v. HPSA* 972 P. 2d 658 (1998).

The first three causes of action are similar, requiring a plaintiff to prove outrageous, wilful or wanton conduct by the defendant before liability can be attached.[174] The plaintiff is also required to show that he or she was the immediate focus of the defendant's outrageous conduct.[175] In other words, the plaintiff must be aware of the defendant's outrageous conduct.

These requirements make these causes of action unattractive to a plaintiff. For example, some courts held that the requirements were not met when the defendant's conduct was merely negligent,[176] where the alleged desecration was done in execution of a public policy embodied in a statute,[177] or where the defendant had atoned for his wrongdoing by pre-litigation compensation to the plaintiff.[178] As a result, a plaintiff offended by the abuse of the dead body of a relative was left without a remedy, even though a remedy was theoretically available in US jurisprudence. Under negligent infliction of emotional distress, there is no comprehensive protection to a plaintiff.[179] To recover for this tort, some US jurisdictions require that damages for emotional distress be accompanied by a contemporaneous physical or pecuniary loss.[180] Because a plaintiff, complaining of the desecration of a dead relative's body, rarely suffers a physical harm or pecuniary loss,[181] he or she was left at the mercy of this anomalous rule.[182] While some jurisdictions allowed recovery without proof of physical and pecuniary loss, they often limited the class of potential plaintiffs by imposing the 'Bystander's rule', which, in part, required a plaintiff to witness injury to a third party.[183]

Because there is no uniform practice among US courts on the matter,[184] a plaintiff has to ascertain whether his or her jurisdiction recognizes such a remedy. If not,

---

174 *Christensen v. Superior Court* 820 P. 2d 181, at 202 (1991).

175 *Ibid.*, at 202–203. This requirement is ably criticized by Mosk, J., at 204.

176 *Culpepper v. Pearl Street BLDG. Inc.* 877 P. 2d 877, at 883 (1994).

177 *Ramirez v. HPSA* 972 P. 2d 658 (1998); *Wallin v. University of Cincinnati Hospital* 698 N.E. 2d 530 (1998).

178 *Jaynes v. Strong-Thorne Mortuary Inc.* 954 P. 2d 45 (1997).

179 *Criswell v. Brentwood Hospital* 551 N.E. 2d 1315, at 1318 (1989).

180 *Sanford v. Ware* 60 S.E. 10 (1950); *Criswell v. Brentwood Hosp.* 551 N.E. 2d 1315 (1989).

181 Except in cases like *Sanford v. Ware* 60 S.E. 10 (1950), where the plaintiff, in addition to mental distress, incurred additional expenses in engaging another undertaker to carry out the re-interment of her deceased husband.

182 In *Allen v. Jones* 163 Cal. Rptr. 445 (1980), the defendant negligently lost in transit the remains of the plaintiff's deceased brother. The court held that the plaintiff could recover for mental distress unaccompanied by any physical harm. In a trenchant criticism of the distinction between damages accompanied by physical loss and others not so accompanied, Justice Gardner observed that the 'distinction is not only gossamer, it is whimsical'. *Ibid.*, at 451. Also, *Mason, supra*, note 38.

183 *Janicki v. Hospital of St Raphael* 744 A. 2d 963, at 973–4 (1999); *Christensen v. Superior Court* 820 P. 2d 181, at 209 (1991).

184 As Eggleston, J. observed in *Sanford v. Ware, supra*, note 180, at 12–13:

When we reach the question as to whether mental pain or suffering is a proper element of damages in such cases [that is, desecration of a corpse] the courts are in hopeless conflict. Upon the principle, prevailing in some jurisdictions, that mental pain and

he or she might be left without a remedy. Thus, a cause of action based on the negligent infliction of emotional distress hardly provides a plaintiff with adequate remedy. Therefore, plaintiffs have sought alternative recourse by way of legal fiction of quasi-property.[185]

Concept of Quasi-Property in a Dead Body Due to the difficulties inherent in tort claims, plaintiffs and US courts often resorted to the concept of quasi-property in a corpse. Many times, the intent is to avoid the requirements of proving wilful or wanton conduct by the defendant, or the similar problem of proving accompanying physical or pecuniary loss.

The concept of quasi-property is an ingenious invention by the US courts to help a deserving plaintiff. It is a legal fiction.[186] It has no relationship with property in the ordinary sense of that word.[187] The concept of quasi-property is a judicial contrivance that provides a legal basis for judicial remedy.[188] It does not mean that a plaintiff has property interest in a corpse in the traditional sense of property right.[189] Rather, the concept of quasi-property merely embodies the next of kin's sepulchral rights, which do not sound in property, such as the right to possession and custody of the corpse for burial.[190] It also gives a right to determine the time, place and manner of burial, and the right to have the deceased delivered to the next of kin in the same way as it was when life left it.[191]

---

suffering alone do not constitute a basis for the recovery of substantial damages, some courts deny a recovery for mental suffering, unaccompanied by pecuniary loss, where the wrongful act of the defendant amounts to mere negligence. Others take the opposite view. In a third class of cases a recovery is allowed for mental pain and suffering alone resulting from a wrongful act which is willful or wanton or amounts to gross negligence.

185 *Carney v. Knollwood Cemetary Assn* 514 N.E. 2d 430, at 434 (1986).

186 *Ibid.*, at 434–5.

187 *Scarpaci v. Milwaukee County* 292 N.W. 2d 816 (1980); *Pierce v. Proprietors of Swan Point Cemetery* 14 Am. Rep. 667 (1872).

188 In *State v. Powell* 497 So. 2d 1188, at 1192 (1986), Overton, J. referred to the concept of quasi-property as a:

[d]ubious 'property right' to the body, [vesting] usually in the next of kin, which did not exist while the decedent was living, cannot be conveyed, can be used only for the one purpose of burial, and not only has no pecuniary value but is a source of liability for funeral expenses. It seems reasonably obvious that such 'property' is something evolved out of thin air to meet the occasion, and that it is in reality the personal feelings of the survivors which are being protected under a fiction likely to deceive no one but a lawyer.

189 *Ibid.*, at 1192.

190 *Whitehair v. Highland Memorial Gardens* 327 S.E. 2d 438, at 441 (1985); *Diebler v. American Radiator and Standard Sanitary Corporation* 92 N.Y.S. 2d 356, at 358 (1949).

191 For more detailed analysis of the concept of sepulchral rights: R.N. Nwabueze, 'The Concept of Sepulchral Rights in Canada and the U.S. in the Age of Genomics: Hints from Iceland' (2005) 31 *Rutgers L. & Tech. L.J.* 217.

The concept of quasi-property has been used in both a jurisdictional and remedial sense.[192] It has proven to be a handy jurisdictional device to grant standing to a plaintiff.[193] A strict application of the British no-property rule denies standing where a plaintiff does not suffer any detriment by the desecration of property he or she has no right to. In *Ritter v. Couch*, the US quasi-property concept recognizes that a plaintiff has an analogous property interest in a dead body that, if desecrated, would give him or her standing.[194] In *Ritter v. Couch*, the plaintiffs objected to the defendant's acquisition of an old cemetery containing their relatives' burial sites.[195] Since the plaintiffs did not pay for the burial plots and merely had a licence to bury their relatives there, the defendant contended that the plaintiffs had no standing.[196] The court, using the quasi-property concept, held that the plaintiffs had standing. According to the court, 'while a dead body is not property in the strict sense of the common law, it is a quasi property, over which the relatives of the deceased have rights which our courts of equity will protect'.[197]

The use of the quasi-property concept occurs more in the remedial context.[198] This concept is usually a last resort when a plaintiff's tort claim fails for the reasons already given. Thus, in *Blanchard v. Brawley*,[199] the court held that Louisiana law did not allow recovery of damages on account of a third party's injury[200] and instead resorted to the general rule of quasi-property to find for the plaintiffs.[201] The remedial or substantive use of the concept was also evident in most of the cases already cited. The concept of quasi-property may not, however, provide a remedy for a plaintiff in some circumstances. Arguably, this concept avails only the closest next of kin with the result that a more distant relative (for example, a grandchild) is denied standing.[202] In some jurisdictions, standing has been recognized for more distant relatives, as in *Carney v. Knollwood Cemetery Assn*.[203] While some US courts have

---

192 *Whitehair, supra*, note 190, at 440–41.

193 *Ibid.*, at 438.

194 *Ritter*, 76 S.E., at 428.

195 *Ibid.*, at 428–9.

196 *Ibid.*, at 429.

197 *Ibid.*, at 430.

198 *Blanchard v. Brawley* 75 So. 2d 891, at 893 (1954).

199 *Ibid.*

200 *Ibid.*, at 893.

201 *Ibid.*

202 *Carney v. Knollwood Cemetery Assn* 514 N.E. 2d 430, at 433 (1986). Compare *Christensen v. Superior Court* 820 P. 2d 181 (1991), where the majority held that a funeral service contract was made for the benefit of all family members, not just the contracting family member, with the exception of unborn family members or those who were not aware of the decedent's death or the nature of the funeral contract. Consequently, the majority held that all the family members for whose benefit a funeral service contract was made were entitled to or had standing to sue for the negligent infliction of mental distress as a result of the desecration of a deceased relative's body. However, Justice Kennard, at 206, was prepared to limit the right of standing to only those family members statutorily entitled to control the disposition of a deceased relative. Other family members, according to Justice Kennard, would have to show that they witnessed the deceased's desecration: at 207, 213.

203 *Ibid.*, at 434–6.

shown the greatest accommodation to a plaintiff, using the quasi-property concept, others have refused to resort to the concept when the plaintiff is required to show pure ownership or a right of possession, as in actions for conversion or detinue. In such cases, the quasi-property concept is stripped of its fictional property characteristics, and reduced to its sepulchral signification.[204]

For instance, in *Crocker v. Pleasant*,[205] the plaintiffs asserted an infringement of their due process right under the 14th Amendment of the United States Constitution and failed. The constitutional infringement alleged by the plaintiffs was that the defendant buried the plaintiffs' son without any notification to the plaintiffs. The court held that the plaintiffs did not have property interest in the corpse of their son and, therefore, were not deprived of their right under the 14th Amendment of the US Constitution.[206] Similarly, in *Keyes v. Konkel*,[207] the plaintiff's possessory claim of a relative's dead body, allegedly detained by an undertaker, also failed.[208] Montgomery, J. observed that, 'no return of the property can be ordered in case of the replevin of a dead body',[209] and that the concept of quasi-property did not apply to 'damage to the corpse as property, but damage to the next of kin by infringement of his right to have the body delivered to him for burial'.[210] Also, in *Culpepper v. Pearl Street BLDG. Inc.*,[211] the plaintiffs used the concept to argue conversion of their son's corpse due to mistaken cremation by the defendant.[212] The court rejected 'the fictional theory that a property right exists in a dead body that would support an action for conversion'.[213]

US courts also found the quasi-property concept unfavourable in an organ donation context because it subjects organ procurement officers to liability in circumstances that vitiate the 'gift of life' laws.[214] In *Green v. Southern Transplant Service Inc.*,[215] the plaintiff's quasi-property claim was upheld even though it involved harvesting

---

204 *Ritter*, 76 S.E. 428; *Blanchard*, 75 So. 2d 891; *Carney*, 514 N.E. 2d 430; *Crocker v. Pleasant* 727 So. 2d 1087 (1999); *Keyes v. Konkel* 78 N.W. 649 (1899); *Culpepper v. Pearl St. Bildg., Inc.* 877 P. 2d 877 (1994) (these cases show how the concept of quasi-property was stripped of its fictional characteristics).

205 727 So. 2d 1087 (1999).

206 *Ibid.*, 1089.

207 78 N.W. 649.

208 *Ibid.*

209 *Ibid.*

210 *Ibid.*

211 877 P. 2d 877, at 882 (1994).

212 *Ibid.*, at 880.

213 *Ibid.*, at 882.

214 *Ramirez v. HPSA* 972 P. 2d 658 (1998); *State v. Powell* 497 So. 2d 1188 (1986); but in the same circumstance, a similar claim was held to be constitutionally valid in *Brotherton v Cleveland* 923 F. 2d 477 (1991), *Whaley v. Saginaw Co.*, 941 F. Supp. 1483 (1996), and *Dampier v. Wayne County* 592 N.W. 2d 809 (1999). However, Klein, J., in *Crocker v. Pleasant* 727 So. 2d 1087, at 1089 (1999), held that the ratio in *Brotherton's* case, *supra*, was contrary to the holding in *Powell's* case. For a criticism of *Brotherton's* case, see Micahel H. Scarmon, 'Brotherton v. Cleveland: Property Rights in the Human Body – Are the Goods Oft Interred with their Bones' (1992) 37 *South Dakota L. Rev.* 429.

215 698 So. 2d 699 (1997).

the deceased's bone and tissue for transplantation.[216] Unlike in *Ramirez v. Health Partners of S. Ariz.*,[217] where the defendants merely went beyond the plaintiff's authorization to harvest additional tissue,[218] the plaintiffs in *Green's* case did not give authorization and the defendants did not plead immunity under the *Uniform Anatomical Gift Act*.[219]

In conclusion, much as most US court decisions are revolutionary in their use of the quasi-property concept as a significant basis for US law on dead bodies, the quasi-property concept does not offer comprehensive protection to a plaintiff. The continuing debate on this subject and its potential solutions tend to obviate the defects present in the current tort-based causes of action. As such the suggested solution found in the *American Restatement of Law 2d, Torts, 274*, becomes relevant.[220]

American Restatement of Law 2d, Torts Section 868 of the Restatement sets out the cause of action for interference with dead bodies and provides:

Interference with Dead Bodies

One who intentionally, recklessly, or negligently removes, withholds, mutilates or operates upon a body of a dead person or prevents its proper interment or cremation is subject to liability to a member of the family of the deceased who is entitled to the disposition of the body.[221]

This proposed section condenses all tort and quasi-property forms of action into a single cause of action.[222] This section, however, renounced the onerous requirements associated with actions already discussed. For example, a plaintiff seeking damages for negligent infliction of emotional distress due to desecration of a dead relative's body could file a suit under Section 868, which would not require proof of a contemporaneous physical or pecuniary loss, or wilful and wanton conduct by the defendant, or the existence of a quasi-property right to the corpse.[223] *Wallin v. University of Cincinnati Hospital*[224] tends to suggest that the traditional requirements associated with a tort action on dead bodies are not part of Section 868 of the American Restatement. Although Section 868 was a lethal weapon for plaintiffs, it was not a statute and did not bind the courts.[225] Additionally, Section 868 represented a minority view, especially when applied in an organ donation context,

---

216 *Ibid.*, at 701.

217 *Ramirez*, 972 P. 2d at 658.

218 *Ibid.*, at 660.

219 *(1987) 8A U.L.A.* 19.

220 *American Restatement (Second) of Torts: Interference with Dead Bodies § 868* (Minn.: American Law Institute Publishers, 1982), at 274.

221 *Ibid.*

222 *Ibid.*

223 *Ibid.*

224 698 N.E. 2d 530, at 531 (1998) (holding that an action under Section 868 of the American Restatement does not require proof of a contemporaneous physical or monetary loss).

225 *Ramirez v. HPSA* 972 P. 2d 658, at 665 (1998).

or where its application would be onerous on a defendant whose conduct was almost without reproach.[226] The result was that in the rejected cases, the courts still required the plaintiff to prove the onerous requirements under the causes of action already discussed.[227]

Section 868 also restricted recovery and standing to 'a member of the family of the deceased who is entitled to the disposition of the body'.[228] Under present priority rules in the United States, the surviving spouse, in the absence of the deceased's direction, has the right of disposition against other members of the deceased's family.[229] Where the decedent had a surviving spouse and children, only the spouse would have standing and right to recover.[230] This would be unfair to family members who might not have a right to the disposition of the deceased's body, but nevertheless suffered no less mental pain and distress than the person with a right to disposition. Close associates of the deceased, also severely distressed by the deceased's desecration, are beyond the contemplation of Section 868.[231] Based on these considerations, a later amendment to the *Restatement Second* removed the limitation on standing and recovery by family members.[232] Lastly, if Section 868 represents a synthesis of the various causes of action, then its semantic formulation presents difficulties for interpreting and seeking a remedy. In other words, a strict literal construction of the section would limit its application to cases of physical interference with a dead body.[233] For example, an unjustified exhibition of a decedent's autopsy picture would not come within the terms of the section.[234]

Florida's District Court of Appeal, Fifth District, confronted a similar problem in *Williams v. City of Minneola*,[235] which was a case of first impression. There, the investigating police officers took pictures and videotape of anatomical examination, during an autopsy of the plaintiff's deceased child, who died suspiciously.[236] The pictures and videotape, disseminated to non-members of the police team in a private

---

226 For those reasons, the section was rejected in *Ramirez v. HPSA, supra*, note 225; *Culpepper v. Pearl Street Building Inc*. 877 P. 2d 877 (1994); *Wallin v. University of Cincinnati* 698 N.E. 2d 530 (1998).

227 *Ramirez*, 972 P. 2d, at 663; *Culpepper*, 877 P. 2d, at 881; *Wallin*, 698 N.E. 2d, at 432.

228 *Restatement (Second) of Torts: Interference with Dead Bodies § 868* (1982).

229 *Felipe v. Vega* 570 A. 2d 1028, at 1030 (1989). Similar rules apply in Canada; see, for instance, *Re: the Estate of Linda Darlene Popp* (2001) BCSC 183.

230 *Ibid.*

231 *Restatement (Second) of Torts: Interference with Dead Bodies § 868* (1982). But see *Christensen v. Superior Court* (1991) 820 P. 2d 181, at 206. The dissenting opinion of Justice Mosk held that a close business associate of the deceased should be allowed to recover for the infliction of mental distress resulting from the abuse of the deceased's body. *Ibid.*

232 *American Restatement of the Law 2d, Torts, Appendix,* Section 868 (Minn.: American Law Institute Publishers, 1982), 75, Reporter's Note.

233 In *Dampier v. Wayne County* 592 N.W. 2d 809, at 816 (1999), Justice Whitbeck observed: '[a] cognizable claim for the mutilation of a dead body is not sufficiently broad to encompass a claim for its decomposition, which does not involve the active incision, dismemberment, or evisceration of the body…'

234 *Williams v. City of Minneola* 575 So. 2d 683, at 695 (1991).

235 575 So. 2d 683 (1991).

236 *Ibid.*, at 685–6.

gathering and later published in a newspaper, captured the plaintiff's attention.[237] The plaintiff brought an action for damages for the negligent infliction of emotional distress and tortuous interference with a dead body.[238] Though the majority found for the plaintiff for the negligent infliction of emotional distress, it held that a cause of action for interference with a dead body was not proved under Section 868. The court held:

> This theory [that is, interference with a dead body] must fail simply because the appellees did not interfere with a dead body. An invariable component of the tort is some action affecting the physical body itself, such as removing it, withholding it, mishandling it, or preventing its proper burial...Publication of a photograph does not, in the absence of a showing of actionable trespass on the body as such, amount to an interference with the possessory or burial rights of another.[239]

Thus, the majority interpreted Section 868 to establish a single tort, but held that the element of physical interference was lacking.[240] The majority was only able to find a remedy for the plaintiff by recourse to pre-Section 868 tort-based categories. Justice Griffin's dissent, however, held that an unjustified publication of a decedent's autopsy picture was an interference within the terms of Section 868.[241] This minority judgement is more consistent with the perceived central objectives of this section as establishing a single tort, embodying the positive sides of the previous categories and renouncing their obstacles. These advantages will be lost in an interpretation that imposes a requirement of physical interference with a dead body. That requirement will limit the reach of this section. Interestingly, the Supreme Court of Canada held in *R v. Moyer*,[242] that physical interference with a corpse was not a necessary element of the offence of interfering with a dead body under the *Canadian Criminal Code*.

Physical interference need not be the basis of a cause of action recognized by Section 868 and this is illustrated by *Finn v. The City of New York*.[243] In *Finn*, the plaintiff suffered mental anguish when the City of New York, due to a lapse in its system of reporting deaths, failed to notify the plaintiff of her husband's death until eight days after his demise.[244] Meanwhile, the deceased was deposited in a morgue under the control of the city.[245] There was no question of physical abuse or any indignity inflicted upon the dead body; the cause of action was based on the negligent withholding of the death information.[246] This case, however, was not treated significantly differently from cases of tortuous withholding of a dead body, and Justice Sullivan observed:

---

237 *Ibid.*, at 686.
238 *Ibid.*
239 *Ibid.*, at 688–9.
240 *Ibid.*
241 *Ibid.*, at 695–6.
242 *R v Moyer* (1994) 2 S.C.R. 899.
243 335 N.Y.S. 2d 516 (1972).
244 *Ibid.*
245 *Ibid.*
246 *Ibid.*, at 520.

But what of a situation where, as here, the anguish and torment were caused not by withholding the body but by withholding the fact of death. It is a fact that throughout the eight days of her husband's disappearance, the plaintiff nurtured the hope and belief that he was still alive; she had no knowledge that he was dead and that his corpse was at the morgue in the custody of the City. Thus, her anguish was the result not of being deprived of the possession of his remains for proper burial, an injury which for its existence must be based on knowledge of the fact that death has occurred, but of not knowing of such occurrence. If the principle that one may not tortiously withhold a deceased's body is to have efficacy, then the law must recognize as a corollary thereof, and this court so holds, that one may not tortiously withhold notification of death.[247]

Though this case was not decided under Section 868, or even explicitly cited, the court suggested that the *ratio* should inspire its interpretation.[248] It showed the futility of the distinction between emotional distress resulting from physical interference versus non-physical interference that, nevertheless, might be of 'much greater severity'.[249] The intent of tort law was to provide a remedy for emotional distress resulting from unjustifiable actions toward a dead body.[250] Limiting a remedy to cases of physical interference with a corpse detracted from this laudable legal objective.[251]

The result is that approaches and solutions with regard to the law on dead bodies are still very much unsettled in US jurisprudence, as in most other places in the world. It also shows that the US aversion to the British traditional no-property rule has its limits. This puts the current debate in proper perspective. Although the quasi-property concept provides some succour to a plaintiff through a fictitious property interest in a dead body or tissue, it does not afford protection to a plaintiff in certain circumstances that have already been analysed. Can a limited property rule provide an escape from the defects already inherent in the current legal categories or forms of action? What will be the conceptual framework for finding a limited property right in a human body? Is our global community ready for such a legal perspective, and what are the bases of possible objection to the objectification of the human

---

247 *Ibid.*, at 521.

248 *Ibid.*

249 *Ibid.*, at 522.

250 *Ibid.*

251 It seems the law is gradually de-emphasizing the fact of physical interference as a basis for a cause of action relating to a dead body. It should be recalled that in *Wallin v. University of Cincinnati Hospital* 698 N.E. 2d 530 (1998), the mental distress resulted mainly from the publication of a false report of the deceased's HIV status. There was no physical abuse of the deceased's body. However, the court held that the plaintiffs failed to prove the defendant's negligence or that the defendant was responsible for the publication of the false report in that case. Again, in *Crocker v. Pleasant* 727 So. 2d 1087 (1999), the mental distress resulted from the defendant's negligence, in not notifying the plaintiffs of the death of their son, who was found dead in a county in Florida and buried by the defendant without adequate notification of the plaintiff/parents. The court, at page 1089, held that a case for tortious interference with a dead body was made out. However, the plaintiffs did not claim in tort but brought a constitutional claim under the 14th Amendment. The court held that the property element of the 14th Amendment was not established and, therefore, affirmed the lower court's dismissal of the plaintiffs' case.

body? Does recent technology justify a finding of limited property interest in a dead body or human tissue?

These are some of the concerns expressed in the subsequent pages. Because of this book's argument in favour of a limited property interest in the human body, there is need to explore briefly the conceptual framework of property and its accommodation of new forms of property that evolved from biotechnology.

The Dominant Paradigms of Property

Chapter 1 showed that although various models of property have been proposed, there are two dominant models for understanding 'property': as right to a thing, which is the reified perspective, and as a bundle of rights.[252] This section examines how the application of these two dominant paradigms of property plays out in the context of the human body.

The Reified Perspective of Property

Generally, a person is said to own or have a right of property in a thing that belongs to that person, such as a chair, book, car or pen. This is referred to as the reified perspective of property because it seems to limit property to a right over a physical object.[253] This is the way that most writers of the last century and before understood property. The reification of property excludes some of what we now generally regard as property, for example, intellectual property. Compared to the bundle of rights

---

252 The concept of property has been used to explain certain relations, such as personhood. The personhood conception of property views property as the embodiment or extension of a person's personality. On this perspective, therefore, property is entitled to the best protection of law: M. Radin, 'Property and Personhood' (1982) 34 *Stan. L. Rev.*, 957; T.O. Elias, *The Nature of African Customary Law* (Manchester: The University of Manchester Press, 1956), 169–70. Applying the personhood analysis to the human body, it is argued that since the human body is most representative of a person's identity and sense of being, it therefore qualifies as property and is entitled to legal protection on that basis: Michelle B. Bray, 'Note, Personalizing Personality: Toward a Property Right in Human Bodies' (1990) 69 *Texas Law Rev.* 209, at 215. However, if property is a mere embodiment or extension of one's personality, then it is doubtful whether a person's personality or the human body will satisfy the criteria of identifiability, permanence and transferability, which are the hallmarks of a property interest. These criteria will be examined in this chapter. But Radin has argued that some property, such as personhood property, could be protected with a regime of market inalienability. See Margaret J. Radin, 'Market-Inalienability' (1987) 100 *Harv. L. Rev.* 1849. For further discussion of the concept of property, see Jeremy Waldron, 'What Is Private Property?' (1985) 5 *Oxford Journal of Legal Studies* 313; Michael A. Heller, 'The Dynamic Analytics of Property' (2001) 2 *Theoretical Inquiries in Law* 79; Daphna Lewinsohn-Zamir, 'Contemporary Property Law Scholarship: A Comment' (2001) 2 *Theoretical Inquiries in Law* 97; Hanoch Dagan and Michael A. Heller, 'The Liberal Commons' (2001) 110 *Yale Law Journal* 549.

253 Douglas Litowiz, 'Reification in Law and Legal Theory' (2000) 9 *S. Ca. Interdis. L.J.* 401.

perspective, the reified concept of property is a narrow concept. Strahan, writing in 1895, observed:

> The next point to be noted in this description of the right of ownership is that it must subsist over a thing; and the thing it subsists over must be a determinate thing, that is, an actually existing physical object...We cannot in this sense own a debt, or a patent, or a copyright, all of which are mere creations of the law, without any physical embodiments over which physical power can be exercised. Accordingly, strictly speaking, such rights are not property...[254]

John Austin,[255] William Blackstone[256] and some judicial decisions[257] espoused the reified perspective of property. The basis that the above perspective restricted property right to physical and tangible things was its theoretical anchorage in control and dominion over things. The reified perspective operated on the principle that once control or dominion exists over a thing, then it is your property.[258] However, Jennifer Nedelsky has observed that the presence of control and decision-making authority does not always translate to a property right.[259] How does the reified view of property treat rights relating to dead bodies and body parts? We may start this inquiry by noting a significant statement by John Locke.

In his analysis of the labour-added theory of property, Locke postulated that every person had a proprietary interest in his or her body. He said:

> Though the earth, and all inferior creatures, be common to all men, yet every man has a *property* in his *person*: this nobody has any right to but himself. The labour of his body, and the *work* of his hands, we may say, are properly his. Whatsoever then he removes out of the state that nature hath provided, left it in, he hath mixed his *labour* with and joined to it something that is his own, and thereby makes it his property. It being by him removed from the common state nature hath placed it in, it hath by this labour something annexed to it, that excludes the common right of other men: for this labour being the

---

254 J.A. Strahan, *Law of Property* (London: Stevens & Sons, Ltd., 1901, 3rd ed.), at 3.

255 J. Austin, *The Province of Jurisprudence Determined* (London: John Murray, Albemarle Street, 1863), Lecture xlvii.

256 W. Blackstone, *Commentaries on the Laws of England, Vol. 2* (Chicago: The University of Chicago Press, 1979).

257 For instance, *Gibson v. United States* 166 U.S. 269.

258 As Strahan rationalized:
> material things, however, of which physical possession has been taken by no one, are the property of no one (*res nullius*). Thus, wild birds, wild beasts, fish in rivers or in the sea, belong to nobody until they are captured, when they become, as a rule, the property of the captor...As long as he keeps possession of them his property in them continues; but should they escape completely out of his possession they are again *res nullius*, and will become the property of the first person who recaptures them.

Strahan, *supra*, note 254, at 4.

259 Nedelsky, *supra*, note 28, at 362: 'Decision-making authority is not the same as ownership...[t]he law confers a wide range of powers of control and decision-making authority upon parents with respect to their children. Yet we do not mistake children for property. Of course children are not "things".'

unquestionable property of the labourer, no man but he can have a right to what that is once joined to…[260] (Italics in the original)

Locke's statement could be a foundation for a property right in the human body. It is also possible that Locke was not thinking of human ownership but was trying to justify private property right in the product of one's labour.[261] In other words, because X has property in its own body, X also has property in the products of its labour. The reified perspective's idea of control as a basis for property right may be problematic when applied to the human body and its parts. Some writers in the eighteenth, nineteenth and twentieth centuries who supported the reified perspective did not think that it was applicable to the human body. For instance, while Austin was willing to restrict right of property to things, he could not ascribe proprietary interest to the human body except by way of analogy: 'I have a right in my own person which is analogous to the right of property in a determinate thing.'[262] Thus, the reified perspective of property offers no consensus that a human body or tissue could be the subject of property.[263]

A view of property restricted to a right over physical things is narrow and likely to be unworkable in a dynamic and modern society where technological development has tremendously pushed the frontiers of property beyond its objectified conception. This era has witnessed new forms of property, which are intellectual creations and knowledge-based.[264] A significant proportion of the new forms of property is intangible and may be difficult to protect under the reified perspective. However,

---

260 John Locke, *Second Treatise of Government* (Indianapolis: Hackett Publishing Co., 1980; ed. by C.B. Macpherson, and originally published in 1690), 19.

261 John Stuart Mill made a similar point: J.S. Mill, *Principles of Political Economy* (New York: Appleton, 1887), 172: 'The essential principle of property being to assure to all persons what they have produced by their labor and accumulated by their abstinence, this principle can not apply to what is not the produce of labor, the raw material of the earth.' Earlier, at 171, he observed:

> The institution of property, when limited to its essential elements, consists in the recognition, in each person, of a right to the exclusive disposal of what he or she have produced by their own exertions, or received either by gift or by fair agreement, without force or fraud, from those who produced it…together with his right to give this to any other person if he chooses, and the right of that other to receive and enjoy it.

262 Austin, *supra*, note 255, Lecture xlviii, 7. Again, Strahan opined:

> Physical objects alone, then, are subjects of ownership. But all physical objects cannot be owned. For example, there cannot by English law be any property in a human body, living or dead, though the executors of a dead testator are entitled to possession of his body for the purpose of burial….With this exception, however, it may be said generally that any material thing of which physical possession can be taken, may be owned.

Supra, note 254, at 4.

263 *Ibid.*

264 Lester Thurow, 'Globalization: The Product of a Knowledge-Based Economy' (2000) 570 *The Annals* 19; Molly A. Holman and Stephen R. Munzer, 'Intellectual Property Rights in Genes and Gene Fragments: A Registration Solution for Expressed Sequence Tags' (2000) 85

some of the new forms of property resulting from biotechnology have physical characteristics and may be amenable to protection under the reified theory.

Biomedical inventions and research materials, such as gametes, cell-lines and tissue samples, take physical form. Accordingly, it is arguable that the reified conception of property offers the greatest protection to a deserving plaintiff with respect to biomedical innovations that take physical forms.[265] Because of the narrowness of the reified perspective, similar protection might not be available to biomedical inventions that do not have physical characteristics. In contrast, protection under the bundle of rights approach may depend on one's view of the controversy relating to the juridical nature of rights that constitute the bundle of rights.[266] If we accept the very expansive and flexible view of the bundle of rights approach, as highlighted in Chapter 1, then property protection under that approach is unquestionable. On the other hand, if we accept the limitations imposed by the British House of Lords in *National Provincial Bank Ltd. v. Ainsworth*,[267] then property protection under the bundle of rights approach becomes more problematic.[268] The 'bundle of rights' perspective entails a complete abstraction and disaggregation of property.[269] It is capable of admitting all valuable interests, including interests relating to corpses and parts of them, to the category of property. The point is that, in contrast to the reified perspective of property, protection offered by the bundle of rights metaphor does not depend on control over physical entities. Despite the narrowness of the reified view of property, the courts often find it to be of some practical utility and have in a good number of cases resorted to the reified conception of property when human tissue is involved.[270]

Historically, the reified perspective of property was applied to purely physical and non-human objects of property. Courts have recently applied the reified view of property to new forms of property created by biomedical technology. These cases show judicial ingenuity by adapting a legal concept cast in different historical

---

Iowa L. Rev. 735; Richard H. Stern, 'The Bundle of Rights Suited to New Technology' (1986) 47 *U. Pitt. L. Rev.* 1229.

265 Kojo Yelpaala, 'Owning the Secret of Life: Biotechnology and Property Rights Revisited' (2000) 32 *McGeorge L. Rev.* 111, at 154.

266 The difficulty may include such questions, for instance, as whether all the rights in the property bundle are transferable for value? Because rights to the human body are not usually transferable for value, it is arguable that the bundle of rights approach may not protect such rights as property rights. But as Chapter 1 shows, such restrictions need not be imposed on the bundle of rights perspective. It is flexible enough to potentially accommodate rights over the human body as property rights. The nature of property rights will be considered later.

267 *National Provincial Bank Ltd. v. Ainsworth* (1965) A.C. 1175.

268 This is discussed in detail later.

269 Thomas C. Grey, 'The Disintegration of Property' in J. Roland Pennock and John W. Chapman, eds, *Property: Nomos XXII69* (New York: New York University Press, 1980); J.E. Penner, 'The "Bundle of Rights" Picture of Property' (1996) 43 *UCLA L. Rev.* 711; Jeanne L. Schroeder, 'Chix Nix Bundle-o-Stix: A Feminist Critique of the Disaggregation of Property' (1994) 93 *Mich. L. Rev.* 239.

270 For example, *Brotherton v. Cleveland* 923 F. 2d 477, at 482 (1991).

circumstances to present day economic and scientific realities,[271] although it should be mentioned that this adaptation is made possible by the physical features of some biotechnological inventions.

In *Cornelio v. Stamford Hospital*,[272] the plaintiff brought an action in detinue to recover possession of a pathology slide that contained the tissue sample used in testing her for cancer. She alleged that the tissue sample was her property and was wrongly detained by the defendant.[273] Although the case was decided using a Connecticut statute under which the plaintiff was not entitled to her non-duplicable medical record,[274] the majority assumed that the plaintiff had a property interest in her body tissue.[275] The dissent was more eager to a find a property interest in the plaintiff's body. The dissent held that property protection was necessary to protect the plaintiff's privacy interest, which was endangered by biomedical science and technology.[276]

In *Janicki v. Hospital of St Raphael*,[277] the plaintiffs brought an action after their stillborn foetus was dissected against their expressed wishes. The court held that a 19-week-old stillborn foetus was neither property nor mere tissue; rather it occupied a position of special respect entitled to legal protection.[278] The court applied the concept of quasi-property and property-like analysis to award damages to the mother.[279] Similarly, the court in *Green v. Southern Transplant Service*[280] held that the deceased's mother, stepfather and siblings had a cause of action for the unauthorized harvesting of the deceased's bone and tissue. It is unclear, however, what type of theoretical analysis the court proffered.

In *U.S. v. Arora*,[281] the personal animosity between two scientists employed by the National Institute of Health reached its peak when one of them maliciously destroyed cultured human cells produced by the other. The United States brought a civil action for conversion against the delinquent researcher. The court, using a pure property analysis, held that the cell, though a product of a living body, was property capable of conversion:

> The court thus sees no reason why a cell line should not be considered a chattel capable of being converted. Indeed, if such a cause of action is not recognized, it is hard to conceive what civil remedy would ever lie to recover a cell line that might be stolen or destroyed, including one with immense potential commercial value, as this one apparently had and has.[282]

---

271 *Brotherton*, 923 F.2d, at 480–82.
272 717 A. 2d 140 (1998).
273 *Ibid.*, at 143.
274 *Ibid.*, at 148.
275 *Ibid.*, at 143–144.
276 *Ibid.*, at 149.
277 744 A. 2d 963 (1999).
278 *Ibid.*, at 971.
279 *Ibid.*, at 967–70.
280 698 So. 2d 699 (1997).
281 *United States v. Arora* 860 F. Supp. 1091 (1994).
282 *Ibid.*, at 1098–9.

These cases illustrate the court's efforts to protect the human body and parts, and also protect our sentiment towards the dead by extending the application of a property concept grounded in common law. This protection is imperative because of the currently intense demand for human body parts and tissues by some biomedical and scientific researchers.[283] As a result of this demand, an outrageous trend exists where crematory and mortuary officials are becoming major merchants in body organs, illegally harvested from cadavers,[284] with some researchers, biomedical research companies and scientists as ready buyers.[285]

This judicial inclination towards protection was evident in *John Moore v. The Regents of the University of California, et al.*[286] The plaintiff underwent a splenectomy for the treatment of hairy-cell leukaemia.[287] In the course of treatment, his physician, also a medical researcher, noticed that the plaintiff had unique cells that were valuable for scientific research.[288] The physician appropriated the plaintiff's excised cells and, under the guise of treatment, obtained more cell samples from the plaintiff.[289] The physician, along with his associates, used the plaintiff's cells to produce a cell-line with enormous potential for producing therapeutic and pharmaceutical products.[290]

Among other causes of action, the plaintiff brought an action for conversion of his bodily materials.[291] The defendants raised a preliminary objection to the plaintiff's suit, contending that the plaintiff's pleading disclosed no reasonable cause of action (demurrer). For the purpose of ruling on the defendants' objection, the court assumed that the facts pleaded by the plaintiff were established. The plaintiff's conversion argument could only succeed if he established a property interest in his bodily materials.[292] The trial court dismissed the plaintiff's action because the plaintiff did not prove any property interest in his body to support an action for conversion.[293] The plaintiff appealed to the Court of Appeal. The Court of Appeal, using the reified perspective of property, held:

> Plaintiff's spleen, which contained certain cells, was something over which plaintiff enjoyed the unrestricted right to *use, control and disposition* [sic]. The rights of dominion over one's own body, and the interests one has therein, are recognized in many cases.

---

283 Ronald Campbell, *et al.*, 'Researchers' Use of Bodies Stirs Emotion, Controversy' (2000) *Dallas Morning News*, 21 April 2000, at A37.

284 Michael Perry, '"Body-Parts Supermarket" Causes Uproar in Australia', *National Post*, 20 March 2001, at A13.

285 That strange scenario was witnessed in *Christensen v. Superior Court* 820 P. 2d 181 (1991).

286 793 P. 2d 479 (1990, Supreme Court of California decision).

287 *Ibid.*, at 230.

288 *Ibid.*

289 *Ibid.*

290 *Ibid.*, at 481, n. 2.

291 *Ibid.*, at 482, n. 4.

292 *Ibid.*, at 488–9.

293 For an excellent review of *Moore's* case: Dickens, *supra*, note 27.

These rights and interests are so akin to property interests that it would be a subterfuge to call them something else.[294] [Italics mine]

The reference to unrestricted use, control and disposition as being akin to property interests is not unproblematic and characterizes the challenge of the reified theory.[295] If property in one's body or tissue was really based on control and dominion, we may revert to early civilization when one could have human property by sheer force, control, domination, or subjugation.

The Court of Appeal seemed to realize this by limiting the property right to one in which every person has a property interest in only his or her body.[296] In other words, a person cannot have a property interest in the body of another person. The fear of commodification or objectification,[297] much as it is legitimate and potentially realizable, does not seem compelling enough to militate against the finding of a limited property interest in the human body.[298] In fact, 'propertization' of the human body may be an effective way to check unauthorized harvesting of human organs and prevent commodification.[299] We saw this reasoning in *Arora's* case.[300]

It is arguable that the reified concept of property is contradictory. If control and dominion over a thing is a sufficient basis for acquiring property, why does person A have no property interest in person B when person B is under the control and dominion of person A? Why is it that parents who have control over their children do not own such children?[301] In defence of the reified perspective, it may be argued that this apparent absurdity is justified by the compelling interest of giving heightened protection to the human body and its privacy interests when those interests are capable of invasion by recent biomedical technology.

---

294 202 Cal. Rptr. 494, at 505 (1988); the court also stated: 'The essence of a property interest – the ultimate right of control – therefore exists with regard to one's own body', at 506. See Tanya Wells, 'The Implications of a Property Right in One's Body' (1990) 30 *Jurimetrics Journal* 371. For a criticism of the Court of Appeal's judgement, see Jennifer Lavoie, 'Ownership of Human Tissue: Life After Moore v. Regents of the University of California' (1989) 75 *Virginia L. Rev.* 1363.

295 Patricia A. Martin and Martin L. Lagod, 'Biotechnology and the Commercial Use of Human Cells: Toward An Organic View of Life and Technology' (1989) 5 *Santa Clara Computer & High Tech. L. J.* 211, at 238–41.

296

> We have approached this issue with caution. The evolution of civilization from slavery to freedom, from regarding people as chattels to recognition of the individual dignity of each person, necessitates prudence in attributing the qualities of property to human tissue. There is, however, a dramatic difference between having property rights in one's body and being the property of another. To our knowledge, no public policy has ever been articulated, nor is there any statutory authority, against a property interest in one's own body.

Moore, supra, note 294, at 494.

297 The Court of Appeal expressed such concerns in the above quotation, *Moore, ibid.*

298 This point is further developed below.

299 *United States v. Arora* 860 F. Supp. 1091, at 1099 (1994).

300 *Ibid.*

301 Nedelsky, *supra*, note 28, at 362.

The Court of Appeal's decision in *Moore* was appealed to the Supreme Court of California.[302] For policy reasons, the California Supreme Court held that *Moore* did not prove his claim for conversion.[303] The court was concerned about the negative impact of upholding *Moore's* property claim on scientific activities of public importance.[304] The Supreme Court of California, however, anticipated the possibility of a future decision in favour of property interests in one's own body.[305] It stated that *Moore* established a cause of action based on lack of informed consent.[306] Broussard and Mosk, JJ., in their dissenting judgement, were prepared to hold that the plaintiff established a property interest in his bodily tissue, based on his exercise of control and dominion.[307]

Disputes over frozen embryos, pre-embryos or sperm further illustrate interesting applications of the reified perspective of property to biological materials.[308] A few Australian, English and American cases relating to post-mortem access to the sperm of a deceased person are germane.[309] The facts of *Re Gray*[310] and *Baker v. State of Queensland*,[311] decided by the Supreme Court of Queensland in Australia, are similar, except that in *Re Gray* the applicant was married to the deceased and they had a child, though they both wished to have another child before the deceased's death. But in *Baker's* case, the applicant was only engaged to the deceased and had no child for him, though they had lived together for five years and had strong desires for children. In both cases, the applicants sought an order of the court authorizing the post-mortem harvesting of the sperm of the deceased persons for the purpose of posthumous procreation. Both Chesterman, J. in *Re Gray* and Muir, J. in *Baker's* case held that the court lacked jurisdiction to authorize interference with the body of the deceased persons and that, in addition to the difficulties involved in ascertaining

---

302 For a good analysis of *Moore's* decision in the Court of Appeal and Supreme Court of California, and also for a support of the no-property framework with regards to the human body, see Debra Mortimer, 'Proprietary Rights in Body Parts: The Relevance of Moore's Case in Australia' (1993) 19 *Monash Uni. L. Rev.* 217.

303 *Moore*, 793 P. 2d at 497.

304 *Ibid.*, at 487–8.

305 *Ibid.*, at 493. Gilmour commented on this judicial prospect as follows:

Although the Supreme Court disclaimed any suggestion that its holding meant excised cells could never be property for any purpose whatsoever, its rejection of the various bases on which a property right was asserted by the human source was so thorough and wide ranging that its claim to still leave the possibility of property analysis open in some unspecified instance seems no more than an empty rhetorical flourish, included only out of an abundance of caution.

Gilmour, *supra*, note 20, at 122.

306 *Moore*, *supra*, note 303, at 483.

307 *Ibid.*, Broussard, J. at 502; and Mosk, J. at 509.

308 See *Davis v. Davis* 842 S.W. 2d 588 (1992); *Kass v. Kass* 696 N.E. 2d 174 (N.Y. 1998); *York v. Jones* 717 F. Supp. 421 (E.D. Va. 1989); *Del Zio v. Columbia Presbyterian Hospital* No. 74-3558, 1978 U.S. Dist. LEXIS 14450 (S.D.N.Y. Nov. 14, 1978).

309 See Belinda Bennett, 'Posthumous Reproduction and the Meanings of Autonomy' (1999) 23 *Melbourne Uni. L. Rev.* 286.

310 *Re Gray* (2001) 2 QDR 35.

311 *Baker v. State of Queensland* (2003) QSC 002.

the wishes of the deceased persons in the circumstances, there were strong policy arguments against such judicial interference.[312] Though there was not much property talk in the two cases, it is interesting that the applicant's lawyer in *Baker's* case made a property analogy to the effect that the strong desire of the parties to procreate was analogous to an enforceable contract to deal with property. Muir, J. rejected this submission, holding that the law of contract was not an appropriate framework for dealing with emotionally laden issues arising from intimate relationships and that in any case, the 'creation and disposition of property and rights in property bears little semblance to the desire to create a human being and to nurture the person in a particular relationship'.[313]

In *Re Denman*,[314] however, Atkinson, J. of the same Supreme Court of Queensland refused to follow the two earlier decisions of the court. As in the above cases, Mrs Denman sought an order of court permitting appointed medical personnel to posthumously harvest the sperm of her deceased husband. The judge held that *Gray* and *Baker's* cases were not binding on him and that the court had inherent jurisdiction to entertain the matter. The court also held that there was no express statutory prohibition of the course of conduct sought by Mrs Denman (which conduct should be assumed lawful) and that public policy on the issue was not decisive and could go either way. The court drew a distinction between the issue of whether a post-mortem harvesting of sperm should be permitted and the juridically different issue of whether the use of that sperm or actual post-mortem procreation should be allowed. The court postponed its decision on the second issue and held in favour of the applicant on the first issue. Interestingly, the court referred to *Doodeward v. Spence*,[315] affirming that property could exist in a corpse in certain circumstances, but anchored its decision on the liberal tradition of a state's non-interference in the private lives of its citizens except to prevent harm to others. Accordingly, Atkinson, J. held that 'where there is no express statutory prohibition then in my view, the harvesting of Mr Denman's spermatozoa ought to be permitted in the absence of any suggestion of harm to others'.[316]

The question of posthumous access to the reproductive material of a deceased person arose in the English case of *R v. Human Fertilization and Embryology Authority, ex parte Blood*,[317] a case of first impression, though the decision was largely based on statutory construction rather than the framework of property. In that case, Mrs Blood and the deceased, after three years of marriage, started making efforts to have a child. But before Mrs Blood could conceive, Mr Blood contracted meningitis and became comatose. Mrs Blood, however, secured the extraction (and subsequent storage) of Mr Blood's sperm by means of electro-ejaculation shortly

---

312 This outcome would seem to support the relational analysis offered by Bennett, *supra*, note 309.

313 *Baker's* case, *supra*, note 311.

314 *Re Denman* (2004) QSC 070.

315 *Doodeward v. Spence* (1908) 6 CLR 406.

316 *Re Denman*, *supra*, note 314.

317 *R v. Human Fertilization and Embryology Authority, ex parte Blood* (1997) 2 All ER 687.

before his death. The Human Fertilization and Embryology Authority (UK), pursuant to its statutory powers, denied Mrs Blood permission to use her deceased husband's sperm for fertility treatment in the UK for want of Mr Blood's prior formal consent; the Authority also refused to exercise its discretion to permit the export of the sperm to Belgium for the treatment of Mrs Blood. Her application for a judicial review of the Authority's decision was dismissed by the trial court and she appealed to the Court of Appeal, where Lord Woolf, MR. observed: 'The absence of the necessary written consent means that both the treatment of Mrs Blood and the storage of Mr Blood's sperm would be prohibited by the 1990 Act. The authority has no discretion to authorise treatment in the United Kingdom.'[318] Lord Woolf, however, opined that the Authority wrongly exercised its discretion in refusing to permit the export of the sperm to Belgium by not considering that such a refusal would amount to an impediment of cross-border services under the European Community law, and that cases like the present one are not likely to occur in the future, since sperm storage can only be done with prior formal consent of the donor.[319] The effect of this decision seems to be that the Court of Appeal was prepared to bestow on Mrs Blood the rights of access and control over Mr Blood's reproductive material for the purpose of posthumous procreation. This is the type of outcome that a property analysis would have yielded.

In *Hecht v. Superior Court*,[320] the deceased's partner, in attempting to posthumously procreate, sought judicial assistance to release the deceased's cryogenically preserved sperm to the plaintiff.[321] The deceased's children opposed the release of their father's sperm, arguing it was against public policy to artificially inseminate a single woman with a deceased's sperm for posthumous procreation.[322] The court held that there was no such public policy.[323] Because the dispute was litigated in probate court, where jurisdiction is mainly limited to a decedent's property,[324] the court determined whether it had jurisdiction over the deceased's sperm.[325] The court reasoned that because the deceased had authority over his sperm during his lifetime, the sperm was property.[326] The court further stated that the decedent's frozen sperm was a 'unique type of "property"', and therefore part of his estate.[327] In *Hecht*, the court made a conscious effort to expand an existing category of property to include a new form of property, such as genetic or reproductive material.[328] *Hecht* also endorsed the earlier

---

318 *Ibid.*, at 697.

319 *Ibid.*, at 702–703.

320 20 Cal. Rptr. 2d 275 (1993).

321 *Ibid.*, at 276.

322 *Ibid.*, at 284.

323 *Ibid.*, at 287.

324 *Ibid.*, at 280.

325 *Ibid.*, at 281.

326 *Ibid.* Jennifer L. Collins, 'Hecht v. Superior Court: Recognizing A Property Right in Reproductive Material' (1995) 33 *Uni. Louisville Jour. Fam. L.* 661.

327 Hecht, *supra*, note 320, at 283.

328 *Ibid.*, at 290–91. Three years later the court further limited the unique property it found to exist in that case and stated that it is the property of one person; in other words,

case of *Davis v. Davis*,[329] holding that a couple's decision-making authority over the disposition of pre-embryos was similar to a property interest.[330]

The above decisions, notwithstanding the defects of the reified perspective of property, are justified by the imperatives of this biomedical age. The reified perspective of property is again used in the Supreme Court of Western Australia case of *Roche v. Douglas*.[331] The case was a paternity suit where the plaintiff applied for a DNA analysis of the deceased's tissue sample.[332] The success of the plaintiff's application turned on whether the deceased's body tissue qualified as property.[333] The court, per Master Sanderson, noted that most British and Australian decisions concerning dead bodies were inapplicable because they did not take account of recent biomedical technology, such as DNA techniques.[334] The court stated that, in addition to the procedural advantages of finding a proprietary interest in the deceased's tissue (that is, saving in time, cost and quantum of evidence), 'it defies reason to not regard tissue samples as property. Such samples have a real physical presence. They exist and will continue to exist until some step is taken to effect destruction. There is no purpose to be served in ignoring physical reality.'[335]

The Bundle of Rights Perspective

Property has increasingly been recognized as a 'bundle of rights'.[336] These rights or interests recognized as property are often intangible and include intellectual property rights, right of way,[337] the duty not to dilute the salinity level in water above one's leased sea bed,[338] and right of access to a navigable river.[339] In the US Supreme Court case of *Scranton v. Wheeler*,[340] Justice Shiras observed: 'The term "property," standing alone, includes everything that is the subject of ownership. It is a *nomen generalissium* extending to every species of valuable right and interest,

---

that person has no rights of transfer or alienation with respect to the property. See *Hecht v. Superior Court* 59 Cal. Rptr. 2d 222 (Cal. Dist. App. Ct. 1996).

329 842 S.W. 2d 588 (1992).

330 *Ibid.*, at 597.

331 (2000) WASC 146, or http://www.austlii.edu.au/au/cases/wa/WASC/2000/146.html.

332 *Ibid.*

333 *Ibid.*

334 *Ibid.*; also on the legal impact of DNA techniques: Sharon McEldowney and Lynda M. Warren, 'The New Biology: A Challenge To Law' (1998) 1 *International Journal of Biosciences and the Law* 315.

335 *Supra*, note 331.

336 Hohfeld's analysis of jural correlatives provides an example of the fragmentation of property as abstract rights: Wesley N. Hohfeld, 'Some Fundamental Legal Conceptions as Applied in Judicial Reasoning' (1911) 23 *Yale L.J.* 16; Wesley N. Hohfeld, 'Fundamental Legal Conceptions as Applied in Judicial Reasoning' (1917) 26 *Yale L.J.* 710; see, generally, D.C. Jackson, *Principles of Property* (Sydney: The Law Book Co. Ltd., 1967), at 10; B. Ziff, *Principles of Property Law* (Toronto: Carswell Publication, 1993), at 1–3.

337 *Preseault v. U.S.* 100 F. 3d 1525 (1996).

338 *Avenal v. U.S* 100 F. 3d 933 (1996).

339 *Yates v. Milwaukee* 10 Wall. 497.

340 179 U.S. 141 (1900).

including things real and personal, easements, franchises, and other incorporeal hereditaments.'[341] Property encompasses a great variety of intangible rights and interests.[342] The greatest exercise of these rights is what constitutes 'ownership'.[343] As Jackson observed: 'A synonym for a proprietary interest is "ownership," which, however, is sometimes said to describe the highest possible such interest rather than the concept in general.'[344]

Identifying property as representative of a bundle of rights, however, does not solve the definitional problem. Does every piece in the bundle of rights qualify as property? A person may have some interest or right in his or her body, but does that right qualify as property? These questions require an inquiry into the nature and prerequisites of a 'right' of property.

Nature of Proprietary Interests and Rights

It seems that in order to qualify as a right of property, the alleged right or interest should possess a particular nature[345] (such as being identifiable, transferable, devisable and monetarily valuable), otherwise the right might not legally qualify as a property right.[346] Some scholars need not agree on these qualifications or characteristics of rights of property.[347] The famous exposition of the principle relating to the nature of property rights remains Lord Wilberforce's *dictum* in *National Provincial Bank Ltd. v. Ainsworth.*[348]

In *Ainsworth*, a deserted wife remained on the matrimonial property that was mortgaged by her husband to a bank.[349] She argued that being the mortgagor's wife gave her an interest in the matrimonial property even though it was legally owned

---

341 *Ibid.*, at 170.

342 Generally, Hohfeld, *supra*, note 336. For a useful criticism of the bundle of rights' neglect of the thingness of property, see Thomas W. Merrill and Henry E. Smith, 'What Happened to Property in Law and Economics?' (2001) 111 *Yale L.J.* 357; Craig Anthony Arnold, 'The Reconstitution of Property: Property as a Web of Interests' (2002) 26 *Harv. Envi. L. Rev.* 281.

343 S.N.C. Obi, *The Ibo Law of Property* (London: Butterworths, 1963), at 43.

344 Jackson, *supra*, note 336, at 11.

345 The identifiability or peculiarity of property rights belies Arnold's observation that: 'It is true that the bundle of rights concept itself tends to disintegrate in its image of property as a bundle of abstract legal rights that have no characteristics to distinguish them from other rights or human relationships generally.' Arnold, *supra*, note 342, at 331.

346 *National Provincial Bank Ltd. v. Ainsworth* (1965) A.C. 1175, at 1247–8 (H.L.).

347 For instance, Radin, *supra*, note 252, at 1903 observed that: '[w]e must cease thinking that market alienability is inherent in the concept of property.' Similarly, Harris argued that the inalienability of whiteness does not disqualify it as property. Cheryl I. Harris, 'Whiteness As Property' (1993) 106 *Harv. L. Rev.* 1709, at 1734: '[t]he inalienability of whiteness should not preclude the consideration of whiteness as property. Paradoxically, its inalienability may be more indicative of its perceived enhanced value, rather than its disqualification as property.'

348 Ainsworth, *supra*, note 346, at 1175.

349 *Ibid.*, at 1176.

by her husband.[350] She claimed that this interest was sufficient to override the bank's legal mortgage.[351] Thus, the case turned on the nature of the property interest asserted by the wife. Lord Wilberforce declared:

> Before a right or an interest can be admitted into the category of property, or of a right affecting property, it must be definable, identifiable by third parties, capable in its nature of assumption by third parties, and have some degree of permanence or stability. The wife's right has none of these qualities, it is characterised by the reverse of them.[352]

The above reasoning does not stand alone, as it has been applied in other jurisdictions and seems to be supported by academic writers.[353] In *First Victoria National Bank v. United States*,[354] Goldberg, J. of the United States Court of Appeals, Fifth Circuit, observed:

> An interest labeled 'property' normally may possess certain characteristics: it can be transferred to others; it can be devised and inherited; it can descend to heirs at law; it can be levied upon to satisfy a judgment; it comes under the jurisdiction of a bankruptcy court in a bankruptcy proceeding; it will be protected against invasion by the courts; it cannot be taken away without due process of law.[355]

Justice Goldberg, however, added a caveat to the otherwise settled proposition on the nature of property interest:

> An interest may qualify as 'property' for some purposes even though it lacks some of these attributes. For example, an individual can have a 'property' right in his job...so that he cannot be fired without appropriate procedural safeguards; yet the job is not assignable, transferable, descendible, or devisable. The 'right to publicity' is transferable during life...but may not be devisable.[356]

It seems that the most lucid application of *Ainsworth's* principle is shown by cases dealing with the property status of university degrees.[357] This often arises in a divorce situation where a spouse asserts that a university degree or professional qualification

---

350 *Ibid.*

351 *Ibid.*

352 *Ibid.*, at 1247–8. But, see the *Matrimonial Homes Act 1967, UK, C. 75.*

353 For instance, Jackson stated:
> The distinction between proprietary and personal interests may be said to rest either on whether or not the holder is given the ability: (i) to 'deal with' the interest by transferring it to another, or (ii) to recover the interest should he lose it, or (iii) bring an action with respect to the interest against a person or persons other than the grantor.

Supra, note 336, at 16.

354 620 F. 2d 1096 (1980).

355 *Ibid.*, at 1103–1104.

356 *Ibid.*, at 1104.

357 Wilbur M. Roadhouse, 'The Problem of the Professional Spouse: Should an Educational Degree Earned During Marriage Constitute Property in Arizona?' (1982) 24 *Ariz. L. Rev.* 963.

acquired by the other spouse during the marriage is community property subject to division upon the dissolution of marriage.[358]

In the Canadian case of *Berghofer v. Berghofer*,[359] Legg, J. of the Alberta Court of Queen's Bench, relying on the earlier Ontario High Court decision of Van Camp, J., in *Caratun v. Caratun*[360] (later overruled by the Ontario Court of Appeal[361]) held that a university degree obtained during the marriage of the couple was an asset that should be considered in an action under the *Matrimonial Property Act*.[362] This was notwithstanding the fact that a university degree, by its intrinsic nature, does not possess the factors stipulated by Lord Wilberforce in the *Ainsworth* case.[363] Beyond relying upon the Ontario High Court decision in *Caratun*, Legg, J. did not provide any theoretical anchorage for holding that a university degree qualified as property.[364] Furthermore, the precedential value of that decision is limited because it was later overruled for holding that a university degree qualified as property.[365]

Another case that ascribed proprietary value to a university degree, though it is not commercially transferable, is *Woodworth v. Woodworth*.[366] The issue was whether the plaintiff's law degree was marital property subject to distribution.[367] The case confronted the social and economic realities of a wife who gave her husband moral support and stood by him in the course of his studies. The court observed:

> Plaintiff contends that his law degree is not such a marital asset. We disagree. The facts reveal that plaintiff's law degree was the end product of a concerted family effort. Both parties planned their family life around the effort to attain plaintiff's degree. Toward this end, the family divided the daily tasks encountered in living. While the law degree did not preempt all other facets of their lives, it did become the main focus and goal of their activities. Plaintiff left his job in Jonesville and the family relocated to Detroit so that plaintiff could attend law school. In Detroit, defendant sought and obtained full time employment to support the family.
>
> We conclude, therefore, that plaintiff's law degree was the result of mutual sacrifice and effort by both plaintiff and defendant. While plaintiff studied and attended classes, defendant carried her share of the burden as well as sharing vicariously in the stress of the experience known as the 'paper chase.'
>
> We believe that fairness dictates that the spouse who did not earn an advanced degree be compensated whenever the advanced degree is the product of such concerted family investment. The degree holder has expended great effort to obtain the degree not only for him- or herself, but also to benefit the family as a whole. The spouse has shared in this

---

358 *Ibid.*, at 963–5.
359 (1988) Alta. L.R. (2d) 186.
360 (1987) 43 D.L.R. (4th) 398.
361 *Caratun v. Caratun* (1992) 96 D.L.R. (4th) 404.
362 *Berghofer, supra*, note 359, at 188.
363 *Ainsworth, supra*, note 346, at 1247–8.
364 *Berghofer, supra*, note 359, at 188.
365 *Caratun, supra*, note 361, at 414–15.
366 (1983) 337 N.W.2d 332.
367 *Ibid.*, at 333.

effort and contributed in other ways as well, not merely as a gift to the student spouse nor merely to share individually in the benefits but to help the marital unit as a whole.[368]

It is evident that this view does not make any conceptual analysis of property before holding that a university degree qualified as such. The court, in characterizing a university degree as property, without subjecting it to a strict application of the concept of property, was primarily concerned with preventing a miscarriage of justice.[369] Moreover, the cases of *Berghofer v. Berghofer*,[370] and *Woodworth v. Woodworth*[371] are completely limited by other cases holding that a professional certificate does not qualify as property.[372] In *Caratun v. Caratun*,[373] it was argued that a dental licence acquired by a spouse in the course of the marriage was property for the purpose of *Family Law Act, 1986, S.O., c. 4*. The Ontario Court of Appeal overruled the decision of the trial court and observed:

> One of the traditional *indicia* of property is its inherent transferability. That transferability may, of course, be precluded either by law or contract. In contrast, the right or licence to practise a particular profession is by its very nature a right personal to the holder, incapable of transfer,….[r]ights or things which are inherently non-transferable, such as the right to practise a profession, clearly do not constitute property in any traditional sense.[374]

Similarly, Lee, J. in the Supreme Court of Colorado case of *In re Marriage of Graham*[375] observed:

> An educational degree, such as an M.B.A., is simply not encompassed even by the broad views of the concept of 'property.' It does not have an exchange value or any objective transferable value on an open market. It is personal to the holder and is not inheritable. It cannot be assigned, sold, transferred, conveyed, or pledged. An advanced degree is a cumulative product of many years of previous education, combined with diligence and hard work. It may not be acquired by the mere expenditure of money. It is simply an intellectual achievement that may potentially assist in the future acquisition of property. In our view, it has none of the attributes of property in the usual sense of that term.[376]

---

368 *Ibid.*, at 334.

369 *Ibid.*, at 335.

370 *Supra*, note 359.

371 *Supra*, note 366.

372 For example, *Lesman v. Lesman* 452 N.Y.S. 2d 935 (1982); *Mahoney v. Mahoney* 182 N.J. Super. 598 (1982); *Wisner v. Wisner* 631 P. 2d 115 (1971); *Frausto v. Frausto* 611 S.W. 2d 656 (1980); *Nastrom v. Nastrom* 262 N.W. 2d 487 (1978); *Muckleroy v. Muckleroy* 498 P. 2d 1335 (1972); *Todd v. Todd* 78 Cal. Rptr. 131 (1969); *In re Marriage of Sullivan* 184 Cal. Rptr. 796 (1982); *In re Marriage of Goldstein* 423 N.E. 2d 1201 (1981); *In re marriage of McManama* 399 N.E. 2d 371 (1980).

373 *Caratun, supra*, note 361, at 404.

374 *Ibid.*, at 409–10.

375 574 P. 2d 75 (1978).

376 *Ibid.*, at 77.

Thus, in order to qualify as property, a right must be assignable, transferable, capable of being sold or pledged, reasonably permanent and identifiable.[377] The question, for the purposes of this chapter, then becomes: does right to a human tissue, body or corpse satisfy the above requirements? The answer is no, if the *Ainsworth* principle is applied and a blind eye is turned to scientific and economic realities.[378] Similarly, Harris suggested that though property talk of self-ownership can be justified rhetorically, it should not be taken literally, since self-ownership is not caught within the defining elements of the institution of property, which he identified as trespassory rules and ownership spectrum.[379] Harris also argued that what we rhetorically call self-ownership rights are, properly speaking, rights that arise from the bodily-use freedom principle, which in turn are derived from the array of our fundamental freedoms and not from the institution of property.[380] Accordingly, Harris observed that:

> Rhetorical invocations…of body ownership are an optional extra. We do not need to appeal to the analogy with property in resources in order to make points which follow from the bodily-use freedom principle. Nevertheless, such invocations may add pithiness and force to what would otherwise seem laboured and tame. They are not intended to be taken literally, for, if they were, they would prove too much. The ownership interest recognized both by law and by societal norms in ordinary chattels lies at the upper end of the ownership spectrum – full-blooded ownership. If I own a book it follows that I may scribble in it, use it to prop up the leg of a rickety table, burn it, lend or sell it to whom I will, or give it away inter vivos or by will. Someone invoking body ownership, rhetorically, is not committed to claiming the same panoply of use-privileges, control-powers and transmission powers over each person's body.[381]

If, however, we rejected *Ainsworth's* principle, which also underpins Harris' comments above, then the bundle of rights perspective is capable of accepting rights relating to dead bodies into the category of property.[382] In Chapter 1, we saw that the

---

377 This contrasts with Craig Arnold's contention: Arnold, *supra*, note 342.

378 Note, however, that with respect to the human body, certain rights are proprietorial in nature; for instance, rights relating to the sale of blood (though some jurisdictions regard it as service rather than sale): *Perlmutter v. Beth David Hospital* 123 N.E. 2d 792 (N.Y. 1954)), contrast with: *Green v. Commissioner* 74 T.C. 1229 (1980), *Carter v. Interfaith Hospital of Queens* 304 N.Y.S. 2d 97 (N.Y. Sup. Ct. 1969), semen, ova and the right of publicity. Other body rights of a proprietorial nature include the power to make transfers recognized under Anatomical Gift Statues (though such transfers are not for value) and cadaveric donations recognized under Anatomy Acts. Other rights relating to or arising from a living human body are personal rights, such as right to life, right to bodily security, right to free speech, right to reputation and right against unjustifiable searches. See Stephen R. Munzer, *A Theory of Property* (New York: Cambridge University Press, 1990), at 44–52.

379 Harris, J.W. 'Who Owns My Body' (1996) 16 *Oxford Journal of Legal Studies* 55–84.

380 *Ibid.*, at 62.

381 *Ibid.*, note, at 63.

382 Note, however, Harris' contention that to the extent that self-ownership could be conceded, then such property rights lie at the lowest rung of the ownership spectrum and might need to be regarded as a unique type of property. See, Harris, *ibid.*, at 65.

bundle of rights concept of property is very flexible and expansive and capable of protecting every valuable interest as a property right. Thus, property is conclusory in nature and as Weinrib observed, it is 'a statement that the court has chosen to assign a particular form of protection to the interest in question'.[383] Similar observations were made by Dean Acheson who noted that:

> [t]he all-absorbing legal conception of the (19th) century (was) that of the property right. Everything was thought of in terms of property – reputation, privacy, domestic relations – and as new interest required protection, their viability depended upon their ability to take on the protective coloring of property.[384]

Nevertheless, *Ainsworth's* principle appears to have been adopted by the Supreme Court of Colorado in *Culpepper v. Pearl Street Building Inc*.[385] The plaintiffs' deceased son was mistakenly cremated by the defendant.[386] The success of the plaintiff's claim, which included damages for conversion of the deceased's body,[387] depended on whether the plaintiffs could show a property interest in their dead son's body.[388] The court dismissed the claim on the basis that the plaintiffs had no property interest in their son's corpse.[389] The court explained that a dead body is not commercially transferable, has no monetary value and, therefore, is not property.[390] The measure of damages for conversion depends on the market value of the converted good, which, in a corpse, is unascertainable.[391] Therefore, the principle in *Ainsworth* excludes rights in dead human bodies or body parts from the legal category of property because they inherently lack the indicia of a property right.[392]

Ainsworth's Case and Biomedical Technology

The proposition in *Ainsworth* was cast in the mould of common law during a period that had not witnessed the tremendous biotechnological advances of today.[393] Marketability and commercial transferability are no longer the touchstones of an object's value. The non-market value of corpses was part of the reasons that the common law failed to recognize corpses as property. But things have changed and common law may not have caught up with the realities of today.

First, corpses, thought to be intrinsically non-transferable or commercially unviable, have now acquired pecuniary value as important raw materials in biomedical

---

383 Arnold S. Weinrib, 'Information and Property' (1988) 38 *Uni. Tor. L.J.* 117, at 120.
384 Dean G. Acheson, 'Book Review' (1919) 33 *Harv. L. Rev.* 329, at 330.
385 877 P. 2d 877 (1994).
386 *Ibid.*
387 *Ibid.*, at 879.
388 *Ibid.*, at 880.
389 *Ibid.*, at 882.
390 *Ibid.*, at 880.
391 *Ibid.*
392 *Ainsworth*, *supra*, note 346, at 1247–8.
393 *Onyeanusi v. Pan Am* 952 F. 2d 788 at 792 (1992).

research.[394] Second, though human body parts may be considered intrinsically non-commodifiable, biomedical technology has jeopardized their safety[395] such that substantial legal protection, analogous to the protection given to property, is now desirable.[396] For the law to serve society as an instrument of social engineering, it must be able to respond meaningfully to changing socio-economic dynamics.[397] The law has shown this adaptability and flexibility in the past by acknowledging a property interest in one's job or personality.[398]

Mary Ann Glendon[399] chronicled the socio-economic considerations underpinning the movement towards property rights in one's job and the judicial recognition of such rights.[400] Since the 1970s, there has been a significant increase in the number of people employed.[401] These people's lives depend on wages and other employment benefits. For some people, salary and employment benefits have come to represent wealth and economic security.[402] Glendon argues that to maintain this new form of

---

394 *Ibid.*; in *Pettigrew v. Pettigrew* 56 A. 878 (1907), it was even held that a corpse satisfied the criteria of ownership, in that it could be the subject of custody, control and disposition by the next of kin. For the importance of body parts in biomedical research, see Peter Furness, 'Consent to Using Human Tissue: Implied Consent Should Suffice' (2003) 327 *BMJ* 759–60.

395 As in the case of *Moore*, 793 P. 2d 497, where a body tissue was taken from a patient without his consent, for use in biomedical research; or in *Christensen, supra*, note 183, where a biomedical company engaged in illegal trade on cadaver organs; or in *R v. Stillman* (1997) 1 S.C.R. 607, where the police authorities obtained a detainee's mucous tissue, without his consent, for DNA testing.

396 To the same effect is the dissenting judgement of McDonald, J. in *Cornelio v. Stamford Hospital* 717 A. 2d 140, at 149 (1998). See also, Churchill, *supra*, note 25, at 281–2.

397 *Moore*, 793 P. 2d at 507.

398 Donald H. J. Herman and Yvonne S. Sor, 'Property Rights In One's Job: The Case For Limiting Employment-At-Will' (1982) 24 *Ariz. L.Rev.* 763; Peter L. Felcher and Edward L. Rubin, 'The Descendibility of the Right of Publicity; Is There Commercial Life After Death?' (1980) 89 *Yale L.J.* 1125–32.

399 M.A. Glendon, *The New Family and the New Property* (Toronto: Butterworths, 1981), at 101–245.

400 *Ibid.*, at 143–70. See, also, Roy Vogt, *Whose Property? The Deepening Conflict Between Private Property and Democracy in Canada* (Toronto; University of Toronto Press, 1999) at 143–95.

401 *Ibid.*

402 Charles Reich made a similar argument for property protection of government largess:

> Eventually those forms of largess which are closely linked to status must be deemed to be held as of right. Like property, such largess could be governed by a system of regulation plus civil or criminal sanctions, rather than a system based upon denial, suspension and revocation. As things now stand, violations lead to forfeitures – outright confiscation of wealth and status. But there is surely no need for these drastic results. Confiscation, if used at all, should be the ultimate, not the most common and convenient penalty. The presumption should be that the professional man keeps his license, and the welfare recipient his pension. These interests should be 'vested'.

Charles A. Reich, 'The New Property' (1964) 73 *Yale L.J.* 733, at 785.

wealth, the law should ensure reasonable stability in employment.[403] The movement toward property rights in one's job contributed to the limitations on the employer's right to arbitrarily terminate an employee's employment in the United States and in many other countries.[404] Many courts facilitated the needed protection by defining employee's rights as property.[405] Thus, an employee had a property interest in his or her job, not because it was transferable, but rather to align the law with the economic realities of employment.[406]

At present, the main source of wealth for biotech companies is knowledge.[407] Raw materials for biomedical research include cells and tissue samples. Biomedical research has contributed to health and social well-being. To maintain social value,[408] the law should provide sufficient and balanced protection to the raw materials and products of biomedical research.[409] The law has already allowed patent protection to biological products, previously thought to be unpatentable.

For example, in *Diamond v. Chakrabarty*[410] the court held that genetically engineered bacteria was patentable. Furthermore, in *President and Fellows of Harvard College v. Canada (Commissioner of Patents)*,[411] the Canadian Court of Appeal held that an oncomouse, a transgenic non-human mammal genetically engineered for use in cancer studies, was patentable.[412] However, the majority of the Supreme Court of Canada, in overruling the Court of Appeal decision, held that the oncomouse was a higher life form and was not patentable.[413] The above cases reveal the efforts of courts in several jurisdictions to align the law with the present realities of science and everyday life.[414]

These recent decisions show that *Ainsworth* does not provide an immutable criterion for property[415] and applying such a rule is counterproductive to biological

---

403 Glendon, *supra*, note 399, at 163. Similarly, Joseph W. Singer, 'The Reliance Interest in Property' (1988) 40 *Stan. L. Rev.* 614.

404 Glendon, *supra*, note 399, at 150–53.

405 Herman and Sor, *supra*, note 398, at 778–80.

406 *Ibid.*

407 Yelpaala, *supra*, note 265, at 154.

408 Emanuel J. Ezekiel, *et al.*, 'What Makes Clinical Research Ethical?' (2000) 283(20) *Jour. Am. Med. Ass.*, 2701.

409 *U.S. v. Arora* 860 F. Supp. 1019 (1994).

410 447 U.S. 303.

411 (2000) D.L.R. 385.

412 *Ibid.*, at 400.

413 *Commissioner of Patents v. President and Fellows of Harvard College* (2002) SCC 76.

414 Generally, *Diamond*, 447 U.S. 303.

415 Jeremy Waldron drew a distinction between a 'concept' and a 'conception' of property. He suggested that alienability was not part of the concept of property and, therefore, might not be recognized by a particular legal system's conception of property:

> The *concept* of ownership is the very abstract idea described in section 5: a correlation between individual names and particular objects, such that the decision of the person whose name is on the object about what should be done with that object is taken as socially conclusive. The detailed rules of particular legal systems (whether real or imaginary) assigning rights, liberties, powers, immunities and liabilities to people in regard to particular resources amount to *conceptions* of that abstract concept. They

forms of property. In considering whether 'whiteness' qualified as property despite its inalienability, Harris posited that 'the inalienability of whiteness should not preclude the consideration of whiteness as property'.[416] Similarly, Radin cautioned that 'we must cease thinking that market alienability is inherent in the concept of property'.[417] Therefore, whether a right over a corpse or human tissue qualifies as property ought not to depend solely on its intrinsic monetary value or allied considerations, but on the social, economic and privacy considerations engendered by biomedical technology. This raises the question of whether (and how) the court should articulate a limited property interest in the human body.[418]

Suggested Routes to Finding a Property Interest in the Human Body

It is possible for courts to find the existence of a limited property interest in a dead human body or tissue by drawing analogies from various areas of law where similar rights are firmly established.[419] Courts have found, in some instances, that property interests do exist in a corpse or in bodily materials such as cells.

Autonomy and Right to Bodily Self-Determination

When examining situations where courts have enforced a person's right to bodily self-determination, it is apparent that courts have indirectly enforced rights

---

indicate ways in which the abstract idea of ownership has been or may be realized concretely in particular societies. [Italics in the original]

'What Is Private Property?' (1985) 5 *Oxford Journal of Legal Studies* 313, at 340.

416 Harris, *supra*, note 347, at 1734.

417 Radin, *supra*, note 252, at 1903.

418 Michelle B. Bray, 'Note, Personalizing Personality: Toward a Property Right in Human Bodies' (1990) 69 *Texas L. Rev.* 209 (suggesting the existence of market-inalienable property right in a corpse and living body parts). Other commentators have also suggested some form of limited property rights or compensatory model; see Thomas P. Dillon, 'Source Compensation for Tissues and Cells Used in Biotechnical Research: Why a Source Shouldn't Share in the Profits' (1989) 64 *Notre Dame L. Rev.* 628; Gina M. Grandolfo, 'The Human Property Gap' (1992) 32 *Santa Clara L. Rev.* 957; Hannah Horsley, 'Reconsidering Inalienability for Commercially Valuable Biological Materials' (1992) 29 *Harvard Journal on Legislation* 223; Catherine A. Tallerico, 'The Autonomy of the Human Body in the Age of Biotechnology' (1990) 61 *Uni. Col. L. Rev.* 659.

419 This analogical approach was favoured by Hardiman who proposed the drawing of:

An analogy to the property right known as the 'right of publicity' that protects the pecuniary value of a public figure's name, voice, and appearance. Like the right of publicity, the right of commerciality would recognize only the commercial value of the body, preventing the misappropriation of that value by others and prohibiting their unjust enrichment…By comparison, the value protected by the right of commerciality originates in the inheritance of genetic traits or the chance infection by some agent that increases the commercial value of one's cells. One could argue that the essence of one's identity is the information of one's cells.

Hardiman, *supra*, note 1, at 260.

similar to property rights. It is well settled that an individual has authority over his or her body and the right to determine what is done to it.[420] This principle of bodily self-determination is best exemplified in the context of the physician-patient relationship.[421] Except in the case of emergency or statutory authorization, medical intervention may only be undertaken with the consent of the patient; otherwise, the physician will be liable for battery.[422] Even when consent is given, the physician has a duty to give the patient adequate information on all the potential and likely risks of medical intervention.[423] A breach of this duty may result in a claim for negligence or medical malpractice.[424]

The common law right of a patient to consent to treatment also includes a right to refuse or withdraw from medical treatment.[425] This right is now constitutionally protected.[426] Thus, a patient may legally refuse life-saving treatment even when death is imminent.[427] Therefore, it may be argued that some legal systems permit a person to terminate his or her life by foregoing life-saving treatment. In other words, disease naturally causes the resultant death.[428] The patient has a choice to be either treated or abstain from treatment. The latter is a deliberate termination of life. Suicide, however, has ceased to be a criminal offence in America,[429] Canada[430] and some other legal systems. The point is that law may be unwittingly facilitating an act of self-destruction.

---

420 *Schloendorff v. N.Y. Hosp.* 105 N.E. 2d 92, at 93 (1914). See, generally, Michael Freeman, 'A Time to be Born and a Time to Die' (2003) 56 *Current Legal Problems* 603–49 (exploring the use of principles of autonomy and dignity in resolving diverse problems arising from existing reproductive technologies).

421 *Ibid.*

422 *Ibid.*, at 92; *Parmley v. Parmley* (1945) 4 D.L.R. 81; *Marshall v. Curry* (1933) 3 D.L.R. 260.

423 *Reibl v. Hughes* (1981) 114 D.L.R. (3d) 1.

424 *Ibid.*

425 *Ciarlariello v. Schacter* (1993) 2 S.C.R. 119.

426 *Ibid.*; *Krischer v. McIver* 697 So. 2d 91, at 102 (1997); *Cruzan v. Director, Missouri Department of Health* 497 U.S. 261 (1990); *Sue Rodriguez v. A.G. of Canada* (1993) 3 S.C.R. 519, at 587–9.

427 *Malette v. Shulman* (1990) 72 O.R. (2d) 417, where the patient was held entitled to refuse a medically necessary blood transfusion, even though the refusal was based on her religious belief.

428 There is a fruitful judicial and juristic distinction of the difference between causation and intent or between refusal of treatment and assisted suicide: Amy L. Jerdee, 'Breaking Through The Silence: Minnesota's Pregnancy Presumption And The Right To Refuse Medical Treatment' (2000) 84 *Minn. L. Rev.* 971; David Orentlicher, 'The Alleged Distinction of Euthanasia and the Withdrawal of Life-Sustaining Treatment: Conceptually Incoherent and Impossible to Maintain' (1998) *Uni. Illi. L. Rev.* 837; Trudo Lemmens, 'Towards the Right to be Killed? Treatment Refusal, Assisted Suicide and Euthanasia in the United States and Canada' (1996) 52 *British Med. Bulletin* 341; *Gilmore v. Finn* 527 S.E. 2d 426 (2000); *Washington v. Glucksberg* 117 S. Ct. 2258 (1997); *Vaco v. Quill* 117 S. Ct. 2293 (1997); *Nancy B. v. Hotel-Dieu de Quebec* (1992) 69 C.C.C. (3d) 450.

429 *Washington v. Glucksberg* 117 S. Ct. 2258 (1997).

430 *Sue Rodriguez v. A.G. of Canada* (1993) 3 S.C.R. 519.

In *McFall v. Shimp*,[431] the plaintiff needed a bone marrow transplant to survive. The defendant, who was the plaintiff's cousin, refused to donate the matching bone marrow. The plaintiff's action to compel the donation under a mandatory injunction failed.[432] The court implicitly recognized a type of property right in the defendant's bone marrow, in holding that the defendant's tissues could not be harvested without his consent.[433] Similarly, in *R v. Stillman*,[434] the Supreme Court of Canada held that it was not permissible for the police to surreptitiously obtain a mucous sample of a detainee for DNA analysis.[435] As such, these cases enforced property-like protections, though they were basically decided on the law of consent as they were all concerned with a living human body.

Transformation of a Corpse or Human Tissue by Work and Skill

Australian courts have recently crystallized an exception, first enunciated in Australia in 1908,[436] that an expenditure of work and labour on a corpse may make it worthy of property protection.[437] This seems to be a judicial recognition of Locke's[438] and Stuart Mill's[439] theses, which state that the product of a person's labour is the property of that person.

In *Doodeward v. Spence*,[440] which involved a right to the possession of a double-headed still-born foetus, Griffith, C.J., of the High Court of Australia, observed:

> I entertain no doubt that, when a person has by the lawful exercise of work or skill so dealt with a human body or part of a human body in his lawful possession that it has acquired some attributes differentiating it from a mere corpse awaiting burial, he acquires a right to retain possession of it, at least as against any person not entitled to have it delivered to

---

431 10 Pa. D. & C. 3d 90 (1978).

432 *Ibid.*, at 92.

433 It is interesting to note that Professor Guido Calabresi's comment on the above case seems to have proceeded on the assumption that there is a property right in one's body: G. Calabresi, 'Do We Own Our Bodies?' (1991) 1 *Health Matrix* 5.

434 (1997) 1 S.C.R. 607.

435 In the above case, the majority reasoned that the mucous sample was not abandoned since it was obtained in the context of detention, and against the explicit prior refusal of the defendant to give bodily samples. It was therefore a conscripted evidence. Nevertheless, it held that the mucous sample was discoverable through an alternative non-conscriptive means, and was obtained with minimal breach of the appellant's dignity. On those grounds, it was therefore admissible: at 675.

436 *Doodeward v. Spence* (1908) 6 C.L.R. 406. Approvingly referred to in the Canadian case of *Miner v. C.P.R.* 409, at 413, the American case of *Janicki v. Hospital of St Raphael* 744 A. 2d 963, at 968 (1999), and the recent English cases of *Dobson v. North Tyneside Health Authority* (1997) 1 W.L.R. 596, and *R v. Kelly (*1998) 3 All E.R. 741.

437 *Doodeward v. Spence* (1908) 6 C.L.R. 406–407.

438 Locke, *supra*, note 260.

439 Mill, *supra*, note 261.

440 *Doodeward*, 6 C.L.R. at 406.

him for the purpose of burial, but subject, of course, to any positive law which forbids its retention under the particular circumstances.[441]

For the above exception to apply, the initial possession of the dead body, or part of it, must be lawful.[442] Also, such possession must not affront public health or decency.[443] Therefore, a researcher who broke into a morgue and stole body parts which were subsequently preserved by the exercise of scientific skill and labour cannot claim the exception. In *R v. Kelly*,[444] the British Court of Appeal held that an artist, who surreptitiously obtained body parts scientifically preserved at the Royal College of Surgeons, was guilty of theft.[445] The court envisaged future legal protection for body parts intended for transplantation or DNA analysis, even when these parts had not been subjected to the application of labour and skill.[446] It has been suggested that the *Doodeward* exception has engulfed the general no-property rule in dead bodies.[447]

With respect to living body parts, *Moore* presents a latent application of the work and skill exception. In *Moore*[448] the plaintiff's excised cell was transformed into a patentable and lucrative cell-line by the use of scientific skill and labour.[449] The court held that the patent belonged to the researchers, even though ownership of the patent was not in issue.[450] It is possible that the investment of scientific labour on Moore's cell contributed to the dismissal of his cause of action for conversion.

Utility

Biomedical technology gives corpses and body parts a utility that was not present when the no-property rule emerged. For instance, before anatomy emerged as a method of medical practice corpses had no medical or commercial value.[451] The emergence of anatomy as a branch of medicine and its systematic regulation by the British *Anatomy Act of 1832*,[452] made cadavers profoundly useful for medical training in the act of surgery. The medical value of cadavers underpinned the activities of grave-robbers, who stole newly buried corpses and sold them to physicians.[453] The

---

441 *Ibid.*, at 414.

442 *Ibid.*, at 406–407.

443 *Ibid.*, at 413.

444 *R v. Kelly* (1998) 3 All E.R. 741 (C.A.).

445 *Ibid.*

446 *Ibid.*, at 750.

447 Stephen White, 'The Law Relating To Dealing With Dead Bodies' (2000) 4 *Med. L. Int.* 145, at 167.

448 *Moore*, 793 P. 2d 479.

449 *Ibid.*, at 481–2.

450 *Ibid.*, at 492.

451 S.M. Shultz, *Body Snatching: The Robbing of Graves for the Education of Physicians* (North Carolina: McFarland & Co., 1992), discussing the grave-robbing activities that took place to satisfy the demands of cadavers for medical education.

452 *Anatomy Act 1832*, Cap. 75, 2 & 3 Williams IV.

453 M.P. Hutchens, 'Grave Robbing and Ethics in the 19th Century' (1997) 278 *JAMA* 1115.

medical value of cadavers also led to a shift in the attitude of British judges toward human corpses.[454] The observation of Willes, J. remains on point:

> [B]ut in modern times the requirements of science are larger than formerly, and when they are so extensive it seems to me that we ought not to entertain any prejudice against the obtaining of dead bodies for the laudable purpose of dissection, but we ought to look at the matter with a view to utility…[455]

Today, the utility of a corpse, or parts of it, has apparently transcended those envisaged by Judge Willes.[456] For instance, cadavers and cadaver parts preserved by a process of plastination[457] could be exhibited for the anatomical and health education of laypeople and to serve as a reminder of our immortality.[458] The preservation technique known as plastination was developed by a German professor, Gunther von Haggens, who has gone to some European countries and Japan for the purpose of exhibiting plastinated cadavers and body parts.[459] Haggens succeeded in carrying out body exhibition in London despite initial opposition from some members of the public.[460] In addition, body parts are currently being used in DNA analysis, artistic casts, researching predictive testing technique for genetic disorders and organ transplants. It is interesting that though artistic utilizations of cadaver and body parts have rich historic precedents, there is surprisingly no current regulatory or legal framework on artistic access to cadavers.[461] Thus, it was suggested that this legal uncertainty was partly responsible for cadaveric abuses by artists, as was witnessed in *Kelly's* case.[462] It seems, therefore, that the progressive utility of the human body might justify a limited property protection to enable a deserving plaintiff to obtain relevant judicial remedies.[463]

---

454 *R v. Feist* (1858) 169 E.R. 1132, at 1135.

455 *Ibid.*

456 For a discussion of more extensive modern utilization of the human body: Lori B. Andrews, 'Harnessing the Benefits of Biobanks' (2005) 33 *J. L. Med. & Ethics* 22.

457 This involves draining away the body fluids and impregnating the body with a type of polymer.

458 Body Words: http://www.bodyworlds.com/en/pages/ausstellungsziel.asp (last accessed on 29 July 2005); 'Corpses Show Not Illegal', BBC News, 20 March 2002: http://news.bbc.co.uk/1/hi/entertainment/arts /1883396.stm (last accessed on 3 December 2004).

459 BBC, *supra.*

460 BBC, *supra.* Mark Lawson, 'Our Bodies, Our Deaths, Our Decisions: At Least the Corpses in the Show of Flayed Flesh were Donated', *The Guardian*, 23 March 2002 (page unknown); Andy Miah, 'Dead Bodies for the Masses: The British Public Autopsy and the Aftermath', www.ctheory.net/printer.asp?id=363 (last accessed on 1 August 2005).

461 Institute of Ideas, *Morbid Fascination: The Body and Death in Contemporary Culture* (Conference organized by the Institute of Ideas on 16 May 2003). See www.instituteofideas.com.

462 *Ibid.*

463 As emphasized in the beginning and later in this chapter, the property protection I propose is not intended to underpin a market in cadavers or body parts.

Characterization under Certain Statutes

When construing certain statutes, some courts have held that the human body is an object of property. While these statutes deal with special circumstances, they are not irrelevant. For example, in *Onyeanusi v. Pan Am*[464] the Court of Appeal held that the plaintiff's deceased mother qualified as 'goods' under *The Warsaw Convention*.[465] Thus, the plaintiff's delay in giving the required statutory notice precluded him from recovering damages for the defendant's nine-day delay in delivering the corpse at the contracted destination.[466] Justice Cowen's observation sets forth the general principle of this case:

> Human remains can have significant commercial value, although they are not typically bought and sold like other goods. Medical schools and hospitals commonly use human cadavers for training and experiments. Human tissue and organs which are taken from the recently deceased have inestimable value in transplant operations. Although remains which are used for these medical and scientific purposes are usually donated, rather than bought and sold, this does not negate their potential commercial value. Onyeanusi argues that many states prohibit commerce in human remains or organ. Notwithstanding the legality of selling some parts of the body, most notably blood and sperm, we believe these state laws against organ and tissue sales are premised on moral and ethical, rather than economic, considerations. In fact, the very existence of these state laws indicates that there would be a market for human remains in the absence of government intervention.[467]

As noted above, statutes like *The Human Tissue Gift Act*,[468] *Human Organ Transplant Act*,[469] and *Uniform Anatomical Gift Act*,[470] though prohibiting sales in transplantable organs, implicitly recognize their proprietary characteristics.[471] Market transactions in regenerative body parts like blood,[472] hair, fingernails, toenails[473] and

---

464 952 F. 2d 788 (1992).

465 *Ibid.*, at 792–3.

466 *Ibid.*, at 793.

467 *Ibid.*, at 792. However, it was held in *Bourne v. Norwich Crematorium Ltd* (1967) All E.R. 576 that 'it would be a distortion of the English language to describe the living or the dead as goods or materials'.

468 *Human Tissue Gift Act, R.S.O. 1990, c. H. 20.*

469 *Human Organ Transplant Act 1989, c. 31* [U.K.].

470 *Uniform Anatomical Gift Act 1987, 8A U.L.A. 19.*

471 Similarly, Dickens, *supra*, note 27, at 126, argued that: 'Legislation prohibiting commerce, affecting purchase and sale of tissue, may indicate that, in the absence of such laws, and in areas or circumstances where they do not apply, property interests exist. Even the prohibition of purchase and sale does not preclude the application and enforcement of other incidents of property rights.' See, also, Barbara Cavuoto, 'Do We Have Both Personal and Proprietary Rights Over Our Own Bodies?' (2001) 6 *QMW L.J.* 43, at 43–4.

472 *Perlmutter v. Beth David Hospital* 123 N.E. 2d 792 (1954); *Carter v. Inter-Faith Hospital of Queens* 304 N.Y.S 2d 97 (1969); *Walker Estate v. York Finch General Hospital* (2001) SCC 23.

473 Regarded as property in *Venner v. Maryland* 354 A. 2d 483 (1976).

bone marrow are already well-known;[474] though in the case of blood it is sometimes regarded as 'service' rather than sale.[475]

Anatomy legislation recognizes that a corpse is property capable of donation for anatomical examination.[476] Donations can be made by persons who have lawful possession of the corpse or by the deceased prior to his or her death.[477] It is pertinent that the first case decided under the British *Anatomy Act of 1832* confirmed this opinion.[478] In *R v. Feist*,[479] Willes, J. observed that: '*[t]he Anatomy Act* has altered the common law, and has rendered the selling of a dead body for the purpose of dissection lawful under certain circumstances'.[480] Society has tolerated, in various forms, some property interests in the human body. Therefore, a full judicial or statutory recognition of a limited property interest in the human body may not be shocking.

Why Not Property in the Human Body?

The strongest argument against the recognition of a property right in the human body is the slippery slope argument that it would cause devaluation, objectification and commodification of life.[481] It is also arguable that propertization of the human body negatively implicates fetal research and abortion. For instance, the conferment of property protection on tissue sources might promote the procurement of abortion for profit for the purpose of harvesting medically needed but scarce fetal tissues.[482] This argument also surfaces in the debate on the patenting of human genes. Some fear that unconscionable scientists will prey upon vulnerable communities that possess unique genes. These fears are exacerbated by the current market for stem cells, harvested from fresh embryos, which sell for as much as US$5,000.[483] Although the no-property argument is often guilty of inattention to the entrepreneurial and market contexts of medical research and corporatization of medical practice,[484] the

---

474 Griggs, L. 'The Ownership of Excised Body Parts: Does an Individual Have the Right to Sell?' (1994) 1 *Journal of Law & Medicine* 223.

475 Rao, *supra*, note 168, at 371–86.

476 For example, Nigeria's *Anatomy Act, Cap. 11*, which is based on the English *Anatomy Act of 1832*.

477 *Ibid.*

478 *R v. Fiest* (1858) 169 E.R. 1132.

479 *Ibid.*

480 *Ibid.*, at 1135.

481 B. Williams, 'Concepts of Personhood and the Commodification of the Body' (1998/99) 7 *Health L. Rev.* 11.

482 Nancy E. Field, 'Evolving Conceptualizations of Property: A Proposal to De-Commercialize the Value of Fetal Tissue' (1989) 99 *Yale L.J.* 169.

483 Margaret Munro, 'A Vision of Spare Parts', *National Post*, 29 March 2001, A15; Brad Evenson, 'Door Opened To Research With Embryos', *National Post*, 30 March 2001, A4.

484 For analysis of the historical connection between medical research, medical practice and markets: Melissa M. Perry, 'Fragmented Bodies, Legal Privilege, and Commodification in Science and Medicine' (1999) 51 *Maine L. Rev.* 169.

uneasiness generated by recent instances of commodification of the human body entitles it to a much closer scrutiny.

In 2001, a newspaper reported that human tissues from a decommissioned anatomy lab at the University of Toronto were being sold at an antique auction.[485] Serious concerns have also been voiced with respect to the existence of markets for human kidneys.[486] Recently, the South African police broke an international organ trafficking ring that matched kidney sellers from Brazil with buyers from Israel for a transplant operation in South Africa.[487] It is estimated that the average price for kidneys in the nefarious global organ trade is US$6,000.[488] In the USA, the director of the willed body programme of the UCLA medical school was accused of selling a total of 496 cadavers for over $704,600 to a middleman who sold them to biotech and pharmaceutical companies, including Mitek, a subsidiary of Johnson & Johnson.[489] Each cadaver was estimated to cost about US$1,400.[490] In a related development, authorities of the Tulane University suspended a distributor of its donated bodies for unlawfully selling seven cadavers to the Army (for about US$25,000–US$30,000), which destroyed them during a test of protective footwear against land mines.[491] The prices of the various parts of the human body, such as head, torso, knee, cornea, fingernails and toenails, are now well known by those who participate in the horrible cadaver black market.[492]

Above are some of the instances of the commodification and objectification of life, which a property regime may potentially exacerbate. Note, however, that recognition of a limited property interest in the human body provides some safeguards against the concerns raised by advocates of a no-property regime. As Chapter 5 demonstrates, it is in the remedification of injuries resulting from misuse or misappropriation of corpses or body parts that the no-property argument becomes glaringly indefensible and absurd. Such no-property arguments encounter frustrating

---

485 Heather Sokoloff, 'Human Tissue on Sale at Auction', *National Post*, 16 April 2001, A4. See, also, Deborah Josefson, 'US Hospitals to Ask Patients for Right to Sell Their Tissue', (2000) 321 *BMJ* 658.

486 Goyal, *supra*, note 46 (reports the existence of such a market in India).

487 Abraham McLaughlin, Ilene R. Prusher and Andrew Downie, 'What is a Kidney Worth?', *The Christian Science Monitor*, 9 June 2004: www.csmonitor.com/2004/0609/p01s03-wogi.html (last accessed on 25 July 2005).

488 *Ibid.*

489 Charles Ornstein and Richard Marosi, '$704,600 Billed for Cadavers', *Los Angeles Times*, 9 March 2004: www.latimes.com/news/local/la-me-bodies9march09,1,416222. story?coll=la-home-headlines; Charles Ornstein and Alan Zarembo, 'UCLA Suspends Body-Donor Program After Alleged Abuses', *Los Angeles Times*, 10 March 2004: www.latimes. com/news/local/la-me-bodies10march10,1,416222.story?coll= la-home-headlines.

490 *Ibid.*

491 *Associated Press*, 'Donated Bodies Used in Land Mine Tests', *The New York Times*, 11 March 2004 (page unknown).

492 John Broder, 'In Science's Name: Lucrative Trade in Body Parts', *The New York Times*, 12 March 2004 (page unknown).

roadblocks when faced with the prospects of avoidable injustice to a plaintiff. That apparently was the experience of Professor Loane Skene in an interesting article.[493]

After unmistakably disavowing a tissue source's right of property and affirming the same right in the receiver, Loane Skene reiterated that upon the assurance of a duly informed consent, a tissue source 'should not have a proprietary right in relation to body parts and tissue removed with consent'.[494] She opined that the 'person or institution holding the body parts or tissue should have a proprietary right over them, but it should be subject to an obligation to use them for medical or scientific purposes and to observe proper ethical standards'.[495] Apart from the conceptual deficiency of this distinction and the absurdity of denying the very source of tissues proprietary rights that are recognized in the tissue receiver, Loane Skene made a tellingly disquieting proposition when she remedially suggested that a 'breach of these requirements (i.e. use of tissues for medical, scientific, and ethical purposes) should be actionable by the person from whom the body part or tissue came, to recover damages'.[496] Could it not be said that the effect of Loane Skene's last statement is to completely implode her no-property thesis. Is it not fantastical that after denying the tissue source ongoing control powers associated with a property right, she turned around to paradoxically bless him or her with a remediable cause of action for damages? Upon what theory of liability would the proposed action for damages be based (recall that consent had already been given by the donor)? Could we say with one breath that a hospital or scientific researcher is the owner of a tissue, and in another breath say that the tissue owner (hospital or scientific researcher) could be sued for the misuse of its property (body tissue) by a person who is no longer the owner and who has relinquished all ongoing control? Have I the right to control the uses to which my car is put after I have sold it to another person? Better still, can I sue for unacceptable uses of my car after its disposition? Outside considerations relating to nuisance[497] and compliance with statutory provisions, how could the hospital be answerable to a person who, according to Loane Skene, no longer has continuing control over, or property right to, his or her tissues?

These absurdities exist because of the denial that a tissue source has property right therein. Loane Skene implicitly admitted, and rightly too, that a tissue source should in some situations be able to bring an action against the receiver, but her no-property framework hopelessly fails to attain that desirable end. Recognition of limited property rights in body parts, as suggested in this book, would alleviate the remedial and conceptual difficulties confronted by Loane Skene and other apologists of the no-property rule. Under a limited property rule, markets in cadavers and body parts could be prohibited, and protection against the abuse of one's body could be provided. A plaintiff would be able to use judicial remedies that are currently unavailable, for instance, remedies relating to tort actions for conversion and detinue,

---

493 Loane Skene, 'Proprietary Rights in Human Bodies, Body Parts and Tissue: Regulatory Contexts and Proposals for New Laws' (2002) 22 *Legal Stud.* 102.

494 *Ibid.*, at 120.

495 *Ibid.*

496 *Ibid.*

497 Every property owner is subject to the law of nuisance.

or constitutional action for an infringement of a property right. A plaintiff would also be able to claim a right to share in the profits resulting from the successful commercialization of research results based on his or her tissue.[498]

Some of the issues which a limited property rule can resolve include how to recover possession and damages from a person who opens a grave, takes the body and refuses to deliver it;[499] what remedies are available to an organ bank when useful human organs in its possession are wilfully destroyed or stolen. How do we recover urine and blood samples unlawfully removed from a police station?[500] Finally, the question arises of how a researcher may recover possession of human cells, lawfully acquired and used in a socially useful activity, from a thief who has stolen them.[501] Similarly, the court in *Ritter v. Couch* asked:[502]

> The world does not contain a tribunal that would punish a son who should resist, even to death, any attempt to mutilate his father's corpse, or tear it from the grave for sale or dissection; but where would he find the legal right to resist, except in his peculiar and exclusive interest in the body?[503]

It seems from the quotation above that if we fail to recognize some 'peculiar and exclusive interest in the body', a plaintiff may not have a standing to sue in court. This chapter suggests that this interest (in the body) should be accepted into the legal category of property, because of the relative merits of that category, though it should be qualified as a limited property. *Ritter's* case suggests that a valuable approach would be to recognize a limited property right in the human body and its parts. Below, an attempt is made to explain how property rights in the human body could be limited.

Statutory Limitation of Property Right in the Human Body

Legitimate objections and concerns regarding the proposed recognition of property rights in the human body and parts of it can be taken care of by appropriate legislation. This legislation should prohibit market in cadavers but recognize that living relatives have limited property rights in corpses for the purpose of obtaining effective and

---

498 Note that the licensing system suggested by M.T. Danforth as a basis for source compensation is based on the recognition of some property rights in the human body: Mary T. Danforth, 'Cells, Sales, and Royalties: The Patient's Right to a Portion of the Profits' (1988) 6 *Yale Law & Policy Rev.* 179.

499 As in *Keyes v. Konkel* 78 N.W. 649 (1899), where any right to recover possession of a corpse was denied.

500 The court confronted that issue in *R v. Welsh* (1974) RTR 478 and *R v. Rothery* (1976) RTR 550.

501 Such consideration inspired the decision in *U.S. v. Arora* 860 F. Supp. 1091 (1994), holding that a cultured human cell was property.

502 76 S.E. 428 (1912).

503 *Ibid.*, at 430.

sufficient judicial remedy.[504] A property-oriented legislative framework could also provide legal protection to living persons against the abuse of their bodies by various biotechnological applications. The legislation proposed here may be similar to those relating to organ transplants and should deal with specific cases of abuse of property rights, like the sordid market in body parts existing in some developing countries.[505] Justice Cowen referred to this nefarious market in *Onyeanusi v. Pan Am.*[506]

Legislative intervention, along the lines proposed in this chapter, would mean that only limited property rights are recognized in cadavers and body parts. This limitation of property right partly results from the prohibition on alienability. It may be asked: why still use the legal category of property after eliminating some of the most important incidents of property? Why not choose other legal categories? The introduction to this chapter outlined problems relating to tort, consent, criminal law, human rights, and constitutional law frameworks, and the cases discussed in this chapter exemplify these problems. Using a property framework is a strategic choice because of its relative powers of protection. A report prepared for the Canadian Royal Commission on New Reproductive Technologies had to consider the legal category under which to protect 'stages of potential life'.[507] According to this report:[508]

> If we decide that, as a matter of policy, the gamete donors ought to have joint control, we may also view property law as an appropriate mechanism by which to achieve that policy. Property law has the capacity to recognize that the gamete donors have joint 'ownership' of the frozen embryo. However, it does not necessarily follow that the 'owners' should be able [to] sell their property (indeed, existing law precludes this), or pass it on to their heirs, or consent to its being used for scientific research. These issues give rise to different policy considerations, and may require different legal responses.[509]

In the context of the above quotation, Jennifer Nedelsky argued that the elimination of substantial incidents of property makes the choice of property framework unsuitable. She asked: 'Why would we invoke the concept of property here, when almost none of the usual incidents of property seems likely to be appropriate?'[510] She opined that the application of a property framework, with respect to stages of potential life, might distort the issues at stake. With reference to stages of potential life, Nedelsky argued

---

504 I already discussed the comparative advantages of property protection over other legal categories, for instance, tort, criminal law, constitutional law and human rights.

505 Madhav Goyal, *et al.*, 'Economic and Health Consequences of Selling a Kidney in India' (2002) 288 *JAMA* 1589–93; Jane Parry, 'Chinese City Outlaws Sale of Human Organs' (2003) 327 *BMJ* 520; Sanjay Kumar, 'Police Uncover Large Scale Organ Trafficking in Punjab' (2003) 326 *BMJ* 180; Judy Siegel-Itzkovich, 'Israeli Women Can Buy Ova From Abroad' (2002) 324 *BMJ* 69; Judy Siegel-Itzkovich, 'Sale of Organs to be Investigated' (2001) 322 *BMJ* 128.

506 958 F. 2d 788, at 792 (1992), footnote 6.

507 This is the phrase used by Nedelsky to re-characterize what is commonly known as reproductive material. See, Nedelsky, *supra*, note 28, at 343.

508 Royal Commission on New Reproductive Technologies, *Reproductive Technology: A Property Law Analysis* (Ottawa: Research Branch of the Library of Parliament, 1992).

509 *Ibid.*, at 61.

510 Nedelsky, *supra*, note 28, at 360.

that one of the values we would like to protect is our attachment to the potential life. She thinks that in protecting that value, a relational approach would better solve the problem than a property framework:

> The complex issues of control and decisional authority should be addressed as such without the distortions of the conceptual framework of property. The entire process of inquiry will be facilitated by a direct inquiry into the values we want to promote by permitting and protecting certain kinds of control. If we articulate why we think powers of decisional authority are appropriate, it will not be hard to specify them in legislation. The concept of property will add nothing and will continually skew the inquiry toward the very dangers we must try to avoid: commodification, exploitation, and alienation. Some of these problems will be so difficult to overcome in any legal framework for the potential life NRTs (i.e., new reproductive technologies) have made possible, that it is crucial that we not select a legal concept that will exacerbate the problem rather than facilitate its solution.[511]

Similarly, the Supreme Court of California in the case of *Moore v. The Regents of the University of California*[512] thought that the elimination of significant incidents of property makes the property category unsuitable:

> [t]he statute's (California Health and Safety Code) practical effect is to limit, drastically, a patient's control over excised cells. By restricting how excised cells may be used and requiring their eventual destruction, the statute eliminates so many of the rights ordinarily attached to property that one cannot simply assume that what is left amounts to 'property' or 'ownership' for purposes of conversion law.[513]

Joan Gilmour expressed concern that the adoption of a property framework may inexorably lead to the realization of other incidents of property.[514] She, therefore, suggested a new legislation that 'could permit the exercise of some of the powers commonly associated with a property right, but need not incorporate all of the economic component that accompanies the institution of property in the normal

---

511 *Ibid.*, at 362.
512 *Moore, supra*, note 23.
513 *Ibid.*, at 492.
514 Gilmour, *supra*, note 20, at 132:

> Categorizing something as 'property' does not stop with or signify only the right to control; it also carries with it expectations of a market model and market behaviour as the norm. The property, whatever it may be, becomes something it is thought appropriate to buy and sell through a market. Once one adopts the language of property in order to obtain its strong protection for the right of control, one cannot necessarily control all the associations that the institution of property will bring with it – expectations of economic exchange value, rights of alienability, and so on. Even though legislation can limit the rights generally ascribed to an owner of property (and this is typical in many contexts – property rights are not absolute), there is often a sense that in doing so, one is taking away something that is rightfully the owner – diminishing the owner's entitlements somehow – rather than enhancing or refining the ability to achieve the policy goals intended in recognizing a property interest in the first place.

course'.[515] She emphasized that the 'nonproperty regulatory system'[516] she proposed should not employ property terms, even if serving the same functions of property. It seems, therefore, that the potentiality of a property framework degenerating into a market for body parts underpins its criticism.

The limited property framework proposed here need not lead to a market in cadavers. A market in cadavers or their parts would be proscribed. The framework (limited property) rather serves some functional purposes, for instance, enabling a plaintiff to sue for an infringement of a constitutionally or legally protected property right, and to bring successful tort actions for conversion and detinue.[517] It is arguable that a property framework is appropriate even when some of the incidents of property are eliminated. A piece of property may still be regarded as such though some important incidents, for instance, alienability and devisability, are not present. With respect to personhood and whiteness, Radin[518] and Harris[519] have shown that a property framework is appropriate even in the absence of alienability. In fact, in both cases, inalienability seems to be the required norm. Right to publicity, or one's personality, is of significant commercial value, yet it is not devisable or descendible.[520] Some cases have shown that I can have a property right in my job though it is not transferable.[521]

Similarly, a property right may exist in professional certificates, though such certificates cannot be bought and sold. The law may preclude an owner of a historic building from selling or destroying the building; nevertheless, the building remains the property of the owner. It is trite that property rights are not absolute. The right to use one's property as one sees fit does not entitle one to cause a nuisance. A legislative diminution of some of the incidents of property would be in keeping with the principle of non-absolutism of property rights. The proposed legislation on property rights to the human body will not be different from the law's treatment of other items of property, because property rights have always been subject to state interest and to the interests of others. In contrast, the current situation of no-property rule perpetuates injustices.

Recognizing a limited property right to the human body may pave the way for constitutional protection.[522] It is certainly arguable that constitutional protection

---

515 *Ibid.*, at 137.

516 *Ibid.*, at 138.

517 It has been argued that the theory of conversion is properly applicable to non-consensual exploitation of a person's body parts: Aaron C. Lichtman, 'Commercial Exploitation of DNA and the Tort of Conversion: A Physician May Not Destroy a Patient's Interest in her Body-Matter' (1989) 34 *New York Law Sch. L. Rev.* 531.

518 Radin, *supra*, note 252.

519 Harris, *supra*, note 347.

520 Felcher and Rubin, *supra*, note 398.

521 Glendon, *supra*, note 399; Vogt, *supra*, note 400.

522 The limited property right proposed by this chapter seems to be supported by some writers. For instance: Hardiman, *supra*, note 1, at 262–3:

> Finally, the right of commerciality would appease those offended by the notion of selling the human body or its parts. Unlike the sale of a commodity, the right of commerciality would focus on negotiations and contracts defining the relative

should be accorded to rights exercisable by the next of kin over a corpse or parts of a corpse.[523] Such protection was attempted in *Crocker v. Pleasant*,[524] where the plaintiffs claimed that the defendant's interment of their son's dead body, without sufficient notice to them, was a breach of their property right under the 14th Amendment of the United States Constitution.[525] The claim failed and the court did not recognize any property interest in a dead body.[526] As noted already, the plaintiff's right to possess a corpse for the purpose of burial does not support an action for conversion or detinue. Some of the cases held that since there is no property in a corpse, a plaintiff would not succeed in an action for conversion that depends on the existence of a property right for its success. The requirement that a plaintiff must prove accompanying physical or pecuniary loss makes the tort action for intentional or negligent infliction of emotional distress a difficult one for a plaintiff. It appears that the benefits of allowing a limited property right in the human body outweigh the disadvantages.

Conclusion

Recent advances in biomedical technology have intensified the question of property rights in a human body or corpse. The common law of England does not generally recognize property rights in corpses, though it does recognize the right of certain persons (for example, executors, administrators and next of kin) to possession of a corpse for the sole purpose of burial. It is a misdemeanour under common law to disinter a corpse without authority or to prevent the burial of a corpse. This common law offence was directed at grave-robbers, a common phenomenon in the eighteenth and nineteenth centuries. However, the common law does not recognize an action for conversion or detention of a corpse because common law does not consider a corpse as property. Recent Court of Appeal cases in England have, however, recognized significant exception to the common law no-property rule. For instance, where a

---

proportion of each party's financial stake in a new product. Most people would probably feel more comfortable with these images than with the image of a salesman bartering off a human kidney. While the reality may not be very different, public acceptance would be vastly simplified.

Similarly, Churchill, *supra*, note 25, at 282, suggested:

It is suggested that the legislature act now to protect the sanctity of the human person by recognizing limited property rights in the human body, which vest in the possessor. These rights would protect the human body from the kind of unauthorized intrusion experienced by Moore through, among other things, the establishment of a right to bodily privacy. The recognition of these rights would still permit the possessor to alienate his or her body or portions thereof as gifts, and not for any form of valuable consideration (in example organ and/or tissue donation during life or at death).

523 Erik S. Jaffe, 'She's Got Bette Davis['s] Eyes: Assessing the Nonconsensual Removal of Cadaver Organs under the Takings and Due Process Clauses' (1990) *Columbia L. Rev.* 528.

524 727 So. 2d 1087 (1999).

525 *Ibid.*, at 1088.

526 *Ibid.*, at 1089.

corpse has undergone some scientific work and labour for the purpose of medical education and exhibition, it is considered a piece of property.

Common law jurisdictions in Canada generally follow the English no-property rule in dead bodies with limited rights of possession for burial, though Quebec appears to follow a limited property rule based on the decision in *Phillips v. Montreal General Hospital*. Section 182 of the *Canadian Criminal Code* prohibits interference with dead bodies. In the USA, many courts did not like the British no-property rule in dead bodies and were prepared to adopt a contrary approach. Thus, some of the USA courts evolved multiple remedial strategies to circumvent the English rule. For instance, the USA courts used the concept of quasi-property and tort principles to grant relief to some deserving plaintiffs. However, the USA approach did not amount to recognition of full property rights in corpses.

Some recent judicial and scholarly opinions tend to support the existence of property interests in the human body tissue or corpses. The two dominant senses of property consider it as 'a right to a thing' and as a 'bundle of rights'. The extent to which the dominant paradigms of property right accommodate the existence of property interests in the human body is not clear. Recognition of such interests has become imperative due to enormous advances in science and technology, which have the potentials of invading the human body. Furthermore, our everyday experience shows that the human body and parts are already being propertized and commodified. For instance, there is an existing market for blood, though payment is characterized as service rather than sale. There is an illegal market for kidney and other body organs in some parts of the developing world. There is also a market for sperm, ova and hair. The current no-property rule does not seem capable of preventing this market. However, an unlimited property rule may exacerbate the emerging markets in body parts. Thus, appropriate legislation should be passed to prohibit a market in body parts and recognize a limited property right in the human body for the purposes of obtaining a judicial relief. The courts, in addition to methods already in use, could find a limited property interest in the human body by drawing analogies from areas of law that affirm property-like rights in the human body. The limited property framework proposed here is intended to provide a remedial basis of action for a plaintiff who complains of the invasion of his or her bodily integrity by the application of biomedical technology. Similarly, it enables a plaintiff to obtain appropriate judicial relief where the cause of action alleges interference with a corpse. The no-property rule makes it difficult for the plaintiff to succeed in an action for conversion, detinue or breach of constitutional right of property with respect to a corpse. A limited property rule will be in accordance with the principle that property rights are not absolute. The proposed legislation can alleviate ethical and religious concerns regarding commodification and objectification of the human body.

Chapter 3

Cultural and Ontological Contexts of Biotechnology and the Human Body

'Ay, my little God. Where are my corpses?
That's all I want to know so I can bury them.'
Miguel Angel Ortega, El Salvador earthquake victim.[1]

Introduction

This chapter examines the existence and desirability of a limited property interest in the human body in the context of non-Western cultures and societies, using Nigeria as a case study. It shows how cultural conditions may affect the choice of legal category under which to protect interests in the human body. It also explores the benefits and disadvantages of a property rule in the peculiar circumstances of Nigerian culture.

In reference to the evolution of modern philosophy from the seventeenth century, Bertrand Russell observed: 'Social cohesion and individual liberty, like religion and science, are in a state of conflict or uneasy compromise throughout the whole period.'[2] The conflictual interaction of science and religion manifests remarkably in the Nigerian milieu, where the peoples' traditional transcendental beliefs inexorably reject the interference of biomedical and biotechnological applications. The pursuit of scientific inquiry within indigenous communities has often resulted in the devastation of their social organization and devaluation of their spirituality. Recently, Patrick Tierney, in his controversial book, examined how some American scientists, pursuing the theoretical connection between violence and reproduction and the effect of radiation on genetic materials, allegedly contributed to the cultural and spiritual impoverishment of the Yanomami of Venezuela and utterly dislocated, if not annihilated, their political and social institutions.[3] Tierney's accusations are

---

1 N. Price, 'Neighbourhood Flattened', *National Post* (15 January 2001) A3.

2 B. Russell, *A History of Western Philosophy* (London: Unwin Paperbacks, 1946), at 15.

3 P. Tierney, *Darkness in El Dorado: How Scientists and Journalists Devastated the Amazon* (New York: W. W. Norton & Company, 2000). Patrick Tierney's book has been criticized by some writers and scientific associations. See, for instance: University of California, Santa Barbara, *Preliminary Report on the Neel/Chagnon Allegations* (Santa Barbara: UCSB, Department of Anthropology, 2001]; Kim Hill, 'Comments on Patrick Tierney's Book, Darkness in El Dorado', posted on www.psych.ucsb.edu/research/cep/eldorado/kimhill.html (last accessed on 13 November 2003), concluding that: '[a]lthough the Tierney book raises important issues about anthropological fieldwork ethics, policies toward remote and isolated indigenous populations and the current state of native South Americans,

controversial, and his account of scientific activities conducted by some Western scientists in the Yanomami region is not generally accepted by anthropologists. Tierney's book, however, serves to illustrate some of the difficult issues that can arise from biomedical research in an indigenous setting.[4]

The contribution of science to contemporary civilization and well-being is arguably axiomatic, but it is not the only social good or value worthy of pursuit. Respect for the dead and religious beliefs are legitimate and equally important social goods meritorious of pursuit. Though present scientific knowledge dismissively consigns traditional religious beliefs to the category of superstition, it is well known that most indigenous peoples continue to be ordered and regulated by their cosmovision. For them, biomedical technologies pose a dilemma: do they tenaciously protect the integrity of their ontology and forfeit or reject the benefit of any conflicting biomedical innovations, or do they accept these innovations even when they entail some spiritual devaluation? This dilemma is a recurrent theme of this chapter, which puts in perspective the contending forces of science and religion, potentially emergent in any biomedical research in Nigeria, and attempts to craft possible ways of achieving reconciliation.

While most Western legal systems have fertile judicial or scholarly commentaries on the nature and extent of rights that inhere in the dead body of a human being or parts of it, there is neither a systematic legal discussion of the subject in the Nigerian context nor a reported Nigerian case law that directly discusses the existence of a property interest in a dead body or human tissue.[5] Some ideas, however, can be

---

the false accusations, ideological persecution, and sheer maliciousness of this book undermines much of the good that could have come from reporting about the Yanomamo situation'; Jane Lancaster, 'A Critique of Darkness in El Doraldo', posted on www.anth.ucsb.edu/discus/html/messages/62/100.html?975960218 (last accessed on 11 November 2003); Diane Paul and John Beatty, 'Darkness in El Doraldo, and Eugenics: The Missing Context', posted on http://groups.yahoo.com/group/evolutinary-psychology/message/8370; The American Society of Human Genetics, 'Response to Allegations Against James V. Neel in Darkness in El Doraldo, by Patrick Tierney', (2002) 70 *Am. J. Hum. Genet.* 1–10; Bruce Alberts (President, National Academy of Sciences), 'Setting the Record Straight Regarding Darkness in El Doraldo', posted on www.nationalacademies.org (last accessed on 13 November 2003).

4   Similar ethical conflict between the value of scientific research and indigenous mortuary tradition was excellently explored by Phillip L. Walker, 'Bioarchaelogical Ethics: A Historical Perspective on the Value of Human Remains', in Katzenberg, M.A. and Saunders, S.R., eds, *Biological Anthropology of the Human Skeleton* (New York: Wiley-Liss, Inc., 2000), 3–39.

5   My review of the subject index of cases reported in various law reports in Nigeria did not reveal a case on point. *Egbe v. Onogun* (1972) 1 All N.L.R. 95 [hereinafter *Egbe*] would have been the first reported Nigerian case to discuss the law on dead bodies but the case eventually turned on procedural issues. The plaintiff had instituted an action against the defendant for trespass to the plaintiff's father's grave. The plaintiff also asked for an interim injunction to restrain further acts of trespass pending the determination of the substantive suit. The learned trial judge, in dismissing the application for an interim injunction, held that the plaintiff had no possessory interest in the father's grave entitling him to the relief claimed. On appeal to the Nigerian Supreme Court, the issue was whether the learned trial judge directed himself properly on the principles governing the grant of an interim injunction. The Supreme

gleaned from the literature on customary family law, although it has to be kept in mind that the following analysis is speculative and not based on precedent. This chapter attempts to construct the legal status of a dead human body and its parts under customary law based on a rationalization of the Ibo ontological and religious traditions, its anthropology and sociology, and some literary works of fiction that depict Ibo communitarian and mortuary tradition. 'Ibo' is used both linguistically and ethnically. It depicts the predominant ethnic group or nationality that indigenously inhabits south-eastern Nigeria. It also refers to the language spoken by this group. Ibo is the starting-point of this chapter's analysis, though conclusions here may be generalizable to other nationalities in Nigeria and other parts of Africa, which share the Ibo's ontological tradition.

Analysis of the Ibo worldview supplies the foundation of this chapter's proposition on the property interest that exists in a corpse or body parts in Nigerian customary law. This proposition is juxtaposed with the relevant statutory and received laws in Nigeria, to bring into relief the latter's shortcomings. Throughout, this chapter grapples with the impact of customary law's apparent propertization of the human body on scientific and biotechnological activities. At each stage of this chapter, helpful comparisons are made with the relevant laws in the United States of America and England. The necessity for adoption or rejection of the English or American view on some aspects of the subject will also be canvassed. This chapter concludes with a suggestion on how the Nigerian law on dead bodies could be tailored to meet the demands of modernization and technological development.

Worldview of the Ibos

The worldview of Nigerians is spiritual. Nigerians, like many other Africans, have a spiritual perception of the world and things around them. The social, economic and political structures are intertwined in a complex web of religion. Religion is the engine that propels every aspect of life in traditional Nigerian society. This explains their spiritual conception of the heavenly bodies and natural phenomena.[6] African religious manifestations come in various and equally applicable forms, and are therefore theistic, dynamistic and spiritistic.[7] These spiritual attitudes engender Africans' proclivity to the veneration of the phenomenal. While a Caucasian's experimental instincts would be aroused by the sight of a phenomenal entity, like

---

Court held that the decision of the trial judge on sepulchral right was premature and therefore set aside the lower court's decision. Because of the way the Supreme Court framed the issue for determination, it lost the opportunity to discuss the law on dead bodies in Nigeria.

  6   R.T. Parsons, *Religion in an African Society* (Leiden: E.J. Brill, 1964), at 159.

  7   I adopt Parsons' definition of these terms, *ibid.*, at 163:

      Theism…is the belief in and the practices and rules of conduct, associated with the belief in a supreme being. Dynamism is the belief in, and the ritual and rules of conduct associated with a belief in, an impersonal, all-pervasive force, operating in 'medicines,' charms, taboos, omens and curses. Spiritism is the belief in, and the practices and rules of conduct associated with the belief in spirits, whether disembodied human spirits or nature-spirits that were never human.

an unusually large tree, and would naturally want to investigate the scientific cause of the strange size, an African would immediately spiritualize such a phenomenon. As said:

> In his environment anything in nature that inspires awe either by its glow or brilliance like the moon or the sun; or anything that extorts his veneration by its massiveness or giddy height like the mountain; or anything that is dreadful from its cast or general look like a very thick cluster of tall wooded dark forest; or anything that appears horrible from its sound like the 'rapid' or the 'fall' of a river, is deemed to house a small god that should be adored and worshipped.[8]

Pope Paul VI recognized this African spirituality when he observed:

> The constant and general foundation of African tradition is the spiritual view of life. Here we have more than the so-called 'animistic' concept, in the sense given to this term in the history of religions at the end of the last century. We have a deeper, broader and more universal concept which considers all living beings and visible nature itself as linked with the world of the invisible and the spirit. In particular, it has never considered man as mere matter limited to earthly life, but recognizes in him the presence and power of another spiritual element, in virtue of which human life is always related to the after-life.[9]

Consequently, religion permeates all aspects of the African life,[10] and is the foundation of most customary legal rules. In some African societies, like the Ibos of south-eastern Nigeria, some actions, like incest and murder of a kinsman or woman, are considered offences against the earth deity. Green has characterized such offences as being 'against a supernatural power'. Such offences demand propitiation, as physical or penal punishment would not be sufficient in the circumstances.[11] There is a

---

8   Account of F.O. Isichei, in E. Isichei, *Igbo Worlds: An Anthology of Oral Histories and Historical Descriptions* (Philadelphia: Institute For The Study Of Human Issues, 1978), at 179.

9   Pope Paul VI, 'Message of His Holiness Pope Paul VI to all the Peoples of Africa for the Promotion of their Religious, Civil and Social Good of their Continent', in E.C. Amucheazi, ed., *Readings In Social Sciences: Issues In National Development* (Enugu: Fourth Dimension Publishers, 1980), at 325.

10   Rt. Rev. Msgr. S.N. Ezeanya admirably observed in 'The Contribution of African Traditional Religion to Nation Building', in Amucheazi, *ibid.*, at 324:

> For the African, life is religion and religion is life. It is unimaginable for the African, following his traditional environment and culture, to think of human life divorced from religion. For the African, there is nothing like a person becoming converted to embrace a religion because life is impossible for anyone who is not religious from birth. There cannot be existence, not to talk of a person making any headway in life if he divorces himself from religion. Man has innate obligation to be religious. It is unnatural for the African that man should be otherwise than religious from cradle or rather, conception to grave. The African lives, moves and has his being in a religious atmosphere, in an atmosphere controlled by countless invisible powers both good and evil that steer the course of human destiny.

11   M.M. Green, *Ibo Village Affairs*, 2nd ed. (New York: Frederick A. Praeger, 1964), at 99–100.

general belief in reincarnation, which is demonstrated in burial ceremonies and rites. For instance, if it is intended that a man should be a genius upon his reincarnation, a very resourceful person in the community is procured to perform an aspect of his burial rites.[12] Abuse, dissection or mutilation of the dead is strictly prohibited. Here, African mortuary tradition shows a deep conflict with laws of most Western countries that allow, in some circumstances, autopsy on the dead or dissection of the dead for medical or scientific purposes.

Reincarnation and Mutilation of the Dead

The belief in reincarnation provides anchorage for the supposition that mutilation of the dead, for whatever purpose, will lead to disablement or physical disfigurement upon reincarnation.[13] As we shall see, this type of mortuary tradition constitutes a bulwark against biomedical and anthropological research. Mutilation of a dead body is allowed, probably, in a single instance, that is, where a mother experiences recurrent birth and death of an infant child. Typically of the African worldview, the death of an infant or baby is considered abnormal and is spiritually interpreted.[14] The traditional rationalization is that the dead child was an *Ogbange*: a child who entered a bond with a group in the spirit world, undertaking not to live to age of maturity. Such children are believed to die as soon as they are born or a few years after their birth, only to be reborn again. As soon as such recurrent birth and death is noticed, the child is characterized an *Ogbange*, and steps are taken to outwit it. One step is that the corpse of an *Ogbange* is mutilated so that it could easily be identified upon rebirth. It is believed that an *Ogbange* dreads recognition and will likely live a full life if it became aware of its recognition. The villages are replete with stories of children born with mutilation marks given to them upon their previous death. Mutilation is also believed to discourage such children from continuing their interminable circle of death and rebirth.

Another step is to prevent the mother from sleeping in her home on the night following the death of her baby, because it is believed that such children 're-enter' their mother's womb on the night of their death, preparing to be born again.[15] The mother, on that night, could sleep outside her home, usually with a relative. Such relocation deceives the *Ogbange* and makes it difficult for it to be conceived by the mother. Save in the case of *Ogbange*, mutilation of a corpse is not allowed because

---

12 *Ibid.*, at 87. Writing in different cultural and historical contexts, Oestigaard similarly observed that: 'The way in which the dead humans are offered to the god(s) influences either the destiny of the deceased or that of the descendents.' Terje Oestigaard, 'Sacrifices of Raw, Cooked and Burnt Humans' (2000) 33 *Norwegian Archaeological Review* 41, at 44.

13 The African belief in after-life and integrity of the body as a basis for the salvation of the soul and continued relationship of the living with the dead seems to be evident in Western religious traditions. See Walker, *supra*, note 4.

14 For non-African cultural and archaeological perspective on the bodies of children, see Kirsi O. Lorentz, 'Cultures of Physical Modifications: Child Bodies in Ancient Cyprus' (2003) 2 *Stanford Journal of Archaeology* 17.

15 O.A.C. Anigbo, *Commensality and Human Relationship among the Igbo* (Nsukka: University of Nigeria Press, 1987), at 135.

of its adverse physical consequences on the after-life, and for constituting total irreverence to the dead.

Customary Law's Conception of Death

For an Ibo, life does not end with death[16] and a man's manner of life on earth will heavily impact on his life after death.[17] Death is seen as the commencement of a journey to the spirit world of the ancestors. It is therefore customary to enclose in the deceased's casket certain items of food and clothing that it will use in that journey. As Anigbo observed: '[P]utting food, clothing and even walking sticks in the coffin can illustrate how the Igbo conceive life beyond the grave. For them life after death entails essentially the same experiences as are had in this world.'[18] Accordingly, the dead continues to relate with living relatives through the medium of dreams, ghostly apparitions and shamanic séances.[19] It is on account of this that the customary laws of some African communities recognize that the deceased could still marry after his death, and his posthumous wife could legally give birth to children in his name.[20] Under such customary law, as in Onitsha of south-eastern Nigeria, a deceased's family consented to a marriage contracted for and on behalf of the deceased, thirty years after his death, by his two sisters.[21]

Thus, in *Okonkwo v. Okagbue*,[22] all the three courts, High Court, Court of Appeal and Supreme Court of Nigeria, affirmed the existence of this custom, which was established by the evidence of expert witnesses on the point. Though the plaintiff argued against the existence of this custom, his witnesses, in agreement with the defendant's, gave evidence in support of the custom.[23] While the High Court and Court of Appeal accepted the legality and enforceability of the custom, the Supreme

---

16 Parsons, *supra*, note 6, at 24. See, also, G.B.A. Coker, *Family Property Among the Yorubas* (London: Sweet & Maxwell, 1966), at 3:

> The whole life of the Yorubas (inhabiting the western part of Nigeria) is dominated by religion and the conception of a man by the Yorubas is essentially religious. This conception involves an acceptance common to the Yorubas of the possession by man of both a material and an ethereal body, the latter capable after his death of continuing existence. Unless it is understood that his belief is fundamental among the Yorubas, it may be difficult to appreciate many of the rules which apply not only to the preservation of family properties but also to the distribution of properties generally in Yorubaland. Once it is realized that the deceased ancestor continues to exist in another form and that from such state of existence he is still capable of watching the affairs of those still alive in the flesh, it is natural to maintain only a course of conduct which would not only benefit the off springs but also to a greater extent placate the living spirit of the deceased.

17 Ezeanya, *supra*, note 10, at 327.

18 Anigbo, *supra*, note 15, at 142.

19 Howard Williams, 'Death Warmed Up: The Agency of Bodies and Bones in Early Anglo-Saxon Cremation Rites' (2004) 9 *Journal of Material Culture* 263, at 266.

20 *Okonkwo v. Okagbue* (1994) 9 N.W.L.R. 301 [hereinafter *Okonkwo*].

21 *Ibid.*

22 *Ibid.*

23 *Ibid.*, at 317–18 and 328–9.

Court, however, struck it down for being contrary to natural justice, equity and good conscience.[24] Throughout the length of the judgement, the Supreme Court acted on the Western concept of marriage, which requires that the parties must be in existence.[25] No regard was had to African philosophical abstraction of man, as articulated in this chapter.[26]

The Ibo's non-materialistic philosophy of existence is shared by the American Indians, who have been described as 'America's first citizens'.[27] The American Indians equally believe that the universe is governed by forces and spirits.[28] The utilization of such forces or spirits could largely be determined by the Indian peoples' worship and attitude. There is also a belief in the continuity of life after death. Consequently, death does not end existence and legal personality. This explains a recent case, *Na Iwi O Na Kupuna O Mokapu v. Dalton*,[29] brought by some American Indians in the name of some human remains.[30] In denying standing to the human remains, Ezra, J., observed:

> The Mokapu remains were intended as Plaintiffs in their own right. Hui Malama asserts that according to Hawaiian custom, human remains are spiritual beings that possess all of the traits of a living person. The Federal Defendant's physical examination of the remains was, they contend, a violation and desecration of the remains. As a result, the remains have allegedly suffered an injury to their spiritual well-being and have standing to bring suit.

> However, as the Federal Defendant contends, neither the provisions of *NAGPRA* nor the common law afford standing to the Mokapu remains. ... The court finds no sound legal basis for granting standing to human remains. Even the cases cited by Hui Malama refer to living organisms or dynamic ecosystems that are generally recognized as capable of suffering real injury in terms of physical or demonstrable detriment. Objects or entities

---

24 *Ibid.*

25 *Ibid.*, at 324, 343 and 346.

26 Indeed, many African customary law systems allow posthumous, levirate, sororate, and 'ghost' marriages that have the effect of perpetuating the deceased's name: K.S.A Ebeku, 'The Legal Status of Nigerian Children Born by a Widow: *Chinweze v. Masi* Revisited' (1994) 38 *J. African L.* at 46; C.O. Akpamgbo, 'A "Woman to Woman" Marriage and the Repugnancy Clause: A Case of Putting New Wine into Old Bottles' (1974–77) 14 *African L. Stud.*, at 87. Consequently, the legal father of resultant children may not be their biological father: *Ibrahim v. Amalibini*, (1978) 1 G.L.R. 368.

27 Statement of Senator D. Inuoye, quoted in J.F. Trope and W.R. Echo-Hawk, '*The Native American Graves Protection and Repatriation Act*: Background and Legislative History' (1992) 24 *Ariz. St. L.J.* 35, at 59.

28 M. Battiste and J.Y. Henderson, *Protecting Indigenous Knowledge and Heritage: A Global Challenge* (Saskatoon: Purich Publishing Ltd., 2000), at 42–3.

29 894 F. Supp. 1397 (1995).

30 Compare the suggestion that inanimate natural objects, for instance, trees, rivers and forests, should be granted legal rights: Christopher D. Stone, 'Should Trees Have Standing? – Toward Legal Rights for Natural Objects' (1972) 45 *S. Cal. L. Rev.* 450. See, also, Matthew H. Kramer, 'Do Animals and Dead People Have Legal Rights?' (2001) 14 *Can. J.L. & Juris.* 29.

without any attributes of life in the observable or provable sense are generally not afforded a legally–protected interest for standing purposes.[31]

However, the court considered the above an *obiter dictum*, since 'it is unclear whether this court could even reach the issue of the remains' eligibility for legal standing'.[32] Therefore, the case was, in part, decided on the basis that the remains had not met the common law's three requirements for standing.[33] The intermixture of the American Indian social, economic and political life with religion is demonstrated in the dissenting judgement of Justice Brennan in *Lyng v. Northwest Indian Cemetery Protective Assn.*[34] There, the defendant, relying on the 1ˢᵗ Amendment's Free Exercise Clause, sought to stop the government from constructing a road across a sacred forest or near that forest in a way that burdened the defendant's religious activities. In demonstrating the inability of the Supreme Court's majority judgement to capture the spiritual essence of the plaintiff's claim, Justice Brennan, in his dissenting judgement, observed:

> As the Forest Service's commissioned study, the Theodoratus Report, explains, for Native Americans religion is not a discrete sphere of activity separate from all others, and any attempt to isolate the religious aspects of Indian life 'is in reality an exercise which forces Indian concepts into non-Indian categories.' App. 110; D. Theodoratus, Cultural Resources of the Chimney Rock Section, Gasquet-Orleans Road, Six Rivers National Forest (1979). Thus, for most Native Americans, '[t]he area of worship cannot be delineated from social, political, cultural, and other areas of Indian life-style.' American Indian Religious Freedom, Hearings on S.J. Res. 102 before the Senate Select Committee on Indian Affairs, 95th Cong., 2d Sess., 86 (1978) (statement of Barney Old Coyote, Crow Tribe). A pervasive feature of this life-style is the individual's relationship with the natural world; this relationship, which can accurately though somewhat incompletely be characterized as one of stewardship, forms the core of what might be called, for want of a better nomenclature, the Indian religious experience. While traditional Western religions view creation as the work of a deity 'who institutes natural laws which then govern the operation of physical nature,' tribal religions regard creation as an on-going process in which they are morally and religiously obligated to participate. ... Native Americans fulfil this duty through ceremonies and rituals designed to preserve and stabilize the earth and to protect humankind from disease and other catastrophes. Failure to conduct these ceremonies in the manner and place specified, adherents believe, will result in great harm to the earth and to the people whose welfare depends upon it. ... Where dogma lies at the heart of Western religions, Native American faith is inextricably bound to the use of land. The site-specific nature of Indian religious practice derives from the Native American perception that land is itself a sacred, living being.[35]

---

31 *Ibid.*, at 1406–1407 [citations omitted].

32 *Ibid.*, at 1407.

33 Stipulated in *Lujan v. Defenders of Wildlife* 504 U.S. 555, at 559–61 (1992), as follows: 1. The plaintiff must have suffered an 'injury in fact', that is, an invasion of a legally protected interest; 2. There must be a causal connection between the injury and the conduct complained of, that is, the injury must be fairly traceable to the challenged action of the defendant; and 3. It must be likely that the injury will be redressed by a favourable decision.

34 485 U.S. 439 (1987).

35 *Ibid.*, at 460–61.

Disinterment of a Corpse

Ibos' reverence for the dead, belief in reincarnation, and continuity of life after death dictate that once buried, a corpse is not to be disinterred. Disinterment is believed to be a mark of disrespect to the deceased and capable of obstructing its journey to the spirit world of its ancestors; or after finishing such journey, disinterment can destroy the deceased's socialization with fellow ancestors. The laws of most Western countries equally prohibit disinterment, except for compelling reasons, having regard to public health, the filial relationship of the parties with the deceased, and the particular circumstances of a case.

Among the Ibo of south-eastern Nigeria, disinterment is allowed for the purpose of exorcizing the spirit of the dead, which is then magically and ritualistically imprisoned, and therefore rendered impotent. This expedient is resorted to when the deceased continues to afflict the living relations with pains and sufferings. This usually occurs with the spirits of dead relatives who died prematurely or in terrible circumstances. Instead of joining the ancestors, they hover around the world harming, or threatening to harm, their living relatives, as if to vent their anger arising from the circumstances of their death. Such spirits are considered evil. They are therefore exorcized and, in traditional parlance, chained. But exorcism is only resorted to after elaborate rituals and divinations, because living relatives are most reluctant to regard the spirit of a dead relative as evil. With this exception, the Ibo regards as sacred and untouchable the graves of departed loved ones.

Disinterment, in African ontology, is capable of leading to the destruction of the metaphysical force of the deceased and, except as indicated above, is strictly prohibited. As a scholar in African Philosophy observed:

> A deceased who has just brought injury to the life of members of the clan, or who, by exercising a pernicious influence on strangers, is compromising the clan which is responsible for his deed, will be called among the Baluba 'mufu wa kizwa,' a bad departed, a wanton, petulant deceased ('wa nsikani'). ... Vital restitution making good the evil wrought can only, in such cases, consist in a struggle which the living members of the clan will undertake against this pervert brother. This is the self-defence of life against the principle of destruction. They insult and injure such a deceased: an attempt will be made to drive him away; if necessary, recourse will be had to 'manga,' that is to say, to 'natural forces'; and, if that is not enough, the ministrations of the 'manga' man will be sought, to get him to take away from the deceased such force as may remain in him, to paralyse his harmful actions, to prevent him from having further dealings with the living; and by preventing his rebirth, which is the utmost diminution of vitality. It is possible even to go so far as to disinter the corpse, to burn it and to scatter the ashes. ... The deceased is then completely 'dead,' cut off from the living. And so ordered existence is restored in face of trouble, perversion, disorder. An ontological purification of the clan has taken place.[36]

---

36 Rev. P. Tempels, *Bantu Philosophy*, trans. Rev. C. King (Paris: Presence Africaine, 1959), at 103–104.

Legal Implications of the Ibo Worldview

The major legal consequence of the Ibos' non-materialistic conception of the world is that the human body, whether living or dead, is a limited property[37] owned by the particular person and his or her family. This analogized proposition seems the best medium to demonstrate the immeasurable interest that an Ibo family has in the life, death and corpse of its relative. When the juridical concept of property is reduced to its pragmatic signification,[38] it becomes obvious that it does not fully capture the

---

37 Professor Trudo Lemmens has ably suggested to me that a *sui generis* categorization may better reflect the Nigerian position than the idea of property. He may be right and the idea of *sui generis* is implicit in decisions like *Davis v. Davis* 842 S.W. 2d 588 (1992) and *Janicki v. Hospital of St Raphael* 744 A. 2d 963 (1999) [hereinafter *Janicki*], which held that human embryo or pre-embryo occupies a middle position between property and personhood, which makes it entitled to a special respect. Also, D. Gracia, 'Ownership of the Human Body: Some Historical Remarks', in H. Ten Have, *et al.*, eds, *Ownership of the Human Body: Philosophical Considerations on the Use of the Human Body and its Parts in Healthcare* (Dordrecht: Kluwer Academic Publishers, 1998), at 68–9, in examining the attitude of Roman Law towards the ownership of the human body, observed:

> The living human body was considered in Roman Law as a constitutive element of each person, and not a 'thing.' Only the dead body was considered a 'thing,' *res*, but *res religiosa*, and therefore *sui generis*, neither appropriable (*res extra patrimonium*) nor salable (*res extra commercium*).

I have emphasized, however, in the subsequent paragraphs that I am not strictly deploying 'property' here as the resultant ethno-conceptualization of the human body. Since customary law does not thrive in the familiar English categorization of private law, with well-defined concepts, 'property' is only used by way of analogy as the most suitable Western legal term that conveys the idea of an Ibo's interest in the human body. While this interest is arguably *sui generis* in its Western legal reduction, it is a term, and legal attitude that has not enjoyed comparable legal definition, certainty and juristic commentary as property. In any case, its use in analogy, rather than property, does not seem to capture the profundity of that interest which an Ibo man has in the corpse of his relative. Even in English and Australian laws, the human body parts have been propertized in a way that makes a *sui generis* characterization somewhat inopportune: *Dobson v. North Tyneside Health Authority* (1997) 1 W.L.R. 596 [hereinafter *Dobson*]; *R v. Kelly* (1998) 3 All E.R. 741 [hereinafter *Kelly*]; *Roche v. Douglas* (2000) W.A.S.C. 22 [hereinafter *Roche*]. Property has increasingly become a fluid concept of utility that serves to protect a highly regarded interest, even when it does not possess traditional proprietary characteristics. Thus, it has been suggested that 'whiteness' is property since it gives rise to racialized privileges and expectations of social, economic and political benefits, which the law expressly and implicitly protect and gratify: C.I. Harris, 'Whiteness as Property' (1993) 106 *Harv. L. Rev.* 1709–91. Thus, the property analogy is not out of place.

38 A right of property ought to be of commercial value, transferable, devisable, tangible, inheritable and permanent: *National Provincial Bank Ltd. v. Ainsworth* (1965) A.C. 1175; *First Victoria National Bank v. United States* 620 F. 2d 1096 (1980). Similarly, A.M. Honoré posited in 'Ownership', in A.G. Guest, ed., *Oxford Essays in Jurisprudence* (Oxford: Oxford University Press, 1961), at 113:

> Ownership comprises the right to possess, the right to use, the right to manage, the right to the income of the thing, the right to the capital, the right to security, the rights or incidents of transmissibility and absence of term, the prohibition of harmful

essence of an Ibo family's interest in the corpse of a member of the family. The sepulchral right of an Ibo family is ampler, and approximates more to proprietary interest, than an equivalent right exercised over a corpse in England, Canada and America. In these legal systems, it seems settled that a corpse is not the subject of property, except where it has been transformed by the application of skill and labour, though possessory right of custody is given to the next of kin for the purpose of burial. This right terminates upon burial.[39] A slightly different formulation of this rule, in terms of 'quasi-property' is of no practical relevance, since it gives exactly the same non-proprietary rights as the general statement of the rule.

While most Western legal systems are still struggling with the scope and ambit of the interests of the 'next of kin', Ibo customary law is spared such controversy, with all its niceties and nuanced distinctions.[40] When a person dies in an Ibo community, the death is a loss to the family in particular and the community in general. These two have standing with respect to matters concerning the deceased and priority depends on a particular issue and is well known. For instance, if another community caused the death, the community of the deceased, as a political entity, seems to have standing, with respect to disputes arising therefrom, in preference to the deceased's family.[41] Generally, no relation of the deceased, notwithstanding the nearness or otherwise of the pedigree, is denied standing. This brings in bold relief the cohesion that animates an African society, where the biblical injunction – love your neighbour as your self – is not only the customary norm but also a common feature of daily life.

Therefore, property seems to be the nearest Western legal concept that best expresses the profundity of interest exercisable over a corpse by an Ibo family. The corpse, both before and after burial, remains the property of the family, which has a sacred duty to protect it against mutilation, disinterment and desecration, and ensures its reunion with the ancestors in the world beyond. An accomplished African scholar, Ollennu, was right when, in the context of customary family law, he observed:

> Belonging to a family includes the concept of the individual being owned by and under the control of the family, and extends to family ownership of all properties which the individual acquires by his personal exertions, mental and otherwise. So long as the individual is mentally capable of managing his affairs, the family leaves him in absolute control of himself and his property with powers of alienation *inter vivos* or by will. The individual's authority, or his mandate to manage his affairs, ceases upon the happening of

---

use, liability to execution, and the incident of residuarity: this makes eleven leading incidents.

39 But in *Dobson, supra*, note 37, at 600, Gibson, L.J., of the English Court of Appeals, doubted whether, apart from executors, administrators and parents of an infant child, a next of kin had a right to the custody and possession of a corpse of a deceased relative.

40 For instance, the struggle for the exercise of burial rights between natural parents and adopting parents in *Smith v. Tamworth City Council* (1997) 41 N.S.W.L.R. 680 (Supreme Court of New South Wales) [hereinafter *Smith*]; or between the father of the deceased and deceased's partner in *Felipe v. Vega* 570 A. 2d 1028 (1989) [hereinafter *Felipe*].

41 P. Contini, 'The Evolution of Blood-Money for Homicide in Somalia' (1971) 15 *J. African L.* 77.

any event which incapacitates him, e.g., upon his becoming insane, or upon his death. In any of these eventualities the family resume full control of his person and property, which are theirs, and administer them.[42]

Exception to the Property Rule Under Ibo Customary Law

Clearly, with respect to dead bodies, a limited property rule seems applicable under Ibo customary law. One exception ought to be noted, and relates to the concept of 'Evil Forest', especially among the Ibos of south-eastern Nigeria. The Evil Forest was, and where it still survives is, a huge forest, usually at the outskirts of a village, where people believed to have died from unnatural causes were, or are, thrown into and not buried. For instance, a sick condition which left a person's abdomen swollen or bloated before his or her death is attributed to the wrath of the gods.[43] The person's death is seen as an abomination and a pollution of the earth, belonging to the earth deity.[44] In such situations, the indigenous mortuary law demands cleansing the earth, which entails dumping the deceased on the Evil Forest, without burial.

Similar treatment is accorded the corpse of one who committed suicide, the corpse of an *Ogbange*, already mentioned, dead bodies of twins,[45] and the corpse of one who died during the Week of Peace, that is, a week immediately before the commencement of planting season, observed by some Ibo communities, during which absolute peace is decreed and any quarrel or violence attracts very severe penalty. As Zahan observed:

> These and other such customs [that is, allegedly barbaric customs] encountered in Africa
> have often provoked the indignation of researchers, who have denounced them as cruel

---

42 N.A. Ollennu, 'The Changing Law and Law Reform in Ghana' (1971) 15 *J. African L.* 132, at 150.

43 O.M. Ejidike, 'Human Rights in the Cultural Traditions and Social Practice of the Igbo of South-Eastern Nigeria' (1999) 43 *J. African L.* 71, at 75.

44 Compare Justice Whitbeck's judgement in *Dampier v. Wayne County* 592 N.W. 2d 809 (1999), that defendant's alleged action which led to the decomposition of the deceased, plaintiff's relative, did not amount to mutilation of a dead body.

45 The reason for some of these examples seems to lie in the Ibos' belief in the perfection of creation: a woman gives birth to a child at a time, only animals can give birth to more than one at a time; therefore, sharing an animal's characteristic was most awful, unnatural and a sign of evil visitation. Also, a person after birth is expected to grow through to maturity and ripe old age. Death in-between was an abomination and a pollution of the earth. If the corpse of a person who died prematurely or committed suicide was buried in the ground, or twins were left to live, it was believed that the whole community would be afflicted with the wrath of the gods. One discovers that the life of an Ibo is characterized by a series of ritualistic transitions from the time of birth to death at an old age, when the deceased makes the final transition to the world of the ancestors. Because the early missionaries and colonists did not appreciate the socio-religious bases of what they regarded as barbaric customs, they readily depicted African ancestors as mere bloodthirsty savages. It should, however, be pointed out that traditional beliefs as to the 'abnormality' of twins have changed, and modern Nigerian culture regards twins as normal babies.

and inhuman. But these denunciations have constituted a rather quick judgment without accomplishing beforehand the necessary unravelling of the intricacies which order these practices.[46]

Unravelling this metaphysical order, which animates the purported barbaric practices of the African people, was the intellectual challenge ably confronted by Reverend Father Placide Tempels in his seminal book.[47]

Tempels ontologically abstracted the African, all animate and inanimate things around him, as metaphysical forces, which animate and orient the African. These forces inter-lock and influence one another and differ in their metaphysical strength, depending on their vital rank in the ontological hierarchy of forces. The Supreme Being stands at the apex of this hierarchy, followed by the dead ancestors, and ends with plants and animals. Those forces are designed to empower the African.[48] The single most important aim of an African is to gain metaphysical power, and not diminish his vital force. Real death, in contradistinction to physical death, is associated with a total diminution of one's force to a zero level. 'Abnormality' in birth, that is, twins,[49] or unusual physical deformities might be traced to a disturbance in the hierarchy of forces, which, if left to exist, could lead to a diminution of a living African's force:

> Every unusual phenomenon, every abnormal being is called by the *Baluba* 'bya malwa,' and these eccentricities they hold to be disturbances in the natural order, forces out of the ordinary, bizarre. Besides, if all forces find themselves in relationships of influence according to their vital rank, it is but a step to the conclusion that a force, abnormal in itself, will usually if not necessarily have a disordering influence upon the forces upon which it exercises its action. A monstrosity does not constitute, any more than any other being, an autonomous force; but, like every other force, it will have a vital influence and this influence will be logically monstrous.[50]

Chinua Achebe, in *Things Fall Apart*,[51] that famous novel, made copious references to the Evil Forest phenomenon. The novel itself is both a fictional and historical expression of the anthropological and sociological underpinnings of the Ibo society, and derives juristic relevance from its systematic dramatization and configuration of the Ibo customary law. Achebe observed:

---

46 D. Zahan, *The Religion, Spirituality, and Thought of Traditional Africa*, trans. K.E. Martin and L.M. Martin (Chicago: The University of Chicago Press, 1979), at 46.

47 Tempels, *supra*, note 36, at 86. Tempels' work has been criticized by some African philosophers. For instance, see, Paulin J. Hountondji, *African Philosophy: Myth and Reality* (London: Hutchinson & Co. Ltd., 1976); M. Akin Makinde, *African Philosophy, Culture, and Traditional Medicine* (Ohio: Ohio University Center for International Studies, 1988).

48 O.M. Ejidike has suggested that these forces work in a parallel, rather than in a hierarchical and vertically downwards, manner: 'Human Rights in the Cultural Traditions and Social Practice of the Igbo of South-Eastern Nigeria' (1999) 43 *J. African L.* 71, at 95–6.

49 As I stated earlier, modern Nigerian culture regards twins as normal babies.

50 Temples, *supra*, note 36, at 86.

51 C. Achebe, *Things Fall Apart* (London: Heinemann Educational Books Ltd., 1958).

When a man was afflicted with swelling in the stomach and the limbs he was not allowed to die in the house. He was carried to the Evil Forest and left there to die. There was the story of a very stubborn man who staggered back to his house and had to be carried again to the forest and tied to a tree. The sickness was an abomination to the earth, and so the victim could not be buried in her bowels. He died and rotted away above the earth, and was not given the first or the second burial.[52]

Consequently, corpses that were thrown into the Evil Forest belong to nobody, and, just like in English, Canadian and American laws, a no-property rule seems to apply to such corpses, subject to the law of trespass.[53]

Effect of the Received English Law on the Law of Dead Bodies

English law was received in Nigeria for the first time in 1863 following the cession of Lagos. In that year the British colonial government established formal colonial administration in Lagos and by legal instrument received English common law, equity and statutes of general application in force in England into Lagos. In 1900 the other parts of Nigeria also received the English law. The reception of English law continues to be a feature of the Nigerian legal system, long after the end of colonial rule in 1960, when the country gained its independence from Britain. A paradigmatic reception statute is s. 45 of the *Interpretation Act*:

> 45(1) Subject to the provisions of this section and except in so far as other provision is made by any Federal law, the common law of England and the doctrines of equity, together with the statutes of general application that were in force in England on the 1st day of January, 1900, shall be in force in Lagos and, in so far as they relate to any matter within the exclusive legislative competence of the Federal legislature, shall be in force elsewhere in the Federation.[54]

We therefore have an apparently contradictory situation of English common law, recognizing no property in a corpse,[55] applying alongside Ibo customary law that maintains an opposite proposition. However, as evident from s. 26(1) and

---

52 *Ibid.*, at 16–17. Similar incidents are also found at 28–9, 71, and 186–7.

53 Sir W. Blackstone, *Commentaries on the Laws of England*, vol. 2 (Chicago: The University of Chicago Press, 1979), at 429, stated more than 200 years ago:

> But though the heir has a property in the monuments and escutcheons of his ancestors, yet he has none in their bodies or ashes; nor can he bring any civil action against such as indecently at least, if not impiously, violate and disturb their remains, when dead and buried.

54 *Interpretation Act, c. 89.*

55 In *Kelly, supra*, note 37, the English Court of Appeals, criminal division, laid down an exception to the general rule; to the effect that where a corpse has been preserved, by the application of skill and labour, for the purpose of exhibition or medical training, then it becomes property capable of being stolen.

(2) of the *High Court Law*,[56] where the deceased and the parties to the case, or one of such parties, are natives, it seems that the customary mortuary law will apply, save if it is repugnant to natural justice, equity and good conscience.[57] With the rate some recent Nigerian Supreme Court decisions have denounced some customary law principles, as being contrary to justice, equity and good conscience,[58] it will be most interesting, and now left to imagination, to see how the Nigerian Supreme Court, or any Nigerian court for that matter, will assess a rule of customary law allowing ownership of a dead body by the deceased's family.

American and English Distinctions Between the 'Dead Body' or 'Corpse' and Skeletal Remains

American jurisprudence maintains a distinction between a dead body or corpse and the skeletal remains. The words 'corpse' and 'dead body' are interchangeable.[59] A corpse, in its American legal signification, characterizes a dead human being, whose body has not undergone a complete process of dissolution or decomposition. Upon complete decomposition of a dead body, the dead ceases to be known as a 'corpse'

---

56 *High Court Law, c. 60, Laws of Lagos State 1994*:
26(1) The High Court shall observe and enforce the observance of customary law which is applicable and is not repugnant to natural justice, equity and good conscience, nor incompatible either directly or by implication with any law for the time being in force, and nothing in this Law shall deprive any person of the benefit of customary law. (2) Customary law shall be deemed applicable in causes and matters where the parties thereto are natives and also in causes and matters between natives and non-natives where it may appear to the court that substantial injustice would be done to either party by a strict adherence to any rules of law which would otherwise be applicable.

57 A similar internal choice of law provision was interpreted by the Nigerian Supreme Court in *Zaidan v. Mohssen* (1973) 1 All N.L.R. 86.

58 In *Meribe v. Egwu* (1976) 1 All N.L.R. 266, the Supreme Court held that a 'woman to woman' marriage, an otherwise established customary law phenomenon, was repugnant to natural justice, equity and good conscience. The case was ably criticized by Akpamgbo, *supra*, note 26. In *Peter Chinweze v. Masi* (1989) A.N.L.R. 1, the same court held *obiter* that a custom which allowed a deceased man to have posthumous children, through his wife's sexual relationship with another man, was 'contrary to the course of nature' and therefore unenforceable. This decision was also justifiably criticized by Ebeku, *supra*, note 26. In *Okonkwo, supra*, note 20, it was held by the same court that a custom which allowed a woman's marriage to a deceased person, contracted after the deceased's death, was repugnant to natural justice, equity and good conscience. In *Mojekwu v. Mojekwu* (1997) 7 N.W.L.R. 283 and *Mojekwu v. Ejikeme* (2000) 5 N.W.L.R. 402, the Nigerian Court of Appeal held that a custom which allowed a surviving male member of a deceased's family to inherit the deceased's estate as against the deceased's female child was contrary to natural justice, equity and good conscience. These cases are criticized in R.N. Nwabueze, 'The Dynamics and Genius of Nigeria's Indigenous Legal Order' (2002) 1 *Indigenous L.J.* 153.

59 *Carter v. City of Zanesville* 52 N.E. 126 (1898) [hereinafter *Carter*].

or 'dead body'.[60] Upon merging with the soil a dead body loses its identity.[61] There is no rule of positive law that prescribes the time for the decomposition of the dead body. That depends on particular soil characteristics and climatic conditions.[62] After decomposition, the human body loses legal signification under the above distinction. It becomes part of the land wherein it is interred, and attracts the application of land law. Its subsequent reference as skeletal remains is of no legal significance, except, probably, under law relating to antiquities, as we shall see below.

This alleged distinction between a corpse and skeletal remains raises profound consequences. It is, therefore, pertinent to examine the cases that allegedly introduced the distinction into American and English jurisprudence. The first direct decision on point seems to be *Carter v. Zanesville.*[63] The plaintiff, an administratrix, complained that the defendants, proprietors of a cemetery, disinterred and took into their possession, the 38-year-old remains of the plaintiff's daughter, without the plaintiff's permission or consent. This civil action was brought under an Ohio statute that damnified in damages any person 'having unlawful possession of the body of any deceased person ...'[64] It seems that the real ratio of the case is that by the very nature of their duty, cemetery proprietors cannot be in unlawful possession of remains buried in their cemetery: 'Nor is the penalty imposed by it [the Ohio statute] directed against cemetery associations (or their trustees) where such remains may be quietly reposing.'[65] However, the court did not stop at that. It went on to postulate that:

> This statute is directed against such persons, *etc.*, as have unlawful possession of a 'body' of a deceased person. The section further refers to the 'body' as such 'corpse.' The terms 'body' and 'corpse,' found in this statute, do not include the remains of persons long buried and decomposed.[66]

As already stated, this distinction was not necessary for the actual decision in that case, that is, that cemetery proprietors or trustees were not within the contemplation of the statute. Nevertheless, it has been the foundation and inspiration of subsequent cases.

In *State v. Glass*,[67] a developer bought large acres of land, a small portion of which was previously used as a cemetery,[68] where four people had been buried about 125 years before the commencement of the case.[69] In the course of development, he

---

   60 It was suggested in an Australian case that a monstrous stillbirth may not qualify as a 'corpse': Barton, J.'s concurring judgement in *Doodeward v. Spence* 6 C.L.R. 406, at 415 (1908) [hereinafter *Doodeward*].
   61 *Gilbert v. Buzzard* (1820) 161 E.R. 761, at 768 [hereinafter *Gilbert*].
   62 *Ibid.*
   63 *Carter, supra,* note 59.
   64 *Ibid.*
   65 *Ibid.*
   66 *Ibid.*
   67 273 N.E. 2d 893 (1971) [hereinafter *Glass*].
   68 This portion was excluded from his deed.
   69 *Glass, supra,* note 67, at 896.

employed an undertaker to disinter and re-inter these bodies in another cemetery, albeit without all the required permits.[70] He was therefore charged under a grave-robbing statute that criminalized any 'willfully and unlawfully open[ing] [of] a grave or tomb where a corpse has been deposited'.[71] In delivering the majority judgement, and heavily relying on *Carter v. Zanesville*,[72] Justice Gray offered this syllogism: the statute penalizes the unlawful removal of a corpse; a completely decomposed body is not a corpse; the bodies in that case were long completely decomposed;[73] therefore (1) there was no corpse in that case, as required by the statute, (2) since there was no corpse, there was no grave that was robbed.[74] On this logic, the defendant was discharged of the offence of grave-robbing.[75]

First, the main precedential justification of *State v. Glass*, that is, *Carter v. Zanesville*, is distinguishable. Second, Justice Gray's logic became problematic when he nevertheless convicted the defendant under the second count, for the unlawful removal of a gravestone.[76] Unless we do serious damage to the meaning of 'gravestone',[77] how could there have been a gravestone marking a grave unless there was a grave, which was denied by the learned justice.

The truth is that the majority was under a heightened and self-imposed pressure to discharge the defendant,[78] whom it found to have duly re-buried the bodies, tried to secure all the necessary approvals, did not harvest any burial goods from the graves,[79] and even undeservedly underwent a sanity examination for 60 days, under the order of the lower court.[80] The minority judgement of Stephenson, J. agreed with the distinction between a corpse and a completely decomposed body, that is, skeletal remains, but maintained that the distinction did not obliterate the equally strong distinction between a 'corpse' and 'grave', so that a grave remains in existence and could be robbed even after the complete decomposition of its content.[81] Therefore, *State v. Glass* provides a unanimous judgement on the point of distinction between a corpse and a completely decomposed body.

---

70 *Ibid.*, at 895.

71 *Ibid.*, at 898.

72 *Carter, supra,* note 59.

73 He held them to be about 125 years. Though Stephenson, J. in his dissenting judgement held that the complete decomposition of the bodies or their ages were not proved by the record and were based on mere supposition: *Glass, supra,* note 67, at 900.

74 *Ibid.*, at 898.

75 *Ibid.*

76 *Ibid.*

77 It is defined as: 'a stone marking a grave': *The Oxford Encyclopedic English Dictionary* (Oxford: Clarendon Press, 1991) *s.v.* 'gravestone'; also *R v. Moyer* (1994) 2 S.C.R. 899, at 908–909.

78 The judgement did not state the punishment the defendant received for conviction on the second count.

79 *Glass, supra,* note 67.

80 *Ibid.*, at 897.

81 *Ibid.*, at 900.

It is pertinent to comment on the English decision, and second case,[82] relied upon by the majority in *State v. Glass*. Justice Gray rationalized *Gilbert v. Buzzard*[83] as holding that, 'the right of burial extends in time no farther than the period needed for complete dissolution [of the corpse]'.[84] If this means that the rights which relatives have over a corpse expire upon its decomposition, then it is tantamount, with respect, to an imperfect rendition of the ratio in *Gilbert v. Buzzard*. There, the plaintiff, a parishioner of an English church, claimed a right to have his deceased wife, equally a parishioner, buried in the church cemetery in an iron coffin.[85] The church refused to accept the burial in an iron coffin, unless the plaintiff was willing to pay higher burial fees. The stalemate raised a serious pandemonium and chaos resulting in the temporary deposition of the deceased's body in a 'bone-house'.[86] The plaintiff therefore brought an action against the church, for the common law offence of obstructing the interment of a dead body.[87] Plaintiff's counsel argued that the sanctity and inviolability of the grave was 'among the most ancient and universal rights'.[88] It was therefore contended that the protection of this right demanded that once a cemetery spot was appropriated to a particular burial, then it remained irreversibly allocated to the deceased therein buried, so that no subsequent burial could be had on the same spot.[89]

The church, defendant, contended that its increasing population, limited burial grounds, and high mortality rate of about 800 persons per year, required that after complete decomposition of a corpse, it should be able to use the same spot for another burial. This objective, it further contended, would be defeated if burial in an iron coffin was allowed, at no extra cost, since iron coffins would delay and prolong the natural decomposition of the remains.[90]

In answering the plaintiff's contention, on the irrevocable appropriation of a spot for a particular corpse, Sir William Scot reasoned that the contention falsely assumed the imperishability of a corpse as, 'there can be no inextinguishable title, no perpetuity of possession belonging to a subject which itself is perishable'.[91] His Lordship maintained that a corpse completely decomposes, after an indefinable period of time, and merges with the soil.[92] Consequently, a parishioner buried in a particular spot of the church cemetery relinquished the possession thereof upon complete decomposition of the body, in which case the living and future parishioners became entitled to succeed to the same spot.[93]

---

82 *Gilbert, supra*, note 61.

83 *Ibid.*

84 *Glass, supra*, note 67, at 898.

85 The resort to an iron coffin was a protective device to guard against the depredations of grave-robbers.

86 *Gilbert, supra*, note 61, at 763.

87 *Ibid.*

88 *Ibid.*

89 *Ibid.*, at 762.

90 *Ibid.*, at 762.

91 *Ibid.*, at 768.

92 *Ibid.*

93 *Ibid.*

It seems, therefore, that the decomposition of a corpse becomes relevant only with respect to the above right of succession; that is, in determining when it arises.[94] This point seems, with respect, to have eluded Justice Gray in *State v. Glass*. Sir William Scot never set out to say, as implied in the American distinction, that flesh is everything and bones are nothing.

Incidentally, a recent American decision, *State v. Redd*,[95] which did not mention the above cases, has held that there is no legal difference between long decomposed remains, about 1000 years old in that case, and yet-to-be decomposed dead bodies. Justice Zimmerman of the Supreme Court of Utah therein observed:

> [I]t may be that reading this statute [Utah Code Ann. S. 76-9-704(1)(a) (1995)] as protecting partial remains of a thousand-year-old Anasazi will not accord with the expectations of some persons ... But a moment's reflection should demonstrate the soundness of the broader public policy our interpretation advances. It will protect the partial remains of many with whom people can readily identify, such as pioneers buried long ago in crude graves, or of war dead, or of victims of horrendous accidents, or crimes.[96]

However, the above distinction has become so ingrained in American jurisprudence[97] that it can hardly admit of the dilution suggested in this chapter, though more cases like *State v. Redd* may ultimately make the necessary in-road. Several consequences flow from the distinction.

First, it seems that the various rights of possession, custody and burial, given by law to surviving relatives, characterized as 'quasi-property' in American law,[98] extinguish upon the complete decomposition of the dead body of their deceased relative.[99] These valuable rights, which enable relatives to maintain an action for abuse of a deceased relative's body, will no longer avail them upon the translation of the deceased from 'corpse' to 'skeletal remains'.[100] Second, a completely

---

94 The American case of *Wilson v. Read* 74 N.H. 322 (1907) seems to reach a similar result when it refused to interfere with the burial of a woman in a spot where an infant was buried 49 years previously.

95 992 P. 2d 986 (1999).

96 *Ibid.*, at 991.

97 F.J. Ludes, *et al.*, eds, *Corpus Juris Secundum* (St. Paul, Minnesota.: West Publishing Co., 1966), at 488; 21 A.L.R. 2d 472, at 476–7 (1952); B. Swartz, 'Property – Nature of Rights in Dead Bodies – Right of Burial' (1939) *Southern Cal. L. Rev.* 435.

98 *Carney v. Knollwood Cemetery Assn.* 514 N.E. 2d 430 (1986).

99 M.B. Bowman recognized this point and therefore argued against the distinction between a corpse and skeletal remains: 'The Reburial of Native American Skeletal Remains: Approaches to the Resolution of a Conflict' (1989) 13 *Harv. Env. L. Rev.* 147, at 169.

100 However, it is evident from the majority of cases decided by the American courts in the past 150 years that relatives of the deceased were awarded damages for unauthorized or wrongful disinterment, in circumstances where it was reasonable to hold that the deceased's body had been completely decomposed. An example is the famous American case of *Re Beekman Street* 4 Bradf. 506 (1856), where an old cemetery was acquired by the City of New York, for a public purpose and upon payment of compensation. One of the claimants of this money was the daughter of a man who had been buried for more than 50 years, and ought ordinarily to have been completely decomposed. In fact, his remains were identified

decomposed body loses its identity and falls within the meaning of land, and would only be protected by the law regulating trespass to land.[101] Therefore, an owner of land becomes owner of the skeletal remains, except as provided under antiquities or similar applicable laws. Again, since the remains have merged with the land, a court would not have *in rem* jurisdiction to order exhumation of a corpse buried outside its territorial jurisdiction.[102] Third, the skeletal remains of a completely decomposed body might be free for the taking, except as limited by positive law. This was the result reached in *Carter v. Zanesville*,[103] where the defendants who took possession of the remains in that case were held entitled to do so, against the wishes and protests of the deceased's family. Fourth, the alleged distinction would lead to despoliation and desecration of old graves. It was for the same reason that the court in *Charrier v. Bell*[104] refused to hold that burial goods could be abandoned. If burial goods were deserving of protection against acquisition by a stranger,[105] then skeletal remains of a completely decomposed body are much more sacrosanct, and merit an even higher degree of protection.

In any case, the alleged distinction is strange, at least in the Nigerian context, and is not likely to become part of its law. As already noted, African philosophy conceives a corpse as a force existing within the hierarchy and community of other forces, animate and inanimate, living and dead. The flesh and skeletal remains are the material embodiment of a deceased's force, with spiritual and ritual significance.

---

only with a ribbon. Nevertheless, it was held that she was entitled to indemnity for the cost of disinterring and reintering the remains. Logically, this indemnity would not have been possible if the legal significance of the remains had been lost upon the decomposition of the body. It could well be that such cases are explainable on the ground that the damages awarded attached not to interference with the remains, which arguably have no legal significance, but to interference with the grave, which housed the remains. R.F. Martin, *Dead Bodies* (1952) 21 A.L.R. 2d 472, at 477, seems to make the same point:

> A grave is nothing more than a place where a body (or ashes of a cremated body) is buried. It continues to be a grave as long as it is recognized or recognizable as such. This may extend over centuries, long after the interred body and its trappings have merged with the soil and have become altogether indiscernible. Against such a grave acts of desecration may be perpetrated ... In the majority of cases an unlawful or unauthorized disinterment and removal constitutes an offense against both the grave and the cadaver. In a sizable number of cases it is not clear what the transgressor offended – whether it was the grave, the corpse, or both.

The injury to the grave, as opposed to the remains, captures the essence of the dissenting judgement of Stephenson, J. in *Glass, supra,* note 67, at 893, who held, with respect to an about 125-year-old grave, that the defendant was guilty of interference with a grave, as opposed to the remains. But whether you are looking at the body as separate from the grave, or the grave as separate from its decomposed content, the point still remains that, apart from the law of trespass to land or antiquity, a decomposed body is given little or no legal protection.

101 *Meagher v. Driscoll* 99 Mass. 281 (1868); *Thirkfield v. Mountain View Cemetery Association* 41 P. 564 (1895); *R v. Sharpe* (1857) 169 E.R. 959, at 960 [hereinafter *Sharpe*].

102 *In re Estate of Medlen* 677 N.E. 2d 33 (1997) [hereinafter *Medlen*].

103 *Carter, supra,* note 59.

104 496 So. 2d 601, at 605 (1986).

105 *Ibid.*

Where the spirit of the dead unjustifiably terrorizes its relatives, it is exorcized. A ritual in which the remains are disinterred and completely burnt accomplishes this, and the spirit is 'chained'. This is a complete destruction of a 'force', by the destruction of its remains. A distinction that trivializes human remains, and unintentionally renders them free for the taking, would, if applied in the African context, wittingly or unwittingly impinge on African spirituality, and may lead to annihilation of the metaphysical constitution of the African people.[106]

Is a Stillborn a Dead Body?

A related issue is the characterization of a stillborn foetus. Is it a dead body and therefore subject to the law on dead bodies? There does not seem to be judicial unanimity on the point. An answer to the above question may determine the extent of protection available to the relatives of a stillborn. It is probable that the first case on the subject is *Doodeward v. Spence*,[107] which was an action to recover possession of a double-headed stillborn foetus. While Griffith, C.J. and Higgins, J. seemed to have accepted that the stillbirth in that case was a corpse or dead body, Barton, J., however, held that the monstrous stillbirth was not a corpse.[108] The status of a stillborn for the purposes of the law relating to dead bodies is now statutorily regulated in many Australian jurisdictions.[109]

Recently, the Superior Court of Connecticut was presented with a similar problem in *Janicki v. Hospital of St Raphael*.[110] The plaintiff gave birth to a 19-week-old non-viable foetus, which was dissected by the defendants against the plaintiff's express instruction. She claimed, in addition to other causes of action, damages for negligent infliction of mental distress, resulting from the unauthorized dissection of the foetus. The court's decision turned on whether the foetus was a 'tissue' or 'child'; if the latter, the law on dead bodies would apply.[111] However, the court did not explicitly resolve this problem of characterization, but it held that a stillborn foetus was neither a tissue nor a child.[112] It seems, however, that the court's affirmation of the existence of the plaintiff's 'quasi-property' right over the foetus,[113] a concept applicable to dead human bodies, is an arguable ground for concluding that it recognized a foetus as a dead body.[114]

---

106 This would apply only to some Africans that still believe in African traditional spirituality.

107 *Doodeward, supra*, note 60.

108 *Ibid.*, at 414–15.

109 Queensland Law Reform Commission. *A Review of the Law in Relation to the Final Disposal of a Dead Body* (Queensland: Queensland Law Reform Commission, Working Paper No 58, 2004).

110 *Janicki, supra*, note 37.

111 *Ibid.*, at 965.

112 *Ibid.*

113 *Ibid.*, at 967–9.

114 It should be emphasized that the court only applied the 'quasi-property' concept by analogy, and maintained that a stillborn foetus, like a pre-embryo, occupied a middle position

In Nigeria, it seems that the courts would have recourse to available statutes for guidance in the resolution of the above characterization problem. An example of such statutes is the *Births, Deaths and Burials Law*.[115] While the birth of a stillborn is not registrable,[116] its death is.[117] The duty of burial, with respect to a stillborn,[118] is imposed on some persons by that law.[119] Consequently, it is suggested that since statutory law already accords some sepulchral rights and duties, with respect to a stillbirth, it should be admitted to the characterization of a dead body.

Nigerian Statutory Laws Affecting the Human Body and its Remains

Nigerian Criminal Code

The customary law's position on a dead body would likely have a serious impact on the interpretation of the offence of stealing under Nigeria's *Criminal Code*.[120] Section 390 of the *Criminal Code* provides: 'Any person who steals anything capable of being stolen is guilty of a felony, and is liable, if no other punishment is provided, to imprisonment for three years.' However, things 'capable of being stolen' are defined as including:

> Every inanimate thing whatever which is the *property of any person*, and which is movable, is capable of being stolen. Every inanimate thing which is the *property of any person*, and which is capable of being made movable, is capable of being stolen as soon as it becomes movable, although it is made movable in order to steal it …[121]

'Property' is further defined to include 'everything, animate or inanimate, capable of being the subject of ownership'.[122] Therefore, to be convicted under this section, the prosecutor must prove that what the accused has stolen amounts to property in law and owned by another person. The question then becomes: is a corpse, under the Nigerian *Criminal Code*, a property of another?

There does not seem to be any Nigerian decision on point.[123] The general legal position in England, subject to the exception introduced by *R v. Kelly*,[124] is that there is no property in a corpse; with the result that an accused can hardly be convicted for the theft of a corpse. However, the English common law recognizes the offence of

---

of 'special respect', that is, neither person nor tissue.

115 *C. 13, Laws of Lagos State, 1994.*

116 *Ibid.*, at s. 3(3).

117 Combined effects of ss. 18, 31 and 36(2).

118 *Ibid.*, at s. 35.

119 *Ibid.*, at s. 40.

120 *Criminal Code, c. 42* [hereinafter *Criminal Code*].

121 *Ibid.*, at s. 382 (emphasis added).

122 *Ibid.*, at s. 1(1).

123 In *Egbe, supra*, note 5, the Nigerian Supreme Court held that the trial court's finding that there was no possessory right over a grave was premature in the circumstances of that case.

124 *Kelly, supra*, note 37.

desecration of a grave, which is a misdemeanour. That is the only way by which the common law protects a grave and, indirectly, its content.[125] That protection, however, does not extend to the corpse itself. As stated by Sir James Stephen: 'The dead body of a human being is not capable of being stolen at common law.'[126]

It seems that a Nigerian court confronted with a charge of stealing a corpse will embark on a jurisprudential exercise of localizing the English common law, by casting it in the mould of African ontological and religious abstraction of man, whether dead or alive, as a contagious force which is owned by a community of forces, including the living and dead members of a man's family. As already stated, the implication is that an African is the property of his or her family and community. Consequently, it seems that a Nigerian court might hold an accused guilty of stealing a corpse, under the relevant section of its *Criminal Code*. In doing so, it would be stating as its own general rule what might be regarded as an exception under the English common law, recently introduced by the English Court of Appeal's decision in *R v. Kelly*.[127] However, the general rule suggested for Nigeria will be wider than *R v. Kelly*'s exception, since the case is limited to the transformation of a corpse by the application of scientific skill and labour.

In that case, an artist, desirous of making casts or moulds of some old anatomical specimens[128] in the premises of the Royal College of Surgeons, lured a junior technician of the College to surreptitiously remove some of the anatomical specimens, which were then given to the artist. Both the artist and technician knew they were not entitled to remove the specimens from the premises of the College; nevertheless, they thought that the College was not entitled to legal possession of the specimens.[129] They therefore claimed to have acted honestly, on a charge of stealing the specimens. On the defendants' submission that the parts were not property which could be stolen, the Court of Appeal, relying on the Australian case of *Doodeward v. Spence*,[130] observed: 'Parts of a corpse are capable of being property within s. 4 of the *Theft Act*, if they have acquired different attributes by virtue of the application of skill, such as dissection or preservation techniques, for exhibition or teaching purposes.'[131] It seems that the Court of Appeal deliberately set out to change, or at least modify, the common law no-property rule because, as it observed, 'the common law does not stand still'.[132] It also realized that the current exception based on preservation of a corpse for exhibition or medical training may not be ample enough[133] and, therefore, envisaged a more elastic future exception:

---

125 *Sharpe*, *supra*, note 101, at 960.

126 Sir J. Stephen, *A Digest of the Criminal Law*, 7th edn (London: Sweet & Maxwell, 1926), at 307. It was stated at note 6, at 307 that: 'It [the dead body] is not property, though it may have value.' Also, *R v. Haynes* (1614) 2 East P.C. 652.

127 *Kelly*, *supra*, note 37.

128 The judgement showed that the specimens were at least 20 years old.

129 *Kelly*, *supra*, note 37, at 743–4.

130 *Doodeward*, *supra*, note 60.

131 *Ibid.*, at 749–50.

132 *Ibid.*, at 750.

133 That was partly why the exception was not applied in the earlier case of *Dobson*, *supra*, note 37, because the preservation in that case, as observed by Justice Gibson at 601,

It may be that if, on some future occasion, the question arises, the courts will hold that human body parts are capable of being property for the purposes of s.4, even without the acquisition of different attributes, if they have a use or significance beyond their mere existence. This may be so if, for example, they are intended for use in an organ transplant operation, for the extraction of DNA or, for that matter, as an exhibit in a trial.[134]

The above observation seems to have prophesied the recent decision of the Supreme Court of Western Australia in *Roche v. Douglas*.[135] It was a civil case in which the plaintiff's paternity was in issue. The plaintiff claimed to be the biological daughter of the deceased and therefore entitled to inherit from the deceased's estate. The executor of the deceased contended that the plaintiff was an adopted daughter of the deceased's mother, and was therefore the deceased's sister. To prove that the deceased was her father, the plaintiff sought an order of the court allowing a DNA analysis of the deceased's tissue sample, obtained and preserved during a medical procedure on the deceased during his lifetime. Under the prevailing Rules of Court, the judge was only entitled to make the order if the tissue sample qualified as property. After a detailed review of some Australian and English authorities touching on the point, Master Sanderson held that a human tissue qualified as property. The judge considered that it was necessary to conform the law to scientific developments, such as DNA analysis techniques; moreover, the DNA evidence would save the court enormous time and expense. No doubt, this case is an important precedent that is likely to inspire others, as it attunes the law to biomedical reality. It seems that a general rule in Nigeria that the dead body is a limited property, on the basis of customary law, will even find support in the above recent cases.

Burial in Homes and Within Living Places

Section 246 of the *Criminal Code*[136] is also pertinent to the analysis undertaken in this chapter. It provides:

> Any person who without the consent of the Governor-General [now President] or a Governor buries or attempts to bury any corpse in any house, building, premises, yard, garden, compound, or within a hundred yards of any dwelling-house, or in any open space situated within a township, is guilty of a misdemeanour, and is liable to imprisonment for six months.

The above section contradicts African mortuary tradition. African metaphysical conception of the dead and the belief in continued relationship with a dead relative explains the burial of dead relatives in their homes or within the premises of living relatives. As such, when married women die, they are taken to their paternal homes

---

was not for medical teaching or exhibition, but pursuant to the performance of a statutory duty under the coroner's law.

134 *Doodeward, supra*, note 60, at 750.

135 *Roche, supra*, note 37.

136 *Criminal Code, supra*, note 120.

for burial, so that their spirits could reunite with their own biological relatives.[137] This practice, burial in the homes, was observed by Rev. Samuel Johnson: 'The Yorubas [a Nigerian tribe] do not bury their dead in graveyards or cemeteries, but in their houses. ... The graves of aged people are dug generally in the piazza or in one of the sleeping rooms.'[138]

The *Nigerian Criminal Code* was originally drafted and enacted by the British colonial administration in 1904, for Northern Nigeria, and was made applicable to the whole country in 1916,[139] following the amalgamation of northern and southern Nigeria in 1914, by Lord Lugard.[140] That amalgamation created the political entity known today as Nigeria. In historical perspective, one can understand such provisions, like s. 246, which the British colonial government used to infuse Western mortuary practice[141] into the mortuary tradition of Nigerian society. But the real surprise is that long after independence in 1960, this section is still statutory criminal law in Nigeria. One can appreciate the health arguments in support of s. 246, that is, the need to prevent the spread of diseases likely to be caused by such burial practice;[142] but the fact that burial in or around homes is still the general practice in Nigeria shows how tenaciously the philosophy that animates that practice is held. No wonder there does not seem to be any reported case on s. 246 of the *Criminal Code*.

The Antiquities Act

The *Nigerian Antiquities Act*[143] contains provisions that are relevant to the exploration of Nigerian law relating to dead bodies. As the analysis below will show, some of the

---

137 Anigbo, *supra*, note 15, at 145 states:
>   The custom is that when she dies her remains must be brought back ceremonially for burial in her lineage land. Burial in her lineage land thereby becomes a confirmation of her membership of the group. Therefore members of her lineage must receive back her remains with dignity and honour due to a member of the lineage.

138 S. Johnson, *The History of the Yorubas* (Lagos: CSS Bookshops Ltd., 1921), at 137.

139 For an excellent historical account of Nigerian criminal law, see C.O. Okonkwo, *Criminal Law In Nigeria*, 2nd edn (London: Sweet & Maxwell, 1980), at 4–17.

140 For a detailed discussion of the administrative, economic and social factors giving rise to the amalgamation see Lord F. Lugard, *The Dual Mandate in British Tropical Africa*, 5th edn (Connecticut: Archon Books, 1965), at 94–113.

141 *Gilbert, supra*, note 57, at 764–5.

142 Health reasons account for the initial absolute prohibition, by the common law, of burial within churches, cities and large towns. Burial within churches or in the churchyard began to be allowed from the time of Pope Gregory I; so that church members could, upon the view of the sepulchres, pray for their departed members. The common law's prohibition was in turn based on the Roman law. As Mr Justice Abney observed in *John Andrews v. Thomas Cawthorne* (1744) 125 E.R. 1308, at 1309 [hereinafter *Andrews*]:
>   Now it is most notorious and certain that all burials by the Roman laws were prohibited not only within the temples but even in cities and large towns ... and this prohibition was founded on a prudent state policy, to prevent infection, from a great number of corrupt corpses lying contiguous in putrefaction; and it is well known that the poorer sorts in great parts of the Kingdom are buried in shrouds without coffins even to this day.

143 *Antiquities Act, c. 12.*

provisions of the *Antiquities Act* need amendment to better reflect the legislation's rationale and give stronger protection to dead bodies. The *Antiquities Act*[144] came into force on 1 August 1954 and was originally promulgated by the British colonial government in Nigeria, for the preservation of antiquities found in Nigeria, which may, with the necessary permit, be exported out of Nigeria.[145] The Act exhaustively defined an antiquity:

'Antiquity' means

a. any object of archaeological interest or land in which any object is believed to exist or was discovered; or

b. any relic of early European settlement or colonisation; or

c. any work of art or craftwork, including any statue, modelled clay figure, figure cast or wrought in metal, carving, housepost, door, ancestral figure, religious mask, staff, drum, bowl, ornament, utensil, weapon, armour, regalia, manuscript or document, if such work of art or craftwork is of indigenous origin and

i. was made or fashioned before the year 1918; or

ii. is of historical, artistic or scientific interest, and is or has been used at any time in the performance, and for the purposes of, any traditional African ceremony[146]

Paragraph (a) above seems to interest us most; consequently, an 'object of archaeological interest' is defined as 'any *fossil remains of man* or of animals found in association with man', or 'any ancient structure, erection, memorial, causeway, bridge, cairn, tumulus, *grave*, shrine, excavation, well, water tank, artificial pool, monolith, group of stones, earthwork, wall, gateway or fortification'.[147] The unfortunate result is that the sacred remains of our ancestors are characterized as objects of antiquity, potentially exportable,[148] and a veritable object of archaeological inquisition.

The Act established an Antiquities Commission,[149] to implement its provisions, and consists of 16 members appointed pursuant to its provisions.[150] Among other things, the Antiquities Commission is given power to accept any gift, loan, devise or bequest of any antiquity; to enter upon and inspect any monument, public museum or archaeological excavation, or any land where excavations or similar operations are being carried out for archaeological purposes;[151] and to grant permits for

---

144 *Antiquities Act*, c. 12.
145 *Ibid.*, at s. 22.
146 *Ibid.*, at s. 2.
147 *Ibid.* There are four other definitions of the phrase, which are not relevant to this discussion (emphasis added).
148 *Ibid.*, at s. 22.
149 *Ibid.*, at s. 3.
150 *Ibid.*, at s. 4.
151 *Ibid.*, at s. 9(1).

archaeological excavations.[152] The Director of Antiquities Service is given power, for the purpose of discovering antiquities in any area, to carry out excavations with the consent of the local government authority of that area.[153]

With the objectification of our ancestral remains, under the *Antiquities Act*, contrary to African mortuary tradition and philosophy, the questions become: can a Nigerian family lawfully stop a proposed or ongoing excavation of the grave of its ancestor? In other words, can such a family stop the Antiquities Commission from issuing a permit for the excavation of an ancestral grave? Again, in whom does the *Antiquities Act* vest ownership of the contents of such grave?

The answers to these questions seem to depend on the interpretation of ss. 23, 24 and 25 of the Act. Section 23(1) provides: 'No person shall by means of excavation or similar operations search for any antiquity unless authorised by a permit issued by the Commission with the consent of the local government authority of the place where the search is to be carried out.' Such permits are to be issued to persons who are competent by training and experience to carry out the operations for which the permit is required, and have the financial or other support of an archaeological or scientific society or institution of good repute.[154] By s. 23(1) above, only the consent of a local government authority is required for the Commission's permit, apparently excluding the need for the consent of the family, whose ancestral grave might be the object of the permit. Taken alone, this section would devastate a family's traditional and metaphysical relationship with a deceased member.

However, s. 23(3)(c) seems to confer some protection to such family: 'A permit issued under this section shall not of itself confer any right to enter upon any land without the consent of the person entitled to grant such consent.' Therefore, it seems that notwithstanding a permit granted by the Antiquities Commission, with the consent of a local government authority, a family can still use the law of trespass to prevent the abuse and desecration of its ancestral grave. Consequently, a permit duly granted by the Antiquities Commission does not ensure, by itself, access to an ancestral grave. But what happens where illegal access, that is, without a family's consent, is gained to an ancestral grave, say by an archaeologist, and the grave is excavated, and the contents taken away? Apart from possible damnation of the trespasser in damages for trespass, does the Act establish any framework for return of the contents of the excavated grave, or does the Act vest sufficient ownership in the family to enable it to claim the return of such items?[155]

It is arguable, under s. 23(5), that a 'grave robber', subject only to damages in trespass, can keep the objects of his robbery. This seems to follow from the fact that s. 23(5) only penalizes illegal excavation by a fine or imprisonment or both:

---

152 *Ibid.*, at s. 23(1).

153 *Ibid.*, at s. 13(a).

154 *Ibid.*, at s. 23(2).

155 It is interesting to point out that a court in Kenya is now faced with determining ownership of the fossilized remains of a hominid, dating back about six million years, excavated in Kenya by a team of French scientists: P. Calamai, 'Skull Find in Kenya Shakes Evolution Tree', *The Toronto Star* (22 March 2001) A1.

Any person who contravenes the provisions of subsection (1) or subsection (4) of this section or fails to comply with any condition [that is, given under Section 23(3)(a)] subject to which he has been granted a permit under this section shall be guilty of an offence and liable to a fine not exceeding one hundred pounds [now 200 naira] or to imprisonment for a term not exceeding six months, or to both such fine and such imprisonment.

The above section applies only when a valid permit was not obtained, but not when the landowner's consent was not obtained under s. 23(3)(c), which does not come within the express terms of the penalty section above. Then, what happens in the case of a tresparous despoliation of a grave, albeit pursuant to a valid permit? Since the excavator may not be convicted for illegal excavation under s. 23(5), can the family, apart from resort to trespass, claim a return of the skeletal remains or any cause of action based on ownership?

This sets the stage for an application of the limited property rule as suggested above. Under this rule, an excavator who, in spite of a family's refusal, excavated a grave merely on the basis of a valid permit will, apart from damages for trespass, be ordered to return the skeletal remains to the 'owners' or pay appropriate damages for their conversion. Even in cases of illegal excavation, the criminal punishment under s. 23(5) does not include a return of the grave contents. But the court may exercise its equitable jurisdiction to order their return, regard being had to the customary law on dead bodies.

Again, when s. 25 is read in conjunction with s. 23, there seems to be a vesting of ownership in a family, with respect to its ancestral grave, enabling it to claim the return of any grave item:

25.(1) When any object of archaeological interest is discovered after the commencement of this Act, the local government authority of the place where the object is discovered may, if it thinks fit, constitute itself the guardian of the object.

(2) Save as otherwise provided in this Act, *the owner of, and any other person having an estate or interest in, any object of archaeological interest of which a local government authority has become the guardian under this section shall have the same right and title to, and estate and interest in, the object* in all respects as if the local government authority had not become the guardian thereof.

(3) A local government authority which has become the guardian of an object of archaeological interest under this section may maintain the object and may have access at all reasonable times by its officers or other employees or any person duly authorised by it to the object for the purpose of inspecting it and doing such acts and things as may be required for the maintenance thereof; and, in the case of a movable object, may, unless the owner refuses his consent, remove the object to, and keep it in, an approved museum. (Emphasis added)

Certainly, as argued in this chapter, a family is such an owner having an interest or estate in an ancestral grave or its contents, and despite the designation of a local authority as a guardian of the contents of an excavated grave, the Act, by s. 25(2), certainly gives a family superior title. Consequently, though the Act infelicitously characterized the ancestral graves of Nigerians and their contents as 'antiquities' and 'objects of archaeological interest', it seems that a proper interpretation of the Act gives some protection against the desecration of an ancestral grave, and enables a family to claim the return of a grave item. As already noted, contrary interpretations are possible. The *Antiquities Act* needs an amendment[156] to eliminate its obnoxious formulation, eliminate ambiguities, and enhance the protection of Nigerian ancestral graves. It may be remarked that there does not seem to be any Nigerian case law on the *Antiquities Act*. This probably shows how much archaeologists and the Antiquities Commission appreciate the sanctity and philosophy that surround a grave in Nigeria.

The *American Antiquities Act 1906*,[157] seems to be the American equivalent of the *Nigerian Antiquities Act*, but both differ in their import and reach. The American Act allows the excavation, with permission, of 'any object of antiquity',[158] 'archaeological sites'[159] or the 'gathering of objects of antiquity'.[160] These characterizations have been lampooned as a most disrespectful description of Native American human remains and sacred objects.[161] So characterized, ownership of Native American human remains is vested in the government, quite unlike the Nigerian Act, because the American Act provides that such objects of antiquity shall be gathered 'for permanent preservation in public museums',[162] Today, the *American Antiquities Act, 1906* is largely replaced by several similar statutes[163] passed thereafter, which are to be read subject to the *Native American Graves Protection and Repatriation Act* ('*NAGPRA*').[164] Even before the passage of the *American Antiquities Act*, there was a shameful scramble for Native American human remains and sacred objects by archaeologists, anthropologists, art collectors, grave-robbers and even the American government.

In 1868, the American government, through its Army Surgeon-General, made a call for the collection of Indian crania for the Army Medical Museum. This led to the decapitation of fallen Native American soldiers and wide-scale excavation

---

156 The *Nigerian Antiquities Act* is not reproduced in the latest revised laws of the Federal Republic of Nigeria 1990. It may not be an omission as the 1999 *Nigerian Constitution*, Second Schedule, Part 2(3) puts it in the concurrent legislative list, that is, giving states legislative competence with reference to antiquities.

157 *American Antiquities Act, 1906, 16 U.S.C. 431–433* [hereinafter *American Antiquities Act*].

158 *Ibid.*, at s. 1.

159 *Ibid.*, at s. 3.

160 *Ibid.*

161 R.M. Kosslak, '*The Native American Graves Protection and Repatriation Act*: The Death Knell for Scientific Study?' (1999–2000) 24 *American Indian L. Rev.* 129, at 134–6.

162 *American Antiquities Act*, *supra*, note 157, at s. 3.

163 An excellent account of the subsequent statutes is given by M.B. Bowman, 'The Reburial of Native American Skeletal Remains: Approaches to the Resolution of a Conflict' (1989) 13 *Harv. Env. L. Rev.* 147, at 185–96; J.B. Winski, 'There Are Skeletons in the Closet: The Repatriation of Native American Human Remains and Burial Objects' (1992) 34 *Ariz. L. Rev.* 187, at 194–8.

164 *25 U.S.C. 3001–3013 (1991)* [hereinafter *NAGPRA*].

of Native American burial sites.[165] Again, Thomas Jefferson, who became the third president of the United States, desecrated a Native American burial ground, albeit before becoming president. He wanted to satisfy his curiosity and unravel a myth surrounding a particular burial mound, but at the spiritual expense of the Native Americans.[166]

Archaeologists, like the famous, if not infamous, Dr Morton, were the worst Native American grave desecrators. They were involved in cranial studies that sought to prove a horrendous and now defunct racial theory that portrayed Native Americans, and also Blacks, as intellectually inferior to Whites. This study led to increased demand for Native American human remains and sustained the activities of grave-robbers and desecrators who wanted to satisfy the increasing market demand.[167] Of course, the above situation drew the ire of Native Americans and some writers, who roundly condemned the desecration and contempt meted out to Native American human remains and sacred objects.[168] This effort bore some fruit when the American government enacted, in 1991, the *Native American Graves Protection and Repatriation Act*,[169] to redress decades of cultural and spiritual injustice to Native Americans.

NAGPRA established a system that requires museums, funded or partly funded by the American government, that have Native American human remains, and cultural or sacred objects,[170] and other public agencies that discovered such remains or objects, to compile an inventory thereof,[171] with a view to repatriating them to Native Americans.[172] *NAGPRA* vests ownership of a cultural item, depending on its nature, in the lineal descendants of the Native American, an Indian tribe or Native

---

165 J. Riding In, 'Without Ethics and Morality: A Historical Overview of Imperial Archaeology and American Indians' (1992) 24 *Ariz. St. L.J.* 11, at 19–20.

166 *Ibid.*, at 15–17.

167 Winski, *supra*, note 163; G.A. Marsh, 'Walking the Spirit Trail: Repatriation and Protection Of Native American Remains and Sacred Cultural Items' (1992) 24 *Ariz. St. L.J.* 79; Riding In, *supra*, note 165.

168 There is a huge amount of literature on the subject which, in addition to sources already cited, includes: J.F. Trope and W.R. Echo-Hawk, '*The Native American Graves Protection and Repatriation Act*: Background and Legislative History' (1992) 24 *Ariz. St. L.J.* 35; S. Hutt, 'Illegal Trafficking in Native American Human Remains and Cultural Items: A New Protection Tool' (1992) 24 *Ariz. St. L.J.* 135; R.W. Johnson and S.I. Haensly, 'Fifth Amendment Takings Implications of the 1990 *Native American Graves Protection and Repatriation Act*' (1992) 24 *Ariz. St. L.J.* 151; S.D. Brooks, 'Native American Indians' Fruitless Search for First Amendment Protection of their Sacred Religious Sites' (1990) 24 *Valparaiso University L. Rev.* 521; P. D'Innocenzo, '"Not in My Backyard!" Protecting Archaeological Sites on Private Lands' (1997) 21 *Am. Ind. L.J.* 131; J. Brady, 'Land is Itself a Sacred, Living Being: Native American Sacred Site Protection on Federal Public Lands Amidst the Shadows Of oBear Lodge' (1999–2000) 24 *Am. Ind. L.J.* 153.

169 *NAGPRA*, *supra*, 164.

170 *NAGPRA* uses the phrase 'cultural items', which is given a wide definition in s. 3001 as meaning 'human remains' and including all the various objects mentioned in the section.

171 *NAGPRA*, *supra*, note 164, at s. 3003.

172 *Ibid.*, at s. 5.

Hawaiian organization.[173] *NAGPRA* imposes penalties on museums for failing to comply with its provisions,[174] which are enforceable in the United States district courts.[175] *NAGPRA* has been described as 'human rights legislation',[176] which

> finally recognizes that Native American human remains and cultural items are the remnants and products of living people, and that descendants have a cultural and spiritual relationship with the deceased. Human remains and cultural items can no longer be thought of as mere 'scientific specimens' or collectibles.[177]

The interpretative problem that can arise under *NAGPRA* emerged, five years later, in the case of *Bonnichsen v. U.S. Dept. of the Army*.[178] There, part of the question was whether *NAGPRA* applied to human remains which were about 9000 years old. The court, however, did not decide this question but remitted the case[179] back to the Army Corps, with a list of questions and issues it should consider before arriving at any decision concerning the ancient remains in that case. As directed by the court, the first issue the Corps should consider was: 'Whether these remains [about 9000 years old] are subject to *NAGPRA*, and why (or why not).'[180]

In 2000, the Secretary of the Interior, on behalf of the Army Corps, determined pursuant to its investigation that the remains were biologically ancestral to present-day American Indians and, therefore, liable to repatriation for burial. The scientists who wanted to study the remains opposed the decision of the Secretary and brought a fresh action in court. The scientists/plaintiffs were successful both at the District Court and the Court of Appeal. The Court of Appeal's judgement in *Bonnichsen v. U.S.*[181] has shed more light on *NAGPRA*'s provisions. It held that suits under *NAGPRA* could be brought by plaintiffs who are not American Indians or Indian Tribes, so that the court had jurisdiction to entertain the suit brought by non-Indian scientists.[182] The court also held that *NAGPRA* unambiguously requires that 'human remains bear some relationship to a *presently existing* tribe, people, or culture to be considered Native American'.[183] Since there was no evidence that the human remains in that case were biologically ancestral to any existing Indian Tribe or otherwise bore any relationship to any present-day indigenous tribe in the USA, the Court of Appeal vacated the Secretary's repatriation order and permitted the scientists to study the remains of Kennewick Man. This latest decision shows that remains that pre-date recorded history are unlikely to be categorized as ancient human remains repatriatable under the provisions of *NAGPRA*. It should be noted that *NAGPRA*

---

173 *Ibid.*, at s. 3002.
174 *Ibid.*, at s. 3007.
175 *Ibid.*, at s. 3013.
176 Trope and Echo-Hawk, *supra*, note 27, at 59.
177 *Ibid.*, at 76.
178 969 F. Supp. 614 (1997).
179 *Bonnichsen v. U.S. Dept. of the Army* 969 F. Supp. 628 (1997).
180 *Ibid.*, at 651.
181 *Bonnichsen v. U.S.* 357 F. 3d 962 (9th Cir. 2004).
182 *Ibid.*, at 971.
183 *Ibid.*, at 972.

achieves for Native Americans a position similar to that obtainable under Nigerian customary law, which is largely maintained by the *Nigerian Antiquities Act*.

The Anatomy Act

The *Nigerian Anatomy Act*[184] was modelled after the *English Anatomy Act of 1832*,[185] which is repealed and replaced by the *Anatomy Act* 1984.[186] While the *Anatomy Act 1984*[187] provides for anatomical examination of a whole corpse or complete parts of a corpse, the *Human Tissue Act, 1961*[188] is mainly concerned with the use of a specified part or some specified parts of a corpse for therapeutic purposes and purposes of medical education and research.[189] The purpose of the *Anatomy Act* could be gleaned from the preamble of the English Act of 1832.[190]

This preamble becomes more meaningful in its historical context. Common law prohibits disinterment of dead bodies, even for purposes of anatomical examination.[191] This rule significantly limited the availability of cadavers for medical research purposes, partly resulting in wide illegal and notorious practices of delaying burials to enable dissections to be performed.[192] The prohibition hardly abated the

---

184 *Anatomy Act, c. 17* [hereinafter *Anatomy Act*].

185 *Anatomy Act, 1832 (U.K.), 2 & 3 Williams, c. 75* [hereinafter *Anatomy Act* (1832)].

186 *Anatomy Act 1984 (U.K.), 1984, c. 14, s. 13(2)* [hereinafter *Anatomy Act* (1984)].

187 *Ibid.*

188 *Human Tissue Act, 1961 (U.K.), 9 & 10 Eliz. II, c. 54* [hereinafter *Human Tissue*].

189 The Preamble and s. 1 of the *Human Tissue Act, ibid.*

190 *Anatomy Act (1832), supra*, note 185:

> WHEREAS a knowledge of the causes and nature of sundry diseases which affect the body, and of the best methods of treating and curing such diseases, and of healing and repairing divers wounds and injuries to which the human frame is liable, cannot be acquired without the aid of anatomical examination: And whereas the legal supply of human bodies for such anatomical examination is insufficient fully to provide the means of such knowledge: And whereas, in order further to supply human bodies for such purposes, divers great and grievous crimes have been committed, and lately murder, for the single object of selling for such purposes the bodies of the persons so murdered: And whereas therefore it is highly expedient to give protection, under certain Regulations, to the study and practice of Anatomy, and to prevent, as far as may be, such great and grievous crimes and murder as aforesaid … .

The *Anatomy Act (1984), supra*, note 186, contains a similar preamble:

> An Act to make provision about the use of bodies of deceased persons, and parts of such bodies, for anatomical examination and about the possession and disposal of bodies of deceased persons, and parts of such bodies, authorised to be used for anatomical examination, and for connected purposes.

191 *R v. Lynn* (1788) 100 E.R. 394, at 395 [hereinafter *Lynn*]. Willes, J. in *R v. Feist* (1858) 169 E.R. 1132, at 1135 [hereinafter *Feist*] stated that: 'It is clear that at common law it is a misdemeanour to take up a corpse out of a burial ground and sell it even for the purpose of dissection.'

192 It is an offence under common law to delay the burial of a dead body, which will likely result in a health hazard: *Lynn, ibid.*; *Feist, ibid.*; *R v. Stewart* (1840) 113 E.R. 1007; *Andrews, supra*, note 142; *R v. Cheere* (1825) 107 E.R. 1294.

horrendous activities of the 'resurrection men'[193] and likely contributed to the crime of murder mentioned in the preamble to the 1832 Act. Before the 1832 Act, the main legitimate source of cadavers for anatomical examination were the bodies of convicted and hanged murderers, which were, under a 1752 Act,[194] liable to be sent to a surgeon, by the court's Sheriff, for compulsory anatomical examination.[195]

The 1752 Act was meant to discourage the then rising crime of murder by imposing the punishment of dissection, in addition to the sentence of death. It therefore required the judge to expressly state the sentence of dissection in the judgement.[196] However, breaches of peace often arose from a struggle between Sheriffs and surgeons, on one hand, and relatives of the convicted and hanged murderers, on the other hand. These parties struggled over possession of the dead bodies of the convicts after execution of the sentence of death. The pandemonium often resulted in dire consequences for the convicts' relatives, as the 1752 Act provided that persons who rescued or tried to rescue such bodies after execution 'shall be deemed and adjudged to be guilty of felony, and shall be liable to be transported to some of his Majesty's colonies or plantations in America for the term of seven years'.[197] It was probably due to social problems and breaches of the peace resulting from the execution of the 1752 Act that led to its repeal by s. 16 of the 1832 Act.[198] In other words, the repeal pertains only to the additional sentence of dissection, which was no longer in force as the 1832 Act directed that the body should be buried after execution.[199]

Only recently, some archaeologists, in search of Roman and Anglo-Saxon artefacts at an excavation site previously occupied by Oxford University medical school in the eighteenth century, discovered a pit dug in 1767 and containing more than 2000 bones believed to be skeletal remains of condemned murderers dissected under the 1752 Act, and those of infants whose bodies were believed to be stolen by grave-robbers.[200] The nature of the bones is believed to offer a clue as to the anatomical methods employed by surgeons and medical students during the embryonic period of medicine.[201]

The *Anatomy Act 1832* was meant to remedy the above defects by establishing a licensing system for the practice of anatomy, and a voluntary and non-commercial system of cadaver donation by persons mentioned in the Act, that is, person in lawful possession of the corpse; the deceased, by decision to that effect made during his

---

193 A characterization for men in the eighteenth century who illegally disinterred and marketed dead bodies for anatomical purposes. An excellent historical account of the depredations of the ressurection men is given by Shultz: S.M. Shultz, *Body Snatching: The Robbing of Graves for the Education of Physicians* (North Carolina: McFarland & Co., 1992).

194 *Anatomy Act, 1752 (U.K.) 25 Geo. II, c. 37, vol. 20.*

195 *Ibid.*, at ss. 2 and 5.

196 *Ibid.*, at s. 3.

197 *Ibid.*, at s. 10.

198 *Anatomy Act* (1832), *supra*, note 185.

199 *Ibid.*

200 S. Bisset and R. Syal, 'Scientists Find Dissected Remains in Oxford Pit: Former Medical School', *National Post* (21 February 2001) A14.

201 *Ibid.*

life time; or an executor. It was even thought by Willes, J., wrongly though, that 'the *Anatomy Act* [that is, of 1832] has altered the common law, and has rendered the selling of a dead body for the purpose of dissection lawful under certain circumstances'.[202] It is easily noticed that none of the 21 sections of the 1832 Act is crafted in the language of commodification. Rather, the dominant words or phrases used in that Act were mainly of a non-commercial nature. They include 'to permit the body ... undergo anatomical examination',[203] 'direct ... his body ... examined anatomically',[204] 'shall nominate'.[205] These phrases do not evince a commercial transaction for value.

It may be that His Lordship was influenced by the facts of that case where a master of a workhouse, and in lawful possession of the dead bodies of some paupers, sent the bodies for dissection and received some remuneration for his efforts. The court, in the circumstances examined below, held that the 1832 Act justified his actions. It seems that the remuneration was not a purchase price for the dead bodies but paid as 'gratuities for his [accused] trouble in going through the formalities and giving the notices and obtaining the certificates, in respect of each of the bodies, required by the *Anatomy Act* [1832]'.[206] Therefore, much as the *Anatomy Act 1832* created a system that facilitated the supply of cadavers for anatomical purposes, it does not seem that it sought to do so by legalizing the commodification of cadavers.

Although the *Nigerian Anatomy Act* did not reproduce the preamble of the English Act, and in fact does not contain any preamble, it is suggested that its nearly complete reproduction of the substantive provisions of the English 1832 Act makes the above preamble a relevant aid in the interpretation of the *Nigerian Anatomy Act*.[207] Neither the Nigerian Act nor the English 1832 Act defined the phrase 'anatomical examination', which was repeated in most of their provisions; though the meaning could be deduced from the preamble of the English 1832 Act. However, the *English Anatomy Act of 1984*,[208] which replaced the 1832 Act defines 'anatomical examination':

'[A]natomical examination' means the examination by dissection of a body for purposes of teaching or studying, or researching into, morphology; and where parts of a body are separated in the course of its anatomical examination, such examination includes the examination by dissection of the parts for those purposes.[209]

---

202 *Feist, supra*, note 191, at 1135.

203 *Anatomy Act (1832), supra*, note 185, at s. 7.

204 *Ibid.*, at s. 8.

205 *Ibid.*

206 *Feist, supra*, note 191, at 1132.

207 In fact, ss. 2, 3, 4, 5, 6, 7, 8, 9, 10 and 11 of the Nigerian Act were respectively taken from ss. 2, 7, 8, 9, 10, 12, 13, 14, 15 and 18 of the 1832 English Act.

208 *Anatomy Act (1984), supra*, note 186.

209 *Ibid.* This Act does not apply to Nigeria and is only relevant as an aid to interpretation.

It seems reasonably clear that the purposes of the *Nigerian Anatomy Act* are to ensure a licensed practice of anatomy and an adequate supply of cadavers for medical research and education.

Consequently, the Nigerian Act establishes a voluntary system of donation of dead bodies for anatomical examination. The deceased, while alive, could, either in writing or verbally in the presence of two or more witnesses during the illness that caused his death, donate his dead body to any school of anatomy for anatomical examination.[210] But what happens where the deceased made a donation of his body during a particular illness but died of another unrelated illness? The deceased's surviving spouse or known relative can, however, defeat a donation by the deceased, resulting in the interment of the deceased without anatomical examination.[211]

An executor or other person in lawful possession[212] of the deceased's body could make a donation of the dead body to a school of anatomy, unless the deceased had indicated, either in writing during his lifetime or verbally in the presence of two or more witnesses during his last illness, that the body should not undergo anatomical examination. The executor's power to donate the deceased's body, or the power of a person in lawful custody to make such a donation could also be defeated by the objection of the deceased's surviving spouse or known relative, resulting in the body being interred without an anatomical examination.

Section 7 of the English 1832 Act, which is similar to s. 3 of the Nigerian Act, was interpreted in *R v. Feist*.[213] There, the defendant, master of a workhouse at Newington, played a trick on the relatives of some deceased paupers and, as a result, obtained their dead bodies, sent them to a hospital for dissection, and received certain payments for his efforts. Defendant's counsel relied on s. 7 of the *Anatomy Act 1832*, which gave lawful possession of the bodies to the master of the workhouse, to contend that in the absence of express request of burial from the deceased relatives, the master of the workhouse could dispose of the bodies for dissection. The jury convicted the defendant for unreasonable delay of burial with a view to dissection. The conviction was set aside on appeal. Pollock C.B. opined:

> We are all of opinion that this conviction cannot be sustained, and the ground on which I believe we all proceed is, that what was done by the defendant was done according to law. He had legal possession of the body, and he did with it that which the law authorised him to do. It may be that he prevented the relatives from requiring the body to be interred without undergoing an anatomical examination by acting a lie; but if that was wrong in the eye of the law, he should have been prosecuted for that wrong.[214]

Similarly, Bramwell, B. observed:

---

210 *Anatomy Act, supra*, note 184, at s. 4.

211 *Ibid.*

212 In *Feist, supra*, note 191, it was held that the master of a workhouse is a person having lawful possession of the bodies of deceased paupers. Certainly, an African family has lawful possession of the body of its deceased member.

213 *Feist, supra*, note 191.

214 *Ibid.*, at 1134.

I assume that, except for the statute [*Anatomy Act (1832)*, s. 7], this indictment would be good at common law. Then, is the defendant protected by the statute? He was justified by the statute in what he did, unless some relative required the body to be buried without dissection. Mr. Robinson [the Prosecutor] admits that none of the relatives did this in terms, and that in fact the idea of dissection never entered their minds; but he contends that their conduct with respect to the burial, and the defendant's fraud in concealing the intention to dissect, are equivalent to a requirement; but this is not so. I think the Act means that there must be an affirmative requirement. The only doubt I have had has been this – the Act seems to mean that the relatives shall have an opportunity of requiring, and for this purpose they must have a reasonable time to do so; and I have had a doubt whether this reasonable time had been afforded them; but I think it had: a reasonable time could not be longer than that which ought to intervene between the death and the burial. The relatives had the whole of this period to make the requirement, and during a portion of this time there had been no fraud. The truth is; a wrong has been done to the relatives by the concealing from them by fraud what they ought to have been made acquainted with. It may be that this would afford a cause of action, but I cannot think that it forms a ground for this indictment.[215]

It is pertinent to emphasize that under the Nigerian Act, and the English 1832 Act, the deceased's surviving spouse, and in fact 'any known relative', can override the deceased's decision to have his body submitted for an anatomical examination. This is in conformity with Nigerian customary law which vests ownership of a person and the dead body in his or her family. This veto power, though contained in the Nigerian Act and the English 1832 Act, is conspicuously missing in the *English Anatomy Act 1984*.[216] Section 4(1)(2), above, is similar to s. 4 of the *Nigerian Anatomy Act* and s. 8 of the *English Anatomy Act 1832*. The major point of departure is that while the Nigerian and English [that is, 1832] Acts give a surviving spouse or known relative

---

215 *Ibid.*, at 1135–6.

216 *Anatomy Act (1984)*, *supra*, note 186. Section 4 provides:

Subsection (2) applies if a person, either in writing at any time or orally in the presence of two or more witnesses during his last illness, has expressed a request that his body be used after his death for anatomical examination.

If the person lawfully in possession of the body after death has no reason to believe that the request was withdrawn, he may authorise the use of the body in accordance with the request.

Without prejudice to subsection (2), the person lawfully in possession of a body may authorise it to be used for anatomical examination if, having made such reasonable inquiry as may be practicable, he has no reason to believe:

that the deceased, either in writing at any time or orally in the presence of two or more witnesses during his last illness, had expressed an objection to his body being so used after his death, and had not withdrawn it, or

that the surviving spouse or any surviving relative of the deceased objects to the body being so used.

a right to override the deceased's anatomical donation, the quotation above does not seem to reproduce such a right. Section 4(3)(a)(b), which makes mention of such a right, seems to create a different right – objection to an executor's anatomical donation – and seemingly should not be read together with s. 4(1) and (2).

Section 4(3)(a)(b) is a reproduction of s. 8 of the English 1832 Act, which was copied into s. 3 of the Nigerian Act. The last two statutes, as well as s. 4(3)(a)(b) of the 1984 Act, give a separate and distinct[217] right to an executor or person in lawful possession of the deceased's body, other than possession as an undertaker, to make a donation of the deceased's body for anatomical examination, except the deceased, during his lifetime, verbally in the presence of witnesses or in writing, objected to such an examination. The power of an executor or person in lawful custody of the corpse to make such a donation could also be overridden by the objection of a surviving spouse or known relative of the deceased.

Therefore, what the 1984 English Act seems to have done is to enact in one section, that is, s. 4, the two separate sections in the 1832 Act, ss. 7 and 8, and the two separate sections in the Nigerian Act, ss. 3 and 4, but without reproducing the right given by s. 4 of the Nigerian Act, and s. 8 of the 1832 Act, to a surviving spouse or known relative of a deceased person to override the deceased's donation of his own body for anatomical examination. The omission of this power in the 1984 English Act (which is now repealed and replaced with the *Human Tissue Act, 2004*) seems to be deliberate and justified by the apparently growing need to make more cadavers available for medical research.

The difference between the *English Anatomy Act of 1984* and its Nigerian equivalent, with regard to the power of a surviving spouse or known relative to override the deceased's anatomical donation, is a material one founded on fundamental religious difference and philosophical orientation. Again, we find here an inhibition to medical research flowing from tradition and spiritualism.

Since the philosophy that animates Nigerian perspective on dead bodies ensures, or potentially ensures, inadequate supply of cadavers for anatomical examination, which can lead to medical breakthroughs, one wonders how the various teaching hospitals in Nigeria have managed to source their raw materials for anatomical examination. It seems the bulk of teaching hospitals' supply of cadavers has come from unclaimed dead bodies, or persons with unknown relatives who died in the

---

217 This right is different from the deceased's own right to make such a donation. As already stated, he can make such a donation in his lifetime to take effect after his death.

hospital.[218] It would appear that in such situations, the hospital qualifies as a person in lawful possession of a dead body,[219] under s. 3 of the *Nigerian Anatomy Act*.[220]

The Coroner's Act[221]

Legislative competence with respect to coroners is vested, by the *1999 Nigerian Constitution*, in the states of the Nigerian federation.[222] Although all the states of the federation now have their own coroners' laws, their provisions were copied from the *Coroners Act*,[223] which previously applied to the whole federation, but to northern Nigeria with some modifications.[224] Consequently, the analysis here shall concentrate on the federal legislation.

A coroner[225] is a person who investigates a sudden, unnatural, or violent death;[226] or a death that occurs in prison and police custody,[227] or in suspicious circumstances. The investigation of a coroner is called an inquest, which, though not defined by the Act, covers all the coroner's activities in his capacity as such.[228] Every magistrate in Nigeria is a coroner; however, other persons may be appointed as a coroner.[229] It seems a coroner acts in a judicial capacity, even though an inquest is a fact-finding exercise.[230] A coroner's judicial powers, however, are not as wide as those of a judge,

---

218 Compare s. 1(6) of the Nigerian *Corneal Grafting Act, c. 69* [hereinafter *Corneal Grafting*]:

> In the case of a body lying in a hospital, any authority under this section may be given on behalf of the person having the control and management of the hospital by any officer or person so designated in that behalf.

219 Stephen, J., was of the same opinion in *R v. Price* (1884) 12 Q.B. 247, at 251 [hereinafter *Price*]. In Hungary, where presumed consent is the controlling doctrine, a cadaver can freely be used for organ transplantation and anatomical purposes, unless the deceased made a contrary request during his or her lifetime: B. Blasszauer, 'Autopsy', in H. Ten Have, *et al.*, eds, *Ownership of the Human Body: Philosophical Considerations on the Use of the Human Body and its Parts in Healthcare* (Dordrecht: Kluwer Academic Publishers, 1998) at 19–26.

220 *Anatomy Act, supra* note 184.

221 A very useful and fascinating exposition of the law and practice of the coroner is the article of an experienced London coroner, J. Burton, 'Is There any Future for Inquests and Inquiries' (1999) 67 *Medico-Legal J.* 91.

222 *Constitution of the Federal Republic of Nigeria, 1999*, s. 4 [hereinafter *Nigerian Constitution*].

223 *Coroners Act, c. 41* [hereinafter *Coroners Act*].

224 *Ibid.*, at s. 1(2) and 3.

225 *Ibid.*, at s. 2: '"coroner" means any person empowered to hold inquests under this Ordinance.'

226 *Ibid.*, at s. 5.

227 *Ibid.*, at s. 7.

228 *Davidson v. Garret, (*1899) 5 C.C.C. 200, at 205 [hereinafter *Davidson*].

229 *Coroners Act, supra*, note 223, at s. 4.

230 *Ibid.*, at s. 17:

> 17(1) A coroner holding an inquest shall have and may exercise all the powers of a magistrate with regard to summoning and compelling the attendance of witnesses and

and may only be exercised for the purpose of ascertaining the identity, time, place and manner of the deceased's death.[231]

A coroner does not investigate a matter which is already a subject of criminal proceedings;[232] and must stay the inquest where it becomes apparent that evidence with respect to the death has been disclosed against a particular person. This is to enable criminal proceedings to be instituted against that person.[233] A coroner has all the powers of a magistrate, for the purpose of the inquest, and may issue summons and warrants, and compel the attendance of witnesses.[234] A coroner is statutorily barred from returning a verdict of guilt against anybody.[235] The coroner's verdict is limited to identifying the deceased, the place, time, nature and circumstances of death.[236] A coroner, in the course of an inquest, may engage a medical practitioner to determine the cause of the deceased's death, and such medical practitioner may dissect the deceased.[237] Although s. 13 requires the post-mortem request to be in writing, it seems that an oral request may be valid, even if made before the formal commencement of the inquest.[238] Consequently, a dissection by a medical practitioner, pursuant to a coroner's request, will not give rise to a cause of action by the deceased's relatives.[239] It has been held that where some body parts of a fatal accident victim were inadvertently left at the scene of the accident by a company acting as an agent of the medical examiner or coroner, such omission was protected by official immunity for the performance of a discretionary duty.[240]

A coroner may not have sufficient legal possession of the deceased's body to make a gift of it for medical education,[241] but he or she has lawful possession for the purpose of, and throughout the duration of, the inquest.[242] After the coroner has viewed the body, it has to be buried.[243] Preservation of a deceased's body pursuant to an inquest, does not amount to scientific application of skill and labour[244] necessary for the application of the exception in *Doodeward v. Spence*,[245] or *R v. Kelly*.[246]

---

requiring them to give evidence, and with regard to the production of any document or thing at such inquest.

See, also, Burton, *supra*, note 221, at 101.

231 *Coroners Act, supra*, note 223.

232 *Ibid.*, at s. 5(b).

233 *Ibid.*, at s. 24.

234 *Ibid.*, at s. 17.

235 *Ibid.*, at s. 27.

236 *Ibid.*, at ss. 15 and 26.

237 *Ibid.*, at ss. 13 and 14.

238 *Davidson, supra*, note 228.

239 *Ibid.*

240 *Guerrero v. Tarrant County Mortician Services Co.* 977 S.W. 2d 829 (1998).

241 *Anatomy Act, supra*, note 184, at s. 10; S. White, 'The Law Relating to Dealing With Dead Bodies' (2000) 4 *Med. L. Intl.* 145, at 163–4.

242 Burton, *supra*, note 221, at 95.

243 *Coroners Act, supra*, note 223, at s. 16.

244 *Dobson, supra*, note 37, at 601–602.

245 *Doodeward, supra*, note 60.

246 *Kelly, supra*, note 37.

However, ss. 6 and 10 of the *Coroners Act* are very relevant to this chapter. Section 6 allows exhumation or disinterment of bodies buried without an inquest, in circumstances where the Act requires an inquest to be held. The section applies 'notwithstanding any law or custom to the contrary'. Section 10 entitles the coroner to prohibit any burial or cremation, in respect of a death for which an inquest has to be held. These sections, especially s. 6, are targeted at the relevant customary laws in most parts of Nigeria. Most deaths in Nigerian traditional society, especially those resulting from rituals or initiations into a traditional cult, in those old days, and which might have been accidental, would clearly come under the jurisdiction of the coroner. Burial, for such deaths, is usually done without contacting the coroner; in fact, tradition may prohibit the presence of such a stranger. The result is that performance of such a traditional burial duty would now attract a penal sanction under the *Coroners Act*.[247] Again, the sections allow a coroner to exhume a dead body, in circumstances which would be considered a desecration by the relatives, and spiritually offensive. However, a coroner may not exhume a body 'where there is no reasonable probability of a satisfactory result being obtained'.[248] It is expected that in the context of Nigeria, coroners will give more weight to this proviso than the main rule.

Births, Deaths and Burials Law

The regulation of births, deaths and burials is within the legislative competence of the states,[249] though most state legislation on the matter is copied from an old federal statute that previously applied throughout the country.[250] The analysis here shall be based on Lagos State's *Births, Deaths and Burials Law*.[251] This law makes it compulsory to register births[252] and deaths[253] occurring within the state. This obligation must be discharged by certain persons mentioned in the enactment, for example, parents, relatives, guardians, or occupiers of certain premises, and within the period stipulated by the law.[254]

The law expects that, subject to coronial jurisdiction,[255] burial should take place within three or four days of the death of the deceased.[256] This seems to be a safeguard against the putrefaction of the corpse and consequent health hazard, but it does not

---

247 *Coroners Act, supra*, note 223, at s. 33.

248 *Ibid.*, at s. 6.

249 *Nigerian Constitution, supra*, note 222, at s. 4.

250 *Births, Deaths and Burials Act, c. 23, Laws of the Federation of Nigeria and Lagos, 1958.*

251 *Births, Deaths and Burials Act, c. 13, Laws of Lagos State, 1994* [hereinafter *Births, Deaths and Burials*].

252 *Ibid.*, at s. 3.

253 *Ibid.*, at s. 18.

254 Births should be registered within 21 days of birth (s. 9), and deaths should be registered within two days of its occurrence (s. 18).

255 *Ibid.*, at ss. 23, 31, 32 and 33.

256 This follows from a combined reading of s. 18 which requires registration of death within two days of its occurrence; s. 31 which obliges the registrar to issue a certificate of

seem to reflect current biomedical technology, which makes it possible to safely preserve a corpse for a much longer time. Again, except with the written consent of a divisional officer, every burial must take place within a designated public burial ground.[257] Thus, the law is brought into conflictual interaction with the custom of most Nigerian nationalities, pursuant to which corpses are buried in or near dwelling houses of the living relatives.[258] Presumably, the custom facilitates the deceased's reunion with his or her ancestral relatives. This probably explains why in *Onyeanusi v. Pan Am*,[259] the plaintiff, an Ibo of south-eastern Nigeria whose mother died while on a visit to the United States,[260] had to make every effort to have the mother's corpse taken to his homeland for burial. Unfortunately, due to nine days' flight delay, the corpse became partially decomposed before the plaintiff could receive it, and he therefore sued for damages. The Court of Appeals, Third Circuit, however, affirmed a district court's ruling dismissing the plaintiff's claim for want of the required notice under the *Warsaw Convention*, applicable to claims against air carriers.[261] Because of the court's willingness to protect Pan Am in accordance with the declared objective of the *Warsaw Convention*,[262] it did not give much attention to the plaintiff's claim that the mishandling of his deceased mother's remains was bound to bring misfortune upon him, his family, and 'tribe'.[263]

The deceased's executor, and in his absence, each and every relative of the deceased has the duty of burial. If there is no known relative, the occupier of the building where the body lies has the duty of burial.[264] In most Western legal systems, the question of who has the duty, and the correlative right, of burial is often a controversial issue,[265] which seems to have been statutorily settled in the case of Nigeria.[266] After burial, and subject to a coroner's order,[267] the law does

---

burial immediately upon registration of any death; and s. 35 which requires burial to take place within 24 hours of the issuance of a burial certificate.

257 *Births, Deaths and Burials*, *supra*, note 251, at s. 39.

258 This aspect of Yoruba custom is well documented by Rev. S. Johnson, *The History of the Yorubas* (Lagos: CSS Bookshops Limited, 1921), at 137.

259 952 F. 2d 788 (1992) [hereinafter *Onyeanusi*].

260 *Ibid.*, at 789.

261 *Ibid.*, at 795.

262 *Ibid.*, at 792–4.

263 *Ibid.*, at 790.

264 *Births, Deaths and Burials*, *supra*, note 251, at s. 40.

265 *Smith*, *supra*, note 40; *Felipe*, *supra*, note 40.

266 In traditional Ibo society, of south-eastern Nigeria, the custom requires, but does not oblige, the eldest male child to bury the father and bear the cost of funeral expenses; partly because he inherits most of the deceased's estate. A younger son who discharges this custom, in the case of refusal or impecuniosity of the eldest male child, is expected to receive more than his traditional share of the deceased's estate. It is interesting to note something of a convergence of this custom with s. 40 of *Births, Deaths, and Burials*, *supra*, note 251. However, s. 40, unlike provisions relating to registration of birth and death (s. 45), does not impose any penalty for failure to discharge the duty of burial.

267 *Coroners Act, supra*, note 223 at s. 6.

not allow exhumation of a corpse, except with the written permission of the State Commissioner.[268]

Certain general observations may be made with respect to this law. It partly deals with burials and imposes the duty of 'causing the body of a deceased person to be buried' on certain persons under s. 40; but it does not define what amounts to burial.

Does cremation, instead of burial, amount to compliance with the law? Unlike most countries in the West, cremation is not a popular burial practice in Nigeria, and has yet to be statutorily regulated. However, there does not seem to be any statute prohibiting it. It is arguable that since the English common law is part of the received law in Nigeria, the court may hold that a duly performed cremation is lawful and complies with the enactment under consideration.[269] Again, unless the coroner otherwise orders, the law allows exhumation only pursuant to the Commissioner's written permission. Does this mean that the jurisdiction over exhumation of dead bodies exercised originally by the Ecclesiastical Courts, and now secular courts in most Western legal systems,[270] is unavailable in Nigerian courts?

First, the decision of the Commissioner will be subject to judicial review by the courts, since it involves the exercise of discretion by a public official. Second, it seems that the original jurisdiction of the High Court under s. 272 of the *1999 Constitution of Nigeria*, and its inherent powers under s. 6(6)(a) of the same Constitution, are expansive enough to include jurisdiction over exhumation or disinterment of dead bodies. Also, the *Birth, Death, and Burial Law* seems to have outlawed the religious and traditional practice of exorcism, mentioned earlier in this chapter, which involves exhumation of a corpse. The Commissioner, however, is not precluded from giving his written consent to exhumation merely because it relates to exorcism.

Impact of African Mortuary Law on Scientific and Biomedical Research

The implications for scientific research of customary law's affirmation of some property interest in the human body are potentially enormous. Certain questions beg for answers. Will the Nigerian law on dead bodies not interfere with some anthropological and scientific investigations of human remains? Does its mortuary tradition not exclude anatomical examinations which are often a crucial component of new biomedical research, and thereby hinder scientific breakthroughs? Does its spiritualization of the body not interfere with the modern administration of justice, under which post-mortem and coronial inquisition may be undertaken in certain cases? Does its unyielding attitude concerning the integrity of the human body not interfere with the performance of ethically unproblematic biomedical research using human research subjects?[271]

---

268 *Births, Deaths and Burials, supra*, note 251, at s. 44.

269 Cremation was held to be a lawful means of disposing of a corpse under common law: *Price, supra*, note 219; *Home Undertaking Co. v. Joliff* 19 P. 2d 654, at 655 (1933).

270 *Medlen, supra*, note 102.

271 The conflict which can result from the juxtaposition of the African worldview and sentimentalization of the dead with scientific inquiry that is propelled by a different belief

Fortunately for Nigeria, it has no recorded history of pothunters, grave-robbers and desecrators, which are part of the history of Native Americans. As we have seen, the desecration of Native American remains was partly inspired by the quest for scientific knowledge by anthropologists and archaeologists, who were not concerned about the feelings of the living relatives of the objects of their scientific inquisition. Though such intrusive research has not been witnessed in Nigeria, it does not seem that the situation will remain so for a long time. In fact, Nigeria and most other developing African countries have recently become the brides of researchers. This may not be unconnected with the relative availability of research subjects, the illiteracy of a majority of the population, and the low-income level of these countries, which render them easy prey to some unconscionable Western researchers.

Just recently, *The Washington Post* published a report of Pfizer's 1996 clinical trial of its drug trovafloxacin in Nigeria.[272] The trial sought to determine the drug's safety and efficacy in the treatment of epidemic meningococcal meningitis; a disorder which leads to degeneration of the brain and spinal cord. Many children who participated in the trial either died or were physically deformed. *The Washington Post* report shows that the trial was conducted in circumstances of doubtful compliance with ethical requirements and principles of biomedical research.[273] Pfizer has denied any unethical conduct with respect to the trial, and asserted that the deaths or deformities were the natural result of the disease, rather than the trial drug.[274] The fact that Nigeria, instead of the USA, was chosen for the trial remains pertinent for the analysis here, and exemplifies the in-roads that scientific activities, which may be destructive, are making in Nigeria.

Nigerian mortuary law's conception of a corpse (as proposed in this book), and even the living, as the limited property of its living relatives will likely serve as a bulwark against any disrespectful excavation of graves and disinterment of remains by scientists. The property concept will help in maintaining the sanctity of these graves and preserving the spiritual communion between the dead and living.[275] Consequently, archaeologists, anthropologists and other researchers may be denied an important tool of their trade. Unfortunately, this may be so even when such activities may be socially useful and needed to meet the demands of a technological, globalizing, and dynamic world. Because scientific efforts, when ethical and properly channelled, could be beneficial to the public, it may be appropriate for developing

---

system is observed by Walker: 'Bioarchaeologists do not view human remains primarily as symbols. Instead they value them as sources of historical evidence that are key to understanding what really happened during the biological evolution of our species. This lack of concern with symbolic issues is in stark contrast to the richness of the symbolic connotations human skeletons have for most people. This conflict in worldviews is especially acute in areas of the world that were subjected to European colonization.' Walker, *supra*, note 4.

272 J. Stephens, 'The Body Hunters: As Drug Testing Spreads, Profits and Lives Hang in Balance', *The Washington Post* (17 December 2000) A1.

273 *Ibid.*

274 Pfizer, on 17 December 2000, posted its defence to *The Washington Post's* allegation on its website.

275 Customary law recognizes only a limited property interest in a corpse and this does not include the power or right to sell a corpse.

countries like Nigeria to embark upon a search on the ways to balance the competing interests of African spirituality and scientific research. Dr Ogbu made a poignant observation on the impediment that African spirituality represents for scientific research and development.[276]

To balance the demands of religion, spirituality and science, Nigeria may find it beneficial to learn from the similar experience of Native American Indians, where several statutes, like *NAGPRA*, have been used to maintain a reasonable balance. It is also true that the Nigerian legislature, by laws regulating anatomy, antiquities, coroners, births, deaths and burials, tried to free the country from the tenacious hold of traditionalism. These laws, however, apart from leaning towards traditionalism in some of their provisions, are yet to be judicially interpreted by the courts. It is feared that any interpretation that is anchored on the traditional mortuary law, without regards to the compelling interest of science, may leave us behind the technological world.

What seems to be needed at this point is intense public education. Peoples' religion and philosophy cannot be effectively wiped out by a legislative fiat. But with education, given formally and informally, citizens would come to realize the counterproductive aspects of our philosophy. It is true that rapid urbanization, interstate and international commercial transactions, communication and travel have brought about a loosening of the walls of traditional religion and philosophy. Yet, the majority of Nigerian citizens live in the rural areas and are, to some extent, still traditional. Even a good percentage of the elite, including the well-educated

---

276 O.U. Ogbu, 'Religion as a Factor in National Development', in Amucheazi, *supra*, note 9, at 315:

> In the new fad of cultural revival some may take a romantic attitude towards the religion of our forefathers. Admittedly theirs was a viable and an alive universe. Core values such as sanctity of life, respect, good character, obedience, honesty, achievement, solidarity of kin group, primacy of the family, loyalty to the group, bravery and industry were held in high regard. But it was a precarious world: evil spirits terrified the living, even good spirits were capricious, priest craft held sway and the movement of time was in an endless cycle. It was a closed society. Numerous rituals engrained brutality. Harsh nature bred hard human beings. Competition for survival and for public acclaim bred exploitation. To a very large extent, traditional African societies lacked sensitivity. Raw nature was too near and proved indomitable. We must admit that some of our concerns about pollution, exploitation, clean surroundings and so on are in fact acquired sensibility. Our traditional societies practised ritual murders and slavery without any qualms and within an ethical system which made sense. The African traditional world had its joys, music, drama and relaxation. But the pace of change was slow; so, also was the concept of technological growth or the deliberate re-fashioning of the environment. To this extent religion in our traditional environment bred order, served as an explanation system and a means of controlling space-time events. But it hardly provided an avenue for progress. The agricultural seasons and the lives of communities flowed in an endless cycle. Folk memory saw no possibilities of a different way of doing things. Rapid change was impeded by traditionalism.

ones living in the West,[277] are still guided by their traditional philosophy. Unless we embark upon such a public enlightenment campaign and open our doors to legitimate scientific enterprise, we may find ourselves many years behind the current biotechnological world.[278]

Conclusion

It is interesting to note that Nigeria does not yet have the equivalent of laws like the *Human Tissue Act*,[279] *Human Organ Transplant Act*,[280] *Uniform Anatomical Gift Act*[281] and *Human Tissue Gift Act*.[282] It is only a demonstration of the state of medical care and technology in Nigeria.[283] When that fact is juxtaposed with a strict interpretation of our worldview, with its propertization of the human body, it becomes more evident that we may miss the biotechnology train as we have already missed the information highway that flourished in the 1970s and 1980s. This chapter attempted to analyse the worldview of the Ibo people of Nigeria, shared by most African people, to show that though it furnishes a veritable foundation for a moral and communitarian life, it conflicts, or potentially conflicts, with the demands of science and technological development. This is partly done by analysis of some of the Nigerian statutes having an impact on the human body and their effect on the worldview of Nigerian citizens. This chapter also suggested that a conscious and articulated public education may help in liberating us from the clutches of undesirable aspects of our traditionalism.

It is true that we are yet to witness intense scientific activity but, as suggested, we do not have to wait for such scientific activities to occur before taking steps to remove possible obstacles to such enterprise. This chapter is not a global condemnation of our mortuary tradition, the benefits of which have been underscored. It only suggests that every aspect of our mortuary tradition and philosophy does not seem to be good, and may well be counterproductive to the interest of scientific research that can be of potential benefit to Nigerians.

---

277 It will be remembered that the claim of the Nigerian Ibo plaintiff in *Onyeanusi*, *supra*, note 259, at 790, was partly based on the traditional belief that the mishandling of the deceased's body would bring misfortune upon the plaintiff, his family and village.

278 The change in traditional attitude suggested here is not simply to accommodate biomedical research, but rather to make room for socially useful modern activities that would not otherwise be possible.

279 *Human Tissue, supra*, note 188.

280 *Human Organ Transplant Act 1989, c. 31.*

281 *Uniform Anatomical Gift Act, 8A U.L.A. 19 (1987).*

282 *Human Tissue Gift Act, R.S.O. 1990, c. H-20.*

283 However, Nigeria has the *Corneal Grafting Act, supra*, note 218, which regulates the harvesting of eyes from deceased persons for therapeutic purposes.

Chapter 4

DNA Banks and Proprietary Interests in Biosamples and Genetic Information

Introduction

Property issues may arise with respect to the collection, retention, use and access to biological or genetic samples in a tissue bank or DNA bank. In order to study the genetic and environmental factors of some common diseases, some countries including Iceland, the Kingdom of Tonga, Estonia, the United Kingdom, and the province of Newfoundland, have established DNA banks. DNA banks may not be a recent phenomenon, though the modern generation of DNA banks involve larger population and are different in size, scope and format.[1] For instance the proposed United Kingdom Population Biomedical Collection will be based on samples and genetic information from 500,000 adults aged between 45 and 69 years.[2] The UK collection will be used in investigating the genetic and environmental causes of diseases such as cancer and cardiovascular conditions.[3] The establishment of a DNA bank can be controversial, especially when established in a developing country at the instance of a commercial company from a developed country.[4] This situation raises the issue of commercial exploitation. A report for the World Health Organization observed that:

---

1   A report for the World Health Organization stated that:

    The concept of genetic databases is not new. For the last 30 years it has been common practice to establish registers of patients with genetic diseases, aimed at providing genetic services to families with these conditions. For example, the Register for the Ascertainment and Prevention of Inherited Disease in Edinburgh, Scotland offered members of families with genetic disease active counseling as soon as they reached adulthood. Similarly, a register centered at the University of Utah, UT, USA was based on the family register of the Mormon Church to identify individuals with autosomal dominant hypercholesterolemia, a condition with a high risk of early myocardial infarction and death. Recently, a national database for families with thalassaemia has been established in the United Kingdom.

   World Health Organization, *Genomics and World Health* (Geneva: WHO, 2002), at 113–14.

    2   J.V. McHale, 'Regulating Genetic Databases: Some Legal and Ethical Issues' (2004) 12 *Med. Law Rev.* 70; Jane Kaye and Paul Martin, 'Safeguards for Research Using Large Scale DNA Collections' (2000) 321 *BMJ* 1146.

    3   *Ibid.*

    4   Kaye and Martin, *supra*, note 2.

Another major issue about the establishment of large-scale databases is that some developing countries are establishing collections of this type often at the behest of companies from the developed world. Because of the lack of appropriate regulatory and ethical bodies in some of these developing countries these problems become much more serious and the dangers of inequitable commercial exploitation are even more acute.[5]

Apart from health research purposes, DNA banks may be established for forensic uses in connection with criminal investigation and prosecution.[6] The forensic application of DNA databases raises another set of issues.[7] Forensic DNA databases should not be conflated with DNA banks dedicated to health research. This chapter is mainly concerned with property issues arising or potentially arising from health-related DNA banks, though reference is made to forensic DNA banks where necessary.

In addition to questions relating to property rights and exploitation, a DNA bank may raise other concerns, such as access, privacy and confidentiality.[8] These concerns may implicate the application of other legal categories.[9] But the relevant question is whether it is possible to protect the privacy interest of tissue sources by giving them a limited property interest in their tissues.[10] Recently, the Australian Law

---

5   WHO, *supra*, note 1, at 117.

6   Trevor R. McDonald, 'Genetic Justice: DNA Evidence and the Criminal Law in Canada' (1998) 26 *Man. L. J.* 1.

7   In this connection, a report for WHO observed:

Many countries now have DNA databases containing DNA from convicted criminals. The use of DNA testing for forensic purposes also raises a number of important issues which have yet to be settled. Just some of these are: should DNA testing be compulsory for those being investigated for criminal activities?; How long should samples be stored in databases?; Should members of the public be asked to donate DNA for 'elimination' purposes?

WHO, *supra*, note 1, at 118.

8   For analysis of some of these issues: Graeme Laurie, *Genetic Privacy: A Challenge to Medico-Legal Norms* (Cambridge: Cambridge University Press, 2002); Mark A. Rothstein, ed., *Genetic Secrets* (New Haven: Yale University Press, 1997); Trudo Lemmens, 'Selective Justice, Genetic Discrimination, and Insurance: Should We Single Out Genes in Our Laws?' (2000) 45 *McGill L. Jour.* 347.

9   In reference to the DNA bank in Iceland, a report for WHO noted:

It must be acknowledged that concerns have been raised over the proposed resource by a number of commentators from academic and clinical medicine both in Iceland and internationally. Particular concerns include the appropriateness of presumed consent, the effects that the opt-out procedure will have on representativity, the lack of public debate in the initial drafting of the Database Act and the extent to which Icelandic academics will be able to access the data.

WHO, *supra*, note 1, at 115.

10   Patricia Roche has suggested that the use of multiple legal categories is possible:

What all these rules (in the Model Genetic Privacy Act) are about is control – control of individually identifiable DNA samples and control of private genetic information. Placing primary control with the individual sources of samples and information cannot be accomplished with any one rule or regulation. Instead, it requires a comprehensive set of rules that not only grants basic rights to individuals, but institutes clear mechanisms and procedures that facilitate the exercise of those rights.

Reform Commission (ALRC) considered regulation of the collection, storage, use of, and access to genetic samples.[11] Though the ALRC recommended that most of the issues that arise could be solved by an amendment of the country's *Privacy Act*,[12] it nevertheless considered 'whether the privacy of genetic samples and information could be more adequately protected by allowing any property rights, other than possession, to be exercised over genetic samples'.[13]

It is possible that a limited property framework may enable a tissue source to claim a portion of profit derived from the commercial exploitation of tissues in a DNA bank.[14] A limited property framework may also give a tissue source sufficient control over the use of tissue sample by others. Patricia Roche suggests that '[d]enying individuals a property interest in DNA is not advisable…if protection of genetic privacy as well as support for legitimate research and commerce is a primary legislative goal'.[15] Some of the commentators on the ethical and legal issues arising from DNA banks have rarely focused on a property approach to the problems that are involved.[16] Accordingly, this chapter proposes to examine in detail the provisions of law establishing DNA banks in some countries such as Iceland, Estonia and the Kingdom of Tonga. The purpose is to see the extent, if any, to which these laws recognize the existence of property rights in biological samples stored in DNA banks. In the absence of such recognition, this chapter examines the desirability of adopting a limited property regime towards resolving some of the issues raised by the existence of DNA banks.

P. Roche, '*Caveat Venditor*: Protecting Privacy and Ownership Interests in DNA', in Bartha M. Knoppers, *et al.*, eds, *Human DNA: Law and Policy* (The Hague: Kluwer Law International, 1997), at 36. Similarly, Moe Litman suggested the use of hybrid legal categories: 'Such material (i.e., genetic material) may be regarded as private property, common property, person, or information. My view is that it would be a mistake to conceptualize genetic materials as fitting solely within any one of these traditional legal categories. It is both possible and advisable to characterize human genetic material as a hybrid of all of these categories.' M. M. Litman, 'The Legal Status of Genetic Material', in Knoppers, *ibid.*, at 17.

11 Australian Law Reform Commission, *Essentially Yours: The Protection of Human Genetic Information In Australia* (Australia: ALRC, March 2003).

12 *Ibid.*, at 261–88.

13 *Ibid.*, at 526.

14 ALRC, *supra*, note 11, at 530, observing that: 'Property rights include rights to the income and the capital of an object. Allowing individuals to seek financial returns on the use of their tissue would enable them to share in the profits that are sometimes made from treatments that result from research.'

15 P. Roche, in Knoppers, *supra*, note 10, at 33.

16 For instance: Kaye and Martin, *supra*, note 2; Ruth Chadwick, 'The Icelandic Database – Do Modern Times Need Modern Sagas?' (1999) 319 *BMJ* 441; Jeffery P. Khan, 'Attention Shoppers: Special Today – Iceland's DNA' Ethics Matters, CNN Interactive, 22 February 1999; posted on: http://www.cnn.com/HEALTH/bioethics/9902/iceland.dna/template.html (last accessed on 3 November 2003).

Some of the Uses of DNA Banks

Genetic technology has encouraged the creation of DNA banks.[17] DNA banks house systematically collected tissue samples for research[18] and forensic identification purposes.[19] These tissue samples are sequenced and used in linkage studies, or undergo DNA analysis and the resultant information is stored in DNA databases, which can be used for forensic identification and public health research purposes. Because DNA samples contain unique information about the sample sources, such as predisposition to disease, behavioral traits, race, height and identity, considerable privacy and confidentiality concerns are implicated,[20] in addition to property issues. Unauthorized use of a person's DNA information could lead to stigmatization and discrimination in employment and insurance. These problems are accentuated in multicultural societies where there are potentials to use DNA techniques to reinforce existing stereotypes or to contradict indigenous beliefs conditioned by historical traditions and cultural practices. A potentially explosive genetic stigmatization case is already brewing up in the United States District Court for Arizona.[21]

In the *Havasupai* case, an indigenous tribe in the State of Arizona collaborated with medical researchers interested in the genetic link to diabetes, a common disease among members of the tribe, by providing 400 blood samples. The tribe claimed that the researchers surreptitiously used the genetic samples to study schizophrenia, inbreeding and population migration without the authority or consent of the members of the tribe. They alleged that the unauthorized study would stigmatize the tribe and contradict their creation story. Accordingly, the tribe has brought an action against the defendants for (1) breach of fiduciary duty and lack of informed consent; (2) fraud and misrepresentation/fraudulent concealment; (3) intentional or negligent infliction of emotional distress; (4) conversion; (5) violation of civil rights; and (6) negligence, gross negligence and negligence *per se*.[22] Judgement in the case is eagerly awaited and promises to define the relationship between biomedical researchers and indigenous people and the duty surrounding a sensitive use of DNA samples. It was for similar reasons that an indigenous group in the USA opposed scientific

---

17 Kaye and Martin, *supra*, note 2; Jean E. McEwen, 'DNA Data Banks', in Mark A. Rothstein, ed., *Genetic Secrets* (New Haven: Yale University Press, 1997), at 231.

18 Such as the population study by the Human Genome Diversity Project, which involves the collection of tissue samples from some representative population groups: Henry T. Greely, 'Human Genome Diversity Project', in Thomas H. Murray, *et al.*, eds, *Encyclopedia of Ethical, Legal, and Policy Issues in Biotechnology* (New York: John Wiley & Sons, 2000, vol. 2), at 552.

19 See *R v. Love* (1995) 102 C.C.C. (3d) 393 (Alta. CA), where the Alberta Court of Appeal relied mainly on DNA evidence to convict the accused person, Love.

20 Joseph Waldbaum, 'DNA Databanks in Massachusetts: Will the Declaration of Rights Provide the Nation's First Successful Constitutional Challenge?' (1999) 3 *J. L. & Soc. Challenges* 179–214.

21 *Havasupai Tribe v. Arizona State University*, civil docket no. 3:04-CV-1494 (D.Ariz. 2004); *Tilousi v. Arizona State University*, civil docket no. 3:04-CV-1290 (D.Ariz. 2004).

22 For a defence of the *Havasupai* researchers' action: Rex Dalton, 'When Two Tribes Go to War' (2004) 430 *Nature* 500.

determination of the age and origin of ancient human remains washed down from the Columbia River at Kennewick, Washington.[23] Initial testing of the remains, known as 'Kennewick Man', estimated the age to be 8340 to 9200 years. Scientist wanted to study the remains to gain invaluable evidence on early American populations, including their origin, social and cultural patterns and migratory history. But the US Interior Department and some American Indian Tribes opposed the proposed study and sought repatriation of the remains on religious grounds for the purpose of burial. They alleged that the spirit of the remains would continue to be in a state of unrest until properly buried.

There was a political angle that was latent in the litigation: analysis of the ancient remains and probable proof of non-aboriginal origin would have far reaching political results on the claims of Native Americans to be the first settlers in the USA and owners of the land therein. As far as the indigenous population is concerned, their claim of being the original settlers is validated by oral tradition and needs no further proof. They, thus, view present scientific attempts at their origin as further efforts to disempower them. In the recent case of *Bonnichsen v. United States of America*,[24] however, the US Court of Appeals, Ninth Circuit dealt a blow to the case of indigenous tribes by refusing repatriation of the Kennewick Man and holding that there was no evidence that the Kennewick Man was related to any presently existing Indian Tribe. The Court of Appeal allowed scientists to study the Kennewick Man. The point, therefore, is that there is no gainsaying the enormous power that control and possession of DNA samples and information affords. This justifies the search for a potent legal metaphor in the nature of property as an appropriate protective framework.

The United States Defense Department maintains a huge DNA bank, containing tissue samples of the United States' military men and women.[25] DNA analysis of these tissue samples is used to identify soldiers missing in action and otherwise unidentifiable. This will significantly reduce the number of soldiers buried as 'unknown soldiers'. It could potentially be used in the criminal investigation of cases involving physically unidentifiable soldiers. Concerns have therefore been raised recognizing the need to put limits on the use of such military DNA bank.

Canada[26] and not less than 48 states in the USA[27] also have laws creating forensic DNA banks to assist in the investigation of cases without suspects, but in which biological samples were left on the crime scene, such as sperm, hair, saliva and

---

23 *Bonnichsen v. United States of America* 357 F. 3d 962 (2004).

24 *Ibid.*

25 Kenneth Kipnis, 'DNA Banking in the Military: An Ethical Analysis', in Robert F. Weir, ed., *Stored Tissue Samples: Ethical, Legal and Public Policy Implications* (Iowa: University of Iowa Press, 1998), at 329–44; Victor Walter Weedn, 'Stored Biologic Specimens for Military Identification: The Department of Defense DNA Registry', in Weir, ed., *ibid.*, at 345–57.

26 *The DNA Identification Act, S.C. 1998, c.37*. This legislation came into force on 30 June 2000.

27 Waldbaum, *supra*, note 20, at 182.

blood.[28] In the context of criminal investigations and the administration of justice, the Canadian Act permits the collection of DNA samples from persons convicted of certain offences, usually involving violence and with a high repeat rate.[29] The samples and their DNA profiles are permanently stored in a forensic DNA bank for comparison with profiles of DNA artefacts left on crime scenes.[30]

In the USA, the federal *DNA Identification Act*[31] seeks to give financial support to states having forensic DNA banks, to set and monitor standards, and facilitate the exchange of DNA information between states. Generally, these laws require that either at the stage of conviction or release, a prisoner should give a tissue sample for a DNA analysis. The resultant DNA profile of the prisoner is then stored in a computerized database. The rationale is that when an offence is committed in the future in which biological materials are left at the scene of the crime, as in rape, but without any known suspect, the DNA analysis of such biological evidence is compared with the DNA profiles already in the database, with a view to identifying the likely offender.[32] State DNA laws are based on the theory that some violent crimes, like rape and murder, have a high rate of recidivism, and that such laws will facilitate the investigation and prosecution of such crimes. However, some states' DNA laws cover even crimes of a non-violent nature, where the repeat rates are low.[33] It is not surprising, therefore, that some of these laws have been challenged on constitutional grounds.[34] Although the cases have generally upheld the constitutionality of forensic DNA banks,[35] some of them have restricted the ambit of their application.

An innovation in DNA banking is the creation of nationwide DNA banks, such as the ones in Estonia[36] and Iceland,[37] Tonga, and the one proposed for the United Kingdom.[38] In some countries, this involves statutory authorization for a population-wide collection of DNA samples and medical records for purposes of research and public health, subject to the terms of the statute. As mentioned earlier, this chapter

---

28 Julianne Parfett, 'Canada's DNA Databank: Public Safety and Private Costs' (2002) 29 *Man. L. J.* 33–79.

29 *Ibid.*

30 *Ibid.*

31 *DNA Identification Act, 42 U.S.C. § 14132 (1994).*

32 The limitations in the presentation of DNA evidence, using Bayesian theory, is discussed by Christian Jowett, 'Lies, Damned Lies, and DNA Statistics: DNA Match Testing, Bayes' Theorem, and the Criminal Courts' (2001) 41 No. 3 *Med. Sci. Law* 194.

33 Waldbaum, *supra*, note 20, at 206.

34 *Ibid.*

35 *Johnson v. Com.* 529 S.E. 2d 769 (2000); *Smith v. State* 744 N.E. 2d 437 (2001); *Kellogg v. Travis* 728 N.Y.S. 2d 645 (2001); *L.S. v. State* 805 So. 2d 1004 (2001). See, generally, Michael J. Markett, 'Genetic Diaries: An Analysis of Privacy Protection in DNA Data Banks' (1996) 30 *Suffolk University Law Rev.* 185; Jennifer N. Mellon, 'Manufacturing Convictions: Why Defendants Are Entitled to the Data Underlying Forensic DNA Kits' (2001) 51 *Duke L.J.* 1094.

36 *The Human Genes Research Act 2000*: posted on http://www.medinfo.cam.ac.uk/ phgu/info_database/ELSI/genet-database.asp (last visited 9 April 2004).

37 *Icelandic Health Sector Database Act 1998*: http://brunnur.stjr.is/interpro/htr.nsf/ pages/gagngr-log-ensk (last visited 9 April 2002).

38 Kaye and Martin, *supra*, note 1.

is concerned with such civil application of DNA banks. Below is a review of the general provisions of the statutes in the above-mentioned jurisdictions. Such general examination provides a context for the subsequent analysis of attendant property problems.

The Iceland Health Sector Database

The Icelandic *Health Sector Database Act 1998*[39] was promulgated into law by the Iceland legislature in December 1998. However, its legislative history dates back to 1994 when Kari Stefansson visited Iceland to collaborate in a study on multiple sclerosis.[40] The study sought to unravel any possible genetic link to the multiple sclerosis disease.[41] Subsequently, Kari Stefansson, a Harvard medical academic, formed the idea of a centralized computer health database in Iceland, which could be used for various biomedical and health-related research activities and could facilitate the tailoring of drugs to suit individual genetic profiles, otherwise known as pharmacogenomics. Pursuant to these objectives, he incorporated a company, deCODE Genetics, Inc.,[42] in Delaware, USA, but which has its physical existence in Iceland. He also persuaded the Icelandic government to give statutory support to the proposed health database, and his efforts led to the *Act on a Health Sector Database no. 139/1998* (1998 Act), which was passed by the Iceland parliament, Alpingi, on 17 December 1998.[43]

Provisions of the HSD

The 1998 Act sought to improve the delivery of health services in Iceland by the creation and operation of a centralized health sector database, which is fed with non-personally identifiable medical data from the medical records of Icelandic citizens.[44] Information collected and recorded in the health sector database would be used to 'develop new or improved methods of achieving better health, prediction, diagnosis and treatment of disease, to seek the most economic ways of operating health services, and for making reports in the health sector'.[45] The Act does not apply to the collection and use of tissue samples,[46] a matter dealt with by another legislation. Health institutions and self-employed health workers in Iceland are permitted to

---

39 Posted on http://brunnur.stjr.is/interpro/htr.nsf/pages/gagngr-log-ensk (last visited on 5 September 2005).

40 Hilary Rose, *The Commodification of Bioinformation: The Icelandic Health Sector Database* (London: The Wellcome Trust, 2001), at 8.

41 *Ibid.*

42 http://www.decode.is/company.

43 For a good overview of the Act, see: Jamaica Potts, 'At Least Give the Natives Glass Beads: An Examination of the Bargain Made Between Iceland and deCode Genetics with Implications for Global Bioprospecting' (2002) 7 *Va. J.L. & Tech.* 8.

44 HSD, *supra*, note 39, art. 1.

45 *Ibid.*, art. 10.

46 *Ibid.*, art. 2.

release information from patients' medical records to the Act's licensee for entry into the Health Sector Database (HSD),[47] though such information should be stripped of personal identifiers before transfer to the HSD.[48]

Consent of the database subjects is presumed, though any person that has reached the age of consent can opt out.[49] Such persons can also opt out on behalf of minors and incompetent persons under their legal authority.[50] A request to opt out must be made by filling and submitting the relevant form to the Director General of Public Health.[51] Persons who exercised the opting out option within six months of the Act[52] could prevent the transfer of their medical records to the HSD.[53] However, after that time-frame medical information already in the database could not be withdrawn, even if a patient subsequently exercised the option to opt out.[54] As at 30 June 2003, it was estimated that over 20,426 Icelandic citizens had opted out of the HSD.[55]

The HSD is operated under a licensing scheme. Pursuant to an application, the Minister of Health is authorized to grant a licence to create and operate the HSD in accordance with the Act.[56] The licensee would pay the cost of preparing and issuing the licence as well as a yearly fee to defray the cost incurred in connection with the database.[57] The Act created a committee to supervise the operation of the HSD and ensure that it is in accordance with the Act and the terms of the licence.[58] The licence shall be exclusive and granted for not more than 12 years at a time.[59] However, the government is to have free access to the database for statistical information.[60] Independent researchers also may be given access to the HSD, provided their activities do not conflict with the licensee's interest.[61]

---

47 *Ibid.*, art. 7.

48 *Ibid.*

49 *Ibid.*, art. 8.

50 Rose, *supra*, note 40, at 20.

51 *Ibid.*

52 HSD, *supra*, note 39, art. 19.

53 Rose, *supra*, note 40, at 24.

54 Henry T. Greely, 'Iceland's Plan for Genomics Research: Facts and Implications' (2000) 40 *Jurimetrics* 153, at 172; Rose, *supra*, note 40, at 24.

55 http://www.mannvernd.is/english/ (last visited on 19 November 2005).

56 HSD, *supra*, note 39, art. 4.

57 *Ibid.*

58 *Ibid.*, art. 6.

59 *Ibid.*, art. 5.

60 *Ibid.*, art. 9.

61 Hróbjartur Jónatansson, 'Iceland's Health Sector Database: A Significant Head Start in the Search for the Biological Grail or an Irreversible Error?' (2000) 26 *Am. J.L. & Med.* 31, at 62.

Criticism of the HSD

The HSD has been both criticized[62] and supported[63] with regards to its provisions on privacy, presumed consent, and the small amount of the licence fee compared to the huge profits that would potentially accrue to the licensee of the HSD. For instance, J.C. Bear estimates that access to the DNA of Iceland's 280,000 people is worth about $14 billion. He argues that potential research participants should negotiate aggressively, or require their governments to do so, with corporate interests wishing to access their DNA.[64] With regard to the consent provisions of the HSD, David Winickoff argues that Iceland has lost an opportunity to bring clear and ethically sound standards to the use of human biological samples in the deCODE database. He further observes that the HSD has extended a notion of 'presumed consent' from the use of medical records to the use of patients' biological samples, and that the Act has made it possible or more likely that a donor's wish to withdraw his/her sample will be ignored.[65] Similarly, Einar Árnason argues that it is both right and reasonable to obtain *a priori* consent of patients for the transfer of their health data to the database and that anything less is unreasonable.[66] Some Icelandic doctors insist that they will not hand over data on their patients unless the patient requests to participate in writing.[67] The HSD provisions have also been criticized for having some potential to impair independent scientific research. This book, however, is concerned with its potential effect as a state's assumption of ownership over, and commercialization of, its citizens' bioinformation.[68]

Icelandic Biobanks Law

The HSD was mainly concerned with the collection of medical information, not genetic materials or tissue samples.[69] So, if the HSD commercialized anything, it is not human materials but medical information in the database, though this information may be genetic in character.[70] However, some genetic studies may warrant linking the medical information on HSD to related genetic materials or samples. Article 10 of the HSD foresaw such linkage and provides that the licensee shall ensure

---

62 Greely, *supra*, note 54.

63 Jónatansson, *supra*, note 61.

64 J.C. Bear, *What is a Person's DNA Worth? Fair Compensation for DNA Access* (Vienna: 10th International Congress of Human Genetics, 2001).

65 David E. Winickoff, 'Biosamples, Genomics, and Human Rights: Context and Content of Iceland's Biobanks Act' (2000) 4 *J. Biolaw & Bus.* 11, at 11–17.

66 Einar Árnason, 'Personal Identifiability in the Health Sector Database' (2001) 87 *Icelandic Medical Journal* 807, at 807–16.

67 Lopeti Senituli and Margret Boyes, *Whose DNA? Tonga and Iceland, Biotech, Ownership and Consent* (Adelaide: Australasian Bioethics Association Annual Conference, 2002), at 2.

68 Rose, *supra*, note 40, at 5.

69 HSD, *supra*, note 39, art. 2.

70 *Ibid.*, art. 3(6)(7).

confidentiality in 'connecting information from the Health Sector Database with the database of genealogical information and with the database of genetic information'. Apparently, there was a need to create a tissue bank to complement the HSD, and this led to the *Act on Biobanks no. 110/2000*,[71] passed by the Icelandic Parliament on 13 May 2000.

Provisions of Biobanks Law

Like the HSD, the Biobanks law sets up a licensing scheme for the creation and operation of a biobank. The objective of the legislation is to authorize the collection, keeping, handling and utilization of biological samples from human beings, with sufficient protection for their privacy and confidentiality.[72] The Minister of Health, based on recommendations from the Director General of Public Health and the National Bioethics Committee, is authorized to grant a licence to a person to create and operate a biobank.[73] The biobank would be operated by a board of not less than three persons, and appointed by the licensee.[74] The board shall keep the Director General of Public Health, the Data Protection Authority and the National Bioethics Committee informed regarding the biological samples and operations of the biobank.[75] The *Biobank Act* uses both informed and presumed consent for the collection of tissue samples in the biobank.

Where a tissue sample was collected in a clinical setting, that is, in connection with a patient's treatment, the Act presumes the patient's consent for the permanent storage of his or her tissue in the biobank.[76] The patient is, however, allowed to withdraw his or her presumed consent by filling and delivering the necessary notice of withdrawal to the Director General of Public Health.[77] After such notification, already collected tissue samples may not be automatically destroyed but can 'only be used in the interests of the donor of a biological sample or by his/her specific permission'.[78] The Director General of Public Health is under a statutory duty to ensure that the general public is aware of their right to opt out.[79]

In a non-clinical setting, tissue samples should be collected only on the basis of free and informed consent, given in writing by the donor after she or he had been 'informed of the objective of the sample collection, the benefits, risks associated with its collection, and that the biological sample will be permanently stored at a biobank for use as provided in art. 9'.[80] Consent of a donor may be withdrawn at any

---

71 Posted on http://www.mannvernd.is/english/laws/Act.Biobanks.html (last visited on 5 September 2002).

72 *Ibid.*, art. 1.

73 *Ibid.*, art. 4.

74 *Ibid.*, art. 6.

75 *Ibid.*

76 *Ibid.*, art. 7.

77 *Ibid.*, art. 7.

78 *Ibid.*, art 7.

79 *Ibid.*, art. 13.

80 *Ibid.*, art. 7.

time and biological samples already collected shall be destroyed, but not information obtained from such samples.[81]

Tissue samples in the biobank shall be labelled and secured, and stored without personal identification.[82] The non-personally identifiable samples in the biobank may only be used for lawful purposes, which include the diagnosis of diseases, quality control and development of methods and tuition.[83] A donor of a biological sample shall not suffer discrimination on grounds of information or data got from the biological sample.[84] Access to the samples for scientific study is conditioned upon permission from the Data Protection Authority, and approval of research protocol by the National Bioethics Committee or ethics committee of the relevant health institution.[85] Biological samples may be used for purposes other than those for which they were collected, provided approval is given by the Data Protection Authority and the National Bioethics Committee, and the potential benefits to the donor outweigh the potential harm.[86] The Act came into force on 1 January 2001.[87]

Ownership Issues under the Icelandic Legislation

Laws creating and regulating the operation of databanks, whether of medical information or tissue samples, usually raise controversies, some of which touch on the proprietary right to bioinformation. The government of Iceland has been criticized for using the instruments of HSD and Biobank law to nationalize and commercialize its citizens' bioinformation. Thus, Article 10 of the HSD permitted the licensee 'during the period of the license to use the data on the database for purposes of financial profit'. And Article 10 of the *Biobank Act* authorizes the licensee to 'take a fee for a biological sample, or access to a biological sample'. Some people may find propertization and commercialization of human body parts or information derived from it as amounting to devaluation and objectification of life. However, this holistic view of the human body may be at odds with the increasing use and commodification of the human body by numerous biotechnological applications. Biotechnology has given huge monetary value to things that were not previously commodifiable. Without attempting to resolve the debate on commodification, it is sufficient to observe that the commercial value of the human body and parts of it has become a reality, and this will likely lead to assertions of proprietary interests in one's own body. For instance, the estimated huge monetary value[88] of access to the HSD could motivate some Icelandic citizens to assert ownership of their bioinformation and claim appropriate compensation.[89]

---

81 *Ibid.*, art 7.
82 *Ibid.*, art. 8.
83 *Ibid.*, art. 9.
84 *Ibid.*, art. 1.
85 *Ibid.*, art. 9.
86 *Ibid.*
87 *Ibid.*, art. 18.
88 Bear, *supra*, note 64.
89 *Ibid.*

What is striking in the commercialization of biosamples in Iceland is that only the sample source is excluded from commercial benefits accruing from the DNA banks. This could be seen as grossly unfair, since without the sample source no genetic information or any invention based on it would materialize. Although the Icelandic legislation gives some protection for the privacy and confidentiality of the sample sources, it seems that the sample sources are unable to exercise continuing control over the samples, once transferred. They are also unable to claim a share in the proceeds resulting from the commercial application of the samples. These are some of the limitations of informed consent and privacy frameworks, which call for an application of a limited property approach that would give the sample sources not only a continuing control over the samples and information in the DNA bank, but also a share in the profits emanating from the research.[90] Because the type of property argument above could be avoided by explicit legislative stipulation, it is important to see the manner and extent, if any, to which the Icelandic legislation treated the property question.

The *HSD Act* did not expressly deal with the question of ownership of the medical information that was transferred to the Health Sector Database. The question seems, however, to have arisen in 1997 when the Icelandic government promulgated the patients' right law. At the initial stage of the *Patient Act*, the Icelandic government seemed to have asserted ownership over medical data in its health system.[91] Sustained protests accompanying the patients' right law led the Icelandic government to abandon its proprietary position in favour of custodianship.[92] Thus, neither the government nor the patients were owners of medical information in the conventional sense of ownership.[93] It is believed that this compromise, which saw the Icelandic government as custodians of health information, underpinned the HSD.[94]

In contrast, the *Biobank Act* apparently took a different position on ownership. It seems that the sufficient control and autonomy accorded a tissue source under Article 7 is property-like, at least for the purpose of the donor's effective protection and self-determination.[95] This observation may not be applicable to samples taken

---

90 Graeme, *supra*, note 8, at 299–328.
91 Jónatansson, *supra*, note 61, at 58.
92 *Ibid.*
93 *Ibid.*
94 *Ibid.*
95 *Ibid.*, article 7 provides:

Art. 7. Consent of donor of a biological sample and withdrawal of consent.

In connection with collection of a biological sample for preservation in a biobank, the free, informed consent of the person giving the biological sample shall be sought. This consent shall be given freely and in writing after the donor of a biological sample has been informed of the objective of the sample collection, the benefits, risks associated with its collection, and that the biological sample will be permanently stored at a biobank for use as provided in art. 9. In addition the provisions of art. 20 of the Act on personal privacy and handling of personal data shall be observed where applicable.

A donor of a biological sample can at any time withdraw his/her consent under the terms of para. 1, and the biological sample shall then be destroyed. Material that has

in a clinical context for which presumed consent applies, unless a donor opts out. This regime of presumed consent may be evidence of the Icelandic government's assertion of some proprietary interest in tissue samples taken by its health institutions in the context of medical treatment. However, Article 10 provides that the licensee 'shall not be counted as the owner of the biological samples, but has rights over them, with limitations laid down by law'. Consequently, the licensee shall not 'pass the biological samples on to another party, nor use them as collateral for financial liabilities, and they are not subject to attachment for debt'.

It is arguable that the Biobank law clearly distributes rights relating to the biobank by denying the licensee any proprietary right to the biological samples in the biobank, and gives donors, especially donors in non-clinical settings, some property-like interest (sufficient control) in their tissues.[96] The Biobank law also gave the Icelandic government some property interest in tissue samples collected in clinical settings. Despite the proprietary implications of presumed consent, with respect to tissues collected in a clinical context, the *Biobank Act* seems to give the Icelandic government only a decisional authority with respect to tissues in the bank. This seems to be supported by Article 10 which provides that after the termination or revocation or expiration of a licence under the Act, the Minister shall 'decide on the future of the biobank, taking into account the wishes and proposals of the licensee'.

---

been produced from a biological sample by performance of a study or the results of studies already carried out shall, however, not be destroyed.

If biological samples have been collected for the purpose of clinical tests or treatment, the consent of the patient may be assumed for the storage of the biological sample in a biobank for use as provided in art. 9, provided that general information on this is provided by a health care professional or health institution.

A donor of a biological sample may at any time withdraw his/her assumed consent for his/her biological sample to be stored in a biobank for use as provided in art. 9, in which case it shall thereafter only be used in the interests of the donor of a biological sample or by his/her specific permission, but see also para. 4 art. 9. The request of a donor of a biological sample may apply to all biological samples which have been taken or may be taken from him/her. Such a request must be complied with. The donor of a biological sample shall inform the Director General of Public Health of his/her request. The Director General of Public Health shall be responsible for preparation of forms for giving such notice, and shall ensure that these are available at health institutions, and at the premises of self-employed health care professionals. The Director General of Public Health shall ensure that a coded register of those who have opted out in this way shall always be available to the boards of biobanks. Staff of the Director General of Public Health who carry out this work are subject to an obligation of confidentiality regarding information they may become aware of in the course of their work, which should remain confidential by law or by its nature. Such staff shall sign an oath of confidentiality before their employment begins. The obligation of confidentiality remains in force after employment ceases.

96 *Ibid.*, article 7.

Judicial Analysis of the HSD

In *Ragnhildur Guðmundsdóttir v. The State of Iceland*,[97] the Supreme Court of Iceland made important pronouncements concerning the constitutional implications of the HSD. The decision, however, draws attention to non-constitutional issues that may become controversial in future cases; for instance, how to determine the conflicting interests of a deceased's children with respect to the transfer of a deceased's medical or genetic information to the HSD. This case further raises the potential question of whether in addition to the constitution or any other relevant statutory law, the quasi-property rights of a next of kin under common law includes the right to control the dissemination and use of the deceased's medical and genetic information. The case is of first impression and provided the Supreme Court of Iceland the opportunity to interpret various sections of the HSD. The facts are uncontroversial and straightforward. The plaintiff was born in 1985 and had two brothers who did not object to the prosecution of this case.[98] The plaintiff's father died on 12 August 1991. On 16 February 2000, the plaintiff applied through her guardian, under Article 8 of the HSD, to the Medical Director of Health in Iceland requesting that genealogical and genetic information contained in her father's medical records should not be transferred to the HSD.[99] After the Medical Director of Health had obtained legal opinion on the matter, he refused the plaintiff's application on 21 February 2001.[100] On 30 April 2001, the plaintiff brought an action in the District Court challenging the decision of the Medical Director of Health. The District Court dismissed the plaintiff's claim and confirmed the decision of the Medical Director of Health. The plaintiff then appealed to the Supreme Court of Iceland.

Very early in the proceedings, the plaintiff's standing was in issue since Article 8 neither expressly permits living relatives to prevent the transfer of a deceased's medical information into the HSD nor directly prohibits them from doing so. Thus, the plaintiff had to show a personal right of action or an authority to bring the action as the deceased's proxy. Because personal rights generally expire upon death, the Supreme Court of Iceland held that the 'appellant cannot…exercise the right provided for in this statutory provision (Article 8) as her deceased father's substitute'.[101] To prove standing, the plaintiff, therefore, had to show that the transfer of her deceased father's genetic information directly implicated her privacy and gave her a personal right of action. The Supreme Court of Iceland extensively reviewed the nature and content of information in a patient's medical records[102] and, accordingly, agreed that the plaintiff had a standing to bring the action, since she demonstrated:

---

97 *Ragnhildur Guðmundsdóttir v. The State of Iceland* No. 151/2003. This decision was rendered on 27 November 2003, but its English translation was only published in April 2004. A copy of the English translation is on the Mannvernd website, *supra*, note 55.

98 *Ibid.*, at 4.

99 *Ibid.*, at 3–4.

100 *Ibid.*, at 4.

101 *Ibid.*, at 4.

102 For instance, the court observed:

As may be inferred from the above, extensive information is entered into medical records on people's health, their medical treatment, lifestyles, social circumstances,

[a] personal interest in preventing the transfer of data from her father's medical records to the Health Sector Database, as it is possible to infer, from the data, information relating to her father's hereditary characteristics which could also apply to herself. The Defendant has not submitted to the court any expert testimony to rebut this contention of the Appellant. In light of this, and with reference in other respects to the reasoning of the District Court, the argument of the Appellant is accepted that, for reasons of personal privacy, she may have an interest in preventing information of this sort about her father from being transferred into the database, and therefore her right to make the claims that she is making in the case is admitted.[103]

After detailed analysis of the provisions of the HSD, particularly those relating to the encryption and protection of information in the medical records and its transfer to the HSD, the Supreme Court of Iceland opined that the HSD did not adequately protect the plaintiff's privacy up to the constitutionally required level. Short of declaring the HSD unconstitutional,[104] the Supreme Court of Iceland upheld the plaintiff's right to prevent the transfer of her father's genealogical and genetic information into the HSD and observed:

Individual provisions in the Act No. 139/1998 (the HSD) refer repeatedly to the fact that health information in the Health Sector Database should be non-personally identifiable. In light of the rules discussed above concerning the issues addressed in Articles 7 and 10 of the Act, however, the achievement of this stated objective is far from being adequately ensured by the provisions of statutory law. Owing to the obligations imposed on the legislature by Paragraph 1 of Article 71 of the Constitution to ensure protection of privacy, as outlined above, this assurance cannot be replaced by various forms of monitoring of the creation and operation of the Health Sector Database, monitoring which is entrusted to public agencies and committees without definite statutory norms on which to base their work. Nor is it sufficient in this respect to leave it in the hands of the Minister to establish conditions in the operating licence or appoint other holders of official authority to establish or approve rules of procedure concerning these matters, which at all levels could be subject to changes within the vague limits set by the provisions of Act No.

---

employment and family. They contain, moreover, a detailed identification of the person that the information concerns. Information of this kind can relate to some of the most intimately private affairs of the person concerned, irrespective of whether the information can be seen as derogatory for the person or not. It is unequivocal that the provisions of Paragraph 1 of Article 71 of the Constitution apply to information of this kind and that they guarantee protection of privacy in this respect. To ensure this privacy the legislature must ensure, *inter alia*, that legislation does not result in any actual risk of information of this kind involving the private affairs of identified persons falling into the hands of parties who do not have any legitimate right of access to such information, irrespective of whether the parties in question are other individuals or government authorities.

Ibid., at 7–8.

103 *Ibid.*, at 4–5.

104 This decision is wrongly interpreted to have declared the HSD unconstitutional. See, for instance, Robert McKie, 'Iceland DNA Project Hit By Privacy Storm', *The Observer*, 16 May 2004; http://www.mannvernd.is/greinar/guardian0504.html (last accessed on 7 July 2004).

139/1998...Based on the above, it is impossible to maintain that the provisions of Act No. 139/1998 will adequately ensure, in fulfillment of the requirements deriving from Paragraph 1 of Article 71 of the Constitution, attainment of the objective of the Act of preventing health information in the database from being traceable to individuals.[105]

Though this recent decision of the Supreme Court of Iceland is relevant to other jurisdictions that operate or intend to operate a centralized health or DNA database, and presumably vindicated the position of some human rights activists that vigorously opposed the HSD, it is jurisprudentially relevant to England, Canada and the USA in unique ways that are conditioned by the existence of their vibrant and rich common law heritage. For instance, in determining the legal source of a plaintiff's authority to bring the action, the Supreme Court of Iceland observed:

> The previously mentioned Article 8 of the Act No. 139/1998 does not provide for the right of descendants or other relatives of deceased persons to request, on their behalf, that information in their medical records should be withheld from the Health Sector Database. *No such rule can be inferred from any other sources of law.*[106] (Italics supplied)

Though the Supreme Court eventually found that the plaintiff's constitutional right of privacy justified the action, the issue in common law countries is likely to be whether, in the event of a similar situation, a court could hold that limited or quasi-property rights of sepulchre include the right to control the use and dissemination of a decedent's genealogical or genetic information? Could the common law relating to burial rights be a source of the rule empowering a next of kin to prevent the biomedical exploitation of a deceased relative's genealogical and genetic information? Quasi-property rights of burial would be meaningless in this genomic age unless they extend to the raw materials of the biotechnology industry; for instance, human biological samples and genetic information obtained from them. Since a next of kin can assert quasi-property rights to prevent the unauthorized dissection of a deceased relative for medical research purposes, it seems to follow without argument that such rights should also avail the next of kin when the genetic information and DNA samples of the deceased are involved. It is suggested, therefore, that the concept of property, especially limited forms of property rights existing under laws relating to dead bodies, is relevant to the interpretation and operation of the HSD. If this is accepted, it would seem to mean that in addition to potential uses of property metaphor to claim shares in the commercial profits arising from the operation of the HSD, sample sources can also use common law quasi property-rights of burial to control the use of a deceased's relatives DNA samples and genetic or medical information.

---

105 *Ragnhildur Guðmundsdóttir, supra*, note 97, at 9.
106 *Ibid.*, at 4.

The Estonian Gene Banking Project

The Estonian DNA banking project contrasts in many respects with the earlier pieces of legislation in Iceland.[107] Both countries, however, have the same objective of creating and maintaining a centralized computer database of health and genetic information of their citizens. The governmental establishment of medical and genetic databases in Iceland and Estonia, and the grant of exclusive commercial and managerial licences over the databases to commercial firms,[108] shows similarity in both countries' public-private partnership approach to genetic research. The Estonian legislation, in contrast, benefited from the wide publicity and criticism heaped upon the earlier Icelandic Acts and, therefore, avoided provisions that infringed or eroded the law and convention on informed consent. It also gave donors and public researchers free access to the database.[109]

Provisions of the HGRA

The *Human Genes Research Act, 2000*[110] was passed into law by the Estonian government on 13 December 2000 and came into force on 8 January 2001. Its objective is to stimulate genetic research in Estonia by the establishment of a Gene Bank with information capable of generating 'more exact and efficient drug development, new diagnostic tests, improved individualised treatment and determination of risks of the development of a disease in the future'.[111] The Act intends to achieve its objectives in the context of highest regards for patients' or donors' right of confidentiality, privacy, autonomy and freedom from genetic discrimination.[112] Section 3(3) of the *Human Genes Research Act*[113] (Act) authorizes a statutory authority, designated by the Act as a 'chief processor', to establish and maintain a Gene Bank. A 'Gene Bank' is defined as a database 'consisting of tissue samples, descriptions of DNA, descriptions of state of health, genealogies, genetic data and data enabling the identification of gene donors'.[114]

This model of database comprising the medical records, genealogy, tissue samples and genetic information makes more statutory economic sense than the Icelandic paradigm that created separate databases (by different pieces of legislation) for each of the above three classes of medical and genetic information. The Estonian Gene Bank is created with tissue samples collected from donors (with their voluntary

---

107 Michael J. Smith, 'Population-Based Genetic Studies: Informed Consent and Confidentiality' (2001) 18 *Santa Clara Comp. & High Tech. L.J.* 57, at 79–89.

108 DeCODE for Iceland, and Egeen Inc. for Estonia.

109 Leone Frank, 'Estonia Prepares for National DNA Database' (2000) 290 *Science* 31.

110 Posted on the website of the Estonian Genome Foundation: http://www.genomics.ee/.

111 Estonian Genome Foundation: http://www.genomics.ee/index. php?lang=eng&show=20 (last visited on 12 September 2002).

112 *Supra*, note 110, s. 1.

113 HGRA, *supra*, note 110.

114 *Ibid.*, s. 2(10).

consent and in accordance with the Act), the donor's statement on state of health and medical treatment, and the donor's medical data stored in medical institutions.[115]

The Gene Bank would be established and managed by a chief processor, which must be a non-profit foundation founded by the Estonian government.[116] Pursuant to this provision, the Government of the Republic of Estonia founded the 'Estonian Genome Project Foundation' (EGV) in 2001, as the chief processor under the Act. The EGV is mandated to: 1. promote the development of genetic research; 2. collect information on the health of the Estonian population and genetic information concerning the Estonian population; and 3. use the results of genetic research to improve public health.[117] The chief processor has a board of nine members,[118] and can delegate processing rights, other than coding and decoding functions, to an authorized processor.[119]

Chapter two of the Act enacts detailed provisions for the protection of sample sources: 'a person who provides a tissue sample in accordance with this Act and with regard to whom a description of state of health and genealogy are prepared.'[120] Instead of the somewhat uneasy opting out form of consent under the Icelandic HSD, the Estonian Act prohibits the collection of tissue samples, genealogy, and description of state of health except under the authority of a prior informed consent, given in writing and signed by the sample source without any undue influence.[121] The consent form must include the particulars of the sample source, and the health provider who would procure the tissue sample, the manner of obtaining the tissue and the part of the body from which the tissue would be taken.[122] The consent must be informed in that the donor must be informed that: 1. the consent is voluntary; 2. no payment is to be made to the tissue donor; 3. the results of genetic research may be unpleasant; 4. the donor has the right to know or not to know his or her genetic data; 5. the donor has a right to apply for the destruction of his or her genetic data, and if identity of donor is compromised, there is a further right to apply for destruction of tissue sample; 6. the donor has the right to withdraw his or her consent pending the coding of his or her tissue sample and genetic information; and 7. the donor has a right to receive a copy of the consent form.[123] Incompetent persons are not allowed to be donors, but persons with restricted legal capacity could consent to be donors through their legal representatives and guardians.[124]

As already noted, a person who has given his or her consent can apply at anytime to withdraw the consent and have the data destroyed.[125] Upon request, the data must

---

115 *Ibid.*, s. 14.
116 *Ibid.*, s. 3.
117 *Ibid.*, s.3.
118 *Ibid.*, s. 4.
119 *Ibid.*, s. 5.
120 *Ibid.*, s. 2(4).
121 *Ibid.*, ss. 9 and 12.
122 *Ibid.*, s. 12.
123 *Ibid.*
124 *Ibid.*, s. 13.
125 *Ibid.*, ss. 10 and 12.

be destroyed within two weeks thereof.[126] However, there is no automatic right to have tissue samples duly donated destroyed. A right to the destruction of tissue samples only arises if the identity of the donor was unlawfully disclosed.[127] In that case, the samples must be destroyed within one month of the receipt of a request in that regard.[128] But the chief processor may prevent such destruction if it proves that the sample donor was responsible for the disclosure of his or her identity.[129] It seems that the Act's reluctance to give a sample source some flexibility with regard to tissue samples duly donated and collected is consistent with its declaration of ownership over the tissue samples in favour of the chief processor.[130]

The Act also granted a sample source free access to personal data in the Gene Bank, except the genealogical aspect.[131] Donors also have the right to genetic counselling upon such access, right to supplement personal information in the Gene Bank, and right to prevent such supplementation.[132] Donors should be identifiable only through coding,[133] and the chief processor is permitted to disseminate genetic information from the Gene Bank only in coded form.[134] The Act prohibits discrimination based on a person's DNA,[135] and the use of data from the Gene Bank in connection with employment,[136] insurance,[137] civil and criminal proceedings.[138] Accordingly, the Gene Bank can only be used for scientific research, research on donor's diseases, public health research, statistical purposes,[139] research to study and describe the links between genes, the physical and social environment and the lifestyles of people.[140] Also permitted are researches that would yield therapeutic products for the treatment of diseases, and diagnostic and predictive tools.[141]

The Act attempts to balance the Estonian government's commercial interest in generating money through the Gene Bank and the need to give private and public researchers access to the Gene Bank. It gives the chief processor power to grant genetic researchers free access to genetic information in the Gene Bank, or to charge a fee for such access.[142] Section 19 further makes such access free for public researchers in Estonia: 'The chief processor shall grant gene researchers who are

---

126 *Ibid.*, s. 21.
127 *Ibid.*, s.10(2).
128 *Ibid.*, s. 21.
129 *Ibid.*
130 *Ibid.*, s. 15.
131 *Ibid.*, s. 11.
132 *Ibid.*
133 *Ibid.*, s. 8.
134 *Ibid.*, s. 20.
135 *Ibid.*, s. 25.
136 *Ibid.*, s. 26.
137 *Ibid.*, s. 27.
138 *Ibid.*, s. 16.
139 *Ibid.*
140 *Ibid.*, s. 6.
141 *Ibid.*
142 *Ibid.*, s.19.

legal persons in public law or state agencies of the Republic of Estonia the right to use descriptions of DNA or parts thereof without charge.'

Ownership of Tissue Samples under the Estonian Legislation

In contrast to the legislation in Iceland, the *Estonian Human Genes Research Act* boldly confronted the proprietary issue concerning ownership of tissue samples and bioinformation. After giving potential donors full latitude in deciding whether to donate their genes and medical information or not, the Act expressly provides that upon the donation of a tissue sample and medical information, it becomes the property of the state, through the state-created chief processor.[143]

Unlike other rights of property, the chief processor is not allowed to transfer its statutory right of property over the samples.[144] Despite the susceptibility of the Act's ownership provision to the accusation that it nationalized the Estonian human gene pool, the Act, through the explicit property provisions above, avoided a lot of potential litigation over ownership rights in donated biosamples and research results. In this sense, the Estonian legislation avoids the ambiguity in the Icelandic Acts with respect to property questions. To put the matter beyond cavil, section 15(3) provides that a 'gene donor is not entitled to request a fee for providing a tissue sample, preparation and study of a description of his or her state of health or genealogy, or use of the research results'. The acceptance of this seemingly expropriatory provision, judging from its relative lack of criticism, was facilitated by the Act's highest respect for the principles of informed consent and individual autonomy.

Tonga DNA Sale

Another interesting model of DNA banking is represented by the genetic data banking agreement between Autogen Limited, an Australian corporation and the Kingdom of Tonga's Ministry of Health. For reasons stated later, it is probable that the subject matter of the above agreement is now abandoned by Autogen. The Kingdom of Tonga is a small island in the South Pacific, with a population of about 108,000. Its small and homogenous population, similar to those of Iceland and Estonia, is ideal for genetic studies. In about November 2000, Tonga's Ministry of Health entered into an agreement with Autogen, which would enable the latter to create a genetic database from tissue samples collected from the Kingdom of Tonga's population.[145]

It seems, however, that tissue samples would be collected only from Tongan people suffering from or prone to diseases which are of interest to Autogen.[146] The genetic database would be used to identify genes that are responsible for predisposition to diseases like obesity, diabetes, cardiovascular disease, hypertension, cancer and

---

143 *Ibid.*, s. 15.

144 *Ibid.*

145 Smith, *supra*, note 107, at 70.

146 Kim Griggs, 'Tonga Sells Its Old, New Genes', Wired News, 27 November 2000: http://www.wired.com/news/privacy/0,1848,40354,00.html (last visited on 13 September 2002).

stomach ulcers. Since obesity and diabetes are common in Tonga, Autogen's focus of research on local diseases seems beneficial to Tonga and the tissue donors.

Under the agreement, Autogen would establish a research facility in Tonga. This would benefit Tonga's economy by creating opportunities for technical training and employment for Tonga's scientists. Moreover, at the expiration of Autogen's project, its modern equipment would be transferred to hospitals in Tonga.[147] In consideration of the agreement, Autogen would provide annual research funding to Tonga's Ministry of Health and pay the Kingdom's government a part of any revenue that accrued from the commercialization of its research results.[148] Additionally, any therapeutic product that results from Autogen's research in Tonga would be distributed free of charge to the people of Tonga.[149] Autogen would have exclusive access to the database,[150] though it seems to deny the exclusivity provision.[151] Genetic samples for the database would be collected on condition of prior informed and voluntary consent.[152]

Though Autogen would have no property right to the biological samples it collected, those samples would be owned by the government of Tonga, and not the donors.[153] This evidences a growing international trend, as witnessed in Estonia and partially in Iceland, towards governmental assumption of ownership of its citizens' gene pool. It may be that allowing individual ownership rights in tissue samples would increase the cost of bargaining and private investment on gene banks. Such disincentive may be too costly for governments wishing to jump-start biotechnology and genetic research in their countries. Policy considerations, therefore, may underpin this apparent genetic nationalization.

Autogen's agreement with the Tongan Ministry of Health has come under intense criticism. The criticism is partly based on the fact that 'the implications of the Agreement have never been discussed publicly either through the media or in Tonga's Legislative Assembly'.[154] In addition, Autogen's ethical policy was flawed for not situating its informed consent process in Tonga's particular historical and socio-cultural context, which requires a group consent approach rather than the model in societies characterized by individualism. As Senituli and Boyes observed:

> Another major weakness (of Autogen's Tonga project) is that it fails to address the unique processes for group decision making in a tightly knit but acutely status-conscious Tongan society. The Ethics Policy (of Autogen for Tongan bioprospecting) provides for voluntary and prior informed consent from individual volunteers but fails to acknowledge that in the tightly knit Tongan society the extended family grouping (ha'a or matakali) will definitely have a say on whether its individual members be permitted to give prior informed consent

---

147 *Ibid.*

148 *Ibid.*

149 *Ibid.*

150 *Ibid.*

151 Megan Howe, 'Australian Company Buys Rights to Tonga Gene Pool' (2001) 2 *Lancet Oncology* 7.

152 *Ibid.*; Griggs, *supra*, note 146.

153 *Ibid.*

154 Senituli and Boyes, *supra*, note 67, at 4.

in the full knowledge that the serum and genetic material donated is reflective of the extended family's genetic make up. In other words, genetic research such as Autogen's is in fact group research but the Ethics Policy is not equipped to address group rights, but only caters for individual members' rights.[155]

Similarly, the Tonga Human Rights and Democracy Movement issued a Press Release[156] on 24 November 2000, condemning Autogen's agreement with the Tonga Ministry of Health in the following terms:

The very thought that one human being (or company or government) can own the intellectual property rights over the parts of another human being's body conflicts with the sanctity of human life and the basic tenet of the Tongan's Christian faith that we were created in God's image.[157]

In about August 2001, Autogen withdrew its genetic research proposal in Tonga due to intense and unfavourable public criticism.[158]

Newfoundland and Labrador

It may also be pertinent to mention the genomic research and 'gene hunting' in Newfoundland and Labrador that are triggered by the Province's unique gene pool.[159] Newfoundland and Labrador, with a population of about 550,000 people, is becoming Canada's favourite spot for genetic researchers due to its relatively small 'gene pool'. Newfoundland's genetic research relevance stems from the fact that its original settlers from Britain and Ireland, between the 1600s and the 1840s, were small in number and that probably entailed a smaller number of particular genes. Newfoundland's unique genetic legacy has not changed much since the first settlers arrived about 300 years ago.[160] According to Staples, 'large families (in Newfoundland) within close-knit isolated coves created enduring pockets of virtually undiluted gene pools. Since many of those early immigrants came from isolated hamlets to start, the so-called founder effect is remarkably strong.'[161] Thus, Newfoundland has become interesting to researchers investigating the genetic underpinnings of some diseases. Some of the common diseases prevalent in Newfoundland include psoriasis, rheumatoid arthritis, Bardet Biedl Syndrome and diabetes.

Some biotech corporations are also beginning to invest in genomic research in Newfoundland and Labrador. For instance, in 2000, Gemini Holdings plc, a clinical genomics company, announced the signing of an agreement with Lineage

---

155 *Ibid.*, at 5.

156 Press Release of 24 November 2000, posted on http://lists.essential.org (last visited on 3 February 2003).

157 *Ibid.*

158 Senituli and Boyes, *supra*, note 67, at 5.

159 Sarah Staples, 'Human Resource: Newfoundland's 300-year-old Genetic Legacy has Triggered a Gold Rush' (2000) 17 *Business Magazine* 117–20.

160 *Ibid.*

161 *Ibid.*, at 117.

Biomedical Inc., of St John, Newfoundland, to establish a joint venture for the purpose of identifying genes for common diseases using the unique population resources of Newfoundland. The joint venture, Newfound Genomics, will establish a genetics-based research facility in Newfoundland and Labrador with the aim of identifying disease-causing genes.[162] There are fears, however, that researchers and biotech corporations, rather than local patients, will reap most of the benefits of genomic research in Newfoundland.

The fears mentioned above were probably vindicated by a research incident that occurred in Newfoundland in 1998. In that year, some scientists from Texas' Baylor College of Medicine came to St John, Newfoundland, to study an extended family that suffered from ARVC, a form of congenital heart disease that renders victims prone to cardiac arrest from an early age. After a weekend of collecting DNA samples, the scientists left without giving any form of follow-up treatment and genetic counselling. Also, local physicians and researchers were not given access to the data collected by the Baylor's scientists. Although Baylor eventually issued a qualified apology, some Newfoundlanders consider the action of Baylor's scientists as 'biopiracy'.[163] Newfoundlanders may appropriately resort to seeking sufficient compensation for their DNA samples. Thus, in the context of Newfound Genomics' (Gemini and Lineage Biomedical's joint venture in Newfoundland) commercial genomic investigation of common disorders in Newfoundland through local advertisements, with little or no government involvement, J.C. Bear has argued that potential research subjects should, instead of volunteering, negotiate directly for compensation for access to their DNA.[164]

Ownership of DNA and Genetic Data outside Statutory Context

Arguably, it is better for legislation or agreement, like those in Iceland, Estonia, and Tonga, to settle ownership issues with respect to genetic materials and DNA banking. The controversial nature of proprietary interest in the human body and genetic materials, however, does not often make the topic amenable to statutory resolution. Leaving the matter to common law, on the other hand, does not produce any easy solution. Because human dignity has an incomparable worth, property rights over human genetic materials might affront our sense of dignity.[165] A property approach, therefore, tends to objectify and commodify the human body. It has been observed that commodification of the human body 'may alter community attitudes towards bodies and their parts, and as a result alter how communities perceive and treat living humans'.[166] A probable response to the argument against a property approach is that contemporary social and economic facts have already witnessed the

---

162 http://snowdeal.org.

163 Staples, *supra*, note 159, at 2.

164 Bear, *supra*, note 64.

165 Stephen R. Munzer, 'Human Dignity and Property Rights in Human Body Parts', in J.W. Harris, ed., *Property Problems: From Genes to Pension Funds* (The Hague: Kluwer Law International Ltd., 1997), at 25–38.

166 ALRC, *supra*, note 11, at 531.

commodification of the human body and parts of it, and that an optimal approach would be to focus attention on regulating the emerging market.[167] The market for human body parts has risen tremendously due to the growth of the biotechnology industry. Biotechnology has made human biological materials exceedingly useful. Human biological materials are potential sources of therapeutic products and services.

There are many advantages associated with a limited property protection of human biological samples. Property protection would complement existing privacy and informed consent protections by giving sample sources continuing control even after transfer of their samples to a researcher or biobank. Such control power would make it easier for the sample source to partake in the profits derived from the commercial utilization of his or her tissues. Moreover, the sample source could prevent uses that violate his or her cultural or religious beliefs. Property protection also operates to the benefit of a biotech company. For instance, lack of property protection may endanger biological raw materials that are lawfully obtained by biotechnology companies.

The legal and ethical arguments concerning commodification of the human body are profound and varied, and unlikely to be resolved by any single piece of writing. As some commentators have said, the 'body is a site of growing struggles'.[168] Whether we own our body so as to control its transfer and disposition, or lack such ownership so that some parts of our body are available to those in need, is certainly a question that current legal theories are likely to answer differently.[169] What seems to be required, however, is a sustained public debate in each country. The proposed debate may lead to the formation of a clear and relevant policy which, ultimately, would be enshrined in a statute. During the Patients' law that preceded the Icelandic HSD, Iceland had a wide public debate and resolved not to give its government ownership rights over its citizens' medical records and tissue samples. The compromise was in favour of custodial rights to the Icelandic government. This position was adopted by the HSD. Public policy in Estonia and the Kingdom of Tonga was apparently in favour of governmental ownership of tissue samples. This was apparently possible because of the elaborate protection of donors' rights and autonomy. Absent statutory provision or clear policy guidance, however, one might need to know how ownership of a genetic data or sample would be resolved. The courts have a duty to resolve ownership issues whenever they arise with respect to tissue samples. In resolving this issue, the courts would, of course, give sufficient consideration to the desirability of conferring ownership or proprietary rights over human body tissues and the ethical and social consequences of such an approach.

---

167 Julia D. Mahoney, 'The Market for Human Tissue' (2000) 86 *Va. L. Rev.* 163–223.

168 Dorothy Nelkin and Lori B. Andrews, 'Introduction: The Body, Economic Power and Social Control' (1999) 75 *Chicago-Kent L. Rev.* 3, at 3.

169 For a critical examination of different theoretical approaches to the question of ownership of the human body and parts of it: Guido Calabresi, 'An Introduction to Legal Thought: Four Approaches to Law and to the Allocation of Body Parts' (2003) 55 *Stan. L. Rev.* 2113.

Currently, the courts seem to prefer the language of privacy, confidentiality and consent, to property when called upon to consider legal rights in connection with DNA banks, genetic testing and research. Extant judicial approaches are, of course, legitimate but give the false impression that they are mutually exclusive with a limited property framework. The proper legal metaphor applicable to tissue samples and genetic information is often a debatable issue and may depend on the circumstances of a particular case. But it is pertinent to consider that, whether we are thinking of the entitlement of the insurer, employer, researcher or physician to access and use one's genetic data or tissue samples, there is always the lurking question of whether a person has such sufficient ownership of his or her genetic data as to exclusively control its dissemination and use. Formulated in the form of ownership of tissue samples or genetic data, one is offered a different but complementary way of looking at the issues of privacy, confidentiality and control of genetic information. In adopting this complementary proprietary analysis, we have to differentiate between our genetic sample and the information obtained from it through DNA analysis or genetic testing. Do we own our genes?

Ownership of Tissue Samples, Genes and Genetic Information

Genes are a minute and near-invisible (cannot be seen with naked eyes unaided) part of the human body and contain codes of a person's characteristics.[170] In deploying a property framework to genes, we should note a distinction between human tissue samples and the genetic information derived from them. Tissue samples are tangible but the genetic information derived from them is intangible and more readily recognizable as mere data. Because of the tangible and physical features of a tissue sample, it is easier to argue that it is an item of property and such argument would find favour with cases such as *Roche v. Douglas*,[171] where it was held by the Western Australian Supreme Court that a deceased's excised body tissue was property because of its physical quality. Genes or genetic information, however, do not share such obvious physical characteristics and argument for their property protection could proceed from different perspectives: first, it could be argued that genes, though intangible, are analogically physical and worthy of the protection of property law; and second, that even if genes are not physical entities, they could attract property protection as valuable pieces of information. Both perspectives are explored in detail.

---

170 '[t]he biologic unit of heredity, self-reproducing and located at a definite position on a particular chromosone. The concept of gene is still evolving. From the standpoint of function, genes are conceived of as structural, operator, and regulator genes. From another standpoint, they are conceived of as cistrons, mutons, and recons.' *The Sloane-Dorland Annotated Medical-Legal Dictionary* (New York: West Publishing Co., 1990), at 310–11.

171 *Roche v. Douglas* (2000) WASC 146.

Genes as Physical Entities

It is perfectly legitimate to analogize genes to other physical parts of the body and protect them as such. Moreover, it might not make much sense to respect and legally protect the external physical manifestations of the body but not its internal and fundamental hereditary blocks.[172] The Australian Law Reform Commission seemed to recognize that human tissue 'includes the genetic material that may be extracted from almost all human cells'.[173] Despite the inorganic characterization of genes in the *Relaxin Case*[174] as a mere 'chemical substance which carries genetic information',[175] some people would still consider genes to be body parts due to the intimate, personal and unique information they carry.[176] If genes qualified as body parts or tissues, they would be legally protected by the recognition of limited property rights in them.[177] It has even been argued that it is possible to regard genes as an extension of the human person to which non-property legal categories could apply.[178] For instance, genes could be protected by laws that deal with issues concerning the human body, notably the laws of tort and privacy (in the case of a living human being), and the law on dead bodies, in the case of dead persons.[179]

Based on the analogy to human body and body parts, genes may be entitled to the current protection accorded to genetic materials or biological samples by the law relating to autonomy and bodily self-determination, and the law on informed consent. Generally, medical treatment can only be given with a person's consent and withdrawn at his or her pleasure. Also a person cannot be forced to be a research subject or participate in research without full and informed consent. Though these legal protections significantly ensure the inviolability of the living human body, the

---

172 Barbara Looney observed that 'genes clearly fall under the category of human body parts'. B.L. Looney, 'Should Genes be Patented? The Gene Patenting Controversy: Legal, Ethical, and Policy Foundations of an International Agreement' (1996) 28 *Intellectual Property Review* 101, at 133.

173 ALRC, *supra*, note 11, at 526.

174 (1995) E.P.O.R. 541.

175 *Ibid.*, at 551.

176 As a commentator observed: 'Genes and DNA sequences are "mid-range" parts of the body in that they are much larger than atoms, such as carbon or nitrogen, but much smaller than tissues or organs.' David Resnik, 'DNA Patents and Human Dignity' (2001) 29 *Jour. L.M. & Ethics* 152, at 158.

177 As Professor Litman observed: 'A Property lawyer might be forgiven for characterizing genetic material as property. After all, though sub-cellular and therefore invisible to the naked eye, genetic material has a physical existence. Almost all tangible things, other than human beings, are property. And, at least in theory, there are very sound reasons for this being so', in Knoppers, *supra*, note 10, at 18.

178 Litman also stated that: 'It is certainly possible for the law to regard such material as an extension of its human source, even if it is not *per se* a human being. Human genetic material emanates from, and is integral to human beings. It is also of profound importance in the biological process of constituting human beings. Accordingly, it would not be illogical to legally characterize genetic material as "person" rather than "property"', in Knoppers, *supra*, note 10, at 19.

179 Radhika Rao, 'Property, Privacy, and the Human Body' (2000) 80 *B.U.L. Rev.* 359.

law has not clearly gone to the extent of conferring self-ownership over one's body,[180] though the possibility of a limited property protection is not excluded.[181] It is possible to extend these current legal protections (autonomy and right to self-determination) to genes.[182] It should be an interference with bodily autonomy and self-determination to sequence a person's genes or DNA without his or her consent. The privacy of our genes and DNA samples deserves adequate protection, as they are the gateway to a person's unique characteristic. A person's unique features encoded in his or her genes or DNA samples could be put to prejudicial uses unless the law provides sufficient protection.[183] Some research guidelines have also adopted the principles of informed consent and autonomy in the protection of genetic materials.[184]

For instance, the Council for International Organizations of Medical Sciences (CIOMS) *International Ethical Guidelines for Biomedical Research Involving Human Subjects* affirm the individual's autonomy over his or her body tissues, by observing in the commentary to Guideline 4 that 'research protocol should include a separate section for clinical-trial subjects who are requested to provide their consent for the use of their biological specimens for research';[185] and that patients 'have a right to know that their records or specimens may be used for research'.[186] Similarly, the Tri-Council Policy Statement,[187] a Canadian research policy document (jointly produced by the Medical Research Council; Natural Sciences and Engineering Research Council; and Social Sciences and Humanities Research Council), provides in Article 10.3(a): 'When identification is possible, researchers shall seek to obtain free and informed consent from individuals, or from their authorized third parties, for the use of their previously collected tissue.'

The protections given to genetic materials under the provisions of the CIOMS guidelines above emphasize individual autonomy and do not amount to the recognition of property rights in genetic materials. But should limited property rights be recognized in an individual's genetic materials?[188] This issue was considered in the Model Genetic Privacy Act (MGPA) proposed for the USA by Patricia Roche,

---

180 Chapters 2 and 3 argued for a limited property interest in one's body.

181 *John Moore v. The Regents of the University of California* (1990) 793 P. 2d 497.

182 As argued below, it is also possible to protect genes by the recognition of limited property interests in them.

183 I. Ellis and G. Mannion, 'Humanity versus Utility in the Ethics of Research on Human Genetic Material' (2001) 1 No. 5 *Genetics Law Monitor* 2: 'human DNA, especially in terms of the public's perception of its potential should be subject to stringent safeguards.'

184 Council for International Organizations of Medical Sciences (CIOMS): *International Ethical Guidelines for Biomedical Research Involving Human Subjects*, 2002 Revised Draft posted on http://www.cioms.ch/guidelines_sept_2002_fp.htm (last visited on 20 September 2002).

185 CIOMS, *ibid.*

186 *Ibid.*

187 *Tri-Council Policy Statement on Ethical Conduct for Research Involving Humans* (Medical Research Council, Natural Sciences and Engineering and Social Sciences and Humanities Research Council of Canada: Ottawa, 1998).

188 The Australian Law Reform Commission recognized the benefits of a property approach:

Leonard Glantz and George Annas in 1996.[189] The MGPA was proposed as a federal legislation and intended to serve as a model for states in the USA that would want to regulate the collection, storage and analysis of identifiable DNA samples.[190] Section 104(a) of the MGPA provided that 'an individually identifiable DNA sample is the property of the sample source'. The authors of the MGPA stated that:

> By establishing an individually identifiable sample as the property of the sample source, the GPA (Genetic Privacy Act) serves not only the interest of those who would want to maintain exclusive control over their DNA, but also enables those who desire to share or transfer such control to do so. This ability is particularly important to individuals who are concerned with preserving their own samples for the future use and benefit of relatives and descendants…Owning one's own DNA sample allows transfer of control in accordance with property law principles.[191]

The MGPA is influential and has inspired legislation in some of the states of the USA. In 1996, Governor Christie Whitman of New Jersey vetoed a New Jersey bill that recognized an individual's property rights in his or her genetic information.[192] In 1995, a similar legislation was passed in the state of Oregon recognizing the existence of property rights in one's genetic materials.[193] In 2001, however, Oregon amended its law to withdraw the recognition of property interest in genetic materials.[194] By virtue of the amendment, interests in genetic materials would now be protected under laws relating to privacy.[195] The protection of genetic materials under a property framework raises problems relating to the objectification and commodification of the body. Recognition of property rights in the human body may lead to the exploitation of the poor. For instance, some poor people might feel compelled to sell their body parts to meet their needs for subsistence. But the poor could see this argument as unduly paternalistic. Where the only means of surviving is selling a non-life threatening body part, is it ethical to prevent the poor from doing so?

The Australian Law Reform Commission considered the appropriateness of a property framework to genetic materials and observed that 'if full property rights

---

> [t]he Inquiry considers it important to regulate the use of human genetic samples in order to ensure adequate protection of genetic information. In seeking to meet this goal, property rights have some clear benefits; they clarify the legal rights of donor and recipient; they facilitate on-going control by the donor until such time as the property is alienated; they enable the donor or other property owner to seek legal remedies for unlawful interference with propriety rights; and they enable a donor to share in the financial benefits that may accrue from use of the tissue.

ALRC, *supra*, note 11, at 534.

189 P. Roche, L. Glantz and G. Annas, 'The Genetic Privacy Act: A Proposal for National Legislation' (1996) 31 *Jurimetrics* 1.

190 P. Roche, in Knoppers, *supra*, note 10, at 34.

191 G. Annas, L. Glantz and P. Roche, 'Drafting the Genetic Privacy Act; Science, Policy and Practical Considerations' (1995) 23 *Journal of Law, Medicine and Ethics* 360, at 363.

192 P. Roche, in Knoppers, *supra*, note 10, at 33.

193 *Oregon Genetic Privacy Act, 1995 (US) § 4(1).*

194 Roche, in Knoopers, *supra*, note 10, at 33.

195 See *§ 15 Senate Bill 114 of 2001 (Oregon).*

existed in genetic material, its owner could sell it to the highest bidder'.[196] The ALRC was also worried that a property approach would adversely affect 'the current system of altruistic donation of samples for research, a situation might develop whereby researchers would have to bid for access to genetic material'.[197] Moreover, the ALRC was concerned that the liability to execution, which is an important incident of a property right, would not exist with respect to tissue samples since 'it is unlikely that the legal system would countenance seizure of someone's genetic material to satisfy a judgment debt'.[198] The ALRC also observed that the inalienability of genetic samples might make property protection inappropriate.[199] As argued in Chapter 2, some of the objections above can be taken care of by establishing only a limited property right in the human genetic material by excluding some of the incidents of property, such as the right of sale.[200] Though the ALRC considered the possibility of eliminating some of the unwanted incidents of property, it nevertheless adopted an approach that favours protection of human genetic materials under the Australian *Privacy Act*.[201]

Genes as Information

If, on the other hand, we fail to analogize genes or DNA data to tissue samples and genetic materials, it is still possible to argue that genes are mere information or data that are properly recognizable as informational property. Are there property rights to genetic information? The existence and extent of property in information is hugely controversial, and much more so in the context of genetics. The approach under this issue is first, to consider the status of genetic information under some biomedical research guidelines and practice; the possibility of regarding genetic information as

---

196 ALRC, *supra*, note 11, at 529.

197 *Ibid.*, at 529.

198 *Ibid.*, at 529.

199 *Ibid.*, at 529.

200 The suggestion for a limited property right to the human body was analysed in detail in Chapter 2. In support of a property rule, it has been observed that:

> From the perspective of protecting genetic privacy, it may be more effective to recognize ownership in regard to DNA samples, however, and not simply focus on the information derived from them. Rather than deter individuals from participating in research, particularly when it has commercial objectives, a recognized property interest in one's own DNA sample could give individuals an incentive to participate in research and experiments that would otherwise be of no possible benefit to them and ultimately benefit research and industry.

Roche, in Knoppers, *supra*, note 10, at 37.

201 It observed that: 'Some alternative property models proposed in submissions addressed a number of specific concerns by removing various incidents of property from the "bundle of rights" usually associated with property. However, once all the desirable limitations are imposed to obviate the adverse consequences of full ownership, the effect is very similar to the changes to the Privacy Act.' ALRC, *supra*, note 11, at 535. Recall that in Chapter 2, I addressed a similar problem by arguing that the elimination of some of the incidents of property is not incompatible with the use of a property approach.

family property; and then to consider current judicial and juristic analysis of property right in information.

Status of Genetic Information under Biomedical Research Guidelines and Practice

Biomedical research guidelines and practice draw a distinction between anonymized and non-anonymized genetic information and tissue sample. The protection given to a genetic material or information may vary depending on its nature, for example, whether it is anonymized or non-anonymized, the likelihood of cure for a particular genetic disorder that is tested, the likelihood of stigmatization arising from disclosure, and the familial character of the information. In recognizing the potential social and economic harms arising from genetic disclosures, Guideline 18 of CIOMS provides that the 'investigator must establish secure safeguards of the confidentiality of subjects' research data. Subjects should be told the limits, legal or other, to the investigators' ability to safeguard confidentiality and the possible consequences of breaches of confidentiality.'[202] Also, Article 8.2 of the *Tri-Council Policy Statement*[203] provides:

> The researcher and the REB shall ensure that results of genetic testing and genetic counselling records are protected from access by third parties, unless free and informed consent is given by the subject. Family information in databanks shall be coded so as to remove the possibility of identification of subjects within the bank itself.

Consequently, the researcher should 'inform the REB as to how the publication of data or other handling of such information will be accomplished. In particular, the researcher should clarify how subjects will be made aware of limitations to the protection of confidentiality.'[204]

It would appear that where a person's genetic information is anonymized, and there is no risk of his or her identification with the genetic data, such data may be used in a clinical or research setting without the need for an express consent or prior consent of the subject of the data.[205] As the commentary to Guideline 18 of CIOMS observed:

---

202 CIOMS, *supra*, note 184,

203 Tri-Council, *supra*, note 187.

204 *Ibid.*, commentary to Article 8.2.

205 This seems to be the practice adopted by some public health institutions with respect to stored tissue samples. For instance, Karen K. Steinberg, *et al.*, 'Use of Stored Tissue Samples for Genetic Research in Epidemiologic Studies', in Weir, ed., *supra*, note 25, at 82–8. But this principle may be unfair to a sample source where the genetic material is commercially valuable or was the subject of commercial research. Accordingly, it may make better sense to restrict the principle to cases of anonymized data used for public research purposes. It seems that one can consistently support the existence of limited property interest in the human body and argue for the unconsented use of anonymized genetic material. For instance, Patricia Roche, a co-author of the Model Genetic Privacy Act, observed:

> These prohibitions and restrictions on collection and analysis of DNA apply to activities involving *identifiable* DNA sample, including research. Consequently, enactment of these rules (Genetic Privacy Act – recognizing the existence of property

[b]efore performing a genetic test that is of known predictive value or gives reliable information about a known heritable condition, and individual consent or permission has not been obtained, investigators must see that biological samples are fully anonymized and unlinked.[206]

Article 10.3(b) of the *Tri-Council Policy Statement* is also in point:

When collected tissue has been provided by persons who are not individually identifiable (anonymous and anonymized tissue), and when there are no potential harms to them, there is no need to seek donor's permission to use their tissue for research purposes, unless applicable law so requires.

The UK Human Genetics Commission[207] and the English Court of Appeal[208] have taken a similar view on the question of proper use of anonymized data.

It is true that unauthorized disclosure of genetic information is likely to prejudice and impact on the privacy of the data subject and could harm him or her in other respects, for example, insurance and employment, but these detriments would mostly occur when the genetic data subject is sufficiently identifiable from the data. It would seem, therefore, that once anonymization is sufficiently accomplished, the privacy and confidentiality of the data subject is secured, and further objection to the use of the data based on property rights would be suspect.[209] Health and biomedical research, which aim at increasing the store of scientific knowledge and improving peoples' health, will be severely limited by a contrary rule. Under some prevailing research guidelines and practice, the property expectations of the source of an anonymized tissue sample or genetic information are, if they exist at all, significantly reduced. Because of this far-reaching conclusion, Ellis and Mannion have suggested that: '[I]f research is to occur on genetic samples that have come from unconsented sources, the samples must be anonymised and restricted to "passive" studies of the DNA sequence and subject to research ethics review.'[210]

---

rights in genetic materials) would not affect use of non-identifiable DNA samples for research because there are no privacy issues involved when samples are not and cannot be linked to an individual. (Italics in the original)

Roche, in Knoppers, *supra*, note 10, at 35–6.

206 CIOMS, *supra*, note 184.

207 Human Genetics Commission, *Inside Information: Balancing Interests in the Use of Personal Genetic Data* (A Report by the Human Genetics Commission, May 2002) at 91–101.

208 *R v. Department of Health, ex parte Source Informatics Ltd*, (2000) 1 All E.R. 786.

209 In this connection, Litman observed:

In the United States, proposed genetic privacy legislation characterizes 'individually identifiable' human genetic material as 'property' of its 'source'. Setting aside the wisdom of labeling human genetic material as property it is readily apparent that this legislation does not establish the legal character of non-identifiable human genetic material. While the legislation is not explicit on this matter, it seems to imply that non-identifiable human genetic material is something other than property.

Litman, in Knoppers, *supra*, note 10, at 18.

210 Ellis and Mannion, *supra*, note 183, at 3.

It should be noted that anonymization, despite its clear benefits, does not provide a complete and unproblematic solution to the ethical issues surrounding genetic research.[211] Even when anonymization is secured, Ellis and Mannion would rather restrict the research to 'passive studies', or usage, meaning that the 'DNA sample is only to be studied for its sequence data', and to be distinguished from 'active usage', which seeks to manipulate, transfer and replicate a DNA for commercial purposes.[212] According to them, the active use of an anonymized DNA sample from unconsented sources should be subject to more restrictions.[213] The commentary to Article 10.3 of the *Tri-Council Policy Statement* further underscores the ethical issues that may arise from unconsented use of an anonymized DNA sample or information:

> Though it may not be possible to identify the individuals who provided the tissue, other ethical issues may warrant scrutiny. Some individuals may not want their tissue used for any research purposes regardless of anonymity. The interests of biological relatives or members of distinct cultural groups or other communities may be adversely affected through research uses of their anonymous tissue. Issues may also arise concerning any duties, in extraordinary circumstances, to make traceable tissue identifiable for purposes of providing significant or beneficial information to those who have provided the tissue. Researchers should address such issues to the satisfaction of the REB.[214]

Despite the acknowledged ethical problems associated with the legitimate use of anonymized tissue samples and information derived from them, it seems clear that biomedical research practice and guidelines give little support to a litigant wishing to assert property rights to non-personally identifiable genetic information. But could such property support come from a familial analysis of genetic information?

Genetic Data as a Family Property

Family considerations may influence the attitude of law towards the protection of genetic information. By its intrinsic nature, genetic information usually carries a significant amount of a family's genetic secret. Some linkage studies may not be possible without the cooperation of members of a family, and a person may be in dire need of a family member's genetic information so as to make sufficient health care management plans. In these and similar circumstances, would it be reasonable to deny family members access to the genetic profile of one another? Can a person claim such sufficient ownership and control of his or her genetic data that would exclude its access by family members? It may be reasonable to regard a family's genetic make-up as a shared 'property' or 'family property'.

A person acquires his or her genetic profile because of biological membership of a given family. An exclusionary right given to a family member, with respect to his or her genetic data, would have the effect of converting what was part of the 'commons'

---

211 Jean E. McEwen, 'Storing Genes to Solve Crimes: Legal, Ethical, and Public Policy Considerations', in Weir, ed., *supra*, note 25, at 324.

212 Ellis and Mannion, *supra*, note 183, at 2.

213 *Ibid.*

214 Tri-Council, *supra*, note 187.

to a 'private' property. The familial nature of genetic information is recognized in Article 8 of the *Tri-Council Policy Statement*: 'Because genetic material is by its very nature shared by biological relatives, identifying a genetic causative agent has implications beyond the individuals. Thus, issues of privacy and confidentiality may affect the individual, the family and the group to which the individual belongs.'

In considering the liability of a physician or researcher for genetic disclosures to biological family members, it is desirable that the familial nature of the genetic information should outweigh the personal or private interests of a particular member.[215] The consent of a family member, however, should first be sought and obtained before genetic disclosure. The CIOMS Guidelines would seem to place an individual's consent above other family members' interest in a piece of genetic information. The commentary to Guideline 18 observes:

> Investigators should not disclose results of diagnostic genetic tests to relatives of subjects without the subjects' consent. In places where immediate family relatives would usually expect to be informed of such results, the research protocol, as approved or cleared by the ethical review committee, should indicate the precautions in place to prevent such disclosure of results without the subjects' consent; such plans should be clearly explained during the process of obtaining informed consent.[216]

Loane Skene has advocated a 'family model' approach to genetic data,[217] though Bell and Bennett[218] would prefer that the matter be left to common law[219] and legislation. In accordance with a family-centred approach, refusal by a family member to voluntarily disclose his or her genetic profile to another family member would justify a physician or researcher in making the needed genetic disclosures without incurring legal liability, provided that the genetic disorder involved is treatable or its risk of occurrence could be reduced or obviated by a timely health management plan. The advantage of a family approach to genetic disclosures is that it avoids some common law requirements, which would prohibit a good deal of genetic disclosures. As Loane Skene observed:

> I have some doubts about the adequacy of this little-tested principle [public interest exception to the confidentiality rule] in relation to genetic testing. First, the legal principle is narrower than that suggested by the Australian Medical Association's Code of Ethics...

---

215 Similarly, Litman observed that: 'It may even be that in exceptional circumstances persons other than the human sources of the genetic information, such as family members or First Nation polities, would be regarded as having a sufficient privacy interest to enforce confidentiality.' Litman, in Knoppers, *supra*, note 10, at 20.

216 CIOMS, *supra*, note 184.

217 Loane Skene, 'Genetic Secrets and the Family: a Response to Bell and Bennett' (2001) 9 *Medical Law Review* 162, at 165. Also L. Skene, 'Patients' Rights or Family Responsibilities? Two Approaches to Genetic Testing' (1998) 6 *Medical Law Review* 1.

218 D. Bell and B. Bennett, 'Genetic Secrets and the Family' (2001) 9 *Medical Law Review* 130.

219 As applied in *Tarasoff v. Regents of the University of California* 551 P. 2d 334 (1976); *W v. Egdell* (1990) 1 Ch. 359; *Pate v. Threlkel* 661 So. 2d 278 (1995); *Safer v. Pack* 677 A. 2d 1188 (1996).

The Code authorizes disclosure 'where the health of others is at risk.' The law [that is, common law] requires the risk to be serious and imminent. It is difficult to imagine a situation in which a genetic risk would be of this type. Take FAP (Familial Adenomatous Polyposis), for example, where in my view disclosure is most arguably justified. The risk is serious; it is a potentially lethal condition. The diagnosis is certain. And there is effective intervention (monitoring and surgery if needed). Yet the risk could not be described as imminent. For these reasons I do not believe the common law exception is sufficient.[220] (Brackets in the original)

The point, therefore, is that genetic information should be legally protected as a unique type of property: family property.

Judicial and Juristic Analysis of Information as Property

Finally, it is possible to argue that genes or genetic data are legally recognizable informational property. Larry Palmer has equally recommended the recognition of blood and genetic samples as data or information with potentially useful knowledge.[221] Unlike the view taken in this book, Larry Palmer opined that genetic information or data should be protected under existing liability rules whose flexibility confers on courts the special advantage of exploring the social contexts of research and the relationship between researchers and subjects.[222] The question, then, is whether genetic information, as distinct from genetic samples, is a legally protectable property?

Some legal systems have, of course, given protection to certain pieces of information in certain circumstances. For instance, civil law has consistently protected commercially valuable trade secrets and information given in confidence. It is not, however, easy to discern the basis upon which courts protect confidential information against disclosure. Even more difficult is the question of what constitutes confidential information. Ungoed-Thomas, J. recognized the difficulties in this area when he observed that English law on confidential information was not 'a well-developed jurisdiction'[223] and that the courts lack 'guides and tests to aid in exercising it'.[224] Despite this difficulty, the courts have been able to clearly articulate the elements of the cause of action for breach of confidence, though its theoretical underpinnings are far from settled.[225] Megarry, J. observed in *Coco v. A.N. Clark (Engineers)* that a claimant in an action for breach of confidence must establish that the information had the quality of confidence; the defendant knew or ought to have known that the information was confidential; and that the defendant used the

---

220 Skene, *supra*, note 217, at 168–9.

221 Larry I. Palmer, 'Should Liability Play a Role in Social Control of Biobanks' (2005) 33 *Journal of Law, Medicine & Ethics* 70.

222 *Ibid.*, at 76–7.

223 *Duchess of Argyll v. Duke of Argyll* (1967) Ch. 302, at 330.

224 *Ibid.*

225 *Saltman Engineering Con Ltd. v. Campbell Engineering Co. Ltd.* (1948) 65 R.P.C. 203; *Terrapin Ltd. v. Builders' Supply Co. (Hayes) Ltd.* (1960) R.P.C. 128.

information without authority and to the detriment of the plaintiff.[226] These principles were earlier adumbrated by Lord Denning in *Seager v. Copydex Ltd,*[227] where the learned justice seized the opportunity to rationalize the juridical basis of the law on confidential information. Accordingly, Lord Denning observed that the 'law on this subject (confidential information) does not depend on any implied contract. It depends on the broad principle of equity that he who has received information in confidence shall not take unfair advantage of it.'[228] Two years later in *Fraser v. Evans,*[229] Lord Denning re-echoed the themes of conscience and fairness as the bases of judicial intervention in actions relating to breach of confidence. He opined that the jurisdiction of courts in cases of confidential information is neither based on property nor contract but on the duty to be of good faith.[230] This apparent consistency in judicial analysis is thwarted by the unexplored proprietorial theme that crept into the reasoning of Lord Denning in *Seager v. Copydex Ltd. (No. 2),*[231] and tends to blur the otherwise clear picture of equitable intervention based on conscience: 'The property so far as there is property in it (confidential information), would vest in them (defendants after paying damages). They would have the right to use that confidential information for the manufacture of carpet grips and selling them.'

What apparently could be described as Lord Denning's powerful instincts for property protection of information in *Seager's* case (No. 2) received a much fuller analysis and exposition in the famous House of Lords case of *Boardman v. Phipps.*[232] In that case, the appellants (a solicitor to a trust and a beneficiary under the trust) acted in a representative capacity for the trustees of a certain trust, in the course of which they obtained valuable information regarding a private company. Honestly believing that the trustees were not interested in the commercial exploitation of that information, the appellants used the information to their own financial advantage by making profitable investments in the private company. One of the beneficiaries of the trust sued the appellants for an account of profit as constructive trustees. Part of the issues raised in the House of Lords was whether the information obtained by the appellants was trust property for which they were liable to account as constructive trustees? Although the House of Lords eventually decided against the appellants by a majority of three to two (Viscount Dilhorne and Lord Upjohn dissenting), an equal majority of the House of Lords decided in favour of information as property. It is interesting to observe that though Viscount Dilhorne and Lord Upjohn agreed in their dissenting judgements that the appellants were not, in the circumstances, liable as constructive trustees, the two justices nevertheless disagreed on the question of whether information could be characterized as property. On that question, Lords Hodson, Guest and Viscount Dilhorne gave an affirmative answer. Viscount Dilhorne

---

226 *Coco v. A.N. Clark (Engineers) Ltd.* (1968) F.S.R. 415, at 419; *Attorney General v. Guardian Newspapers Ltd (No. 2)* (1990) 1 A.C. 109, at 281 (HL).

227 *Seager v. Copydex Ltd* (1967) 1 W.L.R. 923.

228 *Ibid.,* at 932.

229 *Fraser v. Evans* (1969) 1 All E.R. 8, at 11.

230 See Assafa Endeshaw, 'Theft of Information Revisited' (1997) *Jour. Bus. L.* 187 (arguing that jurisdiction relating to confidential information should be based on property).

231 *Seager v. Copydex Ltd. (No. 2)* (1969) 1 W.L.R. 809.

232 *Boardman v. Phipps* (1967) 2 A.C. 46.

was of the view that: 'While it may be that some information and knowledge can properly be regarded as property, I do not think that the information supplied...and obtained by Mr Boardman as to the affairs of that company is to be regarded as property of the trust.'[233] Lord Hodson put it even more emphatically:

> I dissent from the view that information is of its nature something which is not properly to be described as property. We are aware that what is called 'know-how' in the commercial sense is property which may be very valuable as an asset. I agree...that the confidential information acquired in this case which was capable of being and was turned to account can be properly regarded as the property of the trust.[234]

Lord Guest also concurred with the above observations, holding that: 'I see no reason why information and knowledge cannot be trust property.'[235] This bright picture of support for information as property is dimmed by the dissenting judgements of Lords Cohen[236] and Upjohn (on the issue of whether information was property). Lord Upjohn very clearly articulated the view that information is not property:

> In general, information is not property at all. It is normally open to all who have eyes to read and ears to hear. The true test is to determine in what circumstances the information has been acquired. If it has been acquired in such circumstances that it would be a breach of confidence to disclose it to another then courts of equity will restrain the recipient from communicating it to another. In such a case such confidential information is often and for many years has been described as the property of the donor, the books of authority are full of such references; knowledge of secret processes, 'know-how,' confidential information as to the prospects of a company or of someone's intention or the expected results of some horse race based on stable or other confidential information. But in the end the real truth is that it is not property in any normal sense but equity will restrain its transmission to another if in breach of some confidential relationship.[237]

The lack of unanimity in *Boardman's* case does not provide sufficient anchorage for the proposition that English law regards valuable information as property. In fact, any hope that future development of English law on confidence will be in the direction of property was dashed by the observation of Sir Nicholas Browne-Wilkinson V.-C. (as he then was) in *Stephens v. Avery*[238] that 'the basis of equitable intervention to protect confidentiality is that it is unconscionable for a person who has received information on the basis that it is confidential subsequently to reveal that information'.

Rather than property, the *Human Rights Act, 1998* is now the driving force of current developments relating to English law on confidential information. The *Human Rights Act, 1998* incorporated Articles 8 and 10 of the *European Convention for the Protection of Human Rights and Fundamental Freedoms*. Articles 8 and 10 of the Convention, however, show some tension in that while Article 8 protects

---

233 *Ibid.*, at 89–90.
234 *Ibid.*, at 107.
235 *Ibid.*, at 115.
236 *Ibid.*, at 102–103.
237 *Ibid.*, at 127–8.
238 *Stephens v. Avery* (1988) Ch. 449, at 456.

private and family life, Article 10 protects the freedom of expression. What appears, however, to be clear is that any judicial analysis of the law of confidence ought to be in the context of right to privacy and freedom of expression granted by the *Human Rights Act*. It seems, therefore, that modern English law on confidence is based on the twin, though paradoxical, need to protect an individual's right to privacy, and freedom of expression. The privacy rationalization of confidence has received both enormous judicial approval and academic criticism.[239] In *A v. B Plc*,[240] the Court of Appeal had to consider the propriety of an injunction prohibiting the publication of the claimant's sexual relationship with two women. The injunction had earlier been obtained on the ground that the information was confidential and protected by Article 8 of the Convention. Lord Woolf, C.J observed:

> The application for interim injunctions have now to be considered in the context of articles 8 and 10 of the European Convention for the Protection of Human Rights and Fundamental Freedoms. These articles have provided new parameters within which the court will decide, in an action for breach of confidence, whether a person is entitled to have his privacy protected by the court or whether the restriction of freedom of expression which such protection involves cannot be justified. The court's approach to the issues which the application raises has been modified because, under section 6 of the 1998 Act, the court, as a public authority, is required not to act 'in a way which is incompatible with a Convention right.' The court is able to achieve this by absorbing the rights which articles 8 and 10 protect into the long-established action for breach of confidence. This involves giving a new strength and breadth to the action so that it accommodates the requirements of those articles.

Lord Woolf's privacy approach to confidential information was endorsed by the House of Lords in *Campbell v. MGN Ltd.*,[241] and again by the Court of Appeal in *Douglas v. Hello! Ltd.*[242]

Much as the analysis above shows judicial disinclination to the use of a property framework as a basis for the law on confidence, the question remains as to whether there is a compelling need to protect information as property? Are the cases above convincing? Property right to information is emerging as a hotly debated area of law. This is not surprising since we live in a knowledge-based global economy. As argued in this book, there seems to be no reason in principle why the flexible qualities of property should not be applicable to commercially or medically valuable information; such pieces of information can be transferred for value and thus possess an essential characteristic of property rights. Thus, Catherine Barrad was right in her suggestion that genetic information is a legally protectable property because it

---

239 Jonathan Morgan, 'Privacy in the House of Lords, Again' (2004) 120 *L.Q. R.* 563.

240 *A v. B Plc* (2003) QB 195. Professor Phillipson has criticized this decision for failing to develop a specific right to privacy under English law: Gavin Phillipson, 'Judicial Reasoning in Breach of Confidence Cases under the Human Rights Act: Not Taking Privacy Seriously' (2003) *European H. R. L. Rev.* 53.

241 *Campbell v. MGN Ltd.* (2004) 2 A.C. 457.

242 *Douglas v. Hello! Ltd* (2005) 3 W.L.R. 881, at 905.

shares some of the characteristics of property and scales through the justificatory theories of property.[243]

Property is an ingenious legal device that is sufficiently malleable to meet the needs of a fast-growing and information-oriented global society. It is essentially a 'legal characterisation, a statement that the court has chosen to assign a particular form of protection to the interest in question'.[244] Accordingly, it appears that upon the acceptance that a piece of information is worthy of protection because of its social, commercial or personal importance, nothing conceptually prevents the court from assigning it to the category property and the protection that comes from that description.

Today many companies thrive on their commercially valuable information. A company's competitive edge over others may depend on its possession of certain informational assets. The courts routinely protect corporations' assets, such as buildings, machinery and products. It is obviously absurd that judicial protection is available to a company's physical building and machinery but not its informational capital.[245] It is for similar reasons that Arnold Weinrib has suggested in a tightly argued article that a 'legal system that fails to recognize that information itself can be stolen is simply out of touch with the role of information in modern commercial practice'.[246] Information relating to certain genes provides the bedrock of biotechnology industries and is usually protected under patent legislation. Though such pieces of information qualify as property under patent law, it is only after the satisfaction of patent criteria relating to novelty, non-obviousness, industrial application and subject-matter patentability. There is still need, therefore, to determine whether genetically valuable information could be protected outside the confines of intellectual property law. It seems that a sophisticated legal system would be too anachronistic not to recognize the dynamics of modern business and the role of information in the digital age.

The courts, however, have not always treated information as property. We saw that from an examination of some of the English cases relating to confidence. Regrettably, even cases decided outside the law of confidence seem to be to the same effect. *Oxford v. Moss*[247] is one of the earliest commonwealth cases where the question of a property right in information was directly in issue. In that case, a former undergraduate civil engineering student at the University of Liverpool dishonestly obtained an engineering examination question paper ahead of the examination. He read the questions and returned the examination paper. It was accepted by all sides and the court that there was no intention to steal the paper itself, which was the property of the Senate of the University of Liverpool. So, the only question was whether the accused stole the confidential information that the examination paper contained.

---

243 Catherine M. V. Barrad, 'Genetic Information and Property Theory' (1993) 87 *Nw. U.L. Rev.* 1037.

244 Arnold S. Weinrib, 'Information and Property' (1988) 38 *U.T.L.J.* 117, at 120.

245 For a similar analysis and suggestion for the criminalization of theft of information: Jon Lang, 'Secrets, Strategies, and Proposals for Reform in the United Kingdom' (2002) 8 *C.T.L.R.* 193.

246 Weinrib, *supra*, note 244, at 142.

247 *Oxford v. Moss* (1979) 68 Cr. App. R. 183.

The trial magistrate acquitted the accused on the basis that information was not intangible property capable of being stolen under the *English Theft Act 1968*. The prosecutor's appeal against the order of acquittal was dismissed by the Divisional Court. *Oxford's* case provided clear guidance in the commonwealth until the middle 1980s when divisions on the appropriate legal characterization of information began to emerge in Canada.

The Canadian position was initially stated by *R v. Stewart*.[248] The accused had persuaded an employee of a company to surreptitiously obtain for the accused personnel information stored in the company's computer. He was charged with counselling the offence of theft under the *Canadian Criminal Code*. He was acquitted by the trial court, but the Ontario Court of Appeal reversed the acquittal, holding that misappropriation of confidential information can be the basis of a charge of theft under the *Canadian Criminal Code*. Three years later, the Alberta Court of Appeal in *R v. Offley*[249] refused to follow the earlier decision in *Stewart's* case and held that information was not property capable of being stolen. These conflicting precedents were the source of great uncertainty on the proprietorial character of information in Canada until the Supreme Court's decision in *R v. Stewart*.[250] The Supreme Court of Canada, in reversing the Ontario Court of Appeal, upheld the trial court's decision that information was not property under the *Canadian Criminal Code*. The Supreme Court of Canada explored policy challenges attendant upon the recognition of information as property for criminal purposes and opined that the matter is more amenable to legislative, rather than judicial, solution.[251] It could be said now, on the basis of the Supreme Court's decision in *Stewart's* case, that Canada and England share the same position on the question of property right to information.

A recent English case, *R v. Department of Health, ex parte Source Informatics Ltd*,[252] further supports the proposition that there is no property right to information. Source Informatics was a data company concerned with gathering medical prescription information that could be helpful in studying the prescription habits of medical doctors. It usually sold this type of information to pharmaceutical companies, which could use it for more effective marketing of their products. To obtain the prescription information, Source Informatics cooperated with medical doctors and pharmacists, who were modestly remunerated. The pharmacists supplied Source Informatics with all the information on the medical prescription forms of patients, save the patients' names, that is, the information was anonymized. Source Informatics would then process the information, put it in its database and ultimately sell it to pharmaceutical companies.

The Department of Health (UK) issued a policy statement indicating that the pharmacists and doctors cooperating with Source Informatics risked breaching their duty of confidentiality to their patients. Source Informatics therefore sought a

---

248 *R v. Stewart* (1983) 149 D.L.R. (3d) 583.

249 *R v. Offley* (1986) 28 C.C.C. (3d) 1.

250 *R v. Stewart* (1988) N.R. 171 (SCC).

251 Grant Hammond, 'Theft of Information' (1988) *LQR* 527; William L. Hayhurst, 'Confidential Information – No Theft of Intellectual Property' (1989) 11 *E.I.P.R.* 42.

252 (2000) 1 All E.R. 786.

declaration that: 'disclosure by doctors or pharmacists to a third party of anonymous information, that is information from which the identity of patients may not be determined, does not constitute a breach of confidentiality.'[253] The trial court refused to grant the declaration holding, *inter alia*, that anonymization does not obviate the duty of confidence owed to patients by doctors and pharmacists.[254] On Appeal to the Court of Appeal, Civil Division, Simon Brown, L.J., in overruling the trial court, observed:

> What interest, one must ask, is the law here concerned to protect? In my judgment the answer is plain. The concern of the law is to protect the confider's personal privacy. That and that alone is the right at issue in this case. The patient has no proprietorial claim to the prescription form or to the information it contains. Of course he can bestow or withhold his custom as he pleases – the pharmacist, note, has no such right: he is by law bound to dispense to whoever presents the prescription. But that gives the patient no property in the information and no right to control its use provided only and always that his privacy is not put at risk. I referred earlier to Mr Sales' plea for respect for 'the patient's autonomy.' At first blush the submission is a beguiling one. My difficulty with it, however, is in understanding how the patient's autonomy is compromised by Source's scheme. If, as I conclude, his only legitimate interest is in the protection of his privacy and if that is safeguarded, I fail to see how his will could be thwarted or his personal integrity undermined. By the same token that, in a case concerning government information, 'the principle of confidentiality can have no application to it…once it has entered…the public domain (per Lord Goff), so too in a case involving personal confidences I would hold by analogy that the confidence is not breached where the confider's identity is protected.[255]

Recently, in *Douglas v. Hello! Ltd.*,[256] the English Court of Appeal confirmed its rejection of a property approach to information in favour of privacy. In that case, the defendants published wedding photographs of Mr and Mrs Douglas without their consent. The couple had taken serious steps to make their wedding a private affair and, in order to avoid a media frenzy, they granted OK! Ltd. an exclusive licence to publish selected wedding photographs. The plaintiffs brought an action for breach of confidence, and unlawful interference with their commercial interest in their wedding photographs. In the course of the judgement at the Court of Appeal, Lord Phillips of Worth Matravers, MR had to consider whether confidential information possessed the characteristic of property:

> The starting point is to consider the nature of the rights enjoyed by the Douglases. As we have already indicated, their interest in the private information about events at the wedding did not amount to a right of intellectual property. The right to protection of that interest does not arise because they have some form of proprietary interest in it. If that were the nature of the right, it would be one that could be exercised against a third party

---

253 *Ibid.*, at 788.
254 *Ibid.*, at 789.
255 *Ibid.*, at 797.
256 *Douglas v. Hello! Ltd.* (No.3) (2005) 3 W.L.R. 881.

regardless of whether he ought to have been aware that the information was private or confidential. In fact, the right depends upon the effect on the third party's conscience.[257]

In contrast, the position in the USA is still evolving. One of the memorable cases that touch on the proprietary character of genetic information is *Pioneer Hi-Breed International v. Holden Foundation Seeds*.[258] In that case, the defendant improperly appropriated the genetic information imbedded in the plaintiff's hybrid corn seeds to develop its own inbred parent seed lines. Both the District Court and the Court of Appeal gave judgement for the plaintiff. In his concurring Court of Appeal judgement, Arnold, J. observed that 'Holden got the benefit of misappropriated property, and Pioneer lost the benefit of that property, when Holden infringed Pioneer's property rights in its trade secret'.[259] Though *Pioneer's* case arguably stands as an authority for the recognition of property rights in genetic information, its precedential value is limited by the use of trade secret as its theory of liability. Generally, a trade secret law covers information that is: 1. a trade secret; 2. secret acquired as a result of a confidential relationship; and 3. a secret used in an unauthorized manner.[260] It follows that information outside the confines of the itemization above is not protected, such as important genetic information without economic value, and genetic information improperly acquired from a patient or harvested from a tissue sample without the authority of the donor. For the same reason, it has been held that donated medical and genetic information compiled and stored in a Registry for specific medical research is not a trade secret.[261]

More recently, the United States District Court of Florida had the opportunity of considering the legal nature of genetic information in the case of *Greenberg v. Miami Children's Hospital Res. Inst.*[262] In that case, parents of children suffering from Canavan disease collaborated with researchers seeking to isolate the Canavan gene. The research also aimed at developing a prenatal and carrier test and, eventually, to find a cure for the disease. In pursuit of these objectives, the plaintiffs mobilized families suffering from Canavan disease and persuaded them to donate tissue samples and money for the research. The plaintiffs also opened a Canavan Registry: a confidential database and compilation containing epidemiological, medical and other information about the families of people with Canavan disease.

The plaintiffs, however, complained that after the successful isolation of the Canavan gene, the defendants patented the results of the research without the plaintiffs' knowledge or consent. The plaintiffs further complained that the defendants' restrictive licensing practices with regards to carrier and prenatal testing for Canavan disease were detrimental to the plaintiffs. Consequently, the

---

257 *Ibid.*, at 918. See John Hull and Sarah Abbott, 'Property Rights in Secrets – Douglas v. Hello! In the Court of Appeal' (2005) 27 *E.I.P.R.* 379.

258 *Pioneer Hi-Breed International v. Holden Foundation Seeds* 35 F. 3d 1226 (8th Cir. 1994).

259 *Ibid*, at 1247.

260 *Pioneer's* case, at 1235.

261 *Greenberg v. Miami Children's Hospital Res. Inst.* 264 F. Supp. 2d 1064 (S.D. Fla 2003), at 1077.

262 *Ibid.*

plaintiffs sought damages based on lack of informed consent; breach of fiduciary duty; unjust enrichment; fraudulent concealment; conversion; and misappropriation of trade secrets. The defendants' motion to dismiss the plaintiffs' claims succeeded, except with regards to the claim of unjust enrichment. Though it is true that the court refused to entertain the claim for conversion of genetic information contained in the Canavan Registry, it is pertinent to appreciate the basis of its decision and to determine whether it amounts to a denial of a property right to genetic information. A close reading of the *Greenberg's* Court decision on the conversion claim does not seem to offer an incontrovertible authority that there is no property right in genetic information or tissue samples.

On the contrary, it seems that the *Greenberg* Court recognized or indirectly accepted the existence of a property right in genetic samples and information but held, on the facts of that case, that any existing property right had been voluntarily and properly transferred to the defendants (tantamount to an abandonment of right). Accordingly, the *Greenberg* Court characterized the alleged body tissues and genetic information as 'donations to research without any contemporaneous expectations of return'.[263] The semantic formulation in terms of 'donation', which implies or expresses a 'gift', is meaningless absent underlying acceptance that only property can be donated. Certainly, the language of donation and gift is inexorably connected to property even in the context of body parts. As J.V. McHale observed, the 'links between the language of "gift" and the recognition that individuals have property in their human material have not gone unnoticed in the academic literature'.[264] On the basis that only items of property could be the subject of donation, *Greenberg's* case could be rationalized as holding that the plaintiffs, by their donation, had validly transferred their property right in the genetic samples and information to the defendants. This is supported by Justice Moreno's distinguishing of cases purporting to uphold property rights in body parts on the ground that those 'cases, however, do not involve voluntary donations to medical research'.[265] Even the donation rationale of the *Greenberg* Court is open to challenge since, according to Donna Gitter, the donation in that case could not be said to be voluntary absent prior information as to the true uses to which the research result was put.[266] Accordingly, the USA position is still evolving, and the *Havasupai* Court,[267] where the issue of conversion of genetic samples is raised, would most likely have the opportunity of revisiting the proprietorial character of genetic samples and information.

---

263 *Ibid.*, at 1074.

264 McHale, *supra*, note 2.

265 *Greenberg*, *supra*, note 261, at 1075.

266 Donna M. Gitter, 'Ownership of Human Tissue: A Proposal for Federal Recognition of Human Research Participants' Property Rights in their Biological Material' (2004) 61 *Wash. & Lee L. Rev.* 257, at 337.

267 *Havasupai* case, *supra*, note 21.

Conclusion

We have seen that the practice of DNA banking is increasing, and takes the pattern of private–public collaboration, especially in population-based studies. DNA banking has the potential of generating revenue, technical skills, jobs and modern scientific equipment for participating states. It may also stimulate the development of new therapies and new forms of genetic testing which would benefit the local population. There are also potential risks to DNA banking, such as those relating to exploitation, privacy, confidentiality and discrimination. These risks of harm become more acute in the context of a DNA bank in a developing country established at the instigation of a commercial corporation in an industrialized country. DNA banking also involves intricate property questions. Our earlier case studies show that the success of a particular DNA bank would partly depend on the extent of its respect for the above issues, and the degree of public participation through wide dissemination of relevant information and public debates. It is desirable for legislation establishing a DNA bank to specifically deal with the question of property rights to genetic samples and data. In the absence of such statutory resolution, the courts would have to deal with the issue whenever it arises. Current legal protection of genetic materials relies on the law relating to individual autonomy and informed consent. It is possible, however, to apply a property framework. To give a tissue source sufficient control over a genetic material, it is suggested that the law should recognize limited property rights in genetic materials and information.

Anonymized tissue samples from unconsenting sources could be used regardless of any potential property claims to them, though such uses should be passive. Anonymization secures the privacy interest of a sample source and thus performs part of the functions of a limited property rule. In other words, one may not need the operation of a property rule where there is sufficient anonymization of a tissue. Commercial and unconsented uses of anonymized genetic materials, however, may be unfair to the source of the material, though his or her privacy interest is secured. Thus, the unconsented use of anonymized materials may be restricted to public health research or non-commercial research and in other circumstances a sample source should be imbued with a limited property right. Genetic information should also be regarded as a shared family property. This would allow genetic disclosures to interested family members without an individual's consent, or upon that person's refusal to make a voluntary disclosure.

The Estonian case study suggests that some people may be willing to relinquish property rights over their tissues to their government for the purpose of DNA banking, provided full and informed consent is obtained from them. But the commercial profits potentially realizable from DNA banks suggest that some citizens may be eager to claim property rights over their samples in order to obtain a share of the profits. Any country wishing to nationalize its citizens' biologic samples through a DNA bank and without regard to their prior and informed consent would better learn from the Icelandic experience, where opposition to the Health Sector Database was centred on its provisions relating to presumed consent. Thus, it is suggested that population-based genetic studies should be preceded by adequate public debate on the attendant issues, including the resolution of property rights over DNA samples.

Finally, despite current judicial aversion to the notion of informational property, it is suggested that there is nothing conceptually extraordinary in recognizing, at least, a limited property right in valuable information.

Chapter 5

Remedies for Interference with Dead Bodies and Body Parts: Property and Non-Property Approaches

Introduction

It was suggested in the previous chapters that the remedial difficulties faced by a litigant complaining of interference with his or her body part or that of a deceased relative justify the recognition of a limited property interest in the human body. This chapter, therefore, proposes to consider both property and non-property remedies available to a potential plaintiff, with a view to highlighting their comparative advantages and weaknesses. These remedies include liability for nervous shock or psychiatric injury, privacy, human right or constitutional law remedies, consent and informed consent, unjust enrichment and conversion. The remedies are not, however, mutually exclusive and a plaintiff is strongly advised to pursue the whole range of remedies available to him or her, both proprietary and non-proprietary.

Nervous Shock or Psychiatric Injury

It is not difficult to imagine that mistreatment of a dead body or a part of it would cause acute emotional grief or some psychiatric injury to concerned relatives. Redress for such complaints comes through tort law relating to the infliction of nervous shock or psychiatric injury.[1] The guiding principles, however, are shrouded in an artificiality that is driven by policy considerations. That cautious pragmatism, rather than principle, is the goal in this area of law is underscored by the declaration of Lord Hoffmann in *White v. Chief Constable of South Yorkshire*:[2] 'It seems to me that in this area of the law, the search for principle was called off in *Alcock v. Chief Constable of Yorkshire Police*…No one can pretend that the existing law, which your Lordships have to accept, is founded upon principle.' Accordingly, it is appropriate to sketch the development of the law on nervous shock to see how policy considerations have shaped the courts' practical approach.

Nervous shock is the apprehension of a sudden terror that results in provable or recognizable psychiatric illness. According to Lord Ackner in *Alcock v. Chief*

---

1   Nicholas J. Mullany and Peter R. Handford, *Tort Liability for Psychiatric Damage: The Law of Nervous Shock* (Sydney: The Law Book Company Ltd., 1993).

2   *White v. Chief Constable of South Yorkshire* (1999) 2 A.C. 455, at 511.

Constable of South Yorkshire Police,[3] it 'involves the sudden appreciation by sight or sound of a terrifying event, which violently agitates the mind'. Thus, nervous shock would not include cases of 'cumulative shock', such as where the assault on the nervous system was caused by the accumulated effects of a negligent conduct.[4] The infliction of nervous shock or psychiatric injury could be intentional or negligent. Intentional infliction of nervous shock derives its existence, as a cause of action, from the case of *Wilkinson v. Downton*,[5] where in furtherance of a practical but expensive joke, the defendant told the plaintiff that the plaintiff's husband broke his legs in an accident, and was lying in hospital wanting the plaintiff to come and fetch him. In consequence of these deliberate but false statements, the plaintiff sent some people by rail to get her husband. She suffered violent attack on her nervous system and became seriously ill. She sued the defendant for damages. Because there was no precedent for plaintiff's claim, Wright, J. was challenged in formulating a legal basis for plaintiff's redress. In stating that the case was not one of fraudulent deceit, because of the remoteness of damage, Wright, J. observed that the plaintiff would succeed if she proved that the defendant had 'wilfully done an act calculated to cause physical harm to the plaintiff, that is to say, to infringe her legal right to personal safety, and has in fact thereby caused physical harm to her'.[6] He found on the facts that these elements were proved and that the plaintiff was entitled to judgement.

It is important to emphasize the elements of the cause of action established in *Wilkinson's* case because of their possible extension to cases involving dead bodies and body parts. *Wilkinson v. Downton* was a pure case of an intentional tort for which proof of a deliberate and intentionally tortious conduct is fundamental. As in all intentional torts, the court would be concerned with showing that, on the evidence, the defendant acted intentionally rather than negligently. As Wright, J. observed in *Wilkinson's* case, the test of intention is 'whether the defendant's act was so plainly calculated to produce some effect of the kind which was produced that an intention to produce it ought to be imputed to the defendant'.[7] This is not a test of foreseeability of harm in negligence, but a question of intention determined by an inquiry relating to whether the defendant desired (as opposed to foreseeing) the consequences of his conduct or realized with substantial certainty that those consequences would follow. The defendant's liability in *Wilkinson's* case was not based on any foresight of injury but on the imputed knowledge that psychiatric harm was certain to happen. Accordingly, Lord Jauncey of Tullichettle in *Page v. Smith*[8] seems, with respect, to have misconceived the above quotation when he observed in reference thereto: 'I take from this passage that the judge thought it appropriate to apply the foreseeability test in the context of a person of normal susceptibility to such an act.'[9] It is, however,

---

3   *Alcock v. Chief Constable of South Yorkshire Police* (1992) 1 A.C. 310, at 401.

4   K.J. Nasir has argued that type of nervous shock should be recoverable: K.J. Nasir, 'Nervous Shock and Alcock: The Judicial Buck Stops Here' (1992) 55 *M.L.R.* 705, at 709.

5   *Wilkinson v. Downton* (1897) 2 Q.B. 57.

6   *Ibid.*, at 58–9.

7   *Ibid.*, at 59.

8   *Page v. Smith* (1996) A.C. 155.

9   *Ibid.*, at 177.

arguable that *Wilkinson's* case was one of negligence and not intentional tort. The House of Lords decision in *Wainwright v. Home Office*[10] probably supports such a contention. In that case, the plaintiffs complained that they suffered emotional distress (and psychiatric injury by one of them) as a result of being strip-searched by prison officers. They (plaintiffs) argued that the prison officers acted intentionally to the detriment of the plaintiffs and that they were entitled to succeed under the rule in *Wilkinson v. Downton*. Lord Hoffmann rejected this argument and underscored the negligence basis of *Wilkinson v. Downton*: 'Downton obviously did not intend to cause any kind of injury but merely to give Mrs Wilkinson a fright.'[11] Though this observation conflicts with the finding of imputed intent by Wright, J. in *Wilkinson v. Downton*, and the view of some academic commentators that *Wilkinson's* case created an intentional tort,[12] Lord Hoffmann firmly opined that it was a case of negligence:

> By the time of *Janvier v Sweeney* (1919) 2 KB 316, therefore, the law was able comfortably to accommodate the facts of *Wilkinson v Downton*…in the law of nervous shock caused by negligence. It was unnecessary to fashion a tort of intention or to discuss what the requisite intention, actual or imputed, should be. Indeed, the remark of Duke LJ to which I have referred suggests that he did not take seriously the idea that Downton had in any sense intended to cause injury.[13]

It may be too early to dismiss *Wilkinson's* case as creating a category of an intentional tort, since the House of Lords in *Wainwright's* case accepted that the prison officers acted in good faith and that their unacceptable conduct was only sloppy.[14] In other words, *Wainwright's* case was not, on the facts, an appropriate case for the application of the decision in *Wilkinson v. Downton*.

Although *Wilkinson's* case was decided in the context of verbal declarations or spoken words, the *ratio* is capable of application to situations where psychiatric harm results from acts rather than words. For instance, liability might arise where a defendant maliciously and unlawfully opens the grave of a plaintiff's relative. In *Purdy v. Woznesensky*,[15] the plaintiff suffered nervous shock as a result of witnessing a violent assault on her husband by the defendant. The court held that the plaintiff was entitled to damages, although the language used was more appropriate to negligent infliction of nervous shock:

> [t]he defendant must be presumed to know of the vital concern which a wife instinctively feels for the safety of her husband and the serious physical reactions which an attack upon him threatening injuries to his person would in all likelihood produce in her. Hence I think he should have foreseen that by causing her to witness such a sudden and violent assault

---

10 *Wainwright v. Home Office* (2004) 2 A.C. 406.

11 *Ibid.*, at 424.

12 John G. Fleming, *The Law of Torts*, 9th edn (Sydney: LBC Information Services, 1998) 37–41; Lewis Klar, *Tort Law*, 3rd edn (Toronto: Carswell, 2003) 72–7.

13 Wainwright, *supra*, note 10, at 435.

14 *Ibid.*, at 427.

15 *Purdy v. Woznesensky* (1937) 2 W.W.R. 116 (Sask. CA).

as he made upon her husband he would probably upset her nervous system in such a way as to cause her some physical harm.[16]

Finally, a plaintiff must prove that he or she suffered some recognizable damage that was not remote. This proved to be a radical point in *Wilkinson's* case and the solution it adopted has contributed to the significance of the decision. Before *Wilkinson's* case, damages sounding in fright, grief and sorrow were not recognized even if resulting in some psychiatric injury. These primordial judicial attitudes are exemplified by both House of Lords and Privy Council's decisions. In *Lynch v. Knight*,[17] the plaintiff's step-brother slandered her before her husband by alleging that the plaintiff was guilty of gross levity before her marriage and was nearly seduced by another man. Acting on this slander, the plaintiff was sent away by her husband and she sued the defendant (her step-brother) for defamation. Because her action for slander was not actionable except on proof of a special damage, she alleged that her loss of consortium was a special damage sufficient to constitute an action for slander. Although Lord Chancellor Campbell, Lords Brougham and Cranworth were content to dismiss the action on the ground that loss of consortium was in the circumstances remote since no reasonable husband would be expected to chase away his wife on the same facts, Lord Wensleydale anchored his decision on a more doctrinal ground. He observed that English law recognized only material and pecuniary damages but not mental or sentimental injury. After noting that there were circumstances in which a wife could be likened to a servant and therefore capable of suffering some pecuniary injury, he opined that:

> It is to the protection of such material interests that the law chiefly attends. Mental pain and anxiety the law cannot value and does not pretend to redress, when unlawful act complained of causes that only; though, where a material damage occurs connected with it, it is impossible a jury, in estimating it, should altogether overlook the feelings of the party interested. For instance, where a daughter is seduced, however deeply the feelings of the parent may be affected by the wicked act of the seducer, the law gives no redress, unless the daughter is also a servant, the loss of whose service is a material damage which a jury has to estimate, and they cannot avoid considering the injured honour and wounded feelings of the parent in making that estimate.[18]

The non-recognition of psychiatric damage was also evident in the earlier House of Lords case of *Allsop v. Allsop*,[19] where it was held that mental suffering or psychiatric illness produced by slanderous words was not damage sufficient to sustain an action for slander. This proposition was approved in *Lynch v. Knight*.[20]

The infamous case of *Victorian Railways Commissioners v. Coultas*[21] puts the Privy Council on par with the House of Lords as regards damages for psychiatric injury. In that case, the plaintiffs were driving in a buggy when they got to a railway

---

16 *Ibid.*, at 119.
17 *Lynch v. Knight* (1861) 11 All E.R. 854 (HL).
18 *Ibid.*, at 863.
19 *Allsop v. Allsop* (1860) 5 H & N 534.
20 *Lynch v. Knight*, *supra*, note 17, per Lord Chancellor Campbell.
21 *Victorian Railways Commissioners v. Coultas* (1888) 13 App Cas 222.

level crossing. The gatekeeper (the defendant's employee) negligently allowed the plaintiffs to cross the line when a train was fast approaching. Fearing that they were in danger of imminent death, the female plaintiff fainted and suffered serious illness. Sir Richard Couch of the Privy Council dismissed the plaintiff's claim for damages:

> According to the evidence of the female plaintiff her fright was caused by seeing the train approaching, and thinking they were going to be killed. Damages arising from mere sudden terror unaccompanied by any actual physical injury, but occasioning a nervous or mental shock, cannot under such circumstances, their Lordships think, be considered a consequence which, in the ordinary course of things, would flow from the negligence of the gate-keeper. If it were held that they can, it appears to their Lordships that it would be extending the liability for negligence much beyond what that liability has hitherto been held to be.[22]

The Privy Council was obviously aware that it was making a practical decision based on policy considerations, such as the difficulties associated with the establishment and proof of mental distress and the likelihood of a floodgate of claims. For instance, it observed that the 'difficulty which now often exists in case of alleged physical injuries of determining whether they were caused by the negligent act would be greatly increased, and a wide field opened for imaginary claims'.[23] Although some of these reasons are no longer tenable, they proved very formidable at the time when *Wilkinson v. Downton* came for decision. In confronting the precedents above, Wright, J. (in *Wilkinson's* case) held that the *Victorian* case was not relevant since no wilful conduct was involved, and the cases of *Lynch* and *Allsop* were not controlling because they involved special considerations (special damages for slander) which were not relevant to *Wilkinson's* case. He remarked that the psychiatric injury in *Wilkinson's* case was 'so direct and natural a consequence of the defendant's conduct'[24] that the plaintiff was entitled to succeed. It is arguable that *Wilkinson's* case was not really a case of recognition of psychiatric injury since Wright, J. found as a fact that the plaintiff suffered actual physical harm. Wright, J. did not, however, base his decision on this narrow ground and was more inclined to a legal recognition of psychiatric injury that is a direct and probable consequence of the defendant's atrocious conduct:

> Suppose that a person is in a precarious and dangerous condition, and another person tells him that his physician has said that he has but a day to live. In such a case, if death ensued from the shock caused by the false statement, I cannot doubt that at this day the case might be one of criminal homicide, or that if a serious aggravation of illness ensued damages might be recovered.[25]

In summary, therefore, a plaintiff complaining of intentional infliction of nervous shock or psychiatric injury must establish that the defendant's acts or words

---

22 *Ibid.*
23 *Ibid.*
24 *Wilkinson, supra*, note 5, at 60.
25 *Ibid.*, at 60–61.

were intended or calculated to cause harm to the plaintiff. Before exploring the circumstances in which nervous shock could result from intentional mistreatment of corpses or body parts, it is proposed to examine the neighbouring cause of action known as negligent infliction of psychiatric injury.

As shown below, cases of negligent infliction of nervous shock or psychiatric injury are more preponderant than its intentional counterpart. Much as nervous shock or psychiatric injury has become a recognized category of negligence, it is still subject to the same principles that generally apply to actions for negligence. Thus, the plaintiff must prove that she suffered damage as a result of a breach of duty owed her by the defendant. In essence, the plaintiff must prove the existence of a duty of care, scope of the duty and its breach, causation, and damages that are not remote. In applying these principles to nervous shock, the courts are, however, guided more by practical considerations of policy and the need to ensure that the defendant's liability is not disproportionate to his fault. In *White v. Chief Constable of South Yorkshire Police*,[26] Lord Steyn adumbrated major policy factors that differentiate nervous shock cases from those of physical injury, and which make them deserving of special treatment in law. These factors include the difficulty of establishing psychiatric injury and the complexity of drawing a line between recoverable psychiatric injury and non-recoverable mental grief; the negative impact of litigation on recovery from psychiatric illness; increase in the class of potential plaintiffs (floodgates argument); and the prospect of liability that is disproportionate to fault. These considerations have underpinned judicially crafted controls on recovery popularly known as 'control mechanisms'. The artificiality and essentially pragmatic nature of the control mechanisms is echoed by Lord Hoffmann in *White's* case, where he observed that the 'control mechanisms' are 'more or less arbitrary conditions which a plaintiff had to satisfy and which were intended to keep liability within what was regarded as acceptable bounds'.[27] A look at the major cases on nervous shock would show how limitations on recovery were judicially developed in response to the dynamics of time, judicial attitude and medical knowledge.

In *Dulieu v. White*,[28] the plaintiff was pregnant and was behind the bar of a public house owned by her husband when a pair-house van was violently and negligently driven into the public house by the defendant's employees. Out of fear for her own safety, the plaintiff suffered severe nervous shock. She became seriously ill and subsequently gave birth to a premature baby. The defendant objected that the statement of claim did not disclose any cause of action and that the plaintiff's damage was too remote. The court rejected as unreasonable and contrary to authority a contention that psychiatric injury was not recoverable when it was the direct and probable consequence of a nervous shock caused by the defendant's negligence. In affirming the reality and seriousness of psychiatric injury, Kennedy, J. asked: 'Why is the accompaniment of physical injury essential?...I should not like to assume it to be scientifically true that a nervous shock which causes serious bodily illness is

---

26 *White, supra*, note 2, at 493–4.
27 *Ibid.*, at 502.
28 *Dulieu v. White* (1901) 2 K.B. 669 (KBD).

not actually accompanied by physical injury.'[29] Though the court allowed recovery in *Dulieu's* case, Kennedy, J. was anxious not to open a floodgate of litigation in this area:

> It is not, however, to be taken that in my view every nervous shock occasioned by negligence and producing physical injury to the sufferer gives a cause of action. There is, I am inclined to think, at least one limitation. The shock where it operates through the mind must be a shock which arises from a reasonable fear of immediate personal injury to oneself.[30]

Twenty-four years later the Court of Appeal shifted the boundary of recovery in *Hambrook v. Stokes Brothers*,[31] where a mother suffered nervous shock and serious illness when she saw an unmanned vehicle run down a hill, close to where her children were playing around the corner. Her shock was not provoked by fear for her own safety; she was concerned about the safety of her children. Eventually only one of them was hurt but the injury was not serious. The majority of the Court of Appeal held that she was entitled to succeed and that it was absurd to make a distinction between nervous shock suffered by a mother as a result of concern for her own safety and that resulting from concern for the safety of her child.

The first case to get to the House of Lords on nervous shock was *Bourhill v. Young*.[32] The plaintiff in that case alighted from a tram when she heard a collision involving a motor-cyclist and a car. The plaintiff later came to the scene of the accident and saw some blood on the road. She suffered nervous shock and claimed damages. Because she did not see the accident, the House of Lords held that it was not reasonably foreseeable that she would suffer nervous shock. *Bourhill's* case seemed to have emphasized the necessity for a plaintiff to be within sight of an accident, a requirement that was obviously meant to control the number of potential actions. In *McLoughlin v. O'Brian*,[33] however, the House of Lords seemed to have gradually liberalized the law on recovery for psychiatric injury claims. In that case, the plaintiff's husband and three children were involved in an accident which resulted in the death of the plaintiff's youngest child. Within an hour or two of the accident, the plaintiff was informed of the accident and she rushed to the hospital where her family members had been taken. She saw the husband and children in almost the state in which they were at the scene of accident and was informed that one of her children was dead. The plaintiff suffered severe shock resulting in psychiatric illness. If the House of Lords were to be faithful to earlier authorities, the plaintiff in *McLoughlin's* case would have failed since she neither witnessed the accident nor was within earshot of the accident (she was two miles away from the accident). The House of Lords, however, opined that logical progression of the common law demanded that presence at the scene of an accident would include coming upon its immediate aftermath. Lord Wilberforce recognized that an extension of common

---

29 *Ibid.*, at 677.
30 *Ibid.*, at 673.
31 *Hambrook v. Stokes Brothers* (1925) 1 K.B. 141.
32 *Bourhill v. Young* (1943) A.C. 92.
33 *McLoughlin v. O'Brian* (1983) 1 A.C. 410.

law was warranted where 'the plaintiff does not see or hear the incident but comes upon its immediate aftermath'.[34] The principles developed in *McLouglin's* case and previous cases were consolidated in *Alcock v. Chief Constable of South Yorkshire Police*.[35] *Alcock's* case was the judicial outcome of the Hillsborough football stadium disaster in 1989 which claimed 96 lives and caused injury to more than 400 people. The crushing resulted from the defendant's negligent crowd-control measures, a fact that was admitted by the defendant. The plaintiffs were relatives of the victims who learned about the accident from third parties, heard it on the radio, saw broadcast of the accident on the television (though pictures of suffering individuals were not shown) or were present in another part of the stadium. Conscious of the need to reduce the defendant's undue exposure to liability, the House of Lords held that foreseeability of psychiatric injury alone was not sufficient to found liability. In addition to foreseeability, the plaintiff must establish certain proximity factors which include: a. close tie of love and affection with the primary victim, such as exists between a husband and wife, and parent and child; b. the plaintiff must establish proximity to the accident in time and space, by being within sight and sound of the accident or coming upon its immediate aftermath; and c. the plaintiff must have directly perceived the accident and not have been merely informed of it by third parties. Because each of the plaintiffs in *Alcock's* case lacked one or two of these factors, their action was dismissed.

Another opportunity to pronounce on nervous shock presented itself to the House of Lords in *Page v. Smith*.[36] The plaintiff in that case, who was already suffering from chronic fatigue syndrome, was involved in a moderately severe accident with the defendant. Although their cars were damaged, nobody suffered any physical injury, and the plaintiff was able to drive home in his car after the accident. The plaintiff, however, suffered a recrudescence of his illness and sued for damages for the infliction of psychiatric injury. It was established that though the defendant foresaw physical injury to the plaintiff (which never materialized), he could not have foreseen any psychiatric harm. It was, therefore, argued by the defendant that foreseeability of psychiatric harm was required and that ought to militate against plaintiff's recovery. Lord Lloyd of Berwick rejected this submission by introducing the famous distinction between primary and secondary victims. He observed that in all the previous cases decided by the House of Lords on the matter, 'the plaintiff was the secondary victim of the defendant's negligence. He was or she was in the position of a spectator or bystander. In the present case, by contrast, the plaintiff was a participant. He was himself directly involved in the accident, and well within the range of foreseeable physical injury. He was the primary victim.'[37] The classification as to primary and secondary victims bears enormous legal consequences.[38] The most important one is that a primary victim is not subject to the control mechanisms: 'None

---

34 *Ibid.*, at 418.

35 Alcock, *supra*, note 3.

36 *Page v. Smith, supra*, note 8.

37 *Ibid.*, at 184.

38 Chris Hilson, 'Nervous Shock and the Categorisation of Victims' (1998) 6 *Tort L. Rev.* 37.

of these mechanisms are required in the case of a primary victim.'[39] Accordingly, it has become advantageous for plaintiffs to argue that they are primary victims of a negligent conduct. Because the House of Lords was not committed to any strict definition of these terms in *Page v. Smith* their applications in subsequent cases have been far from easy. For instance, in *White v. Chief Constable of Yorkshire Police*, an action brought by police officers who were involved in the Hillsborough disaster, the House of Lords was divided on the question of whether these police officers, who acted both in the course of their employment and as rescuers, qualified as primary victims. The majority of the House of Lords held that since the police officers were not exposed to any physical danger, they did not qualify as primary victims and were subject to the control mechanisms. Lord Steyn admitted that the 'law on the recovery of compensation for pure psychiatric harm is a patchwork quilt of distinctions which are difficult to justify'.[40] He alluded to the potential arbitrariness in the allocation of a plaintiff to the primary or secondary victim category, according to the dictates of justice and the need to forestall further expansion of law in this area: 'In my view the only sensible general strategy for the courts is to say thus far and no further. The only prudent course is to treat the pragmatic categories as reflected in authoritative decisions…as settled for the time being but by and large to leave any expansion or development in this corner of the law to Parliament.'[41] More recently in *W v. Essex County Council*,[42] where psychiatric illness was alleged to have resulted from the negligent placement of a young sexual abuser with the plaintiffs, the House of Lords cautioned that the 'categorisation of those claiming to be included as primary or secondary victims is not…finally closed'. This means that the law in this area is still evolving.

To summarize, for a plaintiff to succeed in an action for negligent infliction of nervous shock or psychiatric injury, he or she must prove to be a primary victim not subject to the control mechanisms. Otherwise, a plaintiff must establish: 1. a tie of love and affection between the plaintiff and the primary victim; 2. proximity in time and space to the accident or its immediate aftermath; 3. personal perception of the incident, rather than knowledge of it from a third party; 4. foreseeability of physical injury to a person of normal fortitude.

Having outlined the law relating to intentional and negligent infliction of nervous shock or psychiatric injury, the next task is to see how the analysis applies in the unique area of dead bodies and body parts. For this purpose, it is proposed to categorize the circumstances in which interference with a dead body or a part of the body could arguably give rise to nervous shock or psychiatric injury:

1. Where a defendant unlawfully opens the grave of a plaintiff's relative for the purpose of stealing grave goods or the corpse buried therein. This category would cover cases of grave-robbing that took place in the eighteenth and early nineteenth centuries (explored in Chapters 2 and 3). During that period a

---

39 *Page, supra*, note 8, at 189.
40 *White, supra*, note 2, at 500.
41 *Ibid.*
42 *W v. Essex County Council* (2001) 2 A.C. 592.

group of professional grave-robbers called resurrectionists stole freshly buried corpses which were sold to medical establishments for medical research and education. It would also cover any case where the disturbance of a grave is intended to annoy, provoke or cause acute emotional trauma. A case in point is the rude, unlawful and malicious disinterment of the body of 82-year-old Gladys Hammond by animal rights activists.[43] The body was unlawfully and maliciously taken from St Peter's churchyard in Yoxall, Staffs, where she was buried. The activists (the Animal Rights Militia) carried out the desecration of Mrs Hammond's corpse as a protest against her son-in-law, Mr Christopher Hall, who was involved in the breeding of guinea pigs for medical research.

2. Where a defendant interferes with a plaintiff's right to the possession of a corpse for the purpose of burial. This is a very important right for living relatives of a deceased person, since if physical possession of a corpse is not gained, disposition of the remains would be hampered. A person could be dispossessed of a corpse in a number of imaginable ways that result in nervous shock. For instance, a funeral director or crematory agency could detain a corpse for debts owed.[44] As we saw in Chapter 2, British common law once recognized the right of a creditor to detain the dead body of a debtor for debts due, though the rule was abolished in the early nineteenth century. Disagreements among family members concerning the disposition of the remains of a deceased person could result in the dispossession of a person legally entitled to possession of the corpse for burial.[45] Dispossession may also occur if the remains of a decedent are lost.[46]

3. Where a defendant interferes with a plaintiff's right to possess the deceased in the condition it was when life left it. Right to possession of a corpse for the purpose of burial would be meaningless in the absence of entitlement to the whole corpse the way it was at the time of death. This category of interference would include the mutilation of the corpse by way of unauthorized autopsy,[47] unauthorized retention of parts of a body after post-mortem,[48] and unauthorized harvesting of body organs and tissues from cadavers.[49] A plaintiff is also likely to suffer nervous shock when a corpse is negligently allowed to decompose and therefore becomes significantly different from the way it was at the time

---

43 BBC News, 'Search Resumes in Body Theft', posted on http://news.bbc.co.uk/2/hi/uk_news/england/Staffordshire/4553507.stm (last visited on 5 July 2006).

44 *Jefferson County Burial Society v. Scott* 188 So. 644 (1928); *Kirksey v. Jernigan* 45 So. 2d 188 (Fla. 1950); *Snyder v. Holy Cross Hosp.* 352 A. 2d 334.

45 *Andrews v. McGowan* 739 So. 2d 132 (Fla. Ct. App. 1999).

46 *Correa v. Maimonides Medical Center* 629 N.Y.S. 2d 673 (Sup. Ct. 1995).

47 *Miner v. C.P.R.* (1911) Alta. L.R. 408.

48 *AB v. Leeds Teaching Hospital NHS* (2005) 2 W.L.R. 358.

49 *Bauer v. North Fulton Medical Center* 527 S.E. 2d 240 (Ga. Ct. App. 1999).

of death.[50] This category also covers cases where a corpse was run over after death,[51] or incinerated negligently.[52]

4. Where a defendant interferes with a plaintiff's right to determine the time, manner and place of burial. Right to determine the time, place and manner of burial is a very important right, and deprivation thereof might result in psychiatric illness.[53]

5. Where a plaintiff was not notified of the deceased's death by the defendant. The withholding of death information from a person so entitled could result in mental anguish and psychiatric illness. In certain circumstances, a deceased's next of kin is entitled to reasonable notice of the deceased's death and unjustifiable failure to give this notice could result in legal liability for any consequent psychiatric harm. For instance, in *Finn v. The City of New York*,[54] the plaintiff suffered mental anguish when the City of New York, due to a lapse in its system of reporting deaths, failed to notify the plaintiff of her husband's death until eight days after his demise. Judge Sullivan observed:

But what of a situation where, as here, the anguish and torment were caused not by withholding the body but by withholding the fact of death. It is a fact that throughout the eight days of her husband's disappearance, plaintiff nurtured the hope and belief that he was still alive; she had no knowledge that he was dead and that his corpse was at the morgue in the custody of the City. Thus, her anguish was the result not of being deprived of the possession of his remains for proper burial, an injury which for its existence must be based on knowledge of the fact that death has occurred, but of not knowing of such occurrence. If the principle that one may not tortiously withhold a deceased's body is to have efficacy, then the law must recognize as a corollary thereof, and this court so holds, that one may not tortiously withhold notification of death.[55]

6. Where there is an interference with the right of repose. This refers to the right not to disturb the deceased's remains after burial by way of disinterment and re-interment, otherwise known as respect for the sanctity of the grave.[56] Psychiatric harm is conceivable where the remains of a deceased are disinterred even for lawful purposes, such as judicially sanctioned disinterment. This will be especially so where a mistreatment of the remains took place in the process of disinterment.[57]

Of all the six categories above, only the first category is most likely to give rise to the *Wilkinson v. Downton* cause of action for intentional infliction of psychiatric injury. The other categories, as shown by cases cited in their support, mainly raise

---

50 *Siver v. Rockingham Memorial Hospital* 48 F. Supp. 2d 609 (W.D. Va. 1999).

51 *Blanchard v. Brawley* 75 So. 2d 891 (La. Ct. App. 1954).

52 *Ibid.*

53 *Pyle v. Pyle* 531 S.E. 2d 738 (Ga. Ct. App. 2000).

54 *Finn v. The City of New York* 335 N.Y.S. 2d. 516 (1972).

55 *Ibid.*, at 521.

56 *Case of Elli Poluhas Dödsbo v. Sweden*, Application no. 61564/00 (judgement of the European Court of Human Rights (Second Section) on17 January 2006).

57 *Whitehair v. Highland Memorial Gardens* (1985) 327 S.E. 2d 439.

issues of negligent infliction of psychiatric injury. Even for the first category, the success of a *Wilkinson* claim depends on whether courts would accept that acts, as opposed to statements, could give rise to a *Wilkinson* claim. This is an important point for dead bodies litigation, since mistreatment of corpses usually arises from acts rather than statements. Despite academic support for the inclusion of 'acts' within the rubric of a *Wilkinson*-type claim,[58] the House of Lords seems to take a contrary view. For instance, Lord Hoffmann in *Wainright v. Home Office* agreed with the Court of Appeal that '*Wilkinson v. Downton* has nothing to do with trespass to the person'.[59] Although it is imaginable that certain false and malicious statements concerning a person's dead relative could give rise to mental distress, it is likely that the courts would regard any alleged psychiatric injury as remote. In contrast, malicious acts, such as the desecration of Mrs Hammond's grave, are likely to be construed by the courts as capable of giving rise to psychiatric illness. The point, however, is that success of a *Wilkinson*-type claim for mistreatment of a dead body is far from certain.

Since the remaining five categories sound in negligence, the plaintiff must prove all the elements of negligence in order to succeed. Most importantly, the plaintiff, except he or she is a primary victim, is subject to the control mechanisms, which impose limits on liability. This is a huge impediment to recovery by plaintiffs who bring an action for interference with the dead bodies of their relatives. Even where a plaintiff proves that he or she is a primary victim, the court could still deny recovery on the basis of a factual application of foreseeability test. Some of these difficulties are illustrated by the recent case of *AB v. Leeds Teaching Hospital NHS*.[60] This group action is the judicial upshot of the paediatric organ removal and retention scandal that rocked the UK between 1999 and 2000. The case was fought on the basis of three lead claims. All the plaintiffs were parents of deceased children whose organs were removed, retained and finally disposed of after post-mortem. Although the parents consented to the post-mortem, they allegedly did not consent to the removal and retention of their children's organs. They also claimed that during the consent process for post-mortem, they were not informed that organs would be removed and retained. Gage, J. also found as a fact that some of the parents expressly requested that they wanted the body of their children returned as a whole after post-mortem. Consequently, the plaintiffs claimed damages for unlawful interference with their children's dead bodies and for a breach of duty of care in negligence. Gage, J. accepted that the plaintiffs suffered a recognizable psychiatric injury in the form of adjustment disorder. With respect to the claim for unlawful interference with the body, Gage, J. held that it was in the nature of conversion of paediatric organs. He opined that conversion of the human body is not a recognized cause of action in England:

> Assuming that my conclusions are correct that the claimants have no right of burial and possession of organs lawfully removed at post mortem and retained, in my judgment,

---

58 For instance, Fleming, *supra*, note 12, at 37–41.

59 *Wainright v. Home Office*, *supra*, note 10, at 426.

60 *AB v. Leeds Teaching Hospital NHS*, *supra*, note 48.

there can be no action for wrongful interference with the body of the child. If, on the other hand, a parent or parents when consenting to a post mortem specifically asked for the return of an organ I can see that in certain circumstances it might be arguable that a cause of action based on conversion exists, if conversion is what is being alleged by the claimants in this group action. But in the absence of such a cause of action in respect of the body of a deceased person being recognised by an English court I am not prepared to hold that one does exist.[61]

Gage, J. recognized that the claimants' efforts to construct a novel cause of action for unlawful interference with the human body might have been borne by a desire to avoid the control mechanisms inherent in a negligence action: 'In those circumstances, where a claim for negligence can arise, I see no reason or justification for constructing another cause of action which is not subject to the various common law controls inherent in any claim in negligence.'[62] As regards the claim in negligence, the claimants alleged that they were primary victims not subject to the control mechanisms. On the other hand, the defendants claimed that the claimants were secondary victims and were not entitled to recover on the basis of applicable control mechanisms. In resolving this issue in favour of the claimants, Gage, J. observed:

> The question of whether a claimant is a primary or secondary victim is 'essentially a question of fact': per Lord Goff in the *Frost* case...Guided by the various passages in the above decisions my conclusion is that they properly fall into the category of primary victims. In reaching this conclusion the following factors are, in my opinion, relevant and important. First, unlike the secondary victims in the *Alcock* and *Frost* cases the foreseeability test in these claims can be applied before the event, the event being the obtaining of consent for a post mortem by the doctors. They are not cases where the test can only be conducted ex post facto. The claimants, at all times before and after that event are readily identifiable. Secondly, in my view there is force in the argument that the children were not primary victims. Neither the clinicians nor the pathologists could have owed any duty of care to them after their death. In my opinion, it follows that if claimants are victims at all they must be primary victims. Thirdly, if, but for this argument, there would exist a doctor-patient relationship, in my judgment, these claims fit more clearly into category 1 of Hale LJ's four categories than any of the other three...In these claims, the alleged negligence of the clinicians in obtaining consent from the claimants, is the very thing which, it is alleged, caused the psychiatric injury.[63]

Although the three reasons given by Gage, J. for classifying the claimants as primary victims are persuasive, they hardly give any guarantee that in all cases where a post-mortem gives rise to psychiatric injury that claimants would be treated as primary victims. This uncertainty is mainly due to two reasons. First, classification still depends on factual considerations and it is open to another judge to arrive at a different conclusion by assessing the facts differently. Second, it is apparent that though Gage, J. held that the claimants were primary victims on the facts, he did not operate on the basis of any judicial definition of the term, and to the extent that he

---

61 *Ibid.*, at 397.
62 *Ibid.*, at 397.
63 *Ibid.*, 405–406.

did so, he relied on the dissenting judgement of Lord Goff in *White's* case, despite his reference to being guided 'by the various passages in the above decisions'. It is clear that if we accept the observation of Lord Hoffmann, who was part of the majority in *White's* case, that 'primary victims' must be 'within the range of foreseeable physical injury',[64] then the claimants in *AB v. Leeds* must be regarded as secondary victims. On the facts of *AB v. Leeds*, it can neither be contended that the defendants' negligence created any foreseeable physical harm to the claimants nor that the claimants were within the zone of physical harm created by the defendants' negligence. In any event, Gage, J. dismissed two of the lead claims on the ground that it was not foreseeable that the claimants would suffer psychiatric injury and upheld only one of the three lead claims on the contrary ground that psychiatric injury was foreseeable. If the claimants in *AB v. Leeds* were treated as secondary victims, none of their claims would have survived the application of current control mechanisms.[65] It hardly needs saying that the uncertainty that surrounds this area of law due to judicially developed control mechanisms and evolving policy considerations means that it is not a first choice remedy for a plaintiff complaining of interference with the body of a deceased relative.[66]

Invasion of Privacy

Could mistreatment of a dead body or parts of the human body amount to an invasion of privacy? The answer depends on the existence, meaning and function of a 'right to privacy'. On a definitional level, privacy is an amorphous and broad term that is hardly contained within Warren and Brandeis' seminal conceptualization as the 'right to be let alone'.[67] Privacy is a concept whose contents depend on the particular culture, society, political system and technological evolution.[68] This makes enunciation of a principle that covers every aspect of privacy practically impossible, a fact recognized by Lord Hoffmann in *Wainwright v. Home Office*, when he doubted the 'value of any high-level generalisation which can perform a useful function in enabling one to deduce the rule to be applied in a concrete case'.[69] It is, however, more appropriate to regard privacy as a high-order principle of generality bereft of specific rules to govern individual cases.[70] It has been suggested that Warren and

---

64 *White, supra*, note 2, at 509.

65 There was considerable lapse of time between the time of the alleged negligence and the time the plaintiffs had knowledge of it.

66 It has also been argued that the uncertainty engendered by current English law on nervous shock militates against early pre-trial resolution of dubious cases and gives little guidance to lawyers and judges: David W. Robertson, 'Liability in Negligence for Nervous Shock' (1994) 57 *M.L.R.* 649–63.

67 Samuel D. Warren and Louis D. Brandeis, 'The Right to Privacy' (1890) 4 *Harv. L.R.* 193.

68 Peter Burns, 'The Law and Privacy: The Canadian Experience' (1976) 54 *Can. Bar. Rev.* 1–64.

69 *Wainwright v. Home Office, supra*, note 10, at 419.

70 P.A. Freund, 'Privacy: One Concept or Many' (1971) 13 *NOMOS* 182, at 197.

Brandeis' 'right to be let alone' should be understood at this level of generality.[71] Specific, gap-filling, rules that give content to privacy are provided by statutes, judicial decisions and constitution. Nevertheless, privacy has its informational and substantive usages and may, in the former sense, be reckoned as a person's right to control access to information about that person.[72] Howsoever defined, privacy is not recognized as a separate tort in Anglo-Canadian jurisprudence.[73] Common law protects the values of privacy through other heads of action, such as trespass to land, defamation, injurious falsehood, trespass to chattels, trespass to the person, nuisance and, more importantly, breach of confidence.

In England, following the introduction of the *Human Rights Act, 1998*, incorporating Article 8 of the European Convention on Human Rights which specifically protects the right of privacy, it was thought by many that a new tort of privacy had become part of English law. Such expectation was soon dashed by a string of House of Lords and Court of Appeal decisions denying the existence of a new tort of privacy and preferring the incremental expansion of the action for breach of confidence.[74] Although the original formulation of an action for breach of confidence protected only disclosures made in breach of a confidential relationship,[75] the courts have since dispensed with that requirement in order to accommodate private information disclosed outside confidential relationships. Instead of asking whether there is a confidential relationship between the claimant and defendant, the courts now seek to find whether a defendant obtained information in circumstances in which he or she knew or ought to have known that the information was confidential. This new test was developed by Lord Goff of Chieveley in *Attorney General v. Guardian Newspapers Ltd. (No 2)* when he observed that 'a duty of confidence arises when confidential information comes to the knowledge of a person...in circumstances where he has notice, or is held to have agreed, that the information is confidential'.[76]

---

71 Burns, *supra*, note 68, at 11.

72 Gavin Phillipson and Helen Fenwick, 'Breach of Confidence as a Privacy Remedy in the Human Rights Act Era' (2000) 63 *M.L.R.* 660, at 662.

73 Klar, *supra*, note 12, at 77–80 (summarizing the Canadian cases on point); some Canadian provinces, however, have enacted *Privacy Acts* that provide civil remedy in damages for an invasion of privacy, though none of the legislation defined the concept of privacy. The provinces with privacy legislation are British Columbia, Manitoba, Newfoundland, Nova Scotia and Saskatchewan. Judicial examination of the British Columbia privacy legislation was made in *Hollingsworth v. BCTV* (1999) 6 W.W.R. 54 (B.C.C.A.). English decisions given before the *Human Rights Act, 1998* which rejected the existence of a separate tort of privacy include: *Kaye v. Robertson* (1991) FSR 62; *R v. Khan* (1997) A.C. 558; *Malone v. Metropolitan Police Comr.* (1979) Ch 344; *Khorasandjian v. Bush* (1993) QB 727.

74 *Douglas v. Hello!* (No 3) (2005) 3 W.L.R. 881; *Campbell v. MGN Ltd.* (2004) 2 A.C. 457; *Garry Flitcroft v Mirror Group Newspapers* (formerly known as *A v. B & C Ltd*) (2002) EWCA Civ 337. In *Wainwright v. Home Office*, *supra*, note 10, at 423, Lord Hoffmann foreclosed the possibility of such recognition on the basis of the *Human Rights Act, 1998*: 'Furthermore, the coming into force of the Human Rights Act 1998 weakens the argument for saying that a general tort of invasion of privacy is needed to fill gaps in the existing remedies. Sections 6 and 7 of the Act are in themselves substantial gap fillers.'

75 *Coco v. A.N. Clark (Engineers) Ltd.* (1969) RPC 41.

76 *Attorney General v. Guardian Newspapers Ltd. (No 2)* (1990) 1 A.C. 109, at 281.

This expansion of confidential information to include invasions of privacy raises doubts as to the propriety of the continued use of the label of breach of confidence to describe that cause of action in its recently expanded form. As Lord Nicholls of Birkenhead observed in *Campbell v. MGN Ltd.*:[77]

> The continuing use of the phrase 'duty of confidence' and the description of the information as 'confidential' is not altogether comfortable. Information about an individual's private life would not, in ordinary usage, be called 'confidential.' The more natural description today is that such information is private. The essence of the tort is better encapsulated now as misuse of private information.

Despite this problem of characterization, it is now firmly established in English jurisprudence that the values of privacy, as specifically enshrined in the *Human Rights Act, 1998*, would be protected through the cause of action for breach of confidence.[78] In *Campbell v. MGN*, the defendant published information, along with the claimant's photograph, relating to the claimant's drug therapy. The claimant is a celebrity and a well-known fashion model. The publication showed: 1. the fact that Miss Campbell was a drug addict; 2. the fact that she was receiving treatment for her addition; 3. the fact that treatment which she was receiving was provided by Narcotics Anonymous; 4. the details of the treatment, for instance, how long, how frequently and at what times of day she had been receiving it, the nature of it and extent of her commitment to the process; and 5. a visual portrayal by means of photographs of her when she was leaving the place where treatment had been taking place.[79] In these circumstances, Miss Campbell sued for damages for breach of confidence. It was argued, and accepted by the House of Lords, that facts 1 and 2 above could not be treated as protectable privacy interests since Miss Campbell had previously publicly denied that she was a drug addict and that the press was entitled to set the record straight. Although the House of Lords was unanimous on the question of applicable legal principles, they differed on the resolution of the facts, especially facts 3–5 above. Lords Nicholls of Birkenhead and Hoffmann held that Miss Campbell was not entitled to succeed because the publication of facts which concededly were not in breach of her privacy justified publication of the extra facts, regards being had to the margin of appreciation accorded to journalists. The majority, however, held that publication of facts 3–5 was disproportionate to the harm done to Miss Campbell by the invasion of her privacy. For present purposes, the point is that privacy is not a free-standing tort in English law but relies for its protection on the old cause of action for breach of confidence, a point given forceful expression by Lord Nicholls of Birkenhead in *Campbell's* case:

> The time has come to recognise that the values enshrined in articles 8 and 10 are now part of the cause of action for breach of confidence. As Lord Woolf CJ has said, the courts have been able to achieve this result by absorbing the rights protected by articles

---

77 *Campbell v. MGN Ltd* (2004) 2 A.C. 457, at 465.

78 This approach was also suggested by Phillipson and Fenwick, *supra*, note 72, at 660–93.

79 *Campbell, supra*, note 77, at 481.

8 and 10 into this cause of action: *A v. B plc* (2003) QB 195…Further, it should now be recognised that for this purpose these values are of general application. The values embodied in articles 8 and 10 are as much applicable in disputes between individuals or between an individual and a non-governmental body such as a newspaper as they are in disputes between individuals and a public authority.[80]

The question, then, is how do we recognize the circumstances in which privacy values are implicated? What are the interests that should be legally protected as privacy interests? When is an interference with a dead body or body parts a breach of the right to privacy? Answers to these questions are greatly illumined by the American approach to privacy where, unlike Canada and the UK, it is recognized as a separate tort and has been judicially developed over the years.[81] The value of American privacy jurisprudence is not entirely lost on the current English approach since it is capable of demonstrating privacy values that underpin application of the cause of action for breach of confidence.

In the USA, privacy is not a unitary cause of action in tort, but is a common term that describes four distinct torts that protect four separate interests. American courts have largely followed Prosser and Keeton's categorization of privacy interests:

> [i]t (privacy) is not one tort, but a complex of four. To date the law of privacy comprises four distinct kinds of invasion of four different interests of the plaintiff, which are tied together by the common name, but otherwise have almost nothing in common except that each represents an interference with the right of the plaintiff 'to be let alone.'[82]

These four categories of privacy have been identified by *Prosser and Keeton on Torts* as:

a. Appropriation of the plaintiff's name, likeness or personality for the defendant's benefit or advantage, such as non-consensual use of the plaintiff's name or picture to advertise the defendant's product. Since there is no exclusive right to one's name, the protection is accorded not to the plaintiff's name as such but to the plaintiff's name as representative of his or her identity.[83] This category of privacy was recognized in Canada by *Krouse v. Chrysler Canada Ltd.*,[84] where the plaintiff, a professional footballer, alleged that the defendant infringed his privacy by the use of the plaintiff's likeness in the promotion of the defendant's products. Estey, J.A. of the Ontario Court of Appeal observed that 'from the foregoing examination of the authorities in the several fields of tort related to the allegations made herein…the common law does contemplate a concept in the law of torts which may be broadly classified as an appropriation of one's personality',[85] The courts, however, attempt to

---

80 *Ibid.*, at 465.

81 William L. Prosser, 'Privacy' (1960) 48 *Cal. L. Rev.* 383.

82 W. Page Keeton, *et al.*, *Prosser & Keeton on Torts*, 5th edn (St Paul, Minnesota: West Publishing, 1984).

83 *Ibid.*, at 852.

84 *Krouse v. Chrysler Canada Ltd* (1974) 1 O.R. (2d) 225 (Ont. C.A).

85 *Ibid.*, at 238.

balance the plaintiff's right to his or her personality with the defendant's right to free speech by construing the requirement of appropriation strictly. For instance, a plaintiff will not succeed under this head where he or she was incidentally mentioned in the alleged publication or where instead of commercial exploitation the motive is to use the plaintiff as a subject of the offending book.[86] The likelihood for recognition of this aspect of privacy in England is remote since Baroness Hale of Richmond unequivocally affirmed in *Campbell v. MGN Ltd.* that 'in this country we do not recognise a right to one's own image'.[87]

b. Intrusion upon the plaintiff's solitude or seclusion. This is an intentional interference in the form of eavesdropping on private conversations through wiretapping, microphones, invasion of the plaintiff's home, peeping into the windows of the plaintiff and incessant and unwanted telephone calls.[88]

c. Public disclosure of private facts. *Prosser and Keeton* noted that three elements are required for this head of privacy to apply: 1. the disclosure must be public; 2. the facts publicly disclosed must be private; 3. the disclosure must be one that is highly offensive to a reasonable person of ordinary sensibilities.[89] It has been suggested that the private/public dichotomy underpinning these requirements are not opposites and should not be taken literally.[90] A good example of this category of privacy is *Melvin v. Reid,*[91] where the plaintiff, a former prostitute and murder defendant, was entitled to recover for an invasion of her privacy when a film revealed her present identity and whereabouts. To succeed under this head of privacy, American courts now require the presence of fault or wrongdoing on the part of a defendant beyond mere publication of private information that is not newsworthy. Thus, in *Anderson v. Fisher Broadcasting Company Inc.,*[92] where embarrassing photographs of an accident victim were published in a newspaper, the Oregon Supreme Court observed that:

[t]he truthful presentation of facts concerning a person, even facts that a reasonable person would wish to keep private, and not newsworthy, does not give rise to common law tort liability for damages for mental or emotional distress, unless the manner or purpose of the defendant's conduct is wrongful in some respect apart from causing the plaintiff's hurt feelings.[93]

---

86 *Gould Estate v. Stoddert Publishing Co.* (1998) 161 D.L.R. (4th) 321 (Ont. C.A.); *Horton v. Tim Donut Ltd.* (1997) 75 C.P.R. (3d) 467 (Ont. C.A.).

87 *Campbell v. MGN Ltd, supra,* note 77, at 501.

88 Keeton, *supra,* note 82, at 854–6.

89 *Ibid.,* at 856–7.

90 Elizabeth Paton-Simpson, 'Private Circles and Public Squares: Invasion of Privacy by the Publication of "Private Facts"' (1998) 61 *M.L.R.* 318–40.

91 *Melvin v. Reid* 112 Cal. App. 285 (1931). Compare with *Florida Star v. BJF* 105 L.Ed 2d 443 (1989) where the disclosure of the identity of a rape victim was held not to justify recovery on the ground that the matter had already become publicly available.

92 *Anderson v. Fisher Broadcasting Company Inc.* 712 P. 2d 803 (Ore. Sup. Ct., 1986).

93 *Ibid.*

d. Putting the plaintiff in a false light in the public eye. This category would include circumstances where a plaintiff is falsely associated with a publication that is objectionable and offensive to a reasonable person of ordinary sensibilities. Instances would include publicly attributing a spurious book or article to the plaintiff or using the plaintiff's name, without his or her authority on a petition or suit filed in court.[94]

For the purpose of this book, however, the question is whether the above categories or forms of privacy interests capture interferences or mistreatment of dead bodies and body parts?

From the standpoint of personal autonomy which privacy partly seeks to protect, there is no doubt that the law of privacy is more relevant to the living body than dead bodies. In the case of living bodies, the law of privacy has been deployed as the foundation of abortion law.[95] Privacy law is also relevant to sundry issues that might arise from various applications of health or DNA databases, a current feature of the modern genetic age.[96] For instance, in the Icelandic case of *Ragnhilder Guðmundsdóttir v. The State of Iceland*,[97] the plaintiff was able to prevent the transfer of her deceased father's tissue and medical information to a health database on the ground that genetic analysis of the decedent's medical data and tissue will reveal private and personal information relating to the plaintiff. The limitation of privacy law to living persons, tissues of such persons, and *Ragnhilder*-type of cases means that there is no remedy in the vast majority of cases concerning the mistreatment of a decedent's remains. More specifically, it means that a plaintiff cannot rely on the remedial framework of privacy where the complaint relates to any of the six categories of interference with dead bodies already identified under the analysis of nervous shock or psychiatric injury. Although there is a dearth of authorities in this area of privacy, some American cases put it beyond cavil that a dead body or parts of a dead body are not entitled to the protection of privacy. In *Armstrong v. H & C Communications*,[98] the skull of the plaintiffs' 6-year-old daughter was found and taken into possession by the police authorities two years after the girl's abduction and murder. Florida's Channel 2 station made a videotape of the skull and broadcast it to its viewers, including the plaintiffs/parents. The plaintiffs were outraged and complained that the broadcast was an invasion of their privacy. Cobb J. for the majority of Florida's District Court of Appeal dismissed the plaintiff's privacy claim on the ground that matters covered by the broadcast were already in the public domain following the public limelight attendant upon the abduction and murder of the plaintiffs' daughter. More importantly, Cobb, J. observed that the 'factual disclosure by Channel 2 does not fit into any of the four general categories

---

94 Keeton, *supra*, note 82, at 863–4.

95 *Griswold v. Connecticut* 381 U.S. 479 (1965); *Roe v. Wade* 410 U.S. 113 (1973).

96 Genetic Interest Group, *Human Rights, Privacy and Medical Research: Analysing UK Policy on Tissue and Data* (Genetic Interest Group, 2006).

97 *Ragnhilder Guðmundsdóttir v. The State of Iceland* No. 151/2003 (Sup. Ct. 2003) – fully explored in Chapter 4.

98 *Armstrong v. H & C Communications* 575 So. 2d 280 (Dist Ct App., 1991).

comprising the tort of invasion of privacy as recognized by Prosser in his Law of Torts'.[99] For similar reasons a privacy remedy was denied in the case of *Waters v. Fleetwood*,[100] where the plaintiff complained about the sale and publication of a photograph of the dead body of a 14-year-old girl.

Interferences with the body parts of a deceased person offer another interesting example of the challenges faced by the law of privacy as a remedy in this area of law. In *Hubenschmidt v. Shears*,[101] the plaintiffs' decedents were killed in an accident allegedly caused by the defendants' negligence (it was a consolidated action). The defendants sought to prove contributory negligence by the deceased persons by relying on alcoholic test results of blood samples taken from the decedents. The plaintiffs (legal representatives of the decedents) opposed the admissibility of the alcoholic test results on the basis of the decedents' right to privacy. The court held that the evidence was relevant and admissible, and that a dead person has no enforceable right to privacy:

> The removal of blood from a dead body for purposes of testing was not unreasonable under the circumstances and does not shock the conscience or our sense of justice…We are not concerned in these cases with issues of search and seizure/right to privacy, security of person or statutory construction which were raised in *Lebel v. Swincicki*, 93 N.W.2d 281 (1958) and *McNitt v. Citco Drilling Co.*, 245 N.W.2d 18 (1976). Both of those cases dealt with extraction of a blood sample from a person still alive. Indeed, in *Lebel,* it is noted that: 'the right to privacy is a personal one which ends with the death of the person to whom it is of value, and it may not be claimed by his estate or by his next of kin.'…Likewise, we can find no legitimate basis for the argument that a decedent's representative can claim, in a civil case, that the non-consensual blood extraction from an already dead body amounted to an illegal search and seizure. Certainly there is no possible claim concerning the constitutional protection against self-incrimination.[102]

Hubenschmidt's case was approved by other cases such as *Bufford v. Brent*[103] and *McLean v. Rogers*.[104] In *Bufford's* case, the Michigan Court of Appeals observed that while non-consensual blood extraction does 'not violate any right that may be claimed by the estate of the decedent', a living person, in contrast, might 'argue that the result of a Breathalyzer test should not be admitted into evidence at a civil trial on account of the right of privacy'.[105] To summarize, therefore, the right of privacy is construed as a personal right available only to the living and not the dead.[106] A relational right of privacy is not available to living relatives to sue for infringement of a dead relative's privacy rights. Living relatives, however, can sue for invasion

---

99 *Ibid.*, at 282.

100 *Waters v. Fleetwood* 212 Ga. 161 (1956).

101 *Hubenschmidt v. Shears* 270 N.W. 2d 2 (1978, Sup. Ct. Mich.).

102 *Ibid.*, at 4.

103 *Bufford v. Brent* 320 N.W. 2d 323 (1982, Ct. App. Mich).

104 *McLean v. Rogers* 300 N.W. 2D 389 (1980, Ct. App. Mich.).

105 *Bufford, supra,* note 103, at 325. Other relevant cases include *Smith v. City of Artesia* 772 P. 2d 373 (Ct App. New Mexico, 1989); *Reid v. Pierce County* 961 P. 2d 333 (Wash. Sup. Ct., 1998).

106 *Silkwood v. Kerr-McGee Corp.* 637 F. 2d 743 (1980).

of their own privacy rights if interference with the deceased exposes them to shame, embarrassment and humiliation, or in some other manner discloses personal details of theirs that they would like to keep secret. It is fair to conclude that these limitations of privacy law make it an inadequate remedial framework for a plaintiff complaining of mistreatment of a deceased relative's dead body.

Consent and Informed Consent

Very few cases have dealt with the problems of consent and informed consent in the context of dead bodies. The reason seems obvious: a dead person has neither the capacity to give consent nor the autonomy that informed consent animates. Consent is the cornerstone of health care law and often analysed against the background of medical treatment or post-mortem. The law of consent recognizes our right to bodily self-determination. It accentuates a living person's autonomy through the protection of his or her interests in physical security and bodily well-being.[107] Consent safeguards our right to be in charge of or, at least, be part of the medical decision-making process that might have enormous consequences for our health.

It is well settled that every adult person of sound mind is entitled to accept or reject treatment for good or bad reasons or for no reason at all. Thus, a physician is not authorized to provide a medical procedure to a patient without his or her consent, except in an emergency or other limited exceptions recognized in law. Where treatment is lawfully refused, it is immaterial that the patient's decision was unreasonable or involved fatal consequences.[108] Likewise, a person has a right to withdraw from treatment already lawfully commenced by a physician.[109] Failure to obtain a patient's consent before treatment amounts to trespass and is redressed by the common law action for battery.[110] Such will also be the case where the treatment rendered is different from the one consented to or where extensive and unnecessary treatment is deliberately given to a patient.[111] However, a complaint that a physician failed to disclose material risks associated with proposed treatments or viable alternative treatments sounds in negligence and not battery.[112] Though of unsure provenance, the doctor–patient relationship is uncontroversially accepted as giving

---

107 Marjorie M. Shultz, 'From Informed Consent to Patient's Choice: A New Protected Interest' (1985) 95 *Yale L.J.* 219.

108 *Malette v. Schulman* (1987) 67 D.L.R. (4ᵗʰ) 321 (Ont. C.A.). Decision to refuse treatment must, however, be based on sufficient information, otherwise a physician might be liable: *Truman v. Thomas* 611 P. 2d 902 (Cal. 1990); Bernard Dickens, 'Informed Consent', in Jocelyn Downie and Timothy Caulfied, *Canadian Health Law and Policy* (Toronto: Butterworths, 1999), at 141.

109 *Ciarlariello v. Schacter* (1993) 100 D.L.R. (4ᵗʰ) 609 (S.C.C.).

110 *Chatterton v. Gerson* (1981) Q.B. 432.

111 *Appleton v. Garrett* 34 BMLR 23 (Q.B.D.).

112 *Sidaway v. Board of Governors of the Bethlem Royal Hospital and the Maudsley Hospital* (1985) A.C. 871 (HL); *Chester v. Afshar* (2004) 3 W.L.R. 927 (HL); *Reibl v. Hughes* (1981) 114 D.L.R. (3d) 1 (S.C.C.).

rise to a duty of care.[113] This duty includes a doctor's obligation to provide a patient with the information necessary to found a judgement as to rejection or acceptance of a recommended therapy. Breach of this duty does not, however, automatically result in liability. As in other areas of negligence, a patient must also prove other elements such as causation and remoteness of damages. These elemental requirements ensure that a plaintiff faces serious challenges to recovery of damages for a physician's negligent failure to disclose material risks.[114]

In the area of dead bodies and body parts, the law of consent has not witnessed as much judicial analysis as in other areas. As already indicated, it is nonsensical to talk about consent by a dead person. Personal rights of action, such as an action for battery, die with a person. Thus, mutilation of a corpse, through autopsy or other means of interference, cannot give rise to an action for battery. Living relatives cannot sue either since there is no such thing as a relational right of battery. A right of action accrues to living relatives only by showing that the defendant's unacceptable conduct towards the dead has injuriously affected them in some way. An effective demonstration of this connection gives rise to an action in negligence. For instance, the deceased's living relatives could show that they suffered provable psychiatric injury or nervous shock as a result of interference with the deceased and are therefore entitled to bring an action in negligence. This remedial prospect is, however, dimmed by the policy limitations on recovery that hedge actions for nervous shock. *AB v. Leeds*[115] is both a quintessential example of the few cases raising problems of consent in a cadaveric setting and the difficulties associated with legal recovery for damages in negligence. There, the plaintiffs complained that they were not given informed consent before post-mortem was carried out on their deceased children and that paediatric organs removed and retained in the post-mortem process (which were subsequently disposed of) were done without their authority. Although Gage, J. found that the parents suffered provable psychiatric injury and that there was a duty of care arising from a doctor–patient relationship,[116] he nevertheless held that only one of the three sets of plaintiffs was entitled to recover in negligence on grounds of foreseeability of injury.

Nevertheless, the issue of consent could become controversial when a part of the living body is extracted or harvested for diagnostic or research purposes. If, for instance, a doctor obtains a patient's blood with consent for diagnostic purposes, is the patient entitled to be informed of the particular tests? Should the patient be told that the blood test is for the presence of the HIV virus?[117] Is a doctor liable when a patient's blood is tested for susceptibility to schizophrenia when consent was only

---

113 Andrew Grubb, 'Consent to Treatment: The Competent Patient', in A. Grubb and J. Laing, eds, *Principles of Medical Law*, 2nd edn (Oxford: Oxford University Press, 2004) 179–80.

114 Emily Jackson, *Medical Law: Text, Cases and Materials* (Oxford: Oxford University Press, 2006) 267–312.

115 *AB v. Leeds, supra*, note 48.

116 The doctor–patient relationship which existed between the doctors and the infant children (while alive) was extended to the mothers of the deceased children.

117 Similar problems were analysed by John Keown, 'The Ashes of AIDS and the Phoenix of Informed Consent' (1989) 52 *M.L.R.* 790.

given for a diabetic test? Whatever standard of disclosure is used to approach these questions,[118] even if the doctor is found to be in breach of his duty of disclosure, the burden on the plaintiff to prove causation might be practicably insurmountable. This is a heavy obstacle for plaintiffs who complain of interference with their living body parts and seek to rely on the framework of informed consent. Causation in negligence means establishing a factual connection between a defendant's negligence and the injury suffered by a plaintiff. In other words, that the defendant's negligent conduct in fact caused the plaintiff's injury. Where the complaint relates to non-disclosure of a medical risk which eventually materializes, it is difficult to establish causation, especially if the plaintiff would have undergone the treatment in any event.[119] As Emily Jackson observed, 'actually proving that the inadequate disclosure caused the claimant's injury is fraught with difficulty and…in practice represents a significant obstacle to the chances of bringing a successful action in negligence. Inadequate disclosure of risks will seldom result in any physical injury at all, and hence will usually be immune from potential liability in negligence.'[120] In the case of testing a tissue for a purpose other than the one consented to, a negligence action is sure to fail for want of injury, except provable psychiatric injury is established. A claimant could, however, arguably bring an action for battery. But this will be a novel application of the law of battery. The situation is even more problematic where the nondisclosure relates to economic or financial matters. For instance, where a patient's tissue was obtained with consent in the context of a therapy but later applied in a lucrative medical research. In such cases, it is difficult to see how injury or causation, both essential for successful negligence actions, would be established. Moreover, complaint about the nondisclosure of economic and financial interests of a physician/researcher would in the circumstances sound fantastical. Can we say, without an abuse of the English language, that a financial interest is a material risk that directly flows from a medical procedure? Even at that, are economic interests of physicians legally disclosable? While it is easy to concede that disclosure of financial interests in the context of treatment or research is an ethical imperative, its legal enforceability is doubtful.[121] Thus, in *Greenberg v. Miami Children's Hosp.*, where the plaintiffs complained that the defendant/medical researchers did not disclose their economic interests (patenting and licensing of research results) before obtaining the plaintiffs' tissues for research on Canavan disease, Moreno, J. opined that the court 'agrees and declines to extend the duty of informed consent to cover a researcher's economic interests'.[122] *John Moore v. The Regents of the University*

---

118 While the UK operates the test of conformity with a responsible body of medical opinion, Canada uses the test of a reasonable and prudent person in the plaintiff's position.

119 In *Chester v. Afshar*, *supra*, note 112, the majority of the House of Lords in a similar situation held that for policy reasons causation was established.

120 Jackson, *supra*, note 114, at 304.

121 Sheldon Krimsky, 'The Ethical and Legal Foundations of Scientific "Conflict of Interest"', in Trudo Lemmens and Duff R. Waring, eds, *Law and Ethics in Biomedical Research* (Toronto: University of Toronto Press, 2006) 63–81.

122 *Greenberg v. Miami Children's Hosp.* 264 F. Supp. 2d 1064, at 1070 (S.D. Fla. 2003).

of California[123] provides another interesting example. Moore suffered from a hairy cell leukaemia and needed a splenectomy. For that purpose, his tissues were obtained for diagnosis. The doctors treating him discovered that Moore's cells were unique and, in furtherance of their medical research, obtained more tissues from Moore, but without disclosing their commercial objectives. The tissues were used to produce a lucrative commercial cell-line. Although Moore' surgery was successfully carried out, he sued for conversion of his tissue, among other causes of action. The Court of Appeal of California decided in his favour on the count of conversion, but the California Supreme Court set it aside for policy reasons and held, rather, that Moore had a cause of action for breach of informed consent and remitted the case for trial. Though this case was subsequently settled out of court, it is difficult to see how Moore would have succeeded on the count of informed consent. Did he suffer any recognizable injury? Although Moore was arguably mentally distressed by discovering the commercial research on his tissue and the mode of obtaining it, that would be short of the legally required provable psychiatric injury. In any case, since proper disclosure of his doctors' research/commercial interests would hardly have prevented Moore from undergoing a highly needed therapeutic surgery, it is hard to see how he could have proved causation. As Larry I. Palmer correctly observed, a 'patient such as John Moore, who was successfully treated for a serious form of leukaemia, would have a hard time convincing a jury that he would not have undergone the treatment had he been aware of the research interests or the financial interests of his treating physician'.[124]

Similar problems arise even where the use of a living person's body part took place outside the contexts of therapy and diagnosis. For instance, if researchers obtained X's body part with consent for inclusion in a DNA database dedicated to studies on malaria. What is X's remedy if the researchers turn around to use the body part in a way that embarrasses or humiliates X? Or sells the body part to other researchers for pure economic gain? In addition to the difficulties confronting X in proving the elements of negligence, X is particularly challenged by the fact that consent as a legal framework does not provide the continuing control needed in such situations. As such, once a person gives consent to the harvesting of his or her body part, it is difficult for that person, outside contract, to determine or control what is subsequently done with the tissue. This type of ongoing control is advantageously provided by a property regime. The inability of consent to empower a claimant with respect to an excised body part is vividly demonstrated by Laurie:

> While no individual will be forced to give samples – and in most cases the only ethically and legally appropriate approach is to seek informed consent to the provision of a sample – the individual retains no continued relationship with the sample in either a factual or a legal sense once consent has been obtained and the sample surrendered. Thus, the focus on consent renders the participatory process disempowering...In sum, the fundamental

---

123 *John Moore v. The Regents of the University of California* 793 P. 2d 479 (Cal. Sup. Ct. 1990).

124 Larry I. Palmer, 'Should Liability Play a Role in Social Control of Biobanks?' (2005) 33 *Journal of Law, Med. & Ethics* 70, at 73.

problem with the consent model is that it does not provide a means by which the subject can exercise *continuing control* of her materials.[125]

For the same reasons that Emily Jackson suggested that 'there is an increasing need to think seriously about abandoning the pretence that tort law offers any protection at all to patients' interests in access to information about their medical treatment',[126] it will be a mistake to suppose that the law of consent or informed consent is of any significant help in the area of dead bodies and body parts.

Constitutional and Human Rights Protection

An interference with a dead body or body parts could possibly engage the protections conferred by a constitution on the exercise of certain freedoms. These include rights to property, privacy and religion. Constitutional protection for dead bodies could be raised under provisions similar to the 14th Amendment of the US Constitution which prohibits states from depriving 'any person of life, liberty, or property without due process of law', or under the 1st Amendment which protects freedom of religion. It is pertinent, however, to separate arguments relating to constitutional protection of a decedent's right qua decedent and the juridically different argument over the constitutional protection of living relatives' rights in respect of the deceased. As regards the deceased, the question then is whether a dead person could bring an action (or one brought on its behalf) for alleged constitutional infringements occurring after death? Could unauthorized autopsy or other forms of non-consensual mutilation of a corpse amount to deprivation of the decedent's privacy, dignity, property or other freedoms and rights protected by a constitution? The issue arose in some US jurisdictions. In *Silkwood v. Kerr-McGee Corporation*,[127] the estate of Karen Silkwood, a former employee of the defendant/corporation, claimed that officials of the corporate defendant and agents of the Federal Bureau of Investigation (FBI) conspired to prevent Karen and other employees from organizing a labour union. It was alleged that this conspiracy violated Karen's (deceased) 1st and 14th Amendment rights by employing acts such as illegal surveillance; unlawful entering of her home, automobile and other private places; wiretapping of her telephones; and physically endangering her life and safety upon the public highways. It was also alleged that Karen's rights to freedom of speech, travel, association and assembly were violated by the defendants. The trial court found that the FBI allegedly became involved in the conspiracy only after the death of Karen and could not, therefore, have violated her constitutional rights. In upholding the trial court's judgement, the United States Court of Appeal (Tenth Circuit) observed:

---

125 Graeme Laurie, *Genetic Privacy: A Challenge to Medico-Legal Norms* (Cambridge: Cambridge University Press, 2002), at 312.

126 Emily Jackson, 'Informed Consent to Medical Treatment and the Impotence of Tort', in Sam McLean, ed., *First Do No Harm* (Aldershot: Ashgate, 2006).

127 *Silkwood v. Kerr-McGee Corporation* 637 F. 2d 743 (Tenth Cir. 1980).

The conspiracy's alleged purpose was two-fold: to violate the rights of Silkwood and others, and to cover up these violations. We agree…that the civil rights of a person cannot be violated once that person has died…It is clear then that the FBI agents could not have violated the civil rights of Silkwood by cover-up actions taken after her death. Additionally, with the death of Silkwood, the conspiracy to violate her rights terminated. Thus, the FBI defendants could not he held liable for the prior violations of Silkwood's constitutional rights even if a *Bivens* claim encompasses a relation back theory of conspiracy law.[128]

Similarly, in *Guyton v. Phillips*,[129] the plaintiff, whose son (Tyrone Guyton) was killed by three of the defendant police officers, claimed that the alleged murderers conspired with the Chief of Police of the City of Emeryville and other persons to cover-up the alleged wrongdoing and shield the police officers from proper prosecution. The plaintiff claimed that the alleged conspiracy violated Tyrone Guyton's (deceased) constitutional rights protected by the 5th, 6th, 8th, 9th and 14th Amendments of the United States Constitution. The court defined the issue presented to it as being whether the 'Civil Rights Act affords a cause of action on behalf of a deceased for acts occurring after the death of that person'.[130] It answered this question in the negative, observing that the 'Civil Rights Act…does not provide a cause of action on behalf of a deceased based upon alleged violation of the deceased's civil rights which occurred after his death';[131] and that the definition of a 'person' for the purposes of constitutional rights does not encompass a deceased person.

Since it appears clear that a corpse cannot legally complain against unconstitutional acts of interference with it, the remaining question is whether living relatives can do so. Given that constitutional rights are personal and not relational in operation, living relatives can only show a constitutional cause of action if they prove that an interference with a dead relative's body injuriously affected their own constitutionally protected rights. For instance, it might be possible to argue that a living relative's freedom of religion under a constitution is violated by unauthorized autopsy on a deceased relative contrary to the parties' religious beliefs. American courts have expressed conflicting decisions on the availability of constitutional protection for next of kin's sepulchral rights. In *Montgomery v. County of Clinton*,[132] the plaintiffs' 16-year-old son (Sannie) was killed in the course of a high-speed police chase and was autopsied pursuant to mandatory statutory requirements. Although the plaintiffs were immediately notified of the accident, they were neither told about the autopsy nor consented to it. Under Michigan law, a medical examiner is required to investigate violent deaths and may order autopsy whether or not the next of kin consents. The plaintiffs sued in damages, claiming that the high-speed chase constituted an excessive use of force and amounted to unreasonable seizure and deprivation of life without due process. But more interesting is the claim of the deceased's mother. Being Jewish, she claimed that autopsy and other forms of mutilation of a cadaver were not permitted by her religion. Accordingly, she contended that the unauthorized

---

128 *Ibid.*, at 749.
129 *Guyton v. Phillips* 606 F. 2d 248 (C.A.Cal., 1979).
130 *Ibid.*, at 250.
131 *Ibid.*, at 250.
132 *Montgomery v. County of Clinton* 940 F. 2d 661 (6th Cir. Mich. 1991).

autopsy on her deceased son infringed her right under the 1ˢᵗ Amendment freely to exercise her religion. The trial District Court obtained evidence on the alleged religious custom, including affidavits from religious scholars, but held that there was no contravention of the plaintiff's faith. The Court of Appeal affirmed the trial court's decision: 'the proof does not establish that plaintiff's religion forbids autopsies but rather appears to allow them in these circumstances. Moreover, even if such an autopsy is inconsistent with plaintiff's religious practices, the District Court did not err in analyzing the state's superior interest.'[133] In *State v. Powell,*[134] the 22-year-old Anthony Powell died in a motor accident in July 1983 and his body was mandatorily autopsied under the relevant legislation in Florida. Pursuant to the legislation, his corneal tissue was removed for transplantation without the consent of his parents. The legislation presumes consent of next of kin and prohibits removal of corneal tissue only if the medical examiner became aware of any objection by decedent's next of kin. The parents of Anthony brought an action alleging that the harvesting of their son's corneal tissue was a deprivation of their constitutionally protected rights of privacy and property. In respect of the privacy claim, Anthony's parents argued that the various rights of sepulchre (recall the six categories noted earlier in the analysis of nervous shock) conferred on them by the law of torts were in the nature of constitutionally protected privacy matters affecting a family. The Supreme Court of Florida dismissed this argument holding that constitutional protection of privacy extends only to freedom of choice in personal maters 'involved in existing, ongoing relationships among living persons as fundamental or essential to the pursuit of happiness by free persons'.[135] The court held that a sepulchral right does not 'rise to the constitutional dimension of a fundamental right traditionally protected under either of the United States or Florida Constitution'.[136] The Supreme Court of Florida equally dismissed the plaintiffs' argument that the non-consensual extraction of their son's corneal tissue was a deprivation of their constitutionally protected property rights to possession and custody of Anthony's remains for the purpose of burial. It noted that Florida law did not recognize property rights in the dead body of another person and the 'right to bring an action in tort does not necessarily invoke constitutional protections'.[137]

In contrast to the above decisions denying constitutional protection to rights in a dead body, the United States Court of Appeals (Sixth Circuit) came to a different conclusion in *Brotherton v. Cleveland.*[138] The plaintiff's husband was found 'pulseless' in a car and was pronounced dead on arrival at Bethesda North Hospital in Cincinnati, Ohio. Because suicide was suspected as the possible cause of death, the body of the deceased was statutorily required to undergo autopsy. The statute also allowed a coroner to harvest a decedent's corneal tissue for the purpose of transplantation except the coroner was aware of an objection from the next of kin.

---

133 *Ibid.,* at 662.
134 *State v. Powell* (1986) 497 So. 2d 1188.
135 *Ibid.,* at 1193.
136 *Ibid.*
137 *Ibid.,* at 1192.
138 *Brotherton v. Cleveland* 923 F. 2d 477 (1991).

At the Bethesda North Hospital, the plaintiff was asked whether she would make an anatomical gift of her husband's corneas, but she declined and a record of her refusal was made on the death report. During the autopsy, however, the coroner got a technician from the Cincinnati Eye Bank to harvest the deceased's corneas without inquiring whether there was an objection or not from the deceased's family. The Bethesda North Hospital also failed to notify the coroner of the plaintiff's objection to making an anatomical gift. Because the Ohio statute presumes consent to anatomical gift of cornea except an objection is known, the coroner adopted a practice of not obtaining the next of kin's consent and not inspecting the medical records or hospital records before removing corneas. The plaintiff, therefore, claimed that her rights to the custody and possession of her deceased husband's body for burial were property rights protected by the 14th Amendment of the US Constitution and infringed by the unauthorized anatomical gift. The trial court dismissed the plaintiff's claim on the ground that Ohio did not recognize property interest in a dead body though certain rights of living relatives were protected by the law of tort. The United States Court of Appeal, Sixth Circuit, agreed that Ohio laws determined the existence and nature of rights claimed by the plaintiff. It, however, held that federal law alone determined whether a legal interest or right rose to the level of a constitutionally protected legitimate claim of entitlement:

> Thankfully, we do not need to determine whether the Supreme Court of Ohio would categorise the interest in the dead body granted to the spouse as property, quasi-property or not property. Although the existence of an interest may be a matter of state law, whether that interest rises to the level of a 'legitimate claim of entitlement' protected by the due process clause is determined by federal law…This determination does not rest on the label attached to a right granted by the state but rather on the substance of that right.[139]

This division of judicial function enabled the Sixth Circuit of the United States Court of Appeal to overcome the obstacle posed by Ohio precedents such as *Carney v. Knollwood*[140] and *Everman v. Davis*,[141] where it was clearly held that there was no property or quasi-property right in a corpse, though tortious interferences might be remedied by an action in negligence.[142] The Sixth Circuit therefore held that the plaintiff's rights in her deceased husband's body were constitutionally protected property rights, and that these rights were violated by the defendant's act and procedure which encouraged intentional ignorance:

> Ohio Rev. Code § 2108.02 (B), as part of the Uniform Anatomical Gift Act governing gifts of organs and tissues for research or transplants, expressly grants a right to Deborah Brotherton to control the disposal of Steven Brotherton's body. *Everman* expresses the recognition that Deborah Brotherton has a possessory right to his body…*Carney* allows a

---

139 *Ibid.*, at 481–2.

140 *Carney v. Knollwood* (1986) 514 N.E. 2d 430.

141 *Everman v. Davis* 561 N.E. 2d 547.

142 The decision in *Brotherton* has been criticized for not following Ohio precedents refusing to recognize property rights in the human body: Michael H. Scarmon, 'Brotherton v Cleveland: Property Rights in the Human Body – Are the Goods Oft Interred with their Bones?' (1992) 37 *South Dakota L. Rev.* 429.

claim for disturbance of his body…Although extremely regulated, in sum, these rights form a substantial interest in the dead body, regardless of Ohio's classification of that interest. We hold the aggregate of rights granted by the state of Ohio to Deborah Brotherton rises to the level of a 'legitimate claim of entitlement' in Steven Brotherton's body, including his corneas, protected by the due process clause of the Fourteenth Amendment.

Though *Brotherton's* decision could impact negatively on the availability of organs for transplantation, it strongly protects the next of kin's universally shared sentiments towards the dead. However, the *Brotherton's* decision seems to be a tiny property island on a non-property ocean. It is contrary to other Court of Appeals decisions such as *Tillman v. Detroit Receiving Hospital*,[143] and *Georgia Lions Eye Bank v. Lavant*.[144] *Brotherton's* ruling was also recently disapproved by the Florida District Court of Appeal in *Crocker v. Pleasant*,[145] for being contrary to the Florida Supreme Court decision in *State v. Powell*.[146] In sum, it does appear that any hope for the deployment of a constitutional or human rights framework to remedy interferences with cadavers and body parts of deceased persons is bound to be a forlorn one indeed.

Unjust Enrichment

Greenberg v. Miami Children's Hospital[147] invites a consideration of whether the law of unjust enrichment is applicable to the human body and body parts. In that case, the plaintiffs (parents of children suffering from Canavan disease and non-profit organizations that fund research on Canavan disease) and the defendants collaborated on a medical research that was intended to identify and develop genetic tests for Canavan disease, a rare genetic abnormality that frequently occurs in Ashkenazi Jewish families. For the research, the plaintiffs provided body tissues (blood, urine and autopsy samples) and financial support which the defendants accepted. The defendants successfully identified the gene responsible for Canavan disease and developed appropriate carrier and prenatal testing for the disorder. The Canavan gene and accompanying testing kit were patented by the defendants without the knowledge of the plaintiffs. The plaintiffs complained that the defendants' restrictive licensing practice limited the availability of Canavan disease testing, contrary to the expectations of the plaintiffs. They therefore sued the defendants for damages and injunction based on six causes of action: lack of informed consent; breach of fiduciary duty; unjust enrichment; fraudulent concealment; conversion; and misappropriation of trade secrets. The defendants' motion to dismiss the plaintiffs' suit for disclosing no reasonable cause of action was allowed by Moreno, J. except with respect to the action for unjust enrichment:

> The complaint has alleged more than just a donor-donee relationship for the purpose of an unjust enrichment claim. Rather, the facts paint a picture of a continuing research

---

143 *Tillman v. Detroit Receiving Hospital* 360 N.W. 2d 275 (Mich. Ct. App. 1984).

144 *Georgia Lions Eye Bank v. Lavant* 335 S.E. 2d 127 (Ga. 1985).

145 *Crocker v. Pleasant* 727 So. 2d 1087 (1999).

146 *State v. Powell, supra*, note 134.

147 *Greenberg v. Miami Children's Hospital* 264 F. Supp. 2d 1064 (S.D.Fla. 2003).

collaboration that involved plaintiffs also investing time and significant resources in the race to isolate the Canavan gene. Therefore, given the facts as alleged, the court finds that plaintiffs have sufficiently pled the requisite elements of an unjust enrichment claim.[148]

Since this ruling only sanctioned trial but not judgement on the unjust enrichment claim, it is still an open question whether an unjust enrichment framework is amenable to body parts. Through restitution the law of unjust enrichment reverses enrichment or gains obtained by the defendant at the expense of the plaintiff. It is mainly concerned with recovery of money payments, as money paid for a non-existent debt.[149] Birks observed that the 'law of unjust enrichment is the law of all events materially identical to the mistaken payment of a non-existent debt'.[150] With this monetary emphasis, it would appear counterintuitive to apply the law of unjust enrichment to the human body and body parts. *Greenberg v. Miami Children's Hospital*, therefore, accentuates the need for a closer examination of the relevance of unjust enrichment to the human body and body parts.

A claimant who wishes to assert a restitutionary remedy based on unjust enrichment must establish that: a. the defendant was enriched; b. at the expense of the plaintiff; and c. it is unjust for the defendant to retain the benefit.[151] These elemental requirements are equally mandatory where the claimant alleges that the defendant's enrichment resulted from an interference with a dead body or body parts. This can happen in a given number of situations. *Moore v. Regents of the University of California*-type of cases would be typical. In *Moore's* case a physician/researcher surreptitiously obtained Moore's bodily tissues after performing a medically needed splenectomy (removal of Moore's diseased spleen). Moore's unique tissues were subsequently applied in a medical research that yielded a therapeutic product of enormous commercial value, running into millions of dollars. Although *Moore's* case concerned the body part of a living person, body parts of a deceased relative could also be reduced to a similar scientific application, with potentials for financial gain or benefit. Even absent actual scientific research on a body part, the defendant could obtain a benefit by selling it to DNA banks or biotechnology companies for a fee. It is too late today to argue that body parts of the dead or a living body have no recognizable value other than food for worms. The inutility of corpses was part of the reason why common law recognized no property rights in dead bodies. But things have changed and developments in medical sciences have pushed the value of corpses and body parts beyond common law's contemplation. Modern biotechnology has enhanced both the utility and commercial value of dead bodies and body parts. Developments and improvements in transplantation technology mean that many more

---

148 *Ibid.*, at 1072–3.

149 *Kelly v. Solari* (1841) 152 E.R. 24. This monetary aspect of unjust enrichment was emphasized by Stoljar when comparing unjust enrichment action to tort: 'The fact remains that whereas unjust enrichment seeks the recovery of money, tort is more concerned with things. It is a very simple difference which accordingly seems minor; yet it is a most significant difference nonetheless.' Samuel Stoljar, 'Unjust Enrichment and Unjust Sacrifice' (1987) *M.L.R.* 603, at 606.

150 Peter Birks, *Unjust Enrichment*, 2nd edn (Oxford: Oxford University Press, 2005), at 3.

151 *Ibid.*, at 39.

human organs would be needed for the relief of those in need. Body parts are needed to feed the demands of DNA banks which are increasing in number and widening the scope of their scientific inquiry. Dead bodies are needed for medical education, as a source of organs for transplants, for test of auto crashes or land-mine boots, for artistic casts, and for display. With these uses in mind, it might be wondered whether any legal system could reasonably hold that body parts obtained by the defendant at the expense of the plaintiff does not constitute a benefit. But this concern just pre-empts a question that requires analysis. The question is whether a human body part constitutes a benefit for the purpose of the law of unjust enrichment?

To succeed in an action for unjust enrichment, the plaintiff must first establish that the defendant was enriched since, according to Lord Millet in *Foskett v. McKeown*, 'he (defendant) cannot have been unjustly enriched if he has not been enriched at all'.[152] But the difficulty lies in defining 'enrichment' for the purpose of an unjust enrichment action. Does it include non-money benefits? This is very crucial for body parts. Being non-monetary by nature, body parts cannot be subject to the law of unjust enrichment unless by definition they are included within the term 'enrichment'. Monetary enrichment is not problematic since money is a measure of value. Receipt of money enlarges the recipient's wealth construed as a single fund measurable in money.[153] Any doubts on enrichment, therefore, give way when the subtraction from a plaintiff sounds in money. A problem arises, however, in the case of non-money subtractions, such as pure services or benefits with no exchange value. If I give you a part of my body that enabled you to carry out an important scientific research that resulted in academic publication, you have no doubt benefited from my body part, but have you been enriched? Although Beatson[154] has argued that only enrichments with exchange value suffice, Virgo thinks that it is too restrictive a definition and does not cover practical instances where enrichment might be conceded absent the possibility of market exchange.[155] Virgo suggests, therefore, that enrichment is better construed as a 'benefit' so as to cover cases of receipt of pure services. Virgo's view seems to be more acceptable and supported by cases where services[156] and non-money benefits[157] were held to constitute enrichment. Courts use both objective and subjective tests to determine the value of non-money benefits. Objectively, the question is whether what the defendant received is something reasonable people would value and pay for; the subjective analysis respects the defendant's autonomy and freedom to set his or her priorities by ascertaining the value placed on the receipt

---

152 *Foskett v. McKeown* (2000) 2 W.L.R. 1299, at 1324.

153 Birks, *supra*, note 150, at 71.

154 Beatson, J. *The Use and Abuse of Unjust Enrichment* (Oxford: Clarendon Press, 1991), at 29–32.

155 Graham Virgo, *The Principles of the Law of Restitution*, 2nd edn (Oxford: Oxford University Press, 2006), at 62–4.

156 *Rowe v. Vale of White Horse DC* (2003) EWHC 388 (concerning the supply of sewage services).

157 *McDonald v. Coys of Kensington* (2004) 1 W.L.R. 2775 (concerning a personalized registration mark).

by the defendant. This is known as subjective devaluation.[158] Subjective devaluation is displaced by a showing of free acceptance and incontrovertible benefit.

On this analysis, Virgo has identified four categories of enrichment which do not include body parts: money, property, services and payment made to a third party on behalf of the defendant.[159] Some remarks could be made. First, Virgo was not concerned with problems of unjust enrichment in the unique area of body parts; and the subject as a whole, as evident from analysis of other commentators, is hardly within the contemplation of the law of unjust enrichment. Few books on restitution and unjust enrichment mention body parts. Second, although Virgo has not expressly included body parts as an example of enrichment, the categories he identified are not closed and do not conceptually exclude body parts. Third, it is arguable that body parts clearly come within the meaning of enrichment. The biotechnological contexts of body parts utilization make this argument very persuasive. It can hardly be said that no benefit is obtained from the use of a body part in a scientific research with potentials for commercial gain. The incontrovertible benefit does not make a room for subjective devaluation. The scientific researchers in *Moore* and *Greenberg's* cases could not credibly have argued that they obtained no benefit from the use of the plaintiffs' tissues. Less clear, however, are cases where the research led only to academic publication, or was not successful at all. In such cases, it is difficult to see the gain or enrichment by reference to which restitution must be made. For how can you be unjustly enriched if you were not enriched at all?[160] Many cases of interference with the human body would belong to this category. Interferences like those in *Moore* and *Greenberg* capable of yielding reversible benefits are completely outweighed by the preponderant complaints of 'non-beneficial' interferences with the human body such as: interference with the right to possession and custody of a corpse for the purpose of burial; right to have the corpse delivered in the way it was when life left it; right to determine the time, place and manner of burial; right to notification of death; and right of repose. What this means is that although body parts could constitute 'enrichment' for the purpose of the law of unjust enrichment, it is only with reference to applications of the human body that yield or are capable of yielding commercial gain. If this view is accepted, then a plaintiff complaining of interference with his body part or that of a deceased relative is still outside the remedial confines of unjust enrichment if the body part was used in a pure scientific and non-commercial research. For instance, where an autopsy was performed on a deceased person without authority, or where a corpse was mutilated or parts of it taken for the purpose of medical education, a plaintiff cannot claim in unjust enrichment. Such a plaintiff must have failed the first hurdle.

The second element 'at the expense' of the plaintiff is also not free from difficulties when applied to the human body. It means that the benefit must have come directly from the plaintiff or indirectly from him or her if the principles of interceptive subtractions are applicable.[161] For plaintiffs like *Moore* or *Greenberg*,

---

158 Virgo, *supra*, note 155, at 65–7.
159 *Ibid.*, at 69–72.
160 *Foskett v. McKeown*, *supra*, note 152, Lord Millet.
161 Birks, *supra*, note 150, at 75–8.

the requirement is easily satisfied. Moore's physician surreptitiously obtained Moore's body parts directly from him. Greenberg and other Canavan disease families directly gave their body parts to the researchers. Complexities arise, however, in two instances. First, a human body part might be obtained by a researcher from other researchers in the course of sharing of data and materials that characterize the scientific landscape. Sharing of biological raw materials is very well known and encouraged by the scientific community. In some instances materials can be shared across regions and continents. Slices of Einstein's brain are known to have been shared and distributed among some scientists in the world.[162] It was the need not to hinder this scientific tradition that partly inspired the majority's decision in *Moore's* case. But the tradition itself poses serious challenges to proving that a body part was subtracted from the plaintiff. Take a case where P's body part was taken by X and then passed through many other scientific hands until it reached D who used it in a lucrative scientific research without knowing the provenance of the original raw material. Could D then be said to be enriched at the expense of P? It seems that policy rather than law would infuse this type of analysis; and would be dominated by the need to promote rather than inhibit scientific research. Therefore, in a case of long transactional or ambiguous chain involving a body part, a court is more likely to hold that the enrichment was not at the expense of the plaintiff. Second, where the body part is not directly obtained from the plaintiff but from the body of a deceased relative, the case for unjust enrichment is likely to be weak. In unjust enrichment, a plaintiff must prove that, before the transfer to the defendant, the 'enrichment' belonged to him or her.[163] If you sell a car which does not belong to you and the purchase price is recovered after the transaction is terminated, you cannot sue the purchaser to recover for the use he or she made of the car in the period up to the termination of the transaction.[164] The car did not belong to you and the enrichment obtained by the purchaser was not at your expense. It was at the expense of the true owner. So also is the case of a deceased relative's body part. With the present state of the law recognizing no property interest in the dead body of a relative, a plaintiff would have a hard time proving that the beneficial use of a dead relative's body part was at his or her expense. The body part simply did not belong to the plaintiff. Although use of a decedent's body part is concededly 'at the expense' of living relatives, such as devaluing next of kin's sentiments toward the dead, Birks argued that such broad conceptions of the phrase (at the expense of) are wrong and that its meaning is restricted to the subtractive sense.[165] This would mean that many cases of interference with the human body, the majority of which concerns the bodies of deceased relatives, would be outside the reach of an unjust enrichment claim. The gist of such cases is the protection of the sentiment of the living towards the dead.

---

162 Lori Andrews and Dorothy Nelkin, *Body Bazaar: The Market for Human Tissue in the Biotechnology Age* (New York: Crown Publishers, 2001), at 9–11.

163 Andrew Burrows, 'Proprietary Restitution: Unmasking Unjust Enrichment' (2001) 117 *L.Q.R.* 412, at 415.

164 *Rowland v. Divall* (1923) 2 K.B. 500.

165 Birks, *supra*, note 150, at 74.

Desecration of the dead is simply not a subtraction for the purposes of the law of unjust enrichment.

Another challenge with the element of 'at the expense' of the plaintiff relates to the establishment of loss. It is still a controversial matter whether the plaintiff is required to show that he or she suffered a loss at all or one that exactly corresponds to the defendant's gain. Birks argued strongly that 'English law appears not to insist that the claimant must have suffered one (loss)' and cited instances where benefits could be gained without a corresponding loss.[166] After analysing the contending perspectives, Virgo opined that exact correspondence should not be required, though some loss must be shown. Accordingly, he preferred 'that some very limited form of the correspondence principle is recognized, but only in the sense that the defendant's gain is reflected by a loss suffered by the claimant'.[167] The case for the presence of a loss is strengthened by *Re BHT (UK) Ltd*,[168] though it decided in favour of the correspondence principle. It would appear that at the minimum, the plaintiff is required to demonstrate some loss. If loss is construed monetarily, as is typical of many unjust enrichment claims that involve receipt of money, or as requiring physical impact or the valuation of property, then a plaintiff complaining of interference with a human body part has a big hurdle. Apart from probable diminishment of autonomy or privacy, what loss does a person suffer when his or her body part or that of a relative is used in scientific research? Mental distress is possible; but as we saw in the treatment of nervous shock, it is unlikely that the courts would import the difficulties in the assessment of psychiatric injury into the law of unjust enrichment. Except the courts accept Birks' thesis on the irrelevance of the loss element, a plaintiff complaining of an interference with a body part can hardly prove a recognizable legal loss for the purposes of unjust enrichment.

The final element is that it must be unjust for the defendant to retain the enrichment. A defendant may be justly enriched at the expense of the plaintiff. It is important that the unjust factor be established. English common law recognizes certain restitutionary factors. Thus, Lord Mansfield in *Moses v. Macferlan* observed that an action 'lies for money paid by mistake; or upon a consideration which happens to fail; or for money got through imposition, (express or implied) or extortion; or oppression; or an undue advantage taken of the plaintiff's situation, contrary to laws for the protection of persons under those circumstances'.[169] Though Lord Mansfield's formulation of restitutionary grounds apparently relate to money enrichment, they are equally applicable to non-money benefits. For as Virgo has observed there is 'no reason why the application of any of the grounds of restitution should depend on the nature of the enrichment which the defendant has received'.[170] Examining these factors from the plaintiff's perspective means that there would be restitution whenever it is established that the plaintiff's intention was impaired. This impairment was raised by the *Greenberg* plaintiffs who argued that they would not have provided

---

166 *Ibid.*, at 78.

167 Virgo, *supra*, note 155, at 114.

168 *Re BHT (UK) Ltd* (2004) EWHC 201 (Ch).

169 *Moses v. Macferlan* (1760) 97 E.R. 676, at 681.

170 Virgo, *supra*, note 155, at 126.

the defendants with their body parts if they had known that the defendants would commercialize their genetic materials through patenting and restrictive licensing. In other circumstances involving an interference with dead bodies and body parts, it is relatively easy for a plaintiff to prove absence of consent, undue influence or exploitation. For instance, in *AB v. Leeds*, the plaintiffs were able to prove that the retention of their children's body parts after autopsy was without their consent; and in *Moore v Regents of the University of California*, the court held that the harvesting of the plaintiff's bodily tissues infringed the rules of informed consent. It is difficult to see how an abuse, mutilation or exploitation of a dead body or body part would not come within one of the recognized grounds of restitution. Provided a plaintiff is able to scale the difficult but first two elements of an action for unjust enrichment, the third element of an unjust ground is relatively easy to establish.

Property Remedy

It is apparent that the deficiencies inherent in all the remedies examined above still leave a potential plaintiff in a vulnerable position. It is therefore pertinent to consider whether a property-based approach would alleviate the remedial difficulties faced by a plaintiff complaining of interference with a dead body or body part. But a property relief would not be available except the law recognizes a property interest in a dead body or body part. No doubt, English common law does not generally recognize a property interest in the human body. This general rule is, however, living dangerously and is threatened to be engulfed by some judicially crafted exceptions. Restriction of the no-property rule in the human body started with the Australian case of *Doodeward v. Spence*[171] where the plaintiff brought an action to recover possession of a double-headed foetus seized by the police and used for public display. The plaintiff had previously purchased the monstrous birth from a physician who preserved it by the application of work and skill. The High Court of Australia was divided on the question of whether the stillborn foetus was capable of being property of the plaintiff. Griffith, C.J. for the majority held that:

> [W]hen a person has by the lawful exercise of work or skill so dealt with a human body or part of a human body in his lawful possession that it has acquired some attributes differentiating it from a mere corpse awaiting burial, he acquires a right to retain possession of it, at least as against any person not entitled to have it delivered to him for the purpose of burial.[172]

The *Doodeward* exception was incorporated into English law by the Court of Appeal's decision in *Dobson v. North Tyneside H.A.*[173] In that case, the plaintiff, an administratrix of the deceased, with a view to a medical malpractice action, sought to obtain the brain tissues of the deceased removed by the defendant after an autopsy ordered by a coroner. Because the defendant destroyed the brain tissues after the post-

---

171 *Doodeward v. Spence* (1908) 6 C.L.R. 406.

172 *Ibid.*, at 414.

173 *Dobson v. North Tyneside H.A.* (1997) 1 W.L.R. 596.

mortem, the plaintiff brought an amended claim for conversion of her property interest in the deceased's tissues. The Court of Appeal observed that while an administratrix has a right to possession and custody of a deceased person for burial, the plaintiff could not succeed because she was appointed an administratrix shortly before the commencement of the suit in 1994 and long after the destruction of the brain, giving rise to the cause of action, had taken place. Equally unsuccessful was her claim as a next of kin because English law, according to the Court of Appeal, did not recognize any duty on the next of kin to bury a deceased person from which a corollary right of possession might arise. Even if a next of kin were to have that right, it terminates on burial of the deceased. Since the plaintiff's decedent in this case had been buried before the case began, her claim as next of kin, even if interpreted benevolently, was, therefore, bound to fail. In other words, disposition of a deceased person is fatal to any possible claim by the next of kin. Ultimately, the plaintiff argued that the fixing of the brain by the defendant came within the exception in *Doodeward* and was sufficient to grant her a property interest in the deceased's tissues for the purpose of conversion. Although the Court of Appeal recognized the *Doodeward* exception, it held that the work and skill in this case (mere fixing of the brain) was not sufficient to trigger that exception:

> Does this mean that it is arguable that when Dr. Perry fixed the brain in paraffin, he thereby transformed it into an item the right to possession of which or the property in which belonged to the plaintiffs? For my part, I do not think so…There is nothing in the pleading or evidence before us to suggest that the actual preservation of the brain after the post mortem was on a par with stuffing or embalming a corpse or preserving an anatomical or pathological specimen for a scientific collection or with preserving a human freak such as a double-headed foetus that had some value for exhibition purposes.[174]

The *ratio* in *Dobson's* case was approvingly referred to in *R v. Kelly*,[175] which recognizes that in some circumstances a property interest might exist in the human body. In that case, an artist dishonestly obtained 35–40 body parts belonging to the Royal College of Surgeons and used for medical education. Kelly wanted the parts for drawing of anatomical specimens. He was charged with theft under the *Theft Act 1968*. He argued, among other things, that a dead body or parts of a dead body belonged to no one and are not capable of being stolen. The Court of Appeal rejected the existence of this wide proposition, observing that 'parts of a corpse are capable of being property within s 4 of the Theft Act, if they have different attributes by virtue of the application of skill, such as dissection or preservation techniques, for exhibition or teaching'.[176] More interestingly, Rose, L.J. anticipated a more expansive future exception that would go beyond *Doodeward* by allowing property rights in body parts that have some use despite the absence of any work and skill on them:

---

174 *Ibid.*, at 601.
175 *R v. Kelly* (1998) 3 All E.R. 741.
176 *Ibid.*, at 749–50.

Furthermore, the common law does not stand still. It may be that if, on some future occasion, the question arises, the courts will hold that human body parts are capable of being property for the purpose of s 4, even without the acquisition of different attributes, if they have a use or significance beyond their mere existence. This may be so if, for example, they are intended for use in an organ transplant operation, for the extraction of DNA or, for that matter, as an exhibit in a trial.[177]

Recently in *AB v. Leeds*, Gage, J. affirmed that property rights can exist in a corpse or part of it in certain circumstances. In that case, parents of deceased children complained that retention of their children's tissues after autopsy was unauthorized and was an unlawful interference with their deceased infants' bodies. The court held that to the extent that the plaintiffs' claim sounded in conversion, they were bound to fail because English law did not recognize an action for conversion of the body of a dead person.[178] The court, however, held that the slides and blocks produced with the retained paediatric parts were the property of the defendants due to the skill and work required for their preparation:

> In my judgment the principle that part of a body may acquire the character of property which can be the subject of rights of possession and ownership is now part of our law. In particular, in my opinion, the Kelly case establishes the exception to the rule that there is no property in a corpse where part of the body has been the subject of the application of skill such as dissection or preservation techniques. The evidence in the lead cases shows that to dissect and fix an organ from a child's body requires work and a great deal of skill, the more so in the case of a very small baby such as Rosina Harris. The subsequent production of blocks and slides is also a skilful operation requiring work and expertise of trained scientists.[179]

Gage, J. therefore concluded that as against the parents/plaintiffs, the pathologists 'became entitled to possess the organs, the blocks and slides at least until a better right is asserted'.[180] This is an important conclusion since it debunks the erroneous assumption that a property rule would always work against medical institutions and biotechnology companies who are engaged in useful activities that have potentials to improve human health. Medical institutions and biotech companies are currently the greatest beneficiaries of the *Doodeward* exception because of their ability to transform a corpse or body part through the application of work and skill. It is suggested that a properly formulated property rule for dead bodies and body parts will not only protect plaintiffs complaining of interference with their bodies or that of their dead relatives, but also biotech companies that utilize body parts as raw materials for their products. More importantly, total rejection of a property approach to the human body does not reflect the widening exceptions increasingly recognized by the courts. The question should not be whether a property interest exists in the human body (as it does); rather, the inquiry should focus on the extent to which property interests should be recognized in the human body. More specifically, and as recognized

---

177 *Ibid.*, at 750.
178 *AB v. Leeds, supra*, note 48, at 398.
179 *Ibid.*, at 395.
180 *Ibid.*, at 396.

by Rose, L.J. in *R v. Kelly*, analytical attention should now be diverted to those circumstances outside work and skill which merit the recognition of a property right. For instance, the law might wish to recognize that a plaintiff's right to possession and custody of a corpse for the purpose of burial approximates to a property right sufficient to underpin an action for conversion. It is for this purpose that this book has suggested the recognition of a limited and remedially-based property interest in the human body. On the basis of the existence and recognition of a limited property right in the human body, the most important avenue for its vindication is an action for conversion.

Conversion

A claim in conversion protects a plaintiff against any intermeddling or interference with his or her property rights. Conversion exists despite the absence of complete ownership. It is sufficient that a plaintiff has actual possession or right to possession of the converted good. Thus, Patterson, J. observed in *Rogers v. Kennay* that any 'person having a right to the possession of goods may bring trover in respect of the conversion of them, and allege them to be his property: and lien, as an immediate right of possession, was held to constitute such a property.'[181] The centrality of possession in an action for conversion is evidenced by cases such as *Costello v. Chief Constable of Derbyshire*,[182] where the possessor of a stolen car was held, as against the police, to be entitled to it; and *Parker v. British Airways Board*,[183] where the finder of a gold bracelet at the executive lounge of Heathrow Airport was held to have title superior to that of the occupiers. But the mere dispossession of a plaintiff does not automatically amount to conversion; he or she must show that the defendant exercised acts that were inconsistent with the plaintiff's title. Acts of interference must be substantial and not trivial. Thus, it was held that conversion was not established in *Fouldes v. Willoughby*[184] when, due to an argument between the plaintiff and defendant, after the latter had embarked on the plaintiff's boat with his horses, the plaintiff put the horses to the shore upon the defendant's refusal to get off the boat. Conversion is a strict liability tort. This means that a deliberate and voluntary act is sufficient, such as where D voluntarily receives from X goods belonging to P without knowing of the defects in X's title.[185] Diplock, L.J. observed in *Marfani & Co. v. Midland Bank Ltd.*:[186]

> At common law one's duty to one's neighbour who is the owner...of any goods is to refrain from doing any voluntary act in relation to his goods which is usurpation of his proprietary or possessory rights in them. Subject to some exceptions...it matters not that

---

181 *Rogers v. Kennay* (1846) 9 Q.B. 594, at 596.
182 *Costello v. Chief Constable of Derbyshire* (2001) 1 W.L.R. 1437.
183 *Parker v. British Airways Board* (1982) Q.B. 1004.
184 *Foulides v. Willoughby* (1841) 8 M. & W. 540.
185 The voluntary nature of acts of conversion was emphasized by the British Columbia Supreme Court in *Poy v. Law Society* (1985) 68 B.C.L.R. 224 (B.C. Sup. Ct.).
186 *Marfani & Co. v. Midland Bank Ltd* (1968) 1 W.L.R. 956, at 971.

the doer of the act of usurpation did not know, and could not by the exercise of any reasonable care have known of his neighbour's interest in the goods. This duty is absolute; he acts at his peril.

The measure of damages for conversion is generally determined by the value of the goods at the date of conversion, and any consequential loss suffered by the plaintiff.

Because of its relative advantage, the framework of conversion recommends itself to a plaintiff contemplating litigation in relation to the human body or parts of it. A few problems arise, however, both from the defendant's and plaintiff's perspectives. As regards the defendant, a strict liability conversion claim in respect of a human body part may result in injustice. Consider the wide sharing and distribution of human biological material in the scientific milieu. If conversion were to be accepted in this area of law, a researcher might be held liable for conversion of a human body part obtained from other scientists without knowledge of the original source of the material. This consideration featured heavily in the majority's reasons for rejecting a conversion claim in *Moore's* case. In contrast to the defendant, the hurdles faced by a plaintiff suing for conversion of a human body part are even more challenging. Currently, many Western legal systems do not generally recognize a property interest in the human body. But, theoretically, this should not be a problem since a plaintiff does not need to establish a property right at the level of ownership to succeed in conversion. Possession is sufficient. Ordinarily one would think that having a right to possession and custody of a deceased person for burial is sufficient for a decedent's close relative to bring an action for conversion. After all, is it not settled law that an executor or the next of kin, as the case may be, is entitled to immediate possession of the deceased for burial? Is this not a possessory right? Unfortunately, many of the cases reviewed in this book suggest that this type of possessory interest is not sufficient to underpin an action for conversion. This is a quintessential instance of gap between practice and theory: the theory of possessory right in dead bodies and the practice of denying conversion for its protection. But it is a weird kind of gap. If the possession of a finder (*Parker's* case) and that of a receiver of a stolen car (*Costello's* case) were sufficient to ground conversion, then there is no reason for denying such a cause of action to a person who is clearly considered by law to have possession of a deceased person for the purpose of burial. This shows that decisions in this area are clearly influenced by sometimes unanalysed public policy. To the extent that such policies are analysed, as in *Moore's* case where anchorage was found in support for biotechnology activities, they do not consider the contradiction of vesting in a defendant the same property right not acceded to a plaintiff. In England, similarly, it will be wrong to construe recent decisions on the point as deciding that there can be no conversion for dead bodies and body parts outside the work and skill exception. Though Gage, J. in *AB v. Leeds* held that English law does not recognize an action for conversion of body parts, it is pertinent to analyse that decision in the context of *Dobson's* case, the first decision in England to consider whether conversion exists for dead bodies and body parts. Gibson, L.J. in *Dobson's* case accepted that the plaintiff's amended claim was for conversion of the decedent's brain, but held that the plaintiff failed for reasons other than non-recognition of conversion claims for body parts in English law. Gibson, L.J.'s judgement was rather based on the fact that the plaintiff, having being appointed an administratrix after the cause of action had arisen, failed to establish a possessory right to the deceased's brain, a necessary ingredient of conversion. If anything, the Court of Appeal in *Dobson's* case recognized that a conversion claim was arguable but not available on the particular facts of that case. On this premise, it is suggested that Gage, J. in *AB v. Leeds* went beyond the bounds of *Dobson's* case in holding that conversion of body parts is not a recognized claim in English law. Nevertheless, some commentators still treat dead bodies and body parts as being outside the law of conversion. For instance, while Rogers identified property capable of conversion as any 'corporeal, movable property', which presumably includes a body part, he nevertheless excluded body parts and dead bodies by observing that: 'There is no property in a corpse (as opposed to e.g. a preserved specimen or skeleton prepared for anatomical purposes).'[187] Could this last quotation not be taken to assume that a right of ownership or property is required for an action for conversion? The impression is misleading; and Rogers made it clear he was not committed to that misconception by warning against the uncritical use of expressions such as 'a right of property in the thing and a right of possession' in respect of conversion:

> If 'right of property' means 'ownership', this might lead one to infer that no one can sue for conversion except an owner in possession at the date of the alleged conversion. But that is not so, for a bailee has only possession and not ownership (which remains in the bailor), and yet the bailee can sue a third party for conversion. And...one who has mere possession at the date of the conversion can generally sue, and so can one who has no more than a right to possess.[188]

This suggests that the elimination of body parts and dead bodies from the realm of conversion is arbitrary and distorts the possession requirement for an action in conversion. To reiterate, it is suggested that just as mere possession is sufficient for conversion of an ordinary chattel, possession of a dead body for burial or right to possession of one's body part should also be sufficient for an action in conversion.

Another challenge facing a potential plaintiff relates to damages for conversion, which is the value of the converted goods. This is presumably the market value. With no current market value for body parts, a plaintiff may find a conversion claim unavailable. This is a real but not insuperable difficulty. In *Culpepper v. Pearl Street Building*,[189] the plaintiffs' son was mistakenly cremated and they brought an action for conversion of their son's body. The majority of the Supreme Court of Colorado rejected the plaintiffs' conversion claim on the additional ground that a dead body had no compensable value, making it difficult to assess damages for conversion measured by the value of the converted property at the date of conversion. But this view may not be entirely accurate in view of recent developments in biotechnology. As we saw in Chapter 2, there is an increasing standardization of the prices of various body parts

---

187 W.H.V. Rogers, *Winfield and Jolowicz on Tort*, 16th edn (London: Sweet & Maxwell, 2002), at 596.

188 *Ibid.*, at 605.

189 *Culpepper v. Pearl Street Building* 877 P. 2d 877, at 882 (Colo. Sup Ct. 1994).

through market channels that are currently unlawful. Recognition of some property rights in body parts will allow for a proper market valuation of various body parts even in the teeth of moral repugnance of the resultant commodification. Moreover, the courts have a lot of experience with the valuation of things without exchange value, such as a wedding ring, or mental distress or damages for psychiatric injury. It is a diminution of this judicial experience to deny a conversion claim for body parts merely on the ground of difficulties associated with the assessment of damages. In summary, it is urged that a conversion claim should be available for interference with dead bodies and body parts, either on the basis of rights to possession and custody of a deceased person for burial, or on the basis of recognition of a limited property interest in the human body.

Conclusion

Much as strong support has been shown both for the recognition of limited property rights in dead bodies and body parts, and the availability of property-based remedies, such as conversion, to plaintiffs complaining of interference with their body parts or that of their dead relatives, it should not be forgotten that the property and non-property remedies considered in this chapter are not mutually exclusive. In other words, a plaintiff should, and is encouraged to, make non-property claims such as negligence claims for nervous shock or infliction of psychiatric injury, breach of privacy, consent or informed consent, deprivation of a constitutionally protected interest, and unjust enrichment. All these should be in addition to a property claim for conversion of a dead body or body parts. Property claims in conversion are attractive for their ease of application and ability to provide relief in circumstances where a plaintiff would have failed despite the injustice suffered by him or her. Because of the requirements associated with the non-property remedies, claims relating to dead bodies and body parts are susceptible to failure. Despite their weaknesses, however, the non-property claims remain important and might provide a safety net for a plaintiff whose property claims are rejected by a court.

Chapter 6

Property and Traditional Knowledge

Introduction

While the previous chapters analysed the challenges faced by property in the areas of dead bodies, body parts, genes and genetic information, this chapter examines a similar challenge to the concept of property but in the different area of traditional knowledge. It explores various issues at the intersection of property and traditional knowledge, especially how the concept of property can be used to protect traditional knowledge. At this stage, the pertinent question is whether the argument for the protection of dead bodies, body parts, genes and genetic information with a limited property regime could be equally applicable to the protection of traditional knowledge? Traditional knowledge is a term that embraces very diverse subjects such as folklore, folk art, folk song, folk music, folk medicine, folk tales, and farmers' varieties of seeds. Traditional knowledge has both tangible and intangible aspects, and its dual forms may appeal to an understanding of property as a 'right to a thing' as well as a 'bundle of rights'. Traditional knowledge, especially knowledge relating to medicine and agriculture, is substantially used by a significant proportion of developing countries' population; and its popularity is increasing in developed countries.[1]

Modern biotechnology has drawn more attention to the potentials of traditional knowledge, especially in the industrialized world. Some pharmaceutical companies in the North use traditional knowledge as one of the tools of their drug discovery efforts. Traditional knowledge and medicinal plants from the South provided the foundation for some drugs developed in the North and now yielding huge income to the pharmaceutical corporations, with little or no returns to traditional knowledge holders.[2] The increasing importance of traditional knowledge and associated products partly justifies their conservation and sustainable use. The conservation of medicinal plants, and biodiversity in general, is threatened by a number of factors including urbanization and various development projects in the South,[3] and inadequate or zero compensation to traditional knowledge holders for the commercial use of traditional knowledge by some multinational corporations.

---

1   Robert Crouch, Richard Elliot, Trudo Lemmens and Louis Charland, *Complementary/Alternative Health Care and HIV/AIDS: Legal, Ethical and Policy Issues in Regulation* (Canadian HIV/AIDS Legal Network, 2001), at 11–13 (observing that between 1990 and 1997 there has been a significant increase in the percentage of Canadians using complementary/alternative health care).

2   Erin B. Newman, 'Earth's Vanishing Medicine Cabinet: Rain Forest Destruction and its Impact on the Pharmaceutical Industry' (1994) 20 *AM. J. L & M* 479.

3   *Ibid.*

Some developing countries also complain that the use or commercialization of some aspects of traditional knowledge and associated products, for instance, the display of some sacred or spiritually relevant traditional artefacts in some Western museums and the depiction of sacred images on commercial products, devalue indigenous peoples' spirituality and dilute their culture.[4] Some of the above issues have underpinned the debate for the protection of traditional knowledge.[5] Thus, in addition to the challenges brought about by the products and processes of new technology, ancient art, for instance folklore and folk techniques, has also challenged the application of property law.[6]

This chapter rethinks some of the objectives of protection of traditional knowledge and the frameworks that are available or potentially available to achieve the desired protection. For instance, is it possible to protect traditional knowledge using existing forms of intellectual property rights (patents, copyright, trademark, industrial design, trade secret and geographical indication) or is the design of a unique framework more appropriate? This chapter highlights the potential and actual difficulties associated with intellectual property rights (IPR) protection and suggests the framing or designing of *sui generis* protection for traditional knowledge. Samples of existing *sui generis* frameworks are analysed. Other protective devices, such as the formulation of a regime to avoid misappropriation and the use of private contracts, are explored. This chapter also examines efforts at the international forum that impact on the protection of traditional knowledge, and suggests that national and regional approaches may be pursued first, and experience gained may later inspire an international solution.

The Meaning, Nature and Relevance of Traditional Knowledge

It is difficult to provide a precise definition of traditional knowledge (hereafter, TK) due to its diverse components, the heterogeneous nature of its constituents, and the different applications of its elements. For instance, TK embraces knowledge of the medicinal properties of plants and animals, knowledge relating to agriculture, folklore,

---

4   *Milpurrurru v. Indofurn Pty. Ltd.* (1994) 54 F.C.R. 240 (Australia), holding that the depiction of aboriginal sacred images on the defendant's imported carpets was a violation of the copyright of the plaintiffs/aboriginal artists in their indigenous work.

5   Lucy M. Moran, 'Intellectual Property Law Protection for Traditional and Sacred Folklife Expressions – Will Remedies Become Available to Cultural Authors and Communities?' (1999) 6 *U. Balt. Intell. Prop. L.J.* 99, at 103–104:

> The need for protection of folklore expressions arises from rapid development of technologies and from the globalization of market economies. Each facilitates the commercialization of folklore…Appropriated works are often distorted or mutilated to adapt to market demands, or copied or distributed out of context without due respect for the cultural and economic interests of the communities in which they originate. No authorization is sought from the communities, no appellation of origin is attached to appropriated works, and no share of the returns from the exploitation is conceded to the communities who have developed and maintained it.

6   Christine H. Farley, 'Protecting Folklore of Indigenous Peoples: Is Intellectual Property the Answer?' (1997) 1 *Connecticut Law Review* 1, at 2.

art, music, dance, literature, designs, marks, names and symbols. TK is part of the cultural manifestation of its holders.[7] The continued use of TK and its modification in response to societal dynamics of its holders is relevant for the perpetuation of the culture, identity and lifestyles of its custodians. In this context, a precise definition of TK would require an exact explication of the associated lifestyle, culture, belief and way of life of its holders. TK could be described as including information, practice, creativity, innovation and invention that is tradition-based.[8]

WIPO has suggested that a precise definition of TK is not as important as defining the criterion for its protection.[9] The New African Initiative (NAI) of the Organization of African Unity (now African Union) defines TK (though it adopts the term 'indigenous knowledge'[10]) in a manner similar to WIPO's definition.[11] In a

---

7 WIPO, *Intellectual Property Needs and Expectations of Traditional Knowledge Holders: WIPO Report on Fact-Finding Missions on Intellectual Property and Traditional Knowledge, 1998–1999* (Geneva: WIPO, 2001), at 26, observing that, 'traditional knowledge is, in turn, a subset of the broader concept of heritage'.

8 WIPO uses TK to refer to:

tradition-based literary, artistic or scientific works; performances; inventions; scientific discoveries; designs; marks, names and symbols; undisclosed information; and all other tradition-based innovations and creations resulting from intellectual activity in the industrial, scientific, literary or artistic fields. 'Tradition-based' refers to knowledge systems, creations, innovations and cultural expressions which: have generally been transmitted from generation to generation; are generally regarded as pertaining to a particular people or its territory; and are constantly evolving in response to a changing environment. It should be emphasized, however, that a precise definition of traditional knowledge is not a crucial requisite for establishing a system for its protection. Actually, most patent laws do not define inventions. Likewise, most trademark laws do not define signs. The crucial element for the protection of any subject-matter is the identification of some characteristics that it must meet as a condition for protection – such as novelty, inventiveness and susceptibility of industrial application, for inventions, and distinctiveness, for trademarks. The same criterion could be applied to traditional knowledge as well.

WIPO International Forum, *Intellectual Property and Traditional Knowledge: Our Identity, Our Future* (Conference organized by WIPO and the Government of the Sultanate of Oman, 21–22 January 2002).

9 *Ibid.*

10 Mugabe has suggested that TK is much broader than 'indigenous knowledge', and means the 'totality of all knowledge and practices, whether explicit or implicit, used in the management of socio-economic and ecological facets of life'. John Mugabe, 'Intellectual Property Protection and Traditional Knowledge: An Exploration in International Policy Discourse' (1998) posted on: www.acts.or.ke.

11 The NAI uses 'indigenous knowledge' to refer to 'tradition-based literary, artistic and scientific works, performances, inventions, scientific discoveries, designs, marks, names and symbols, undisclosed information and all other tradition-based innovations and creations resulting from intellectual activity in the industrial, scientific, literary or artistic fields. The term also includes genetic resources and associated medicinal knowledge.' Organization of African Unity, *The New African Initiative: A Merger of the Millennium African Renaissance Partnership Programme (MAP) and the Omega Plan* (OAU, Lusaka Summit, Zambia, July 2001).

similar but slightly more functional manner, the African Model Provisions defines TK (though using the term 'indigenous knowledge') as follows: 'Community or indigenous knowledge is the accumulated knowledge that is vital for conservation and sustainable use of biological resources and/or which is of socio-economic value, and which has been developed over the years in indigenous/local communities.'[12] TK is characterized by its collective nature, inter-generationality and continuous evolution, and is largely undocumented.

TK is usually owned collectively by a particular community, and rarely exclusively claimed by individual members of the community.[13] The generation of TK is usually the result of a conscious or subconscious response to the custodian's cultural environment and then passed from generation to generation. Thus, indigenous/traditional works that are apparently the products of individual efforts, or TK in the possession of individuals, may still be regarded as part of the collective property of a particular community.[14] Similarly, aspects of TK in the possession of only a few members of the community (such as knowledge and skills for making sacred artefacts), or in the possession of a particular group of its members (such as ritual and healing aspects of TK possessed by tribal healers or shamans) remain the collective property and heritage of present TK holders, and liable to be passed from generation to generation. However, the collective nature of TK, which probably facilitated its widespread non-exclusionary use in certain societies, is one of the factors that militates against its full protection under modern intellectual property systems that are designed to accommodate private ownership of intellectual property.

---

12 *African Model Legislation for the Protection of the Rights of Local Communities, Farmers and Breeders, and for the Regulation of Access to Biological Resources* (OAU, 2000) posted on www.grain.org, art. 1.

13 However, it is possible to witness the existence of unique individual creations in certain indigenous/traditional societies that belong to the individual rather than the community. As Downes observed: '[w]hile it is true that many indigenous cultures appear to develop and transmit knowledge from generation to generation within a communal system, individuals in local or indigenous communities can distinguish themselves as informal creators or inventors, separate from the community.' David R. Downes, 'How Intellectual Property Could Be a Tool to Protect Traditional Knowledge' (2000) 25 *Columbia Journal of Environmental Law* 253, at 258.

14 Carlos Correa, *Protection and Promotion of Traditional Medicine: Implications for Public Health in Developing Countries* (Geneva: South Centre, 2002), at 4, observed with reference to traditional medicine:

> Possession of knowledge by individuals, in effect, does not mean that such knowledge is perceived by communities as not belonging to them. Though at any one time, the knowledge may only be held by a handful of people with special roles in the community, in the course of history of that community it is essentially communally held knowledge. Those with the special knowledge do not 'own' it as such, and many have obligations to share the knowledge within the community at different intervals. There may exist, for instance, community standards for when the information must be passed, such as during initiation rituals. These features indicate slight but important differences between the meaning of individual property in Western culture, and knowledge held by individuals within a non-Western community context.

TK is said to have existed before the emergence of modern intellectual property rights and represents the lifestyles of peoples regulated by it.[15]

TK is also inter-generational, which means that it was developed and passed from one generation to another, and continues to be improved upon by the present generation of its custodians. This also means that no one generation can claim exclusive ownership or authorship of TK.[16] The issue of author specificity with respect to TK also has implications for designing its protection, whether under an intellectual property regime or a non-intellectual property regime.

TK is in continuous evolution.[17] WIPO has cautioned that the word 'traditional' used to qualify knowledge should not be equated with ancient.[18] TK continues to be improved upon, and new elements of it created, by its current holders in response to the dynamics of their cultural environment.[19]

Some elements of TK are verbal and largely undocumented; for instance, folk literature, music, performance, dance, medicinal knowledge, and knowledge relating to plant variety and agriculture. However, some elements or products of TK are fixed, documented, or in tangible form, such as folk paintings, cultural objects and other works of art, textile designs and Ayurveda traditional medicine.[20]

TK is generally relevant as an important therapeutic tool for its holders; it is also relevant for sustaining the agricultural systems of many indigenous communities and has played a significant role in the global drug industry. In some indigenous communities and developing countries, where access to modern health care is limited by socio-economic factors, significant reliance is placed upon traditional medicine and associated knowledge in fulfilling the primary health needs of the population. The World Health Organization estimates that 80 per cent of people in developing countries rely on traditional medicine for their various health needs.[21] Traditional medicine (hereinafter TM) is much more integrated in the health care systems of some countries like China, Japan and India. TM constitutes up to 30 to 50 per cent of total medicinal consumption in China.[22] Between 1974 and 1989, there was a fifteen-fold increase in traditional medicine consumption in Japan, which was said to have the

---

15 *African Model Legislation, supra,* note 12, Preamble.

16 But it is also possible to have an individually distinctive work in a traditional community. Such works would belong to the individual authors.

17 David R. Downes and Sarah A. Laird, 'Community Registries of Biodiversity-Related Knowledge: The Role of Intellectual Property in Managing Access and Benefit Sharing', in Rosemary Coombe, *Intellectual Property, Human Rights and Development* (Toronto: University of Toronto Press, 2000), 271, at 372.

18 WIPO, *supra,* note 8.

19 *Ibid.*

20 Carlos M. Correa, *Traditional Knowledge and Intellectual Property: Issues and Options Surrounding the Protection of Traditional Knowledge* (Geneva: The Quaker United Nations Office, 2001), at 4.

21 World Health Organization, Press Release: WHO Launches the First Global Strategy on Traditional and Alternative Medicine, WHO/38/16 May 2002. Posted on: www.who.int (last visited on 5 May 2003).

22 World Health Organization, Fact Sheet N 134, September 1996: Traditional Medicine. Posted on: www.who.int (last visited on 5 May 2003).

world's highest per capita consumption of herbal medicine.[23] Interest in, and use of, TM is also growing in industrialized countries.[24] The WHO estimates that in 'France, 75% of the population has used complementary medicine at least once...and in the United Kingdom, expenditure on complementary or alternative medicine stands at US$2300 million per year'.[25] Twenty-five per cent of modern pharmaceuticals are based on traditional medicinal plants and associated knowledge.[26]

Chronic conditions, like cancer, have been partly tackled with knowledge and medicinal plants derived from developing countries. For instance, vincristine and vinblastine, used in the treatment of cancers like Hodgkin's disease and pediatric lymphocytic leukaemia, were derived from the medicinal properties of Madagascar's rosy periwinkle and yield about US$100 million annually to US-based Eli Lilly.[27] It is in recognition of the importance of traditional medicinal knowledge that the World Health Organization has recently released a detailed strategy for the evaluation of the safety, efficacy, regulation and evidence of TM and the legal protection of traditional medicinal knowledge.[28]

TM and associated knowledge also play a significant role in the global drug trade. It is estimated that the value of global trade in herbal drugs amounted to US$60 billion annually.[29] The worth of TM in domestic markets is also enormous and continues to grow. In China, TM generated about US$5 billion in 1999 from the international market and US$1 billion from the domestic market.[30] There has been a significant increase in the sales of some traditional medicinal products in the USA. It was estimated that between 1997 and 1998 the following percentage increase occurred in the sales of popular TM products in the USA: Total herbal supplements 101 per cent, Tchinacea 96 per cent, Garlic 24 per cent, Ginkgo biloba 143 per cent, Ginseng 26 per cent, St John's wort 102 per cent, and other herbs 85 per cent.[31]

TK has been relevant in the generation and improvement of traditional varieties of crops, which form the basis of food and seed supply and have sustained the agricultural systems of some traditional communities. Thus, TK may significantly impact on the food security of indigenous communities and developing countries.[32] It

---

23 *Ibid.*

24 Crouch, *et al.*, *supra*, note 1.

25 WHO, *supra*, note 22.

26 *Ibid.*

27 Shayana Kadidal, 'Plants, Poverty, and Pharmaceutical Patents' (1993) 103 *Yale L.J.*, at 223–4.

28 WHO, *WHO Traditional Medicine Strategy 2002–2005* (Geneva: World Health Organization, 2002).

29 WHO, *supra*, note 22.

30 Correa, *supra*, note 14, at 9.

31 WHO, *supra*, note 28, at 12.

32 For general analysis: Geoff Tansey, *Food Security, Biotechnology and Intellectual Property: Unpacking Some Issues Around TRIPS* (Geneva: Quaker United Nations Office, 2002).

is estimated that about 90 per cent of the world's food crops is derived from farmers' varieties nurtured by TK.[33]

In addition, TK has underpinned the overall cultural life of some traditional societies and has formed the basis of their folklore, arts, designs, music and other artistic manifestations. Paul Kuruk has highlighted the contribution of TK in moulding the African personality through the morale of folktales and songs.[34] Important historical events have been recorded in folk music, also used for festive, burial and ritual purposes, as well as announcing the beginning of hostilities between warring factions or ethnic nationalities.[35] The importance of traditional knowledge is gradually gaining recognition outside the traditional milieu, and the need for its protection has been recently recognized, though differences still exist as to the modalities for such protection.

The Protection of Traditional Knowledge

Though some commentators, NGOs and international bodies, such as WHO, WIPO and FAO, have accepted in principle that TK deserves protection, there does not appear to be a consensus on the particular framework for such protection.[36] While some people opine that TK is best left in the public domain and that developed countries should be encouraged to offer technical assistance to indigenous/traditional communities and developing countries, others think that an intellectual property or other appropriate and effective protection of TK is necessary for its preservation, sustainable use of its products, and the fair and equitable sharing of benefits arising from its utilization. The matter is further complicated by the complex nature of the concept of protection.

Understanding the nature and objectives of protection may be a requisite for designing any effective regime of protection of TK.[37] To protect is 'to shield from injury, danger, or loss; guard; defend'.[38] From the above definition it could be argued that many regimes of IPR, for instance, patent, copyright, trademark, industrial design, which prevent the unauthorized appropriation of intellectual property rights

---

33 Pat Roy Mooney, *The Parts of Life: Agricultural Biodiversity, Indigenous Knowledge, and the Role of the Third System* (Uppsala, Sweden: The Dag Hammarskjöld Centre, 1997), at 94.

34 Paul Kuruk, 'Protecting Folklore Under Modern Intellectual Property Regimes: A Reappraisal of the Tensions Between Individual and Communal Rights in Africa and the United States' (1999) 48 *American University L. Rev.* 769, at 780.

35 *Ibid.*

36 For instance, Kadidal, *supra*, note 27, argued that protection in the context of the *Biodiversity Convention* should be by granting biodiversity-rich countries patent rights in the naturally occurring chemical structure of their biodiversity resources. Though the author lucidly analysed ways the proposed patent right could be structured to overcome the natural product exception to patentability, it is doubtful whether such far-reaching and uncommon patent right would be conceded by some developed countries that may have significant interest in the biodiversity of developing countries.

37 Correa, *supra*, note 20, at 5.

38 *Websters New World Dictionary, Third College Edition*, at 1081.

by third parties,[39] could help in protecting TK.[40] However, IPR is not the only means of protection available to TK. For instance, any regime that tends to prevent the loss of TK, by promoting its use and documentation, would arguably be a vehicle of protection. Correa has suggested that the protection of TK is justified by concerns relating to equity, conservation of biodiversity, preservation of traditional practices and culture, avoidance of biopiracy, and the promotion of the use of TK.[41] Protection may also be necessary for the realization of certain rights under some international human rights documents. Some of the objectives that underpin TK's protection are explored below.

Equity (in the sense of fairness)

Equitable considerations underpin and overlap with other objectives for the protection of TK, and probably offer a strong ground for the protection of TK. For instance, a significant amount of knowledge produced by Western societies has been protected through various forms of intellectual property regimes like patent, copyright, trademark and industrial designs. Global protection of such knowledge was sought and significantly achieved through the Agreement on Trade Related Aspects of Intellectual Property Rights (TRIPS), which requires member countries of the WTO, including developing countries, to grant intellectual property protection to products and processes in all fields of technology, and not below the minimum standard set by TRIPS. Equity and the principle of reciprocity, therefore, would demand that knowledge created by indigenous peoples and traditional societies, mainly living in

---

39 For instance, with respect to patents, it was held in: *Re Legal Protection of Biotechnological Inventions: The Netherlands v. European Parliament and E.C. Council* (2001) 3 C.M.L.R., at 1185:

> Once conferred, a patent merely entitles the holder to prevent others from making, using or selling the patented invention in the territory in which the patent has effect. It confers no right of ownership as *such*, nor any absolute right to manufacture or otherwise exploit the invention. Thus the holder of a patent will still need to comply with national law when he makes, uses or sells his invention. He may, for example, need to obtain a licence or authorisation; he may even patent an invention (a type of weapon for example) the making, use or sale of which is prohibited by national law.

Also, David B. Resnik, 'DNA Patents and Human Dignity' (2001) 29 *J.L. Med. & Ethics* 152, at 157–8.

40 Farley observed:

> Indigenous peoples seek to use these intellectual property laws in an effort to control and restrict the flow of images, thereby securing the meaning of their art. They want to be able to deny certain uses of their art, especially those that would amount to spiritual violations. They also want the ability to authorize certain uses of their art. They want to end the current situation in which only non-indigenous peoples are making money off their culture. Therefore, they want the ability to license certain uses and to collect royalties. They want to be able to authorize those uses of their art that would celebrate their culture and to use certain mass media imagery as a means of articulating their community identity to the outside world.

Farley, *supra*, note 6, at 13–14.

41 Correa, *supra*, note 20, at 5. See, also, WIPO, *supra*, note 8.

developing countries, be given an equally sufficient level of qualitative protection.[42] Doing equity in the area of TK does not necessarily entail the application of IPRs or *sui generis* frameworks; it includes the respect and recognition of TK holders as useful contributors to the global knowledge pool and creative innovators.

Furthermore, TK and associated products have been appropriated and used as the basis of inventions yielding large profits to some Western pharmaceutical corporations and scientists without significant returns to the TK holders.[43] Though in some cases, TK holders have been paid some monetary and other forms of compensation, the value pales in comparison to the total revenue accruing to some Western users of TK and products. Thus, equity, in the broad sense of fairness, requires that TK holders be adequately compensated for their custodianship of TK and TK-based products. For instance, the media reported that the San people of the Republic of South Africa, inhabiting the Kalahari Desert area, discovered through their TK that hoodia cactus (locally known as Xhoba) had medicinal properties that could suppress hunger and thirst.[44] They have traditionally used the plant during long hunting expeditions with little water and food.[45] In 1997, a South African government laboratory derived an appetite suppressant, P57, from the hoodia cactus and patented the compound without the knowledge or inclusion of the San people. The South African government licensed P57 to Phytopharm PLC, a small British firm, which later sub-licensed P57 to Pfizer.[46] Though a royalty agreement has been agreed with the San people, their case partly demonstrates the inequity that could exist in the exploitation of TK and associated products.

Another instance that calls for equitable considerations in the protection of TK is the Mexican Yellow Bean, a farmer's variety in Mexico, which was generated, conserved and continued to be improved upon with TK. The bean was purchased in Mexico in 1994 by Larry Proctor, whose company (POD-NERS) secured a patent over the bean in 1999.[47] With the patent, POD-NERS warned competitors in the USA that importing and selling the Mexican Yellow Bean in the USA without its authority would amount to infringement of its patent. The company subsequently brought suits against two US corporations alleged to have infringed its patent. This resulted in a sharp drop in Mexican export sales by about 90 per cent.[48] Thus, the granting of patent rights over a significantly traditional variety resulted in dire economic consequences for its custodians. Though the Mexican bean itself does not amount to TK, it was TK that helped to generate and conserve it. Furthermore, farmers are not compensated for traditional varieties developed and conserved by them, while

---

42 Comparative and qualitative protection for TK does not necessarily mean the application of IPRs, but may refer to deliberate efforts to design and structure suitable protection for TK in the same way that IPRs were deliberately crafted to achieve their objectives.

43 Correa, *supra*, note 20.

44 Dina Kraft, 'Bushmen, Drug Giant Battle over Royalties: Biopiracy Topic at Development Summit', *The Toronto Star*, 24 August 2002, at A18.

45 *Ibid.*

46 *Ibid.*

47 Rural Advancement Foundation International (now ETC), 'Enola Bean Patent Challenged', News Release, 5 January 2001. Posted on www.rafi.org.

48 *Ibid.*

commercial farmers and seed companies are compensated for new varieties derived from the farmers' varieties, through the grant of plant breeder's rights, and patent protection in some countries. Equitable considerations would help ensure that access to TK and associated products are balanced with fair and just compensation, proper control and recognition of the rights of TK holders.

Conservation of Biodiversity

The protection of TK may provide an incentive for the nurturing and conservation of biodiversity. TK includes critical knowledge of a particular ecosystem, the diversity within and between its species, and the maintenance of its integrity through sustainable uses and sound conservation practices. The biodiversity wealth of some developing countries is currently threatened with industrialization, urbanization and the steady erosion of traditional ways of life. Developing countries' biodiversity has been conserved from time immemorial with the help of TK.[49] For instance, the Tigray community farmers in Ethiopia have used indigenous technology to conserve selected seeds of high quality from various traditional crops.[50] The Tigray farmers continue to select the best performing seeds, which are stored in moisture-free receptacles and put in the care of some women in the community.[51] Some traditional communities have also cultivated various species of plants, including wild varieties, in home or family gardens in order to conserve them.[52] These indigenous conservation efforts, which deserve recognition, promotion and protection, contribute to the maintenance of biodiversity.

Similarly, the intellectual property protection of traditional varieties of seeds may yield revenue that provides an incentive for their nurturing and the concomitant promotion of biodiversity.[53] Protection may also be a way for biodiversity-rich countries to be integrated in the global economy on the basis of their comparative advantage in biodiversity wealth.[54] Biodiversity and the protection of associated knowledge may be a vehicle for development.[55] The biodiversity wealth of some developing countries may generate significant revenue from tourism, processed

---

49 M.S. Swaminathan, 'Farmers' Rights and Plant Genetic Resources' (1998) 36 Biotechnology *and Development Monitor* 544, at 545, observing:

> Before the advent of well-structured government sponsored methods of *in situ* conservation and *ex situ* preservation, the dominant method was *in situ* conservation by local communities. This has resulted in numerous folk varieties and rich inter-specific variability. For example the over 100,000 rice strains preserved cryogenically in gene banks such as at the International Rice Research Institute (IRRI) in the Philippines, are the products of the *in situ* on-farm conservation traditions of farm families.

50 Mugabe, *supra*, note 10, at 101.

51 *Ibid.*

52 Mooney, *supra*, note 33, at 84–5.

53 Correa, *supra*, note 20, at 6.

54 WIPO, *supra*, note 8.

55 Elli Louka, *Biodiversity and Human Rights: The International Rules for the Protection of Biodiversity* (New York: Transnational Publishers, 2002), at 22.

products of biodiversity,[56] and boost industries and commercial activities that make use of biodiversity and associated TK.[57] Thus, protection of TK may help in conserving, maximizing and realizing the potential wealth of biodiversity.

Preservation of Traditional Practices and Culture

It is not only economic or profit incentives that could justify the protection of TK. Concerns for the survival of socio-cultural activities embodying TK are also relevant factors that support the protection of TK. The protection of TK may promote a sense of identity among its holders and fortify their efforts towards self-determination. Protection may also be a means of showing respect and recognition for TK custodians and their culture by other TK users.[58] TK and associated lifestyles, however, are gradually disappearing. For instance, some indigenous languages, which express TK, are becoming extinct. Many indigenous languages are not taught in schools and have become (or would become) extinct.[59] Part of the endangered TK includes knowledge relevant to agriculture, medicine and biodiversity. It may be the objective of any system of protection to promote significant literacy rate in TK. It seems, however, that a more effective way to ensure the preservation of TK is to desist from actions that dislocate indigenous peoples from their ancestral lands and cultural environment,[60] and to promote their interaction within their traditional environments.

Avoidance of Biopiracy

Some countries in the South have complained against the appropriation of their TK and associated products, partly by some Western scientists and multinational corporations, without their consent and/or compensation. Thus, the protection of TK may be driven by the desire to prevent biopiracy. Biopiracy has been defined by the International Chamber of Commerce (ICC).[61] Case studies such as the neem tree, turmeric and ayahausca patents demonstrate instances of biopiracy. For instance,

---

56 *Ibid.*

57 World Tourism Organization & United Nations Environment Program, eds, *Guidelines: Development of National Parks and Protected Areas for Tourism* (WTO and UNEP, 1992).

58 Antony Taubman has suggested the design of a protective framework that embodies and recognizes customary law, as a mark of respect of custodians of TK: Antony Taubman, 'Saving the Village: Conserving Jurisprudential Diversity in the International Protection of Traditional Knowledge', in Keith E. Maskus and Jerome H. Reichman, eds, *International Public Goods and Transfer of Technology Under a Globalized Intellectual Property Regime* (Cambridge: Cambridge University Press, 2005), at 521.

59 Mooney, *supra*, note 33, at 88; Correa, *supra*, note 20, at 6–7.

60 Such displacements were usually motivated by wildlife management projects, nature reserves or biospheres, and some other land management activities. For the impact of such actions on the human rights of indigenous peoples, see, generally, Louka, *supra*, note 55.

61 International Chamber of Commerce: The World Business Organization, 'Policy Statement: TRIPS and the Biodiversity Convention: What Conflict?', Commission on Intellectual and Industrial Property, 28 June 1999:

the neem tree has been historically used in India as a pesticide and toothpaste. The pesticidal quality was extracted by traditional means. Nevertheless, the US Patent and Trademark Office granted W.R. Grace & Co. patent over a similar pesticide based on the neem tree, though this time the extraction was by scientific and technological means.[62] In contrast, a similar patent granted to W.R. Grace & Co. by the European Patent Office was revoked in 2000 on the ground of prior use in India.

Similarly, the people of India have traditionally used the medicinal property of turmeric in the treatment of wounds. Notwithstanding this traditional use, the US Patents and Trademark Office issued in 1993 a patent for turmeric to the University of Mississippi Medical Center. The patent was vigorously and successfully opposed by the Indian Council of Scientific and Industrial Research,[63] relying on an Indian journal published in the middle of the twentieth century, which described the healing qualities of turmeric.

The ayahausca patent is yet another example. The US Patent and Trademark Office (US PTO), in 1986, granted Loren Miller, an American citizen, a plant patent over a variety of ayahausca designated by Miller as Da Vine. Ayahausca has been used by generations of indigenous peoples in the Amazon Basin in religious ceremonies,

---

In our view, a rational definition of 'biopiracy' would focus on activities relating to access or use of genetic resources in contravention to national regimes based on the CBD. Accordingly, a legitimate claim of 'biopiracy' will involve unauthorized access to a controlled genetic resource and using that resource in a manner that contravenes the national regime. In practical terms, this means that (a) the activity in question occurred after the CBD came into force (December of 1993), and (b) the act consists of a party gaining access without the consent of the source country, or in contravention to laws or regulations governing access to or use of genetic resources that the country has established.

The above definition is, however, open to some criticism. First, if states have always had sovereignty over their natural resources, why restrict biopiractical acts to those occurring after the CBD came into force? There may be a reason for this parochial definition. It is likely part of the North's sustained effort to exclude from protection the germplasm collected from developing countries before December 1993, and now stored in international genebanks and research centres under the control of the Consultative Group on International Agricultural Research (CGIAR). It is arguable that these seeds were inappropriately obtained from developing countries, and constitutes an act of biopiracy. The ICC tends to pretend that property regime over natural resources started with the CBD. Second, in the absence of a positive norm of a state violated by a biopirate, is it fair that s/he should keep the fruits of a morally problematic act? Should a biopirate be allowed to keep the financial rewards from the genetic resources s/he harvested with the mere 'consent of the source country', even when there was no informed consent? Is the ICC's standard of consent not contradicted by the requirement of 'prior informed consent' imposed by Article 15(5) of the CBD?

62 See, generally, Emily Marden, 'The Neem Tree Patent: International Conflict over the Commodification of Life' (1999) 22 *Boston College Int. & Comp. L. Rev.* 279.

63 'Turmeric an Indian Discovery, Says US Patent Office', http://www.rediff.com/news/aug/23tur.htm (last visited 6 August 2002); 'India-Trade/Patent Denial Boosts Foes of Bio-Piracy', http://www.iahf.com/piracy.html (last visited 6 August 2002).

and for the treatment of sickness and diseases.[64] The indigenous peoples did not discover the ayahausca patent until 1994, and did so to their uttermost dismay.[65] On 30 March 1999, and on behalf of the concerned tribes, the Center for International Environmental Law (CIEL) launched an attack against the ayahausca patent by requesting its re-examination by the US PTO.[66] The CIEL argued that Da Vine was not new and was anticipated by prior art. More importantly, it argued that it was against public policy and morality to grant a patent to an American citizen over a plant that has medicinal and religious significance to an indigenous group.[67]

On 3 November 1999, the US PTO cancelled the ayahausca patent but on the narrow ground that it was not new, and anticipated by accessioned specimen sheets from the Chicago Field Museum.[68] This victory was momentous and excited indigenous peoples and NGOs all over the world,[69] but it lasted only for a while. On 25 January 2001, the US PTO, pursuant to Loren Miller's request for a reconsideration of its decision, reinstated the ayhausca patent. It based its decision on the 'characteristic distinctions in leaf side and shape between the respective plants (i.e., Da Vine and the alleged prior art), with the foliage of "Da Vine" having a comparably greater length to width ratio, while being slimmer and smaller in overall size'.[70] This latest US PTO decision on ayahausca is likely to ignite another round of protest from indigenous peoples and NGOs.

The above instances arguably make a compelling case for the protection of TK and associated products.[71] Biopiracy may unacceptably lead to a limit on traditional use of a product, even though most patents based on TK and associated products do not actually prohibit traditional uses. More importantly, biopiracy does not seem to respect the contributions of indigenous communities that have used a product or knowledge for a long time. The prevention of biopiracy seems to lie at the core of certain provisions of the *Convention on Biological Diversity*, for instance Articles 3, 8(j), 15, 16, and 19.

---

64 Glenn M. Wiser, 'PTO Rejection of the "Ayahausca" Patent Claim: Background and Analysis' (1999): http://ciel.org/Biodiversity/ptorejection.html (last visited on 3 September 2002).

65 *Ibid.*

66 *Ibid.*

67 *Ibid.*

68 *Ibid.*

69 David Rothschild and Glenn Wiser, 'U.S. Patent Office Admits Error, Rejects Patent on Sacred "Ayahuasca" Plant' (1999): http://ciel.org/Biodiversity/AyahauscaRejectionPR.html (last visited on 30 August 2002).

70 United States Department of Commerce Patent and Trademark Office, 'Notice of Intent to Issue Reexamination Certificate: Statement of Reasons for the Patentability and/ or Confirmation', 25 January 2001: posted on http://ciel.org/Publication/PTO_Examiner_Transcript.pdf (last visited on 30 August 2005).

71 Possible methods of protection are analysed later.

Promoting the Use of Traditional Knowledge

The protection of TK could be motivated by the need to conserve it through the promotion of its use or application. Use of TK is also a form of conservation since it prevents its extinction or loss through non-use. This becomes more apparent in the context of some indigenous languages and associated culture that are gradually disappearing. The World Health Organization has promoted the use of traditional medicinal knowledge and products for the health care of the majority of some developing countries' population. The WHO has recently launched a strategy for evaluating the quality, safety and efficacy of TM and associated knowledge, and to promote the accessibility and availability of TM.[72] Article 8(j) of the *Convention on Biological Diversity* also calls for the 'wider application' of TK. However, monopolistic regimes or IPRs or other forms of property framework may restrict, rather than promote, access to and use of TK.

Human Rights and Traditional Knowledge

The objective of protection may be to give effect to rights granted or implied under some international human rights documents. For instance, Article 27(2) of the *Universal Declaration on Human Rights* provides that 'everyone has the right to the protection of the moral and material interests resulting from any scientific, literary, or artistic production of which he is the author'. Similarly, Article 15 of the *Covenant on Economic, Social and Cultural Rights* (CESCR 1966)[73] provides:

1. The States Parties to the present Covenant recognise the right of everyone : (a) To take part in cultural life; (b) To enjoy the benefits of scientific progress and its applications; (c) To benefit from the protection of the moral and material interests resulting from any scientific, literary or artistic production of which he is the author.
2. The steps to be taken by the States Parties to the present Covenant to achieve the full realization of this right shall include those necessary for the conservation, the development and diffusion of science and culture.

Though TK qualifies as part of these 'moral and material' interests under the provisions above, it is arguably not protected under Article 27(2) of the UDHR and Article 15 CESCR, since both Articles apparently protect individual, rather than collective, rights.[74]

Other Conventions seem to focus more specifically on the protection of collective interests. Some Conventions of the International Labour Organization (ILO), for example, may be interpreted as providing a basis for the protection of TK, though those Conventions were not directly concerned with TK. In 1957, the ILO adopted the *Convention Concerning the Protection and Integration of Indigenous and Other Tribal and Semi-Tribal Populations in Independent Countries* (Convention 107).

---

72 WHO, *supra*, note 28.

73 Posted on http://www.umn.edu/humanrts/instree/b2esc.htm.

74 Jack Donnelly, *Universal Human Rights in Theory and Practice* (New York: Cornell University Press, 1989), at 144.

This Convention sought to protect indigenous people on the basis of assimilation into Western society and its associated lifestyle. In 1989, the revised Convention (ILO Convention 169),[75] adopted a different philosophical basis of protection of indigenous people, recognizing their right to separate identity, lifestyle and culture.

Article 31(1) of ILO Convention 169 provides that 'governments shall respect the special importance of the cultures and spiritual values of the peoples concerned of their relationship with the lands or territories, or both as applicable, which they occupy or otherwise use, and in particular the collective aspects of this relationship'. Of course, the collective aspects of indigenous peoples include their TK, and though ILO Convention 169 was not thematically concerned with the protection of TK, the full realization of the benefits of its provisions is an arguable ground for the protection of TK.

Frameworks for Protecting Traditional Knowledge

The diverse objectives of TK protection imply that no single framework can exclusively provide the desired protection or answers to the policy issues and legal questions concerning TK. For instance, while an IPR regime can be legitimately used to achieve the objective of excluding third parties from the unauthorized appropriation of TK, or used to charge user fees, it does not further the objective of promoting free access and widespread use of TK.[76] Thus, other property, non-property or policy frameworks, in addition to an IPR regime, may be considered in devising the strategy for the protection of TK. Some commentators, however, have argued that TK is better protected by the prevailing IPR regimes or modified and adapted versions of those regimes. IPR protection arguably has some advantages. Potential revenue from an IPR regime would provide the needed incentive for technological application and further development of TK.[77]

An IPR regime could generate economic and financial returns that may encourage biodiversity conservation. Prospects for such returns and its potentially positive impact on biodiversity conservation could be deduced from the success story of the privatization of wildlife management in Zimbabwe and Namibia.[78] Under statutory laws in both countries, local communities are given authority to manage wildlife and benefit from the revenue accruing from such management.[79] The rationale underpinning the statutes was that privately owned animals face less threat of extinction than wild ones; so that similar treatment of wild animals may produce

---

75 Posted on www.usask.ca/nativelaw/ILO169html.

76 For instance, Correa observed in the context of traditional medicine that 'IPRs may be relevant to promote the commercialization of TRM, but not very relevant or completely irrelevant in relation to other possible objectives often mentioned in the literature'. Correa, *supra*, note 14, at 37.

77 Mugabe, *supra*, note 10, at 105.

78 Louka, *supra*, note 55, at 79–85.

79 *Ibid.* While the programme in Zimbabwe is called the Communal Area Management Program for Indigenous Resources (CAMPFIRE), that of Namibia is designated Community-Based Natural Resources Management (CBNRM).

comparable results.[80] Though the communities are given powers to manage the wildlife reserves, they do not, however, own the animals, which remain the property of the state.[81] For Zimbabwe, Louka observed that: 'All the adults in the community are shareholders in the cooperative (i.e., CAMPFIRE) and they receive benefits from employment and dividends from tourism, ivory culling and meat marketing.'[82]

The CAMPFIRE programme has considerably checked poaching and illegal activities that threatened wildlife, and has beneficially impacted on wildlife protection: 'Privatization has done wonders for the protection of the elephants. In 1990 Zimbabwe's elephant population was less than 4,000. Today it is well over 64,000.'[83] Though the prevention of the extinction of some animals is just one aspect of biodiversity conservation, which the above local conservation programmes are meant to achieve, it is arguable that the protection of TK and associated products under an IPR regime would bring about financial returns and biodiversity conservation comparable to the results of the CAMPFIRE and CBNRM programmes.

There are further advantages of an IPR protection of TK. It is arguably easier to accommodate TK under a prevailing IPR regime, for instance, patent, trademark, copyright and industrial design, than it probably is to negotiate, design and agree on some special form of protection either at the domestic or international level.[84]

However, opponents of IPR protection contend that it is inherently unsuitable for TK because of some conceptual incompatibility between an indigenous knowledge system and Western knowledge-oriented IPRs.[85] According to this perspective, care should be taken to avoid uncritical acceptance of such Western-oriented solutions that seem to be based on the theory of possessive individualism. Possessive individualism conceptually defines and identifies an individual by the property he or she possesses.[86] It is a Western concept[87] and provides the theoretical underpinning of most IPR regimes, including patent, copyright, trademark and industrial designs. Possessive individualism is epistemologically unsuitable for community or collective property, for example, ethnobotanical knowledge or plant genetic resources in a particular part of a national territory.[88] Thus, potential remedies available under an

---

80 *Ibid.*, at 79.

81 *Ibid.*

82 *Ibid.*, at 80–81.

83 *Ibid.*, at 82.

84 Kuruk, *supra*, note 34, at 793.

85 Daniel Gervais, 'Traditional Knowledge and Intellectual Property: A TRIPS-Compatible Approach' (2005) *Mich. St. L. Rev.* 137, at 145–6.

86 Richard Handler, 'Who Owns the Past? History, Cultural Property, and the Logic of Possessive Individualism', in Brett Williams, ed., *The Politics of Culture* (Washington: Smithsonian Institution Press, 1991), at 63.

87 C.B. Macpherson, *The Political Theory of Possessive Individualism: Hobbes to Locke* (Oxford: Oxford University Press, 1962).

88 According to Richard Handler:

The problem with these restitutionist arguments [that is, the argument that those dispossessed of their cultural objects have a right to their restitution or reparation] is that they make use of worn-out metaphors – collectivities seen as individuals, culture seen as property – borrowed from the hegemonic culture that the restitutionists are

IPR regime are limited by their apparently contradictory philosophical anchorage. Opponents of an IPR framework also argue that an IPR regime will restrict access to TK and thus undermine the social and historical character of TK.

Apart from IPR, other frameworks are available to achieve protection of TK. For instance, it is possible to use and improve protections available under customary law.[89] However, the effectiveness of customary law is severely limited for a number of reasons, including non-recognition of customary law in a number of legal systems, the limited jurisdiction of customary law (binding only on persons subscribing to it), weaker sanctions of customary law compared to that of a modern state, and the unwritten character of customary law, which make the ascertainment of its provisions and sanctions difficult.[90] Furthermore, it is possible to design a unique or *sui generis* form of protection for TK, provided the dynamics of such a framework and the issues involved are adequately investigated. Whichever framework is adopted would depend on the objectives sought to be achieved or the needs of a particular community or state. Below is an attempt to analyse some of the issues that arise under an IPR and other regimes.

Patent

Since the difficulties arising from protecting TK under a patent regime are mirrored in other intellectual property regimes like copyright, trademark and industrial design, this chapter attempts to give a fuller examination of the issues and problems involved under a patent framework and will briefly discuss copyright, trademark and other IPR regimes.

A patent right is a monopoly granted by the state to an inventor entitling him or her to prevent or exclude others from exploiting the invention, by way of use, sale or manufacture of the patented invention.[91] The monopoly is for a limited period,

---

attempting to resist...It is no longer useful for anthropologists to imagine cultures as collective individuals possessed of property and characterized by that 'identity' so central to the individualistic worldview.

Brett Williams, *supra*, note 86, at 68.

89 Some customary law systems recognize rights analogous to conventional IPRs, as evident in the report of WIPO's fact-finding mission between 1998 and 1999. See, WIPO, *supra*, note 7. Similarly, a commentator observed that: 'some indigenous or traditional societies are reported to recognize various types of intellectual property rights over knowledge, which may be held by individuals, families, lineages, or communities. Discussions of IPRs and traditional knowledge should draw more on the "diversity and creativity of indigenous approaches to IPR issues".' Downes, *supra*, note 13, at 258.

90 Remigius N. Nwabueze, 'The Dynamics and Genius of Nigeria's Indigenous Legal Order' (2002) 1 *Indigenous Law Journal* 153 (discussing the nature, characteristics and enforcement of customary law).

91 Historically speaking, the first patent under common law seems to have been granted by Henry VI to John of Utynam in 1449. The patent related to glass windows that were used for Eton College buildings. In the *Clothworkers of Ipswich Case* (1653) 78 E.R. 147, at 148, the King's Bench Court of England held that the crown could grant a patent to a person who 'hath brought in a new invention and a new trade within the kingdom...or made a new

for example, 20 years.[92] The consideration for this monopoly is that the inventor sufficiently discloses the invention in the specification of the patent application, so that persons skilled in the art could reproduce the invention, that is, following the specification, after the expiration of the patent.[93] As such, reproducibility of an invention is an important condition for the grant of a patent right.[94] Patent embodies a contract between an inventor and society, which aims at increasing the stock of human knowledge, as well as rewarding the inventor for his/her ingenuity. The courts are aware of the tension between patent protection and competition, and tend to resolve it through a purposive interpretation of the claims in a patent application. In *Free World Trust v. Électro Santé Inc. et al.*,[95] the Supreme Court of Canada expounded this interpretive role with respect to patent law. Justice Binnie observed:

> The patent system is designed to advance research and development and to encourage broader economic activity. Achievement of these objectives is undermined however if competitors fear to tread in the vicinity of the patent because its scope lacks a reasonable measure of precision and certainty. A patent of uncertain scope becomes 'a public nuisance'...The patent owner, competitors, potential infringers and the public generally are thus entitled to clear and definite rules as to the extent of the monopoly conferred. This in turn requires that the subjective or discretionary element of claims interpretation (e.g., the elusive quest for the 'spirit of the invention') be kept to the minimum, consistent with giving 'the inventor protection for that which he has actually in good faith invented' (*Western Electric Co. v. Baldwin International Radio of Canada*, [1934] S.C.R. 570 at p. 574, [1934] 4 D.L.R. 129). Predictability is achieved by interpreting those claims in an informed and purposive way.[96] (Brackets in the original)

---

discovery of anything'. And the condition of the grant was that 'he [patentee] only shall use such a trade or trafique for a certain time, because at first the people of the kingdom are ignorant and have not the knowledge or skill to use it: but when that patent is expired, the King cannot make a new grant thereof'. The English *Statute of Monopolies, 1623 21 Jam. 1. C. 3* voided all monopolies in England but preserved a 14-year patent monopoly right to 'the true and first inventor', *ibid.*, section 6, of any 'new manufacturers within this realm'. *Ibid.* In stating the condition of patentability and term of a patent right, the *Statute of Monopolies* marked the provenance of patent legislation in the United Kingdom. However, the first formal patent legislation is the *Venetian Law of 1474*, which granted patents for 'any new ingenious contrivance...reduced to perfection, so that it can be used and exercised'.

Stephen P. Ladas, *Patents, Trademarks, and Related Rights – National and International Protection* (Massachusetts: Harvard University Press, 1975), at 6–7. At this embryonic period of patent law, patents were mainly granted for mechanical and chemical products and processes. This category of inventions reflected society's level of economic and social development at that time. Now, inventions have taken new forms that are beyond the contemplation of patent law as originally conceptualized.

92 Article 33, TRIPS agreement. Posted on WTO website: www.wto.org.

93 *Ibid.*, Article 29.

94 *Kirin-Amgen Inc. v. Roche Diagnostics GMBH* (2002) R. P. C. 1, at 83; *Pioneer Hi-Breed Ltd. v. Canada (Commissioner of Patents)* (1989) 25 C.P.R. (3d) 257, at 266–72. (Supreme Court of Canada).

95 (2000) 9 C.P.R. (4th) 168.

96 *Ibid.*, at 188–9.

Generally, the legal institution of property is an artificial and social construct designed to encourage and protect the investment of labour and capital, and to promote the minimization of waste.[97] Thus, right to a patent, like property rights in general, does not seem to be a natural right.[98] An inventor does not gain automatic patent protection upon the completion of an invention. She or he would have to set the machinery of patent law into motion by filing the prescribed application in a patent office and fulfilling all the conditions precedent to the grant of a patent. This observation is relevant for traditional innovation. Many traditional innovations are the outcome of ingenious contributions from past and present generations of a particular milieu. Though some of these innovations have become relevant for modern biotechnology, they do not have any automatic patent protection, assuming they qualify for such protection. As it were, patent protection for TK and products is not self-executing. This situation has put some of the traditional communities in a quandary, by the knowledge that it may be difficult to prevent, by assertion of a patent right, the exploitation of their traditional innovation by modern biotechnology entrepreneurs.

An applicant would be eligible for patent protection, if his or her invention is new, non-obvious and capable of industrial application.[99] TRIPS does not clearly and specifically define these concepts and a country anxious to protect TK may use innovative judicial interpretation to accommodate TK and associated innovation under the patent criteria.[100] Some TK and associated products and innovations are potentially patentable.[101] For instance, useful herbal remedies or combinations

---

97 Charles A. Reich, 'The New Property' (1964) 73 *Yale L.J.* 733, at 771–2.

98 Though there is no natural right to a patent, common law has long recognized the right of an inventor to a limited monopoly for the exploitation of his/her invention. For instance, in the *Clothworkers of Ipswich Case* (1653) 78 E.R. 147, at 148, the King's Bench Court (UK) held that the crown could grant a patent to a person who 'hath brought in a new invention and a new trade within the kingdom...or made a new discovery of anything'. For Canada, however, the common law right to a patent is not recognized. This is the clear position of the Supreme Court of Canada in *Commissioner of Patents v. Farbwerke Hoechst A.G. vormals Meister Lucius and Bruning* (1963) 25 Fox Pat. C 99, at 107: 'There is no inherent common law right to a patent. An inventor gets his patent according to the terms of the *Patent Act*, no more and no less.' In Nigeria, where common law became applicable to the whole country on 1 January 1900, the courts may adopt a different approach by holding that the prerogative to grant patents for inventions was part of the common law received into Nigeria, and remains in force subject to applicable statutory provisions.

99 Article 27(1) TRIPS.

100 Ruth L. Gana, 'Prospects for Developing Countries under the TRIPS Agreement' (1996) 29 *Vanderbilt Jour. of Transnational Law* 735, at 749–51, suggesting that developing countries could set an interpretative minimum threshold for patentability under article 27, that is, with respect to novelty, inventive step and industrial application. She argued that such an interpretative device would ensure patent protection for local inventions that may not pass a strict test of the patent criteria. According to her, foreigners are unlikely, under the national treatment rule of Article 3, to take advantage of such a lower interpretive standard of patentability, since a near obvious invention may not be patentable elsewhere.

101 Y. Liu, 'IPR Protection for New Traditional Knowledge: With a Case Study of Traditional Chinese Medicine' (2003) 25 *Eur. Intell. Prop. Rev.* 194.

thereof, extracts of active ingredients in medicinal plants and medicinal formulations produced by a skilful utilization of TK may be patentable.[102] In this context, Elizabetsky[103] observed:

> Traditional remedies, although based on natural products, are not found in 'nature' as such; they are products of human knowledge. To transform a plant into a medicine, one has to know the correct species, its location, the proper time of collection (some plants are poisonous in certain seasons), the part to be used, how to prepare it (fresh, dried, cut in small pieces, smashed), the solvent to be used (cold, warm, or boiling water; alcohol, addition of salt, etc), the way to prepare it (time and conditions to be left on the solvent), and finally, posology (route of administration, dosage). Needless to say, curers have to diagnose and select the right medicine for the right patients.[104]

Furthermore, patent potentials may be found in indigenous activities involving considerable technical input, for instance, mining activity, canoe building, construction of musical instruments and cloth-weaving devices.[105]

Traditional use offers potentials for invalidating a patent or precluding the grant of one. Some innovations in biotechnology, especially in the pharmaceutical field, have been based on traditional uses of TK and associated products. It is arguable that such prior traditional uses could form the basis of the defence of anticipation. 'Anticipation' is one of the grounds for opposing the grant of a patent, or revoking one already granted. The defence of anticipation seeks to negate the alleged novelty of a patent, which is necessary for its validity. Anticipation is an allegation that prior use, sale, knowledge, publication or grant renders a patent invalid. As observed by Décary, J., in *Diversified Products Corp. v. Tye-Sil Corp.*,[106] 'the defences of prior knowledge, prior use, prior publication and prior sale are "very much intermingled" and are referred to as "anticipation"'.[107] He continued by stating that 'what is said with respect, for example, to anticipation through prior knowledge is applicable, *mutatis mutandis*, to anticipation through prior publication'.[108] For anticipation to succeed, the prior art relied upon must be able to teach the invention the validity of which is impugned. The prior art must be able to give such directions that would enable a skilful but unimaginative technician to reproduce the invention without undue difficulty.

---

102 Patents granted on TK, especially TM, and related products include, U.S. 4178372 on hypoallergenic stabilized aloe vera gel; U.S. 4725483 on an aloe vera ointment; U.S. 4696819 on material extracted from coca leaves; EP 0513671 on '*commiphora mukul*' extracts; EP 0519777 relating to formulations made out of a variety of fresh plants; and WO 93/11780 on a skin therapeutic mixture containing cold-processed aloe-vera extract: Correa, *supra*, note 14, at 47–8.

103 Elaine Elizabetsky, 'Folklore, Tradition, or Know-How?' (1991) *Cultural Survival Q.* (Summer) 9.

104 *Ibid.*, at 10–11.

105 Kuruk, *supra*, note 34, at 783.

106 (1991) 35 C.P.R. (3d) 350.

107 *Ibid.*, at 360.

108 *Ibid.*, at 360–61.

In *Reeves Brothers Inc. v. Toronto Quilting & Embroidery Ltd.*,[109] Gibson, J. formulated eight tests that the defence of anticipation must satisfy in order to succeed.[110] It appears that satisfaction of any one of them will justify the defence of anticipation.[111] Hugessen, J. A. in *Beloit Canada Ltd. v. Valmet Oy*,[112] defined anticipation:

> It will be recalled that anticipation, or lack of novelty, asserts that the invention has been made known to the public prior to the relevant time. The inquiry is directed to the very invention in suit and not, as in the case of obviousness, to the state of the art and to common general knowledge...anticipation must be found in a specific patent or other published document; it is not enough to pick bits and pieces from a variety of prior publications and to meld them together so as to come up with the claimed invention. One must, in effect, be able to look at a prior, single publication and find in it all the information which, for practical purposes, is needed to produce the claimed invention without the exercise of any inventive skill. The prior publication must contain so clear a direction that a skilled person reading and following it would in every case and without possibility of error be led to the claimed invention.[113]

Pessimism seems to characterize the judicial approach to the defence of anticipation.[114] The court observed in *Wahl Clipper Corp. v. Andis Clipper Co. et al.*,[115] that, 'it is more important to study those developments of the art which are bright with use in the channels of trade than to delve into abandoned scrap heaps of dust-covered books which tell of hopes unrealized and flashes of genius quite

---

109 (1979) 43 C.P.R. (2d) 145.

110 *Ibid.*, at 157:

> As I understand it, in order that there may be a finding of anticipation, the prior art must (1) give an exact prior description; (2) give directions which will inevitably result in something within the claims; (3) give clear and unmistakable directions; (4) give information which for the purpose of practical utility is equal to that given by the subject patent; (5) convey information so that a person grappling with the same problem must be able to say 'that gives me what I wish'; (6) give information to person of ordinary knowledge so that he must at once perceive the invention; (7) in the absence of explicit directions, teach an 'inevitable result' which 'can only be proved by experiments'; and (8) satisfy all these tests in a single document without making a mosaic.

111 *Diversified Products Corp. v. Tye-Sil Corp.*, *supra*, note 106, at 361.

112 (1986) 8 C.P.R. (3d) 289.

113 *Ibid.*, at 297.

114 Thorson, P. stated in *Lovell Mfg. Co. et al. v. Beatty Bros. Ltd* (1962) 23 Fox Pat. C. 112, at 140:

> In view of the severity of the tests which a prior publication must meet before it can be considered as an anticipation of an invention it is not surprising that attacks on the validity of a patent on the ground that the invention covered by it was anticipated by a prior patent so seldom succeed. Indeed, although I have been the President of this Court for more than twenty years, I have not yet heard any patent case in which the validity of the patent involved in the case has been successfully attacked on the ground that the invention covered by it had been anticipated by a prior patent.

115 66 F. (2d) 162; 18 U.S. Pat. Q. 179.

forgotten'. Consequently, anticipation is usually construed narrowly, and in favour of the impugned patent.[116]

The issue here is whether TK could be successfully used as the basis of the defence of anticipation. This potential deployment of TK has become imminent in view of some patents that are already 'anticipated' by prior uses and knowledge in some traditional communities. For instance, the patent granted to W.R. Grace & Co. concerning products based on the neem tree could be said to have been anticipated by traditional uses in India.[117] The European patent for neem products was revoked in 2000 by the European Patent Office.[118] Though it is possible for traditional use to undergird the defence of anticipation in Canada or the UK,[119] it does not generally seem that many Western courts and institutions would readily invalidate a patent based on such traditional uses.[120] In this regard, general apathy towards indigenous institutions and culture would further exacerbate judicial pessimism towards the defence of anticipation.

Moreover, TK is not generally in a printed or published form, and may not be amenable to the defence of anticipation by prior publication.[121] Only very few elements of TK that have been covered by previous publication are entitled to the status of prior publication.[122] For instance, the patent issued for turmeric, a traditional Indian healing medicine, to the University of Mississippi Medical Center was set aside based on an Indian journal published in the middle of the twentieth century, which described the healing qualities of turmeric.

Not many aspects of TK have the privilege of a published description, and may therefore be open to exploitation by entrepreneurs. Some developing countries, like India, are working hard to overcome this difficulty. The strategy includes printed documentation of TK, TK registries and special statutory protection. It is arguable that TK registries and databases may facilitate access to and exploitation of TK,

---

116 *Christiani v. Rice* (1930) 4 D.L.R. 401, at 407-408; *Eli Lilly & Co. v. Marzone Chemicals Ltd.* (1978) 37 C.P.R. (2d) 3, at 32; *Free World Trust v. Électro Santé Inc. et al.* (2000) 9 C.P.R. (4th) 168, at 181–2.

117 Emily Marden, 'The Neem Tree Patent: International Conflict over the Commodification of Life' (1999) 22 *Boston College Int. & Comp. L. Rev.* 279.

118 Vandana Shiva, 'Intellectual Property Protection in the North/South Divide', in Christopher Heath and Anselem K. Sanders, eds, *Intellectual Property in the Digital Age: Challenges for Asia* (The Hague: Kluwer Law International, 2001), at 126–8.

119 Harold G. Fox, *The Canadian Law and Practice Relating to Letters Patent for Inventions* (Toronto: Carswell Co. Ltd., 1969, 4th edn), at 110–16.

120 Wiser, *supra*, note 64.

121 However, Section 28 of the *Canadian Patent Act* no longer requires prior art to be in a printed form.

122 There are emerging progressive steps to document traditional medicinal knowledge in Africa. Maurice M. Iwu, *Handbook of African Medicinal Plants* (Boca Raton, FL.: CRC Press, 1993). The World Health Organization has also published many monographs relating to TM: WHO, *supra*, note 28, at 51.

rather than preventing such. However, such registries and databases may facilitate proof of prior art.[123]

There are further considerable difficulties to the protection of TK under patent law. As observed earlier, the concepts of patent law (and many other components of IPR) are inherently incompatible with the TK system, for instance, with regard to the issue of ownership. While patent law allows for individual ownership or private property right over an invention, TK is a collective property of a group to which members of that group generally have free access. Furthermore, the inter-territorial nature of TK poses another obstacle to its potential patentability. Some elements of TK are commonly shared by indigenous communities demarcated by artificial national boundaries. For instance, knowledge of the medicinal quality of a particular shrub may be common to indigenous peoples of Nigeria, Ghana, Gambia and several other West African countries. The ayahausca plant is central to spiritual healing and religious ceremonies of many indigenous communities in both Brazil and Ecuador.[124] Even within a particular country, inter-state boundaries may be such that a particular indigenous community is split into different states. This situation does not make it easy for the ascertainment of claims of ownership or inventorship.

Similarly, the perpetual protection that TK enjoys in some customary legal systems is inconsistent with the limited monopoly which patent law grants to a patentee. The court had observed in the *Clothworkers of Ipswich Case*[125] that a patent for an unlimited period would amount to a denial of 'free-trade, which is the birthright of every subject'.[126] The impermanence of a patent grant is further underscored by Article 1, Section 8 of the United States Constitution, which is the constitutional anchorage for patent law in the USA. The Section provides that the power of Congress to promote the progress of science and useful arts shall be exercised by 'securing for limited times to authors and inventors the exclusive rights to their respective writings and discoveries'. Canadian cases also emphasize the limited nature of patent monopoly.[127]

Unlimited protection of a patent right would create a pure monopoly and negate the bargain which lies at the heart of a patent law, that is, limited protection in return for the disclosure and availability of the invention for future public use. The rationale of patent law and its term protection was vividly stated by the Supreme Court of the United States in *Kewanee Oil Co. v. Bicron Corp.*[128] However, the nature of TK

---

123 For a discussion of the Indian traditional knowledge registry: Anil K. Gupta, 'Conserving Biodiversity and Rewarding Associated Knowledge and Innovation Systems: Honey Bee Perspective', in Thomas Cottier and Petros C. Mavroidis, eds, *Intellectual Property: Trade, Competition, and Sustainable Development* (Ann Arbor: The University of Michigan Press, 2003), at 373.

124 Wiser, *supra*, note 64.

125 *Supra*, note 91.

126 *Ibid.*, at 148.

127 For instance, *Free World Trust v. Électro Santé Inc.*, *supra*, note 95, at 178.

128 *Kewanee Oil Co. v. Bicron Corp* (1974) 416 US 470, at 480–81:

The stated objective of the Constitution in granting the power to Congress to legislate in the area of intellectual property is to 'promote the progress of Science and useful Arts.' The patent laws promote this progress by offering a right of exclusion for a

does not seem to make it amenable to limited protection, assuming it qualifies for a patent grant. Many elements of TK are an integral part of the life of an indigenous community, and may have spiritual and religious significance. Therefore, any legal protection to them would naturally be for an unlimited term. This is a privilege that many statutes on intellectual property may not afford.

Furthermore, patent protection of TK may be problematic in view of the principle that mere discoveries are not patentable. It is now a well-established principle of patent law that things existing in a state of nature, or the mere discovery of things in their natural state, is not patentable. Likewise, no patent is granted for a scientific principle or abstract theorem.[129] However, where a scientific discovery is coupled with directions as to novel use, then it amounts to a technical contribution and therefore patentable. Article 5(1) of *European Directive 98/44 on the Legal Protection of Biotechnological Inventions*[130] provides that, 'the simple discovery of one of its [that is, the human body] elements, including the sequence or partial sequence of a gene, cannot constitute patentable inventions'. However, subsection 2 of the same Article allows the patentability of an 'element isolated from the human body or otherwise produced by means of a technical process, including the sequence or partial sequence of a gene'. Similarly, Article 27(3)(b) of TRIPS allows member states to deny patents to plants and animals and 'essentially biological processes for the production of plants or animals', but not microorganisms (including genes) and non-biological and microbiological processes.

The principle that mere discoveries are not patentable has been used to challenge many patents on genes. The allegation, usually, is that the sequence of a gene or DNA is mere discovery of that which exists in nature and should not be protected by patent law. However, many of the cases have held that when a gene is isolated and purified, it ceases to exist in nature.[131] Biologically, genes do not naturally exist in an isolated and purified state.

---

limited period as an incentive for inventors to risk the often enormous costs in terms of time, research and development. The productive effort thereby fostered will have positive effect on society through the introduction of new products and processes of manufacture into the economy and the emanations by way of increased employment and better lives for our citizens...When a patent is granted and the information contained in it is circulated to the general public, and those especially skilled in the trade, such additions to the general store of knowledge are of such importance to the public wealth that the Federal government is willing to pay the high price of 17 years of exclusive use for its disclosure, which disclosure, it is assumed, will stimulate ideas and the eventual development of further significant advances on the art.

129 For instance: Section 27(8) *Canadian Patent Act, R.S.C. 1985, c. P-4*, as amended.

130 *(1998) O.J. L213/13.*

131 *In Gale's Application* (1991) R.P.C. 305 at 324: 'Thus, a discovery as such is not patentable as an invention under the Act. But when applied to a product or process which, in the language of the 1977 Act [UK], is capable of industrial application, the matter stands differently.' *Genetech Inc.'s Patents* (1987) R.P.C. 553, at 566: 'It is trite law that you cannot patent a discovery, but if on the basis of that discovery you can tell people how it can be usefully employed, then a patentable invention may result. This in my view would be the case, even though once you have made the discovery, the way in which it can be usefully employed

In the recent case of *Kirin-Amgen Inc. v. Roche Diagnostics GMBH*,[132] the patentee had, for the first time, successfully isolated and patented the gene responsible for the production of erythropoietin, a protein which is responsible for stimulating the production of red blood cells. The isolated gene is relevant for the treatment of anaemia. In an action for infringement of the patent, part of the defendants' argument was that the claims in the patent covering the isolated gene were invalid, since the gene sequence was a discovery of what already existed in nature. In dismissing this argument, Justice Neuberger of the English Patents Court held that, 'while it is obviously the case that the essential feature of 605, and in particular of claim 1, is a "discovery", namely that of the DNA sequence of the EPO gene, or at least a substantial part of that gene…, it was a discovery which clearly made a technical contribution'.[133] He further observed that his judgement, allowing the claims on the isolated gene, was justified by the practice of the European Patent Office and the US Patent and Trademark Office in the previous 20 years.[134]

What may be considered some elements of TK, like genetic resources from plants and animals, are arguably in the state of nature: mere discoveries removed from the zone of patentability.[135] It is not every aspect of TK that is found in the state of nature. For instance, some herbal remedies and traditional therapies involving a skilful application or utilization of TK are not found in nature.[136] Generally, however, patent law does not seem to regard traditional products and processes as technical contributions. In contrast, products and processes derived from these natural resources, mainly by Western corporations and entrepreneurs, are considered to be patentable inventions.[137]

In addition to the above general problems that diminish the potentials for TK protection under patent law, there are difficulties that arise with some specific provisions of patent law. For instance, patent provisions relating to the definition and identification of an 'inventor', and the public disclosure of an invention do not easily accommodate TK and associated innovation.

---

is obvious enough.' *Fujitsu Ltd's Application* (1997) R.P.C. 608, at 614: '[I]t is…a principle of patent law that mere discoveries or ideas are not patentable, but those discoveries and ideas which have technical aspect or make a technical contribution are. Thus the concept that what is needed to make an excluded thing patentable is a technical contribution is not surprising…It is a concept at the heart of patent law.'

132 (2002) R.P.C. 1.

133 *Ibid.*, at 143–4.

134 *Ibid.*, at 144.

135 As Justice Lamer of the Supreme Court of Canada stated in *Pioneer Hi-Breed Ltd v. Canada (Commissioner of Patents)* (1989) 25 C.P.R. (3d) 257, at 264–5: 'The courts have regarded creations following the laws of nature as being mere discoveries the existence of which man has simply uncovered without thereby being able to claim he has invented them.'

136 Elizabetsky, *supra*, note 103.

137 Muria Kruger, 'Harmonizing TRIPS and the CBD: a Proposal from India' (2001) 10 *Minnesota Jour. of Global Trade* 169; Valentina Tejera, 'Tripping over Property Rights: Is it Possible to Reconcile the Convention on Biological Diversity with Article 27 of the TRIPS Agreement?' (1999) 33 *New England L. Rev.* 967.

Patent protection is inventor-specific. This means that the patent application should identify the inventor or inventors that seek patent protection. Usually, the inventor is an individual or a number of persons but not a community, in the sense of an indigenous population or community. It is possible that some components of TK were originally individual creations but were subsequently adopted by a particular group and passed from generation to generation, making it difficult in some cases to identify the original creator.[138] Even when it is possible to identify an individual inventor of a form of TK, the invention would have been largely dictated or influenced by (or was in response to) culture, tradition, and the store of TK, making it difficult for an individual in the community to exclusively claim to be the sole inventor. Thus, absence of specific and identifiable inventors may render patent protection for TK problematic.[139] The problems relating to the statutory provision on inventorship and how it impacts on TK are explored below in the context of Canadian patent legislation, which is similar to patent laws in the USA and the UK. Section 27 of the *Canadian Patent Act* provides for the grant of patent to an inventor.[140]

The *Canadian Patent Act* does not define an 'inventor' but Section 2 thereof defines an 'applicant' to include an inventor. A 'patentee' is also not defined with reference to inventorship but as the 'person for the time being entitled to the benefit of a patent'.[141] Under Section 27, an application for a patent must be filed by an inventor.[142] Patent applications usually name the inventor or joint inventors.[143] Absent statutory definition of an inventor, the courts would have to rely on juristic sources for help. *Hughes and Woodley on Patents* defined an inventor: 'It is the person who conceives the idea, not the one who commercializes it, who is the inventor, having regard to the invention as claimed... Where the wrong person or persons have been

---

138 An informant to the WIPO fact-finding mission (FFM) to North America observed with reference to the traditional tipi designs:

> The tipi designs can only be created through a vision, a spiritual dreaming or as the results of a vision quest. The designs are very limited and they were handed down from years and years ago. We know the original owners of the tipi designs, they transferred the ownership to family friends, who then transferred them to current owners. Anything we have now was transferred and the design cannot be replicated unless it is transferred through a ceremony. Those designs are ancient and sacred.

WIPO, *supra*, note 7, at 59.

139 Richard A. Guest, 'Intellectual Property Rights and Native American Tribes' (1995–1996) 20 *American Indian L. Rev.* 111, at 122–3.

140 *Canadian Patent Act*, *supra*, note 129:

> 27(1) The Commissioner shall grant a patent for an invention to the *inventor or the inventor's legal representative* if an application for the patent in Canada is filed in accordance with this Act and all other requirements for the issuance of a patent under this Act are met.
>
> (2) The prescribed application fee must be paid and the application must be filed in accordance with the regulations *by the inventor or the inventor's legal representative* and the application must contain a petition and a specification of the invention. (Italics supplied)

141 *Patent Act*, *ibid.*, Section 2.

142 *671905 Alberta Inc. v. Q'Max Solutions Inc.* (2001) 14 C.P.R. (4th) 129, at 158.

143 *Patent Act*, *supra*, note 129, Section 31.

named as inventors, the resulting patent will be invalid.'[144] Harold Fox equally stated that an inventor must be 'the first to discover or conceive [a thing] *and* to make it available to the public or file application for patent'.[145] (Italics in original.) This emphasis on the conception of an invention and its reduction to practical shape *by the same person* may disentitle existing indigenous persons to claims of inventorship, since they may not have conceived many inventions within the realm of TK.

Some of the traditional inventions are of immemorial origin, both in their conception and tangible manifestation.[146] A consideration of the intergenerational nature of TK makes it doubtful that current and existing indigenous persons can legally claim to be the inventors of TK, at least for the purpose of a patent application.[147] TK and innovation is not attributable to any particular person or generation of a community.[148] The ideas behind many traditional innovations were conceived by indigenous persons and their ancestors, many of whom cannot be traced.

TK is the achievement and common heritage of a particular community. It belongs not only to the past and present generation but also to the future generation.[149] In expressing the intrinsic opposition of patent law to group achievement, the United States Court of Appeals, District of Columbia, observed: 'We are bound to interpret the patent law in the light of its purpose declared by the Supreme Court, to reward individual and not group achievement.'[150] Moreover, patent commissioners may find it difficult to comprehend a patent application naming an undefined class of unborn persons as co-inventors. Certainly, unborn indigenous persons do not legally qualify as inventors. It is unlikely that a patent office would grant a patent for an invention

---

144 *Hughes and Woodley on Patents* (Markham, ON.: Butterworths, 2002), at 703.

145 Fox, *supra*, note 119, at 225.

146 Even more problematic for traditional innovators is Dr Fox's emphatic statement:

> In order to be the inventor, the applicant for a patent must have invented the thing himself, and not as a result of suggestion by another or as a result of reading. If it has been in previous use and available to the public, or if the applicant himself did not make the invention, or if it did not originate in his own mind, the applicant cannot be considered to be in law the inventor.

Ibid.

147 H.W.O. Okoth-Ogendo, 'Property Systems and Social Organisation in Africa: An Essay of the Relative Position of Women under Indigenous and Received Law', in Peter N. Takirambudde, ed., *The Individual Under African Law* (Swaziland: Swaziland Printing and Publishing Co., 1982), at 50: 'The one fundamental principle underlying the concept of immovable property in such societies [that is, Africa] is that rights over it are transgenerational...The transgenerational nature of property rights therefore excludes the possibility of withholding access to future members of society.'

148 David B. Gordon, 'Square Pegs and Round Holes: Domestic Intellectual Property Law and Native American Economic and Cultural Policy: Can it Fit?' (2000–2001) 25 *American Indian L. Rev.* 93, at 99 (noting with respect to authorship and copyrightability of traditional innovation that: 'Tribal works are infrequently original individual creations. The works created in the tribal community are the result of group participation, as well as generational participation. Each tribal generation adds or takes away from the work, exhausting the opportunity to identify original authors.')

149 Takirambudde, ed., *supra*, note 147.

150 *Potts v. Coe* (1944) 140 F. 2d 470, at 478.

(traditional knowledge and associated products) with indeterminate inventors. However, such an obstacle may be minimized by bringing the patent application in the name of a community and on behalf of its past, present and future citizens. But this suggested solution that sounds in perpetuitous trust would require further investigation and analysis.

Some Canadian judicial decisions highlight the importance of accurate specification of inventor(s) in a patent application. The cases were concerned with the interpretation of Section 53 of the *Canadian Patent Act*.[151] In *Apotex Inc. v. Wellcome Foundation Ltd.*,[152] part of the argument against the validity of the patent (concerning the novel use of AZT in the treatment of HIV) was that two independent scientists who performed some confirmatory tests for the patentee were inventors, and that failure to name them in the patent application as co-inventors voided the patent. In considering the above argument, Sexton, J.A. of the Federal Court of Appeal dealt in details with the law on inventorship, and his analysis may be relevant to the issue of TK. He held that an inventor must not only have conceived the idea of the invention, but must also have devised the means of putting that idea into practical shape.[153] He concluded that: 'In law, then, an inventor is that person (or those persons) whose conception or discovery gives rise to the invention for which a patent is sought. It should thus be equally clear that a person who does not conceive the idea or discover the thing is not an inventor.'[154] (Brackets in the original.) If this ruling were generally applied to TK, then it is doubtful whether present and future custodians of TK could be said to have conceived its idea, even though the present stakeholders can claim to have taken part in putting it into practical shape.

Though the above judicial determination was sufficient to determine the issue in that case, Sexton, J.A. went on to consider whether failure to name a co-inventor in a patent application would void a patent.[155] Since non-disclosure of a co-inventor in a

---

151 Section 53 of the *Canadian Patent Act*:

    53(1) A patent is void if any material allegation in the petition of the applicant in respect of the patent is untrue, or if the specification and drawings contain more or less than is necessary for obtaining the end for which they purport to be made, and the omission or addition is willfully made for the purpose of misleading.

    (2) Where it appears to a court that the omission or addition referred to in subsection (1) was an involuntary error and it is proved that the patentee is entitled to the remainder of his patent, the court shall render a judgement in accordance with the facts, and shall determine the costs, and the patent shall be valid for that part of the invention described to which the patentee is found to be entitled.

152 (2001) 10 C.P.R. (4th) 65.

153 *Ibid.*, at 77.

154 *Ibid.*, at 78.

155 I agree with the trial judge's decision that the failure to mention a co-inventor in a patent petition does not constitute an untrue 'material allegation' sufficient to invalidate a patent in accordance with section 53 of the *Patent Act*. As Addy, J. held in *Procter & Gamble Co. v. Bristol-Meyers Co.*, 'it is really immaterial to the public whether the applicant is the inventor or one of two joint inventors as this does not got [sic] to the term or to the substance of the invention nor even to the entitlement'. In my view, the trial judge thus correctly concluded that failure to name a co-inventor in a petition for a patent does not constitute a 'material

patent application is not material enough to invalidate a patent, it is possible to argue that strict identification and specification of TK innovators (inventors) should not present an insoluble obstacle to patent protection. But even if this hurdle was passed, patent application for TK would still face the general problems examined earlier.

Another illustrative judicial decision concerning inventorship is the recent case of *671905 Alberta Inc. v. Q'Max Solutions Inc.*[156] In this case, part of the defendant's contention was that the true inventor was Rick Smith and not James K. Fleming and Harold C. Fleming as named in the patent application. After holding that Rick Smith was the true inventor,[157] Gibson, J., of the Federal Court, Trial Division, had to consider the effect of that error and concluded: 'I conclude that, by virtue of s-s 53(1) of the Act, the 884 patent is void by reason of an untrue material allegation in the petition, that being the allegation contained therein that James K. Fleming and Harold C. Fleming "made" the invention of the 884 patent.'[158]

The two cases above could not be said to be in irreconcilable conflict. The first dealt with failure to name a co-inventor and the second was concerned with failure to name the true and only inventor. This distinction, which resulted in the different judicial conclusions, was recognized by Gibson, J.,[159] who was also aware of the earlier ruling in *Apotex's* case.[160] In the context of TK, it does not seem that *671905 Alberta's* case will be particularly relevant since inventorship by members of the community is hardly in dispute, though controversy will likely centre on the importance, identification, specification or naming of co-inventors, a point whose legal effect was generally considered in *Apotex's* case. It is suggested, therefore, that failure to name all co-inventors of TK should not be fatal to patent protection, and that it should be sufficient if the patent application is brought on behalf and for the benefit of the concerned community. As earlier pointed out, this solution would require further study.

Another specific statutory requirement that diminishes the chances of patent protection of TK is the exclusion of inventions in the public domain from the protection of a patent. An invention is not patentable if it had been disclosed to the general public before the application for a patent. Section 28 of the *Canadian Patent Act* deals with the disclosure of an invention.[161] Disclosure to a single person may

---

allegation' that results in a patent's invalidity, pursuant to section 53 of the *Patent Act*. *Ibid.*, at 81–2.

156 (2001) 14 C.P.R. (4th) 129.

157 *Ibid.*, at 158.

158 *Ibid.*, at 161.

159 *Ibid.*, at 159–60.

160 *Ibid.*, at 159.

161 Section 28 of the *Canadian Patent Act*:

28.2(1) The subject-matter defined by a claim in an application for a patent in Canada must not have been disclosed

(a) more than one year before the filing date by the applicant, or by a person who obtained knowledge, directly or indirectly, from the applicant, in such a manner that the subject-matter became available to the public in Canada or elsewhere;

(b) before the claim date by a person not mentioned in paragraph (a) in such a manner that the subject-matter became available to the public in Canada or elsewhere.

be sufficient to make an invention available to the public, if that disclosure was not subject to any condition of confidentiality.[162]

It may be difficult for TK to satisfy the test relating to public disclosure. Many elements of TK are known to members of its custodial community, and probably to some foreigners.[163] Codified systems of TK in China and India, for instance, the authoritative books on the Ayurvedic system of medicine, and publications by indigenous and foreign scholars in the fields of history, anthropology, botany and pharmacy, concerning TK or aspects of it, facilitate the disclosure of TK to the public.[164] However, it may be argued that TK is 'private information confined to a select group',[165] and therefore not available to the public. This may be true of traditional medicinal knowledge possessed only by specific members of a traditional or indigenous community, such as TM possessed by traditional healers, birth attendants, canoe builders and iron smelters. In the above cases, the TK concerned is usually held secret and disclosed only to the initiated, such as an apprentice. Thus, it is arguable that not all TK is available to the public. But is knowledge by some members of a group not a public knowledge or knowledge available to the public? The old case of *Plimpton v. Malcolmson*[166] may provide some guidance.[167]

---

162 In *Gibney, et al. v. Ford Motor Co. of Canada Ltd.* (1968) 52 C.P.R. 140, the alleged invention was a car part: a protector for automobile generator, designated in the patent application as 'Protector for Electric Rotary Machines'. *Ibid.*, at 143. The inventor fixed this part in an unidentified customer's car without any condition as to confidentiality or secrecy. The inventor obtained a patent for this invention more than one year after the invention. In an action against the defendant for infringement of the patent, it argued that the invention had already been made available to the public before the application for the patent. Noel, J. held that 'the authorities clearly establish that it is sufficient that one person alone sees the invention…to make it known in a public manner, which is the test (and not use by the public)'. *Ibid.*, at 161 (brackets in original). He also observed that 'one use alone is sufficient to establish public use'. *Ibid.*

163 There are now a significant number of monographs and databases on TK and related products produced by some agencies of the UN (such as the WHO), and some NGOs. These sources increase access to TK and make it available to the public.

164 Correa, *supra*, note 14, at 6.

165 David Vaver, *Intellectual Property Law* (Concord, Ontario: Irwin Law, 1997), at 132.

166 *Plimpton v. Malcolmson* (1876) 3 Ch. D. 531.

167 Jessel, M.R. observed:

> When you say a thing is known to the public and part of common knowledge, of course you do not mean that every individual member of the public knows it. That would be absurd. What is meant is that if it is a manufacture connected with a particular trade, *the people in the trade shall know something about it*; if it is a thing connected with a chemical invention, *people conversant with chemistry* shall know something about it. And it need not go so far as that. You need not show that the bulk, or even a large number, of those people know it. If a sufficient number know it, or if the communication is such that a sufficient number may be presumed, or assumed, to know it, that will do.

Ibid., at 556. (Italics supplied)

It is possible, then, to argue that TK is available to the public, since indigenous people connected with it are conversant with it.[168] On this perspective, it would be immaterial that TK is not known to the larger public. However, if we consider the entire members of a traditional community as inventors of TK, then the obstacle might be diminished, since knowledge by all co-inventors is not knowledge available to the public. Even then, we still have to contend with aspects of TK that are already in the possession of foreigners, in view of the significant publication on TK and the growing number of TK databases and registries.

To summarize, there are aspects of TK that are amenable to patent protection, for instance, herbal remedies and therapies involving a skilful utilization of TK, and technical traditional innovations such as canoe building, mining, making of musical instruments and cloth-weaving. However, potentials for the application of patent law are minimized by legal and interpretive problems relating to ownership, inventorship, duration of protection, notion of discovery, codification and the inter-territoriality of TK. In addition, there are further difficulties resulting from specific statutory criteria relating to public disclosure of an invention and the definition of an inventor. TK understanding of some of the above concepts are different from the meanings attributed to them under patent law. It is partly on account of the above difficulties that a developing country should also consider protection of TK under a *sui generis* framework, which is explored later. Before then, a brief examination of other IPR regimes such as copyright and trademark is necessary.

Copyright[169]

Copyright protects original work of authorship.[170] Protection is for the life of the author and for a period of 50 years (70 years for the UK) after his or her death.[171] Works protected under the *Canadian Copyright Act* are 'every original literary, dramatic, musical and artistic work'.[172] This includes compilations, books, pamphlets, lectures, dramatic, or dramatico-musical works, translations, illustrations, sketches and plastic works relative to geography, topography, architecture or science, tables, computer programs and cinematography.[173] The owner of a copyright[174] has the right, among others, to 'produce or reproduce the work or any substantial part thereof in any material form whatever, to perform the work or any substantial part

---

168 *Ibid.*

169 The use of a copyright system to protect folklore, an aspect of TK, was extensively examined by Farley, *supra*, note 6, at 1–57.

170 *Canadian Copyright Act, R.S.C. 1985, c. C-42*, as amended; *Copyright, Designs and Patents Act, 1988* (UK).

171 *Ibid.*, S. 6.

172 *Ibid.*, S. 5.

173 *Ibid.*, S. 2.

174 'Subject to this Act, the author of a work shall be the first owner of the copyright.' *Ibid.*, S. 31(1).

thereof in public'.[175] The Act provides for both civil[176] and criminal[177] remedies for the infringement of copyright. Like copyright legislation in a significant number of developed countries, the *Canadian Copyright Act* does not expressly protect or contemplate the protection of folklore.

Some elements of TK, however, have features closely resembling works protected under the *Canadian Copyright Act* (and similar legislation in other developed countries), thus making it a potential framework for the protection of TK.[178] A copyright framework appears suitable for the protection of the folkloric aspects of TK.[179] Kuruk observed that 'aspects of folklore that could be regulated under copyright laws include the traditional paintings, sculptures, designs and drawings as artistic works; dramas, dances and folktales as literary works; and folk songs as musical works'.[180]

Despite potentials for the protection of some aspects of TK under most developed countries' copyright legislation, there are practical and conceptual difficulties in accommodating TK under accepted meanings given to copyright concepts such as ownership, originality, duration of protection and fixation.[181] For instance, copyright protects only the work of an author that is in a fixed form. It is difficult, however, to identify such an author, or fixation, with respect to some components of TK. As earlier noted, TK is collectively owned and transmitted from generation to generation, sometimes orally. However, the WIPO/UNESCO Model Provisions on folklore, examined later, attempt to deal with the problems of fixation and collective

---

175 *Ibid.*, S. 3.

176 *Ibid.*, S. 34.

177 *Ibid.*, S. 42.

178 WIPO, *supra*, note 7, at 43.

179 'Of all the existing legal mechanisms, copyright law initially appears to be the best suited to protect indigenous folklore', Farley, *supra*, note 6, at 16. Similarly, Moran observed that:

> What is attractive about extending intellectual property law protection to control 'illicit exploitation' of sacred folklife expressions is that the subject matter material itself, such as songs, artwork, performances, and stories, falls squarely within the protectible subject matter of copyright law. Additionally, the willful or negligent actions giving rise to complaints, including reproducing, copying, broadcasting, performing, or deriving other works from originals, are each well-defined infringements of copyright law.

Supra, note 5, at 112–13.

180 Kuruk, *supra*, note 34, at 792.

181 For instance S. 1(2) of the *Nigerian Copyright Act, Cap. 68, Laws of the Federation of Nigeria, 1990*, provides:

> A literary, musical or artistic work shall not be eligible for copyright unless –
> (a) sufficient effort has been expended on making the work to give it an original character;
> (b) the work has been fixed in any definite medium of expression now known or later to be developed, from which it can be perceived, reproduced or otherwise communicated either directly or with the aid of any machine or device.

See also, Farley, *supra*, note 6, at 17–23.

ownership of folklore. Generally, the problems that confront copyright protection of TK are similar to the ones analysed under patent and need not be repeated here.

Quite unlike the copyright legislation in Canada and some other developed countries, the copyright legislation in some African countries, for instance, Nigeria,[182] Ghana,[183] Congo,[184] Mali,[185] Cameroon,[186] Central African Republic[187] and Senegal[188] has provisions relating to folklore. Section 28(5) of the *Nigerian Copyright Act* protects expressions of folklore including folk poetry, folk riddles, folk songs, folk music, folk dances, folk plays and folk arts.[189] Though the definition of folklore under the Nigerian legislation is broad, it is not comprehensive enough to cover other aspects of TK, such as traditional medicinal knowledge, herbal remedies or traditional therapies, and farmers' varieties.

The Nigerian Act empowers the Nigerian Copyright Council, a statutory body,[190] to protect expressions of folklore.[191] The Act protects expressions of folklore against unauthorized commercial reproduction, public performance, broadcasting, adaptations, translations and other transformations.[192] However, the Act exempts traditional or customary uses, private and domestic use, uses for educational purposes, illustration in original work, and the use of folklore as the basis of original

---

182 *Ibid.*

183 *Copyright Law (Ghana), 1985*, in 21 Copyright: Monthly Rev. World Intell. Prop. Org. (1985), at 423.

184 *Law on Copyright and Neighboring Rights (Congo), 1982*, in 19 Copyright: Monthly Rev. World Intell. Prop. Org. (1983), at 201.

185 *Ordinance Concerning Literary and Artistic Property (Mali), 1977*, in 16 Copyright: Monthly Rev. World Intell. Prop. Org. (1980), at 180.

186 *Law No. 82-18 to Regulate Copyright (Cameroon), [1982]*, in 19 Copyright, *supra*, note 184, at 360.

187 *Ordinance No. 85-002 on Copyright (Central African Republic), 1985*, in 21 Copyright, *supra*, note 183, at 158.

188 *Law on the Protection of Copyright (Senegal), 1973*, in 10 Copyright: Monthly Rev. World Intell. Prop. Org. (1974), at 211.

189 *Nigerian Copyright Act*, S. 28(5), *supra*, note 181:

> For the purpose of this section, 'folklore' means a group-oriented and tradition-based creation of groups or individuals reflecting the expectation of the community as an adequate expression of its cultural and social identity, its standards and values as transmitted orally, by imitation or by other means including –
> (a) folklore, folk poetry, and folk riddles;
> (b) folk songs and instrumental folk music;
> (c) folk dances and folk plays;
> (d) productions of folk arts in particular, drawings, paintings, carvings, sculptures, pottery, terracota, mosaic, woodwork, metalware, jewelry, handicrafts, costumes, and indigenous textiles.

190 *Ibid.*, S. (30).

191 *Ibid.*, S. 28(4).

192 *Ibid.*, S. 28(1).

work of authorship.[193] In the above cases, there should be proper acknowledgment of the source of the folklore.[194]

The *Nigerian Copyright Act*,[195] and similar legislation in some other African countries, has taken significant steps in the protection of the expressions of folklore. It is expected that other African countries would take the same direction, probably leading to a binding regional agreement on the matter. However, the Act does not include other important folkloric rights such as traditional medicinal knowledge and remedies, and traditional varieties of plants. Furthermore, the Act is territorial and applies only in Nigeria. Thus, unauthorized use of folklore abroad would be outside the reach of the legislation, though the Nigerian Copyright Council could cooperate with foreign governments and similar institutions abroad to secure the protection of Nigerian folklore therein.[196] However, this may involve financial resources beyond the budget of the Council, or may not be on the priority list of the Nigerian government which, like some other developing countries, is saddled with social, economic and political problems.

Trademark

A trademark is used to distinguish the goods of one person or services rendered by him or her from those of another person.[197] A trademark is registrable in Canada, and other countries having similar legislation, if it is clearly distinctive.[198] At the rudimentary stage of some traditional societies, when commercial exchange was mainly by means of barter or the direct purchase of goods from individual producers, it was likely that few people were concerned about the use of clearly distinctive and unique marks to distinguish their goods or services from those of others. However, some marks were used (and continue to be used) in traditional societies

---

193 *Ibid.*, S. 28(2).

194 *Ibid.*, S. 28(3).

195 *Ibid.*

196 *Ibid.*, S. (30)(3):

The Council shall –

(a) be responsible for all matters affecting copyright in Nigeria as provided for in this Act;

(b) monitor and supervise Nigeria's position in relation to international conventions and advise Government thereon;

(c) advise and regulate conditions for the conclusion of bilateral and multilateral agreements between Nigeria and any other country;

(d) enlighten and inform the public on matters relating to copyright;

(e) maintain an effective data bank on authors and their works;

(f) be responsible for such other matters as relate to copyright in Nigeria as the Minister may, from time to time, direct.

197 Illustration is given with the *Canadian Trademark Act, R.S.C., 1985, c. T-13*, as amended. Section 2 defines trademark as 'a mark that is used by a person for the purpose of distinguishing or so as to distinguish wares or services manufactured, sold, leased, hired, or performed by him from those manufactured, sold, leased, hired or performed by others'. Also to the same effect, s. 1 *Trade Marks Act, 1994* (UK).

198 *Ibid.*, s. 12 (Canada); s. 3 (UK).

and are potentially protectable under the trademark legislation. These traditional marks would include marks on agricultural implements and carving,[199] and signs and symbols used by traditional societies.[200] There are prospects of TK protection under the *Trademark Act*. For instance, trademarks remain protected as long as they are in use. Thus, there is a possibility for perpetual protection of a trademark. This type of perpetual protection is suitable for TK. In addition, some trademarks, such as collective and certification marks, could be registered and owned by a group of people. This resembles collective ownership of TK. Thus, current trademark law, like copyright, evinces characteristics that are compatible with TK and might supply a useful framework for the protection of TK.

Trade Secret

The regime of trade secret may be a valuable tool for the protection of TK.[201] The law protects trade secrets or confidential commercial information against unauthoriszed disclosure.[202] Unlike some other IPR frameworks (for example, patent), a trade secret is not registrable,[203] and may be protected perpetually. This is a significant economic advantage for poor indigenous societies that may be hard-pressed to finance the application and acquisition of certain intellectual property rights, such as patent. The potential perpetual protection under trade secret law also mirrors the interminable protection of TK under the customary law of most indigenous societies.

It is possible, therefore, to protect traditional medicinal knowledge as a trade secret. To qualify for protection, the information must be a secret.[204] The information held by traditional healers relating to medicinal qualities of plants, preparation and administration of herbal remedies, is usually not known by every member of the community and held in secret by its custodians; thus, it may qualify as a trade secret. The information must also have a commercial value.[205] Knowledge of the medicinal qualities of plants has significant commercial value and has been the basis of drug discovery efforts of some pharmaceutical companies based in some developed countries.[206] Also, some traditional varieties or farmers' varieties have been used by modern and commercial plant breeders in the developed world to generate new or improved varieties. Finally, the person in control of the information must have taken steps to keep it secret.[207] In the case of traditional medicinal knowledge in

---

199 Kuruk, *supra*, note 34, at 793.

200 Correa, *supra*, note 20, at 13.

201 Srividhya Ragavan, 'Protection of Traditional Knowledge' (2001) 2 *Minnesota Intellectual Property Rev.* 1, at 20–22.

202 TRIPS, *supra*, note 92, Article 39; also Ragavan, *supra*, note 201, at 21.

203 TRIPS, *supra*, note 92.

204 *Ibid.*, Article 39(2): an information is a trade secret if it is not ' generally known among or readily accessible to persons within the circles that normally deal with the kind of information in question'.

205 *Ibid.*

206 Ragavan, *supra*, note 201, at 21.

207 TRIPS, *supra*, note 92.

the possession of traditional healers, steps are usually taken to keep it secret and disclosed only to the initiated.[208]

While trade secret laws could protect undisclosed and secret aspects of TK, it is of no avail with respect to TK already in the public domain. Conceptually, information already in the public domain or easily ascertainable is not protectable as a trade secret. Publicly disclosed TK, therefore, would have to rely on another method of protection. Another hurdle is the requirement that a plaintiff in an action for unauthorized disclosure of a trade secret must establish the existence of a confidential relationship in breach of which the disclosure was made. This is an element that is difficult to establish by TK custodians since many TK users obtained the information outside any confidential relationship with TK custodians. For instance, some TK users got TK products, forming the basis of their inventions, from the general markets, or from public international institutions. Fortunately, current trade secret law does not insist on the requirement of a confidential relationship. Though the existence of a confidential relationship is still relevant, it is not a necessary element of a trade secret action. Absent such relationship, it is sufficient if a plaintiff establishes that the secret was obtained improperly.[209] If this were all that mattered in a trade secret action, it would have been of much avail to TK custodians since they can establish, in some cases, impropriety in the acquisition of TK by some of its users. But because of other requirements of trade secret law, which have to be satisfied, it still remains of limited utility to TK holders.

Other IPR Tools

Other potential tools include the use of geographical indications to enhance the value of TK products,[210] the use of industrial designs to protect the shape and design of TK products, the analogical use of Moral Rights (a copyright concept) to recognize indigenous innovators and protect the integrity of their works, and the use of trade names to identify indigenous groups and products. It is likely that the use of a particular IPR tool or a combination thereof, whether in the current or modified form, would be balanced against the objectives sought to be achieved and the cost of acquisition and enforcement of the acquired rights.

The *Sui Generis* Option

Considering the practical and conceptual problems that confront the protection of TK under existing IPR regimes analysed above, it may be useful for a developing country

---

208 However, TK relevant to agriculture, such as farmers' varieties, are traditionally freely used and exchanged, implying a loss of secrecy.

209 *Pioneer Hi-Breed International v. Holden Foundation Seed*, 35 F. 3d 1226, at1238 (8th Cir. 1994).

210 Downes has endorsed creative use of geographical indication in designing solutions to some of the problems relating to the protection of TK: Downes, *supra*, note 13, at 268–73.

to consider the development of a *sui generis* system for the protection of TK.[211] A 'sui generic' system is a unique one.[212] It is a system 'specifically designed to address the needs and concerns of a particular issue'.[213] There does not appear to be any rule of international law or treaty that precludes States from developing a *sui generis* system that sufficiently protects TK and accounts for its unique nature and features compared to knowledge systems protected under existing IPR regimes. TRIPS allows members of the WTO to protect plant varieties by patents or an effective *sui generis* system or by a combination of both.[214] However, it does not define what amounts to *sui generis* or an effective *sui generis* system.[215] The flexibility offered by Article 27 of TRIPS affords any developing country the opportunity of designing a *sui generis* system that responds to its needs and objectives, including the protection of TK and farmers' varieties. This could be done by conceptualizing the subject matter of protection in a way that anticipates the elements of TK and associated products and in a manner that responds to the peculiarity of TK such as its collectivity, perpetuity and enforceability. In fact, a *sui generis* system may be based on the package of intellectual property rights recognized and enforced under particular customary law systems. Even though this approach has some considerable difficulties relating to extra-territorial proof, recognition and enforcement of customary law, it has the advantage of according TK custodians the respect they deserve.[216] The purpose of this section is to examine some of the *sui generis* tools developed nationally, regionally and internationally. The diverse nature of the components of TK make it more complex for a single *sui generis* system to regulate all facets of TK. Thus, some of the *sui generis* systems discussed below focus on one component of TK or another.

The African Model Legislation[217]

The *African Model Legislation* attempts to implement the provisions of the *Convention on Biological Diversity* and, thus, provides a guide to member states of the Organisation of African Unity (now African Union) wishing to promulgate domestic legislation that implements the Biodiversity Convention.[218] Like the

---

211 Kuruk, *supra*, note 34, at 837–41.

212 *Webster's New World Dictionary*, *supra*, note 38, at 1339.

213 WIPO, *supra*, note 7, at 24.

214 TRIPS, *supra*, note 92, article 27(3)(b).

215 For the various papers presented at the International Seminar on Sui Generis Rights: GRAIN and BIOTHAI, eds, *Signposts to Sui Generis Rights: Resource Materials from the International Seminar on Sui Generis Rights* (Thai Network on Community Rights & Biodiversity (BIOTHAI) and Genetic Resources Action International (GRAIN), Bangkok, 1–6 December 1997).

216 Taubman, *supra*, note 58.

217 *African Model Legislation*, *supra*, note 12 (hereafter, Model Legislation).

218 Part of the Preamble states: 'Whereas, there is the need to implement the relevant provisions of the Convention on Biological Diversity, in particular Article 15 on access to genetic resources, and Article 8(j) on the preservation and maintenance of knowledge, innovations and practices of indigenous and local communities.' *Ibid.*

Biodiversity Convention, the main objective of the Model Legislation is to ensure conservation of biological diversity, sustainable use of its components, and equitable distribution of benefits arising from its utilization. It also seeks to protect traditional knowledge of local communities,[219] plant breeders' rights, and to recognize and reward the particular contribution of women to biodiversity.[220]

Part 4 of the Model Legislation establishes 'Community Rights'[221] as the *sui generis* framework for the protection of TK.[222] Under the Model Legislation, the State shall recognize traditional or indigenous societies as legitimate custodians and users of TK, including their right to biological resources, innovations, practices, knowledge and technologies acquired through generations, and the right to collectively benefit from their utilization.[223] Community intellectual rights are inalienable and do not require registration.[224] Such rights are also not defeated by the fact that they are

---

219 The Model Legislation uses the term 'community knowledge' which it defines as follows: 'community knowledge or indigenous knowledge is the accumulated knowledge that is vital for conservation and sustainable use of biological resources and/or which is of socio-economic value, and which has been developed over the years in indigenous/local communities.' *Ibid.*, art. 1.

220 *Ibid.*, Part 1. Thus, paragraph (e) of Part 1 undertakes to ensure 'the effective participation of concerned communities, with a particular focus on women, in making decisions as regards the distribution of benefits which may derive from the use of their biological resources, knowledge and technologies'. The Model Legislation vindicates M.S. Swaminathan's proposal for a legislation or framework that recognizes and rewards the contribution of women to TK:

> Women farmers need special recognition for their contribution to the conservation and improvement of genetic resources. For instance, the FAO sponsored studies conducted by the M.S. Swaminathan Research Foundation in India, Sri Lanka and Maldives showed that women often play a significant role in the selection and saving of seeds. They also conserve biodiversity through their home gradens, containing a wide range of fruits, food and medicinal crops. Moreover, women's involvement in seed conservation practices are highly significant in communities in which women are primarily responsible for food production, as among the Apatanis of Arunachal Pradesh, India and the Garhwalis of the Western Himalayas, or share joint responsibility as among the Mizos, Nagas and some hill tribes in the Western Ghats of India.

M.S. Swaminathan, 'Farmers' Rights and Plant Genetic Resources' (1998) 36 *Biotechnology and Development Monitor* 544, at 547.

221 Defined as 'those rights held by local communities over their biological resources, or parts or derivatives thereof, and over their practices, innovations, knowledge and technologies'. *Supra*, note 12, art. 1.

222 The protection of TK under a 'community intellectual rights' framework had earlier been suggested by some scholars, including Gurdial Singh Nijar, 'Community Intellectual Rights Protect Indigenous Knowledge' (1998) 36 *Biotechnology and Development Monitor* 601.

223 *Supra*, note 12, art. 16.

224 *Ibid.*, article 23(1) and 23(3).

already available to the public or have become part of the public domain.[225] Having defined the nature or types of community rights granted by it, the Model Legislation provides that the extent or scope of such rights, which the State shall recognize and enforce, would be determined by the customary law of the relevant community.[226] Access to any resource or knowledge protected as a community right shall be subject to the prior informed consent of the concerned community and women shall fully participate in the consent process.[227] Consent may be granted conditionally or unconditionally, refused or withdrawn where the proposed activities may prejudice the integrity or sanctity of TK or otherwise adversely affect the life of the local community.[228] Traditional or customary uses by community members, as determined by customary law or local practice, are exempted from the requirement of consent.[229] This provision is significant since requiring consent in that situation would contradict some customary practices.

Where pursuant to consent an element of TK or community right has been commercialized, the benefit accruing therefrom to the State shall be shared between it and the concerned community (or communities),[230] which shall receive at least 50 per cent of the benefits.[231] In partly rewarding the contribution of women to TK, the Model Legislation requires that the distribution of benefits shall treat men and women equitably.[232]

In Part 5, the Model Legislation establishes a *sui generis* regime for the recognition and protection of farmers' rights.[233] Traditional or farmers' varieties shall be protected by the issuance of a variety certificate.[234] Unlike new varieties subject to

---

225 *Ibid.*, 23(4):

> The publication of a written or oral description of a biological resource and its associated knowledge and information, or the presence of these resources in a genebank or any other collection, or its local use, shall not preclude the local community from exercising its community intellectual rights in relation to those resources.

226 *Ibid.*, art. 17.

227 *Ibid.*, art. 18.

228 *Ibid.*, arts. 19 and 20.

229 *Ibid.*, arts 21 and 22.

230 *Ibid.*, art. 12(2): 'The State and the community or communities shall be entitled to a share of the earning derived from when any biological resource and/or knowledge collected generates, directly or indirectly, a product used in a production process.'

231 *Ibid.*, art. 22.

232 *Ibid.*

233 *Ibid.*, art. 24(1):

> Farmers' Rights are recognised as stemming from the enormous contributions that local farming communities, especially their women members, of all regions of the world, particularly those in the centres of origin or diversity of crops and other agro-biodiversity, have made in the conservation, development and sustainable use of plant and animal genetic resources that constitute the basis of breeding for food and agriculture production.

234 *Ibid.*, art. 25(2):

> A variety with specific attributes identified by a community shall be granted intellectual protection through a variety certificate which does not have to meet the criteria of distinction, uniformity and stability. This variety certificate entitles the community to

plant breeders' legislation, farmers' varieties protected under the Model Legislation do not have to meet some specific criteria and only have to be identified by the concerned community as possessing some 'specific attributes'.[235] Farmers' varieties are characteristically unstable and this gives them the ability to respond to changing conditions.[236] Thus, what amounts to 'specific attributes' at the time of registration of the variety may change at the time of any resulting litigation.[237] A certificate for farmers' varieties grants exclusive property rights to the concerned community[238] and may, without more, impinge on the traditional practice of free exchange of seeds. The Model Legislation provides that farmers' rights shall include right to save, use, sell and exchange farm-saved seed and right to make non-commercial use of breeders' varieties.[239]

Though formulation of farmers' rights under the Model Legislation includes the right of local farmers to sell, on a non-commercial scale, the protected varieties of breeders,[240] it is still a much narrower formulation of farmers' rights compared to the

---

have the exclusive rights to multiply, cultivate, use or sell the variety, or to license its use without prejudice to the Farmers' Rights set out in this law.

235 For instance, under UPOV 1991 (posted on http://www.upov.int), for a new plant variety to be protected, it must be new, distinct, uniform and stable. *Ibid.*, arts. 5, 6, 7 and 9. The test of novelty is not as rigorous as that of patent. A plant variety is new if, at the date of application for protection, it has not been sold in the country of application, with the breeder's consent, for a period exceeding one year or four years in another country. *Ibid.*, art. 16. However, an existing variety may still be considered new, notwithstanding expiration of the period above, where a country applies, for the first time, the protection of UPOV to a genus or specie covering that variety. *Ibid.*, art. 16(2). The new variety must be distinct, in the sense that, '...it is clearly distinguishable from any other variety whose existence is a matter of common knowledge'. *Ibid.*, art. 7. It seems to be enough if only one quality distinguishes it from similar varieties of the same genus or specie. A new variety satisfies the test of uniformity if it achieves some homogeneity in '...its relevant characteristics'. *Ibid.*, art. 8., though this may depend on the means of propagation or reproduction.

Where, after successive production or propagation, a new variety retains its essential characteristics, then it is taken to be stable. *Ibid.*, art. 9. The examination of a new plant variety, for the above qualities, entails a high degree of knowledge, skill, experience and expense. The strength of countries in this regard is likely to vary, and some countries may have greater expertise in the examination of a particular genus or specie than others. Consequently, UPOV expects that member countries may enter into agreements with a view to joint utilization of examination services. *Ibid.*, art. 30(2) UPOV 1978. Or a country may, for the purpose of protection in its territory, accept the validity of a test result in another member country with respect to the same variety. *Ibid.*, art. 12.

236 Niels P. Louwaars, 'Sui Generis Rights: From Opposing to Complementary Approaches' (1998) 36 *Biotechnology and Development Monitor* 551, at 553.

237 UPOV, *supra*, note 235.

238 *Ibid.*

239 *Ibid.*, art. 26.

240 *Ibid.*, art 26(2): 'Notwithstanding sub-paragraphs (c) and (d), the farmer shall not sell farm-saved seed/propagating material of a breeders' protected variety in the seed industry on a commercial scale.'

Indian Plant Variety Protection and Farmers' Rights Act, 2001.[241] Farmers' rights under the Indian legislation permit farmers to save and re-use seeds of protected varieties, and to exchange and sell farm-saved seeds without restriction as to the scale of commerciality.[242]

Nevertheless, the farmers' rights provisions of the Model Legislation are a welcome development.[243] It would be interesting to see how some of its provisions

---

241 Suman Sahai, 'India's Plant Variety Protection and Farmers' Rights Legislation', in Peter Drahos and Ruth Mayne, *Global Intellectual Property Rights: Knowledge, Access and Development* (New York: Palgrave MacMillian, 2002), at 214–16.

242 *Ibid.*, at 217–18:

> The new law recognises the farmer not just as a cultivator but also as a conserver of the agricultural gene pool and a breeder who has bred several successful varieties. Farmers' Rights (s.39, clause (iv)), in part reads as follows: 'The farmer...shall be deemed to be entitled to save, use, sow, resow, exchange, share or sell his farm produce including seed of a variety protected under this Act in the same manner as he was entitled before the coming into force of this Act; Provided that the farmer shall not be entitled to sell branded seed of a variety protected under this Act.' Explanation: for the purpose of clause (iii) branded seed means any seed put in a package or any other container and labelled in a manner indicating that such seed is of a variety protected under this Act. This formulation allows the farmer to sell in the way he has always done, with the restriction that this seed cannot be branded with the breeder's registered name.

243 The concept of farmers' rights appears to have emerged during the so-called 'seed wars' of the 1970s and 1980s and could be traced to the legally non-binding *International Undertaking on Plant Genetic Resources* (IU). IU is an international agreement that was adopted by the twenty-second Session of the Conference of Food and Agricultural Organization (FAO) in 1983 by its Resolution 8/83. The Conference also established the Commission on Plant Genetic Resources to administer IU and provide an international forum for the discussion of issues relating to plants' genetic resources. The IU is an international policy framework that articulates issues of plant genetic resource exploration, conservation, sustainable use and sharing of benefits derived from the utilization of plant genetic resources. In 1995, the mandate of the Commission was broadened to include all issues of agro-biodiversity of relevance to food and agriculture. Consequently, the Commission was renamed Commission on Genetic Resources for Food and Agriculture (CGRFA). See http://www.fao.org/ag/cgrfa (last visited May 2002).

In 1983, the IU declared that all plant genetic resources were a common heritage of mankind, thereby giving a free and unhindered access to those resources. *Ibid.*, art. 1. This conception of plant genetic resources as a common property is analogous to John Henry Merryman's construct of 'cultural internationalism', which posits that objects of culture are a common heritage of mankind and should be freely transferable. National cultural property is only a component part of this common heritage and loses its national character in the resultant whole: 'Two Ways Of Thinking About Cultural Property' (1986) 80 *American Journal of International Law* 831. Also, John Henry Merryman, 'The Public Interest in Cultural Property' (1989) 77 *Cal. Law Review* 339.

The I.U's 'common heritage' resources would by interpretation include both traditional varieties in the South and commercially bred lines in the North. See J.R. Kloppenburg, *First the Seed: The Political Economy of Plant Biotechnology, 1492-2000* (Cambridge: Cambridge University Press, 1988), at 173. Thus, plant breeders in the North perceived this declaration

play out in practice.[244] Certain issues would need to be resolved under the legislation. For instance, though the recognition and respect of customary law as a source of law, and as providing the rule of decision, is very revolutionary and welcome, there would be complex difficulties and cost relating to litigation of TK pursuant to the

---

as inimical to their economic interest, resulting in pressures on their governments to ensure the restriction of the reach of IU. See Klaus Bosselman, 'Plants and Politics: The Intenational Legal Regime Concerning Biotechnology and Biodiversity' (1996) 7 *Colorado Jour. Int'l. Envtl. L. & Pol.* 111, at 132–3. This campaign, of plant breeders, was a success and yielded an agreed interpretation to IU, that is, Resolution 4/89, which accepted that plant breeders' rights, as defined in UPOV, were not in conflict with the IU. In order to placate farmers, Resolution 5/89 provided for farmers' rights. Farmers' rights are defined as: '[r]ights arising from the past, present and future contributions of farmers in conserving, improving, and making available plant genetic resources, particularly those in the centres of origin/diversity.' The international community is a trustee of these rights, which are to be realized through a voluntary international fund to support conservation efforts in developing countries.

In 1993, steps were undertaken to do the following: bring the IU into harmony with the *Convention on Biological Diversity* (CBD); make it more responsive to farmers' rights; and provide for access to germplasm not addressed in the CBD. These were issues dealt with, but not resolved, by the First Extraordinary Session of CGRFA, and subsequent meetings. However, the 1996 Leipzig International Technical Conference, convened by the FAO, adopted the Leipzig Declaration and the Global Plan of Action, which set out comprehensive and global modalities, including the financial and technical resources necessary for the realization of the objectives of the IU and urged for its complete revision. NGOs have been active in the revision process of the IU. Their actions have concentrated on advocating a system of multilateral access that removes life forms from patentability, whether under TRIPS or UPOV; ensuring that the IU is a legally binding instrument; and giving more legal teeth to farmers' rights. See 'A Call for Action on the International Undertaking n Plant Genetic Resources', http://www.ukabc.org/IU.htm.

A revised draft of the IU was adopted at the Sixth Extraordinary Session of the Commission on 1 July 2001. The revised IU was approved by the Conference of the FAO on 3 November 2001 as the *International Treaty on Plant Genetic Resources for Food and Agriculture* and was submitted to the Sixth Conference of the Parties to the CBD in 2002. Perhaps the major contribution of this latest treaty is the establishment of a multilateral system of access and benefit sharing, anchored on the sovereignty of states over their resources. Under the multilateral system, states are to allow free and unhindered access to plant genetic resources listed in an appendix to the treaty and selected on the basis of their relevance to food security. However, the resources covered by the multilateral system are not to be subjected to non-food industrial, pharmaceutical and chemical applications, but are to be used only for the purposes of research, breeding and training for food and agriculture. Again, these resources are to be free from intellectual property claims, but it seems that new varieties derived from them or their genetically engineered versions can be propertized. Developing countries and NGOs are likely to be disappointed by this latest treaty, as regards its treatment of farmers' rights. At the international level, farmers' rights is still being treated as a mere concept, an ideal whose realization is left to the whims and caprices of member states. It is yet to proceed beyond its recognitional utility.

244 Swaminathan, *supra*, note 49, at 548, observing that just like the formulation and implementation of breeders' rights have benefited from decades of experience resulting in several revisions of UPOV, farmers' rights may have to go through similar learning for their necessary perfection.

Model Legislation outside the confines of a particular developing country. In a foreign court, customary law, as the source of intellectual property rights, would have to be established as a fact. Thus, there are obvious difficulties associated with cost, proof and ascertainment of customary law, which is largely unwritten.

Similarly, where a particular variety is identified by more than one community, which of them is entitled to the issuance of a variety certificate under Article 25(2) of the Model Legislation? A State implementing its provisions, and already a member of UPOV, may have to take advantage of the provision of UPOV allowing members to make exceptions for farm-saved seeds.[245] However, the formulation of farmers' rights under the Model Legislation, allowing for the sale of protected varieties, though not on a commercial scale, may raise issues of consistency with UPOV.[246] Also, the grant of certificate for farmers' varieties may probably entail some cost and formal application by the local community. A regulatory national authority should nevertheless be competent to handle such incidental issues, including the waiver of fees for local communities.[247]

UNESCO/WIPO Model Provisions

The *UNESCO/WIPO Model Provisions for National Laws on the Protection of Expressions of Folklore Against Illicit Exploitation and Other Prejudicial Actions*[248] (Model Provisions) provides the statutory framework for a *sui generis* protection of expressions of folklore. Folklore is just one of the components of TK.[249] Instead of 'works' used in some copyright legislation to characterize the protected material, the Model Provisions use 'expressions of folklore' to highlight its *sui generis* nature. Although the Model Provisions address and ensure special copyrightability of

---

245 Article 15(20) UPOV 1991, posted on http://www.upov.int, provides:
   Notwithstanding Article 14, each Contracting Party may, within reasonable limits and subject to the safeguarding of the legitimate interests of the breeder, restrict the breeder's right in relation to any variety in order to permit farmers to use for propagating purposes, on their own holdings, the product of the harvest which they have obtained by planting, on their own holdings, the protected variety or a variety covered by Article 14(5)(a)(i) or (ii).

246 Suman Sahai, 'India's Plant Variety Protection and Farmers' Rights Legislation', in Peter Drahos and Ruth Mayne, *supra*, note 241, at 222, similarly observing that: 'It is likely that the new Indian Law, with its reasonably strong farmers' rights, will raise issues of consistency with UPOV. UPOV does not acknowledge strong farmers' rights and granting the right to sell seed of a variety protected by a breeder's right will in all likelihood be inconsistent with UPOV standards.'

247 Model Legislation, *supra*, note 12, art. 57: 'The State shall designate or establish a National Competent Authority which shall implement and enforce the provisions of this legislation.'

248 http://www.wipo.org/traditionalknowledge/pdf/1982-folklore-modelprovisions. Some of the provisions of the Model Provisions were adopted in Nigeria by the *Nigerian Copyright Act, Cap 68, Laws of the Federation of Nigeria, 1990*, Sections 28–29.

249 The earlier attempts in the late 1960s to draft the Model Provisions and its potential benefits for African countries are discussed by Harriet Fran Hunt, 'African Folklore: The Role of Copyright' (1969–1972) 1 *African Law Studies* 87. See, also, Paul Kuruk, *supra*, note 34.

folklore, it does not address other important categories of TK, such as agricultural knowledge, ecological knowledge and medicinal knowledge. However, where the desired objective of protection of any aspect of TK meets the rationale of the Model Provisions,[250] then its framework may be a potentially useful guide.[251]

The inter-generational, communal, oral and unfixed nature of folklore makes copyrightability difficult under the Western copyright system, which is partly characterized by fixation of expression and authorial ownership. The Model Provisions attempt to overcome this difficulty by granting protection to intangible expressions of folklore,[252] the commercial exploitation of which must be preceded by prior authorization[253] given by a competent authority.[254] Traditional, customary, non-commercial and fair uses, for example, education, research, source for a new original work, incidental use, conservation and archiving, are exempted from the requirements of prior authorization.[255] The Model Provisions also provide for both criminal and civil remedies, which may be pursued concurrently.[256] It is, therefore, possible to protect folkloric aspects of TK along the lines of the Model Provisions.[257]

The remedy provided by the Model Provisions (that is, folkloric protection) is based on a special adaptation of Western copyright law. Critics and opponents of IPR over TK may argue that since indigenous peoples and developing countries have blamed the Western intellectual property system for the unjust exploitation of their resources, it is ironic that they should employ the same disliked system as a basis for some solution to the problem. Such opponents may consider that this indicates a conceptual gap in the Model Provisions.

Unlike Western copyright law, which emphasizes authorial ownership, many indigenous ownership systems keep a good deal of tangible and intangible property in the commons. What the Model Provisions seem to have done is to circumscribe access to these commons (for example, folklore) by conferring 'ownership' thereof

---

250 The rationale of the Model Provisions seems to be the avoidance of misappropriation and the payment of compensation for non-traditional use of folklore.

251 The Crucible Group, *People, Plants, and Patents: The Impact of Intellectual Property on Biodiversity Conservation, Trade, and Rural Society* (Ottawa: International Development Research Center, 1994), at 69–70.

252 Model Provisions, *supra*, note 248, section 2. This section shows that the Model Provisions do not protect every aspect of folklore, such as traditional beliefs, but only those that qualify as an artistic heritage.

253 *Ibid.*, section 3.

254 *Ibid.*, sections 9 and 10.

255 *Ibid.*, section 4.

256 *Ibid.*, sections 6, 7 and 8.

257 In 1984, WIPO/UNESCO prepared a draft treaty along the lines of the Model Provisions to give it the character of a binding international instrument, but disagreement among member states, pertaining to the desirability of a binding international instrument on folklore, defeated its adoption. However, in 1997 efforts were made to reintroduce the debate on the international protection of folklore, particularly at the UNESCO/WIPO World Forum on the Protection of Folklore, held in Phuket, Thailand, in April 1997. The Phuket Plan of Action decided, however, to promote the protection of folklore at the national level, and subsequently at the regional level. Experience gained at these levels may provide guidance for possible protection at the international level.

on the person or authority whose prior authorization is needed for their exploitation. This solution, critics may contend, is in the spirit of the intellectual property system of the West, and against the traditional system of free access. Such critics may caution against uncritical acceptance of such Western-oriented solutions that seem to be based on the theory of possessive individualism. Possessive individualism conceptually defines and identifies an individual by the property he or she possesses.[258] It is a Western concept[259] and provides the theoretical underpinning of patent, copyright and some *sui generis* protections. It is arguably epistemologically unsuitable for community or collective property, for example, folklore, ethnobotanical knowledge or plant genetic resources in a particular part of a national territory.[260]

Despite the potential criticism above, the Model Provisions is a step in the right direction, ensuring some *sui generis* protection for folklore, and has already been reflected in the legislation of some African countries, for instance, Nigeria, Ghana, Mali, Senegal, Congo, Cameroon and the Central African Republic.[261] Until indigenous communities acquire sufficient political empowerment, the metaphor of possessive individualism will remain a standard weapon in their fight against the unjust and uncompensated exploitation of their TK, by the hegemonic culture. As Richard Handler observed: 'Those who would assert what they see as their rights against the powers-that-be must articulate their claims...in a language that power understands.'[262]

The Indian Biodiversity Act

In 2001, India passed the *Biodiversity Act, 2001*,[263] which created a bioprospecting authorizing agency known as the National Biological Authority (NBA), with power to protect Indian biodiversity and grant or refuse access thereto to bioprospectors,

---

258 Richard Handler, 'Who Owns the Past? History, Cultural Property, and the Logic of Possessive Individualism', in Brett Williams, ed., *The Politics of Culture* (Washington: Smithsonian Institution Press, 1991), at 63.

259 C.B. Macpherson, *The Political Theory of Possessive Individualism: Hobbes to Locke* (Oxford: Oxford University Press, 1962).

260 According to Richard Handler:
> The problem with these restitutionist arguments [that is, the argument that those dispossessed of their cultural objects have a right to their restitution or reparation] is that they make use of worn-out metaphors – collectivities seen as individuals, culture seen as property – borrowed from the hegemonic culture that the restitutionists are attempting to resist...It is no longer useful for anthropologists to imagine cultures as collective individuals possessed of property and characterized by that 'identity' so central to the individualistic worldview.

In Brett Williams, *supra*, note 86, at 68.

261 *Supra*, notes 181–188. However, the adopting legislation in some of these African countries that pre-dated the Model Provisions appears to be based on the earlier UNESCO/ WIPO Tunis Model Copyright Law, 1976.

262 In Brett Williams, *supra*, note 86, at 70–71.

263 Bhagirath Choudhary, 'Legislation for a Genetic Heritage' (2001) 48 *Biotechnology and Development Monitor* 19–21.

mainly foreigners. Money realized by the NBA from bioprospecting is paid into the National Benefit Fund.[264] The NBA could refuse its consent to any bioprospecting that is inimical to the spiritual welfare of Indians and its clearance is needed for patents based on Indian TK and associated products. The *Indian Biodiversity Act* implements the *Convention on Biological Diversity* and ensures the enforcement of informed consent and benefit-sharing obligations through its complementary role in the patent process. Though the Act mainly relates to biodiversity resources, its provisions nevertheless cover, at least implicitly, TK relevant for biodiversity.

Thailand's Traditional Medicine Intelligence Act

The *Thai Traditional Medicine Intelligence Act* established a *sui generis* regime for the protection of TM.[265] The Thai Act promotes and protects three categories of TM and knowledge thereof: National Formulae; Individual Formulae; and General Formulae.

Formulations belonging to the category of the National Formulae are determined and announced by the Ministry of Public Health.[266] These are formulations crucial to human health and their commercial exploitation is subject to permission from the Thai government.[267] Individual formulations can be registered and belong to the inventor or developer, with exclusive right to exploit the formulation for the lifetime of the inventor and for a further period of 50 years from the date the inventor dies.[268] Third parties require permission from the owner/inventor to use private formulations.[269] General formulations are freely available and not subject to prior authorizations.[270] The Thai Act provides for the protection of medicinal plants, by establishing a list of plants regarded as being close to extinction. Prior permission is needed for any management activities involving such plants.[271] The Act formally established the Institute of Thai Traditional Medicine that functioned informally for a period of seven years, and also distributed registration authority to 75 provincial offices.[272] It is noteworthy that under the Thai Act, traditional healers and the Thai community are permitted to use without payment any of the three categories of formulations, provided the use is domestic and in limited quantity.[273] The Thai approach is markedly different from, and could be contrasted with, the framework of the African Model Provisions examined earlier. Unlike the African Model Provisions, the Thai

264 Ragavan, *supra*, note 201, at 655.

265 World Health Organization (WHO), *Report of the Inter-Regional Workshop on Intellectual Property Rights in the Context of Traditional Medicine* (Bangkok, Thailand, 6–8 December 2000), at 16–17. See, also, Correa, *supra*, note 20, at 13.

266 *Ibid.*
267 *Ibid.*
268 *Ibid.*
269 *Ibid.*
270 *Ibid.*
271 *Ibid.*
272 *Ibid.*
273 *Ibid.*

Act is not based on customary law but adopts the modified version of a Western IPR system.

Other Protection Tools

In addition to potential options under the existing intellectual property rights, and *sui generis* framework, it is possible to design a misappropriation regime that would not entail any form of monopolization.[274] Correa has examined the dynamics of such a regime, which may include the documentation of TK (for instance, the Registries of TK developed in India[275]), an obligation to declare the origin of the TK component of the raw materials used in inventions covered by IPR claims,[276] and the requirement of informed consent.[277] A misappropriation regime would be apposite where exclusionary rights are not sought by TK custodians. For instance, where the objective is to ensure monetary or valuable compensation for the exploitation of TK, the use of bioprospecting contracts may be a handy tool. Recent bioprospecting contracts have revealed useful compensation models, of which Merck and INBio's 1991 agreement is an example. INBio, a Costa Rican, non-profit, private conservation institute, entered into a renewable contract with Merck, a transnational pharmaceutical company, under which INBio initially supplied Merck

---

274 Correa, *supra*, note 20, at 18.

275 Downes and Laird, in Coombe, *supra*, note 17.

276 The *European Directive 98/44/EC on the Legal Protection of Biotechnological Inventions, OJ No. 213, 1998* requires, but does not oblige, European patent applicants to disclose the origin of TK used in the invention. Recently, at the Third Session of the WIPO Intergovernmental Committee on Intellectual Property and Genetic Resources, Traditional Knowledge and Folklore, 13–21 June 2002 (WIPO/GRTKF/IC/3/16), the European Community and its member states supported the disclosure of origin of TK as a possible protective device:

> The preamble to the EU legislation on the legal protection of biotechnology inventions lays down that, if an invention is based on biological material of plant or animal origin, or if it uses such material, the patent application should, where appropriate, include information on the geographical origin of such material, if known; this is without prejudice to the processing of patent applications or the validity of rights arising from granted patents. This provision must be regarded as being an encouragement to mention the geographical origin of biological material in the patent application, along the lines indicated by Articles 16(5) and 11 of the CBD. However, the provision of such information is not an obligation under EU law. Nor does the failure to provide such information have, as such, any legal consequences for the processing of patent applications, nor for the validity of rights arising from the granted patents. The EC and its Member States are willing to discuss the modalities of any system that would allow Member States to keep track, at global level, of patent applications with regards to TK for which access has been granted…The information to be provided by patent applicants should be limited to the information on the origin of TK used in an invention which the applicant knows or has reasons to know.

Apart from European countries that adhere to the above directive, disclosure of origin is also an emerging patent practice in the USA. See, Downes, *supra*, note 13, at 274.

277 Correa, *supra*, note 20, at 18–19.

with 10,000 biosamples or extracts from wild plants, insects and microorganisms for a consideration of US$1.135 million. One million dollars was paid up-front in cash, while US$135,000 represented the value of scientific equipment supplied by Merck.[278] Under the contract INBio would, in addition, be paid a certain percentage of the royalties resulting from any commercialization of the resources it supplied. The money realized by INBio would be applied to conservation efforts, training and capacity-building.[279]

The Letter of Collection (LOC) issued by the US National Cancer Institute (NCI) offers another compensation paradigm. Since 1985, the NCI has been involved in plant collection in the tropics, with a view to discovering anti-cancer and anti-AIDS chemical compounds. Its plant collection is generally done through US professional institutes, like the Missouri Botanical Garden and New York Botanical Garden, known as 'Contractors'. The NCI Contractors enter into a plant-collection agreement with professional institutions in the tropics, for example, universities, known as 'Collaborators'. Such agreements, between Contractors and Collaborators, are based on a model prepared by the NCI and popularly called the LOC.

The LOC generally provides that the result of plant screening will be made available to the Collaborators, who are expected to keep it secret until it is patented by the NCI. The Collaborators are to be offered training in NCI laboratories and would have a share of royalties resulting from any successful commercialization of samples supplied by them. Again, the Collaborators will have the first right of supplying the needed raw materials, which a successful drug development might entail.[280]

As with the Merck/INBio agreement, the LOC neither provides any direct benefit to individuals and local communities nor generally permits their participation in the negotiation process, though they are not intrinsically excluded.[281] This result is produced by the LOC's concentration on institutional entities. It is in this context that the compensation model of Shaman Pharmaceuticals (a San Francisco Company) offers a more interesting example. Shaman is a comparatively young pharmaceutical company, which has blazed the trail in basing its drug discovery effort exclusively on ethnopharmacological knowledge. Before Shaman embarks on any bioprospecting activity, it negotiates with the relevant local community and grants initial

---

278 A detailed analysis of the contract has been done by Christopher J. Hunter, 'Sustainable Bioprospecting: Using Private Contracts and International Legal Principles and Policies to Conserve Raw Medicinal Materials' (1997) 25 *Boston College Envt'l. Aff. L. Rev.* 129, at 151–74; The Crucible Group, *supra*, note 251, at 90–92.

279 *Ibid.*

280 A comprehensive analysis of the LOC is done by Gordon M. Cragg, *et al.*, 'Policies for International Collaboration and Compensation in Drug Discovery and Development at the United States National Cancer Institute, The NCI Letter of Collection', in Tom Greaves, ed., *Intellectual Property Rights for Indigenous Peoples: A Sourcebook* (Oklahoma City: Society for Applied Anthropology, 1994), at 85.

281 This is evidenced by the agreement between the AWA Federation in Ecuador and an NCI Contractor, the New York Botanical Garden: Tom Greaves, ed., *ibid.*, at 92.

compensation based on the immediate needs of such a community.[282] Thus, Shaman repaired and expanded the airstrip used for emergency medical evacuations by the Quichua community in the Ecuadorian Amazon.[283] Shaman funds, and encouraged the founding of, the Healing Forest Conservancy, a biodiveristy conservation NGO. A portion of the profits from any of Shaman's products is paid to the Conservancy, which distributes it amongst the communities, institutions and states from the region where the commercialized product was sourced.[284]

Though these various compensation models show varying degrees of sensitivity to the complaint of biodiversity-rich countries, one should not be unwarily enthusiastic in concluding that they meet the demands of these countries.[285] Private contracts do not always meet all the objectives of TK protection. Very often, the complaint is that commercial exploitation of a religiously useful plant undermines the spiritual values of concerned communities. This was the substance of the opposition directed to the patenting of ayahausca by Loren Miller of the International Plant Medicine Corporation, a US company.[286] Ayahausca is used as a traditional medicine, and in religious ceremonies, by the indigenous peoples of the Amazon River basin. In such a scenario, prohibition on commercial exploitation would seem to meet the demands of indigenous people, thus pitching them against the commercial interest of multinational pharmaceutical companies. Unfortunately, this would seem to involve a conflict between religion and commerce, which the law is generally not equipped to handle.

The International Contexts of Traditional Knowledge

This section briefly analyses the impact of efforts at the international level on the protection of TK. The intention is to highlight the various international fora concerned

---

282 Steven R. King, 'Establishing Reciprocity: Biodiversity, Conservation and New Models for Cooperation Between Forest-Dwelling Peoples and the Pharmaceutical Industry', in Tom Greaves, ed., *supra*, note 280, at 69.

283 *Ibid.*

284 Katy Moran, 'Biocultural Diversity Conservation Through The Healing Forest Conservancy', in Tom Greaves, ed., *supra*, note 280, at 101.

285 For the bioprospecting guidelines of some international institutions, including compensation structure, for instance, that of the Association of Systematics Collections, the Center for Plant Conservation, the International Society of Ethnobiology, the Pew Conservation Fellows and the University Research Expeditions Program, see Katy Moran, *Mechanisms for Benefit Sharing: Nigerian Case Study for the Convention on Biological Diversity* (Washington, DC: The Healing Forest Conservancy, 1998). Also see Maurice M. Iwu, 'Biodiversity Prospecting in Nigeria: Seeking Equity and Reciprocity in Intellectual Property Rights Through Partnership Arrangements and Capacity Building' (1996) 51 *Journal of Ethnopharmacology* 209; Katy Moran, *et al.*, 'Biodiversity Prospecting: Lessons and Prospects' (2001) 30 *Annu. Rev. Anthropol.* 505.

286 According to the Environmental News Service of 5 November 1999, the patent on ayahausca was set aside by the US Patent and Trademark Office on the ground of existing prior publication on ayahausca: 'U.S. Cancels Patent on Sacred Ayahausca Plant', http://www. erowid.org/plants/babisteriopsis_media1.html. However, the patent was later reinstated.

or partly concerned with the protection of TK or aspects of it in order to ascertain some useful model of protection for TK. There is no attempt to analyse in details the programme of work undertaken by the relevant international agencies or bodies considered in this section. These agencies or bodies include: the World Intellectual Property Organization (WIPO), the United Nations Environmental Program (UNEP), the Food and Agricultural Organization of the United Nations (FAO), the United Nations Working Group on Indigenous Populations (WGIP), the United Nations Educational, Scientific, and Cultural Organization (UNESCO), the International Labour Organization (ILO), the World Bank, the World Health Organization (WHO), the United Nations Conference on Trade and Development (UNCTAD), the World Trade Organization (WTO), the United Nations Development Program (UNDP), the United Nations Population Fund (UNFPA), the World Food Program (WFP), and the International Fund for Agricultural Development (IFAD).

Each of the above institutions has its own unique mandate and objectives and approaches the protection of TK or aspects thereof in the context of its mandate and objectives. The different approaches, however, show the complexity of the subject and the richness of divergent views for TK protection. There is room for cooperation between two or more institutions, as evidenced by the WIPO and UNESCO collaboration in developing Model Provisions for the protection of the expressions of folklore against illicit exploitation and other prejudicial actions.[287] Below is an examination of only some of the institutions identified above.

The UNEP and the Convention on Biological Diversity (CBD)

The CBD,[288] which came into force on 29 December 1993, is about the most famous international convention on indigenous knowledge, resource conservation and sustainable utilization.[289] Article 1 states the objectives of the convention to be the '...conservation of biological diversity, the sustainable use of its components and

---

287 *Supra*, note 248.

288 Text of the Convention is posted on http://www.biodiv.org/.

289 It was preceded by earlier international conventions that showed some sensitivity to indigenous knowledge, culture and environment: *International Labour Organization Convention Concerning Indigenous and Tribal Peoples in Independent Countries, June 1989* (ILO Convention 169) provides in Article 31.1 that 'governments shall respect the special importance of the cultures and spiritual values of the peoples concerned of their relationship with the lands or territories, or both as applicable, which they occupy or otherwise use, and in particular the collective aspects of this relationship'. Posted on http://www.usask.ca/nativelaw/ILO169html (last visited 2 January 2002). Article 15 of the *Covenant on Economic, Social and Cultural Rights* (CESCR 1966) provides:

    1. The States Parties to the present Covenant recognize the right of everyone : (a) To take part in cultural life; (b) To enjoy the benefits of scientific progress and its applications; (c) To benefit from the protection of the moral and material interests resulting from any scientific, literary or artistic production of which he is the author (2) The steps to be taken by the States Parties to the present Covenant to achieve the full realization of this right shall include those necessary for the conservation, the development and diffusion of science and culture.

the fair and equitable sharing of the benefits arising out of the utilisation of genetic resources...'. Article 3 vests sovereign rights over genetic resources in their states of origin. Article 8 recognizes the importance of traditional knowledge and methods conducive to biodiversity conservation and urges their generalization, dissemination and compensation. Article 15 obliges contracting parties to provide reasonable access to genetic resources in their sovereign territories on the basis of prior informed consent and equitable sharing of benefits. Article 16 provides that in consideration of access to genetic resources of developing countries, developed countries should facilitate the transfer, to developing countries, of '...technologies that are relevant to the conservation and sustainable use of biological diversity or make use of genetic resources...'. However, access to technologies shall be 'consistent with the adequate and effective protection of intellectual property rights'.[290]

It seems that transferable technology under Article 16 should not be literally and parochially construed. Article 16(1) obliges contracting states to recognize that 'technology *includes* biotechnology'. This inclusionary phraseology should dominate the construction and ascertainment of technology to which the South has access. It seems only fair that since the North is given a virtually unrestrained and unlimited use of the South's genetic resources,[291] the South should also have a qualitatively similar access to the North's technology. The CBD is not a self-executing legislation and signatory States are required to implement its provisions through domestic legislation. However, there seems to be significant debate and uncertainty as to its proper implementational model.[292] Scholars, partly because of the CBD's ambiguous provisions, have yet to agree on whether intellectual property law or participation of indigenous peoples in the formulation of domestic biodiversity policy is the ideal

---

Posted on http://www.umn.edu/humanrts/instree/b2esc.htm (last visited 2 January 2002). Similarly, Chapter 21 of *Agenda 21: Earth's Action Plan* directs that: 'Governments could.... adopt legal instruments that will protect indigenous intellectual and cultural property.' N. Robinson, ed., *Agenda 21: Earth's Action Plan* (New York: Oceana, 1993).

290 CBD, art. 16(2).

291 The only appearance of limitation is the requirement of Article 15(2) that genetic resources should be committed to 'environmentally sound uses'.

292 Another deficiency of the CBD is that it does not, for its non-retroactivity, apply to germplasm collected from developing countries before 1993 and now housed in seed banks under the control of various international agricultural research centres run by the Consultative Group on International Agricultural Research (CGIAR).

or optimal way to implement the Convention.[293] Some countries, like India[294] and Australia,[295] are still experimenting with various legislative and policy options.

The CBD has helped in internationalizing the plight of developing countries, especially with respect to the non-consented and uncompensated exploitation of their ethnobotanical and ethnopharmacological knowledge and genetic resources. The CBD has helped in changing the pre-CBD characterization of developing countries' plants' genetic resources as a common heritage of mankind. Moreover, the CBD has given a significant boost to the recognition and promotion of TK and informal innovation. Article 8(j) provides:

> Each Contracting Party shall, as far as possible and as appropriate: Subject to its national legislation, respect, preserve and maintain knowledge, innovations and practices of indigenous and local communities embodying traditional lifestyles relevant for the conservation and sustainable use of biological diversity and promote their wider application with the approval and involvement of the holders of such knowledge, innovations and practices and encourage the equitable sharing of the benefits arising from the utilization of such knowledge, innovations and practices.[296]

However, it may be incorrect to infer from Articles 3 and 8 of the CBD that TK and informal innovation lacked legitimacy before the Convention. TK derives its validity from epistemological, ecological and indigenous structures outside the context of the CBD.[297]

The Conference of the Parties (COP) to the CBD is the governing body of the Convention. Its tasks include monitoring and advancing the implementation of the Convention's provisions through COP's periodic decisions. The implementation of Article 8(j) of the CBD has been considered in the Conference of the Parties to the CBD in its third session in November 1996, fourth session in May 1998, fifth session in May 2000 and sixth session in April 2002.[298] The COP-3 decided to establish

---

293 For instance, Keith Aoki, 'Neocolonialism, Anticommons Property, and Biopiracy in the (not-so-brave) New World Order of International Intellectual Property Protection' (1998) 6 *Indiana Jour. of Global Legal Studies* 11; Michael Halewood, 'Indigenous and Local Knowledge in International Law: A Preface to Sui Generis Intellectual Property Protection' (1999) 44 *McGill L.J.* 953.

294 David R. Downes and Sarah A. Laird, 'Community Registries of Biodiversity-Related Knowledge: The Role of Intellectual Property in Managing Access and Benefit Sharing', in Rosemary Coombe, *Intellectual Property, Human Rights and Development* (Toronto: University of Toronto Press, 2000), at 597.

295 Michael Blakeney, 'Access to Biological Resources: Domestic and International Developments and Issues' (1998) 5 *Murdoch University Electronic Journal of Law*; http://www.sustain.org/biotech/library/admin/uploadedfiles/Access_to_Biological_Resources_Domestic...

296 CBD, art. 8(j).

297 A theoretical discussion of indigenous knowledge can be fruitfully read in Marie Battiste and James Henderson, *Protecting Indigenous Knowledge and Heritage: A Global Challenge* (Saskatoon: Purich Publishing Ltd., 2000), chapter 2.

298 The various decisions taken at these sessions, some of which impact on the implementation of Article 8(j), are posted on www.biodiv.org.

an intersessional process to work on the implementation of Article 8(j) and related provisions.[299] Pursuant to this process, a Workshop on Traditional Knowledge and Biological Diversity was held in Madrid, Spain in 1997. The Workshop, in its report, recommended the development of a programmatic work plan on Article 8(j). Recalling the above report, the COP-4 established an Ad Hoc Open-ended Inter-sessional Working Group with a mandate to develop a programme of work that implements Article 8(j) and related provisions and to provide advice on the development of legal and other appropriate forms of protection for subject matter covered by Article 8(j).[300]

The Working Group has developed a work programme for the implementation of Article 8(j), and this was endorsed by the COP-5 in 2000.[301] In its latest session, the COP-6 considered and took several decisions relating to the implementation of Article 8(j),[302] including the integration of relevant tasks of the programme of work on Article 8(j) and related provisions into the thematic programmes of the *Convention on Biological Diversity*, evaluation of progress in the implementation of the priority tasks of the programme of work on Article 8(j) and related provisions, and the conduct of cultural, environmental and social impact assessment regarding developments proposed on sacred sites and on waters traditionally occupied or used by indigenous and local communities.

TRIPS and the WTO

Trade Related Aspects of Intellectual Property Rights (TRIPS) is an international agreement with significant economic implications for developing countries.[303] TRIPS seeks to align WTO members' intellectual property laws with the standard set by TRIPS. TRIPS is a corollary of the Uruguay Round of GATT (General Agreement on Trade and Tariffs), which was concluded in 1994. It is patterned after, and probably globalized, the patent law of the United States of America.[304] Because of procedural and substantive concerns, there are reasons why TRIPS has been accused by some developing countries of being a quintessential exercise in economic and legal imperialism.[305]

---

299 *Ibid.*, COP Decision III/14.

300 *Ibid.*, COP Decision IV/9.

301 *Ibid.*, COP Decision V/16.

302 *Ibid.*, COP Decision VI/10.

303 Text of the Agreement is posted on http://www.austili.edu.au/au/other/dfat/treaties/1995/809.htm (last visited 2 January 2002).

304 Vandana Shiva, 'The US Patent System Legalizes Theft and Biopiracy', *The Hindu*, 28 July 1999: http://www.purefood.org/patent/uspatsys.cfm (last visited 3 January 2002).

305 Martin Khor observed:

> [t]he developing countries of today are asked to adhere to IPR standards that would effectively prevent them from taking the same technology path as the developed countries. It is hard to avoid the conclusion that TRIPS is a protectionist device designed not only to advance the monopoly privileges of global corporations but also to prevent developing countries from being successful competitors to developed countries.

By the international law doctrine of specialization, intellectual property is traditionally within the province of the World Intellectual Property Organization (WIPO).[306] However, WIPO did not have the flexibility needed to promulgate a controversial international IP law in the form of TRIPS. GATT, which traditionally handled issues of trade liberalization, assumed jurisdiction over intellectual property, since it had the flexibility, and enforcement mechanism, to secure the passage of TRIPS as a binding international agreement. Furthermore, the acceptance of TRIPS was made a condition precedent for membership of the newly created World Trade Organization (WTO) which replaced GATT. Developing countries that are understandably anxious to have access to foreign markets for their exports, an access facilitated by membership of WTO, therefore found TRIPS irresistible.

Ana Maria Pacon has suggested further reasons that facilitated the successful passage of TRIPS. She observed that developing countries lost their opposition to TRIPS, which was based on the argument that reverse engineering and technological imitation were necessary for their industrial development.[307] There were many reasons for this defeat. First, the USA had, in the late 1980s, brandished its 'Special Clause 301', under the *1988 US Omnibus Trade and Competitiveness Act*, as a lethal weapon against countries, mainly developing countries, which gave little or no protection to US intellectual property. Under the Clause, trade sanctions were imposed against a number of developing countries like Brazil, China and Argentina. The existence of 'Special 301' and its excruciating sanctions painfully reminded developing countries, during the Uruguay Round, that failure to accede to TRIPS might be visited with US trade sanctions.

Second, developing countries witnessed a permeation of neo-liberal economic theory, which significantly diluted their erstwhile economic protectionist policy. The elites and advocates of this emerging economic dispensation were sufficiently persuaded that proper intellectual property protection was a prerequisite for free trade and technological growth. Third, the end of the Cold War meant a loss of bargaining power for developing countries. The US economic pressure no longer finds a counter-force in Russian alliance. Fourth, developing countries could not form a united front, despite India and Brazil's demonstrated opposition to TRIPS. Industrially stronger developing countries, like Taiwan, South Korea and Hong Kong, maintained a passive position, for fear of US sanctions. The US, therefore, had no effective opposition to the passage of TRIPS.

Before the TRIPS agreement, there were some international normative frameworks for intellectual property, for instance, the *Paris Convention of 1883* (PC)

Martin Khor, 'Rethinking Intellectual Property Rights and TRIPS', in Peter Drahos and Ruth Mayne, eds, *Global Intellectual Property Rights: Knowledge, Access and Development* (New York: Palgrave MacMillian, 2002), at 206.

306 WIPO, *supra*, note 7.

307 Ana Maria Pacon, 'What Will TRIPS Do For Developing Countries?', in Friedrich-Karl Beier and Gerhard Schricker, eds, *From GATT to TRIPS – The Agreement on Trade-Related Aspects of Intellectual Property Rights* (Munich: Max Planck Institute for Foreign and International Patent, Copyright and Competition Law, 1996), at 329.

governing patent, trademarks and industrial designs,[308] and the *Berne Convention of 1886*,[309] which regulated copyright.[310] The hallmark of PC was its extension of the national treatment principle to foreign patentees, which meant that foreigners should enjoy the same intellectual property rights accorded by a domestic law to citizens.[311] Unlike TRIPS, the PC did not impose any minimum standard of intellectual property protection. Countries were allowed to adopt their own patent system, which reflected their different economic, technological and social circumstances.[312]

The impact of a patent system on economic development and foreign investment is generally admitted, but the actual effect does not lend itself to exact measurement, at least on the basis of current anecdotal empirical evidence. On the theory that effective intellectual property protection is a condition for economic development,[313]

---

308 The text of the Convention is posted on: http://www.tufts.edu/departments/fletcher/multi/tests/BH004.txt (last visited 2 January 2002).

309 The text of the Convention is posted on http://www.law.cornell.edu/treatise/berne/overview.html (last visited 2 January 2002).

310 Some of the other international IP legislation includes: *Berne Convention for the Protection of Literary and Artistic Works, 1971*; *The International Convention for the Protection of Performers, the Producers of Phonograms and Broadcasting Organizations, 1961 (the Rome Convention)*; *Convention for the Protection of Producers of Phonograms Against Unauthorized Duplication of their Phonograms, 1971 (the Phonogram Convention)*; *The Convention Relating to the Distribution of Programme-Carrying Signals Transmitted by Satellite, 1974 (the Satellite Convention)*; *The Budapest Treaty on the International Recognition of the Deposit of Microorganisms for the Purposes of Patent Procedure, 1980 (the Budapest Treaty)*; *The Patent Cooperation Treaty, 1970, Madrid Agreement Concerning the International Registration of Marks, 1891* and the *Protocol Relating to that Agreement, 1989*; *The Trademark Law Treaty, 1994*; and *The Hague Agreement Concerning the International Registration of Industrial Designs, 1925*.

311 Article 3 of TRIPS substantially re-enacted PC's national treatment principle.

312 Ruth L. Gana, 'Prospects For Developing Countries under the TRIPS Agreement' (1996) 29 *Vanderbilt Jour. of Transnational Law* 735.

313 This is a highly contentious issue and explored in detail by: Robert M. Sherwood, 'Intellectual Property: A Chip Withheld in Error', in Owen Lippert, ed., *Competitive Strategies for the Protection of Intellectual Property* (Vancouver: The Fraser Institute, 1999), at 73; Ulf Anderfelt, *International Patent Legislation and Developing Countries* (The Hague: Martinus Nijhoff, 1971), at 26–64; Edwin Mansfield, 'Unauthorized Use of Intellectual Property: Effects on Investment, Technology Transfer, and Innovation', in Mitchell B. Wallerstein, *et al.*, eds, *Global Dimensions of Intellectual Property Rights in Science and Technology* (Washington, DC: National Academy Press, 1993), at 107; A. Samuel Oddi, 'TRIPS – Natural Rights and a Polite Form of Economic Imperialism' (1996) 29 *Vanderbilt Jour. of Transnational Law* 415; Robert M. Sherwood, 'Why a Uniform Intellectual Property System Makes Sense for the World', in Michael B. Wallerstein, *et al.*, eds, *Global Dimensions of Intellectual Property Rights in Science and Technology* (Washington, DC: National Academy Press, 1993), at 68; Brian Martin, *Information Liberation: Challenging the Corruptions of Information Power* (London: Freedom Press, 1998), chapter 3; Owen T. Adikibi, 'The Multinational Corporation and Monopoly of Patents in Nigeria' (1988) 16 *World Development* 511; Carlos A. Primo Braga and Carsten Fink, 'The Relationship between Intellectual Property Rights and Foreign Direct Investment' (1998) 9 *Duke Journal of Comparative & International Law* 163; Keith E. Maskus, 'The Role of Intellectual Property Rights in Encouraging Foreign Direct Investment

Article 27(1) of TRIPS makes patent available in all fields of technology, subject to universal criteria of novelty, non-obviousness or inventive step and industrial application. Consequently, socially and economically responsive regimes of non-patentability for agricultural and pharmaceutical products, operative in developing countries like India, were overthrown by this maximalist provision. TRIPS does not define concepts like 'inventive step', 'novelty' and 'industrial application', thus giving member states some room for creativity in adapting TRIPS to local needs and circumstances.[314] However, Article 27(2) allows countries to deny patents to inventions whose commercial exploitation will not be conducive to public order or morality or will harm human, animal or plant life or will jeopardize the environment.[315]

The ability of developing countries to creatively utilize these exemptions is limited by the proviso, in the same Article, that the exemptions should not be 'made merely because the exploitation is prohibited by domestic law'. Article 27(3) also exempts the following from patentability: diagnostic, therapeutic and surgical methods for the treatment of plants and animals; plants and animals, and essentially biological processes for the production of plant and animals. However, Article 27(3) allows patent protection for microorganisms and microbiological processes. Under Article 27(3)(b), countries have the option of protecting plant varieties either by patents or a *sui generis* system[316] or a combination of both. Consequently, Article 27

---

and Technological Transfer' (1998) 9 *Duke Journal of Comparative & International Law* 109; F. Scott Kieff, 'Property Rights and Property Rules for Commercializing Inventions' (2001) 85 *Minnesota Law Review* 697.

314 Gurdial Singh Nijar, 'Community Intellectual Rights Protect Indigenous Knowledge' (1998) 36 *Biotechnology and Development Monitor* 601, at 604.

315 On the morality of patents on life forms, see Deryck Beyleveld and Roger Brownsword, 'Patenting Human Genes: Legality, Morality, and Human Rights', in J.W. Harris, ed., *Property Problems: From Genes to Pension Funds* (The Hague: Kluwer Law International Ltd., 1997), at 9–44; Barbara Looney, 'Should Genes be Patented? The Gene Patenting Controversy: Legal, Ethical, and Policy Foundations of an International Agreement' (1996) 28 *Intellectual Property Rev.* 101; The *Plant Genetic Systems Case* (1995) E.P.O.R. 357; *President and Fellows of Harvard College v. Canada (Commissioner of Patents)* (2002) SCC 76.

316 TRIPS neither defines what amounts to an effective *sui generis* system nor mandatorily requires its development on any standardized lines. However, it is generally thought that compliance with TRIPS will require domestic legislation patterned after the *International Convention for the Protection of New Varieties of Plants*, UPOV, signed at Paris on 2 December 1961. For instance, see M.S. Swaminathan, 'Farmers' Rights and Plant Genetic Resources' (1998) 36 *Biotechnology and Development Monitor* 544; Neils P. Louwaars, 'Sui Generis Rights: From Opposing to Complementary Approaches' (1998) 36 *Biotechnology and Development Monitor* 551; Huib Ghijsen, 'Plant Variety Protection in a Developing and Demanding World' (1998) 36 *Biotechnology and Development Monitor* 538; Philippe Cullet, 'Plant Variety Protection in Africa: Towards Compliance with TRIPS Agreement' (2001) 45 *Jour. Afri. L.* 97. The UPOV Convention was revised at Geneva on 10 November 1972, 23 October 1978 and 19 March 1991. See http://www.upov.int for the various UPOV conventions.

UPOV intends to harmonize or unify the laws of member states of the Union for the Protection of New Varieties of Plants with respect to legal protections given to a breeder of a

successfully secured the interests of pharmaceutical, agricultural and biotechnology industries, mainly based in the North.

Several bodies of the WTO, for instance, the Committee on Trade and Environment (CTE), the Council of TRIPS, and the General Council, provide an important platform for discussions on the protection of TK. Some documents prepared by the WTO Secretariat show that TRIPS does not prohibit the development of measures, whether new or existing, to protect TK.[317] In the context of the review of Article 27(3)(b) of TRIPS, some countries, for instance the African Group, have made far-reaching proposals which include the exclusion of life-forms from the regime of patentability, the protection of TK under TRIPS, and harmonization of TRIPS with the *Convention on Biological Diversity* and the FAO International Undertaking on Plant Genetic Resources.[318]

World Intellectual Property Organization (WIPO)

WIPO is a specialized agency of the United Nations dedicated to the promotion and protection of intellectual property rights throughout the world, and administers about 21 international treaties on various aspects of intellectual property. WIPO has been

---

new plant variety. The necessity for UPOV is anchored on the same traditional justifications deployed to sustain a patent regime. (For a defence of the contemporary patent system, see F. Scott Kieff, 'Property Rights and Property Rules for Commercializing Inventions' (2001) 85 *Minnesota L. Rev.* 697) Thus, some people believe that plant breeders need incentive, by means of intellectual property protection, to engage in breeding activities that involve lots of time (between ten and twenty years), and cost a lot money. Plant breeders arguably have a moral right to recoup their investment and profit from a new variety, and to be recognized as innovators. Moreover, with an estimated world population of eight billion by the year 2020, there is need for improved and better yielding varieties that utilize less land. Plant breeders, supporters argue, seem to be in a position to contain the negative impacts of a future population explosion on agriculture and, therefore, demand special protection. Therefore, the activities of plant breeders may be correlative to food security. UPOV 1991 sets the minimum standard for the protection of a new plant variety. By means of bilateral or multilateral agreements, Union members may confer more intellectual property protection on plant breeders, provided such additional protection is not inconsistent with UPOV. The protection given to a breeder of a new variety sounds in prior authorization of that breeder, which may be given conditionally or otherwise. Thus, in respect of propagating material, or harvested material derived from illegitimate use of propagating material, the breeder's prior authorization is required for its production or reproduction, conditioning for the purpose of propagation, offering for sale, selling or other marketing, exporting, importing and stocking for any of the listed purposes. A contracting state may opt to extend the need for a breeder's prior authorization to products of a harvested material of the protected variety. A new variety essentially derived from a protected variety shall not be exploited without the breeder's prior authorization.

317 *Environment and TRIPS* (WT/CTE/W/8/Corr.1); *The Convention on Biological Diversity and the Agreement on Trade-Related Aspects of IP Rights* (WT/CTE/W/50); *The Relationship Between the Convention on Biological Diversity and the Agreement on Trade-Related Aspects of IP Rights, with a Focus on Article 27.3(b)* (WT/CTE/W/125).

318 Martin Khor, 'Rethinking Intellectual Property Rights and TRIPS', in Drahos and Mayne, eds, *supra*, note 241, at 208.

very active in the area of TK, and has collaborated with other UN agencies, NGOs and some other institutions on matters relating to TK. In the 1980s WIPO collaborated with UNESCO to develop a Model Legislation on folklore that was intended to guide national or domestic legislation on folklore. WIPO also collaborated with the United Nations Environmental Program (UNEP) on two case studies that examined the role of IPR in the sharing of benefits arising from the utilization of TK and related biological resources.

In 1997, WIPO established a Global Intellectual Property Issues Divisions (GIPID) to respond to various issues confronting intellectual property in the context of technological change and globalization. The GIPID, as part of its mandate, developed a programme of work, which was approved by WIPO member states as part of the WIPO Program and Budget for 1998–1999 biennium. This work programme included exploration of the needs and expectations of TK holders. Thus, between 1998 and 1999 WIPO organized a fact-finding mission on intellectual property and TK (FFMs). The FFMs worked in a total of 28 countries located in the South Pacific; Southern, Eastern and West Africa; South Asia; North, South and Central America; the Arab countries; and the Caribbean. The FFMs have now produced a report on the needs and expectations of TK holders.[319] WIPO has developed a sample Traditional Knowledge Digital Library (TKDL), and organized regional seminars or workshops on TK or aspects of TK. For instance, in 1999 WIPO conducted four regional consultations on the protection of expressions of folklore,[320] and in 1998, it conducted an Asian regional seminar on intellectual property protection of traditional medicinal knowledge.[321] Between 1998 and 1999 WIPO organized two roundtables on effective protection of TK and, thus, facilitated discussion among various stakeholders.

Partly on account of TK's linkages with many organizations, institutions and issues, such as agriculture, environment, trade and culture, WIPO established in 2000 an Intergovernmental Committee on Intellectual Property and TK, Genetic Resources, and Folklore (Intergovernmental Committee) to deal with matters arising from these issues and to provide solutions for the protection of TK.[322] At the first session of the Intergovernmental Committee in 2001, the USA opined that multilateral solution of the problems related to TK may not be appropriate at this time. It observed that if States were encouraged to develop national (or regional) solutions to the problem, the experience gained may ultimately inform an international solution.[323] However, the submission of the European Community and its member states to the Third Session of the Intergovernmental Committee in June 2002 supported the development of an

---

319 The report is posted on WIPO website: http://www.wipo.org.

320 For instance, the WIPO/UNESCO African Regional Consultation on the Protection of Expressions of Folklore, Pretoria, 23–25 March 1999, posted on http://www.unesco.org.

321 The seminar was conducted in New Delhi, India, in October 1998.

322 Tansey, *supra*, note 32, at 12.

323 General Declaration of the U.S.A. to the First Session of the WIPO Committee, 30 April–3 May 2001; posted on www.wipo.org.

international solution to the issues raised by TK and the use of WIPO as the suitable forum for such an approach.[324]

The United Nations Working Group on Indigenous Populations

In 1982, the Economic and Social Council of the United Nations established the Working Group on Indigenous Populations (WGIP), which is a subsidiary organ of the Sub-Commission on the Promotion and Protection of Human Rights. The WGIP has functions that include the monitoring and review of human rights protection of indigenous peoples by national governments, and the development of international standards on the rights of indigenous peoples. The WGIP has developed several Draft Principles and Guidelines concerning the protection of the rights of indigenous peoples. One such document is the *Draft United Nations Declaration on the Rights of Indigenous Peoples*, Paragraph 29:

> Indigenous peoples are entitled to the recognition of the full ownership, control and protection of their cultural and intellectual property. They have the right to special measures to control, develop and protect their sciences, technologies and cultural manifestations, including human and other genetic resources, seeds, medicines, knowledge of the properties of fauna and flora, oral tradition, literatures, designs and visual and performing arts.[325]

This Declaration was adopted in 1994 by the Sub-Commission on Prevention of Discrimination and Protection of Minorities (now Sub-Commission on the Promotion and Protection of Human Rights), but is not legally binding on member states of the

---

324 The EC and its Member States support further work towards the development of an international *sui generis* model for the legal protection of TK. A broader scope of protection including elements of particular interest to developing countries, and in particular TK, would improve confidence in the international IP system and bring benefit to a broader scope of economic and societal actors. Such an international regulatory framework to protect TK should clearly identify and strictly define the protected subject-matter, determine the beneficiaries of such protection, and extent of rights they enjoy, regulating access to it and possibly modalities as regards the sharing of benefits for the use of technologies derived from TK, while leaving sufficient flexibility to States to adapt this regime to local situations. Indeed, TK can be very diverse in its expressions according to the countries concerned. TK protection would have to be implemented and enforced by government and/or by civil action before a national court. The existence of such requirements should not change the patentability as such of an inventive novel application derived from TK, but they would affect the sharing of benefits from use of it. The EC and its Member States therefore invite those Members which have practical experience with protecting TK at domestic or regional level to share this experience with this Intergovernmental Committee, so as to be able to better determine the possible building blocks for an international *sui generis* model.

Submission of the European Community and its Member States to the Third Session of the WIPO Intergovernmental Committee on Intellectual Property and Genetic Resources, Traditional Knowledge and Folklore, 13–21 June 2002 (WIPO/GRTKF/IC/3/16).

325 *Draft Declaration on the Rights of Indigenous Peoples*, 23 August 1993; posted on http://www.usask.ca/nativelaw/ddir.html (last visited 2 January 2002).

United Nations because it has not been adopted as a treaty. However, its persuasive effects should not be underestimated.

The Food and Agricultural Organization of the United Nations (FAO)

Through its International Undertaking on Plant Genetic Resources (IU), developed in the 1980s and revised on a number of occasions, the FAO has promoted and protected TK relevant for food and agriculture by the development and articulation of the concept of farmers' rights. The IU, however, applies only to a component of TK, for instance farmers' rights, and does not apply to TK relevant to animal genetic resources or traditional medicinal knowledge. Thus, the latest version of IU that was adopted as a treaty by the FAO Conference in Rome in November 2001 is concerned with a narrower aspect of TK by providing for the 'protection of traditional knowledge relevant to plant genetic resources for food and agriculture'.[326]

The World Bank

The World Bank is a significant source of loan and development assistance for many countries of the world, especially developing countries. Recently, the World Bank established a programme on TK, with a view to facilitating discussion among stakeholders on policy issues concerning the promotion and protection of TK.[327] The objectives of the programme are to develop pilot instruments for the capture,

---

326
> 9.1. The Contracting Parties recognize the enormous contribution that local and indigenous communities and farmers of all regions of the world, particularly those in the centres of origin and crop diversity, have made and will continue to make for the conservation and development of plant genetic resources which constitute the basis of food and agriculture production throughout the world.
> 9.2. The Contracting Parties agree that the responsibility for realizing Farmers' Rights, as they relate to Plant Genetic Resources for Food and Agriculture, rests with national governments. In accordance with the needs and priorities, each Contracting Party should, as appropriate, and subject to its national legislation, take measures to protect and promote Farmers' Rights, including:
> (a) protection of traditional knowledge relevant to plant genetic resources for food and agriculture;
> (b) the right to equitably participate in sharing benefits arising from the utilization of plant genetic resources for food and agriculture;
> (c) the right to participate in making decisions, at the national level, on matters related to the conservation and sustainable use of plant genetic resources for food and agriculture.
> 9.3. Nothing in this Article shall be interpreted to limit any rights that farmers have to save, use, exchange and sell farm-saved seed/propagating material, subject to national law and as appropriate.

The International Treaty on Plant Genetic Resources for Food and Agriculture, posted on www.fao.org.

327 World Bank Indigenous Knowledge Program: http://www.worldbank.org/afr/ik/index.htm.

dissemination and application of indigenous/traditional knowledge to development practices; facilitating the sharing of indigenous practices and innovations among local communities through a South-to-South exchange; promoting the integration of indigenous/traditional knowledge in the development process; and establishing partnerships.[328] These objectives are to be achieved through ways that include the development of a database on TK and 'IK Notes', which describe TK solutions to complex problems. The World Bank has also established about 15 TK resource centres in Africa and has integrated TK in many of the World Bank's supported projects in some African countries.[329]

The World Health Organization (WHO)

The WHO is an agency of the United Nations that is dedicated to saving lives and improving the health of all peoples in the world. WHO's focus on TK, however, has been mainly in relation to TM and related products. WHO has collaborated with other organizations[330] on TM and has published a monograph on selected medicinal plants.[331] The WHO monographs are a rich source of scientific information on the safety, efficacy and quality control of some popular medicinal plants and have been used as a model for similar monographs prepared by some national governments.[332] In the context of widespread use of TM by a significant proportion of the population of some developing countries and its increasing popularity in developed countries, WHO released in 2002 its comprehensive strategy for TM. WHO's strategy addressed issues of policy, safety, efficacy, quality, access and rational use of traditional, complementary and alternative medicine.[333] The policy aspect of WHO's strategy includes consideration of intellectual property issues arising from the appropriation and utilization of traditional medicinal knowledge and medicinal plants.[334]

---

328 *Ibid.*

329 *Ibid.*; Thomas Griffiths and Marcus Colchester, *Indigenous Peoples, Forests and the World Bank: Policies and Practice 8-10* (Draft Discussion Document; Workshop on Indigenous Peoples, Forests and the World Bank, 9–10 May 2000).

330 These include: Center for Scientific Research in Plant Medicines, Mampong-Akwapim, Ghana; National Center for Complementary and Alternative Medicine (NCCAM), National Institutes of Health, Department of Health and Human Services, Bethesda, USA; College of Pharmacy, University of Illinois, Chicago; Centre of Research in Bioclimatology, Biotechnologies and Natural Medicine, State University of Milan, Milan, Italy; Academy of Traditional Korean Medicine, Pyongyang, Democratic People's Republic of Korea; Institute of Acupunture and Moxibustion, China Academy of Traditional Chinese Medicine, Beijing, People's Republic of China.

331 WHO, *Monograph on Selected Medicinal Plants, Vol. 1* (Geneva: WHO, 1999); WHO, *Monograph on Selected Medicinal Plants, Vol. 2* (Geneva: WHO, 2001).

332 WHO, *supra*, note 28, at 33.

333 *Ibid.*

334 *Ibid.*, at 21.b.

Conclusion

TK has many components that differ in their significance, nature and use. TK claims cover intangible forms, such as folktales and traditional medicinal knowledge, and physical manifestations of TK, such as works of traditional artists or some cultural objects. Both the tangible and intangible components of TK capture property's dominant forms as a 'right to a thing' and as a 'bundle of rights'.

As this chapter attempted to show, the many issues involved in the protection of TK are not exclusively within the domain of property, though the framework of property is one of the potentially useful remedies and could also inspire *sui generis* protections. However, any protective regime should first articulate the bases and objectives of protection. These objectives include the attainment of equity in dealings between parties that are economically unequal, the conservation and sustainable use of biodiversity and the equitable sharing of benefits arising from its utilization, the preservation of culture, the avoidance of biopiracy, the promotion of the use of TK, and the realization of certain human rights.

The articulation of a country's objectives for the promotion and protection of TK should be informed by an assessment of the needs and expectations of its TK holders. As WIPO's fact-finding mission on TK shows, it is not easy to ascertain the needs and expectations of TK holders, and when such is possible, there are significant differences among TK holders and beneficiaries as to what their needs and expectations are. Some frameworks exist for the realization of the diverse objectives of TK protection. Where the objective is to exclude third parties, there are potentials for the use of existing forms of intellectual property rights, for instance, patents, trademarks, copyright, trade secret, and industrial designs, either in their present form or with some modifications. For instance, some formulations of traditional medicine may be patentable, and copyright may exist in some traditional art works. However, a good deal of TK may not be accommodated under existing IPRs.

There are also other problems with IPR protection of TK. These include the inherent unsuitability of IPR for TK due to differences in epistemology, the collective nature of TK in contrast with the individual-specific (author or inventor-specific) nature of IPRs, and the failure of a good deal of TK to fulfil some statutory criteria of some IPR legislation. As a result of these problems, this chapter suggests the designing of a special or *sui generis* protection of TK, though the dynamics of a particular *sui generis* protection and the issues involved should be properly investigated. It is noteworthy that the emergence and development of *sui generis* regimes partly demonstrate the evolutionary and adaptive nature of property.[335] Outside customary law, TK was largely unrecognized or unprotected by the Western-oriented law of property.[336] In the last few years, however, there has been an increasing debate on

---

335 Similarly, Downes and Laird observed: 'As the evolution of the *sui generis* database right suggests, principles of intellectual property evolve over time, and intellectual property rights take different forms in different places, in response to claims of right or arguments about social welfare.' Downes and Laird, in Coombe, *supra*, note 17.

336 A good chunk of TK was regarded as being in the public domain, despite TK's protection under customary law.

modalities for conferring appropriate legal protection on TK, including its protection under property and *sui generis* frameworks. The debate continues in its intensity and it would not be surprising if property law evolves in the near future to fully accommodate TK.

This chapter explored some *sui generis* instruments like the *African Model Legislation*, the *Thai Traditional Medicine Intelligence Act* and the *Indian Biodiversity Act*. Though none of the above *sui generis* instruments singularly covered all aspects of TK, they represent a step in the right direction and could inspire domestic legislation in many African and developing countries. A regime to avoid misappropriation may also be a handy protective tool where monopolistic rights over TK are not intended. Finally, a developing country may also use contractual instruments to regulate exploitation of its TK and products and also ensure adequate compensation.

This chapter also examined some of the international platforms where issues concerning TK have been considered. The institutions mentioned have different objectives and mandates and have considered TK from each institution's perspective, though collaborations have been possible between some of the institutions. There is no consensus as to whether TK issues should be addressed and solved using an international framework or a domestic one. Considering that domestic experience on TK has not yet crystallized in a significant number of countries, it may be appropriate to adopt a national approach to the issue of TK. This may lead to regional collaboration and, ultimately, the experience gained may inspire an international solution.

Bibliography

Books and Articles

Abbott, Frederick. 'Protecting First World Assets in the Third World: Intellectual Property Negotiations in the GATT Multilateral Framework' (1989) 22 *Vanderbilt Journal of Transnational Law* 689.

_____ 'Commentary: The International Intellectual Property Order Enters the 21st Century' (1996) 29 *Vanderbilt Journal of Transnational Law* 471.

Achebe, C. *Things Fall Apart* (London: Heinemann Educational Books Ltd., 1958).

_____ *The Trouble with Nigeria* (Enugu, Nigeria: Fourth Dimension Publishers, 1983).

Acheson, D.G. 'Book Review' (1919) 33 *Harvard Law Review* 329.

Ackerknecht, Erwin. *Medicine and Ethnology* (Baltimore, Maryland: The Johns Hopkins Press, 1991).

Ackerman, B. *Economic Foundations of Property Law* (Boston: Little, Brown & Co., 1975).

_____ *Private Property and the Constitution* (New Haven: Yale University Press, 1977).

Ackerman, S. 'The White Supremacist Status Quo: How the American Legal System Perpetuates Racism as Seen Through the Lens of Property Law' (1999) 21 *Hamline Journal of Public Law & Policy* 137.

Ackiron, Evan. 'Patents for Critical Pharmaceuticals: The AZT Case' (1991) 17 *American Journal of Law and Medicine* 145.

Adair, J. 'The Bioprospecting Question: Should the United States Charge Biotechnology Companies for the Commercial Use of Public Wild Genetic Resources?' (1997) 24 *Ecology Law Quarterly* 131.

Adamantopoulos, Konstantinos. *An Anatomy of the World Trade Organization* (The Hague: Kluwer Law International, 1997).

Adams, C. (ed.) *The Works of John Adams* (New York: Books for Libraries Press, 1969).

Adams, John. 'Litigation Beyond the Technological Frontier: Comparative Approaches to Multinational Patent Enforcement' (1996) 27 *Law and Policy in International Business* 277.

Adams, Nassau. *Worlds Apart: The North-South Divide and the International System* (London: Zed Books, 1993).

Adelman, Martin and Baldia, Sonia. 'Prospects and Limits of the Patent Provisions in the TRIPS Agreement: The Case of India' (1996) 29 *Vanderbilt Journal of Transnational Law* 507.

Adikibi, O.T. 'The Multinational Corporation and Monopoly of Patents in Nigeria' (1988) 16 *World Development* 511.

Adler, Jonathan. 'Cartagena Protocol: Biosafe or Bio-sorry?' (2000) *The Georgetown International Environmental Law Review* 772.

_____ 'More Sorry than Safe: Assessing the Precautionary Principle and the Proposed International Biosafety Protocol' (2000) 35 *Texas International Law Journal* 173.

Adler, R. 'Controlling the Applications of Biotechnology: A Critical Analysis of the Proposed Moratorium on Animal Patenting' (1988) 1 *Harvard Journal of Law and Technology* 1.

Afifi, F. 'Unifying International Patent Protection: The World Intellectual Property Organization Must Coordinate Regional Patent Systems' (1993) 15 *Loyola L.A. International & Comparative Law Journal* 453.

Agenda 21: The First Five Years (Luxembourg: Office for the Official Publications of the European Communities, 1997).

Akpamgbo, C.O. 'A "Woman to Woman" Marriage and the Repugnancy Clause: A Case of Putting New Wine into Old Bottles' (1974–77) 14 *African Law Studies* 87.

Albanese, Ferdinando. 'Genetics and Human Rights' (1985) 33 *European Yearbook* 73.

Alexander, G.S. 'Time and Property in the American Republican Legal Culture' (1991) 66 *New York University Law Review* 273.

Alford, W.P. 'Don't Stop Thinking About Yesterday: Why There was No Indigenous Counterpart to Intellectual Property Law in Imperial China' (1993) 7 *Journal of Chinese Law* 3.

Alford, W.P. 'Making the World Safe for What? Intellectual Property Rights, Human Rights and Foreign Economic Policy in the Post-European Cold War World' (1996–97) 29 *International Law and Politics* 135.

Alfredsson, D. 'The Rights of Indigenous Peoples With a Focus on the National Performance of the Nordic Countries' (1999) 59 *ZaorRv-Heidelberg Journal of International Law* 529.

Allen, Anita. 'Genetic Testing, Nature, and Trust' (1997) *Seton Hall Law Review* 887.

Allen, R. *How to Save the World: Strategy for World Conservation* (Ontario: Prentice-Hall, 1980).

Allen, R. and Prescott-Allen, Christine. *Genes From the Wild : Using Genetic Resources for Food and Raw Materials* (London: Earthscan Publications, 1988).

Allen, S.W. and Leonard, J.W. *Conserving Natural Resources* (New York: McGraw Hill, 1966).

Allen, Ted. 'The Philippine Children's Case: Recognizing Standing for Future Generations' (1993) 6 *Georgetown Environmental Law Review* 713.

Allen, Tom. 'Commonwealth Constitutions and Implied Social and Economic Rights' (1994) 6 *African Journal of International and Comparative Law* 555.

Allen, Tom. *The Right to Property in Commonwealth Constitutions* (Cambridge: Cambridge University Press, 2000).

Allot, Phillip. 'State Responsibility and the Unmaking of International Law' (1988) 29 *Harvard International Law Journal* 1.

Allyn, Robert. 'Plant Patent Questions' (1933) 15 *Journal of Patent Office Society* 180.

_____ 'More About Plant Patents' (1933) 15 *Journal of Patent Office Society* 963.

Alston, Philip. 'The United Nations' Specialized Agencies and Implementation of the International Covenant on Economic, Social and Cultural Rights' (1979) 18 *Columbia Journal of Transnational Law* 79.

_____ 'Conjuring Up New Human Rights: A Proposal for Quality Control' (1984) 78 *American Journal of International Law* 607.

_____ 'Making Space for New Human Rights: The Case of the Right to Development' (1988) 1 *Harvard Human Rights Yearbook* 3.

_____ 'Revitalizing United Nations Work on Human Rights and Development' (1991) 18 *Melbourne University Law Review* 216.

Alstyne, W.V. 'Cracks in "The New Property": Adjudicative Due Process and the Administrative State' (1977) 62 *Cornell Law Review* 445.

Altieri, M.A. and Rosset, P. *Ten Reasons Why Biotechnology will not Ensure Food Security, Protect the Environment and Reduce Poverty in the Developing World* (Association of Natural Biocontrol Producers, 1999).

American Restatement (Second) of Torts (Minn.: American Law Institute Publishers, 1982).

American Society of Human Genetics. 'Response to Allegations Against James V. Neel in Darkness in El Doraldo, by Patrick Tierney' (2002) 70 *American Journal of Human Genetics* 1.

Amucheazi, E.C. (ed.) *Readings in Social Sciences: Issues in National Development* (Enugu, Nigeria: Fourth Dimension Publishers, 1980).

Anaya, James. 'Environmentalism, Human Rights and Indigenous Peoples: A Tale of Converging and Diverging Interests' (2000) 7 *Buffalo Environmental Law Journal* 1.

Anderfelt, U. *International Patent Legislation and Developing Countries* (The Hague: Martinus Nijhoff, 1971).

Anderson, Frederick *et al.* (eds). *Environmental Protection: Law and Policy* 3rd edn (New York: Aspen Law and Business, 1999).

Anderson, W. *et al.* (eds). *Patents and Progress: The Sources and Impact of Advancing Technology* (Illinois: Richard Irwin, 1965).

Andrea, Gaski and Johnson, Kurt. *Prescription for Extinction: Endangered Species and Patented Oriental Medicines in Trade* (Washington: Traffic USA, 1996).

Andrews, Lori. 'Past as Prologue: Sobering Thoughts on Genetic Enthusiasm' (1997) 27 *Seton Hall Law Review* 893.

Andrews, Lori B. 'Harnessing the Benefits of Biobanks' (2005) 33 *Journal of Law, Medicine & Ethics* 22.

Andrews, L. and Nelkin, D. 'Whose Body Is It Anyway? Disputes Over Body Tissue in a Biotechnology Age' (1998) 351 *Lancet* 53.

Andrews, L. and Nelkin, D. *Body Bazaar: The Market for Human Tissue in the Biotechnology Age* (New York: Crown Publishers, 2001).

Anigbo, O.A.C. *Commensality and Human Relationship among the Igbo* (Nsukka, Nigeria: University of Nigeria Press, 1987).

Annas, G., Glantz, L. and Roche, P. 'Drafting the Genetic Privacy Act; Science, Policy and Practical Considerations' (1995) 23 *Journal of Law, Medicine and Ethics* 360.

Anuradha, R.V. 'In Search of Knowledge and Resources: Who Sows? Who Reaps?' (1997) 6 *Review of European Community and International Law* 263.

_____ 'IPRs: Implications for Biodiversity and Local and Indigenous Communities' (2001) 10 *Review of European Community & International Environmental Law* 27.

Aoki, K. '(Intellectual) Property and Sovereignty: Notes Toward a Cultural Geography of Authorship' (1996) 48 *Stanford Law Review* 1293.

_____ 'Neocolonialism, Anticommons Property, and Biopiracy in the (not-so-brave) New World Order of International Intellectual Property Protection' (1998) 6 *Indiana Journal of Global Legal Studies* 11.

Archer, Heather. 'Effect of United Nations Draft Declaration on Indigenous Rights on Current Policies of Member States' (1999) 5 *Journal of International Legal Studies* 205.

Arlidge, A. 'The Trial of Dr. David Moor' (2000) *Criminal Law Review* 31.

Armstrong, M. 'Race and Property Values in Entrenched Segregation' (1998) 52 *University of Miami Law Review* 1051.

Árnason, E. 'Personal Identifiability in the Health Sector Database' (2001) 87 *Icelandic Medical Journal* 807.

Arnold, C.A. 'The Reconstitution of Property: Property as a Web of Interests' (2002) 26 *Harvard Environmental Law Review* 281.

Arup, Christopher. *Innovation, Policy and Law: Australia and the International High Technology Economy* (Cambridge: Cambridge University Press, 1993).

Asebey, Edgar and Kempenaar, Jill. 'Biodiversity Prospecting: Fulfilling the Mandate of the Biodiversity Convention' (1995) 28 *Vanderbilt Journal of Transnational Law* 703.

Ashton, T.S. *The Industrial Revolution, 1760-1830* (Oxford: Oxford University Press, 1948).

Atapattu, Sumudu. 'Recent Trends in International Environmental Law' (1998) 10 *Sri Lanka Journal of International Law* 47.

Auchincloss, Stuart. 'Does Genetic Engineering Need Genetic Engineers?: Should the Regulation of Genetic Engineering Include a New Professional Discipline?' (1993) 20 *Boston College Environmental Affairs Law Review* 37.

Austin, J. *The Province of Jurisprudence Determined* (London: John Murray, Albermarle Street, 1863).

Australian Law Reform Commission. *Essentially Yours: The Protection of Human Genetic Information In Australia* (Australia: ALRC, March 2003).

Avila, D. 'Assisted Suicide and the Inalienable Right to Life' (2000) 16 *Issues in Law & Medicine* 111.

Ayittey, George. 'How the Multilateral Institutions Compounded Africa's Economic Crisis' (1999) 30 *Law and Policy in International Business* 585.

Aylmer, G.E. 'The Meaning and Definition of "Property" in Seventeenth-Century England' (1980) 86 *Past & Present* 87.

Ayres, I. and Goldbert, P.M. 'Optimal Delegation and Decoupling in the Design of Liability Rules' (2001) 100 *Michigan Law Review* 1.

Babula, J. 'Transgenic Crops: A Modern Trojan Horse' (1999) 3 *Journal of Law and Social Challenges* 127.

Backes, Chris and Verschuuren, Jonathan. 'The Precautionary Principle in International, European, and Dutch Wildlife Law' (1998) 9 *Colorado Journal of Environmental Law and Policy* 43.

Baker, Katharine. 'Consorting with Forests: Rethinking Our Relationship to Natural Resources and How we Should Value their Loss' (1995) 22 *Ecology Law Quarterly* 677.

Bakewell, James. 'The American and British Systems of Patent Law' (1891) 7 *The Quarterly Law Review* 364.

Bakhashab, Omar. 'Islamic Law and the Environment: Some Basic Principles' (1988) 3 *Arab Law Quarterly* 287.

Bale, Harvey. 'Patent Protection and Pharmaceutical Innovation' (1996–97) 29 *International Law and Politics* 95.

Balick, Michael and Cox, Paul Alan. *Plants, People and Culture – The Science of Ethnobotany* (New York: Freeman and Company, 1996).

Balkin, J.M. 'The Hohfeldian Approach to Law and Semiotics' (1990) 44 *University of Miami Law Review* 1119.

Bardales, Cheryl. 'A Primer of Genetic Engineering 1: Basic Structural Components of the Cell' (1994) 4 *Dickinson Journal of Environmental Law and Policy* 7.

Barrad, Catherine M.V. 'Genetic Information and Property Theory' (1993) 87 *Northwestern University Law Review* 1037.

Barron, Brian. 'Chinese Patent Legislation in Cultural and Historical Perspective' (1991) 6 *Intellectual Property Journal* 313.

Barsh, Russel. 'The Right to Development as a Human Right: Results of the Global Commission' (1991) 13 *Human Rights Quarterly* 322.

_____ 'Is the Expropriation of Indigenous Peoples' Land GATT-able?'(2001) 10 *Review of European Community & International Environmental Law* 13.

Bartlett, Robert *et al.* (eds). *International Organizations and Environmental Policy* (Connecticut: Greenwich Press, 1995).

Bastian, Kevin. 'Biotechnology and the United States Department of Agriculture: Problems of Regulation in a Promotional Agency' (1990) 17 *Ecology Law Quarterly* 413.

Battiste, M. and Henderson, J. *Protecting Indigenous Knowledge and Heritage: A Global Challenge* (Saskatoon: Purich Publishing Ltd., 2000).

Beacham, Gwen. 'International Trade and the Environment: Implications of the General Agreement on Tariffs and Trade for the Future of Environmental Protection Efforts' (1992) 3 *Colorado Journal of Environmental Law and Policy* 655.

Bear, J.C. *What is a Person's DNA Worth? Fair Compensation for DNA Access* (Vienna: 10th International Congress of Human Genetics, 2001).

Beatson, J. *The Use and Abuse of Unjust Enrichment* (Oxford: Clarendon Press, 1991).

Bebchuk, L.A. 'Property Rights and Liability Rules: The Ex Ante View of the Cathedral' (2001) 100 *Michigan Law Review* 601.

Behrman, Jack. *Industrial Policies: International Restructuring and Multinationals* (Toronto: Lexington Books, 1984).

Beier, F.K., Crespi, R.S. and Strauss, J. *Biotechnology and Patent Protection: An International Review* (Paris: OECD, 1985).

Beier, Friedrich-Karl. 'The European Patent System'(1981) 14 *Vanderbilt Journal of Transnational Law* 1.

_____ 'One Hundred Years of International Cooperation – The Role of the Paris Convention in the Past, Present and Future' (1984) 15 *International Review of Industrial Property and Copyright Law* 1.

Beier, Friedrich and Schricker, Gerhard (eds). *GATT or WIPO? New Ways in the International Protection of Intellectual Property* (Munich: Max Planck Institute, 1989).

_____ *From GATT to TRIPS – The Agreement on Trade-Related Aspects of Intellectual Property Rights* (Munich: Max Planck Institute for Foreign and International Patent, Copyright, and Competition Law, 1996).

Bell, D. and Bennett, B. 'Genetic Secrets and the Family' (2001) 9 *Medical Law Review* 130.

Belsky, Martin. 'Using Legal Principles to Promote the "Health" of an Ecosystem' (1996) 3 *Tulsa Journal of Comparative and International Law* 183.

Bennett, B. 'Posthumous Reproduction and the Meanings of Autonomy' (1999) 23 *Melbourne University Law Review* 286.

Benoit, Joly and Marie-Angele, de Looze. 'An Analysis of Innovation Strategies and Industrial Differentiation Through Patent Applications: The Case of Plant Biotechnology' (1996) 25 *Research Policy* 1028.

Bently, L. and Sherman, B. 'The Ethics of Patenting: Towards a Transgenic Patent System' (1995) 3 *Medical Law Review* 275.

Bentsi-Enchill, K. *Ghana Land Law: An Exposition, Analysis and Critique* (London: Sweet & Maxwell, 1964).

Bergelson, J. *et al.* 'Promiscuity in Transgenic Plants' (1998) 25 *Nature* 25.

Berkey, Judson. 'The Regulation of Genetically Modified Foods' (1999) *ASIL Insights* (October) 1.

Berkman, Jeffrey. 'Intellectual Property Rights in the P.R.C.: Impediments to Protection and the Need for the Rule of Law' (1996) 15 *Pacific Basin Law Journal* 1.

Bhagwati, Jagdish and Hirsch, Mathias (eds). *The Uruguay Round and Beyond – Essays in Honor of Arthur Dunkel* (Ann Arbor, Michigan: The University of Michigan Press, 1999).

Bhalla, R.S. 'Legal Analysis of the Right to Property' (1981) 10 *Anglo-American Law Review* 180.

_____ 'The Basis of the Right of Property' (1982) 11 *Anglo-American Law Review* 57.

Biagioli, Mario. 'The Instability of Authorship: Credit and Responsibility in Contemporary Biomedicine' (1998) 12 *Life Science Forum* 3.

Bilderbeek, Simone *et al.* (eds). *Biodiversity and International Law – The Effectiveness of International Environmental Law* (Amsterdam: IOS Press, 1992).

Birks, P. *Unjust Enrichment*, 2nd edn (Oxford: Oxford University Press, 2005).

Birnie, P and Boyle, A.E. *International Law and the Environment* (Oxford: Clarendon Press, 1992).

Blackstone, W. *Commentaries on the Laws of England* (Chicago: The University of Chicago Press, 1979).

Blakeney, M. 'Access to Biological Resources: Domestic and International Developments and Issues' (1998) 5 Murdoch University Electronic Journal of Law.

Blomquist, Robert. 'Protecting Nature "Down Under": An American Law Professor's View of Australia's Implementation of the CBD-Laws, Policies, Progress, Institutions, and Plans, 1992-2000' (2000) 9 *Dickinson Journal of Environmental Law and Policy* 237.

Blumm, Michael. 'Wetlands Protection and Coastal Planning: Avoiding the Perils of Positive Consistency' (1978) 5 *Columbia Journal of Environmental Law* 69.

Boardman, Robert. *International Organization and the Conservation of Nature* (Bloomington: Indiana University Press, 1981).

Bodansky, Daniel. 'International Law and the Protection of Biological Diversity' (1995) 28 *Vanderbilt Journal of Transnational Law* 623.

Bogart, H. 'Lockean Provisos and State of Nature Theories' (1985) 95 *Ethics* 834.

Bookchin, M. *The Ecology of Freedom* (California: Cheshire Books, 1982).

Boozang, Kathleen. 'Western Medicine Opens the Door to Alternative Medicine' (1998) 24 *American Journal of Law and Medicine* 12.

Borlaug, N.E. *Feeding a World of Ten Billion People* (London: Norman Borlaug Institute for Plant Science Research of DeMonfort University, 1997).

Bosselman, Klaus. 'Plants and Politics: The International Legal Regime Concerning Biotechnology and Biodiversity' (1996) 7 *Colorado Journal of International Environmental Law and Policy* 111.

Botha, L.B. 'The Protection of New Varieties of Plants in the Republic of South Africa' (1976) *Annual of Industrial Property* 406.

Botkin, D.B. *et al.* (eds). *Changing the Global Environment: Perspectives on Human Involvement* (Boston: Academic Press, 1989).

Boulware, Margaret *et al.* 'An Overview of Intellectual Property Rights Abroad' (1994) 16 *Houston Journal of International Law* 441.

Bowman, M.B. 'The Reburial of Native American Skeletal Remains: Approaches to the Resolution of a Conflict' (1989) 13 *Harvard Environmental Law Review* 147.

Bowrey, Kathy. 'Art, Craft, Good Taste and Manufacturing: The Development of Intellectual Property Laws' (1997) 15 *Law in Context* 78.

Boyce, R.M. 'Organ Transplantation Crisis; Should the Deficit be Eliminated Through Inter Vivos Sales?' (1983) 17 *Akron Law Review* 283–302.

Boyd, Bradley. 'The Development of a Global Market-Based Debt Strategy to Regulate Lending to Developing Countries' (1988) 30 *Georgia Journal of International and Comparative Law* 461.

Boyer, Barry. 'Building Legal and Institutional Frameworks for Sustainability' (1993) 1 *Buffalo Environmental Law Journal* 63.

Bradley, Curtis. 'Biodiversity and Biotechnology' (1995) 7 *Colorado Journal of International Environmental Law and Policy* 107.

Brady, J. 'Land is Itself a Sacred Living Being: Native American Sacred Site Protection on Federal Public Lands Amidst the Shadows of Bear Lodge' (1999–2000) 24 *American Indian Law Journal* 153.

Braga, Carlos Primo. 'The Economics of Intellectual Property Rights and the GATT: A View from the South' (1989) 22 *Vanderbilt Journal of Transnational Law* 243.

Braga, C.A.P. and Fink, C. 'The Relationship between Intellectual Property Rights and Foreign Direct Investment' (1998) 9 *Duke Journal of Comparative & International Law* 163.

Braga, Carlos Primo, *et al. Intellectual Property Rights and Economic Development* (Washington, D.C.: The World Bank. World Bank Discussion Paper No. 412, 2000).

Brams, M. 'Transplantable Human Organs: Should their Sale be Authorized by State Statutes?' (1977) 3 *American Journal of Law & Medicine* 183–95.

Bray, M.B. 'Note, Personalizing Personality: Towards a Property Right in Human Bodies' (1990) 69 *Texas Law Review* 209.

Brazener, R.A. 'Liability in Damages for Withholding Corpse From Relatives' (1973) 48 *American Law Reports (A.L.R.)* 3d 240.

Brazier, M. 'Organ Retention and Return: Problems of Consent' (2003) 29 *Journal of Medical Ethics* 30.

Broad, R. and Cavanagh, J. 'Don't Neglect the Impoverished South' (1995) 101 *Foreign Policy* 18.

Brockway, Lucile. *Science and Colonial Expansion: The Role of the British Botanic Gardens* (New York: Academic, 1979).

Brolman, Catherine *et al.* (eds). *Peoples and Minorities in International Law* (Dordrecht: Martinus Nijhoff, 1993).

Brooks, S.D. 'Native American Indians' Fruitless Search for First Amendment Protection of their Sacred Religious Sites' (1990) 24 *Valparaiso University Law Review* 521.

Brosnan, Deborah. 'Ecosystem Management: An Ecological Perspective for Environmental Lawyers' (1994) 4 *Journal of Environmental Law* 135.

Brown, Batram. 'Developing Countries in the International Trade Order' (1994) 14 *Northern Illinois University Law Review* 347.

Brown, Donald. 'After the Earth Summit: The Need to Integrate Environmental Ethics into Environmental Science and Law' (1992) 2 *Dickinson Journal of Environmental Law and Policy* 1.

Brown, M.F. 'Can Culture Be Copyrighted?' (1998) 39 *Current Anthropology* 193.

Brownlie, Ian. 'Legal Status of Natural Resources in International Law' (1979) *Recueil de Cour* 1.

Brownsword, Roger *et al.* (eds). *Law and Human Genetics: Regulating a Revolution* (Oxford: Hart Publishing, 1998).

Brudner, Alan. 'The Unity of Property Law' (1991) 4 *Canadian Journal of Law & Jurisprudence* 3.

Brush, Stephen and Stabinsky, Doreen (eds). *Valuing Local Knowledge: Indigenous People and Intellectual Property Rights* (Washington/Covelo: Island Press, 1996).

Buchanan, James. 'Between Advocacy and Responsibility: The Challenge of Biotechnology for International Law' (1994) 1 *Buffalo Journal of International Law* 221.

Burchfiel, Kenneth. 'Revisiting the "Original" Patent Clause: Pseudohistory in Constitutional Interpretation' (1989) 2 *Harvard Journal of Law and Technology* 155.

Burhenne, W.E. and Irwin, W.A. *The World Charter for Nature* (Berlin: Erich Scmidt Verlag, 1986).

Burhenne-Guilmin, Francoise and Casey-Lefkowitz, Susan. 'The Convention on Biological Diversity: A Hard Won Global Achievement' (1992) 3 *Yearbook of International Environmental Law* 44.

Burns, P. 'The Law and Privacy: The Canadian Experience' (1976) 54 *Canadian Bar Review* 1.

Burrows, A. 'Proprietary Restitution: Unmasking Unjust Enrichment' (2001) 117 *Law Quarterly Review* 412.

Burton, J. 'Is There any Future for Inquests and Inquiries' (1999) 67 *Medico-Legal Journal* 91.

Burton, Lloyd. 'Indigenous Peoples and Environmental Policy in the Common Law Nation-States of the Pacific Rim: Sovereignty, Survival, and Sustainability' (1998) *Colorado Journal of International Environmental Law and Policy* 129.

Butler, Declan and Smaglik, Paul. 'Celera Genome Licensing Spark Concerns Over Monopoly' (2000) 403 *Nature* 231.

Butterton, Glenn. 'Pirates, Dragons and US Intellectual Property Rights in China: Problems and Prospects of Chinese Enforcement' (1996) 38 *Arizona Law Review* 1081.

Byrne, Noel. 'Plants, Animals, and Industrial Patents' (1985) *Review of Industrial Property and Copyright Law* 1.

Cabanellas, Guillermo. 'Applicable Law Under International Transfer of Technology Regulations' (1994) 15 *International Review of Industrial Property and Copyright Law* 39.

Caillaux, Jorge. 'Biological Resources and the Convention on Biological Resources' (1994) 1 *Journal of Environmental Policy and Law in Latin America and the Caribbean.*

Calabresi, G. 'Do We Own Our Bodies?' (1991) 1 *Health Matrix* 5.

–––––– 'An Introduction to Legal Thought: Four Approaches to Law and to the Allocation of Body Parts' (2003) 55 *Stanford Law Review* 2113.

Calabresi, G. and Melamed, D. 'Property Rights, Liability Rules, and Inalienability: One View of the Cathedral' (1972) 85 *Harvard Law Review* 1089.

Callicott, Baird. 'The Metaphysical Implications of Ecology' (1986) 8 *Environmental Ethics* 301–16.

Cambridge Genetics Knowledge Park and the Public Health Genetics Unit. *A Critique of the Human Tissue Bill: A Discussion Paper* (CGKP, 2004).

Cameron, James and Abouchar, Juli. 'The Precautionary Principle: A Fundamental Principle of Law and Policy for the Protection of the Global Environment' (1991) 14 *Boston College International and Comparative Law Review* 1.

Campbell, Dennis (ed.). *International Environmental Law and Regulations*, vol.2 (Toronto: John Wiley & Sons, 1997).

Campbell, Kenneth. 'On the General Nature of Property Rights' (1992) 3 *Kings College Law Journal* 79.

Canadian Biotechnology Advisory Committee. Patenting of Higher Life Forms and Related Issues (Ottawa: Canadian Biotechnology Advisory Committee, June 2002).

Canadian Biotechnology Advisory Committee. *Improving the Regulation of Genetically Modified Foods and other Novel Foods in Canada* (Ottawa: Canadian Biotechnology Advisory Committee, August 2002).

Carlson, Jonathan. 'Strengthening the Property-Rights Regime for Plant Genetic Resources: The Role of the World Bank' (1996) 6 *Transnational Law and Contemporary Problems* 91.

Carr, Richard. 'Our Patent System Works – A Reply to the Melman Report' (1960) 4 *Patent, Trademark, Copyright Journal of Research and Education* 5.

Carroll, Amy. 'Not Always the Best Medicine: Biotechnology and the Global Impact of U.S. Patent Law' (1994–95) 44 *American University Law Review* 2433.

Carter, Robert and Lasenby, David. 'Values and Ecology: Prolegomena to an Environmental Ethics' (1977) 6 *Alternatives: Perspectives on Society and Environment* 39.

Castel, J.G. 'Legal Implications of Biomedical Science and Technology in the Twenty-First Century' (1973) 11 *Canadian Bar Review* 119.

Catanese, Adrienne. 'Paris Convention, Patent Protection, and Technology Transfer' (1985) 3 *Boston University International Law Journal* 209.

Cate, Fred. 'Sovereignty and the Globalization of Intellectual Property' (1998) 6 *Indiana Journal of Global Legal Studies* 1.

Caulfied, T.A. and William-Jones, B. (eds). *The Commercialization of Genetic Research: Ethical, Legal, and Policy Issues* (New York: Plenum Publishers, 1999).

Cavuoto, B. 'Do We Have Both Personal and Proprietary Rights Over Our Own Bodies?' (2001) 6 *Queen Mary and Westfield Law Journal* 43.

Chadwick, Ruth. 'The Icelandic Database – Do Modern Times Need Modern Sagas?' (1999) 319 *British Medical Journal* 441.

Chakrabarti, Kalyan. *Conservation and Development* (Calcutta: Darbari Prokashan, 1994).

Chalfant, James *et al.* 'Recombinant DNA: A Case Study in Regulation of Scientific Research' (1979) *Ecology Law Quarterly* 55.

Chandler, Melinda. 'The Biodiversity Convention: Selected Issues of Interest to the International Lawyer' (1993) 4 *Colorado Journal of International Environmental Law and Policy* 141.

Chapman, Bruce. 'Rational Environmental Choice: Lessons for Economics from Law and Ethics' (1993) 6 *Canadian Journal of Law and Jurisprudence* 63.

Charney, Jonathan. 'Biodiversity: Opportunities and Obligations' (1995) 28 *Vanderbilt Journal of Transnational Law* 613.

Charney, Jonathan *et al.* (eds). *Politics, Values and Functions: International Law in the 21ˢᵗ Century* (The Hague: Martinus Nijhoff Publishers, 1997).

Chen, J. 'Embryonic Thoughts on Racial Identity as New Property'(1997) 68 *University of Colorado Law Review* 1123.

Chen, Jim. 'Globalization and its Losers' (2000) 9 *Minnesota Journal of Global Trade* 157.

Chisum, Donald. 'Foreign Activity: Its Effect on Patentability Under United States Law' (1980) 11 *International Review of Industrial Property and Copyright Law* 26.

Choudhary, B. 'Legislation for a Genetic Heritage' (2001) 48 *Biotechnology & Development Monitor* 19.

Chowdhury, Subrata *et al.* (eds). *The Right to Development in International Law* (Dordrecht: Martinus Nijhoff, 1992).

Christie, Edward. 'The Eternal Triangle: The Biodiversity Convention, Endangered Species Legislation and the Precautionary Principle' (1993) 10 *Environmental and Planning Law Journal* 470.

Christol, Carl. 'The Common Heritage of Mankind Provision in the 1979 Agreement Governing the Activities of States on the Moon and Other Celestial Bodies' (1980) 14 *International Lawyer* 429.

Churchill, J. 'Patenting Humanity: The Development of Property Rights in the Human Body and the Subsequent Evolution of Patentability of Living Things' (1994) 8 *Intellectual Property Journal* 249.

Chused, R.H. (ed.). *A Property Anthology* (Georgetown: Anderson Publishing Co., 1993).

Clairmonte, F.F. and Cavanagh, J.L. 'Third World Debt: The Approaching Holocaust' (1986) 21 *Economic and Political Weekly* 16.

Clark, C.E. 'Relations, Legal and Otherwise' (1922) 5 *Law Quarterly* 26.

Clarke, Paul. 'Animal Invention' (1988–89) 16 *American Intellectual Property Association Quarterly Journal* 443.

Clarke, W.C. and Munn, R.E. (eds). *Sustainable Development of the Biosphere* (Cambridge: Cambridge University Press, 1986).

Claus-Joerg, Ruetsch and Broderick, Terry. 'New Biotechnology Legislation in the European Community and Federal Republic of Germany' (1990) 18 *International Business Law* 408.

Clech-Lam, Maivan. 'Making Room for Peoples at the United Nations: Thoughts Provoked by Indigenous Claims to Self-Determination' (1992) 25 *Cornell International Law Journal* 603.

Coase, R.H. 'The Problem of Social Cost' (1960) 3 *Journal of Law and Economics* 1.

Cohen, F.S. 'Dialogue on Private Property' (1954) 9 *Rutgers Law Review* 357.

Cohen, Felix. 'The Spanish Origin of Indian Rights in the Law of the United States' (1942) 31 *Georgetown Law Journal* 12.

Cohen, J.I. (ed.). *Managing Agricultural Biotechnology: Addressing Research Program Needs and Policy Implications* (New York: CABI Publishing, 1997).

Cohen, L.R. 'Increasing the Supply of Transplant Organs; The Virtues of a Futures Market' (1989) 58 *George Washington Law Review* 1.

Cohen, M.R. 'Property and Sovereignty' (1927) 13 *Cornell Law Quarterly* 8.

Coker, G.B.A. *Family Property Among the Yorubas* (London: Sweet & Maxwell, 1966).

Colangelo, J. 'Labour Law: *Harrison v. Carswell*' (1976) 34 *University of Toronto Faculty of Law Review* 236.

Colding, Johan and Folke, Carl. 'The Taboo System: Lessons About Informal Institutions for Nature Management' (2000) 12 *The Georgetown International Environmental Law Review* 413.

Coleman, J. 'Medieval Discussions of Property: Ration and Dominium According to John of Paris and Marsilius of Padua' (1983) 4 *History of Political Thought* 209.

Coleman, Jules. *Markets, Morals and the Law* (Cambridge: Cambridge University Press, 1988).

Colin, R. 'Human Tissue Act 2004 and Medical Microbiology' (2004) 126 *Royal College of Pathology Bulletin* 23.

Collins, F.S. and McKusick, V.A. 'Implications of the Human Genome Project for Medical Science' (2001) 285 *Journal of American Medical Association* 540.

Collins, J.L. 'Hecht v. Superior Court: Recognizing a Property Right in Reproductive Material' (1995) 33 University of Louisville Journal of Family Law 661.

Contini, P. 'The Evolution of Blood-Money for Homicide in Somalia' (1971) 15 *Journal of African Law* 77.

Conway, G. 'Genetically Modified Crops: Risks and Promise' (2000) 4(1) *Ecology* 2.

Cook, L.M. *Genetic and Ecological Diversity: The Sport of Nature* (London: Chapman & Hall, 1991).

Cook, Robert. 'Applying the Plant Patent Law' (1931) 13 *Journal of Patent Office Society* 22.

Cook, W.W. 'Comment: The Associated Press Case' (1919) 28 *Yale Law Journal* 387.

Cook-Deegan, R.M. and McCormack, S.J. 'Patents, Secrecy, and DNA' (2001) 293 *Science* 217.

Coombe, R.J. 'The Properties of Culture and the Politics of Possessing Identity: Native Claims in the Cultural Appropriation Controversy' (1993) 6 *Canadian Journal of Law and Jurisprudence* 249.

_____ 'Challenging Paternity: Histories of Copyright' (1994) 6 *Yale Journal of Law and the Humanities* 407.

_____ 'The Cultural Life of Things: Anthropological Approaches to Law and Society in Conditions of Globalization' (1995) 10 *American University Journal of International Law and Policy* 791.

_____ 'Intellectual Property, Human Rights and Sovereignty: New Dilemmas in Intenational Law Posed by the Recognition of Indigenous Knowledge and the Conversation of Biodiversity' (1998) 6 *Indiana Journal of Global Legal Studies* 59.

_____ 'Critical Cultural Legal Studies' (1998) 10 *Yale Journal of Law and the Humanities* 463.

_____ *The Cultural Life of Intellectual Property: Authorship, Appropriation, and the Law* (Durham: Durham University Press, 1998).

_____ *Intellectual Property, Human Rights and Development* (Toronto: University of Toronto Press, 2000).

Corbin, A.L. 'What is a Legal Relation?' (1922) 5 *Law Quarterly* 50.

Corn, Carolyn. 'Pharmaceutical Patents in Brazil: Is Compulsory Licensing the Solution?' (1991) 9 *Boston University International Law Journal* 71.

Cornish, William. 'Patents and Innovation in the Commonwealth' (1983–85) 9 *Adelaide Law Review* 1.

Correa, C.M. *Traditional Knowledge and Intellectual Property* (Geneva: The Quaker United Nations Office, 2001).

_____ *Protection and Promotion of Traditional Medicine: Implications for Public Health in Developing Countries* (Geneva: South Centre, 2002).

Correa, Carlos and Abdulqawi, Yusuf (eds). *Intellectual Property and International Trade* (The Hague: Kluwer Law International, 1998).

Cottier, T. *et al.* (eds). *Strategic Issues of Industrial Property Management in a Globalizing Economy* (Oregon: Hart Publishing, 1999).

Cottier, T. and Mavroidis, P.C. (eds) *Intellectual Property: Trade, Competition, and Sustainable Development* (Ann Arbor: The University of Michigan Press, 2003).

Coval. S., Smith, J.C. and Coval, Simon. 'The Foundations of Property and Property Law' (1986) 45 *Cambridge Law Journal* 457.

Crawford, James (ed.). *The Rights of Peoples* (Oxford: Clarendon Press, 1988).

Crespi, R.S. *Patents: A Basic Guide to Patenting in Biotechnology* (Cambridge: Cambridge University Press, 1988).

Croome, John. *Reshaping the World Trading System – A History of the Uruguay Round* (The Hague: Kluwer Law International, 1999).

Crouch, R., Elliot, R., Lemmens, T. and Charland, L. *Complementary/Alternative Health Care and HIV/AIDS: Legal, Ethical and Policy Issues in Regulation* (Canadian HIV/AIDS Legal Network, 2001).

Crowder, M. *The Story of Nigeria* (London: Faber and Faber, 1962).

Cullet, Philippe. 'Plant Variety Protection in Africa: Towards Compliance With TRIPS Agreement' (2001) 45 *Journal of African Law* 97.

Cuncliffe, M. *The Right to Property: a Theme in American History* (Leicester: Leicester University Press, 1974).

Currier, Andrew. 'To Publish or to Patent, That is the Question' (2000) 16 *Canadian Intellectual Property Review* 337.

D'Innocenzo, P. '"Not in my Backyard!" Protecting Archaeological Sites on Private Lands' (1997) 21 *American Indian Law Journal* 131.

Dagan, H. and Heller, M.A. 'The Liberal Commons' (2001) 110 *Yale Law Journal* 549.

Dalton, R. 'When Two Tribes Go to War' (2004) 430 *Nature* 500.

Danforth, M.T. 'Cells, Sales, and Royalties: The Patient's Right to a Portion of the Profits' (1988) 6 *Yale Law & Policy Review* 179.

Date, V. 'Global "Development" and its Environmental Ramifications –The Interlinking of Ecologically Sustainable Development and Intellectual Property Rights' (1997) 27 *Golden Gate University Law Review* 631.

Davies, Seaborne. 'The Early History of the Patent Specification' (Part 1) (1934) 50 *The Law Quarterly Review* 86.

_____ 'The Early History of the Patent Specification' (Part 2) (1934) 50 *The Law Quarterly Review* 92.

Davis, Michael. 'The Patenting of Products of Nature' (1995) 21 *Rutgers Comparative Technology Law Journal* 293.

De Klemm, Cyril. 'The Convention on Biological Diversity: State Obligations and Citizens Duties' (1989) 19 *Environmental Policy and Law* 50.

De Klemm, Cyril and Shine, Clare. *Biological Diversity Conservation and the Law – Legal Mechanisms for Conserving Species and Ecosystems* (Gland: IUCN, 1993).

Deardoff, Alan. 'Welfare Effects of Global Patent Protection' (1992) 59 *Economica* 35.

Deepa, Francis. 'Bodysnatching in Canada' (2001) 164 *Journal of American Medical Association* 530.

DeGregori, T.R. 'NGOs, Transgenic Food, Globalization, and Conservation' (2002) 13 *Colorado Journal of International Environmental Law & Policy* 115.

Demiray, David. 'Intellectual Property and the External Power of the European Community: The New Extension' (1994) 16 *Michigan Journal of International Law* 187.

Demonet, Paul. 'The Metamorphoses of the GATT: From the Havana Charter to the World Trade Organization' (1995) 34 *Columbia Journal of Transnational Law* 123.

Demsetz, H. 'Toward A Theory of Property Rights' (1967) 57 *American Economic Review* 347.

Department of Health. *Isaacs Report: The Investigation of Events that Followed the Death of Cyril Mark Isaacs* (England: The Department of Health, 2003).

_____ *Proposals for New Legislation on Human Organs and Tissue* (London: DOH, 2003).

Derr, Thomas. 'Religious Responsibility for the Ecological Crisis: An Argument Run Amok' (1975) 18 #1 *Worldview* 43.

Devall, B. and Sessions, G. *Deep Ecology: Living as if Nature Mattered* (Utah: Gibbs Smith, 1985).

Dewar, S. and Boddington, P. 'Returning to the Alder Hey Report and its Reporting: Addressing Confusions and Improving Inquiries' (2004) 30 *Journal of Medical Ethics* 463.

Dickens, B. 'The Control of Living Body Materials' (1977) *University of Toronto Law Journal* 142.

_____ 'Living Tissue and Organ Donors and Property Law; More on Moore' (1992) 8 *Journal of Contemporary Health Law and Policy* 73.

_____ 'Morals and Legal Markets in Transplantable Organs' (1994) 2 *Health Law Journal* 121.

Dietz, Adolf. 'Trends Toward Patent Rights in Socialist Countries?' (1971) 2 *International Review of Industrial Property and Copyright Law* 155.

Dijck, Pitou Van and Faber, Gerrit (eds). *Challenges to the New World Trade Organization* (The Hague: Kluwer Law International, 1980).

Dill, T.M. 'Colonial Development of the Common Law' (1909) 40 *The Law Quarterly Review* 8.

Dillon, Sarah. 'Trade and the Environment: A Challenge to the GATT/WTO Principle of "Ever-Freer Trade"' (1996) 11 *St. John's Journal of Legal Commentary* 351.

_____ 'Fuji-Kodak, the WTO, and the Death of Domestic Political Constituencies' (1999) 8 *Minnesota Journal of Global Trade* 197.

Dillon, T. P. 'Source Compensation for Tissues and Cells Used in Biotechnical Research: Why a Source Shouldn't Share in the Profits' (1989) 64 *Notre Dame Law Review* 628.

_____ 'The World Trade Organization: A New Legal Order for World Trade?' (1995) 16 *Michigan Journal of International Law* 349.

Doane, Michael. 'TRIPS and International Intellectual Property Protection in an Age of Advancing Technology' (1994) *American University Journal of International Law and Policy* 465.

Dobson, Tracy. 'Loss of Biodiversity: An International Environmental Policy Perspective' (1992) 17 *North Carolina Journal of International Law and Commercial Regulations* 277.

Donnelly, J. *Universal Human Rights in Theory and Practice* (New York: Cornell University Press, 1989).

Doorman, Gerald. 'Patent Law in the Netherlands: Suspended in 1869 and Re-established in 1910' (1948) 30 *Journal of the Patent Office Society* 225.

Doremus, Holly. 'Patching the Ark: Improving Legal Protection of Biological Diversity' (1991) 18 *Ecology Law Quarterly* 265.

Douglas, J.A. 'The "Most Valuable Sort of Property": Constructing White Identity in American Law, 1880-1940' (2003) 40 *San Diego Law Review*.

Downes, D.R. 'How Intellectual Property Could Be a Tool to Protect Traditional Knowledge' (2000) 25 *Columbia Journal of Environmental Law* 253.

Downie, J. and Caulfied, T. *Canadian Health Law and Policy* (Toronto: Butterworths, 1999).

Drahos, Peter. 'Global Property Rights in Information: The Story of TRIPS at the GATT' (1995) 13 *Prometheus* 12.

_____ *A Philosophy of Intellectual Property* (Dartmouth: Aldershot, 1996).

_____ 'Indigenous Knowledge and the Duties of Intellectual Property Owners' (1997) 11 *Intellectual Property Journal* 179.

_____ 'Indigenous Knowledge, Intellectual Property and Biopiracy: Is a Global Bio-Collecting Society the Answer? [Opinion]' (2000) 6 *European Intellectual Property Review* 245.

Drahos, Peter and Mayne, Ruth. *Global Intellectual Property Rights: Knowledge, Access and Development* (New York: Palgrave MacMillian, 2002).

Ducor, Phillipe. *Patenting the Recombinant Products of Biotechnology and Other Molecules* (London: Kluwer Law International, 1998).

Duncan, M.L. 'Reconceiving the Bundle of Sticks: Land as a Community-Based Resource' (2002) 32 *Environmental Law* 773.

Dyer, C. 'Group's Legal Action Launched Over Retained Organs' (2001) 322 *British Medical Journal* 1202.

Ebeku, K.S.A. 'The Legal Status of Nigerian Children Born by a Widow: *Chinweze v. Masi* Revisited' (1994) 38 *Journal of African Law* 46.

Edgar, Craig. 'Patenting Nature: GATT on a Hot Tin Roof' (1994) 34 *Washburn Law Journal* 76.

Edsman, Carl-Martin (ed.). *Studies in Shamanism* (Uppsala: Almqvist & Boktryckeri, 1962).

Eisenberg, R. 'Proprietary Rights and the Norms of Science in Biotechnology Research' (1989) 21 *Intellectual Property Law Review* 29.

_____ 'Patenting the Human Genome' (1990) 39 *Emory Law Journal* 721.

Ejidike, O.M. 'Human Rights in the Cultural Traditions and Social Practice of the Igbo of South-Eastern Nigeria' (1999) 43 *Journal of African Law* 71.

Ekins, Paul. *A New World Order: Grassroots Movements for Global Change* (London: Routledge, 1992).

Eleftheriadis, Pavlos. 'The Analysis of Property Rights' (1996) 16 *Oxford Journal of Legal Studies* 31.

Elias, T.O. *The Nature of African Customary Law* (Manchester: The University of Manchester Press, 1956).

_____ *Nigerian Land Law* (London: Sweet & Maxwell, 1971).

Elizabetsky, E. 'Folklore, Tradition, or Know-How?' (1991) *Cultural Survival Quarterly* (Summer) 9.

Ellis, I. and Mannion, G. 'Humanity versus Utility in the Ethics of Research on Human Genetic Material' (2001) 1 Genetics Law Monitor 2.

Ely, J.W. *The Guardian of Every Other Right: A Constitutional History of Property Rights* (Oxford: Oxford University Press, 1992).

Emmert, Frank. 'Intellectual Property in the Uruguay Round – Negotiating Strategies of the Western Industrialized Countries' (1990) 11 *Michigan Journal of International Law* 1317.

Endeshaw, Assafa. 'Theft of Information Revisited' (1997) *Journal of Business Law* 187.

Endres, A.B. 'GMO: Genetically Modified Organism or Gigantic Monetary Obligation? The Liability Schemes for GMO Damage in the United States and the European Union' (2000) 22 *Loyola L.A. International & Comparative Law Journal* 453.

England, Philippa. 'Tree Planting, Sustainable Development and the Roles of Law in Bongo, North-East Ghana' (1995) 39 *Journal of African Law* 138.

Environmental Protection and Sustainable Development – Legal Principles and Recommendations Adopted by the Expert Group on Environmental Law of the World Commission on Environment and Development (London: Martinus Nijhoff, 1986).

Epstein, R.A. 'No New Property' (1990) 56 *Brooklyn Law Review* 747.

_____ 'International News Service v. Associated Press: Custom and Law as Sources of Property Rights in News' (1992) 78 *Virginia Law Review* 85.

_____ 'On the Optimal Mix of Private and Common Property' (1994) 11 *Social Philosophy and Policy* 17.

Ercmann, Sevine. 'Linking Human Rights, Rights of Indigenous People and the Environment' (2000) 7 *Buffalo Environmental Law Journal* 15.

Erramouspe, M. 'Staking Patent Claims on the Human Blueprint: Rewards and Rent-Dissipating Races' (1996) 43 *UCLA Law Review* 961.

Erstling, Jay. 'The Protection of Intellectual Property – of Metaphysics, Motivation, and Monopoly' (1991) 3 *Sri Lanka Journal of International Law* 51.

_____ 'The Role of Licensing and Technology Transfer in the Protection and Management of Intellectual Property: A Developing Country Perspective' (1993) 5 *Sri Lanka Journal of International Law* 21.

Ezeabasili, N. *African Science: Myth or Reality* (New York: Vantage Press, 1977).

Ezekiel, E.J. *et al.* 'What Makes Clinical Research Ethical?' (2000) 283 *Journal of American Medical Association* 2701.

Falk, Richard. 'Toward a World Order Respectful of the Global Ecosystem' (1991–92) 19 *Boston College Environmental Affairs Law Review* 711.

Farley, C.H. 'Protecting Folklore of Indigenous Peoples: Is Intellectual Property the Answer?' (1997) 30 *Connecticut Law Review* 1–57.

Farrington, J. (ed.). *Agricultural Biotechnology: Prospects for the Third World* (London: Overseas Development Institute, Regent's College, London, 1989).

Fecteau, L. 'The Ayahausca Patent Revocation: Raising Questions About Current U.S. Patent Policy' (2001) 21 Boston College Third World Law Journal 69.

Felcher, Peter L. and Rubin, Edward L. 'The Descendibility of the Right of Publicity; Is There Commercial Life After Death?' (1980) 89 *Yale Law Journal* 1125.

Ferre, Frederick and Hartel, Peter (eds). *Ethics and Environmental Policy – Theory Meets Practice* (Athens, Georgia: The University of Georgia Press, 1994).

Fidler, D.P. 'Neither Science nor Shamans: Globalization of Markets and Health in the Developing World' (1999) 7 *Indiana Journal of Global Legal Studies* 191.

Field, N.E. 'Evolving Conceptualizations of Property: A Proposal to De-Commercialize the Value of Fetal Tissue' (1989) 99 *Yale Law Journal* 169.

Firestone, O.J. *Economic Implications of Patents* (Ottawa: University of Ottawa Press, 1971).

Fleming, J.G. *The Law of Torts*, 9th edn (Sydney: LBC Information Services, 1998).

Florencio, P.S. and Keller, R.H. 'End-Of-Life Decision Making: Rethinking the Principles of Fundamental Justice in the Context of Emerging Empirical Data' (1999) 7 *Health Law Journal* 233.

Forsythe, David (ed.). *Human Rights and Development – International Views* (New York: St Martins Press, 1989).

Foster, George. *Traditional Societies and Technologies Change* (Delhi: Allied Publishers, 1973).

Foucault, M. *The History of Sexuality* (New York: Vintage Books, 1990. Translated by Robert Hurley).

Fox, D. 'Enforcing a Possessory Title to a Stolen Car' (2002) 61 *Cambridge LawJournal* 27.

Fox, H.G. *The Canadian Law and Practice Relating to Letters Patent for Inventions* (Toronto: Carswell Co. Ltd., 1969).

Franck, Thomas. *Fairness in International Law and Institutions* (Oxford: Clarendon Press, 1995).

Franck, Thomas and Hawkins, Steven. 'Justice in the International System' (1989) 10 *Michigan Journal of International Law* 127.

Frank, L. 'Estonia Prepares for National DNA Database' (2000) 290 *Science* 31.

Fredland, John. 'Unlabel Their Frankenstein Foods!: Evaluating a U.S. Challenge to the European Commission's Labeling Requirements for Food Products Containing Genetically Modified Organisms' (2000) 33 *Vanderbilt Journal of Transnational Law* 183.

Freeman, M. 'A Time to be Born and a Time to Die' (2003) 56 *Current Legal Problems* 603.

Freestone, D. and Hey, E. (eds). *The Precautionary Principle and International Law: The Challenge of Implementation* (The Hague: Kluwer Law International, 1996).

Frempong, G. 'Priority Setting in Agricultural Research: Comparing Experiences of Ghana and Kenya' (1998) 38 *Biotechnology and Development Monitor* 14.

Fressola, A. 'Liberty and Property' (1981) 18 *American Philosophical Quarterly* 316.

Freund, P.A. 'Privacy: One Concept or Many' (1971) 13 *NOMOS* 182.

Frey, R.G. (ed.). *Utility and Rights* (Minneapolis: University of Minnesota Press, 1984).

Frow, John. 'Public Domain and Collective Rights in Culture' (1998) 13 *Intellectual Property Journal* 39.

_____ 'Public Domain and Public Rights in Culture' (1998) 13 *Intellectual Property Journal* 39.

Fry, Patricia. 'A Social Biosphere: Environmental Impact Assessment, the Innu, and their Environment' (1998) 56 *University of Toronto Faculty of Law Review* 177.

Fryer, William. 'Patent Law Harmonization Treaty Decision is not Far Off – What Course Should the U.S. Take?: A Review of the Current Situation and Alternatives Available' (1989–90) 30 *IDEA* 309.

Furness, Peter. 'Consent to Using Human Tissue: Implied Consent Should Suffice' (2003) 327 *British Medical Journal* 759.

Gadbaw, Michael. 'Intellectual Property and International Trade: Merger or Marriage of Convenience?' (1989) 22 *Vanderbilt Journal of Transnational Law* 223.

Gadbaw, Michael and Richards, Timothy (eds). *Intellectual Property Rights: Global Consensus, Global Conflict?* (Boulder: Westview Press, 1988).

Gana, R.L. 'Has Creativity Died in the Third World? Some Implications of the Internationalization of Intellectual Property' (1995) 24 *Denver Journal of International Law and Policy* 109.

_____ 'Prospects for Developing Countries under the TRIPS Agreement' (1996) 29 *Vanderbilt Journal of Transnational Law* 735.

Ganet, Ronald. 'Communality and Existence: The Rights of Groups' (1983) 56 *Southern California Law Review* 1001.

Gardiner, Richard. 'Industrial and Intellectual Property Rights: Their Nature and the Law of the European Community' (1972) 88 *The Modern Law Review* 507.

_____ 'Language and the Law of Patents' (1994) 47 *Current Legal Problems* 255.

_____ 'Diverse Opinions on Biodiversity' (1999) 6 *Tulsa Journal of Comparative and International Law* 303.

Gates, C. 'Property in Human Tissues: History and Possible Implementations' (1998) 4 *Appeal* 32.

Gathii, J.T. 'The Legal Status of the Doha Declaration on TRIPS and Public Health under the Vienna Convention on the Law of Treaties' (2002) 15 *Harvard Journal of Law & Technology* 291.

Gaythwaite, D.M. 'Patents for Microbiological Inventions in the United Kingdom' (1976) *Annual of Industrial Property Law* 465.

Geisinger, Alex. 'Sustainable Development and the Domination of Nature: Spreading the Seed of the Western Ideology of Nature' (1999) 27 *Environmental Affairs* 43.

Genetic Interest Group. *Human Rights, Privacy and Medical Research: Analysing UK Policy on Tissue and Data* (Genetic Interest Group, 2006).

George, A. *Property in the Human Body and Its Parts: Reflections on Self-Determination in Liberal Society* (San Domenico, Italy: European University Institute, 2001).

Gerber, David. 'Prometheus Born: The High Middle Ages and the Relationship between Law and Economic Conduct' (1994) 38 *St. Louis University Law Journal* 674.

Gerhart, Peter. 'Reflections: Beyond Compliance Theory – TRIPS as a Substantive Issue' (2000) 32 *Case Western Reserve Journal of International Law* 357.

Gervais, D. 'Traditional Knowledge and Intellectual Property: A TRIPS-Compatible Approach' (2005) Michigan State Law Review 137.

Getches, David. 'The Challenge of Rio' (1993) 4 *Colorado Journal of International Environmental Law and Policy* 1.

Ghijsen, H. 'Plant Variety Protection in a Developing and Demanding World' (1998) 36 *Biotechnology and Development Monitor* 538.

Giliker, P. 'A "New" Head of Damages: Damages for Mental Distress in the English Law of Torts' (2000) 20 *Legal Studies* 19.

Gilmour, J.M. ' "Our" Bodies: Property Rights in Human Tissue' (1993) 8 *Canadian Journal of Law & Society* 113.

Ginther, Konrad *et al.* (eds). *Sustainable Development and Good Governance* (Dordrecht: Martinus Nijhoff Publishers, 1995).

Gitter, D.M. 'International Conflicts Over Patenting Human DNA Sequences in the United States and the European Union: An Agreement for Compulsory Licensing and a Fair Use Exemption' (2001) 76 New York University Law Review 1623.

_____ 'Ownership of Human Tissue: A Proposal for Federal Recognition of Human Research Participants' Property Rights in their Biological Material' (2004) 61 Washington & Lee Law Review 257.

Glendon, M.A. *The New Family and the New Property* (Toronto: Butterworths, 1981).

Global Biodiversity Assessment – Published for the United Nations Environment Programme (Cambridge University Press, 1995).

Glowka, L. *et al.* (eds). *A Guide to the Convention on Biological Diversity* (Gland, Switzerland: IUCN, 1994).

Glowka, Lyle. *A Guide to Designing Legal Frameworks to Determine Access to Genetic Resources* (Gland: IUCN, 1998).

Gluckman, M. (ed.). *Ideas and Procedures in African Customary Law* (Oxford: Oxford University Press, 1969).

Gold, E.R. *Body Parts: Property Rights and the Ownership of Human Biological Materials* (Washington, D.C.: Georgetown University Press, 1996).

_____ *Patents in Genes* (Ottawa: Canadian Biotechnology Advisory Committee, 2000).

Golden, J.M. 'Biotechnology, Technology Policy, and Patentability: Natural Products and Invention in the American System' (2001) 50 *Emory Law Journal* 101.

Goldman, Karen. 'Labelling of Genetically Modified Foods: Legal and Scientific Issues' (2000) 12 *The Georgetown International Environmental Law Review* 717.

Goldman, Michael (ed.). *Privatizing Nature – Political Struggles for the Global Commons* (London: Pluto Press, 1998).

Gollin, Michael. 'Using Intellectual Property to Improve Environmental Protection' (1991) 4 *Harvard Journal of Law and Technology* 193.

Gordon, D.B. 'Square Pegs and Round Holes: Domestic Intellectual Property Law and Native American Economic and Cultural Policy: Can it Fit?' (2000–2001) 25 *American Indian Law Review* 93.

Gordon, J. 'Patent Law Reform' (1906) 55 *Journal of the Society of Arts* 26.

Gordon, W.J. 'On Owning Information: Intellectual Property and the Restitutionary Impulse'(1992) 78 *Virginia Law Review* 149.

Gore, Al. 'Essentials for Economic Progress: Protect Biodiversity and Intellectual Property Rights' (1992) October, *The Journal of NIH Research* 5.

Gorove, Stephen. 'The Concept of "Common Heritage of Mankind": A Political, Moral or Legal Innovation?' (1972) 9 *San Diego Law Review* 390.

Goss, J. 'A Postscript to the Trial of Dr. David Moor' (2000) *Criminal Law Review* 568.

Goss, Peter. 'Guiding the Hand that Feeds: Towards Socially Optimal Appropriability in Agricultural Biotechnological Innovation' (1996) 84 *California Law Review* 1395.

Goulet, Michel. 'Novelty Under Canada's Patent Act – A European Accent' (1998) 13 *Intellectual Property Journal* 83.

Goy, R.H.M. 'The International Protection of the Cultural and Natural Heritage' (1973) 4 *Netherlands Yearbook of International Law* 17.

Goyal, M. *et al*. 'Economic and Health Consequences of Selling a Kidney in India' (2002) 288 *Journal of American Medical Association* 1589–93.

Grandolfo, G.M. 'The Human Property Gap' (1992) 32 *Santa Clara Law Review* 957.

Grant, Hammond. 'Theft of Information' (1988) *Law Quarterly Review* 527.

Gratwick, Stephen. 'Having Regard to What Was Known and Used' (1972) 88 *The Law Quarterly Review* 341.

_____ 'Having Regard to What Was Known and Used – Revisited' (1986) 102 *The Law Quarterly Review* 403.

Gravelle, Michelle and Whalley, John. 'Africa and the Uruguay Round' (1996) 6 *Transnational Law and Contemporary Problems* 123.

Gray, J. *Liberalism* (Milton Keynes: Open University Press, 1986).

Gray, K. 'Property in Thin Air' (1991) 50 *Cambridge Law Journal* 252.

Graziano, Karen. 'Biosafety Protocol: Recommendations to Ensure the Safety of the Environment'(1995) 7 *Colorado Journal of International Environmental Law and Policy* 179.

Greaves, T. (ed.). *Intellectual Property Rights for Indigenous Peoples: A Sourcebook* (Oklahoma City: Society for Applied Anthropology, 1994).

Greely, H.T. 'Iceland's Plan for Genomics Research: Facts and Implications' (2000) 40 Jurimetrics 153.

Green, M.M. *Ibo Village Affairs* (New York: Frederick A. Praeger, 1964).

Greenfield, Michael. 'Recombinant DNA Technology: A Science Struggling with the Patent Law' (1993) 25 *Intellectual Property Law Review* 135.

Greif, S. 'Patents and Economic Growth' (1987) 18 *International Review of Industrial Property and Copyright Law* 191.

Grey, T.C. 'Origins of the Unwritten Constitution: Fundamental Law in American Revolutionary Thought' (1978) 30 *Stanford Law Review* 843.

Grey, T.C. 'The Disintegration of Property', in J. Roland Pennock and John W. Chapman, eds, *NOMOS XXII: Property* (New York: New York University Press, 1980).

Griggs, L. 'The Ownership of Excised Body Parts: Does an Individual Have the Right to Sell?' (1994) 1 *Journal of Law & Medicine* 223.

Gross, A.J. 'Litigating Whiteness: Trials of Racial Determination in the Nineteenth-Century South' (1998) 108 *Yale Law Journal* 109.

Grubb, A. and Laing, J. (eds). *Principles of Medical Law*, 2nd edn (Oxford: Oxford University Press, 2004).

Guest, A.G. (ed.) *Oxford Essays in Jurisprudence* (Oxford: Oxford University Press, 1961).

Guest, R.A. 'Intellectual Property Rights and Native American Tribes' (1995–96) 20 American Indian Law Review 111.

Guruswamy, Lakshman, Roberts, Jason and Drywater, Catina. 'Protecting the Cultural and Natural Heritage' (2000) 7 *Buffalo Environmental Law Journal* 47.

Gutowski, Robert. 'The Marriage of Intellectual Property and International Trade in the TRIPS Agreement: Strange Bedfellows or a Match Made in Heaven?' (1999) 47 *Buffalo Law Review* 713.

Gutterman, Alan. 'The North-South Debate Regarding the Protection of Intellectual Property Rights' (1993) 28 *Wake Forest Law Review* 89.

Haar, Paul. 'Revision of the Paris Convention: A Realignment of Private and Public Interests in the International Patent System' (1982) 8 *Brooklyn Journal of International Law* 17.

Hagen, Paul and Weiner, John Barlow. 'The Cartagena Protocol on Biosafety: New Rules for International Trade in Living Modified Organisms' (2000) 12 *The Georgetown International Environmental Law Review* 697.

Halewood, Michael. 'Indigenous and Local Knowledge in International Law: A Preface to Sui Generis Intellectual Property Protection' (1999) 44 *McGill Law Journal* 953.

Halewood, Peter. 'Law's Bodies: Disembodiment and the Structure of Liberal Property Rights' (1996) 81 *Iowa Law Review* 1331.

Hamilton, Marci. 'The TRIPS Agreement: Imperialistic, Outdated, and Overprotective' (1996) 29 *Vanderbilt Journal of Transnational Law* 613.

Hamilton, Neil. 'Why Own the Farm if you can Own the Farmer (and the Crop)? Contract Production and Intellectual Property Protection of Grain Crops' (1994) 73 *Nebraska Law Review* 91.

Hammond, Grant. 'Theft of Information' (1988) *Law Quarterly Review* 527.

Hannig, Mark. 'An Examination of the Possibility to Secure Intellectual Property Rights for Plant Genetic Resources Developed by Indigenous Peoples of NAFTA States: Domestic Legislation under the International Convention for Plant Varieties' (1996) 13 *Arizona Journal of International and Comparative Law* 175.

Hansen, L.C. and Obrycki, J.J. 'Field Deposition of Bt Transgenic Corn Pollen: Lethal Effects on the Monarch Butterfly' (2000) 125 *Oecologia* 241.

Hansmann, H. 'The Economics and Ethics of Markets for Human Organs' (1989) 14 *Journal of Health Politics, Policy, and Law* 57–85.

Haq, Inamul. 'The Problem of Global Economic Inequity: Legal Structures and Some Thoughts on the Next 40 Years' (1979) 9 *Georgia Journal of International and Comparative Law* 507.

Hardiman, R. 'Comment, Towards the Right of Commerciality: Recognizing Property Rights in the Commercial Value of Human Tissue' (1986) 34 *UCLA Law Review* 207.

Hardin, G. 'A Tragedy of the Commons' (1968) 162 *Science* 1243.

Harding, Sandra. *Whose Science? Whose Knowledge? Thinking From Women's Perspectives* (Ithaca, New York: Cornell University Press, 1991).

Hardy, Cheryl. 'Patent Protection and Raw Materials: The Convention on Biological Diversity and its Implications for U.S. Policy on the Development and Commercialization of Biotechnology' (1994) 15 *University of Pennsylvania Journal of International Business Law* 299.

Harper, Bruce. 'TRIPS Article 27.2: An Argument for Caution' (1997) 21 *William & Mary Environmental Law and Policy Review* 381.

Harrington, Laurence. 'Recent Amendments to China's Patent Law: The Emperor's New Clothes?'(1994) 17 *Boston College International & Comparative Law Review* 337.

Harris, C.I. 'Whiteness as Property' (1993) 106 *Harvard Law Review* 1709.

_____ 'Bondage, Freedom and the Constitution: The New Slavery Scholarship and its Impact on Law and Legal Historiography. Part II Contribution: Private Law and United States Slave Regimes' (1996) 18 *Cardozo Law Review* 309.

Harris, J.W. 'Who Owns My Body' (1996) 16 *Oxford Journal of Legal Studies* 55.

_____ (ed.). *Property Problems: From Genes to Pension Funds* (The Hague: Kluwer Law International Ltd., 1997).

Harris, L.J. (ed.). *Nurturing New Ideas: Legal Reports and Economic Roles* (Washington: Bureau of National Affairs, 1969).

Hartridge, David and Subramanian, Arvind. 'Intellectual Property Rights: The Issues in GATT' (1989) 22 *Vanderbilt Journal of Transnational Law* 893.

Hattenbach, Ben. 'GATT TRIPS and the Small American Inventor: An Evaluation of the Effort to Preserve Domestic Technological Innovation' (1995) 10 *Intellectual Property Journal* 61.

Haug, David. 'The International Transfer of Technology: Lessons that East Europe can Learn from the Failed Third World Experience' (1992) 5 *Harvard Journal of Law and Technology* 209.

Hayek, F.A. *New Studies in Philosophy, Politics, Economics, and the History of Ideas* (London: Routledge and Kegan Paul, 1978).

Hayhurst, W.L. 'Confidential Information – No Theft of Intellectual Property' (1989) 11 *European Intellectual Property Review* 42.

Heath, C. and Sanders, A.K. (eds). *Intellectual Property in the Digital Age: Challenges for Asia* (The Hague: Kluwer Law International, 2001).

Hegel, G.W.F. *Hegel's Philosophy of Right* (London: Oxford University Press, 1967. Translated with notes by T.M. Knox).

Heijnsbergen, Van. 'Biodiversity and International Law' (1991) 45 *International Spectator* 681.

_____ *International Legal Protection of Wild Fauna and Flora* (Amsterdam: Ohmsha Press, 1997).

Held, V. (ed.). *Property, Profits, and Economic Justice* (Belmont: Wadsworth, 1980).

Helfgott, Samson. 'Cultural Differences Between the U.S. and Japanese Patent Systems' (1990) 72 *Journal of Patents and Trademark Office Society* 231–8.

Heller, M. and Eisenberg, R.S. 'Can Patents Deter Innovation? The Anticommons in Biomedical Research' (1998) 280 *Science* 698.

Heller, M.A. 'The Tragedy of the Anticommons: Property in the Transition from Marx to Markets' (1998) 111 *Harvard Law Review* 623.

_____ 'The Dynamic Analytics of Property' (2001) 2 *Theoretical Inquiries in Law* 79.

Hellmich, R.L. *et al.* 'Monarch Larvae Sensitivity to Bacillus Thuringiensis-Purified Proteins and Pollen' (2001) 98 *Proceedings of the National Academy of Science* 1295.

Helmholz, R.H. 'Wrongful Possession of Chattels: Hornbook Law and Case Law' (1986) 80 *Northwestern University Law Review* 1221.

Herman, D.H.J. and Sor, Y.S. 'Property Rights in One's Job: The Case for Limiting Employment-At-Will' (1982) 24 *Arizona Law Review* 763.

Hettinger, Ned. 'Patenting Life: Biotechnology, Intellectual Property, and Environmental Ethics' (1995) 22 *Environmental Affairs* 267.

Hey, Ellen. 'Increasing Accountability for the Conservation and Sustainable Use of Biodiversity: An Issue of Transnational Global Character' (1995) *Colorado Journal of International Environmental Law and Policy* 1.

Hildebrand, A.J. 'Masked Intentions: the Masquerade of Killing Thoughts Used to Justify Dehydrating and Starving People in a Persistent Vegetative State and People with other Profound Neurological Impairments' (2000) 16 *Issues in Law & Medicine* 143.

Hillel, S. 'The Natural Right to the Means of Production' (1977) 27 *Philosophical Quarterly* 41.

Hilmert, L.J. 'Cloning Human Organs: Potential Sources and Property Implications' (2002) 77 *Indiana Law Journal* 636.

Hilson, Chris. 'Nervous Shock and the Categorisation of Victims' (1998) 6 *Tort Law Review* 37.

Hirst, M. 'Preventing the Lawful Burial of a Body' (1996) *Criminal Law Review* 96.

Ho, Cynthia. 'Building a Better Mousetrap: Patenting Biotechnology in the European Community' (1992) 3 *Duke Journal of Comparative and International Law* 173.

Hochberg, Michael *et al.* (eds). *Aspects of the Genesis and Maintenance of Biological Diversity* (Oxford: Oxford University Press, 1996).

Hodgskin, T. *The Natural and Artificial Right of Property Contrasted* (New Jersey: Augustus M. Kelly Publishers, 1832).

Hoebel, E.A. 'Fundamental Legal Concepts as Applied in the Study of Primitive Law' (1942) 51 *Yale Law Journal* 951.

Hoelting, Rebecca. 'After Rio: The Sustainable Development Concept Following the United Nations Conference on Environment and Development' (1994) 24 *Georgia Journal of International and Comparative Law* 117.

Hoffmaster, Barry. 'The Ethics of Patenting Higher Life Forms' (1989) 4 *Intellectual Property Journal* 1.

_____ 'Between the Sacred and the Profane: Bodies, Property, and Patents in the *Moore* Case' (1991) 7 *Intellectual Property Journal* 115.

Hohfeld, W.N. 'Some Fundamental Legal Conceptions as Applied in Judicial Reasoning' (1911) 23 *Yale Law Journal* 16.

_____ 'Fundamental Legal Conceptions as Applied in Judicial Reasoning' (1917) 26 *Yale Law Journal* 710.

Holdsworth, W.S. *A History of English Law*, 2nd edn (London: Sweet & Maxwell, 1937, vol 7).

Holland, Donald. 'Can Product-by-Process Patents Provide the Protection Needed for Proteins Made by Recombinant DNA Technology?' (1992) 74 *Journal of Patents and Trademark Office Society* 902.

Holman, M.A. and Munzer, S.R. 'Intellectual Property Rights in Genes and Gene Fragments: A Registration Solution for Expressed Sequence Tags' (2000) 85 *Iowa Law Review* 735.

Holwick, S. 'Developing Nations and the Agreement on Trade-Related Aspects of Intellectual Property Rights' (1999) *Colorado Journal of International Environmental Law and Policy* 49.

Honoré, A.M. 'Rights of Exclusion and Immunities Against Divesting' (1960) 34 *Tulane Law Review* 453.

Horsley, H. 'Reconsidering Inalienability for Commercially Valuable Biological Materials' (1992) 29 *Harvard Journal on Legislation* 223.

Horton, Curtis. 'Protecting Biodiversity and Cultural Diversity Under Intellectual Property Law: Toward a new International System' (1995) 10 *Journal of Environmental Law and Litigation* 1.

Houck, Oliver. 'On the Law of Biodiversity and Ecosystem Management' (1997) 81 *Minnesota Law Review* 869.

House of Commons (UK). *The Royal Liverpool Children's Inquiry* (The House of Commons, 2001).

Howe, M. 'Australian Company Buys Right to Tonga Gene Pool' (2001) 2 *Lancet Oncology* 7.

Huber, Peter. 'Biotechnology and the Regulation Hydra' (1987) 90 *Technology Review 8.*

Hughes and Woodley on Patents (Markham, ON.: Butterworths, 2002).

Hull, J. and Abbott, S. 'Property Rights in Secrets – Douglas v. Hello! In the Court of Appeal' (2005) 27 *European Intellectual Property Review* 379.

Hulme, Wyndham. 'The History of the Patent System under the Prerogative and at Common Law' (1896) 12 *The Law Quarterly Review* 141.

_____ 'On the Consideration of the Patent Grant, Past and Present' (1897) 13 *The Law Quarterly Review* 313.

_____ 'The History of the Patent System under the Prerogative and at Common Law – A Sequel' (1900) 16 *The Law Quarterly Review* 441.

_____ 'On the History of Patent Law in the Seventeenth and Eighteenth Centuries' (1902) 18 *The Law Quarterly Review* 280.

Hulsey, William *et al.* "Recent Development in Patent Law" (1995) *Texas Intellectual Property Law Journal* 99.

Human Genetics Commission. *Inside Information: Balancing Interests in the Use of Personal Genetic Data* (A Report by the Human Genetics Commission, May 2002).

Hunt, G. (ed.). *The Writings of James Madison* (New York: G.P. Putnam's Sons, 1906).

Hunt, H.F. 'African Folklore: The Role of Copyright' (1969–1972) 1 *African Law Studies* 87.

Hunter, Christopher. 'Sustainable Biosprospecting: Using Private Contracts and International Legal Principles and Policies to Conserve Raw Medicinal Materials' (1997) 25 *Boston College Environmental Affairs Law Review* 129.

Hunter, David *et al.* 'Environment and Trade Concepts and Principles of International Law: An Introduction' (1995) 3 *Global Environmental Law Annual* 99.

Hurrell, A. and Kingsbury, B. (eds). *The International Politics of the Environment* (Oxford: Clarendon Press, 1992).

Husserl, Gerhart. 'Public Policy and Order Public' (1938) 25 *Virginia Law Review* 37.

Hutchens, M.P. 'Grave Robbing and Ethics in the 19th Century' (1997) 278 *Journal of American Medical Association* 1115.

Hutt, S. 'Illegal Trafficking in Native American Human Remains and Cultural Items: A New Protection Tool' (1992) 24 *Arizona State Law Journal* 135.

Hutt, Sherry and McKeown, Timothy. 'Control of Cultural Property as Human Rights' (1999) 31 *Arizona State Law Journal* 363.

Hylton, K.N. 'The Law and Economics of Organ Procurement' (1990) 12 *Law & Policy* 197–224.

Ikemoto, Lisa. 'The Racialization of Genomic Knowledge' (1997) 27 *Seton Hall Law Review* 937.

Institute of Ideas. *Morbid Fascination: The Body and Death in Contemporary Culture* (Conference organized by the Institute of Ideas on 16 May 2003).

Irvine, J. 'Some Thoughts on Trespass to Airspace' (1986) 37 *Canadian Cases on the Law of Torts* 99.

Isaac, Erich. *Geography of Domestication* (Prentice-Hall: New Jersey, 1970).

Isichei, E. *Igbo Worlds: An Anthology of Oral Histories and Historical Descriptions* (Philadelphia: Institute for the Study of Human Issues, 1978).

IUCN: Inter-Commission Task Force on Indigenous Peoples and Sustainability – Cases and Actions (Utrecht: IUCN & International Books, 1997).

Iwu, M.M. *Handbook of African Medicinal Plants* (Boca Raton, FL.: CRC Press, 1993).

_____ 'Biodiversity Prospecting in Nigeria: Seeking Equity and Reciprocity in Intellectual Property Rights Through Partnership Arrangements and Capacity Building' (1996) 51 *Journal of Ethnopharmacology* 209.

Iyer, Krishna. 'Wounded Nature versus Human Future' (1995) 19 *Cochin University Law Review* 1.

Jackson, D.C. *Principles of Property* (Sydney: The Law Book Co. Ltd., 1967).

Jackson, E. *Medical Law: Text, Cases and Materials* (Oxford: Oxford University Press, 2006).

Jackson, Fatimah. 'Concerns and Priorities in Genetic Studies: Insights from Recent African American Biohistory' (1997) 27 *Seton Hall Law Review* 951.

Jackson, John. 'The Great 1994 Sovereignty Debate: United States Acceptance and Implementation of the Uruguay Round Results' (1997) 36 *Columbia Journal of Transnational Law* 157.

Jacoby, Craig and Weiss, Charles. 'Recognizing Property Rights in Traditional Biocultural Contribution' (1997) 16 *Stanford Environmental Law Journal* 74.

Jaffe, E.S. 'She's Got Bette Davis['s] Eyes: Assessing the Nonconsensual Removal of Cadaver Organs under the Takings and Due Process Clauses' (1990) 90 *Columbia Law Review* 528.

Jain, Meetal. 'Global Trade and the New Millenium: Defining the Scope of Intellectual Property Protection of Plant Genetic Resources and Traditional Knowledge in India' (1999) 22 *Hastings International and Comparative Law Review* 777.

James, George (ed.). *Ethical Perspectives On Environmental Issues in India* (New Delhi: A.P.H. Publishing Corporation, 1999).

Jarrette, Henry (ed.). *Environmental Quality in a Growing Economy* (Baltimore: Johns Hopkins University Press, 1966).

Jarvis, Mark (ed.). *The Influence of Religion on the Development of International Law* (Dordrecht: Martinus Nijhoff Publishers, 1991).

Jenks, Daniel. 'The Convention on Biological Diversity – An Efficient Framework for the Preservation of Life on Earth?' (1995) 15 *Northwestern Journal of International Law and Business* 636.

Jerdee, A.L. 'Breaking Through the Silence: Minnesota's Pregnancy Presumption and the Right to Refuse Medical Treatment' (2000) 84 *Minnesota Law Review* 971.

Jervis, Herbert. 'Impact of Recent Legal Developments on the Scope and Enforceability of Biotechnology Patent Claims' (1994) 4 *Dickinson Journal of Environmental Law and Policy* 79.

Jewkes, J., Sawers, D. and Stillerman, S. *The Sources of Invention* (London: Macmillan, 1969).

Jlosvay, T. 'Scientific Property' (1953) 2 *American Journal of Comparative Law* 180.

Johnson, Martha (ed.). *Lore – Capturing Traditional Environmental Knowledge* (Ottawa: Dene Cultural Institute and the International Development Research Centre, 1992).

Johnson, R.W. and Haensly, S.I. 'Fifth Amendment Takings Implications of the 1990 *Native American Graves Protection and Repatriation Act*' (1992) 24 *Arizona State Law Journal* 151.

Johnson, S. *The History of the Yorubas* (Lagos: CSS Bookshops Ltd., 1921).

Johnston, Todd. 'The Role of International Equity in a Sustainable Future: The Continuing Problem of Third World Debt and Development' (1998) 6 *Buffalo Environmental Law Journal* 35.

Jónatansson, H. 'Iceland's Health Sector Database: A Significant Head Start in the Search for the Biological Grail or an Irreversible Error?' (2000) 26 *American Journal of Law & Medicine* 31.

Jones, Gareth D.G. 'The Human Cadaver: An Assessment of the Value We Place on the Dead Body' (1995) 47 *Perspectives on Science & Christian Faith* 43.

Jones, Judith. 'Regulating Access to Biological and Genetic Resources in Australia: A Case Study of Bioprospecting in Queensland' (1998) 5 *The Australasian Journal of Natural Resources Law and Policy* 89.

Jones, Kevin. 'United States Dependence on Imports of Four Strategic and Critical Minerals: Implications and Policy Alternatives' (1988) *Boston College Law Review* 217.

Josefson, Deborah. 'US Hospitals to Ask Patients for Right to Sell Their Tissue' (2000) 321 British Medical Journal 658.

Jowett, C. 'Lies, Damned Lies, and DNA Statistics: DNA Match Testing, Bayes' Theorem, and the Criminal Courts' (2001) 41 *Medical Science Law* 194.

Joyner, Christopher. 'Antarctica and the Law of the Sea: Rethinking the Current Legal Dilemmas' (1981) *San Diego Law Review* 415.

———— 'Legal Implications of the Concept of the Common Heritage of Mankind' (1986) 35 *International and Comparative Law Quarterly* 190.

———— 'Biodiversity in the Marine Environment: Resource Implications for the Law of the Sea' (1995) 28 *Vanderbilt Journal of Transnational Law* 635.

Juma, Calestous and Ojwang, J.B. (eds). *In Land we Trust: Environment, Private Property and Constitutional Change* (Nairobi: Initiatives Publishers, 1996).

Jung-Gum, Kim and Howell, John. *Conflict of International Obligations and State Interests* (The Hague: Martinus Nijhoff, 1972).

Kadidal, Shayana. 'Plants, Poverty, and Pharmaceutical Patents' (1993) 103 *The Yale Law Journal* 223.

———— 'Subject-Matter Imperialism? Biodiversity, Foreign Prior Art and the Neem Patent Controversy' (1996–97) 37 *IDEA* 371.

Kameri-Mbote, Annie Patricia and Cullet, Philippe. 'Agro-Biodiversity and International Law – A Conceptual Framework (1999) 11 *Journal of Environmental Law* 257.

Kant, I. *Foundations of the Metaphysics of Morals* (Indianapolis: Bobbs-Merril Educational Pub., 1959. Translated with an introduction by Lewis White Beck).

Karr, James. 'Protecting Ecological Integrity: An Urgent Societal Goal' (1993) 18 *Yale Journal of International Law* 297.

Kastenmeier, Robert and Beier, David. 'International Trade and Intellectual Property: Promise, Risks, and Reality' (1989) 22 *Vanderbilt Journal of Transnational Law* 285.

Katz, S.N. 'Thomas Jefferson and the Right to Property in Revolutionary America' (1976) 19 *Journal of Law and Economics*. 467.

Katzenberg, M.A. and Saunders, S.R. (eds) *Biological Anthropology of the Human Skeleton* (New York: Wiley-Liss, Inc. 2000).

Kaufman, Les and Mallory, Kenneth (eds). *The Last Extinction*, 2nd edn (Cambridge, Mass: The MIT Press, 1993).

Kaye, J. and Martin, P. 'Safeguards for Research Using Large Scale DNA Collections' (2000) 321 *British Medical Journal* 1146.

Keane, Thomas. 'The Patentability of Biotechnological Inventions' (1992) *Irish Law Times* 139.

Keeton, W.P. et al., *Prosser & Keeton on Torts*, 5th edn (St. Paul, Minnesota: West Publishing, 1984).

Kennedy, D. 'The Structure of Blackstone's Commentaries' (1979) 28 *Buffalo Law Review* 209.

Keown, J. 'The Ashes of AIDS and the Phoenix of Informed Consent' (1989) 52 *Modern Law Review* 790.

Ketley, Harriet. 'Cultural Diversity versus Biodiversity' (1994) 16 *Adelaide Law Review* 99.

Khan, Q.K. 'Colonialism Revisited: Insights into the Human Genome Diversity Project' (1999) 3 *Journal of Law & Social Challenges* 89.

Kieff, F.S. 'Property Rights and Property Rules for Commercializing Inventions' (2001) 85 *Minnesota Law Review* 697.

Kiley, Thomas. 'Patents on Random Complementary DNA Fragments?' (1992) 14 *Science* 915.

Kim, Judy. 'Out of the Lab and into the Field: Harmonization of Deliberate Release Regulations for Genetically Modified Organisms' (1993) 16 *Fordham International Law Journal* 1170.

Kimball, Lee. 'The Biodiversity Convention: How to Make it Work' (1995) 28 *Vanderbilt Journal of Transnational Law* 763.

Kindall, M.P.A. 'Talking Past Each Other at the Summit' (1993) 4 *Colorado Journal of International Environmental Law and Policy* 69.

Kirchanski, Stefan. 'Protection of U.S. Patent Rights in Developing Countries: U.S Efforts to Enforce Pharmaceutical Patents in Thailand' (1994) 16 *Loyola L.A. International and Comparative Law Journal* 569.

Kirton, John and Richardson, Sarah (eds). *The Halifax Summit: Sustainable Development, and International Institutional Reform* (Ottawa: National Roundtable on the Environment and the Economy, 1995).

Kitch, Edmund. 'The Nature and Function of the Patents System' (1977) 20 *Journal of Law and Economics* 265.

_____ 'The Patent Policy of Developing Countries' (1994) 13 *Pacific Basin Law Journal* 166.

_____ 'The Japanese Patent System and U.S Innovators' (1996–97) 29 *International Law and Politics* 177.

Klar, Lewis. *Tort Law*, 3ʳᵈ edn (Toronto: Carswell, 2003).

Kloppenburg, Jack Jr. *First the Seed – The Political Economy of Plant Biotechnology, 1492-2000* (Cambridge: Cambridge University Press, 1988).

Knetsch, J.L. *Property Rights and Compensation: Compulsory Acquisition and other Losses* (Boston: Butterworths, 1983).

Knoppers, B.M., *et al.* (eds). *Human DNA: Law and Policy* (The Hague: Kluwer Law International, 1997).

Kocourek, A. 'Plurality of Advantage and Disadvantage in Jural Relations' (1920) 19 *Michigan Law Review* 47.

Kohler, P. 'The Death of Ownership and the Demise of Property' (2000) 53 *Current Legal Problems* 237.

Kometani, Kazumochi. 'Trade and Environment: How Should WTO Panels Review Environmental Regulations Under GATT Articles III and XX?'(1996) 16 *Northwestern Journal of International Law and Business* 441.

Kongolo, Tshimanga. 'The New OAPI Agreement as Revised in February 1999' (2000) 3 *Journal of World Intellectual Property* 5.

_____ 'Towards a More Balanced Coexistence of Traditional Knowledge and Pharmaceuticals Protection in Africa' (2001) 35 No. 2 *Journal of World Trade* 349.

Koning, Martine. 'Biodiversity Prospecting and the Equitable Remuneration of Ethnobiological Knowledge: Reconciling Industry and Indigenous Interests' (1998) 12 *Intellectual Property Journal* 261.

Kosslak, R.M. '*The Native American Graves Protection and Repatriation Act*: The Death Knell for Scientific Study?' (1999–2000) 24 *American Indian Law Review* 129.

Kothari, Ashish and Anuradha, R.V. 'Biodiversity and Intellectual Property Rights: Can the Two Co-exist' (1999) 2 *Journal of International Wildlife Law and Policy* 204.

Kovar, Jeffrey. 'A Short Guide to the Rio Declaration' (1993) 4 *Colorado Journal of International Environmental Law and Policy* 119.

Kramer, M.H. 'Do Animals and Dead People Have Legal Rights?' (2001) 14 *Canadian Journal of Law & Jurisprudence* 29.

Krattiger, Anatole *et al.* (eds). *Widening Perspectives on Biodiversity* (Gland, Switzerland: IUCN, 1994).

Kristeller, P.O. 'Creativity and Tradition' XLIV (1983) *Journal of the History of Ideas* 105.

Krosin, Kenneth. 'Are Plants Patentable Under the Utility Patent Act?' (1985) 67 *Journal of Patents and Trademark Office Society* 220.

Kruger, M. 'Harmonizing TRIPS and the CBD: a Proposal from India' (2001) 10 *Minnesota Journal of Global Trade* 169.

Kuhn, T. *The Structure of Scientific Revolution* (Chicago: University of Chicago Press, 1972).

Kulseth, Reagan. 'Biotechnology and Anima Patents: When Someone Builds a Better Mouse' (1990) 32 *Arizona Law Review* 691.

Kumar, S. 'Police Uncover Large Scale Organ Trafficking in Punjab' (2003) 326 *British Medical Journal* 180.

Kunz-Hallstein, Hans. 'The United States Proposal for a GATT Agreement on Intellectual Property and the Paris Convention for the Protection of Industrial Property' (1989) 22 *Vanderbilt Journal of Transnational Law.*

Kuruk, Paul. 'Protecting Folklore Under Modern Intellectual Property Regimes: A Reappraisal of the Tensions Between Individual and Communal Rights in Africa and the United States' (1999) 48 *American University Law Review* 769.

Kushan, Jeffrey. 'Biodiversity: Opportunities and Obligations' (1995) 28 *Vanderbilt Journal of Transnational Law* 755.

Lachs, Manfred. 'The Development and General Trends of International Law in our Time' (1980) 169 *Recueil Des Cours* 240–41.

Ladas, S.P. *The International Protection of Industrial Property* (Cambridge: Harvard University Press, 1930).

_____ *Patents, Trademarks, and Related Rights – National and International Protection* (Massachusetts: Harvard University Press, 1975).

Laine, J.M. 'Infringement of Patents by Intention' (1901) 17 *The Law Quarterly Review* 201.

Lallas, Peter *et al.* 'Environmental Protection and International Trade: Toward Mutually Supportive Rules and Policies' (1992) 16 *Harvard Environmental Law Review* 271.

Landau, Georges. 'The Treaty for Amazonian Cooperation' (1980) 10 *Georgia Journal of International and Comparative* Law 463.

Landy, David (ed.). *Culture, Disease and Healing – Studies in Medical Anthropology* (New York: Macmillan Publishing Co., Inc, 1977).

Lang, Jon. 'Secrets, Strategies, and Proposals for Reform in the United Kingdom' (2002) 8 *Computer and Telecommunications Law Review* 193.

Lange, David. 'Recognizing the Public Domain' (1981) 44 *Law and Contemporary Problems* 4.

Langley, Winston. 'The Third World: Towards a Definition' (1981) 2 *Boston College Third World Law Journal* 1.

Lantz, C. 'The Anencephalic Infant as Organ Donor' (1996) 4 *Health Law Journal* 179.

Larkin, P. *Property in the Eighteenth Century: With Special Reference to England and Locke* (Dublin: Cork University Press, 1930).

Larschan, Bradley and Brennan, Bonnie. 'The Common Heritage of Mankind Principle in International Law' (1982–83) 21 *Columbia Journal of Transnational Law* 305.

Larsch-Quinn, Elizabeth. 'Commentary: Democracy Should not Have Losers' (2000) 9 *Minnesota Journal of Global Trade* 589.

Laurie, Graeme. *Genetic Privacy: A Challenge to Medico-Legal Norms* (Cambridge: Cambridge University Press, 2002).

Lavoie, J. 'Ownership of Human Tissue: Life After Moore v. Regents of the University of California' (1989) 75 *Virginia Law Review* 1363.

Lawrence, Robert and Litan, Robert. 'The World Trading System after the Uruguay Round' (1990) 8 *Boston University International Law Journal* 247.

Lawson, F.H. and Rudden, B. *The Law of Property*, 3rd edn (Oxford: Oxford University Press, 2002).

Lawton, Anne. 'Regulating Genetic Diversity: A Comparative Study of Legal Constraints in Europe and the United States' (1997) 11 *Emory International Law Review* 365.

Leafer, Marshall. 'Protecting United States Intellectual Property Abroad: Toward a New Multilateralism' (1991) 76 *Iowa Law Review* 273.

Leelakrishnan, P. *et al.* 'Law Fiddles While Forest Habitat Burns' (1988) 12 *Cochin University Law Review* 1.

Lemley, Mark. 'The Economic Irrationality of the Patent Misuse Doctrine' (1990) 78 *California Law Review* 1599.

Lemmens, T. 'Towards the Right to be Killed? Treatment Refusal, Assisted Suicide and Euthanasia in the United States and Canada,' (1996) 52 *British Medical Bulletin* 341.

_____ 'Selective Justice, Genetic Discrimination, and Insurance: Should We Single Out Genes in Our Laws?' (2000) 45 *McGill Law Journal* 347.

Lemmens, T. and Waring, D.R. (eds) *Law and Ethics in Biomedical Research* (Toronto: University of Toronto Press, 2006).

Lesser, William. *Institutional Mechanisms Supporting Trade in Genetic Materials: Issues Under the Biodiversity Convention and GATT/TRIPS* (Geneva: UNEP, 1994).

_____ *Sustainable Use of Genetic Resources Under the Convention on Biological Diversity – Exploring Access and Benefit Sharing Issues* (Oxford: CAB International, 1997).

Letourneau, Ch. *Property: Its Origin and Development* (London: The Walter Scott Publishing Co., Ltd., 1892).

Lewinsohn-Zamir, D. 'Contemporary Property Law Scholarship: A Comment' (2001) 2 *Theoretical Inquiries in Law* 97.

Lewis, Stephen. 'Attack of the Killer Tomatoes? Corporate Liability for the International Propagation of Genetically Altered Agricultural Products' (1997) 10 *Transnational Law* 178–88.

Libby, Ronald Theodore. *The Ideology and Power of the World Bank* (Ann Arbor, Michigan: Unpublished Doctoral Thesis, 1985).

Libling, D.F. 'The Concept of Property: Property in Intangibles' (1978) 94 *Law Quarterly Review* 103.

Lichtman, A.C. 'Commercial Exploitation of DNA and the Tort of Conversion: A Physician May Not Destroy a Patient's Interest in her Body-Matter' (1989) 34 *New York Law School Law Review* 531.

Liddel, K. *et al.* 'Beyond Bristol and Alder Hey: The Future Regulation of Human Tissue' (2005) 13 *Medical Law Review* 170.

Lim, Chin and Elias, Olufemi. 'The Role of Treaties in the Contemporary International Legal Order' (1997) 66 *Nordic Journal of International Law* 1.

Lin, Ruey-Long. 'Protection of Intellectual Property in the Republic of China' (1986–87) 6 *Chinese Yearbook of International Law and Affairs* 120.

Linck, Nancy. 'Patentable Subject Under Section 101– Are Plants Included?' (1985) 67 *Journal of Patents and Trademark Office Society* 489.

Lindley, Mark. *The Acquisition and Government of Backward Territory in International Law: Being a Treatise on the Law and Practice Relating to Colonial Expansion* (New York: Negro Universities Press, 1969).

Lippert, Owen (ed.). *Competitive Strategies for the Protection of Intellectual Property* (Vancouver: The Fraser Institute, 1999).

Lischutz, Ronnie. 'Wasn't the Future Wonderful? Resources, Environment, and the Emerging Myth of Global Sustainable Development' (1991) 2 *Colorado Journal of International Environmental Law and Policy* 35.

Litman, Jessica. 'The Public Domain' (1990) 39 *Emory Law Journal* 968.

Litowiz, D. 'Reification in Law and Legal Theory' (2000) 9 *Southern California Interdisciplinary Law Journal* 401.

Liu, Paul. 'U.S. Industry's Influence on Intellectual Property Negotiations and Special 301 Actions' (1994) 13 *Pacific Basin Law Journal* 87.

Liu, Y. 'IPR Protection for New Traditional Knowledge: With a Case Study of Traditional Chinese Medicine' (2003) 25 *European Intellectual Property Review* 194.

Locke, J. *Second Treatise of Government* (Indianapolis: Hackett Publishing Co., 1980).

Longo, Peter. 'The Human Genome Project's Threat to the Human Constitution: Protections from Nebraska Constitutionalism' (1999) 33 *Creighton Law Review* 3.

Looney, B. 'Should Genes be Patented? The Gene Patenting Controversy: Legal, Ethical, and Policy Foundations of an International Agreement' (1996) 28 *Intellectual Property Review* 101.

Lorentz, Kirsi O. 'Cultures of Physical Modifications: Child Bodies in Ancient Cyprus' (2003) 2 *Stanford Journal of Archaeology* 17.

Losey, J.E. *et al.* 'Transgenic Pollen Harms Monarch Larvae' (1999) 399 *Nature* 214.

Louka, E. *Biodiversity and Human Rights: The International Rules for the Protection of Biodiversity* (New York: Transnational Publishers, Inc., 2002).

Louwaars, N.P. 'Sui Generis Rights: From Opposing to Complementary Approaches' (1998) 36 *Biotechnology & Development Monitor* 551.

Lowe, Vaughan. 'Precluding Wrongfulness or Responsibility: A Plea for Excuses' (1999) 10 *European Journal of International Law* 405.

Lowie, R.H. *Primitive Society* (New York: Routledge, 1920).

Ludes, F.J. *et al. Corpus Juris Secundum* (St. Paul, Minnesota: West Publishing Co., 1966).

Ludlow, P. (ed.). *High Noon on the Electronic Frontier: Conceptual Issues in Cyberspace* (Cambridge, Mass.: MIT Press, 1996).

Lugard, F. The Dual Mandate in British Tropical Africa (Connecticut: Archon Books, 1965).

Lundestad, Geir. *East, West, North South: Major Developments in International Politics 1945-1986* (Norwegian University Press, 1988).

Lutz, Karl. 'A Proper Public Policy on Patents: Are We Adopting the Soviet View?' (1951) 37 *American Bar Association Journal* 943.

Luxemberg, Rosa. *The Accumulation Of Capital* (London: Routledge, 1951).

Mace, Georgina *et al.* (eds). *Conservation in a Changing World* (Cambridge: Cambridge University Press, 1999).

Macer, D. *Shaping Genes* (Tsukuba, Japan: Eubios Ethics Institute, 1990).

Macey, J.R. 'From Fairness to Contract: The New Direction of the Rules Against Insider Trading' (1984) 13 *Hofstra Law Review* 9.

MacGillivary, R. 'Body-Snatching in Ontario' (1988) 5 *Canadian Bulletin of Medical History* 51.

Machlup, Fritz and Penrose, Edith. 'The Patent Controversy in the 19th Century' (1950) 10 *Journal of Economic History* 1.

Mackinnon, K.A.B. 'Giving It All Away? Thomas Reid's Retreat from a Natural Rights Justification of Private Property' (1993) 2 *Canadian Journal of Law & Jurisprudence* 367.

Macleod, C. 'The Paradoxes of Patenting: Invention and Its Diffusion in 18th and 19th Century Britain, France and North America' (1991) *Technology and Culture* 905.

Macpherson, C.B. *The Political Theory of Possessive Individualism: Hobbes to Locke* (Oxford: Oxford University Press, 1962).

_____ *Property: Mainstream and Critical Positions* (Toronto: University of Toronto Press, 1978).

Maggio, Gregory. 'Recognizing the Vital Role of Local Communities in International Legal Instruments for Conserving Biodiversity' (1997–98) 16 *Journal of Environmental Law* 179.

Magnusson, Roger. 'The Recognition of Proprietary Rights in Human Tissue in Common Law Jurisdictions' (1992) 18 *Melbourne University Law Review* 601.

Magraw, Daniel. 'Transboundary Harm: The International Law Commission's Study of "International Liability"' (1986) 80 *American Journal of International Law* 305.

Mahoney, J.D. 'The Market for Human Tissue' (2000) 86 *Virginia Law Review* 163.

Maienschein *et al.* 'Biology and Law: Challenges of Adjudicating Competing Claims in Democracy' (1998) 38 *Jurimetrics Journal* 151.

Malinowski, Michael. 'Globalization of Biotechnology and the Public Health Challenges Accompanying It' (1996) 60 *Albany Law Review* 119.

Maluwa, Tiyanjana. 'Environment and Development in Africa: An Overview of Basic Problems of Environmental Law and Policy' (1989) 1 *La Revue Africaine de Droit International et Compare* 650.

Mandelker, Barry. 'Indigenous People and Cultural Appropriation: Intellectual Property Problems and Solutions' (2000) 16 *Canadian Intellectual Property Review* 367.

Manne, H.H. *The Economics of Legal Relationships: Readings in the Theory of Property Rights* (New York: West Publishing Co., 1975).

Marden, Emily. 'The Neem Tree Patent: International Conflict over the Commodification of Life' (1999) 22 *Boston College International & Comparative Law Review* 279.

Marguiles, Rebecca. 'Protecting Biodiversity: Recognizing International Intellectual Property Rights in Plant Genetic Resources' (1993) 14 *Michigan Journal of International Law* 322.

Markett, Michael J. 'Genetic Diaries: An Analysis of Privacy Protection in DNA Data Banks' (1996) 30 *Suffolk University Law Review* 185.

Marsh, G.A. 'Walking the Spirit Trail: Repatriation and Protection Of Native American Remains and Sacred Cultural Items' (1992) 24 *Arizona State Law Journal* 79.

Marshall, Eliot. 'Patent on HIV Receptor Provokes an Outcry' (2000) 287 *Science* 1375.

Martin, B. *Information Liberation: Challenging the Corruptions of Information Power* (London: Freedom Press, 1998).

Martin, P.A. and Lagod, M.L. 'Biotechnology and the Commercial Use of Human Cells: Toward An Organic View of Life and Technology' (1989) 5 *Santa Clara Computer & High Technology Law Journal* 211.

Martin, R.F. *Dead Bodies* (1952) 21 *American Law Reports* 2d 472.

Martinez, Magdalena. *National Sovereignty and International Organizations* (The Hague: Kluwer Law International, 1996).

Marusky, R.W. and Swain, M.S. 'A Question of Property Rights in the Human Body' (1989) 21 *Ottawa Law Review* 351.

Maskus, K.E. 'The Role of Intellectual Property Rights in Encouraging Foreign Direct Investment and Technological Transfer' (1998) 9 *Duke Journal of Comparative & International Law* 109.

_____ 'Intellectual Property Challenges for Developing Countries: An Economic Perspective' (2001) 1 *University of Illinois Law Review* 457.

Maskus, Keith E. and Reichman Jerome H. (eds) *International Public Goods and Transfer of Technology Under a Globalized Intellectual Property Regime* (Cambridge: Cambridge University Press, 2005).

Matthews, Douglas. 'International Inequality: Some Global and Regional Perspectives' (1988–89) 7 *Wisconsin International Law Journal* 261.

Matthews, P. 'Whose Body? People as Property' (1983) 36 *Current Legal Problems* 193.

Mayer, Christopher. 'The Brazilian Pharmaceutical Industry Goes from Walking Ipanema to Prosperity: Will the New Intellectual Property Law Spur Domestic Investment' (1998) 12 *Temple International and Comparative Law Journal* 377.

Mazzoleni, Roberto and Nelson, Richard. 'The Benefits and Costs of Strong Patent Protection: A Contribution to the Current Debate' (1998) 27 *Research Policy* 273.

McCabe, Kevin. 'The January 1999 Review of Article 27 of the TRIPS Agreement: Diverging Views of Developed and Developing Countries Toward the Patentability of Biotechnology' (1998) 6 *Journal of Intellectual Property Law* 41.

McClearly, R.M. 'The International Communities Claim to Right in Brazilian Amazonia' (1991) 39 *Political Studies* 691.

McCloskey, Michael. 'The Emperor has no Clothes: The Conundrum of Sustainable Development' (1999) 9 *Duke Environmental Law and Policy Forum* 153.

McCorquodale, Robert and Fairbrother, Richard. 'Globalization and Human Rights' (1999) 21 *Human Rights Quarterly* 735.

McDonald, Leighton. 'Can Collective and Individual Rights Coexist?' (1998) 22 *Melbourne University Law Review* 310.

McDonald, T.R. 'Genetic Justice: DNA Evidence and the Criminal Law in Canada' (1998) 26 *Manitoba Law Journal* 1.

McDougal, Myers. 'The Impact of International Law upon National Law: A Policy Oriented Perspective' (1959) 4 *South Dakota Law Review* 25.

McEldowney, S. and Warren, L.M. 'The New Biology: A Challenge to Law' (1998) 1 *International Journal of Biosciences & the Law* 315.

McFetridge Douglas and Smith, Douglas. 'Patents, Prospects, and Economic Surplus: A Comment' (1980) 23 *Journal of Law and Economics* 197.

McGeary, Judith. 'A Scientific Approach to Protecting Biodiversity' (1998–99) 14 *Journal of Natural Resources and Environmental Law* 85.

McHale, J.V. 'Regulating Genetic Databases: Some Legal and Ethical Issues' (2004) 12 *Medical Law Review* 70.

McIntyre, John and Papp, Daniel (eds). *The Political Economy of International Technology Transfer* (New York: Quorum Books, 1986).

McKenzie, Lawson. 'Scientific Property' (1953) 118 *Science* 767.

McKie, Edward. 'Patent Cooperation Treaty: A New Adventure in the Internationality of Patents' (1978–79) 4 *North Carolina Journal of International Law and Commercial Regulation* 429.

McLean, S. (ed.) *First Do No Harm* (Aldershot: Ashgate, 2006).

McLean, Sheila. 'Science's Holy Grail – Some Legal and Ethical Implications of the Human Genome Project' (1995) 48 *Current Legal Problems* 233.

McManis, C.R. 'The Interface between International Intellectual Property and Environmental Protection: Biodiversity and Biotechnology' (1998) 76 *Washington University Law Quarterly* 255.

McNeely, Jeffrey. *Economics and Biological Diversity: Developing and Using Economic Incentives to Conserve Biological Resources* (Switzerland: IUCN, 1988).

McNeely, Jeffrey *et al* (eds). *Protecting Nature: Regional Reviews of Protected Areas* (Gland: IUCN, 1994).

McWhinney, Edward. 'Towards an Empirically-Based New International Economic Order' (1989) 27 *Canadian Yearbook of International Law* 309.

Mehta, M.D. 'Public Perceptions of Genetically Engineered Foods: "Playing God" or Trusting Science' (2001) 12 *Risk, Health, Safety & Environment* 205.

Mellon, J.N. 'Manufacturing Convictions: Why Defendants Are Entitled to the Data Underlying Forensic DNA Kits' (2001) 51 *Duke Law Journal* 1094.

Mendelsohn, Oliver and Baxi, Upendra (eds). *The Rights of Subordinated Peoples* (Delhi: Oxford University Press, 1994).

Merchant, Carolyn. *The Death of Nature: Women, Ecology and the Scientific Revolution* (New York: Harper and Row, 1980).

_____ *Radical Ecology: The Search for a Livable World* (London: Routledge, 1992).

Merges, R. 'Commercial Success and Patent Standards: Economic Perspectives on Innovation' (1988) *California Law Review* 803.

_____ 'Intellectual Property in Higher Life Forms: The Patent System and Controversial Technologies' (1988) 47 *Maryland Law Review* 1051.

_____ 'Battle of Lateralisms: Intellectual Property and Trade' (1990) 8 *Boston University International Law Journal* 239.

_____ 'Intellectual Property Rights and Bargaining Breakdown: The Case of Blocking Patents' (1996) 28 *Intellectual Property Review* 69.

_____ 'Contracting into Liability Rules: Intellectual Property Rights and Collective Rights Organizations' (1996) 84 *California Law Review* 1293.

Merges, Robert and Nelson, Richard. 'On the Complex Economics of Patent Scope' (1990) 90 *Columbia Law Review* 839.

_____ 'A Transactional View of Property Rights' (2005) *Berkeley Center for Law and Technology*, Paper 8.

Merges, Robert and Reynolds, Glenn. 'The Proper Scope of the Copyright and Patent Power' (2000) 37 *Harvard Journal on Legislation* 45.

Merrill, T.W. and Smith, H.E. 'What Happened to Property in Law and Economics?' (2001) 111 *Yale Law Journal* 357.

Merryman, J.H. 'Two Ways Of Thinking About Cultural Property' (1986) 80 *American Journal of International Law* 831.

_____ 'The Public Interest in Cultural Property' (1998) 77 *California Law Review* 339.

Mesevage, Thomas. 'The Carrot and the Stick: Protecting U.S. Intellectual Property in Developing Countries' (1991) 17 *Rutgers Computer and Technology Law Journal* 421.

Meulders-Klein, M.T. 'The Right Over One's Own Body: Its Scope and Limits in Comparative Law' (1983) 6 *Boston College of International & Comparative Law Review* 29.

Meyer, Anja. 'International Environmental Law and Human Rights: Towards the Explicit Recognition of Traditional Knowledge' (2001) 10 *Review of European Community & International Environmental Law* 37.

Meyer, George *et al.* (eds). *Folk Medicine and Herbal Healing* (Illinois: Charles Thomas Publisher, 1981).

Meyers, Gary. 'Surveying the Land, Air, and Water: Features of Current International Environmental and Natural Resources Law, and Future Prospects for the Protection of Species Habitat to Preserve Global Biological Diversity' (1992) 3 *Colorado Journal of International Environmental Law and Policy* 479.

Meyers, Gary and Muller, Simone. 'The Ethical Implications, Political Ramifications and Practical Limitations of Adopting Sustainable Development as National and International Policy' (1996) 4 *Buffalo Environmental Law Journal* 1.

Mgbeoji, Ikechi. 'Patents and Traditional Knowledge of the Uses of Plants: Is a Communal Patent Regime Part of the Solution to the Scourge of Biopiracy?' (2001) 9 *Indiana Journal of Global Legal Studies* 163.

Michael, D. *et al.* (eds). *The Cultural Dimension of Development: Indigenous Knowledge Systems* (London: Intermediate Technology Publications, 1995).

Middleton, Neil *et al.* *The Tears of the Crocodile: From Rio to the Reality in the Developing World* (London: Pluto Press. 1993).

Mill, J.S. *Principles of Political Economy* (New York: Appleton, 1887).

Miller, A.S. 'Pretense and Our Two Constitutions' (1986) 54 *George Washington Law Review* 375.

Miller, H.I. 'Risk and Regulations: The U.N. Offers Swimming Lessons to People in the Sahara' (2002) 12(3) National Review.

Miller, John. 'Globalization and Its Metaphors' (2000) 9 *Minnesota Journal of Global Trade* 594.

Milsom, S.F.C. *Historical Foundations of the Common Law* (London: Butterworths, 1969).

Mitchcam, Allison. 'The Wild Creatures, The Native People, and Us: Canadian Literary-Ecological Relationships' (1977–78) 7 *Alternatives: Perspectives on Society and Environment* 20.

Moldan, Bedrich and Billharz, Suzanne (eds). *Sustainability Indicators: Report on Indicators of Sustainable Development* (Toronto: John Wiley and Sons, 1997).

Monheit, Rivka. 'The Importance of Correct Inventorship' (1999) 7 *Journal of Intellectual Property Law* 191.

Mooney, Harold *et al.* (eds). *Functional Roles of Biodiversity: A Global Perspective* (Toronto: John Wiley & Sons, 1996).

Mooney, P.R. *The Parts of Life: Agricultural Biodiversity, Indigenous Knowledge, and the Role of the Third System* (Uppsala, Sweden: The Dag Hammarskjöld Centre, 1997).

Mooney, Pat. *The Seeds of the Earth: A Private or Public Resource?* (Ottawa: Inter Pares, 1979).

Mooney, Pat and Fowler, Cary. *Shattering: Food, Politics and the Loss of Genetic Diversity* (Tucson: The University of Arizona Press, 1990).

Moran, K. *Mechanisms for Benefit Sharing: Nigerian Case Study for the Convention on Biological Diversity* (Washington, DC: The Healing Forest Conservancy, 1998).

Moran, K. *et al.* 'Biodiversity Prospecting: Lessons and Prospects' (2001) 30 *Annual Reviews Anthropology* 505.

Moran, Lucy M. 'Intellectual Property Law Protection for Traditional and Sacred Folklife Expressions – Will Remedies Become Available to Cultural Authors and Communities?' (1999) 6 *University of Baltimore Intellectual Property Law Journal* 99.

Morgan, Jonathan. 'Privacy in the House of Lords, Again' (2004) 120 *Law Quarterly Review* 563.

Morley, Peter and Wallis, Roy (eds). *Culture and Curing – Anthropological Perspectives on Traditional Medical Beliefs and Practices* (Philadelphia: University of Pennsylvania Press, 1978).

Mortimer, D. 'Proprietary Rights in Body Parts: The Relevance of Moore's Case in Australia' (1993) 19 *Monash University Law Review* 217.

Mossinghoff, Gerald. 'The Importance of Intellectual Property Protection in International Trade' (1984) 7 *Boston College International & Comparative Law Review* 235.

Moya, Olga. 'Adopting an Environmental Justice Ethic' (1996) 5 *Dickinson Journal of Environmental Law and Policy* 215.

Mugabe, John *et al.* (eds). *Access to Genetic Resources – Strategies For Sharing Benefits* (Bonn: IUCN-ELC, 1997).

Mullany, Nicholas J. and Handford, Peter R. *Tort Liability for Psychiatric Damage: The Law of Nervous Shock* (Sydney: The Law Book Company Ltd., 1993).

Munzer, S.R. *A Theory of Property* (New York: Cambridge University Press, 1990).

_____ 'Kant and Property Rights in Body Parts' (1993) 6 *Canadian Journal of Law & Jurisprudence*. 319–41.

Murphy, Sean. 'Biotechnology and International Law' (2001) 42 *Harvard International Law Journal* 47.

Murray, J. 'Owning Genes: Disputes Involving DNA Sequence Patents' (1999) 75 *Chicago-Kent Law Review* 231.

Murray, T.H. *et al.* (eds). *Encyclopedia of Ethical, Legal, and Policy Issues in Biotechnology* (New York: John Wiley & Sons, Inc., 2000).

Myers, Norman. 'The Hamburger Connection: How Central America's Forests Become North America's Hamburgers' (1981) 10 *Ambio* 3–8.

Nanda, Ved. 'Genetically Modified Food and International Law – The Biosafety Protocol and Regulations in Europe' (2000) 28 *Denver Journal of International Law and Policy* 235.

Nanyenya-Takirambudde, Peter. *Technology Transfer and International Law* (New York: Praeger, 1980).

Narveson, J. *The Libertarian Idea* (Philadelphia: Temple University Press, 1988).

Nasir, K.J. 'Nervous Shock and Alcock: The Judicial Buck Stops Here' (1992) 55 *Modern Law Review* 705.

Nedelsky, J. 'Property in Potential Life? A Relational Approach to Choosing Legal Categories' (1993) 6 *Canadian Journal of Law & Jurisprudence*. 343.

Nelkin, D. 'A Brief History of the Political Work of Genetics' (2002) 42 *Jurimetrics Journal* 121.

Nelkin, D. and Andrews, L.B. 'Introduction: The Body, Economic Power and Social Control' (1999) 75 *Chicago-Kent Law Review* 3.

Neufeldt, V. (ed.). *Webster's New World Dictionary* (New York: Simon & Schuster, 1988).

Neumeyer, Frederik. 'Employees' Rights in their Inventions – A Comparison of National Laws' (1962) 44 *Journal of the Patent and Trademark Office Society* 674.

New Developments in Biotechnology (Congress of the United States, Office of Technology Assessment, 1987).

Newman, E.B. 'Earth's Vanishing Medicine Cabinet: Rain Forest Destruction and its Impact on the Pharmaceutical Industry' (1994) 20 *American Journal of Law and Medicine* 479.

Nichols, Philip. 'Corruption in the World Trade Organization: Discerning the Limits of the World Trade Organization's Authority' (1996) 28 *New York University Journal of International Law and Politics* 711.

Nickel, James. 'The Human Right to a Safe Environment: Philosophical Perspectives on its Scope and Justification' (1993) 18 *Yale Journal of International Law* 281.

Nickerson, Brian. 'The Environmental Laws of Zimbabwe: A Unique Approach to Management of the Environment' (1994) 14 *Boston College Third World Law Journal* 189.

Nijar, G.S. 'Community Intellectual Rights Protect Indigenous Knowledge' (1998) 36 *Biotechnology & Development Monitor* 601.

Nolan, R.C. 'Property in a Fund' (2004) *Law Quarterly Review* 109.

Nordle, J.A. *et al.* 'Identification of a Brazil-Nut Allergen in Transgenic Soybeans' (1996) 334 *New England Journal of Medicine* 688.

Nozick, R. *Anarchy, State and Utopia* (Oxford: Blackwell Publisher Ltd., 1974).

Nwabueze, Remigius N. 'Biotechnology and the New Property Regime in Human Bodies and Body Parts' (2002) 24 *Loyola L.A. International & Comparative Law Journal* 19.

_____ 'Spiritualising in the Godless Temple of Biotechnology: Ontological and Statutory Approaches to Dead Bodies in Nigeria, England, and the USA' (2002) *Manitoba Law Journal* 171.

_____ 'The Dynamics and Genius of Nigeria's Indigenous Legal Order' (2002) 1 *Indigenous Law Journal* 153.

_____ 'The Concept of Sepulchral Rights in Canada and the U.S. in the Age of Genomics: Hints from Iceland' (2005) 31 *Rutgers Computer and Technology Law Journal* 217.

O'Neill, Catherine and Sunstein, Cass. 'Economics and the Environment: Trading Debt and Technology for Nature' (1992) 17 *Columbia Journal of Environmental Law* 93.

Obi, S.N.C. *The Ibo Law of Property* (London: Butterworths, 1963).

Oczek, Jeremy. 'In the Aftermath of the "Terminator" Technology Controversy: Intellectual Property Protections for Genetically Engineered Seeds and the Right to Save and Replant Seed' (2000) 41 *Boston College Law Review* 627.

Oddi, A.S. 'The International Patent System and Third World Development: Reality or Myth?' (1987) 63 *Duke Law Journal* 831.

_____ 'Beyond Obviousness: Invention Protection in the Twenty-First Century' (1989) 38 *The American University Law Review* 1097.

_____ 'TRIPS – Natural Rights and a Polite Form of Economic Imperialism' (1996) 29 *Vanderbilt Journal of Transnational Law* 415.

_____ 'Un-Unified Theories of Patents – The Not-Quite-Holy Grail' (1996) 71 *Notre Dame Law Review* 267.

Odek, James. 'The Kenya Patent Law: Promoting Local Inventiveness or Protecting Foreign Patentees?' (1994) 38 *Journal of African Law* 96.

Odum, E.P. 'The Strategy of Ecosystem Development' (1969) 164 *Science* 262.

Oestigaard, Terje. 'Sacrifices of Raw, Cooked and Burnt Humans' (2000) 33 *Norwegian Archaeological Review* 41.

Ojwang, Jackton. 'Kenya's Place in International Environmental Law Initiative' (1993) 5 *African Journal of International and Comparative Law* 781.

Okonkwo, C.O. *Criminal Law In Nigeria*, 2nd edn (London: Sweet & Maxwell, 1980).

Okoro, N. *The Customary Laws of Succession in Eastern Nigeria and the Statutory and Judicial Rules Governing their Application* (London: Sweet & Maxwell, 1966).

Ollennu, N.A. *Principles of Customary Land Law in Ghana* (London: Sweet & Maxwell, 1962).

_____ 'The Changing Law and Law Reform in Ghana' (1971) 15 *Journal of African Law* 132.

On The Road to Brazil – The Earth Summit (Ottawa: National Roundtable on the Environment, 1991).

Onyejekwe, Kele. 'GATT Agriculture, and Developing Countries' (1993) 17 *Hamline Law Review* 77.

Orentlicher, D. 'The Alleged Distinction of Euthanasia and the Withdrawal of Life-Sustaining Treatment: Conceptually Incoherent and Impossible to Maintain' (1998) University of Illinois Law Review 837.

Organization of African Unity. *The New African Initiative: A Merger of the Millennium African Renaissance Partnership Programme (MAP) and the Omega Plan* (OAU Secretariat: OAU, 2000).

Orsinger, Victor. 'Natural Resources of Africa: Conservation by Legislation' (1971–72) 5 *African Law Studies* 29.

Osterborg, Lise. 'Patent Term a la Carte?' (1986) 17 *International Review of Industrial Property and Copyright Law* 60.

Overwalle, Geertrui. 'Patent Protection for Plants: A Comparison of American and European Approaches' (1999) 39 *IDEA* 143.

Palmer, L.I. 'Should Liability Play a Role in Social Control of Biobanks' (2005) 33 *Journal of Law, Medicine & Ethics* 70.

Panjabi, Ranee. 'The South and the Earth Summit: The Development/Environment Dichotomy' (1992) 11 *Dickinson Journal of International Law* 77.

_____ 'Can International Law Improve the Climate? An Analysis of the United Nations Framework Convention on Climate Change Signed at the Rio Summit in 1992' (1993) *North Carolina Journal of International Law and Commercial Regulation* 491.

_____ 'International Law and the Preservation of Species: An Analysis of the Convention on Biological Diversity Signed at the Rio Earth Summit in 1992' (1993) 11 *Dickinson Journal of International Law* 187.

_____ *The Earth Summit at Rio – Politics, Economics, and the Environment* (Boston: Northeastern University Press, 1997).

Pardo, A. *The Common Heritage: Selected Papers on Oceans and World Order 1967-1974* (Malta: Malta University Press, 1975).

Parel, A. and Flanagan, T. (eds). *Theories of Property: Aristotle to the Present* (Waterloo, ON.: Wilfrid Laurier University Press, 1979).

Parfett, J. 'Canada's DNA Databank: Public Safety and Private Costs' (2002) 29 *Manitoba Law Journal* 33.

Park, Julie. 'Pharmaceutical Patents in the Global Arena: Thailand's Struggle Between Progress and Protectionism' (1993) 13 *Boston College Third World Law Journal* 121.

Parry, J. 'Chinese City Outlaws Sale of Human Organs' (2003) 327 *British Medical Journal* 520.

Parsons, R.T. *Religion in an African Society* (Leiden: E.J. Brill, 1964).

Passmore, John. *Man's Responsibility for Nature: Ecological Problems and Western Traditions* (New York: C. Scribner's and Sons, 1974).

Paton-Simpson, E. 'Private Circles and Public Squares: Invasion of Privacy by the Publication of "Private Facts"' (1998) 61 *Modern Law Review* 318–.

Paul, E.F. *et al.* (eds). *Property Rights* (New York: Cambridge University Press, 1994).

Paul, James. 'The Human Right to Development: Its Meaning and Importance' (1992) 25 *The John Marshall Law Review* 235.

Pejovich, S. 'Towards An Economic Theory Of The Creation And Specification Of Property Rights' (1972) 30 *Review of Social Economy* 82.

Penner, J.E. 'The "Bundle of Rights" Picture of Property' (1996) 43 *UCLA Law Review* 711.

Pennock, J.R. and Chapman, J.W. (eds). *Property: Nomos XXII* (New York: New York University Press, 1980).

Penrose, Edith. *The Economics of the International Patent System* (Connecticut: Greenwood Press, 1974).

Perlman, Dan and Adelson, Glenn. *Biological Diversity: Exploring Values and Priorities in Conservation* (Massachusetts: Blackwell Inc, 1997).

Perry, C. 'Human Organs and the Open Market' (1980) 91 *Ethics* 63–71.

Perry, M.M. 'Fragmented Bodies, Legal Privilege, and Commodification in Science and Medicine' (1999) 51 *Maine Law Review* 169.

Persley, G.J. and MacIntyre, R. (eds). *Agricultural Biotechnology: Country Case Studies – A Decade of Development* (New York: CABI Publishing, 2002).

Philbrick, Francis S. 'Changing Conceptions of Property in Law' (1938) 86 University of Pennsylvania Law Review 691.

Philip, A. 'Protection of the Right to Property under the Canadian Charter of Rights and Freedoms' (1986) 18 *Ottawa Law Review* 55–81.

Phillipson, Gavin. 'Judicial Reasoning in Breach of Confidence Cases under the Human Rights Act: Not Taking Privacy Seriously' (2003) *European Human Rights Law Review* 53.

Phillipson, Gavin and Fenwick, Helen. 'Breach of Confidence as a Privacy Remedy in the Human Rights Act Era' (2000) 63 *Modern Law Review* 660.

Pickett, S.T.A. and Ostfeld, R.S. *et al.* (eds). *The Ecological Basis of Conservation: Heterogeneity, Ecosystems, and Biodiversity* (New York: Chapman & Hall, 1997).

Pimental, D. 'Overview of the Use of Genetically Modified Organisms and Pesticides in Agriculture' (2001) 9 *Indiana Journal of Global Legal Studies* 51.

Pizzini, F. 'The Medicalization of Women's Body' http://www.women.it/quarta/workshop/epistemological4/pizzini.htm.

Plant, Arnold. 'The Economic Theory Concerning Patents For Inventions' (1934) 1 *Economic* 67.

Posner, R.A. *Economic Analysis of Law* (Boston: Little, Brown & Co., 1986).

_____ 'Hegel and Employment at Will: A Comment' (1989) 10 *Cardozo Law Review* 1625.

Post, R. (ed.) *Law and the Order of Culture* (California: University of California Press, 1991).

Potts, Harold. 'The Definition of Invention in Patent Law' (1944) 7 *The Modern Law Review* 113.

Potts, J. 'At Least Give the Natives Glass Beads: An Examination of the Bargain Made Between Iceland and deCode Genetics with Implications for Global Bioprospecting' (2002) 7 *Virginia Journal of Law and Technology* 8.

Powell, J.A. 'New Property Disaggregated: A Model to Address Employment Discrimination' (1990) 24 *University of San Francisco Law Review* 363.

Powers, Michelle. 'The United Nations Framework Convention on Biological Diversity: Will Biodiversity Preservation be Enhanced through its Provisions Concerning Biotechnology Intellectual Property Rights?' (1993–94) 12 *Wisconsin International Law Journal* 110.

Prager, Frank. 'The Early Growth and Influence of Intellectual Property' (1952) 34 *Journal of the Patent Office Society* 106.

Prescott-Allen, Robert. *Genes From the Wild* (London: Earthscan, 1988).

Pritchard, Robert. 'The Future is Now – The Case for Patent Harmonization' (1995) 20 *North Carolina Journal of International Law and Commercial Regulation* 291.

Pritchard, Sarah (ed.). *Indigenous Peoples, the United Nations and Human Rights* (London: Zed Books Ltd., 1998).

Prosser, W.L. 'Privacy' (1960) 48 *California Law Review*. 383.

Proudhon, P.J. *What is Property? An Inquiry into the Principle of Right and of Government* (New York: Dover Publications, Inc., 1970, translated from French to English by B.R. Tucker).

Putter, A. (ed.). *Safeguarding the Genetic Basis of Africa's Traditional Crops* (The Netherlands: CTA, 1992).

Putterman, Daniel. 'Model Material Transfer Agreements for Equitable Biodiversity Prospecting' (1996) 7 *Colorado Journal of International Environmental Law and Policy* 149.

Qaim, M., *et al.* (eds). *Agricultural Biotechnology in Developing Countries: Towards Optimizing the Benefits for the Poor* (Dordrecht, The Netherlands: Kluwer Academic Publishers, 2000).

Queensland Law Reform Commission. *A Review of the Law in Relation to the Final Disposal of a Dead Body* (Queensland: Queensland Law Reform Commission, Working Paper No 58, 2004).

Qureshi, Asif. *The World Trade Organization – Implementing International Trade Norms* (Manchester: Manchester University Press, 1996).

Rackleff, Kathryn. 'Preservation of Biological Diversity: Toward a Global Convention' (1992) 3 *Colorado Journal of International Environmental Law and Policy* 405.

Radin, M. "A Restatement of Hohfeld"(1938) 51 *Harvard Law Review* 114.

_____ 'Property and Personhood' (1982) 34 *Stanford Law Review* 57.

_____ 'The Consequences of Conceptualism' (1986) 41 *University of Miami Law Review* 239.

_____ 'Market-Inalienability' (1987) 100 *Harvard Law Review* 1849.

_____ 'Reflections on Objectification' (1991) 65 *Southern California Law Review* 34.

_____ *Reinterpreting Property* (Chicago: The University of Chicago Press, 1993).

_____ *Contested Commodities* (Cambridge, Mass.: Harvard University Press, 1996).

Ragavan, S. 'Protection of Traditional Knowledge' (2001) 2 *Minnesota Intellectual Property Review* 1.

Rai, Kaur Arti. 'Regulating Scientific Research: Intellectual Property Rights and the Norms of Science' (1999) 94 *Northwestern University Law Review* 77.

Rajagopalan, R (ed.). *Common Heritage and the 21st Century* (Malta: International Ocean Institute, 1998).

Rao, R. 'Property, Privacy, and the Human Body' (2000) 80 *Boston University Law Review* 359.

Reeve, A. *Property* (London: Macmillan Education Ltd., 1986).

Reich, C.A. 'The New Property' (1964) 73 *Yale Law Journal* 733.

Reichman, J. H. 'Intellectual Property in International Trade: Opportunities and Risks of a GATT Connection' (1989) 22 *Vanderbilt Journal of Transnational Law* 747.

_____ 'Beyond the Historical Lines of Demarcation: Competition Law, Intellectual Property Rights, and International Trade After the Uruguay Round' (1993) 20 *Brooklyn Journal of International Law* 75.

_____ 'Charting the Collapse of the Patent-Copyright Dichotomy: Premises for a Restructured International Intellectual Property System' (1994) 13 *Cardozo Arts & Entertainment Law Journal* 475.

_____ 'From Free Riders to Fair Followers: Global Competition Under the TRIPS Agreement' (1996–97) 29 *International Law and Politics* 11.

_____ 'The TRIPS Agreement Comes of Age: Conflict or Cooperation With the Developing Countries' (2000) 32 *Case Western Reserve Journal of International Law* 441.

Reid, Walter and Miller, Kenton. *Keeping Options Alive: The Scientific Basis for Conserving Biodiversity* (Washington: World Resources Institute, 1989).

Reid, Walter *et al.* (eds). *Biodiversity Prospecting: Using Genetic Resources for Sustainable Development* (Washington: WRI, 1993).

Renier, Victor. 'Vegetable Novelties and Inventor's Rights' (1960) (Belgium) *Annals of Law and Political Science* 253.

Renton, Wood. 'Patent Right in England and the United States' (1891) 26 *The Law Quarterly Review* 150.

Repetto, Robert (ed.). *The Global Possible* (New Haven: Yale University Press, 1985).

Resnik, D.B. 'DNA Patents and Human Dignity' (2001) 29 *Journal of Law, Medicine & Ethics* 152.

Richardson, Benjamin. 'Environmental Law in Post-Colonial Societies: Straddling the Local-Global Institutional Spectrum' (2000) 11 *Colorado Journal of International Environmental Law and Policy* 1.

_____ 'Indigenous Peoples, International Law and Sustainability' (2001) 10 *Review of European Community & International Environmental Law* 1.

Richardson, J.E. 'Private Property Rights in the Air Space at Common Law' (1953) 31 *Canadian Bar Review* 117.

Riding In, J. 'Without Ethics and Morality: A Historical Overview of Imperial Archaeology and American Indians' (1992) 24 *Arizona State Law Journal* 11.

Riley, Angela. 'Recovering Collectivity: Group Rights to Intellectual Property in Indigenous Communities' (2000) 18 *Cardozo Arts & Entertainment Law Journal* 175.

Ringel, Andrew. 'The Population Policy Debate and the World Bank: Finity v. Supply-Side Demographics' (1993) 6 *Georgetown International Environmental Law Review* 213.

Ritchie, Mark and Dawkins, Kristin. 'WTO Food and Agricultural Rules: Sustainable Agriculture and the Human Right to Food' (2000) 9 *Minnesota Journal of Global Trade* 9.

Ritchie, Mark *et al.* 'Intellectual Property Rights and Biodiversity: The Industrialization of Natural Resources and Traditional Knowledge' (1996) 11 *St. John's Journal of Legal Comment* 431.

Roadhouse, W.M. 'The Problem of the Professional Spouse: Should an Educational Degree Earned During Marriage Constitute Property in Arizona?' (1982) 24 *Arizona Law Review* 963.

Roberts, Colin. 'Human Tissue Act 2004 and Medical Microbiology' (2004) 126 *Royal College of Pathology Bulletin* 23.

Roberts, Dorothy. 'The Nature of Black's Skepticism About Genetic Testing' (1997) 27 *Seton Hall Law Review* 971.

Roberts, Paul. 'International Funding for the Conservation of Biological Diversity: Convention on Biological Diversity' (1992) 10 *Boston University International Law Journal* 303.

Roberts, T. 'Broad Claims for Biotechnological Inventions' (1994) 9 *European Intellectual Property Review* 373.

Robertson, D.W. 'Liability in Negligence for Nervous Shock' (1994) 57 *Modern Law Review* 649.

Robinson, N. (ed.) *Agenda 21: Earth's Action Plan* (New York: Oceana, 1993).

Robinson, R.E., Coval, S.C. and Smith, J.C. 'The Logic of Rights' (1983) 33 *University of Toronto Law Journal* 267.

Roche, P., Glantz, L. and Annas, G. 'The Genetic Privacy Act: A Proposal for National Legislation' (1996) 31 *Jurimetrics* 1.

Rogers, H.J. and Parkes, H.C. 'Transgenic Plants and the Environment' (1995) 46 *Journal of Experimental Botany* 467.

Rogers, Kathleen and Moore, James. 'Revitalizing the Convention on Nature Protection and Wild Life Preservation in the Western Hemisphere' (1995) 36 *Harvard International Law Journal* 465.

Rogers, W.H.V. *Winfield and Jolowicz on Tort*, 16th edn (London: Sweet & Maxwell, 2002).

Rohrbacher, Dana and Crilly, Paul. 'The Case for a Strong Patent System' (1995) 8 *Harvard Journal of Law and Technology* 263.

Roht-Arriaza, Naomi. 'Of Seeds and Shamans: The Appropriateness of the Scientific and Technical Knowledge of Indigenous and Local Communities' (1996) 17 *Michigan Journal of International Law* 940.

Rolston, Holmes III. 'Rights and Responsibilities on the Home Planet' (1993) 18 *Yale Journal of International Law* 251.

Roscoe, L.A. *et al*. 'Dr Jack Kevorkian and Cases of Euthanasia in Oakland County, Michigan, 1990-1998' (2000) 343 *New England Journal of Medicine* 1735.

Rose, C. 'The Comedy of the Commons: Custom, Commerce, and Inherently Public Property' (1986) 53 *University of Chicago Law Review* 720.

Rose, C.M. 'Possession as the Origin of Property' (1985) 52 *University of Chicago Law Review* 73.

_____ 'Canons of Property Talk, or, Blackstone's Anxiety' (1998) 108 *Yale Law Journal* 601.

Rose, Gerald. 'Do you Have a "Printed Publication?" If not, Do you Have Evidence of Prior "Knowledge or Use"?' (1979) 61 *Journal of Patents and Trademark Office Society* 643.

Rose, H. *The Commodification of Bioinformation: The Icelandic Health Sector Database* (London: The Wellcome Trust, 2001).

Rosen, Dan. 'A Common Law for the Ages of Intellectual Property' (1984) 38 *University of Miami Law Review* 769.

Rosenblatt, David. 'The Regulation of Recombinant DNA Research: The Alternative of Local Control' (1982) 10 *Boston College Environmental Affairs* 37.

Ross, T. 'The Rhetorical Tapestry of Race: White Innocence and Black Abstraction' (1990) 32 *William & Mary Law Review* 1.

Rossman, Joseph. 'Plant Patents' (1931) 13 *Journal of Patent Office Society* 7.

Rothman, D.J. 'Ethical and Social Consequences of Selling a Kidney' (2002) 288 *Journal of American Medical Association* 1640–41.

Rothschild, D. and Wiser, G. *U.S. Patent Office Admits Error, Rejects Patent on Sacred Ayahausca* (Center for International Environmental Law, 2002).

Rothschild, Steven and White, Thomas. 'Printed Publication: What is it Now?' (1988) 70 *Journal of Patents and Trademark Office Society* 42.

Rothstein, M.A. (ed.). *Genetic Secrets* (New Haven: Yale University Press, 1997).

Rowat, Malcolm. 'An Assessment of Intellectual Property Protection in LDCs from Both a Legal and Economic Perspective – Case Studies of Mexico, Chile and Argentina' (1993) 21 *Denver Journal of International Law and Policy* 401.

Roy, R. Carl. 'The History of the Patent Harmonization Treaty: Economic Self-interest as an Influence' (1993) 26 *John Marshall Law Review* 457.

Royal College of Physicians of Edinburgh. *Comments on DOH: The Removal, Retention and Use of Human Organs and Tissue; the Law in England and Wales* (www.rcpe.uk/news/consultation_docs/removal_human_organs.html).

Royal Commission on New Reproductive Technologies. *Reproductive Technology: A Property Law Analysis* (Ottawa: Research Branch of the Library of Parliament, 1992).

Royer, Matthew. 'Halting Neotropical Deforestation: Do the Forest Principles Have What it Takes?' (1996) 6 *Duke Environmental Law and Policy Forum* 105.

Rubin, Seymour. 'Economic and Social Human Rights and the New International Economic Order' (1986) 1 *American University Journal of International Law and Policy* 67.

Rudden, Bernard. 'Things as Things and Things as Wealth' (1994) 14 *Oxford Journal of Legal Studies* 81.

Ruhl, J.B. 'Sustainable Development: A Five Dimensional Algorithm for Environmental Law' (1999) 18 *Stanford Environmental Law Journal* 31.

Ruiz, Manuel. 'The Andean Community's New Industrial Regime: Creating Synergies Between the CBD and Intellectual Property Rights' (2000) *Bridges* 12.

Russell, B. *A History of Western Philosophy* (London: Unwin Paperbacks, 1946).

Russell, Clifford. 'Two Propositions About Biodiversity' (1995) 28 *Vanderbilt Journal of Transnational Law* 689.

Ruth, Chadwick. 'The Icelandic Database – Do Modern Times Need Modern Sagas?' (1999) 319 *British Medical Journal* 441.

Ruttan, V.W. 'Biotechnology and Agriculture: A Skeptical Perspective' (1999) 2 *AgBioForum* 54.

Ryan, A. *Property and Political Theory* (Oxford: Basil Blackwell Publisher Ltd., 1984).

Sagoe, Ekua. 'Industrial Property Law in Nigeria' (1992) 14 *The Comparative Law Yearbook of International Business* 312.

Sagoff, M. 'Biotechnology and Agriculture: The Common Wisdom and Its Critics,' (2001) 9 *Indiana Journal of Global Legal Studies* 13.

Saigo, Holly. 'Agricultural Biotechnology and the Negotiation of the Biosafety Protocol' (2000) 12 The *Georgetown International Environmental Law Review* 779.

Salzman, James. 'Valuing Ecosystem Services' (1997) 24 *Ecology Law Quarterly* 887.

Samuels, A. 'Whose Body is it Anyway?' (1999) 39 *Medical Science Law* 285.

———— 'The Doctor, the Patient, and Easing the Passing: the Law' (2000) 68 *Medico-Legal Journal* 38.

Sanders, Barkev. 'The Economic Impact of Patents' (1958) 2 *Patents, Trademark, Copyright Journal of Research & Education* 340.

Sanders, J. 'Justice and the Initial Acquisition of Private Property' (1987) 10 *Harvard Journal of Law & Public Policy* 377.

Sandoval, Rodolpho and Leung, Chung-Pok. 'A Comparative Analysis of Intellectual Property Law in the United States and Mexico, and the Free Trade Agreement' (1993) 17 *Maryland Journal of International Law and Trade* 145.

Sands, Philippe. 'International Law in the Field of Sustainable Development' (1994) 55 *British Yearbook of International Law* 303.

Sanwal, Mukul. 'Sustainable Development, the Rio Declaration and Multilateral Cooperation' (1993) 4 *Colorado Journal of International Environmental Law and Policy* 45.

Sanzo, Michael. 'Patenting Biotherapeutics' (1991) 20 *Hofstra Law Review* 387.

Sarkar, R. 'The Developing World in the New Millenium: International Finance, Development, and Beyond' (2001) 34 *Vanderbilt Journal of Transnational Law* 469.

Sarma, Lakshmi. 'Biopiracy: Twentieth Century Imperialism in the Form of International Agreements' (1999) 13 *Temple International and Comparative Law Journal* 107.

Sawyerr, Akilagpa. 'Marginalisation of Africa and Human Development' (1993) 5 *African Journal of International and Comparative Law* 176.

Sax, J.L. 'Liberating the Public Trust Doctrine From Its Historical Shackles' (1980) 14 *University of California at Davis Law Review* 185.

Scalise, David and Nugent, Daniel. 'International Intellectual Property Protections for Living Matter: Biotechnology, Multinational Conventions and the Exception for Agriculture' (1995) 27 *Case Western Reserve Journal of International Law* 83.

Scarmon, M.H. 'Brotherton v. Cleveland: Property Rights in the Human Body – Are the Goods Oft Interred with their Bones?' (1992) 37 *South Dakota Law Review* 429.

Schalatter, R. *Private Property; The History of an Idea* (London: George Allen & Unwin Ltd., 1951).

Schiff, Eric. *Industrialization Without National Patents – The Netherlands, 1869-1912, Switzerland, 1850-1907* (New Jersey: Princeton University Press, 1971).

Schmid, A.A. *Property, Power, and Public Choice: An Inquiry into Law and Economics* (New York: Praeger, 1978).

Schrecker, Ted and Wellington, Alex. *Patenting Of Biotechnological Innovations Concerning Animals and Human Beings* (Ottawa: Canadian Biotechnology Advisory Committee, 1999).

Schreurs, Miranda and Economy, Elizabeth (eds). *The Internationalization of Environmental Protection* (Cambridge: Cambridge University Press, 1997).

Schrijver, Nico. *Sovereignty Over Natural Resources: Balancing Rights and Duties* (Cambridge: Cambridge University Press, 1997).

Schroeder, J.L. 'Chix Nix Bundle-o-Stix: A Feminist Crtique of the Disaggregation of Property' (1994) 93 *Michigan Law Review* 239.

_____ 'Three's a Crowd: a Feminist Critique of Calabresi and Melamed's One View of the Cathedral' (1999) 84 *Cornell Law Review* 394.

Schultz, D. 'Political Theory and Legal History: Conflicting Depictions of Property in the American Political Founding' (1993) 37 *American Journal of Legal History* 464.

Schuyler, G.W. *Hunger in a Land of Plenty* (Massachusetts: Schenkman Publishing Co. Inc., 1980).

Sease, Edmund. 'From Microbes, to Corn Seeds, To Oysters, To Mice: Patentability of New Life Forms' (1989) 38 *Drake Law Review* 551.

Seay, Nicholas. 'Protecting the Seeds of Innovation: Patenting Plants' (1988–89) 16 *American Intellectual Property Association Quarterly Journal* 418.

Sen, Amartya. *Poverty and Famine: An Essay on Entitlement and Deprivation* (Oxford: Clarendon, 1981).

_____ *The Standard of Living* (Cambridge: Cambridge University Press, 1987).

_____ *The Political Economy of Hunger* (Oxford: Oxford University Press, 1990).

_____ 'Population: Delusion and Reality' (1994) 41 *New York Review of Books* 62.

_____ *Development as Freedom* (New York: Anchor Books, 1999).

Senituli, L. and Boyes, M. *Whose DNA? Tonga and Iceland, Biotech, Ownership and Consent* (Adelaide: Australasian Bioethics Association Annual Conference, 2002).

Sherwin, Emily. 'Two- and Three-Dimensional Property Rights' (1997) 29 *Arizona State Law Journal* 1074.

Sherwood, Robert. *Intellectual Property and Economic Development* (Boulder, Colorado: Westview Press, 1990).

_____ 'The TRIPS Agreement: Implications for Developing Countries' (1996–97) 37 *The Journal of Law and Technology* 491.

_____ 'Human Creativity for Economic Development: Patents Propel Technology' (2000) 33 *Akron Law Review* 1.

Sherwood, Robert *et al.* 'Promotion of Inventiveness in Developing Countries Through a More Advanced Patent Administration' (1999) 39 *IDEA* 473.

Shine, C. and Kohona, P.T.B. 'The Convention on Biological Diversity: Bridging the Gap Between Conservation and Development' (1992) I *Review of European Community and International Environmental Law* 3.

Shiva, V. *Staying Alive – Women, Ecology and Development* (London: Zed Books Ltd., 1988).

_____ *The Violence of the Green Revolution* (London: Zed Books Ltd, 1991).

_____ *Monocultures of the Mind – Perspectives on Biodiversity and Biotechnology* (New Jersey: Zed Books Ltd, 1993).

_____ *Biopiracy: The Plunder of Nature and Knowledge* (Toronto: Between the Lines, 1997).

Shiva, Vandana (ed.). *Biodiversity Conservation: Whose Resource? Whose Knowledge?* (New Delhi: India National Trust for Art & Cultural Heritage, 1995).

Shraga, D. 'The Common Heritage of Mankind: The Concept and its Application' (1986) 15 *Annales D'Etudes Internationales* 45.

Shulman, S. *Owning the Future* (Boston: Houghton Mifflin Co., 1999).

Shultz, Marjorie M. 'From Informed Consent to Patient's Choice: A New Protected Interest' (1985) 95 *Yale Law Journal* 219.

Shultz, S.M. *Body Snatching: The Robbing of Graves for the Education of Physicians* (North Carolina: McFarland & Co., 1992).

Shutkin, William. 'International Human Rights Law and the Earth: The Protection of Indigenous Peoples and the Environment' (1991) 31 *Virginia Journal of International Law* 479.

Sibley, Mulford. 'The Relevance of Classical Political Theory for Economy, Technology and Ecology' (1973–74) 3 *Alternatives: Perspectives on Society and Environment* 14.

Siegel-Itzkovich, J. 'Sale of Organs to be Investigated' (2001) 322 *British Medical Journal* 128.

_____ 'Israeli Women Can Buy Ova From Abroad' (2002) 324 *British Medical Journal* 69.

Silverman, H.W. and Evans, J.D. 'Aeronautical Noise in Canada' (1972) 10 *Osgoode Hall Law Journal* 607.

Simmonds, Norman. *Principles of Crop Improvement* (New York: Longman, 1979).

Simmons, A.J. *The Lockean Theory of Rights* (Princeton: Princeton University Press, 1992).

Singer, J.W. 'The Reliance Interest in Property' (1988) 40 *Stanford Law Review* 614.

Singer, Joseph and Beerman, Jack. 'The Social Origins of Property' (1993) 6 *Canadian Journal of Law and Jurisprudence* 217.

Singer, P.A. and Daar, A.S. 'Avoiding Frankendrugs' (2000) 18(12) *Nature Biotechnology* 1225.

Singer, Romuald. 'The European Patent Enters a New Phase' (1970) 1 *International Review of Industrial Property and Copyright Law* 19.

Singh, Rana. (ed.). *Environmental Ethics – Discourses, and Cultural Traditions* (Varanasa: The National Geographical Society of India, 1993).

Sinha, Rajiv. *Ethnobotany – The Renaissance of Traditional Herbal Medicine* (Jaipur, India: Ina Shree Publishers, 1996).

Skegg, P.D.G. 'Human Corpses, Medical Specimens and the Law of Property' (1975) 4 *Anglo-American Law Review* 412.

_____ 'The No-Property Rule and Rights Relating to Dead Bodies' (1997) 5 *Tort Law Review* 222.

Skene, L. 'Patients' Rights or Family Responsibilities? Two Approaches to Genetic Testing' (1998) 6 *Medical Law Review*. 1.

_____ 'Genetic Secrets and the Family: a Response to Bell and Bennett' (2001) 9 *Medical Law Review* 162.

_____ 'Sale of DNA of People of Tonga' (2001) 1 *Genetic Law Monitor* 7.

_____ 'Proprietary Rights in Human Bodies, Body Parts and Tissue: Regulatory Contexts and Proposals for New Laws' (2002) 22 *Legal Studies* 102.

Sklan, Mark. 'African Patent Statutes and Technology Transfer' (1978) 10 *Case Western Reserve Journal of International Law* 55.

Slater, David. 'Contesting Occidental Visions of the Global: The Geopolitics of Theory and North-South Relations' (1994) (December) *Beyond Law* 97.

Slind-Flor, Victoria. 'Plants Protected by Patents: Federal Circuit's Ruling Clarifies Confusion in the Law' (2000) (January) *The National Law Journal* 1.

Smith, Carrie. 'Patenting Life: The Potential and Pitfalls of Using the WTO to Globalize Intellectual Property Rights' (2000) 26 *North Carolina Journal of Law and Commercial Regulation* 143.

Smith, J.C. 'A Comment on Moor's Case' (2000) *Criminal Law Review* 41.

Smith, M.J. 'Population-Based Genetic Studies: Informed Consent and Confidentiality' (2001) 18 *Santa Clara Computer & High Technology Law Journal* 57.

Sneiderman, B. 'A Do Not Resuscitate Order for an Infant Against Parental Wishes: a Comment on the Case of Child and Family Services of Central Manitoba v. R.L. & L.H.' (1999) 7 *Health Law Journal* 205.

_____ 'The Case of Robert Latimer: a Commentary on Crime and Punishment' (1999) 37 *Alberta Law Review* 1017.

Sneiderman, B. and Verhoef, M. 'Patient Autonomy and the Defence of Medical Necessity: Five Dutch Euthanasia Cases' (1996) 34 *Alberta Law Review* 374.

Solow, Andrew and Broadus, James. 'Issues in the Measurement of Biological Diversity' (1995) 28 *Vanderbilt Journal of Transnational Law* 695.

Soule, Michael (ed.). *Conservation Biology: The Science of Scarcity and Diversity* (Massachussetts: Sinauer Associates, Inc, 1986).

Spaulding, Norman III. 'Commodification and its Discontents: Environmentalism and the Promise of Market Incentives' (1997) 16 *Stanford Environmental Law Journal* 293.

Spence, Michael. 'Patents and Biotechnology' (1997) 113 *Law Quarterly Review* 45.

Spindler, K.A. 'Current Patent Protection Granted for Genetically Modified Organisms under the European Patent Convention and the Scandal of EP 0695351' (2001) *Santa Clara Computer & High Technology Law Journal* 95.

Stanley, Autumn. *Mothers And Daughters of Inventions* (New Jersey: Rutgers, 1993)
Staples, Sarah. 'Human Resource: Newfoundland's 300-year-old Genetic Legacy has Triggered a Gold Rush' (2000) 17 *Business Magazine* 117.

Stark, W. (ed.). *Jeremy Bentham's Economic Writings* vol.1 (London: Allen and Unwin, 1952).

Starr, June and Hardy, Kenneth. 'Not By Seeds Alone: The Biodiversity Treaty and the Role for Native Agriculture' (1993) 12 *Stanford Environmental Law Journal* 85.

Steck, Henry. 'Power and the Liberation of Nature: The Politics of Ecology' (1971) 2 *Alternatives: Perspectives on Society and Environment* 4.

Stedman, John. 'The Employed Inventor, the Public Interest, and Horse and Buggy Law in the Space Age' (1970) 45 *New York University Law Review* 1.

Steinfeld, R.J. 'Property and Suffrage in the Early American Republic' (1989) 41 *Stanford Law Review* 335.

Stenson, Anthony and Gray, Tim. *The Politics of Genetic Resource Control* (London: Macmillan Press, 1999).

Stephen, J. *A Digest of the Criminal Law* (London: Sweet and Maxwell, 1926).

Stephen, W. 'The Law Relating to Dealing With Dead Bodies' (2000) 4 *Medical Law International* 145.

Stern, R.H. 'The Bundle of Rights Suited to New Technology' (1986) 47 *University of Pittsburgh Law Review* 1229.

Stevens, Henry Bailey. *The Recovery of Culture* (New York: Harper & Brothers Publishers, 1949).

Stewart, Terence (ed.). *The GATT Uruguay Round – A Negotiating History* (1986–1992) Vols. 1 & 2 (Boston: Kluwer Law and Taxation Publishers, 1993).

Stiller, C.R. and Abbot, C. 'What Will Increase the Number of Organs for Transplantation? Some Strategies to Consider' (1994) 150 *Canadian Medical Association Journal* 1401.

Stoljar, S. 'Unjust Enrichment and Unjust Sacrifice' (1987) *Modern Law Review* 603.

Stone, C.D. 'Should Trees Have Standing? – Toward Legal Rights for Natural Objects' (1972) 45 *Southern California Law Review* 450.

Strahan, J.A. *Law of Property* (London: Stevens and Sons Ltd., 1901).

Strong, Maurice. 'Beyond Rio: Prospects and Portents' (1993) 4 *Colorado Journal of International Environmental Law and Policy* 21.

Sun, Lin (ed.). *UNEP's New Way Forward: Environmental Law and Sustainable Development* (Nairobi: UNDP, 1995).

Sutherland, Johanna. 'Representations of Indigenous Peoples' Knowledge and Practice in Modern International Law and Politics' (1995) 2 *Australian Journal of Human Rights* 20.

Swaminathan, M.S. 'Farmers' Rights and Plant Genetic Resources' (1998) 36 *Biotechnology & Development Monitor* 544.

Swan, Kenneth. 'Patent Rights in an Employee's Invention' (1959) 75 *The Law Quarterly Review* 77.

Swanson, Timothy (ed.). *The Economics of Biodiversity and Ecology Decline: The Forces Driving Global Change* (Cambridge: Cambridge University Press, 1995).

_____ *Intellectual Property Rights and Biodiversity Conservation: An Interdisciplinary Analysis of the Values of Medicinal Plants* (Cambridge: Cambridge University Press, 1995).

Swartz, B. 'Property – Nature of Rights in Dead Bodies – Right of Burial' (1939) Southern California Law Review 435.

Swayze, F.J. 'The Growing Law' (1915) 25 *Yale Law Journal* 1.

Sweet J. M. 'BRCA1 and the Onset of Disability at the Age of Majority' (1995) 17 *Hamline Journal of Public Law & Policy* 41.

Taft, W.H. 'The Right of Private Property' (1894) 3 *Michigan Law Journal* 215.

Takacs, David. *The Idea of Biodiversity – Philosophies of Paradise* (Baltimore: The Johns Hopkins University Press, 1996).

Takenaka, Toshiko. 'Does a Cultural Barrier to Intellectual Property Trade Exist? The Japanese Example' (1996–97) 29 *International Law and Politics* 153.

Takirambudde, P.N. (ed.). *The Individual Under African Law* (Swaziland: Swaziland Printing and Publishing Co., 1982).

Tallerico, C.A. 'The Autonomy of the Human Body in the Age of Biotechnology' (1990) 61 University of Colorado Law Review 659.

Tansey, G. *Food Security, Biotechnology and Intellectual Property: Unpacking Some Issues Around TRIPS* (Geneva: Quaker United Nations Office, 2002).

Tapp, Richard and Posek, Richard. 'Benefits and Costs of Intellectual Property Protection in Developing Countries' (1990) 24 *Journal of World Trade* 75.

Taylor, C.A. and Silberston, Z.A. *The Economic Impact of the Patent System – A Study of the British Experience* (Cambridge: Cambridge University Press, 1973).

Tejera, Valentina. 'Tripping over Property Rights: Is it Possible to Reconcile the Convention on Biological Diversity with Article 27 of the TRIPS Agreement?' (1999) 33 *New England Law Review* 976.

Temples, P. *Bantu Philosophy* (Paris: Presence Africaine, 1959).

Ten Have, H. *et al.* (eds). *Ownership of the Human Body: Philosophical Considerations on the Use of the Human Body and its Parts in Healthcare* (Dordrecht: Kluwer Academic Publishers, 1998).

Ten Kate, Kerry and Laird, Sarah. *The Commercial Use of Biodiversity: Access to Genetic Resources and Benefit Sharing* (London: Earthscan Publications Ltd, 1999).

The Crucible Group *People, Plants, and Patents: The Impact of Intellectual Property on Biodiversity, Conservation, Trade, and Rural Society* (Ottawa: International Development Research Center, 1994).

_____ Vol. I. *Seeding Solutions: People, Plants, and Patents Revisited* (Ottawa: IDRC, 2000).

_____ Vol. II. *Seeding Solutions: Options for National Laws Governing Access to and Control Over Genetic Resources* (pre-publication version – not for quotation) (Ottawa: IDRC, 2001).

The TRIPs Agreement and Developing Countries (UNCTAD: United Nations, New York and Geneva, 1996).

Thomas, C.M. *Should the Law Allow Sentiment to Triumph Over Science? The Retention of Body Parts* (Auckland: Massey University School of Accountancy Discussion Paper Series 210, 2002).

Thomas, John. 'Litigation Beyond the Technological Frontier: Comparative Approaches to Multinational Patent Enforcement' (1996) 27 *Law and Policy in International Business* 1.

Thomas, W.L. (ed.). *Man's Role in Changing the Face of the Earth* (Chicago: University of Chicago Press, 1956).

Thompson, Amy Guerin. 'An Untapped Resource in Addressing Emerging Infectious Diseases: Traditional Healers' (1998) 6 *Indiana Journal of Global Legal Studies* 257.

Thompson, Patricia. 'Philippines Indigenous Peoples Rights Act' (1998) *Human Rights and the Environment* 3.

Thompson, Paul. 'Globalization, Losers, and Property Rights' (2000) 9 *Minnesota Journal of Global Trade* 602.

Thomson, E.J. 'Ethical, Legal and Social Implications of the Human Genome Project' (1994) 3 *Dickinson Journal of Environmental Law and Policy* 55.

Thomson, J.J. 'Property Acquisition' (1976) 73 *Journal of Philosophy* 664.

Thomson, J.J. *The Realm of Rights* (Cambridge, MA: Harvard University Press, 1990).

Thurow, L. 'Globalization: The Product of a Knowledge-Based Economy' (2000) 570 *The Annals* 19.

Tiefenbrun, Susan. 'Piracy of Intellectual Property in China and the Former Soviet Union and its Effects Upon International Trade: A Comparison' (1998) 46 *Buffalo Law Review* 1.

Tierney, P. *Darkness in El Dorado: How Scientists and Journalists Devastated the Amazon* (New York: W.W. Norton & Co., 2000).

Tillford, David. 'Saving the Blue Prints: The International Regime for Plant Resources' (1998) 30 *Case Western Reserve Journal of International Law* 373.

Tilmann, D.T. 'German Prosecutor Investigates the Removal of Dead Babies' Organs' (2000) 320 *British Medical Journal* 77.

Tinker, Catherine. 'Introduction to Biological Diversity: Law, Institutions, and Science' (1994) 1 *Buffalo Journal of International Law* 1.

―――― 'Responsibility for Biological Diversity Conservation under International Law' (1995) 28 *Vanderbilt Journal of Transnational Law* 777.

Tjahjadi, Riza. *Nature and Farming* (Jakarta: Pan Indonesia, 1993).

Tobin, Brendan. 'Redefining Perspectives in the Search for Protection of Traditional Knowledge: A Case Study from Peru' (2001) 10 *Review of European Community & International Environmental Law* 27.

Tokarczysk, Roman. 'Biojurisprudence: A Current in Jurisprudence' (1996) 7 *Finnish Yearbook of International Law* 341.

Tomasevski, Katarina (ed.). *The Right to Food – Guide Through Applicable International Law* (Dordrecht: Martinus Nijhuff Publishers, 1987).

Torres, Raidza. 'The Rights of Indigenous Populations: The Emerging International Norm' (1991) 16 *Yale Journal of International Law* 127.

Trope, J.F. and Echo-Hawk, W.R. '*The Native American Graves Protection and Repatriation Act*: Background and Legislative History' (1992) 24 *Arizona State Law Journal* 35.

Tuck, R. *Natural Rights Theories – Their Origin and Development* (Cambridge: Cambridge University Press, 1979).

Turpel, Mary Ellen. 'Indigenous Peoples' Right of Political Participation and Self-Determination: Recent International Legal Developments and the Continuing Struggle for Recognition' (1992) 25 *Cornell International Law Journal* 579.

Tweeten, L.G. and McClelland, D.G. (eds). *Promoting Third-World Development and Food Security* (Connecticut: Praeger Publishers, 1997).

Twining, William. 'Globalization and Legal Theory – Some Local Implications' (1996) 49 *Current Legal Problems* 1.

Underkuffler, L.S. 'On Property: An Essay' (1990) 100 *Yale Law Journal* 127.

University of California, Santa Barbara. *Preliminary Report on the Neel/Chagnon Allegations* (Santa Barbara: UCSB, Department of Anthropology, 2001).

Vacchiano, Emanuel. 'It's a Wonderful Genome: The Written-Description Requirement Protects the Human Genome from Overly Broad Patents' (1999) 32 *The John Marshall Law Review* 805.

Van Der Zoon, Ton (ed.). *Biological Diversity* (The Hague: The Netherlands, 1995).

Van Diest, P. and Savulescu, J. 'For and Against: No Consent Should be Needed for Using Leftover Body Material for Scientific Purposes' (2002) 325 *British Medical Journal* 648.

Vanaskie, Thomas. 'The European Patent Conventions: State Sovereignty Surrendered to Establish a Supranational Patent' (1977) 1 *A.S.I.L.S. International Law Journal* 73.

Vandevelde, K.J. 'The New Property of the Nineteenth Century: The Development of the Modern Concept of Property' (1980) 29 *Buffalo Law Review* 325.

Vaver, Donald. 'Intellectual Property Today: Of Myths and Paradoxes' (1990) 69 *Canadian Bar Review* 98.

Vaver, D. *Intellectual Property Law* (Concord, ON.: Irwin Law, 1997).

Vavilov, Nikolai. 'Studies on the Origin of Cultivated Plants' (1925) 16 #2 *Bulletin of Applied and Plant Breeding* 1–248.

Vedaram, S. 'The New Indian Patents Law' (1972) 3 *International Review of Industrial Property and Copyright Law* 39.

Venne, Sharon Helen. *Our Elders Understand Our Rights: Evolving International Law Regarding Indigenous Rights* (Penticton, British Columbia: Theytus Books Ltd, 1998).

Vice, Daniel. 'Implementation of Biodiversity Treaties: Monitoring, Fact-Finding, and Dispute Resolution' (1997) 29 *International Law and Politics* 577.

Virgo, G. *The Principles of the Law of Restitution*, 2nd edn (Oxford: Oxford University Press, 2006).

Vogt, R. *Whose Property? The Deepening Conflict Between Private Property and Democracy in Canada* (Toronto: University of Toronto Press, 1999).

Vosti, Stephen and Thomas, Reardon (eds). *Sustainability, Growth and Poverty Allevaition – A Policy and Agroecological Perspective* (Baltimore: The Johns Hopkins University Press, 1997).

Vukmir, Mladen. 'The Roots of Anglo-American Intellectual Property Law in Roman Law' (1991) 32 *IDEA* 123.

Waldbaum, J. 'DNA Databanks in Massachusetts: Will the Declaration of Rights Provide the Nation's First Successful Constitutional Challenge?' (1999) 3 *Journal of Law and Social Challenges* 179.

Walder, Andrew. 'Harmonization: Myth and Ceremony: A Comment' (1994) 13 *Pacific Basin Law Journal* 163.

Waldron, J. 'Enough and as Good Left for Others' (1976) 29 *Philosophical Quarterly* 319.

_____ 'What is Private Property?' (1985) 5 *Oxford Journal of Legal Studies* 313.

_____ 'Property, Justification and Need' (1993) 2 *Canadian Journal of Law and Jurisprudence* 185.

Walker, William. 'Uruguay Round TRIPS: A Bibliographic Essay' (1989) 22 *Vanderbilt Journal of Transnational Law* 911.

Wallerstein, M.B. *et al.* (eds). *Global Dimensions of Intellectual Property Rights in Science and Technology* (Washington, D.C.: National Academy Press, 1993).

Ward, Barbara. *The Rich Nations and the Poor Nations* (Toronto: Canadian Broadcasting Corporation, 1961).

_____ 'Man or Beast: The Convention on Biological Diversity and the Emerging Law of Sustainable Development' (1995) 28 *Vanderbilt Journal of Transnational Law* 823.

Warren, D.M. *et al.* (eds). *The Cultural Dimensions of Development: Indigenous Knowledge Systems* (London: Intermediate Technology Publications, 1995).

Warren, S.D. and Brandeis, L.D. 'The Right to Privacy' (1890) 4 *Harvard Law Review* 193.

Watkins, Melville. 'North-South Relations' (1975) 5 *Alternatives: Perspectives on Society and Environment* 33.

Watson, A. *Legal Transplants: An Approach to Comparative Law* (Athens: The University of Georgia Press, 1993).

Watson, Irene. 'Law and Indigenous Peoples: The Impact of Colonialism on Indigenous Cultures', *Cross-Currents: Internationalism, National Identity and Law* (La Trobe University Press, 1996) 107.

Weeramantary, C.G. (ed.). *Human Rights and Scientific and Technological Development* (New York: United Nations Press, 1990).

Wegner, Harold. 'Purified Protein Patents: A Legal Process Gone Berserk?' (1990) 12 *European Intellectual Property Review* 187.

_____ 'TRIPS Boomerang – Obligations for Domestic Reform' (1996) 29 *Vanderbilt Journal of Transnational Law* 535.

Wegner, Harold and Pachenberg, Jochen. 'Paris Convention Priority: A Unique American Viewpoint Denying "The Same Effect" to the Foreign Filing' (1974) 5 *International Review of Industrial Property and Copyright Law* 361.

Weidne, Helen. 'The United States and North-South Technology Transfer: Some Practical and Legal Obstacles' (1982–83) 2 *Wisconsin International Law Journal* 205.

Weinrib, Arnold S. 'Information and Property' (1988) 38 *University of Toronto Law Journal* 117.

Weir, R.F. (ed.). *Stored Tissue Samples: Ethical, Legal and Public Policy Implications* (Iowa: University of Iowa Press, 1998).

Weisbrot, Mark. 'Globalization for Whom' (1998) 31 *Cornell International Law Journal* 631.

Weiss, Edith Brown. 'In Fairness to Future Generations and Sustainable Development' (1992) 8 *American University Journal of International Law and Policy* 19.

Welling, B. *Property in Things in the Common Law System* (Gold Coast, Australia: Scribblers Publishing, 1996).

Wells, Michael *et al.* (eds). *Investing in Biodiversity – A Review of Indonesia Integrated Conservation and Development Projects* (Washington: The World Bank, 1999).

Wells, T. 'The Implications of a Property Right in One's Body' (1990) 30 *Jurimetrics Journal* 371.

White, Alan and Warden, J.C. 'The British Approach to "Obviousness" (1977) *Annual of Industrial Property Law* 447.

White, John. 'The New "Investigation" for Patents' (1903) 19 *The Law Quarterly Review* 307.

White, Lynn. 'The Historical Roots of Our Ecological Crisis' (10 March 1967) 155 *Science* 1203.

White, Stephen. 'The Law Relating to Dealing with Dead Bodies' (2000) 4 *Medical Law International* 145.

Whitt, L.A. 'Indigenous Peoples, Intellectual Property and the New Imperial Science' (1998) 23 *Oklahoma City University Law Review* 211.

Wilbrod, L. *Freedom and Property* (Ottawa: University of Ottawa, 1986).

Wilder, Richard. 'The Effect of the Uruguay Round Implementing Legislation on U.S. Patent Law' (1995–96) 36 *IDEA* 33.

Wilkes, Garrison. 'The World's Crop Germplasm – An Endangered Resource' (1977) 33 *Bulletin of the Atomic Scientists* 8–16.

William, Lucy and Barker, Francois. 'Justifying Property and Justifying Access' (1993) 6 *Canadian Journal of Law and Jurisprudence* 287.

Willamson, A.R. 'Gene Patents: Socially Acceptable Monopolies or an Unnecessary Hindrance to Research?' (2001) 17 *Trends in Genetics* 670.

Williams, B. 'Concepts of Personhood and the Commodification of the Body' (1998/99) 7 *Health Law Review* 11.

Williams, B. (ed.) *The Politics of Culture* (Washington: Smithsonian Institution Press, 1991).

Williams, H. 'Death Warmed Up: The Agency of Bodies and Bones in Early Anglo-Saxon Cremation Rites' (2004) 9 *Journal of Material Culture* 263.

Williams, J. 'The Rhetoric of Property' (1998) 83 *Iowa Law Review* 277.

Williams, P.J. 'The Obliging Shell: An Informal Essay on Formal Equal Opportunity' (1989) 87 *Michigan Law Review* 2128.

Williams, R. *The American Indian in Western Legal Thought* (Oxford: Oxford University Press, 1990).

Willison, D.J. and Macleod, S.M. 'Patenting of Genetic Material: Are The Benefits To Society Being Realized?' (2002) 167 *Canadian Medical Association Journal* 259–66.

Wilson, Edward (ed.). *Biodiversity* (Washington, DC: National Academy Press, 1988).

Wilson, Edward. *The Diversity of Life* (Cambridge, Mass.: Harvard University Press, 1992).

Winickoff, D.E. 'Biosamples, Genomics, and Human Rights: Context and Content of Iceland's Biobanks Act' (2000) 4 *Journal of BioLaw & Business* 11.

Winski, J.B. 'There are Skeletons in the Closet: The Repatriation of Native American Human Remains and Burial Objects' (1992) 34 *Arizona Law Review* 187.

Winter, Ryan. 'Reconciling the GATT and WTO with Multilateral Environmental Agreements: Can we Have our Cake and Eat it Too?' (2000) 11 *Colorado Journal of International Environmental Law and Policy* 223.

WIPO. *Intellectual Property Needs and Expectations of Traditional Knowledge Holders: WIPO Report on Fact-Finding Missions on Intellectual Property and Traditional Knowledge, 1998–1999* (Geneva: WIPO, 2001).

WIPO International Forum. *Intellectual Property and Traditional Knowledge: Our Identity, Our Future* (Conference organized by WIPO and the Government of the Sultanate of Oman, 21–22 January 2002).

Wirth, Timothy. 'The Road From Rio – Defining a New World Order' (1993) 4 *Colorado Journal of International Environmental Law and Policy* 37.

Wiser, G.M. *PTO Rejection of the Ayahausca Patent Claim: Background and Analysis* (Center for International Environmental Law, 1999).

Wold, Chris. 'The Futility, Utility, and Future of the Biodiversity Convention' (1998) 9 *Colorado Journal of International Environmental Law and Policy* 1.

Wolfeld, Warren. 'International Patent Cooperation: The Next Step' (1983) 16 *Cornell International Law Journal* 229.

Wolfrun, Rudiger. 'The Principle of the Common Heritage of Mankind' (1983) 43 *ZaorRv-Heidelberg Journal of International Law* 312.

_____ 'The Protection of Indigenous Peoples in International Law' (1999) 59 *ZaorRv-Heidelberg Journal of International Law* 369.

Wood, G.S. *The Creation of the American Republic 1776-1787* (Chapel Hill, Published for the Institute of Early American History and Culture at Williamsburg, VA, by the University of North Carolina, 1969).

Worku, Dereje. 'Patents and the Process of Innovation in East African Countries' (1990) 21 *International Review of Industrial Property and Copyright Law* 38.

World Bank Development Report 1989 (Oxford: Oxford University Press, 1989).

WHO, *Monograph on Selected Medicinal Plants, Vol. 1* (Geneva: WHO, 1999).

WHO, *Monograph on Selected Medicinal Plants, Vol. 2* (Geneva: WHO, 2001).

World Health Organization (WHO). *WHO Traditional Medicine Strategy 2002–2005* (Geneva: WHO, 2002).

_____ *Genomics and World Health* (Geneva: WHO, 2002).

World Tourism Organization & United Nations Environment Program (eds). *Guidelines: Development of National Parks and Protected Areas for Tourism* (WTO and UNEP, 1992).

Yamin, Farhana. *The Biodiversity Convention and Intellectual Property Rights* (A WWF International Discussion Paper, October 1995).

Yano, Lester. 'Protection of the Ethnobiological Knowledge of Indigenous Peoples' (1993) 41 *UCLA Law Review* 443.

Yelpaala, K. 'Owning the Secret of Life: Biotechnology and Property Rights Revisited' (2000) 32 *McGeorge Law Review* 111.

Young, John. *Sustaining the Earth* (Cambridge: Mass.: Harvard University Press, 1990).

Yu, Jianyang. 'Protection of Intellectual Property in the P.R.C.: Progress, Problems, and Proposals' (1994) 13 *Pacific Basin Law Journal* 140.

Yusuf, Abdulqawi. 'International Law and Sustainable Development: The Convention on Biological Diversity' (1995) 1 *African Yearbook of International Law* 109.

Zahan, D. *The Religion, Spirituality, and Thought of Traditional Africa* (Chicago: The University of Chicago Press, 1979).

Ziff, B. *Principles of Property Law* (Toronto: Carswell Publication, 1993).

Ziff, B. and Roa, P. (eds). *Borrowed Power: Essays on Cultural Appropriation* (New Brunswick: Rutgers University Press, 1997).

Zimmerman, K. 'The Deforestation of the Brazilian Amazon: Law, Politics, and International Cooperation' (1990) 21 *Inter-American Law Review* 513.

Newspaper Sources

Abati, Reuben. 'The Whale Hunters of Victoria Island', *The Guardian*, 24 August 2001, page unknown.

Abraham, Carolyn. 'UN Sees Genetics As Boon For Third World', *The Globe & Mail*, 1 May 2002, p. A6.

Adamu, Hassan. 'We'll Feed Our People As We See Fit', *The Washington Post*, 11 September 2000, p. A23.

Adeoye, Seun. 'Provosts Asks Government to Check Brain Drain in Health Sector', *The Guardian*, 15 April 2002, page unknown.

AP. 'Donated Bodies Used in Land Mine Tests', *Associated Press*, 11 March 2004.

Barthos, Gordon. 'Offer Africa that Box of Nails', *The Toronto Star*, 6 June 2002, p. A32.

BBC News, 'Corpse Show Not Illegal', *BBC News*, 20 March 2002: http://news.bbc.co.uk/1/hi/entertainment/arts/1883396.stm.

Bisset, S. and Syal, R. 'Scientists Find Dissected Remains in Oxford Pit: Former Medical School', *National Post*, 21 February 2001, p. A14.

Broder, John. 'In Science's Name, Lucrative Trade in Body Parts', *The New York Times*, 12 March 2004.

Calamai, P. 'Skull Find in Kenya Shakes Evolution Tree', *The Toronto Star*, 22 March 2001, p. A1.

Campbell, Ronald *et al.* 'Researchers' Use of Bodies Stirs Emotion, Controversy', *Dallas Morning News*, 21 April 2000, p. A37.

Canadian Research-Based Pharmaceutical Companies. National Post, 25 September 2002, p. A9 (Advertisement).

Daniel, Alifa. 'Education Fund Raises N40b (forty billion naira) in Seven Years', *The Guardian*, 15 March 2002, page unknown.

Edwards, Michael. 'The Case for NGOs: the Mouse that Roared', *The Globe & Mail*, 3 January 2002, p. A17.

Evenson, Brad. 'Door Opened to Research with Embryos', *National Post*, 30 March 2001, p. A4.

Faiola, Anthony. 'Is It Biopiracy – Or Just Business?', *The Washington Post*, 18 July 1999, page unknown.

Gillis, Charlie. 'Doctor Left Autopsies Unfinished in Halifax: Children's Organs Found in Warehouse', *National Post*, 3 October 2000, p. A8.

Goodspeed, Peter. 'Death on Demand', *National Post*, 3 April 2001, p. A11.

Gorner, Peter. 'Parents Suing over Patenting of Genetic Test: They Say Researchers They Assisted Are Trying to Profit from a Test for a Rare Disease', *Chicago Tribune*, 19 November 2000, p. A1.

Griggs, Kim. 'Tonga Sells Its Old, New Genes', *Wired News*, 27 November 2000, page unknown.

Guardian Editorial. 'African Leaders and NEPAD', *The Guardian*, 16 April 2002, page unknown.

Guccione, J. 'Body Parts Suit Enters Murky Area of the Law', *Los Angeles Times*, 13 March 2004.

Ibrahim, Sani. 'The Return of the Middle Class', *The Guardian*, 16 May 2002, page unknown.

Kebonkwu, Mike. 'Where Are the Enemies', *The Guardian*, 29 August 2001, page unknown.

Kraft, Dina. 'Bushmen, Drug Giant Battle over Royalties: Biopiracy Topic at Development Summit', *The Toronto Star*, 24 August 2002, p. A18.

Kwayera, James. 'Gene Banking: UK Scientists Accused of Biopiracy', *News Wire*, 15 December 1999, page unknown.

Lee-Chua, Queen N. 'Genetically Modified Crops – Actual and Potential Benefits', *Philippine Daily Inquirer*, 15 March 2002, page unknown.

Lawson, Mark. 'Our Bodies, Our Deaths, Our Decisions: At Least the Corpses in the Show of Flayed Flesh were Donated', *The Guardian*, 23 March 2002 (page unknown).

McKie, Robert. 'Iceland DNA Project Hit By Privacy Storm', *The Observer*, 16 May 2004.

Maynard, Roger. 'Row Over Body Parts Erupts in Australia', *The Times*, 2 February 2001.

McLaughlin, A., Prusher, R. and Downie, A. 'What is a Kidney Worth?', *The Christian Science Monitor*, 9 June 2004.

Mittal, Anuradha. 'Enough Food for the Whole World', *The Washington Post*, 15 September 2000, p. A26.

Munro, Margaret. 'A Vision of Spare Parts', *National Post*, 29 March 2001, p. A15.

_____ 'Map of Rice Genome Could End Hunger', *National Post*, 5 April 2002, p. A1.

Njoroge, James. 'New Forum to Lobby for Genomics in Africa', *SciDev. Net*, 12 March 2002, page unknown.

Ornstein, C. 'Sale of Body Parts at UCLA Alleged', *Los Angeles Times*, 6 March 2004.

_____ 'Arrest Made in Cadaver Inquiry', *Los Angeles Times*, 7 March 2004.

Ornstein, C. and Marosi, R. 'Man Says He Sold UCLA'S Cadavers', *Los Angeles Times*, 8 March 2004.

_____ '$704,600 Billed for Cadavers', *Los Angeles Times*, 9 March 2004.

Ornstein, C. and Zarembo, A. 'The UCLA Body Parts Scandal: UCLA Suspends Body-Donor Program After Alleged Abuses', *Los Angeles Times*, 10 March 2004.

Perry, Michael. 'Body-Parts Supermarket Causes Uproar in Australia', *National Post*, 20 March 2001, p. A13.

Price, N. 'Neighbourhood Flattened', *National Post*, 15 January 2001, p. A3.

Raj, Ranjit Dev. 'Biopiracy-Friendly Laws Worry Neem Battle Winner', *Asia Times*, 27 May 2001, page unknown.

Safo, Amos. 'Trouble for Nigerian Crooks', *Accra Mail*, 30 August 2001, page unknown.

Shiva, Vandana. 'The US Patent System Legalizes Theft and Biopiracy', *The Hindu*, 28 July 1999, page unknown.

Sokoloff, Heather. 'Human Tissue On Sale At Auction', *National Post*, 16 April 2001, p. A4.

Sommerville, Margaret. 'The President, the Prime Minister, the Pope and the Embryo', *National Post*, 21 September 2000, p. A18.

Stephens, J. 'The Body Hunters: As Drug Testing Spreads, Profits and Lives Hang in Balance', *The Washington Post*, 17 December 2000, p. A1.

Stewart, Alastair. 'Brazilian Congress Committee Approves GMO Draft Bill', *Dow Jones*, 12 March 2002, page unknown.

Waldie, Paul. 'Husband Sues after Brain Tissue Taken from Dead Wife', *National Post*, 29 January 2000, p. A13.

Wallace, Charles P. 'For Sale: The Poor's Body Parts', *Los Angeles Times*, 27 August 1992, at p. A1.

Warner, Susan. 'South Africa and Drug Industry Settle Suit', *The Inquirer*, 20 April 2001, page unknown.

Zarembo, A. and Garrison, J. 'Illegal Profits Drive Trade in Body Parts', *Seattle Times*, 8 March 2004.

Index